Lecture Notes in Computer Science   12958

More information about this subseries at http://www.springer.com/series/7407

Osvaldo Gervasi · Beniamino Murgante ·
Sanjay Misra · Chiara Garau ·
Ivan Blečić · David Taniar ·
Bernady O. Apduhan · Ana Maria A. C. Rocha ·
Eufemia Tarantino · Carmelo Maria Torre (Eds.)

Computational Science and Its Applications – ICCSA 2021

21st International Conference
Cagliari, Italy, September 13–16, 2021
Proceedings, Part X

Springer

Editors
Osvaldo Gervasi ⓘ
University of Perugia
Perugia, Italy

Beniamino Murgante ⓘ
University of Basilicata
Potenza, Potenza, Italy

Sanjay Misra ⓘ
Covenant University
Ota, Nigeria

Chiara Garau ⓘ
University of Cagliari
Cagliari, Italy

Ivan Blečić ⓘ
University of Cagliari
Cagliari, Italy

David Taniar ⓘ
Monash University
Clayton, VIC, Australia

Bernady O. Apduhan
Kyushu Sangyo University
Fukuoka, Japan

Ana Maria A. C. Rocha ⓘ
University of Minho
Braga, Portugal

Eufemia Tarantino ⓘ
Polytechnic University of Bari
Bari, Italy

Carmelo Maria Torre ⓘ
Polytechnic University of Bari
Bari, Italy

ISSN 0302-9743   ISSN 1611-3349 (electronic)
Lecture Notes in Computer Science
ISBN 978-3-030-87015-7   ISBN 978-3-030-87016-4   (eBook)
https://doi.org/10.1007/978-3-030-87016-4

LNCS Sublibrary: SL1 – Theoretical Computer Science and General Issues

This Springer imprint is published by the registered company Springer Nature Switzerland AG
The registered company address is: Gewerbestrasse 11, 6330 Cham, Switzerland

Preface

These 10 volumes (LNCS volumes 12949–12958) consist of the peer-reviewed papers from the 21st International Conference on Computational Science and Its Applications (ICCSA 2021) which took place during September 13–16, 2021. By virtue of the vaccination campaign conducted in various countries around the world, we decided to try a hybrid conference, with some of the delegates attending in person at the University of Cagliari and others attending in virtual mode, reproducing the infrastructure established last year.

This year's edition was a successful continuation of the ICCSA conference series, which was also held as a virtual event in 2020, and previously held in Saint Petersburg, Russia (2019), Melbourne, Australia (2018), Trieste, Italy (2017), Beijing. China (2016), Banff, Canada (2015), Guimaraes, Portugal (2014), Ho Chi Minh City, Vietnam (2013), Salvador, Brazil (2012), Santander, Spain (2011), Fukuoka, Japan (2010), Suwon, South Korea (2009), Perugia, Italy (2008), Kuala Lumpur, Malaysia (2007), Glasgow, UK (2006), Singapore (2005), Assisi, Italy (2004), Montreal, Canada (2003), and (as ICCS) Amsterdam, The Netherlands (2002) and San Francisco, USA (2001).

Computational science is the main pillar of most of the present research on understanding and solving complex problems. It plays a unique role in exploiting innovative ICT technologies and in the development of industrial and commercial applications. The ICCSA conference series provides a venue for researchers and industry practitioners to discuss new ideas, to share complex problems and their solutions, and to shape new trends in computational science.

Apart from the six main conference tracks, ICCSA 2021 also included 52 workshops in various areas of computational sciences, ranging from computational science technologies to specific areas of computational sciences, such as software engineering, security, machine learning and artificial intelligence, blockchain technologies, and applications in many fields. In total, we accepted 494 papers, giving an acceptance rate of 30%, of which 18 papers were short papers and 6 were published open access. We would like to express our appreciation for the workshop chairs and co-chairs for their hard work and dedication.

The success of the ICCSA conference series in general, and of ICCSA 2021 in particular, vitally depends on the support of many people: authors, presenters, participants, keynote speakers, workshop chairs, session chairs, organizing committee members, student volunteers, Program Committee members, advisory committee members, international liaison chairs, reviewers, and others in various roles. We take this opportunity to wholehartedly thank them all.

We also wish to thank Springer for publishing the proceedings, for sponsoring some of the best paper awards, and for their kind assistance and cooperation during the editing process.

We cordially invite you to visit the ICCSA website https://iccsa.org where you can find all the relevant information about this interesting and exciting event.

September 2021

Osvaldo Gervasi
Beniamino Murgante
Sanjay Misra

Welcome Message from the Organizers

COVID-19 has continued to alter our plans for organizing the ICCSA 2021 conference, so although vaccination plans are progressing worldwide, the spread of virus variants still forces us into a period of profound uncertainty. Only a very limited number of participants were able to enjoy the beauty of Sardinia and Cagliari in particular, rediscovering the immense pleasure of meeting again, albeit safely spaced out. The social events, in which we rediscovered the ancient values that abound on this wonderful island and in this city, gave us even more strength and hope for the future. For the management of the virtual part of the conference, we consolidated the methods, organization, and infrastructure of ICCSA 2020.

The technological infrastructure was based on open source software, with the addition of the streaming channels on YouTube. In particular, we used Jitsi (jitsi.org) for videoconferencing, Riot (riot.im) together with Matrix (matrix.org) for chat and ansynchronous communication, and Jibri (github.com/jitsi/jibri) for streaming live sessions to YouTube.

Seven Jitsi servers were set up, one for each parallel session. The participants of the sessions were helped and assisted by eight student volunteers (from the universities of Cagliari, Florence, Perugia, and Bari), who provided technical support and ensured smooth running of the conference proceedings.

The implementation of the software infrastructure and the technical coordination of the volunteers were carried out by Damiano Perri and Marco Simonetti.

Our warmest thanks go to all the student volunteers, to the technical coordinators, and to the development communities of Jitsi, Jibri, Riot, and Matrix, who made their terrific platforms available as open source software.

A big thank you goes to all of the 450 speakers, many of whom showed an enormous collaborative spirit, sometimes participating and presenting at almost prohibitive times of the day, given that the participants of this year's conference came from 58 countries scattered over many time zones of the globe.

Finally, we would like to thank Google for letting us stream all the live events via YouTube. In addition to lightening the load of our Jitsi servers, this allowed us to record the event and to be able to review the most exciting moments of the conference.

Ivan Blečić
Chiara Garau

Organization

ICCSA 2021 was organized by the University of Cagliari (Italy), the University of Perugia (Italy), the University of Basilicata (Italy), Monash University (Australia), Kyushu Sangyo University (Japan), and the University of Minho (Portugal).

Honorary General Chairs

Norio Shiratori	Chuo University, Japan
Kenneth C. J. Tan	Sardina Systems, UK
Corrado Zoppi	University of Cagliari, Italy

General Chairs

Osvaldo Gervasi	University of Perugia, Italy
Ivan Blečić	University of Cagliari, Italy
David Taniar	Monash University, Australia

Program Committee Chairs

Beniamino Murgante	University of Basilicata, Italy
Bernady O. Apduhan	Kyushu Sangyo University, Japan
Chiara Garau	University of Cagliari, Italy
Ana Maria A. C. Rocha	University of Minho, Portugal

International Advisory Committee

Jemal Abawajy	Deakin University, Australia
Dharma P. Agarwal	University of Cincinnati, USA
Rajkumar Buyya	University of Melbourne, Australia
Claudia Bauzer Medeiros	University of Campinas, Brazil
Manfred M. Fisher	Vienna University of Economics and Business, Austria
Marina L. Gavrilova	University of Calgary, Canada
Yee Leung	Chinese University of Hong Kong, China

International Liaison Chairs

Giuseppe Borruso	University of Trieste, Italy
Elise De Donker	Western Michigan University, USA
Maria Irene Falcão	University of Minho, Portugal
Robert C. H. Hsu	Chung Hua University, Taiwan
Tai-Hoon Kim	Beijing Jaotong University, China

Vladimir Korkhov	St. Petersburg University, Russia
Sanjay Misra	Covenant University, Nigeria
Takashi Naka	Kyushu Sangyo University, Japan
Rafael D. C. Santos	National Institute for Space Research, Brazil
Maribel Yasmina Santos	University of Minho, Portugal
Elena Stankova	St. Petersburg University, Russia

Workshop and Session Chairs

Beniamino Murgante	University of Basilicata, Italy
Sanjay Misra	Covenant University, Nigeria
Jorge Gustavo Rocha	University of Minho, Portugal

Awards Chair

Wenny Rahayu	La Trobe University, Australia

Publicity Committee Chairs

Elmer Dadios	De La Salle University, Philippines
Nataliia Kulabukhova	St. Petersburg University, Russia
Daisuke Takahashi	Tsukuba University, Japan
Shangwang Wang	Beijing University of Posts and Telecommunications, China

Technology Chairs

Damiano Perri	University of Florence, Italy
Marco Simonetti	University of Florence, Italy

Local Arrangement Chairs

Ivan Blečić	University of Cagliari, Italy
Chiara Garau	University of Cagliari, Italy
Alfonso Annunziata	University of Cagliari, Italy
Ginevra Balletto	University of Cagliari, Italy
Giuseppe Borruso	University of Trieste, Italy
Alessandro Buccini	University of Cagliari, Italy
Michele Campagna	University of Cagliari, Italy
Mauro Coni	University of Cagliari, Italy
Anna Maria Colavitti	University of Cagliari, Italy
Giulia Desogus	University of Cagliari, Italy
Caterina Fenu	University of Cagliari, Italy
Sabrina Lai	University of Cagliari, Italy
Francesca Maltinti	University of Cagliari, Italy
Pasquale Mistretta	University of Cagliari, Italy

Augusto Montisci   University of Cagliari, Italy
Francesco Pinna   University of Cagliari, Italy
Davide Spano   University of Cagliari, Italy
Giuseppe A. Trunfio   University of Sassari, Italy
Corrado Zoppi   University of Cagliari, Italy

Program Committee

Vera Afreixo   University of Aveiro, Portugal
Filipe Alvelos   University of Minho, Portugal
Hartmut Asche   University of Potsdam, Germany
Ginevra Balletto   University of Cagliari, Italy
Michela Bertolotto   University College Dublin, Ireland
Sandro Bimonte   INRAE-TSCF, France
Rod Blais   University of Calgary, Canada
Ivan Blečić   University of Sassari, Italy
Giuseppe Borruso   University of Trieste, Italy
Ana Cristina Braga   University of Minho, Portugal
Massimo Cafaro   University of Salento, Italy
Yves Caniou   University of Lyon, France
José A. Cardoso e Cunha   Universidade Nova de Lisboa, Portugal
Rui Cardoso   University of Beira Interior, Portugal
Leocadio G. Casado   University of Almeria, Spain
Carlo Cattani   University of Salerno, Italy
Mete Celik   Erciyes University, Turkey
Maria Cerreta   University of Naples "Federico II", Italy
Hyunseung Choo   Sungkyunkwan University, South Korea
Chien-Sing Lee   Sunway University, Malaysia
Min Young Chung   Sungkyunkwan University, South Korea
Florbela Maria da Cruz   Polytechnic Institute of Viana do Castelo, Portugal
  Domingues Correia
Gilberto Corso Pereira   Federal University of Bahia, Brazil
Fernanda Costa   University of Minho, Portugal
Alessandro Costantini   INFN, Italy
Carla Dal Sasso Freitas   Universidade Federal do Rio Grande do Sul, Brazil
Pradesh Debba   The Council for Scientific and Industrial Research
                             (CSIR), South Africa
Hendrik Decker   Instituto Tecnolčgico de Informática, Spain
Robertas Damaševičius   Kausan University of Technology, Lithuania
Frank Devai   London South Bank University, UK
Rodolphe Devillers   Memorial University of Newfoundland, Canada
Joana Matos Dias   University of Coimbra, Portugal
Paolino Di Felice   University of L'Aquila, Italy
Prabu Dorairaj   NetApp, India/USA
Noelia Faginas Lago   University of Perugia, Italy
M. Irene Falcao   University of Minho, Portugal

Cherry Liu Fang	Ames Laboratory, USA
Florbela P. Fernandes	Polytechnic Institute of Bragança, Portugal
Jose-Jesus Fernandez	National Centre for Biotechnology, Spain
Paula Odete Fernandes	Polytechnic Institute of Bragança, Portugal
Adelaide de Fátima Baptista Valente Freitas	University of Aveiro, Portugal
Manuel Carlos Figueiredo	University of Minho, Portugal
Maria Celia Furtado Rocha	Universidade Federal da Bahia, Brazil
Chiara Garau	University of Cagliari, Italy
Paulino Jose Garcia Nieto	University of Oviedo, Spain
Jerome Gensel	LSR-IMAG, France
Maria Giaoutzi	National Technical University of Athens, Greece
Arminda Manuela Andrade Pereira Gonçalves	University of Minho, Portugal
Andrzej M. Goscinski	Deakin University, Australia
Eduardo Guerra	Free University of Bozen-Bolzano, Italy
Sevin Gümgüm	Izmir University of Economics, Turkey
Alex Hagen-Zanker	University of Cambridge, UK
Shanmugasundaram Hariharan	B.S. Abdur Rahman University, India
Eligius M. T. Hendrix	University of Malaga, Spain/Wageningen University, The Netherlands
Hisamoto Hiyoshi	Gunma University, Japan
Mustafa Inceoglu	EGE University, Turkey
Peter Jimack	University of Leeds, UK
Qun Jin	Waseda University, Japan
Yeliz Karaca	University of Massachusetts Medical School, USA
Farid Karimipour	Vienna University of Technology, Austria
Baris Kazar	Oracle Corp., USA
Maulana Adhinugraha Kiki	Telkom University, Indonesia
DongSeong Kim	University of Canterbury, New Zealand
Taihoon Kim	Hannam University, South Korea
Ivana Kolingerova	University of West Bohemia, Czech Republic
Nataliia Kulabukhova	St. Petersburg University, Russia
Vladimir Korkhov	St. Petersburg University, Russia
Rosa Lasaponara	National Research Council, Italy
Maurizio Lazzari	National Research Council, Italy
Cheng Siong Lee	Monash University, Australia
Sangyoun Lee	Yonsei University, South Korea
Jongchan Lee	Kunsan National University, South Korea
Chendong Li	University of Connecticut, USA
Gang Li	Deakin University, Australia
Fang Liu	Ames Laboratory, USA
Xin Liu	University of Calgary, Canada
Andrea Lombardi	University of Perugia, Italy
Savino Longo	University of Bari, Italy

Tinghuai Ma   Nanjing University of Information Science
                                     and Technology, China
Ernesto Marcheggiani   Katholieke Universiteit Leuven, Belgium
Antonino Marvuglia   Research Centre Henri Tudor, Luxembourg
Nicola Masini   National Research Council, Italy
Ilaria Matteucci   National Research Council, Italy
Eric Medvet   University of Trieste, Italy
Nirvana Meratnia   University of Twente, The Netherlands
Giuseppe Modica   University of Reggio Calabria, Italy
Josè Luis Montaña   University of Cantabria, Spain
Maria Filipa Mourão   Instituto Politécnico de Viana do Castelo, Portugal
Louiza de Macedo Mourelle   State University of Rio de Janeiro, Brazil
Nadia Nedjah   State University of Rio de Janeiro, Brazil
Laszlo Neumann   University of Girona, Spain
Kok-Leong Ong   Deakin University, Australia
Belen Palop   Universidad de Valladolid, Spain
Marcin Paprzycki   Polish Academy of Sciences, Poland
Eric Pardede   La Trobe University, Australia
Kwangjin Park   Wonkwang University, South Korea
Ana Isabel Pereira   Polytechnic Institute of Bragança, Portugal
Massimiliano Petri   University of Pisa, Italy
Telmo Pinto   University of Coimbra, Portugal
Maurizio Pollino   Italian National Agency for New Technologies, Energy
                                     and Sustainable Economic Development, Italy
Alenka Poplin   University of Hamburg, Germany
Vidyasagar Potdar   Curtin University of Technology, Australia
David C. Prosperi   Florida Atlantic University, USA
Wenny Rahayu   La Trobe University, Australia
Jerzy Respondek   Silesian University of Technology Poland
Humberto Rocha   INESC-Coimbra, Portugal
Jon Rokne   University of Calgary, Canada
Octavio Roncero   CSIC, Spain
Maytham Safar   Kuwait University, Kuwait
Francesco Santini   University of Perugia, Italy
Chiara Saracino   A.O. Ospedale Niguarda Ca' Granda, Italy
Haiduke Sarafian   Pennsylvania State University, USA
Marco Paulo Seabra dos   University of Coimbra, Portugal
  Reis
Jie Shen   University of Michigan, USA
Qi Shi   Liverpool John Moores University, UK
Dale Shires   U.S. Army Research Laboratory, USA
Inês Soares   University of Coimbra, Portugal
Elena Stankova   St. Petersburg University, Russia
Takuo Suganuma   Tohoku University, Japan
Eufemia Tarantino   Polytechnic University of Bari, Italy
Sergio Tasso   University of Perugia, Italy

Ana Paula Teixeira	University of Trás-os-Montes and Alto Douro, Portugal
Senhorinha Teixeira	University of Minho, Portugal
M. Filomena Teodoro	Portuguese Naval Academy/University of Lisbon, Portugal
Parimala Thulasiraman	University of Manitoba, Canada
Carmelo Torre	Polytechnic University of Bari, Italy
Javier Martinez Torres	Centro Universitario de la Defensa Zaragoza, Spain
Giuseppe A. Trunfio	University of Sassari, Italy
Pablo Vanegas	University of Cuenca, Equador
Marco Vizzari	University of Perugia, Italy
Varun Vohra	Merck Inc., USA
Koichi Wada	University of Tsukuba, Japan
Krzysztof Walkowiak	Wroclaw University of Technology, Poland
Zequn Wang	Intelligent Automation Inc, USA
Robert Weibel	University of Zurich, Switzerland
Frank Westad	Norwegian University of Science and Technology, Norway
Roland Wismüller	Universität Siegen, Germany
Mudasser Wyne	National University, USA
Chung-Huang Yang	National Kaohsiung Normal University, Taiwan
Xin-She Yang	National Physical Laboratory, UK
Salim Zabir	National Institute of Technology, Tsuruoka, Japan
Haifeng Zhao	University of California, Davis, USA
Fabiana Zollo	University of Venice "Cà Foscari", Italy
Albert Y. Zomaya	University of Sydney, Australia

Workshop Organizers

Advanced Transport Tools and Methods (A2TM 2021)

| Massimiliano Petri | University of Pisa, Italy |
| Antonio Pratelli | University of Pisa, Italy |

Advances in Artificial Intelligence Learning Technologies: Blended Learning, STEM, Computational Thinking and Coding (AAILT 2021)

Alfredo Milani	University of Perugia, Italy
Giulio Biondi	University of Florence, Italy
Sergio Tasso	University of Perugia, Italy

Workshop on Advancements in Applied Machine Learning and Data Analytics (AAMDA 2021)

Alessandro Costantini	INFN, Italy
Davide Salomoni	INFN, Italy
Doina Cristina Duma	INFN, Italy
Daniele Cesini	INFN, Italy

Automatic Landform Classification: Spatial Methods and Applications (ALCSMA 2021)

Maria Danese	ISPC, National Research Council, Italy
Dario Gioia	ISPC, National Research Council, Italy

Application of Numerical Analysis to Imaging Science (ANAIS 2021)

Caterina Fenu	University of Cagliari, Italy
Alessandro Buccini	University of Cagliari, Italy

Advances in Information Systems and Technologies for Emergency Management, Risk Assessment and Mitigation Based on the Resilience Concepts (ASTER 2021)

Maurizio Pollino	ENEA, Italy
Marco Vona	University of Basilicata, Italy
Amedeo Flora	University of Basilicata, Italy
Chiara Iacovino	University of Basilicata, Italy
Beniamino Murgante	University of Basilicata, Italy

Advances in Web Based Learning (AWBL 2021)

Birol Ciloglugil	Ege University, Turkey
Mustafa Murat Inceoglu	Ege University, Turkey

Blockchain and Distributed Ledgers: Technologies and Applications (BDLTA 2021)

Vladimir Korkhov	St. Petersburg University, Russia
Elena Stankova	St. Petersburg University, Russia
Nataliia Kulabukhova	St. Petersburg University, Russia

Bio and Neuro Inspired Computing and Applications (BIONCA 2021)

Nadia Nedjah	State University of Rio de Janeiro, Brazil
Luiza De Macedo Mourelle	State University of Rio de Janeiro, Brazil

Computational and Applied Mathematics (CAM 2021)

Maria Irene Falcão	University of Minho, Portugal
Fernando Miranda	University of Minho, Portugal

Computational and Applied Statistics (CAS 2021)

Ana Cristina Braga	University of Minho, Portugal

Computerized Evaluation of Economic Activities: Urban Spaces (CEEA 2021)

Diego Altafini	Università di Pisa, Italy
Valerio Cutini	Università di Pisa, Italy

Computational Geometry and Applications (CGA 2021)

Marina Gavrilova   University of Calgary, Canada

Collaborative Intelligence in Multimodal Applications (CIMA 2021)

Robertas Damasevicius   Kaunas University of Technology, Lithuania
Rytis Maskeliunas   Kaunas University of Technology, Lithuania

Computational Optimization and Applications (COA 2021)

Ana Rocha   University of Minho, Portugal
Humberto Rocha   University of Coimbra, Portugal

Computational Astrochemistry (CompAstro 2021)

Marzio Rosi   University of Perugia, Italy
Cecilia Ceccarelli   University of Grenoble, France
Stefano Falcinelli   University of Perugia, Italy
Dimitrios Skouteris   Master-Up, Italy

Computational Science and HPC (CSHPC 2021)

Elise de Doncker   Western Michigan University, USA
Fukuko Yuasa   High Energy Accelerator Research Organization
                                   (KEK), Japan
Hideo Matsufuru   High Energy Accelerator Research Organization
                                   (KEK), Japan

Cities, Technologies and Planning (CTP 2021)

Malgorzata Hanzl   University of Łódź, Poland
Beniamino Murgante   University of Basilicata, Italy
Ljiljana Zivkovic   Ministry of Construction, Transport and
                                   Infrastructure/Institute of Architecture and Urban
                                   and Spatial Planning of Serbia, Serbia
Anastasia Stratigea   National Technical University of Athens, Greece
Giuseppe Borruso   University of Trieste, Italy
Ginevra Balletto   University of Cagliari, Italy

Advanced Modeling E-Mobility in Urban Spaces (DEMOS 2021)

Tiziana Campisi   Kore University of Enna, Italy
Socrates Basbas   Aristotle University of Thessaloniki, Greece
Ioannis Politis   Aristotle University of Thessaloniki, Greece
Florin Nemtanu   Polytechnic University of Bucharest, Romania
Giovanna Acampa   Kore University of Enna, Italy
Wolfgang Schulz   Zeppelin University, Germany

Digital Transformation and Smart City (DIGISMART 2021)

Mauro Mazzei   National Research Council, Italy

Econometric and Multidimensional Evaluation in Urban Environment (EMEUE 2021)

Carmelo Maria Torre   Polytechnic University of Bari, Italy
Maria Cerreta   University "Federico II" of Naples, Italy
Pierluigi Morano   Polytechnic University of Bari, Italy
Simona Panaro   University of Portsmouth, UK
Francesco Tajani   Sapienza University of Rome, Italy
Marco Locurcio   Polytechnic University of Bari, Italy

The 11th International Workshop on Future Computing System Technologies and Applications (FiSTA 2021)

Bernady Apduhan   Kyushu Sangyo University, Japan
Rafael Santos   Brazilian National Institute for Space Research, Brazil

Transformational Urban Mobility: Challenges and Opportunities During and Post COVID Era (FURTHER 2021)

Tiziana Campisi   Kore University of Enna, Italy
Socrates Basbas   Aristotle University of Thessaloniki, Greece
Dilum Dissanayake   Newcastle University, UK
Kh Md Nahiduzzaman   University of British Columbia, Canada
Nurten Akgün Tanbay   Bursa Technical University, Turkey
Khaled J. Assi   King Fahd University of Petroleum and Minerals,
                                  Saudi Arabia
Giovanni Tesoriere   Kore University of Enna, Italy
Motasem Darwish   Middle East University, Jordan

Geodesign in Decision Making: Meta Planning and Collaborative Design for Sustainable and Inclusive Development (GDM 2021)

Francesco Scorza   University of Basilicata, Italy
Michele Campagna   University of Cagliari, Italy
Ana Clara Mourao Moura   Federal University of Minas Gerais, Brazil

Geomatics in Forestry and Agriculture: New Advances and Perspectives (GeoForAgr 2021)

Maurizio Pollino   ENEA, Italy
Giuseppe Modica   University of Reggio Calabria, Italy
Marco Vizzari   University of Perugia, Italy

Geographical Analysis, Urban Modeling, Spatial Statistics (GEOG-AND-MOD 2021)

Beniamino Murgante	University of Basilicata, Italy
Giuseppe Borruso	University of Trieste, Italy
Hartmut Asche	University of Potsdam, Germany

Geomatics for Resource Monitoring and Management (GRMM 2021)

Eufemia Tarantino	Polytechnic University of Bari, Italy
Enrico Borgogno Mondino	University of Turin, Italy
Alessandra Capolupo	Polytechnic University of Bari, Italy
Mirko Saponaro	Polytechnic University of Bari, Italy

12th International Symposium on Software Quality (ISSQ 2021)

Sanjay Misra	Covenant University, Nigeria

10th International Workshop on Collective, Massive and Evolutionary Systems (IWCES 2021)

Alfredo Milani	University of Perugia, Italy
Rajdeep Niyogi	Indian Institute of Technology, Roorkee, India

Land Use Monitoring for Sustainability (LUMS 2021)

Carmelo Maria Torre	Polytechnic University of Bari, Italy
Maria Cerreta	University "Federico II" of Naples, Italy
Massimiliano Bencardino	University of Salerno, Italy
Alessandro Bonifazi	Polytechnic University of Bari, Italy
Pasquale Balena	Polytechnic University of Bari, Italy
Giuliano Poli	University "Federico II" of Naples, Italy

Machine Learning for Space and Earth Observation Data (MALSEOD 2021)

Rafael Santos	Instituto Nacional de Pesquisas Espaciais, Brazil
Karine Ferreira	Instituto Nacional de Pesquisas Espaciais, Brazil

Building Multi-dimensional Models for Assessing Complex Environmental Systems (MES 2021)

Marta Dell'Ovo	Polytechnic University of Milan, Italy
Vanessa Assumma	Polytechnic University of Turin, Italy
Caterina Caprioli	Polytechnic University of Turin, Italy
Giulia Datola	Polytechnic University of Turin, Italy
Federico dell'Anna	Polytechnic University of Turin, Italy

Ecosystem Services: Nature's Contribution to People in Practice. Assessment Frameworks, Models, Mapping, and Implications (NC2P 2021)

Francesco Scorza	University of Basilicata, Italy
Sabrina Lai	University of Cagliari, Italy
Ana Clara Mourao Moura	Federal University of Minas Gerais, Brazil
Corrado Zoppi	University of Cagliari, Italy
Dani Broitman	Technion, Israel Institute of Technology, Israel

Privacy in the Cloud/Edge/IoT World (PCEIoT 2021)

Michele Mastroianni	University of Campania Luigi Vanvitelli, Italy
Lelio Campanile	University of Campania Luigi Vanvitelli, Italy
Mauro Iacono	University of Campania Luigi Vanvitelli, Italy

Processes, Methods and Tools Towards RESilient Cities and Cultural Heritage Prone to SOD and ROD Disasters (RES 2021)

Elena Cantatore	Polytechnic University of Bari, Italy
Alberico Sonnessa	Polytechnic University of Bari, Italy
Dario Esposito	Polytechnic University of Bari, Italy

Risk, Resilience and Sustainability in the Efficient Management of Water Resources: Approaches, Tools, Methodologies and Multidisciplinary Integrated Applications (RRS 2021)

Maria Macchiaroli	University of Salerno, Italy
Chiara D'Alpaos	Università degli Studi di Padova, Italy
Mirka Mobilia	Università degli Studi di Salerno, Italy
Antonia Longobardi	Università degli Studi di Salerno, Italy
Grazia Fattoruso	ENEA Research Center, Italy
Vincenzo Pellecchia	Ente Idrico Campano, Italy

Scientific Computing Infrastructure (SCI 2021)

Elena Stankova	St. Petersburg University, Russia
Vladimir Korkhov	St. Petersburg University, Russia
Natalia Kulabukhova	St. Petersburg University, Russia

Smart Cities and User Data Management (SCIDAM 2021)

Chiara Garau	University of Cagliari, Italy
Luigi Mundula	University of Cagliari, Italy
Gianni Fenu	University of Cagliari, Italy
Paolo Nesi	University of Florence, Italy
Paola Zamperlin	University of Pisa, Italy

13th International Symposium on Software Engineering Processes and Applications (SEPA 2021)

Sanjay Misra	Covenant University, Nigeria

Ports of the Future - Smartness and Sustainability (SmartPorts 2021)

Patrizia Serra	University of Cagliari, Italy
Gianfranco Fancello	University of Cagliari, Italy
Ginevra Balletto	University of Cagliari, Italy
Luigi Mundula	University of Cagliari, Italy
Marco Mazzarino	University of Venice, Italy
Giuseppe Borruso	University of Trieste, Italy
Maria del Mar Munoz Leonisio	Universidad de Cádiz, Spain

Smart Tourism (SmartTourism 2021)

Giuseppe Borruso	University of Trieste, Italy
Silvia Battino	University of Sassari, Italy
Ginevra Balletto	University of Cagliari, Italy
Maria del Mar Munoz Leonisio	Universidad de Cádiz, Spain
Ainhoa Amaro Garcia	Universidad de Alcalà/Universidad de Las Palmas, Spain
Francesca Krasna	University of Trieste, Italy

Sustainability Performance Assessment: Models, Approaches and Applications toward Interdisciplinary and Integrated Solutions (SPA 2021)

Francesco Scorza	University of Basilicata, Italy
Sabrina Lai	University of Cagliari, Italy
Jolanta Dvarioniene	Kaunas University of Technology, Lithuania
Valentin Grecu	Lucian Blaga University, Romania
Corrado Zoppi	University of Cagliari, Italy
Iole Cerminara	University of Basilicata, Italy

Smart and Sustainable Island Communities (SSIC 2021)

Chiara Garau	University of Cagliari, Italy
Anastasia Stratigea	National Technical University of Athens, Greece
Paola Zamperlin	University of Pisa, Italy
Francesco Scorza	University of Basilicata, Italy

Science, Technologies and Policies to Innovate Spatial Planning (STP4P 2021)

Chiara Garau	University of Cagliari, Italy
Daniele La Rosa	University of Catania, Italy
Francesco Scorza	University of Basilicata, Italy

Anna Maria Colavitti	University of Cagliari, Italy
Beniamino Murgante	University of Basilicata, Italy
Paolo La Greca	University of Catania, Italy

Sustainable Urban Energy Systems (SURENSYS 2021)

Luigi Mundula	University of Cagliari, Italy
Emilio Ghiani	University of Cagliari, Italy

Space Syntax for Cities in Theory and Practice (Syntax_City 2021)

Claudia Yamu	University of Groningen, The Netherlands
Akkelies van Nes	Western Norway University of Applied Sciences, Norway
Chiara Garau	University of Cagliari, Italy

Theoretical and Computational Chemistry and Its Applications (TCCMA 2021)

Noelia Faginas-Lago	University of Perugia, Italy

13th International Workshop on Tools and Techniques in Software Development Process (TTSDP 2021)

Sanjay Misra	Covenant University, Nigeria

Urban Form Studies (UForm 2021)

Malgorzata Hanzl	Łódź University of Technology, Poland
Beniamino Murgante	University of Basilicata, Italy
Eufemia Tarantino	Polytechnic University of Bari, Italy
Irena Itova	University of Westminster, UK

Urban Space Accessibility and Safety (USAS 2021)

Chiara Garau	University of Cagliari, Italy
Francesco Pinna	University of Cagliari, Italy
Claudia Yamu	University of Groningen, The Netherlands
Vincenza Torrisi	University of Catania, Italy
Matteo Ignaccolo	University of Catania, Italy
Michela Tiboni	University of Brescia, Italy
Silvia Rossetti	University of Parma, Italy

Virtual and Augmented Reality and Applications (VRA 2021)

Osvaldo Gervasi	University of Perugia, Italy
Damiano Perri	University of Perugia, Italy
Marco Simonetti	University of Perugia, Italy
Sergio Tasso	University of Perugia, Italy

**Workshop on Advanced and Computational Methods for Earth Science
Applications (WACM4ES 2021)**

Luca Piroddi	University of Cagliari, Italy
Laura Foddis	University of Cagliari, Italy
Augusto Montisci	University of Cagliari, Italy
Sergio Vincenzo Calcina	University of Cagliari, Italy
Sebastiano D'Amico	University of Malta, Malta
Giovanni Martinelli	Istituto Nazionale di Geofisica e Vulcanologia, Italy/Chinese Academy of Sciences, China

Sponsoring Organizations

ICCSA 2021 would not have been possible without the tremendous support of many
organizations and institutions, for which all organizers and participants of ICCSA 2021
express their sincere gratitude:

Springer International Publishing AG, Germany
(https://www.springer.com)

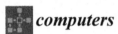

Computers Open Access Journal
(https://www.mdpi.com/journal/computers)

IEEE Italy Section, Italy
(https://italy.ieeer8.org/)

Centre-North Italy Chapter IEEE GRSS, Italy
(https://cispio.diet.uniroma1.it/marzano/ieee-grs/
index.html)

Italy Section of the Computer Society, Italy
(https://site.ieee.org/italy-cs/)

University of Perugia, Italy
(https://www.unipg.it)

University of Cagliari, Italy
(https://unica.it/)

University of Basilicata, Italy
(http://www.unibas.it)

Monash University, Australia
(https://www.monash.edu/)

Kyushu Sangyo University, Japan
(https://www.kyusan-u.ac.jp/)

University of Minho, Portugal
(https://www.uminho.pt/)

Scientific Association Transport Infrastructures,
Italy
(https://www.stradeeautostrade.it/associazioni-e-
organizzazioni/asit-associazione-scientifica-
infrastrutture-trasporto/)

Regione Sardegna, Italy
(https://regione.sardegna.it/)

Comune di Cagliari, Italy
(https://www.comune.cagliari.it/)

Città Metropolitana di Cagliari

Cagliari Accessibility Lab (CAL)
(https://www.unica.it/unica/it/cagliari_
accessibility_lab.page/)

Referees

Nicodemo Abate	IMAA, National Research Council, Italy
Andre Ricardo Abed Grégio	Federal University of Paraná State, Brazil
Nasser Abu Zeid	Università di Ferrara, Italy
Lidia Aceto	Università del Piemonte Orientale, Italy
Nurten Akgün Tanbay	Bursa Technical University, Turkey
Filipe Alvelos	Universidade do Minho, Portugal
Paula Amaral	Universidade Nova de Lisboa, Portugal
Federico Amato	University of Lausanne, Switzerland
Marina Alexandra Pedro Andrade	ISCTE-IUL, Portugal
Debora Anelli	Sapienza University of Rome, Italy
Alfonso Annunziata	University of Cagliari, Italy
Fahim Anzum	University of Calgary, Canada
Tatsumi Aoyama	High Energy Accelerator Research Organization, Japan
Bernady Apduhan	Kyushu Sangyo University, Japan
Jonathan Apeh	Covenant University, Nigeria
Vasilike Argyropoulos	University of West Attica, Greece
Giuseppe Aronica	Università di Messina, Italy
Daniela Ascenzi	Università degli Studi di Trento, Italy
Vanessa Assumma	Politecnico di Torino, Italy
Muhammad Attique Khan	HITEC University Taxila, Pakistan
Vecdi Aytaç	Ege University, Turkey
Alina Elena Baia	University of Perugia, Italy
Ginevra Balletto	University of Cagliari, Italy
Marialaura Bancheri	ISAFOM, National Research Council, Italy
Benedetto Barabino	University of Brescia, Italy
Simona Barbaro	Università degli Studi di Palermo, Italy
Enrico Barbierato	Università Cattolica del Sacro Cuore di Milano, Italy
Jeniffer Barreto	Istituto Superior Técnico, Lisboa, Portugal
Michele Bartalini	TAGES, Italy
Socrates Basbas	Aristotle University of Thessaloniki, Greece
Silvia Battino	University of Sassari, Italy
Marcelo Becerra Rozas	Pontificia Universidad Católica de Valparaíso, Chile
Ranjan Kumar Behera	National Institute of Technology, Rourkela, India
Emanuele Bellini	University of Campania Luigi Vanvitelli, Italy
Massimo Bilancia	University of Bari Aldo Moro, Italy
Giulio Biondi	University of Firenze, Italy
Adriano Bisello	Eurac Research, Italy
Ignacio Blanquer	Universitat Politècnica de València, Spain
Semen Bochkov	Ulyanovsk State Technical University, Russia
Alexander Bogdanov	St. Petersburg University, Russia
Silvia Bonettini	University of Modena and Reggio Emilia, Italy
Enrico Borgogno Mondino	Università di Torino, Italy
Giuseppe Borruso	University of Trieste, Italy

Michele Bottazzi	University of Trento, Italy
Rahma Bouaziz	Taibah University, Saudi Arabia
Ouafik Boulariah	University of Salerno, Italy
Tulin Boyar	Yildiz Technical University, Turkey
Ana Cristina Braga	University of Minho, Portugal
Paolo Bragolusi	University of Padova, Italy
Luca Braidotti	University of Trieste, Italy
Alessandro Buccini	University of Cagliari, Italy
Jorge Buele	Universidad Tecnológica Indoamérica, Ecuador
Andrea Buffoni	TAGES, Italy
Sergio Vincenzo Calcina	University of Cagliari, Italy
Michele Campagna	University of Cagliari, Italy
Lelio Campanile	Università degli Studi della Campania Luigi Vanvitelli, Italy
Tiziana Campisi	Kore University of Enna, Italy
Antonino Canale	Kore University of Enna, Italy
Elena Cantatore	DICATECh, Polytechnic University of Bari, Italy
Pasquale Cantiello	Istituto Nazionale di Geofisica e Vulcanologia, Italy
Alessandra Capolupo	Polytechnic University of Bari, Italy
David Michele Cappelletti	University of Perugia, Italy
Caterina Caprioli	Politecnico di Torino, Italy
Sara Carcangiu	University of Cagliari, Italy
Pedro Carrasqueira	INESC Coimbra, Portugal
Arcangelo Castiglione	University of Salerno, Italy
Giulio Cavana	Politecnico di Torino, Italy
Davide Cerati	Politecnico di Milano, Italy
Maria Cerreta	University of Naples Federico II, Italy
Daniele Cesini	INFN-CNAF, Italy
Jabed Chowdhury	La Trobe University, Australia
Gennaro Ciccarelli	Iuav University of Venice, Italy
Birol Ciloglugil	Ege University, Turkey
Elena Cocuzza	Univesity of Catania, Italy
Anna Maria Colavitt	University of Cagliari, Italy
Cecilia Coletti	Università "G. d'Annunzio" di Chieti-Pescara, Italy
Alberto Collu	Independent Researcher, Italy
Anna Concas	University of Basilicata, Italy
Mauro Coni	University of Cagliari, Italy
Melchiorre Contino	Università di Palermo, Italy
Antonella Cornelio	Università degli Studi di Brescia, Italy
Aldina Correia	Politécnico do Porto, Portugal
Elisete Correia	Universidade de Trás-os-Montes e Alto Douro, Portugal
Florbela Correia	Polytechnic Institute of Viana do Castelo, Portugal
Stefano Corsi	Università degli Studi di Milano, Italy
Alberto Cortez	Polytechnic of University Coimbra, Portugal
Lino Costa	Universidade do Minho, Portugal

Alessandro Costantini	INFN, Italy
Marilena Cozzolino	Università del Molise, Italy
Giulia Crespi	Politecnico di Torino, Italy
Maurizio Crispino	Politecnico di Milano, Italy
Chiara D'Alpaos	University of Padova, Italy
Roberta D'Ambrosio	Università di Salerno, Italy
Sebastiano D'Amico	University of Malta, Malta
Hiroshi Daisaka	Hitotsubashi University, Japan
Gaia Daldanise	Italian National Research Council, Italy
Robertas Damasevicius	Silesian University of Technology, Poland
Maria Danese	ISPC, National Research Council, Italy
Bartoli Daniele	University of Perugia, Italy
Motasem Darwish	Middle East University, Jordan
Giulia Datola	Politecnico di Torino, Italy
Regina de Almeida	UTAD, Portugal
Elise de Doncker	Western Michigan University, USA
Mariella De Fino	Politecnico di Bari, Italy
Giandomenico De Luca	Mediterranean University of Reggio Calabria, Italy
Luiza de Macedo Mourelle	State University of Rio de Janeiro, Brazil
Gianluigi De Mare	University of Salerno, Italy
Itamir de Morais Barroca Filho	Federal University of Rio Grande do Norte, Brazil
Samuele De Petris	Università di Torino, Italy
Marcilio de Souto	LIFO, University of Orléans, France
Alexander Degtyarev	St. Petersburg University, Russia
Federico Dell'Anna	Politecnico di Torino, Italy
Marta Dell'Ovo	Politecnico di Milano, Italy
Fernanda Della Mura	University of Naples "Federico II", Italy
Ahu Dereli Dursun	Istanbul Commerce University, Turkey
Bashir Derradji	University of Sfax, Tunisia
Giulia Desogus	Università degli Studi di Cagliari, Italy
Marco Dettori	Università degli Studi di Sassari, Italy
Frank Devai	London South Bank University, UK
Felicia Di Liddo	Polytechnic University of Bari, Italy
Valerio Di Pinto	University of Naples "Federico II", Italy
Joana Dias	University of Coimbra, Portugal
Luis Dias	University of Minho, Portugal
Patricia Diaz de Alba	Gran Sasso Science Institute, Italy
Isabel Dimas	University of Coimbra, Portugal
Aleksandra Djordjevic	University of Belgrade, Serbia
Luigi Dolores	Università degli Studi di Salerno, Italy
Marco Donatelli	University of Insubria, Italy
Doina Cristina Duma	INFN-CNAF, Italy
Fabio Durastante	University of Pisa, Italy
Aziz Dursun	Virginia Tech University, USA
Juan Enrique-Romero	Université Grenoble Alpes, France

Annunziata Esposito Amideo	University College Dublin, Ireland
Dario Esposito	Polytechnic University of Bari, Italy
Claudio Estatico	University of Genova, Italy
Noelia Faginas-Lago	Università di Perugia, Italy
Maria Irene Falcão	University of Minho, Portugal
Stefano Falcinelli	University of Perugia, Italy
Alessandro Farina	University of Pisa, Italy
Grazia Fattoruso	ENEA, Italy
Caterina Fenu	University of Cagliari, Italy
Luisa Fermo	University of Cagliari, Italy
Florbela Fernandes	Instituto Politecnico de Braganca, Portugal
Rosário Fernandes	University of Minho, Portugal
Luis Fernandez-Sanz	University of Alcala, Spain
Alessia Ferrari	Università di Parma, Italy
Luís Ferrás	University of Minho, Portugal
Ângela Ferreira	Instituto Politécnico de Bragança, Portugal
Flora Ferreira	University of Minho, Portugal
Manuel Carlos Figueiredo	University of Minho, Portugal
Ugo Fiore	University of Naples "Parthenope", Italy
Amedeo Flora	University of Basilicata, Italy
Hector Florez	Universidad Distrital Francisco Jose de Caldas, Colombia
Maria Laura Foddis	University of Cagliari, Italy
Valentina Franzoni	Perugia University, Italy
Adelaide Freitas	University of Aveiro, Portugal
Samuel Frimpong	Durban University of Technology, South Africa
Ioannis Fyrogenis	Aristotle University of Thessaloniki, Greece
Marika Gaballo	Politecnico di Torino, Italy
Laura Gabrielli	Iuav University of Venice, Italy
Ivan Gankevich	St. Petersburg University, Russia
Chiara Garau	University of Cagliari, Italy
Ernesto Garcia Para	Universidad del País Vasco, Spain,
Fernando Garrido	Universidad Técnica del Norte, Ecuador
Marina Gavrilova	University of Calgary, Canada
Silvia Gazzola	University of Bath, UK
Georgios Georgiadis	Aristotle University of Thessaloniki, Greece
Osvaldo Gervasi	University of Perugia, Italy
Andrea Gioia	Polytechnic University of Bari, Italy
Dario Gioia	ISPC-CNT, Italy
Raffaele Giordano	IRSS, National Research Council, Italy
Giacomo Giorgi	University of Perugia, Italy
Eleonora Giovene di Girasole	IRISS, National Research Council, Italy
Salvatore Giuffrida	Università di Catania, Italy
Marco Gola	Politecnico di Milano, Italy

A. Manuela Gonçalves	University of Minho, Portugal
Yuriy Gorbachev	Coddan Technologies LLC, Russia
Angela Gorgoglione	Universidad de la República, Uruguay
Yusuke Gotoh	Okayama University, Japan
Anestis Gourgiotis	University of Thessaly, Greece
Valery Grishkin	St. Petersburg University, Russia
Alessandro Grottesi	CINECA, Italy
Eduardo Guerra	Free University of Bozen-Bolzano, Italy
Ayse Giz Gulnerman	Ankara HBV University, Turkey
Sevin Gümgüm	Izmir University of Economics, Turkey
Himanshu Gupta	BITS Pilani, Hyderabad, India
Sandra Haddad	Arab Academy for Science, Egypt
Malgorzata Hanzl	Lodz University of Technology, Poland
Shoji Hashimoto	KEK, Japan
Peter Hegedus	University of Szeged, Hungary
Eligius M. T. Hendrix	Universidad de Málaga, Spain
Edmond Ho	Northumbria University, UK
Guan Yue Hong	Western Michigan University, USA
Vito Iacobellis	Polytechnic University of Bari, Italy
Mauro Iacono	Università degli Studi della Campania, Italy
Chiara Iacovino	University of Basilicata, Italy
Antonino Iannuzzo	ETH Zurich, Switzerland
Ali Idri	University Mohammed V, Morocco
Oana-Ramona Ilovan	Babeş-Bolyai University, Romania
Mustafa Inceoglu	Ege University, Turkey
Tadashi Ishikawa	KEK, Japan
Federica Isola	University of Cagliari, Italy
Irena Itova	University of Westminster, UK
Edgar David de Izeppi	VTTI, USA
Marija Jankovic	CERTH, Greece
Adrian Jaramillo	Universidad Tecnológica Metropolitana, Chile
Monalisa Jena	Fakir Mohan University, India
Dorota Kamrowska-Załuska	Gdansk University of Technology, Poland
Issaku Kanamori	RIKEN Center for Computational Science, Japan
Korhan Karabulut	Yasar University, Turkey
Yeliz Karaca	University of Massachusetts Medical School, USA
Vicky Katsoni	University of West Attica, Greece
Dimitris Kavroudakis	University of the Aegean, Greece
Shuhei Kimura	Okayama University, Japan
Joanna Kolozej	Cracow University of Technology, Poland
Vladimir Korkhov	St. Petersburg University, Russia
Thales Körting	INPE, Brazil
Tomonori Kouya	Shizuoka Institute of Science and Technology, Japan
Sylwia Krzysztofik	Lodz University of Technology, Poland
Nataliia Kulabukhova	St. Petersburg University, Russia
Shrinivas B. Kulkarni	SDM College of Engineering and Technology, India

Pavan Kumar	University of Calgary, Canada
Anisha Kumari	National Institute of Technology, Rourkela, India
Ludovica La Rocca	University of Naples "Federico II", Italy
Daniele La Rosa	University of Catania, Italy
Sabrina Lai	University of Cagliari, Italy
Giuseppe Francesco Cesare Lama	University of Naples "Federico II", Italy
Mariusz Lamprecht	University of Lodz, Poland
Vincenzo Laporta	National Research Council, Italy
Chien-Sing Lee	Sunway University, Malaysia
José Isaac Lemus Romani	Pontifical Catholic University of Valparaíso, Chile
Federica Leone	University of Cagliari, Italy
Alexander H. Levis	George Mason University, USA
Carola Lingua	Polytechnic University of Turin, Italy
Marco Locurcio	Polytechnic University of Bari, Italy
Andrea Lombardi	University of Perugia, Italy
Savino Longo	University of Bari, Italy
Fernando Lopez Gayarre	University of Oviedo, Spain
Yan Lu	Western Michigan University, USA
Maria Macchiaroli	University of Salerno, Italy
Helmuth Malonek	University of Aveiro, Portugal
Francesca Maltinti	University of Cagliari, Italy
Luca Mancini	University of Perugia, Italy
Marcos Mandado	University of Vigo, Spain
Ernesto Marcheggiani	Università Politecnica delle Marche, Italy
Krassimir Markov	University of Telecommunications and Post, Bulgaria
Giovanni Martinelli	INGV, Italy
Alessandro Marucci	University of L'Aquila, Italy
Fiammetta Marulli	University of Campania Luigi Vanvitelli, Italy
Gabriella Maselli	University of Salerno, Italy
Rytis Maskeliunas	Kaunas University of Technology, Lithuania
Michele Mastroianni	University of Campania Luigi Vanvitelli, Italy
Cristian Mateos	Universidad Nacional del Centro de la Provincia de Buenos Aires, Argentina
Hideo Matsufuru	High Energy Accelerator Research Organization (KEK), Japan
D'Apuzzo Mauro	University of Cassino and Southern Lazio, Italy
Chiara Mazzarella	University Federico II, Italy
Marco Mazzarino	University of Venice, Italy
Giovanni Mei	University of Cagliari, Italy
Mário Melo	Federal Institute of Rio Grande do Norte, Brazil
Francesco Mercaldo	University of Molise, Italy
Alfredo Milani	University of Perugia, Italy
Alessandra Milesi	University of Cagliari, Italy
Antonio Minervino	ISPC, National Research Council, Italy
Fernando Miranda	Universidade do Minho, Portugal

B. Mishra	University of Szeged, Hungary
Sanjay Misra	Covenant University, Nigeria
Mirka Mobilia	University of Salerno, Italy
Giuseppe Modica	Università degli Studi di Reggio Calabria, Italy
Mohammadsadegh Mohagheghi	Vali-e-Asr University of Rafsanjan, Iran
Mohamad Molaei Qelichi	University of Tehran, Iran
Mario Molinara	University of Cassino and Southern Lazio, Italy
Augusto Montisci	Università degli Studi di Cagliari, Italy
Pierluigi Morano	Polytechnic University of Bari, Italy
Ricardo Moura	Universidade Nova de Lisboa, Portugal
Ana Clara Mourao Moura	Federal University of Minas Gerais, Brazil
Maria Mourao	Polytechnic Institute of Viana do Castelo, Portugal
Daichi Mukunoki	RIKEN Center for Computational Science, Japan
Beniamino Murgante	University of Basilicata, Italy
Naohito Nakasato	University of Aizu, Japan
Grazia Napoli	Università degli Studi di Palermo, Italy
Isabel Cristina Natário	Universidade Nova de Lisboa, Portugal
Nadia Nedjah	State University of Rio de Janeiro, Brazil
Antonio Nesticò	University of Salerno, Italy
Andreas Nikiforiadis	Aristotle University of Thessaloniki, Greece
Keigo Nitadori	RIKEN Center for Computational Science, Japan
Silvio Nocera	Iuav University of Venice, Italy
Giuseppina Oliva	University of Salerno, Italy
Arogundade Oluwasefunmi	Academy of Mathematics and System Science, China
Ken-ichi Oohara	University of Tokyo, Japan
Tommaso Orusa	University of Turin, Italy
M. Fernanda P. Costa	University of Minho, Portugal
Roberta Padulano	Centro Euro-Mediterraneo sui Cambiamenti Climatici, Italy
Maria Panagiotopoulou	National Technical University of Athens, Greece
Jay Pancham	Durban University of Technology, South Africa
Gianni Pantaleo	University of Florence, Italy
Dimos Pantazis	University of West Attica, Greece
Michela Paolucci	University of Florence, Italy
Eric Pardede	La Trobe University, Australia
Olivier Parisot	Luxembourg Institute of Science and Technology, Luxembourg
Vincenzo Pellecchia	Ente Idrico Campano, Italy
Anna Pelosi	University of Salerno, Italy
Edit Pengő	University of Szeged, Hungary
Marco Pepe	University of Salerno, Italy
Paola Perchinunno	University of Cagliari, Italy
Ana Pereira	Polytechnic Institute of Bragança, Portugal
Mariano Pernetti	University of Campania, Italy
Damiano Perri	University of Perugia, Italy

Federica Pes	University of Cagliari, Italy
Marco Petrelli	Roma Tre University, Italy
Massimiliano Petri	University of Pisa, Italy
Khiem Phan	Duy Tan University, Vietnam
Alberto Ferruccio Piccinni	Polytechnic of Bari, Italy
Angela Pilogallo	University of Basilicata, Italy
Francesco Pinna	University of Cagliari, Italy
Telmo Pinto	University of Coimbra, Portugal
Luca Piroddi	University of Cagliari, Italy
Darius Plonis	Vilnius Gediminas Technical University, Lithuania
Giuliano Poli	University of Naples "Federico II", Italy
Maria João Polidoro	Polytecnic Institute of Porto, Portugal
Ioannis Politis	Aristotle University of Thessaloniki, Greece
Maurizio Pollino	ENEA, Italy
Antonio Pratelli	University of Pisa, Italy
Salvatore Praticò	Mediterranean University of Reggio Calabria, Italy
Marco Prato	University of Modena and Reggio Emilia, Italy
Carlotta Quagliolo	Polytechnic University of Turin, Italy
Emanuela Quaquero	Univesity of Cagliari, Italy
Garrisi Raffaele	Polizia postale e delle Comunicazioni, Italy
Nicoletta Rassu	University of Cagliari, Italy
Hafiz Tayyab Rauf	University of Bradford, UK
Michela Ravanelli	Sapienza University of Rome, Italy
Roberta Ravanelli	Sapienza University of Rome, Italy
Alfredo Reder	Centro Euro-Mediterraneo sui Cambiamenti Climatici, Italy
Stefania Regalbuto	University of Naples "Federico II", Italy
Rommel Regis	Saint Joseph's University, USA
Lothar Reichel	Kent State University, USA
Marco Reis	University of Coimbra, Portugal
Maria Reitano	University of Naples "Federico II", Italy
Jerzy Respondek	Silesian University of Technology, Poland
Elisa Riccietti	École Normale Supérieure de Lyon, France
Albert Rimola	Universitat Autònoma de Barcelona, Spain
Angela Rizzo	University of Bari, Italy
Ana Maria A. C. Rocha	University of Minho, Portugal
Fabio Rocha	Institute of Technology and Research, Brazil
Humberto Rocha	University of Coimbra, Portugal
Maria Clara Rocha	Polytechnic Institute of Coimbra, Portugal
Miguel Rocha	University of Minho, Portugal
Giuseppe Rodriguez	University of Cagliari, Italy
Guillermo Rodriguez	UNICEN, Argentina
Elisabetta Ronchieri	INFN, Italy
Marzio Rosi	University of Perugia, Italy
Silvia Rossetti	University of Parma, Italy
Marco Rossitti	Polytechnic University of Milan, Italy

Francesco Rotondo	Marche Polytechnic University, Italy
Irene Rubino	Polytechnic University of Turin, Italy
Agustín Salas	Pontifical Catholic University of Valparaíso, Chile
Juan Pablo Sandoval Alcocer	Universidad Católica Boliviana "San Pablo", Bolivia
Luigi Santopietro	University of Basilicata, Italy
Rafael Santos	National Institute for Space Research, Brazil
Valentino Santucci	Università per Stranieri di Perugia, Italy
Mirko Saponaro	Polytechnic University of Bari, Italy
Filippo Sarvia	University of Turin, Italy
Marco Scaioni	Polytechnic University of Milan, Italy
Rafal Scherer	Częstochowa University of Technology, Poland
Francesco Scorza	University of Basilicata, Italy
Ester Scotto di Perta	University of Napoli "Federico II", Italy
Monica Sebillo	University of Salerno, Italy
Patrizia Serra	University of Cagliari, Italy
Ricardo Severino	University of Minho, Portugal
Jie Shen	University of Michigan, USA
Huahao Shou	Zhejiang University of Technology, China
Miltiadis Siavvas	Centre for Research and Technology Hellas, Greece
Brandon Sieu	University of Calgary, Canada
Ângela Silva	Instituto Politécnico de Viana do Castelo, Portugal
Carina Silva	Polytechic Institute of Lisbon, Portugal
Joao Carlos Silva	Polytechnic Institute of Cavado and Ave, Portugal
Fabio Silveira	Federal University of Sao Paulo, Brazil
Marco Simonetti	University of Florence, Italy
Ana Jacinta Soares	University of Minho, Portugal
Maria Joana Soares	University of Minho, Portugal
Michel Soares	Federal University of Sergipe, Brazil
George Somarakis	Foundation for Research and Technology Hellas, Greece
Maria Somma	University of Naples "Federico II", Italy
Alberico Sonnessa	Polytechnic University of Bari, Italy
Elena Stankova	St. Petersburg University, Russia
Flavio Stochino	University of Cagliari, Italy
Anastasia Stratigea	National Technical University of Athens, Greece
Yasuaki Sumida	Kyushu Sangyo University, Japan
Yue Sun	European X-Ray Free-Electron Laser Facility, Germany
Kirill Sviatov	Ulyanovsk State Technical University, Russia
Daisuke Takahashi	University of Tsukuba, Japan
Aladics Tamás	University of Szeged, Hungary
David Taniar	Monash University, Australia
Rodrigo Tapia McClung	Centro de Investigación en Ciencias de Información Geoespacial, Mexico
Eufemia Tarantino	Polytechnic University of Bari, Italy

Sergio Tasso	University of Perugia, Italy
Ana Paula Teixeira	Universidade de Trás-os-Montes e Alto Douro, Portugal
Senhorinha Teixeira	University of Minho, Portugal
Tengku Adil Tengku Izhar	Universiti Teknologi MARA, Malaysia
Maria Filomena Teodoro	University of Lisbon/Portuguese Naval Academy, Portugal
Giovanni Tesoriere	Kore University of Enna, Italy
Yiota Theodora	National Technical Univeristy of Athens, Greece
Graça Tomaz	Polytechnic Institute of Guarda, Portugal
Carmelo Maria Torre	Polytechnic University of Bari, Italy
Francesca Torrieri	University of Naples "Federico II", Italy
Vincenza Torrisi	University of Catania, Italy
Vincenzo Totaro	Polytechnic University of Bari, Italy
Pham Trung	Ho Chi Minh City University of Technology, Vietnam
Dimitrios Tsoukalas	Centre of Research and Technology Hellas (CERTH), Greece
Sanjida Tumpa	University of Calgary, Canada
Iñaki Tuñon	Universidad de Valencia, Spain
Takahiro Ueda	Seikei University, Japan
Piero Ugliengo	University of Turin, Italy
Abdi Usman	Haramaya University, Ethiopia
Ettore Valente	University of Naples "Federico II", Italy
Jordi Vallverdu	Universitat Autònoma de Barcelona, Spain
Cornelis Van Der Mee	University of Cagliari, Italy
José Varela-Aldás	Universidad Tecnológica Indoamérica, Ecuador
Fanny Vazart	University of Grenoble Alpes, France
Franco Vecchiocattivi	University of Perugia, Italy
Laura Verde	University of Campania Luigi Vanvitelli, Italy
Giulia Vergerio	Polytechnic University of Turin, Italy
Jos Vermaseren	Nikhef, The Netherlands
Giacomo Viccione	University of Salerno, Italy
Marco Vizzari	University of Perugia, Italy
Corrado Vizzarri	Polytechnic University of Bari, Italy
Alexander Vodyaho	St. Petersburg State Electrotechnical University "LETI", Russia
Nikolay N. Voit	Ulyanovsk State Technical University, Russia
Marco Vona	University of Basilicata, Italy
Agustinus Borgy Waluyo	Monash University, Australia
Fernando Wanderley	Catholic University of Pernambuco, Brazil
Chao Wang	University of Science and Technology of China, China
Marcin Wozniak	Silesian University of Technology, Poland
Tiang Xian	Nathong University, China
Rekha Yadav	KL University, India
Claudia Yamu	University of Groningen, The Netherlands
Fenghui Yao	Tennessee State University, USA

Contents – Part X

International Workshop on Smart Tourism (SmartTourism 2021)

**International Workshop on Space Syntax for Cities in Theory
and Practice (Syntax_City 2021)**

**International Workshop on Theoretical and Computational Chemistry
and Its Applications (TCCMA 2021)**

International Workshop on Urban Space Accessibility and Safety (USAS 2021)

International Workshop on Smart and Sustainable Island Communities (SSIC 2021)

Practices for an Integrated Planning Between Urban Planning and Green Infrastructures for the Development of the Municipal Urban Plan (MUP) of Cagliari (Italy)

Chiara Garau[1] , Giulia Desogus[1](✉) , Francesca Maltinti[1](✉) ,
Alessandro Olivo[1] , Laura Peretti[2], and Mauro Coni[1]

[1] Department of Civil and Environmental Engineering and Architecture (DICAAR),
University of Cagliari, 09129 Cagliari, Italy
{g.desogus,maltinti}@unica.it
[2] Independent Researcher, LAURA PERETTI Architects, Roma, Italy

Abstract. As underlined by the European Commission in Green Infrastructure (GI) - Enhancing Europe's Natural Capital (2013), in Europe, solutions based on green infrastructures are particularly used in urban areas to reduce pollution and health problems related to population growth, and to the settlement concentration of activities and residences. With this paper, the authors evaluate the link between the old sectoral model of infrastructure planning and a more functional one, based on the new green infrastructure paradigms used in different European cities. The main aim is to understand how these paradigms can improve the viability and the quality of life of the population in a coastal city with a particular frame on sustainability. To this end, starting from national and international examples, the authors outline typologies of integrated planning between urban planning and green infrastructures with particular reference to the relationship between historic city and waterfront in coastal cities. Subsequently, these typologies will be applied to the case study of Cagliari (Sardinia, Italy) as a tool to mitigate the fragmentation and unsustainable use of the soil with a particular frame in achieving the Sustainable Development Goals (SDGs). This allowed not only to study a model for the city of Cagliari for the regeneration of waterfront urban areas, but also for developing a system of green infrastructures capable of minimizing travel times within the city and of increasing the accessibility of slow mobility. This paper shows a first phase of research as part of the ongoing elaboration of the Municipal Urban Plan (MUP) of Cagliari.

This paper is the result of the joint work of the authors. 'Abstract' 'Overpass or Underpass? National and International Practices on Green Infrastructure Connecting City and Waterfront', and 'Proposals for the infrastructural redevelopment of the Cagliari waterfront for the Municipal Urban Plan (MUP)' were written jointly by the authors. Chiara Garau wrote the 'Introduction'. Giulia Desogus wrote the 'Description of the case study of Cagliari (Italy)' and Mauro Coni wrote the 'Conclusions'.

Keywords: Green infrastructure · Accessibility · Slow mobility · MUP · Waterfront · Coastal cities

1 Introduction

Today cities represent less than 2% of the total world territory, but have about 55% of the world population with a level of urbanization that is expected to reach almost 70% by 2050 [1]. Cities also develop through an organized physical layout and a road interconnection system in which roads particularly play a fundamental role, as they interconnect places, people and goods, thus facilitating trade, social interaction and mobility. All of this requires effective management by national and local authorities to make cities and human settlements inclusive, safe, long-lasting and sustainable [2]. In fact, in accordance with the Sustainable Development Goals (SDGs) (particularly with Goal 11), by 2030 cities will have to increase inclusive and sustainable urbanization by providing access not only to safe, sustainable and affordable for all but also to safe and inclusive public green spaces through integrated policies and plans towards inclusion and efficiency [3].

Mobility must therefore become a primary factor also considering social inclusion as a tool for improving the environmental, social and economic well-being of communities and not focusing exclusively on transferring people [3]. From this point of view, in a city the spaces intended for transport infrastructures should be designed on a human scale to perform a collective function through integrated mobility between multiple transport systems to offer people different, efficient and pleasant options. In fact, urban planning strategies, correlated to the smart city model [4, 5], are leading local institutions to use social capital to improve city services [6, 7]. These services are especially related to mobility including urban accessibility, infrastructure of traditional transport communication, the availability of ICT infrastructures, sustainable, innovative and safe transport systems [8, 9]. The infrastructures should therefore be interpreted as socially active connection networks in which the functions of streets and squares must have the aim of improving the needs and perceptions of citizens [4]. They should be thought of as relational spaces in which the interactions of pedestrians become one of the primary objectives of their design. In the United Nations report "Streets as Public Spaces and Drivers of Urban Prosperity", this concept has been highlighted since 2013. It is stated that "streets, as public spaces, have lost importance in terms of shared surface and in their primary role in formation of the culture and history of the city" [10].

These premises lead to think about green infrastructures. Starting from 2011, the European Union recognizes them as a network of natural or semi-natural areas, which, if strategically planned with other environmental elements, can become an effective tool for obtaining ecological, economic and social benefits. Furthermore, they constitute a strategy aimed at reconnecting natural areas with urban centers and at restoring and improving their functional role [11]. The "Green Infrastructure Handbook" [12] argues that green infrastructures vary in the scales at which they can be identified and planned. At the urban level it is possible to design artificial connectivity elements: they are "elements made by man with the aim of facilitating the passage of species in a territory, including green bridges and eco-pipelines to bypass transport infrastructures and stairs for ichthyofauna, where natural movement is prevented by human activities and settlements" [13, p. 9]. The inclusion of these elements in cities would reduce pollution and health problems related to the growth of the population, and would also promote sociability and pedestrian use of the street.

Furthermore, as numerous examples in the world demonstrate (Barcelona, Marseille, etc.), in the case of a coastal city, these elements make possible to connect the built city with water through a sustainable design of the waterfront. In fact, through green infrastructures (eco-pipelines or green bridges) these areas take on a strategic dimension especially in terms of environmental and social sustainability that has increasingly made possible to involve the entire area in the urban system behind it, even on a metropolitan scale. In other words, the seafront with the inclusion of sustainable connection infrastructures can be understood as an integral part of the large urban system and as a hinge and junction of mediation with the static nature of the urban territory.

Starting from these assumptions, the goal of this study is to highlight how it is possible to improve urban mobility, through an integrated design between urban planning and green infrastructure. The intent of this article is to answer the following question: is it possible to read, design, interpret the streets as places of relationship and not exclusively as places of transition or separation?

Therefore, this paper focuses on how, in a coastal city, the design of infrastructures can radically change the relationship between the built city and the waterfront, by favouring the union and interpenetration of the two ones. To do this, this study initially focuses on the description of the Cagliari case study, highlighting the current conformation of the area facing the waterfront (paragraph 2). Subsequently, the authors analyse some national and international projects by comparing the positive and negative aspects of the overpass and underpass to unite city and waterfront (paragraph 3). In light of this, Sect. 4 proposes a functional redevelopment of the viability of the Cagliari waterfront as the first starting point for the development of the Municipal Urban Plan (MUP). The document concludes by emphasizing the need for a functional interplay between port infrastructure, waterfront and urban fabric through a massive change in traffic, projected towards sustainable development.

2 Description of the Case Study of Cagliari (Italy)

The Cagliari case study is a significant example because, as a reference city for the whole of Sardinia, starting from the 1960s the population moved from rural areas to the city, and now 1/4 of the Sardinian population lives in its Metropolitan area [14, 15]. This has had a negative impact of rapid urbanization and high traffic in a city characterized by an urban structure typical of a coastal city [16].

With art. 17 of the Regional Law 4 February 2016, n. 2 "Reorganization of the local autonomy system of Sardinia" the city of Cagliari has become the capital of the metropolitan city of Cagliari (constituted by seventeen municipalities with approximately 432,000 inhabitants). This has caused a further increase in the problems linked to commuting with a high prevalence of private vehicles and with a public transport not adequate to meet the demands [17]. This is also the result of the wrong transport policies of the 1980s when cars were allowed to enter the city by occupying pedestrian areas and squares. "The result of these policies was that until 2010 Cagliari was characterized by the absence of pedestrian areas, restricted traffic areas and cycle infrastructures. At the same time, an important urban tram network was abolished. Consequently, the Cagliari recorded a loss of social relations, culture and peculiarities of the community" [3, p. 557]. Furthermore, Cagliari is the largest city in Sardinia with an area of 85.01 km^2 and a population of approximately 151,000 inhabitants. Cagliari has a strong link with nature not only because it is coastal but above all because within it several Special Protection Areas (SPAs) and Sites of Community Importance (SIC) are present.

This environmental heritage is projected on the Gulf of Cagliari through the port system which becomes (i) the neuralgic center between the built city and its projection on the sea; (ii) an integral part of the vast area; (iii) a hinge and junction of economic mediation with the hinterland of southern Sardinia. These characteristics form a city characterized by a strong link between city and nature which should also be enhanced by considering the relationship that the city has with its metropolitan area.

An emblematic example of the relationship between city and nature is the large area that goes from *piazza Matteotti* to the *Sant'Elia* Stadium (streets, squares and places are deliberately left in Italian throughout the paper, so as not to lose the identity of the places) passing through the Port of Cagliari and *via Roma* which represents a nodal point not only for the city of Cagliari and its metropolitan area, but for the whole of Sardinia (Fig. 1). In fact, it hosts the most important port center in the south of the island where the highest concentration of inhabitants converges, with the most relevant indices of industrialization, of the commercial service sector and production in the agricultural sector [18]. Furthermore, the port front on the *via Roma* is the area of greatest interest both from a historical point of view and for its strong interrelation with the whole city. This area, in recent decades, has undergone various transformations [19] which have significantly improved urban use.

Fig. 1. The waterfront of Cagliari. Relation between historic city and sea. Source: elaboration by the authors

These can be summarized in [18]:

1. The demolition of the separation wall between *via Roma* and the port area subject to customs control has allowed the opening of the seafront to the city. This opening made the water in front of it usable after the construction of the mooring piers for pleasure boats.
2. East side of *via Roma*:

   2.a The arrangement of the Ichnusa Pier with the building of the maritime station, currently used for cultural and recreational activities, and the construction of a long pedestrian walkway over the sea in front of the fence of the naval base to connect the Ichnusa Pier to the Bonaria zone;
   2.b The requalification of the *Su Siccu* pinewood and of the park on the sea in front of the Basilica of Bonaria;
   2.c The ongoing design of the *Su Siccu* strip where the sports clubs are located, the Sant'Elmo Basin and the *Padiglione Nervi*;
   2.d The waterfront equipped with cycle paths to the Sant'Elia district and cultural promotion in the old *Lazzaretto* complex.

3. West side of *via Roma*:

   3.a The *Rinascita* Pier, equipped for the reception of large cruise ships.
   3.b The *Porto Canale* area, with quays equipped for unloading and loading of containers and for secondary handling of goods in transit through transhipment. In it are located, with dedicated basins, the maritime structures of finance and the operational structures of the Harbor Master's Office.
   3.c The start of the ministerial and regional procedure for the establishment of a Customs Free Zone. It should give, through the competitiveness of the *Porto Canale*, new opportunities for international movement and substantial economic implications in the hinterland of the island.

From the list of public works realised in the port complex, the positivity of the system and the connective articulated between land and water can be assessed. But after the realization of these works, it becomes even more important to guarantee in the area a precise policy based on infrastructures that allow, at the same time, a fast traffic flow (to dispose of the traffic linked to the station and the port area with the cruise terminal) and a design for the area with a soft mobility.

These reflections lead the authors to evaluate sustainable solutions for this area that make possible to implement the relationship between water and city. With this in mind, an extensive national and international experience in the transport sector exists [20] on the implementation of green infrastructures linked to the design of underpasses and overpasses. In the waterfront area of Cagliari, these infrastructures can improve the general viability of the area under study, and also can create interdependence with the surrounding environment. This would ensure added value to the city and its relationship between the historic city and the waterfront. For this reason, the authors studied several case studies for the design of the Cagliari waterfront. They are illustrated in the next section and highlighted the positive and negative aspects of the overpasses and underpasses in the cities with similar problems of Cagliari.

3   Overpass or Underpass? National and International Practices on Green Infrastructure Connecting City and Waterfront

At the national and international level, there are several examples of cities that have significantly changed their structure through infrastructures (underpasses and overpasses). These allowed the development of settlements and urbanization to be controlled [21]. With the aim of understanding how these infrastructures can become a tool for sustainable development in a maritime city, the authors focus on the positive and negative aspects of underpasses and overpasses from a perspective of sustainability and connection between city and nature. To do this, five national and international case studies are analysed (Genoa, Naples in Italy, Barcelona and Madrid in Spain and New York in the United States). These case studies allow not only to have a broader framework of how these cities have chosen their infrastructure, but also to understand the opportunities of connecting the historic city with its waterfront. For the overpasses, the Genoa project allows to understand how the infrastructure, through a single hub, can connect the city and the port. The Naples project, on the other hand, allows to reflect on how the relationship above/below the flyover can work as an opportunity for car/pedestrian connection. The underpasses are studied through the projects of Madrid (emblematic example of green connection infrastructure between two well-established city sections), of New York, by considering Central Park (example of connection between urban viability and internal viability of the park) and of Barcelona (example of connection between sliding and local roads through an underpass). This projects and their analysis of the strengths and weaknesses of underpasses and overpasses, therefore, allows to have a more precise framework of the connection methods that identify best practices in relation to two fundamental elements for the objective of this work: [1] the function and intended use of the transport infrastructure [2] and the potential repercussions that a new appearance of the road infrastructure can bring to the relationship between built cities and natural and maritime environment.

Genoa: The Relationship Between the Port and the Historic City Through the Connection of the Flyover Called "Sopraelevata". The "Sopraelevata" inaugurated in 1965, was designed with the aim of disposing the traffic crossing of Genoa which was increasing immeasurably between the end of the fifties and the beginning of the sixties, with the spread of mass motorization. Its construction was already foreseen by the general master plan adopted in 1956 and was definitively approved by the Ministry of Public Works in 1959 [22]. In 2004, for "Genoa European Capital of Culture", a total transformation of the city's waterfront took place, by modifying the previous sense that the Sopraelevata used to have as a dividing element between the city and the port.

In fact, Renzo Piano's project that connects the historic center to the sea has transformed the historic port from a port area to an urban area (Fig. 2) through the design of an urban port park [23–25]. This urban port park moved "the center of gravity of the city towards the sea, with positive repercussions both on the recovery process of the

Fig. 2. Case study 1 _ Genoa. Relation between the port and the historic city through the flyover called "Sopraelevata". Source: elaboration by "LAURA PERETTI_architects"

neighbouring historic center and, above all, on the relationship between the city and the sea. In essence, the city was able to begin to interface with its sea and to create a direct iteration with it" [25, p. 3]. Currently, the "Sopraelevata", which has 3 other levels of roads below the aquarium, is the only pedestrian point of contact between the historic city and the sea.

Naples: The Relationship and Use of the Above and Below the Flyover. The project analyses the function of the infrastructure and in particular the use and intended use of the above and below the elevation. The flyover of Naples highlights the complex pedestrian/car relationship which over the years has transformed into a long strip of decay that entered into the city (Fig. 3) and which has given rise to a sort of no man's land difficult to manage below the infrastructure.

Fig. 3. Case study 2 _ Naples. Relationship and use of the above and below the infrastructure. Source: elaboration by "LAURA PERETTI_architects"

These two projects illustrated some negative and positive aspects of the overpasses.

Table 1 clearly shows that the negatives outweigh the positives ones. The flyover allows a better connection between different parts of the city and between distant points, the possibility of avoiding demolition during construction and the possibility of using the above and below the infrastructure, However, the negative aspects are many, over the high percentage of urban decay that can occur under the flyover (such as in Naples). From the greater acoustic and environmental impact and the difficulties of maintaining the supporting structure, from a landscape point of view the overpass is a linear building that could significantly change the skyline of the city. In addition, in most cases this involves a doubling of the infrastructure on two or more levels.

In coastal cities, this becomes an even bigger problem. In fact, connecting the city and the waterfront, the linear road parallel to the sea creates an element of disconnection and not a union that must be resolved through the connecting hubs (such as Genoa). Furthermore, the structure creates a landscape different from the initial one, not making the city perceive by those arriving from the sea, or the sea by those who live in the city.

Table 1. Positive and negative aspects of the overpasses. Source: elaboration by the authors

Overpass	
Positive aspects	Negative aspects
1. Connection between different parts of the city	1. Significative maintenance of the supporting structure
2. Connection between distant points of the city	2. Acoustic impact amplification
3. Possibility of avoiding demolitions	3. Environmental impact amplification
4. Possibility of connections below	4. Greater dispersion of fine dust
	5. Intrusion in the skyline of a linear artifact
	6. Formation of ramps
	7. Formation of a "world below": urban decay
	8. Usual doubling of the linear infrastructure on two or more levels

Madrid: The Underpass as a Connection Between Parts of the City. The large urban arteries are treated as open rivers and the crossings are hubs that are always equal to the altitude of the city. This system is likewise adopted for pedestrians, creating urban continuity between the parts (Fig. 4). The strategic location of the market on the bridges favours the social and economic exchange between two adjacent districts of the city otherwise separated by the infrastructure.

Fig. 4. Case study 3 _ Madrid. The underpass as a connection between parts of the city. Source: elaboration by "LAURA PERETTI_architects"

New York. Connection Between Environment and City. The park, opened in 1856 with a project by Frederick Law Olmsted, is now characterized by a longitudinal and transversal road system with different functions (Fig. 5). The longitudinal direction is crossed by park ways used for internal uses, for the only passage of pedestrians and cycles. The great urban arteries cross it in a transverse direction. From south to north, they are located on 65th Street, 79th Street, 86th Street and 97th Street. Each street contains two lanes, one in each direction placed below the level of the rest of the park. In the four transversal streets the passage of cars takes place through a slight change in altitude, with the park becoming a sort of "anti-litteram ecoduct". Each of them represents a communication route between one side of the city and the other.

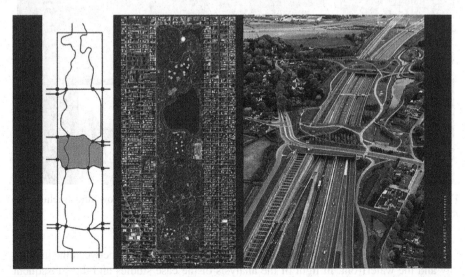

Fig. 5. Case study 4 _ New York, Central Park. Connection between environment and city. Source: elaboration by "LAURA PERETTI_architects"

Barcelona. Relationship and Use of the Above and Below Infrastructure Near the Sea. The case of Barcelona (Fig. 6) is completely different from the case studies previously described. In 1992, the Vila Olímpica, one of the many projects for the major urban restructuring for the Olympic Games, emerged as a hinge between the port and the historic city. Through the complete infrastructural reorganization "the site was enhanced by creating a pedestrian connection space where citizens practice outdoor sports and today it has become an attractive tourist center animated by numerous restaurants and clubs" [26, p. 83]. The project includes large green public areas that connect the city to the sea and it is interesting for the choice of mobility. In fact, the great sliding roadway passes underneath allowing to use the coast with a soft mobility. It is a worthy example of the relationship between two different types of mobility that still leave space for pedestrian use of the coast.

Table 2 shows several positive and negative aspects of the underpasses, highlighted by the analysed projects. Unlike the overpasses, these examples have more positive aspects. In fact, apart from the separation of joint areas and the formation of residual spaces, the underpasses offer better maintenance and better control of the environmental impact. From a landscape point of view, the underpasses maintain the indispensable view for maritime cities, preserving the urban horizon in a waterfront that wants to connect (even visibly) the historic city and water. Moreover, the negative aspects can be easily mitigated thanks to the construction of eco-pipelines that restore continuity between the neighbourhoods and limit the interluded spaces usually destined for urban decay.

Fig. 6. Case study 5 _ Barcelona. Relationship and use of the above and below infrastructure near the sea. Source: elaboration by "LAURA PERETTI_architects"

All case studies analysed allowed to think about the connection between the historic city and the waterfront. In light of the analysis of the case studies and the subsequent study on the strengths and weaknesses of the overpasses and underpasses for designing an infrastructure capable of connecting the historic city to the sea, the authors in the next

Table 2. Positive and negative aspects of the underpasses. Source: elaboration by the authors

Underpass	
Positive aspects	Negative aspects
1. Ease of maintenance	1. Separation between contiguous areas
2. Possibility of connections to the city elevation line	2. Formation of debris spaces for ramps
3. Reduction of acoustic impact	
4. Containment of fine dust	
5. Reduction of environmental impact	
6. Maintenance of the urban horizon	

section propose different proposals of an infrastructure redevelopment of the Cagliari waterfront showing a first phase of a research as part of the ongoing elaboration of the Municipal Urban Plan (MUP) of Cagliari.

4 Proposals for the Infrastructural Redevelopment of the Cagliari Waterfront for the Municipal Urban Plan (MUP)

Figure 7 shows the proposals of the authors, which include the coastal area from *piazza Matteotti* to *via Ferrara*. Seven proposals are foreseen for the functional requalification of the road infrastructure system, coherent and linked each other which will then be further explored in a subsequent phase. Each proposal consists of a critical area and deals with the critical points of the current road network, even disconnected from the sea (Fig. 7, proposals 6–7) but which, for design continuity, deserve no less attention in the relationship between the historic city and the sea.

Proposal 1 *"Piazza Matteotti"*. The piazza is an emblematic center of the city which, due to its presence from the station and the proximity of the cruise terminal, becomes an intermediate center characterised not only by the flow of people arriving from other parts of Sardinia but also by the flow of tourists from Italy and beyond. The proposal provides for pedestrian and vehicular flows between the station, the square (intermodal center) and an underground structure that allows cars to pass over and under pedestrians. The cars, in fact, remain on the surface and are sorted by a roundabout between the station, *piazza Matteotti* and the head of the intermodal center, thus building an underground pedestrian area.

Proposal 2 *"Via Roma"*. This street is characterised by arcaded buildings built between the end of the 19th century and the second half of the 20th century, interspersed with various alleys that rise towards the upper part of the historic city (the Marina district). The current road structure creates a strong separation between the historic city and the port, so as to make an urban redevelopment necessary. It should review the organization of the entire road network to promote the continuity of the space between the historic city

Fig. 7. The infrastructure redevelopment in seven proposals for the Cagliari waterfront. Source: elaboration by the authors

and the arcades of the buildings and between the latter and the port docks. The proposal foresees pedestrian and vehicular flows, transverse crossings and functional continuity of longitudinal flows. To do this, a solution is proposed: the idea is to do a lowering of the *via Roma* for a very limited stretch (250 m), by restoring completely the transversal continuity to the sea through the eco-pipelines.

In addition, restricted access roads for shops and the port may be envisaged in the area. In this way the street could become a unitary square with parking spaces under the street in a simple way, contextually to the excavation. An example of this modality can be found in Barcelona where the connection between the historic city and the port, in a wide band of 130 × 656 (Cagliari 110 × 474), is solved with only 2 crossings and the maintenance of many longitudinal flows both at an altitude of the city than at a slightly lower-level difference.

Proposal 3 "Darsena" (The Dock). It is characterised by a historic urban form which is currently surrounded by modern buildings of uneven quality and size. This context is crossed by the main flows of vehicular traffic coming and going from the city. The rear part of the Darsena has buildings of limited value and consistency. For design continuity, which sees the infrastructure of the area from *piazza Matteotti* to *via Ferrara*, the redevelopment could include the connection of *viale Diaz* and *viale Colombo* through v*ia Pirastu*. This would give the possibility of diverting vehicle flows, thus giving continuity on the transversal promenade on via Roma, increasing the freedom through a roundabout in *piazza Defenu*. Furthermore, this would give the possibility to pedestrianize the area of the Darsena.

Proposal 4 Basilica of the *"Madonna di Bonaria".* This proposal aims to re-join the path from the Basilica of Bonaria to the sea, currently separated from the vehicular flows of *viale Diaz* and *viale Colombo*. This is conceived with a redevelopment of the parking area as an urban place of transition and the organization of the sea urchin market that today takes place in the Bonaria pine forest. The passage that connects the basilica directly to the sea starts next to the monumental staircase. The parking area could be covered and could be used in a multifunctional way: the roof could remain viable as a public space.

Proposal 5 "Fiera and Porto". The proposal sees the connection between parts that today are completely disconnected from each other (the "fiera" complex, the sea and the port) as a continuation of proposal 4 (Madonna di Bonaria) which is part of the transversal crossings that reunite the city with the sea. The goal is to bring the perception of the sea into the city and to the Cagliari "fiera" and vice versa, to project this onto the seafront. This could be done through two eco-pipelines that allow to cross *viale Colombo*, resizing the road network that is now oversized compared to real needs. Along *viale Colombo* the eco-pipelines reconnect the "fiera" and the port according to the new network, with pedestrian and vehicular routes that directly connect the urban fabric to the sea.

The proposed interventions are in total coherence with the initiatives and planning that the port authority is doing around the Nervi pavilion. In this hub a roundabout (Fig. 7, proposal 6) would effectively reconnect the reorganized road axes, increasing the accessibility of the context and the parking facilities. The same hub could accommodate a pedestrian crossing at high altitude by completely integrating the two sectors now divided. It would be extremely useful to envisage a redevelopment of *via Ferrara* (Fig. 7, proposal 7) to connect two important but still separate parts of the area: the stadium and *Sant'Elia* district.

5 Discussion and Conclusions

With this study, the authors have assessed how the functional model of the new paradigms of green infrastructures can radically change the viability of a city, generating important environmental, social and economic effects that comply with the model of smart cities [27–32]. The realised analyses focused on a particularly emblematic area of coastal cities, which sees the water-front as a connection point between the city and the sea. To do this, the document presented a series of both national and international projects.

Firstly, these analyses served to understand how, in the case of a coastal city, the relationship between roads, city and waterfront must be the basis of the redevelopment. In other words, the study of these cities - relating to overpasses (Table 1) and underpasses (Table 2) - constituted an important basis of analysis to identify the positive and negative aspects of these transport infrastructures. Furthermore, these analyses have shown that in these areas the solution of the underpass is much better not only from a viewpoint of sustainability of the infrastructure itself but above all in respect of the landscape and also in the visual connection between the city and the waterfront. In fact, from the analysis of national and international examples it was possible to reflect on two key points related to the viability of a coastal city: [1] the relationship between city, waterfront and water: the viability can allow the waterfront to become the keystone of any social, urban and political process due to the gravitational effects that these structures projected onto the water have on the cities and the territory behind them. The waterfront organized with a double viability (at the city level, soft mobility and vehicle underpasses) becomes the focal point of meeting for citizens, welcoming the needs related to the mobility that the city needs in a port, maritime or railway area.

[2] The visibility of the city by those arriving from the sea and those who live in the city: it is necessary not to damage the visual and landscape connection between city and sea with invasive structures. The underpass, unlike the overpasses, allows in a coastal area to maintain the urban horizon without changing the skyline with a linear building such as that of the infrastructure. Conversely, from the city, the underpass allows to enjoy the maritime area, strengthening the link between city and sea, without creating visual and physical barriers between one area and another.

These reflections made it possible to have a first approach to the Cagliari waterfront redevelopment. This focused on a particularly critical area of the city, from *piazza Matteotti* to *via Ferrara*, which still today, despite the redevelopment works that took place in recent years, shows strong problems of connection and interpenetration between the historic city and the sea. Problems of both perception and mobility. This redevelopment is constituted by seven proposals and is based on a system of road infrastructures capable of minimizing travel times and increasing accessibility to slow mobility.

Furthermore, in the ongoing Municipal Urban Plan (MUP) of Cagliari, the analysis developed in this article with the case study of the Cagliari waterfront can be repeated in other similar contexts. In fact, the authors demonstrate how the relationships between built city and nature require adequate accessibility conditions that speed up the passage of vehicles, facilitate soft mobility and respect the city and nature both from a landscape and environmental point of view.

Future research will be oriented in two complementary directions: the first one, more theoretical, involves the study of actions aimed at improving the overall efficiency of transport, through green infrastructures, in coastal cities which by their nature have similar geographical connotations. The second one wants to extend the methodology to other parts of the city, especially as a link between natural areas and urbanized areas, in order to have a complete picture of the strategies to be implemented for the Municipal Urban Plan (MUP) of Cagliari.

Acknowledgments. This study was supported by the agreement with the Municipality of Cagliari – Strategic and Territorial Planning Service (CUP code: G22C20000080006 - CIG ZEA2E99622) entitled "Innovative methods for participatory urban planning in the drafting of the MUP in adaptation to the RLP and the HSP. Preparation of the preliminary environmental report in the SEA process. Study of the infrastructural structure in the light of the new forms of mobility in line with the drafting SUMPS". This study was developed within the Interdepartmental Center of the University of Cagliari "Cagliari Accessibility Lab".

This study was also supported by the MIUR through the project "WEAKI TRANSIT: WEAK-demand areas Innovative TRANsport Shared services for Italian Towns" (Project protocol: 20174ARRHT_004; CUP Code: F74I19001290001), financed with the PRIN 2017 (Research Projects of National Relevance) programme. We authorize the MIUR to reproduce and distribute reprints for Governmental purposes, notwithstanding any copyright notations thereon. Any opinions, findings and conclusions or recommendations expressed in this material are those of the authors, and do not necessarily reflect the views of the MIUR.

References

1. United Nations Regional Information Center, UN 75 - I grandi temi: Una demografia che cambia - ONU Italia (unric.org). Accessed 13 May 2021
2. Agenzia Italiana per lo sviluppo sostenibile (ASVIS). https://asvis.it/goal-e-target-obiettivi-e-traguardi-per-il-2030/. Accessed 13 May 2021
3. Coni, M., Garau, C., Pinna, F.: How has Cagliari changed its citizens in smart citizens? Exploring the influence of ITS technology on urban social interactions. In: Gervasi, O., et al. (eds.) ICCSA 2018. LNCS, vol. 10962, pp. 573–588. Springer, Cham (2018). https://doi.org/10.1007/978-3-319-95168-3_39
4. Garau, C., Desogus, G., Zamperlin, P.: Governing technology-based urbanism: degeneration to technocracy or development to progressive planning?, pp. 157–174 (2020)
5. Garau, C., Annunziata, A.: Smart city governance and children's agency: an assessment of the green infrastructure impact on children's activities in Cagliari (Italy) with the tool "Opportunities for Children in Urban Spaces (OCUS)." Sustainability 11(18), 4848 (2019). https://doi.org/10.3390/su11184848
6. Garau, C., Nesi, P., Paoli, I., Paolucci, M., Zamperlin, P.: A big data platform for smart and sustainable cities: environmental monitoring case studies in Europe. In: Gervasi, O., et al. (eds.) ICCSA 2020. LNCS, vol. 12255, pp. 393–406. Springer, Cham (2020). https://doi.org/10.1007/978-3-030-58820-5_30
7. Gabrielli, S.: L'accessibilità nelle smart cities. TeMA J. Land Use Mobil. Environ. 7(2), 185–198 (2014)
8. Pinna, F., Masala, F., Garau, C.: Urban policies and mobility trends in Italian smart cities. Sustainability 9(4), 494 (2017)
9. Caragliu, A., Del Bo, C., Nijkamp, P.: Smart cities in Europe. J. Urban Technol. 18(2), 65–82 (2011)
10. Unhabitat. www.unhabitat.org. Accessed 13 May 2021
11. Interreg CENTRAL EUROPE Programme. interreg-central.eu. Accessed 13 May 2021
12. Green Infrastructure Handbook (2019). https://www.interreg-central.eu/Content.Node/MaGICLandscapes-Green-Infrastructure-Handbook.pdf. Accessed 18 May 2021
13. Interreg CENTRAL EUROPE Programme. https://www.interreg-central.eu/Content.Node/MaGICLandscapes-Manuale-sulle-Infrastrutture-Verdi.pdf. Accessed 13 May 2021
14. Coni, M., Garau, C., Maltinti, F., Pinna, F.: Accessibility improvements and place-based organization in the Island of Sardinia (Italy). In: Gervasi, O., et al. (eds.) ICCSA 2020. LNCS, vol. 12255, pp. 337–352. Springer, Cham (2020). https://doi.org/10.1007/978-3-030-58820-5_26
15. Garau, C., Desogus, G., Coni, M.: Fostering and planning a smart governance strategy for evaluating the urban polarities of the Sardinian Island (Italy). Sustainability 11(18), 4962 (2019). https://doi.org/10.3390/su11184962
16. Mistretta, P., Garau, C.: Città e sfide. Conflitti e Utopie. Strategie di impresa e Politiche del territorio. Successi e criticità dei modelli di governance (2013)
17. Comune di Cagliari, Sala controllo della mobilità, Statistiche dati di traffico. http://www.comune.cagliari.it/portale/viabilita/at16_dati_statist_traffico. Accessed 13 May 2021
18. Desogus, G., Mistretta, P.: Nella Città che cambia: la "forma" è strategica per lo sviluppo e la crescita, CUEC, Cagliari (2017)
19. Piano regolatore portuale del porto di Cagliari, BURAS, Legge n. 84/1994, art. 5. http://buras.regione.sardegna.it/custom/frontend/viewInsertionxhtml?insertionId=d37b7f94-97d2-468d-8e67-38421507e938. Accessed 13 May 2021
20. Green Infrastructure and the Transport sector. https://ec.europa.eu/environment/nature/ecosystems/pdf/Green%20Infrastructure/GI_transport.pdf. Accessed 13 May 2021

21. Manuale sulle infrastrutture verdi, Interreg. https://www.interreg-central.eu/Content.Node/ MaGICLandscapes-Manuale-sulle-Infrastrutture-Verdi.pdf. Accessed 13 May 2021
22. Genova 2050. https://www.genova2050.com/nodi-e-vuoti-urbani/sopraelevata-genova. Accessed 13 May 2021
23. Capitale europea della Cultura. https://www.larassegna.it/capitale-europea-della-culturaper-genova-stata-una-svolta/?print=print. Accessed 13 May 2021
24. Atlante architettura contemporanea. https://www.atlantearchitetture.beniculturali.it/acq uario-di-genova/. Accessed 13 May 2021
25. Asosiación para la Colaboración entre Puertos y Ciudades. http://retedigital.com/wp-con tent/themes/rete/pdfs/portus_plus/1_2011/Tem%C3%A1ticas/La_recalificaci%C3%B3n_ de_los_waterfront/03_AndreaConca.pdf. Accessed 13 May 2021
26. Barcellona, architetture e interni URBAN. https://core.ac.uk/download/pdf/141690218.pdf. Accessed 13 May 2021
27. Laurini, R., Las Casas, G., Murgante, B.: Smart city as the city of knowledge. In: Smart Cities and the un SDGs, pp. 211–232. Elsevier (2021)
28. Annunziata, A., Garau, C.: Understanding kid-friendly urban space for a more inclusive smart city: the case study of Cagliari (Italy). In: Gervasi, O., et al. (eds.) ICCSA 2018. LNCS, vol. 10962, pp. 589–605. Springer, Cham (2018). https://doi.org/10.1007/978-3-319-95168-3_40
29. Annunziata, A., Garau, C.: Smart city governance for child-friendly cities. Impacts of green and blue infrastructures on children's independent activities. In: Planning, Nature and Ecosystem Services, pp. 524–538. FedOAPress (2019)
30. Garau, C., Zamperlin, P., Balletto, G.: Reconsidering the Geddesian concepts of community and space through the paradigm of smart cities. Sustainability **8**(10), 985 (2016)
31. Azzari, M., Garau, C., Nesi, P., Paolucci, M., Zamperlin, P.: Smart city governance strategies to better move towards a smart urbanism. In: Gervasi, O., et al. (eds.) ICCSA 2018. LNCS, vol. 10962, pp. 639–653. Springer, Cham (2018). https://doi.org/10.1007/978-3-319-95168-3_43
32. Maltinti, F., et al.: Vulnerable users and public transport service: analysis on expected and perceived quality data. In: Gervasi, O., et al. (eds.) ICCSA 2020. LNCS, vol. 12255, pp. 673–689. Springer, Cham (2020). https://doi.org/10.1007/978-3-030-58820-5_49

Empirical Evaluation of Urban Heat Island Pavements Related. Cagliari Case Study

Mauro Coni[1]([✉]) [iD], Agostino Satta[1], Silvia Portas[2] [iD], and Francesca Maltinti[1] [iD]

[1] Department of Civil and Environmental Engineering and Architecture (DICAAR), University of Cagliari, via Marengo 2, 09123 Cagliari, Italy
mconi@unica.it
[2] So.G.Aer. International Airport of Cagliari, Cagliari, Italy

Abstract. Worldwide, higher temperatures occur in urban areas (UHI - Urban Heat Island) compared to the surrounding countryside, with a considerable impact on people's health and well-being. Extensive use of paved surface and bituminous materials and human activity heat generation are the major causes of the UHI. The paper points out the importance of bituminous pavements on UHI and reports the empirical evaluation performed in Cagliari (Italy). Using thermal data from the Italian SmartRunway located in Cagliari airport, a fitting empirical model developed for bituminous pavement surface (R2 < 0.94) has been extended to other materials used in the urban context. The model input data are a minimum and maximum air temperature and solar irradiation during the day, and output is the surface temperature. The simplified characterization of different kinds of surfaces covering the cities can be operated through visual analysis of orthophotos or a geodatabase. Combining these data, in the paper is proposed a methodology to build temperature profile along a town cross-section. Finally, a zenithally thermal survey has validated the empirical methodology, with a significant correlation (R^2 > 81%).

Keywords: Urban Heat Island · Bituminous surface · UHI mitigation · Urban warming · Asphalt pavements

1 Introduction

UHI is high-temperature levels in urban centers compared to surrounding rural areas. In the last 15 years, extensive research efforts study UHI (Urban Heat Island) phenomenon. Literature review reports hundreds of investigations [1] related to evaluation, impact, and mitigation, starting in 2000. Mitigation methods include green and blue infrastructure, cool roofs and pavements, urban structures, and the use of vegetation coverage. Some states issued regulations and standards to mitigate the UHI effects, and there is continuous progress to incorporate in the technical codes innovation in construction system, strategies, and research results.

In Italy in 2017, a law on minimum environmental criteria fix the SRI (Solar Reflectance Index) for materials at least 29 to moderate the effect of solar radiation

© Springer Nature Switzerland AG 2021
O. Gervasi et al. (Eds.): ICCSA 2021, LNCS 12958, pp. 19–32, 2021.
https://doi.org/10.1007/978-3-030-87016-4_2

on UHI [2]. Nevertheless, a lack of general coherence among public administration, academia, companies, and professional operators is a substantial impediment to the implementation and effectiveness of UHI mitigation strategies in urban and regional plans. In general, the pavements capable of reducing thermal field are designed as "cool pavements". The reduction can be achieved using highly reflective and emissive materials, porous and permeable layers [3]. The "cool pavements", include both conventional (asphalt and concrete), stone pavement [14], and nonconventional pavements (white-colored course, resin-bonded pavements, a porous superficial layer, and micro surfacing) [3, 17]. Several studies investigated the appreciable cooling of reflective pavements [4–8], but some remark that they can adversely affect drivers such as glare and discomfort due to reflected radiation or the moisture reduction cause higher daytime temperature [9–11].

Recent research [12] remarks that the intensity of UHIs is related to population size and mean annual precipitation and, an explanation for this relationship can be reproduced by introducing in large-scale model population, climate, and UHI intensity. Evapotranspiration and convection efficiency are the main factor that explains differences between rural and urban areas (Fig. 1).

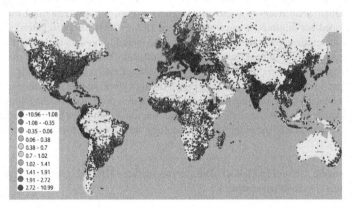

Fig. 1. The intensity of UHI over more than 30,000 world cities according to the model proposed by Manoli, G., Fatichi, S., Schläpfer, M., et al. [12]

Therefore, in dry regions is more efficient to increase vegetation cover and albedo, whereas cities in a tropical climate will require innovative solutions. The results of an online survey in 2020 [2] investigate the perceptions of UHI mitigation approaches and, green infrastructure was selected by most respondents ($\approx$90%), and at the same time, less than 50% consider cool pavement to be effective (Fig. 2). Green infrastructure and stone pavements are widely used for UHI mitigation and environmental and social benefits [7, 35]. Urban vegetation refreshes cities through evapotranspiration and shading, but few papers [15, 16] quantify the urban vegetation's cooling effect. It is fundamental to have forecasting models to evaluate different mitigation actions in urban plans and adaptation strategies to climate change. Several investigations proposed a simulation model to predict the surface temperature of the pavements.

Fig. 2. Different types of "cool pavements": colored, porous (concrete and asphalt), green and stone pavements (Color figure online).

Two linear regression models for predicting the daily minimum and maximum pavement temperatures were developed in 2006 by Diefenderfer et al., using data from Virginia Smart Road [13]. A similar model, developed during the Italian SmartRunway project in 2009 at Cagliari airport, fit empirical data from bituminous pavement surface ($R^2 < 0.98$) over two years [18, 19]. All the models include solar radiation, minimum and maximum ambient temperature, and depth from the surface. Qin [14] in 2015 proposed the following theoretical model

$$T_{s,max} = \Gamma \frac{(1 - R)}{P\sqrt{\omega}} + T_o \tag{1}$$

Where:

Γ = % absorption of the thermal conduction.

R = reflectivity.

I_0 = daily zenith solar irradiation.

w = angular frequency of a sinusoidal wave ($w = 2\pi/24/3600$),

T_0 = constant (period base temperature).

$P = \sqrt{kc\gamma}$ Thermal inertia of the asphalt (k = thermal conductivity, c = heat capacity, and γ = density of the asphalt).

This model addresses the different ways to reduce temperature: increasing reflectivity R (e.g., white coating), increasing thermal inertia P (e.g., dense materials), reducing absorption Γ (e.g., porous materials) and, protection by solar irradiation I_0 (e.g., trees shading). Some authors [20, 21] classify different types of reflective pavements: infrared-reflective paints, coarse aggregates, thermochromic materials and, alternative constituents (i.e., fly ash) and, many studies [22–25] evaluate this reflectance strategy. Porous pavements allow removing heat through evaporative cooling and airflow induced by wind. Phase change materials (PCM) are promising strategies to minimize thermal peaks [26–29]. PCM and various heat-harvesting pavements were also studied to convert the absorbed heat to other forms of energy.

The paper investigates asphalt pavement's contribution to UHI and proposes a simplified empirical evaluation to estimate UHI pavement's related effect. Using thermal data from the Italian SmartRunway located in Cagliari airport, a fitting empirical model developed for bituminous pavement surface ($R^2 < 0.98$) has been extended to other materials used in the urban context. The model input data are a T_{min}, T_{max}, and R_s (Solar Irradiation) during the day, and output is the surface temperature during the 24 h. The methodology allows building temperature profiles along a town cross-section. The aerial thermal survey allows validating the methodology, with a significant correlation ($R^2 > 94\%$).

2 Data and Methodology

The structure of the research (Fig. 3) follows five levels:

1. Development of the thermal asphalt model
2. Model extension to different materials
3. Thermal survey and data gathering over Cagliari town
4. Data analysis and model validation
5. Building a cross-section temperature profile along with the town

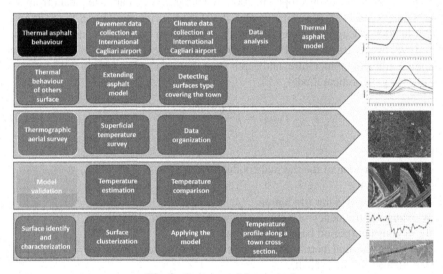

Fig. 3. Structure of the research

2.1 Development of the Thermal Asphalt Model

In 2008 the runway at Cagliari-Elmas International Airport had been reconstructed and, the asphalt pavement od the touchdown area on head 32 was instrumented with a total of 149 instruments: 36 Linear Variable Differential Transformers, 36 pressure cells, four Time Domain Reflectometers, 28 T-thermocouples, and 45 HMA strain gauges (Fig. 4). In particular, the system collected thermal data from April 2009 to December 2011 at regular intervals every 15min, through 2 vertical alignments of T-thermocouples at 14 different depth: 1 cm, 3 cm, 5 cm, 7 cm, 10 cm, 15 cm, 20 cm, 25 cm, 30 cm, 35 cm, 45 cm, 60 cm, 75 cm, and 90 cm.

Figure 5 shows the temperature variability at the top and bottom of HMA layers at Cagliari Airport from May 2009 to December 2010. HMA temperature ranging between 1.2 °C to 56.2 °C at 1.0 cm depth and from 6.2 °C to 42.3 °C at the bottom of the HMA layer (35 cm) with the mean value of 24.7 °C.

Fig. 4. Instrumentation installation at Italian SmartRunway at Cagliari airport

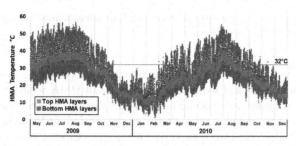

Fig. 5. The temperature of asphalt pavement at Cagliari Airport (2009–2010)

Many approaches have been used to predict the temperature distribution in the HMA layer, such as theoretical, numerical, and statistical methods. The input parameter involves air temperature, solar radiation, wind speed, relative air humidity, heat convection, and heat diffusion. Sometimes the models require complex input, and they are not suitable for practical use. Since 1957 Barber [30] discuss the evaluation of maximum pavement temperatures from weather information to predict pavement temperatures profile, and over the years, many other researchers investigate on temperature distribution in HMA. Only in 2001, some researchers presented models to predict daily temperatures. Park et al. [31] proposed a simple equation to predict temperature inside asphalt layers at any time of the day:

$$T_z = T_{surf} + (-0.3451z - 0.0432z^2 + 0.00196z^3)\sin(-6.3252t + 5.0967) \qquad (2)$$

where:
T_z = temperature at depth z (°C).
T_{surf} = temperature at the surface (°C).
z = depth from the surface (cm).
t = time (fraction of day).

Many other researchers propose to estimate daily maximum and minimum HMA temperature [32–34] based on the daily solar radiation (R_s), air temperature (T_a), and depth from the surface (z). Using climate data at Cagliari-Elmas Airport for 315 days in 2010, these models can predict maximum pavement the observed temperature with reliability between 72.2% < R^2 < 91.7%. Figure 6 shows regression between measured and predicted temperatures at 3 cm, 20, and 35 cm deep during the warm season.

The model proposed in this paper first estimates the daily minimum and maximum temperature of HMA through a regression analysis of climate data provided by C.O.Met. (Italian Ministry of Defence - Air Force - Operational Centre for Meteorology). The

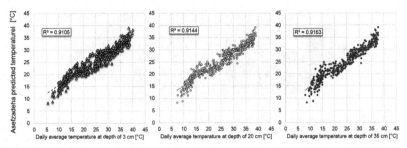

Fig. 6. Predicted versus Cagliari Airport measured HMA temperatures at a depth of 3 cm, 20, and 35 cm during the warm season.

multiple regression based on daily minimum and air temperature and solar radiation give the daily minimum and maximum temperature of HMA with $R^2 = 92\%$. This result has been obtained on a regular day, characterized by no clouds and wind. The assumption allows avoiding high variability during the seasons and the local peculiarity (i.e., buildings shadow and wind tunnel effect in the urban streets). The best-fit equations obtained for the regular day are:

$$T_{Daily-min} = 1.2097 + 0.6754T_{air-min} + 0.37642R_s \tag{3}$$

$$T_{Daily-max} = 10.4875 + 0.6864T_{air-max} + 0.5674R_s \tag{4}$$

where:
$T_{Daily-min}$ = daily minimum temperature of HMA (°C).
$T_{Daily-max}$ = daily maximum temperature of HMA (°C).
$T_{air-min}$ = minimum temperature of air (°C).
$T_{air-max}$ = maximum temperature of air (°C).
R_s = total daily solar irradiation (MJ/m^2).

Considering the periodical trend of daily temperature, a Fourier series development of the phenomenon over the day is very effective. In the research, a high correlation was observed between predicted and measured values. Stopping the development of the Fourier series at the first four terms, R^2 has always been greater than 94.5%

$$T_{surf} = a_0 + \sum_{n=1}^{\infty} (a_n \cos n\omega t + b_n \sin n\omega t) \approx \ldots$$

$$\cdots \approx a_0 + a_1 \cos\omega t + b_1 \sin\omega t + a_2 \cos2\omega t + b_2 \sin2\omega t \tag{5}$$

where:
a_0 = mean daily temperature $T_{Daily-med}$ = ($T_{Daily-max}$ + $T_{Daily-min}$)/2.
a_1 = $T_{Daily-min}$ - $T_{Daily-med}$.
b_1 = $T_{Daily-max}$ - $T_{Daily-med}$.
a_2, b_2 = 2° order coefficient.
ω = angular frequency of a sinusoidal wave (w = 2π /24/3600).

2.2 Model Extension to Different Materials

A simplified approach is implemented to extend the model validated to HMA to others covering materials. The analysis comprises asphalt (HMA), light and dark roofs, concrete, stone material, vegetation, and unpaved areas. In addition, since the city of Cagliari have numerous water surfaces and lagoons, the thermal response of a water surface 2.0 m deep was also considered. In order to extend the model, several daily measurements have been performed in different conditions and areas with the simultaneous presence of asphalt and other covering materials (Fig. 7). Comparing the thermal response of the different surfaces with respect to asphalt allows resizing the proposed model for other materials.

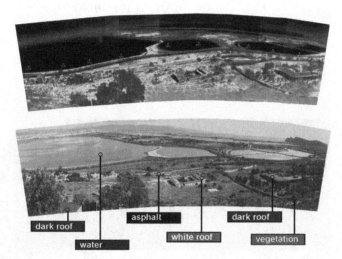

Fig. 7. Thermal measurements in areas with the simultaneous presence of asphalt and other covering materials.

The following Table 1 shows the linear combination coefficient to predict maximum and minimum daily temperature for different materials.

2.3 Thermal Survey and Data Gathering over Cagliari Town

In order to validate the proposed methodology and analyze the UHI phenomenon over the city of Cagliari, an aerial survey was carried out on October 17, 2017, at 4.00 PM.

During the flight, a thermal video was recorded. Twenty images were extracted, relating to different areas of Cagliari, significant since covered by large surfaces of the different materials considered. Figure 8 shows the flight plan, for a total length of 70 km, with a speed of 80 knots (148 km/h) and an altitude of 300 m. The areas analyzed are highlighted with red boxes (250 x 250 m).

The flight was performed in clear-sky conditions in the afternoon, with an air temperature of about 20 °C and low wind speed (11 km/h).

Table 1. Linear combination coefficient of the model

| | $T_{Daily-min}$ | | | $T_{Daily-max}$ | | |
| | $l_1 + m_1 T_{air-min} + n_1 R_s$ | | | $l_2 + m_2 T_{air-max} + n_2 R_s$ | | |
	l_1	m_1	n_1	l_2	m_2	n_2
Asphalt	10.4875	0.6864	0.5674	1.2097	0.6754	0.3764
Dark Roof	10.461	0.640	0.469	1.196	0.644	0.320
White roof	8.462	0.631	0.366	1.195	0.612	0.258
Concrete	8.155	0.622	0.360	1.189	0.615	0.266
Stone	7.136	0.420	0.321	1.190	0.603	0.261
Vegetation	0	1	0	0	1	0
Water	0	1	1	0	1	1
Unpaved	7.050	0.380	0.321	1.209	0.615	0.306

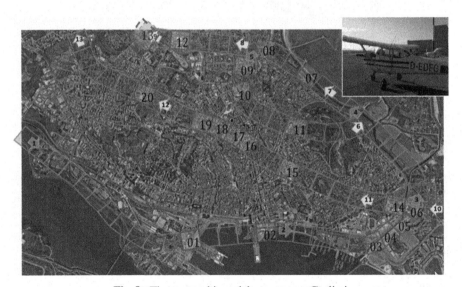

Fig. 8. Thermographic aerial survey over Cagliari

3   Results

3.1   Data Analysis and Model Validation

The twenty areas recorded in the aerial flight were analyzed using both the municipal cartography's orthophotos and the survey on the sites. Figure 9, on the top, shows the results and analysis for zone 20 and Zone 3: temperature distribution an the left, surface type at the centre and, orthophoto on the right. Each area has been segmented into the different types of surfaces present, associating each one with the corresponding thermal images of the fly survey. The surface classification includes the materials type, their color intensity, and coverage area. Next, through a calculation code developed in Matlab R16, the temperature values of the surfaces of each thermal image were extrapolated, and the weighted average of these values in the respective areas was calculated. Figure 9 reports two examples of the areas analyzed.

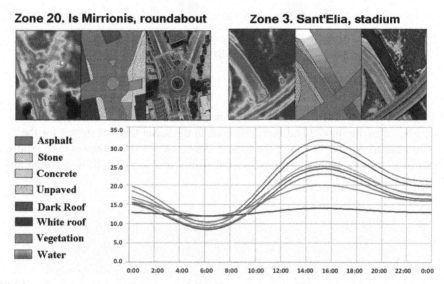

Fig. 9. Two examples of the areas analysed (on the top: temperature distribution an the left, surface type at the centre and, orthophoto on the right) and daily estimated temperature for different materials (on the bottom).

The histogram in Fig. 10 shows higher temperature values for asphalt road pavements and dark roof, which during the survey assume a mean temperature close to 30 °C. Concrete and stone have similar values, lower than those of asphalt by about 4 °C. Vegetation have the lowest temperature values of about 10 °C. The model extension show limited correlation for water surfaces.

3.2 Building a Cross-Section Temperature Profile Along with the Town

The proposed method allows estimating the temperature profile through any cross-section of the urban centre. By extending the section to the more peripheral and rural areas, it is possible to highlight the urban effect of heat islands. The estimation is based on the segmentation of the cross-section of the urban center into cells, evaluating the surface extension of the various covering materials. Inputting data $T_{air-min}$, $T_{air-max}$, R_s, and hour of the day in the model, the temperature of each covering surface is calculated. The mean temperatures of each surface, weighted regarding the extension of the surfaces, allow attributing an average temperature value to each cell.

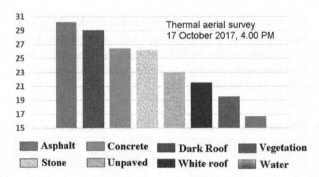

Fig. 10. Temperature distribution on a different surface (October 17 2017, 4:00 PM)

A good correlation ($R^2 = 0.81$) was found between the weighted temperature values predicted by the model and that measured in the aerial thermal survey for the 20 cells considered. Figure 11 shows the cross-section and estimated temperature profile, evaluated in four different situations: typical winter and summer, early morning and afternoon.

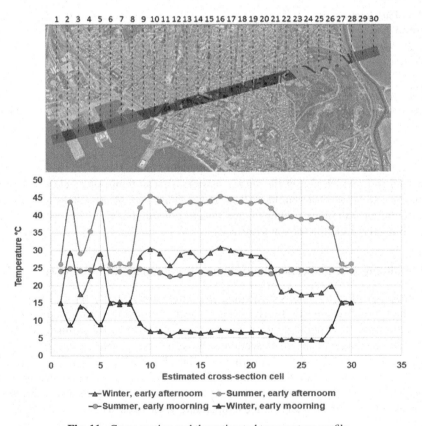

Fig. 11. Cross-section and the estimated temperature profile.

4   Conclusions and Remarks

In urban areas, temperatures are increasingly higher than in the surrounding rural areas. The well-known phenomenon (UHI - Urban Heat Island) has several negative consequences on cities' energy balances and people's health and well-being. Many urban climate change adaptation plans include UHI reduction strategies. The wide use of bituminous materials for road paving is one of the leading causes of UHI due to the thermal properties, mainly high absorbent and low solar reflection index.

The paper proposes an original methodology for the empirical evaluation of UHI, calibrated on Cagliari (Italy), and highlights the importance of bituminous pavements. The authors outline some mitigation strategies to reduce global warming. Main mitigation strategies comprise "cool materials" for the urban context surfaces: roads, parking, squares, dirt field, and buildings. The reduction of asphalted surfaces would significantly benefit since, in medium latitudes, they reach temperatures up to 65 °C. Knowing the thermal behavior of materials in the actual condition is crucial to promoting "cool materials" on roofs and pavements.

An empirical model of the surface temperature of the bituminous pavement ($R2 < 0.98$) was developed in the research. The model has been extended to other materials used in the urban context of Cagliari. For the development of the model were the thermal data of the Italian SmartRunway and the climatic data of the Cagliari airport.

The input data are the minimum and maximum temperatures and solar radiation forecast for the day, and the output is the surface temperature on the pavement. All-day experimental surveys of the temperatures of different materials highlight a behavior very similar to that of bituminous surfaces. The substantial difference is the magnitude of the minimum and maximum peaks. Therefore the rescaling factors were calculated, extending the model to the other materials.

Following a section of the city of Cagliari was divided into cells, identifying the areas of the covering materials, using the available orthophotos. At specific times of the day, the temperatures predicted for these materials were weighted to the calculated average value. Finally, a zenithally thermal survey has validated the empirical methodology, with a significant correlation ($R2 > 81\%$).

Acknowledgments. This study was supported by the MIUR (Ministry of Education, Universities and Research [Italy]) through a project entitled WEAKI TRANSIT: WEAK-demand areas Innovative TRANsport Shared services for Italian Towns (Project protocol: 20174ARRHT_004; CUP Code: F74I19001290001), financed with the PRIN 2017 (Research Projects of National Relevance) program. We authorize the MIUR to reproduce and distribute reprints for Governmental purposes, notwithstanding any copyright notations thereon. Any conclusions, opinions, findings, or recommendations expressed in this paper are those of the authors and do not necessarily reflect the visions of the MIUR.

The research is also supported by Sardinia Regional Administration (Italy) under SRACC (Regional Adaptation Strategy to Climate Change).

The authors also acknowledge the C.O.Met. (Italian Ministry of Defence - Air Force - Operational Centre for Meteorology) which made its meteorological data available for this study, helpful in developing the pavement runway's temperature asphalt model at Cagliari International Airport.

Author Contributions:. Concept and methodology, M.C., A.S., S.P., and F.M.; experimental campaign and validation, M.C., and A.S.; analysis, M.C., A.S., and F.M.; writing, review and editing, M.C., A.S., S.P., and F.M.; project administration, M.C. and F.M. All authors have read and agreed to the published version of the manuscript.

References

1. Wang, W.C., Wang, Z., Kaloush, K.E.: Critical Review and Gap Analysis Of Impacts From Pavements On Urban Heat Island, ASU National Center of Excellence for Smart Innovation, Arizona State University, Final Report, December 2020 (2020). https://ncesmart.asu.edu/wp-content/uploads/2020/12/NAPA-20120-ASU-UHI-Report..pdf
2. Italian Ministry of the Environment and Protection of the territory and the sea. (DM 11.10.2017, 17A07439). Action plan for environmental sustainability. Minimum environmental criteria (2017). https://www.minambiente.it/sites/default/files/archivio/allegati/GPP/GU_259_dm_CAMedilizia.pdf
3. U.S. EPA: Cool Pavements, in: Reducing Urban Heat Islands: Compendium of Strategies, U.S. Environmental Protection Agency (EPA) (2012). https://www.epa.gov/sites/production/files/2017-05/documents/reducing_urban_heat_islands_ch_5.pdf
4. Santamouris, M., et al.: Passive and active cooling for the outdoor built environment – analysis and assessment of the cooling potential of mitigation technologies using performance data from 220 large scale projects. Sol. Energy **154**, 14–33 (2017). https://doi.org/10.1016/j.solener.2016.12.006
5. Yang, J., Wang, Z.-H., Kaloush, K.E.: Environmental impacts of reflective materials: is high albedo a 'silver bullet' for mitigating urban heat island? Renew. Sustain. Energy Rev. **47**, 830–843 (2015). https://doi.org/10.1016/j.rser.2015.03.092
6. Santamouris, M., Synnefa, A., Karlessi, T.: Using advanced cool materials in the urban built environment to mitigate heat islands and improve thermal comfort conditions. Sol. Energy **85**, 3085–3102 (2011). https://doi.org/10.1016/j.solener.2010.12.023
7. Qin, Y.: A review on the development of cool pavements to mitigate urban heat island effect. Renew. Sustain. Energy Rev. **52**, 445–459 (2015). https://doi.org/10.1016/j.rser.2015.07.177
8. Santamouris, M.: Using cool pavements as a mitigation strategy to fight urban heat island, a review of the actual developments. Renew. Sustain. Energy Rev. **26**, 224–240 (2013). https://doi.org/10.1016/j.rser.2013.05.047
9. Li, H.: Evaluation of Cool Pavement Strategies for Heat Island Mitigation. Institute of Transportation Studies, University of California, Davis, CA (2012)
10. Bloch, S.: The Problem with "Cool Pavements": They Make People Hot, CITY-LAB (2019). https://www.citylab.com/environment/2019/10/-cool-pavement-materials-coating-urban-heatisland-research/599221
11. Stempihar, J.J., Pourshams-Manzouri, T., Kaloush, K.E., Rodezno, M.C.: Porous asphalt pavement temperature effects for urban heat island analysis. Transp. Res. Rec. **2293**, 123–130 (2012). https://doi.org/10.3141/2293-15
12. Manoli, G., Fatichi, S., Schläpfer, M., et al.: Magnitude of urban heat islands largely explained by climate and population. Nature **573**, 55–60 (2019). https://doi.org/10.1038/s41586-019-1512-9
13. Diefenderfer, B.K., Al-Qadi, I.L., Diefenderfer, S.D.: Model to predict pavement temperature profile: development and validation. J. Transp. Eng. **132**(2), 162–167 (2006). https://doi.org/10.1061/(ASCE)0733-947X(2006)132:2(162)
14. U.S. Environmental Protection Agency, Basics: What is Green Infrastructure? (2019). https://www.epa.gov/green-infrastructure/what-green-infrastructure. Accessed 29 June 2019

15. Saaroni, H., Amorim, J.H., Hiemstra, J.A., Pearlmutter, D.: Urban green infrastructure as a tool for urban heat mitigation: survey of research methodologies and findings across different climatic regions. Urban Clim. **24**, 94–110 (2018). https://doi.org/10.1016/j.uclim.2018.02.001

16. Gunawardena, K.R., Wells, M.J., Kershaw, T.: Utilising green and blue space to mitigate urban heat island intensity. Sci. Total Environ. **584–585**, 1040–1055 (2017). https://doi.org/10.1016/j.scitotenv.2017.01.158

17. Coni, M.: Ultrathin multi-functional overlay. ASCE Airfield and Highway Pavements Conference 2013, Los Angeles 9, 12 June 2013

18. Al-Qadi, I.L., Portas, S., Coni, M., Lahouar, S.: Runway pavement stress and strain experimental measurements. per il Journal of the Transportation Research Board, No. 2153, January 12, 2010, Vol. 1, pp. 162–169, Scopus Code: 2-s2.0–78651268142, ISI: Pavement Management (2010)

19. Wang, H., Al-Qadi, I.L., Portas, S., Coni, M.: Three-dimensional finite element modeling of instrumented airport runway pavement responses. In: TRB Transportation Research Board, 92th Annual Meeting, Washington, 12–17 January 2013

20. Santamouris, M.: Using cool pavements as a mitigation strategy to fight urban heat island - a review of the actual developments. Renew. Sustain. Energy Rev. **26**, 224–240 (2013). https://doi.org/10.1016/j.rser.2013.05.047

21. Akbari, H., et al.: Local climate change and urban heat island mitigation techniques–state of the art. J. Civ. Eng. Manag. **22**, 1–16 (2016). https://doi.org/10.3846/13923730.2015.111 1934

22. Cao, X., Tang, B., Zhu, H., Zhang, A., Chen, S.: Cooling principle analyses and performance evaluation of heat-reflective coating for asphalt pavement. J. Mater. Civ. Eng. **23**, 1067–1075 (2011). https://doi.org/10.1061/(ASCE)MT.1943-5533.0000256

23. Sha, A., Liu, Z., Tang, K., Li, P.: Solar heating reflective coating layer (SHRCL) to cool the asphalt pavement surface. Constr. Build. Mater. **139**, 355–364 (2017). https://doi.org/10.1016/j.conbuildmat.2017.02.087

24. Tran, N., Powell, B., Marks, H., West, R., Kvasnak, A.: Strategies for designing and constructing high-reflectance asphalt pavements. Transp. Res. Rec. **2098**, 124–130 (2009). https://doi.org/10.3141/2098-13

25. Carnielo, E., Zinzi, M.: Optical and thermal characterization of cool asphalts to mitigate urban temperatures and building cooling demand. Build. Environ. **60**, 56–65 (2013). https://doi.org/10.1016/j.buildenv.2012.11.004

26. Souayfane, F., Fardoun, F., Biwole, P.-H.: Phase change materials (PCM) for cooling applications in buildings: a review. Energy Build. **129**, 396–431 (2016). https://doi.org/10.1016/j.enbuild.2016.04.006

27. Athukorallage, B., Dissanayaka, T., Senadheera, S., James, D.: Performance analysis of incorporating phase change materials in asphalt concrete pavements. Constr. Build. Mater. **164**, 419–432 (2018). https://doi.org/10.1016/j.conbuildmat

28. Meizhu Chen, L., Wan, J.: Effect of phase-change materials on thermal and mechanical properties of asphalt mixtures. J. Testing Eval. **40**(5), 20120091 (2012). https://doi.org/10.1520/JTE20120091

29. Guan, B., Ma, B., Qin, F.: Application of asphalt pavement with phase change materials to mitigate urban heat island effect. Int. Sympos. Water Resour. Environ. Protect. **2011**, 2389–2392 (2011). https://doi.org/10.1109/ISWREP.2011.589374

30. Barber, E.S.: Calculation of Maximum Pavement Temperatures from Weather Reports. Highway Research Board Bull, Washington DC (1957)

31. Park, D.Y., Buch, N., Chatti, K.: Effective layer temperature prediction model and temperature correction via falling weight deflectometer deflections, Transport. Res. Rec. J. Transport. Res. Board **1764**, 97–111 (2001)

32. Minhoto, M., Pais, J., Pereira, P., Picado-Santos, L.: Predicting asphalt pavement temperature with a three-dimensional finite element method, transport. Res. Rec. J. Transport. Res. Board **2005**, 96–110 (1919)

33. Asefzadeha, A., Hashemianb, L., Bayat, A.: Development of statistical temperature prediction models for a test road in Edmonton, Alberta, Canada. Int. J. Pav. Res. Technol. **10**(5), 369–382 (2017)

34. Coni, M., Portas, S., Maltinti, F., Pinna, F.: Sealing of paving stone joints. Int. J. Pav. Res. Technol. (2018). https://doi.org/10.1016/j.ijprt.2018.07.002

35. Coni, M., Garau, C., Pinna, F.: How has Cagliari changed its citizens in smart citizens? Exploring the influence of ITS technology on urban social interactions. In: Gervasi, O. (ed.) Computational Science and Its Applications–ICCSA 2018, pp. 573–588. Springer International Publishing, Cham (2018). https://doi.org/10.1007/978-3-319-95168-3_39

Circular Economy Strategy in the Construction Sector: The Use of Recycle Aggregates in the Sardinian Island

Luisa Pani⬤, Lorena Francesconi⬤, James Rombi⬤, Marta Salis⬤, and Flavio Stochino(✉)⬤

Department of Civil, Environmental Engineering and Architecture,
University of Cagliari, 09123 Cagliari, Italy
`fstochino@unica.it`

Abstract. The recycling of concrete debris to obtain coarse recycled aggregates for structural concrete production represents a model of circular economy in the construction sector. It reduces landfill waste and raw material exploitation. In this applied research, the recycled aggregate, obtained from construction and demolition waste, was used in partial replacement of coarse natural aggregate in structural concrete. The analysis concerns two case studies: production process, and failure mechanism of precast reinforced concrete foundation made with coarse recycled concrete aggregate; method to estimate the demand of recycled aggregates in urban planning in three towns (Calasetta, Carloforte and Portoscuso) in southern Sardinia Island, for new construction, building refurbishment, cycle track, and pedestrian path.

In this context, the circular economy model is the best practice to achieve the sustainable development of the construction sector. The applied research offers an important contribution to the management plan of construction and demolition waste in Sardinia Island.

Keywords: Circular economy · Urban planning · recycled aggregate · Sustainability

1 Introduction

Concrete constructions largely contribute to the exploitation of non-renewable natural resources. For this reason, concrete debris could be recycled to produce recycled concrete aggregates, promoting a circular economy strategy. The use of recycled aggregates represents a valid alternative to natural ones for concrete production, promoting natural resources preservation and reducing landfill disposal.

Maximizing the quantity of recycled materials is an effective approach towards sustainable constructions (Kovler and Roussel 2011; Meyer 2009; Rao et al. 2007, Pepe et al. 2014, Pani et al. 2020). In Italy, following the European Commission guidelines, the Ministry of the Environment and the Protection of the Territory and the Sea has published

© Springer Nature Switzerland AG 2021
O. Gervasi et al. (Eds.): ICCSA 2021, LNCS 12958, pp. 33–43, 2021.
https://doi.org/10.1007/978-3-030-87016-4_3

the National Action Plan on Green Public Procurement (PANGPP), DM 11/10/17 2017. It defines, for all public contracts, the Minimum Environmental Criteria (CAM). They are the environmental requirements defined for the various phases of the purchase process aimed at identifying the best design solutions, products, and services from an environmental point of view throughout the entire life cycle. Applied researches show that there is no technical and scientific limit to the use of recycled concrete aggregate, in structural and non-structural concretes. Some general conclusions can be drawn about the use of coarse recycled aggregate in structural concrete (Ajdukiewicz and Kliszczewicz 2002; Etxeberria et al. 2007; Rahal 2007; González-Fonteboa and Martínez-Abella 2008; Pani et al. 2019, Pepe et al. 2014).

Available experimental data concerning concrete made with Recycled Concrete Aggregate (RCA) are variable (Pacheco et al. 2019, Francesconi et al. 2016, Koenders et al. 2014) and some authors (González-Fonteboa and Martínez-Abella 2008; Kou and Poon 2015; Rahal, 2007; Stochino et al. 2017; Tabsh and Abdelfatah 2009, Pani et al. 2020) found that recycled concrete having medium compressive strength can be produced, regardless of the parent concrete quality. Reinforced concrete columns made with RCA have been studied in the last years (see Xu et al. 2017, Xu et al. 2018, Xu et al. 2019) showing the applications of these materials to full scale structural elements.

In this paper, the use of coarse RCA in precast recycled concrete elements has been analyzed. In the precast concrete industry, the coarse recycled aggregate by crushing and screening of processing waste can be obtained, reducing landfilling costs and raw materials.

An important experimental campaign was carried out with a precast company of reinforced concrete elements (beams, plinths, and hollow core slabs). The research focused the attention on the production of prefabricated plinths, made with recycled concrete, in which the coarse aggregates, were obtained from the crushing of processing waste.

Moreover, this paper analyzed a method to estimate the demand for recycled aggregates in urban planning on the southwest coast of Sardinia.

The analysis conducted aims to define a methodological approach to support decision-making processes in the development of strategies to connect coastal areas, concerning the use of recycled aggregates in local planning. Furthermore, a method is presented to quantify the demand for recycled aggregates in compliance with local planning. The proposed method is implemented in three towns (Calasetta, Carloforte, and Portoscuso) in southern Sardinia Island.

2   Precast Plinth Using Coarse Recycled Concrete Aggregates

Precast reinforced concrete plinths made with natural fine aggregates and coarse recycled aggregates in partial replacement of natural ones were produced and tested. Two recycled concrete mixes with 30% and 50% substitution percentage, by weight, of coarse recycled aggregates were used.

For comparison, a reinforced ordinary concrete plinth, made with natural aggregates, was produced.

The test focus was to determine the mechanism and force of the collapse in precast reinforced recycled concrete plinths. The force on the structure is applied on the top of a precast reinforced concrete column connected to the plinth (Fig. 1). The connection between plinth and column were realized with ordinary concrete (Fig. 2).

Fig. 1. Plinth column element

The precast elements were made by prefabrication company Vibrocemento (Fig. 3). Tests were carried out in the Laboratory of Material Testing, Department of Civil Engineering Environmental and Architecture of the University of Cagliari.

Fig. 2. Connections between precast plinth-column

Fig. 3. Casting of the reinforced concrete plinth

2.1 Materials

Three different concrete mixtures were made: RC0% made with fine and coarse natural aggregates, RC30% made with fine natural aggregates and natural and recycled coarse aggregates (70% by weight of natural aggregates and 30% by weight of recycled aggregates), RC50% with fine natural aggregates and natural and recycled coarse aggregates (50% by weight of natural aggregates and 50% by weight of recycled aggregates). Precast columns were made with RC0%. The concrete mixes are shown in Table 1.

Table 1. Mix design of concrete (1 m^3)

Concrete		RC0%	RC30%	RC50%
Cement CEM 525 RI (kg)		350	356	352
Water (kg)		160	186	215
Fine natural aggregates (kg)	0–2 mm	120	130	120
	0–6 mm	600	595	600
Coarse natural aggregates (kg)	4–10 mm	520	365	255
	8–16 mm	600	415	300
Coarse recycled aggregates (kg)	4–16 mm	0	340	560

The results of natural and recycled aggregate characterization are reported in Table 2, in compliance with the UNI EN 933–1 and UNI EN 12620 standards. Figure 4 shows the aggregate particle size distribution used in the concrete mixes RC0%, RC30% and RC50%.

For each concrete mix, 6 cubic specimens (150 mm) and 1 prismatic specimen (side 160 mm, height 330 mm) were made. In Table 3 the results of compressive strength, tensile strength, and elastic modulus are reported in appliance with UNI EN 12390–3: UNI EN 12390-3 2019, UNI EN 12390-6: UNI EN 12390-6 2010, and UNI EN 12390–13: UNI EN 12390-13 2013. In plinths and columns reinforcing steel bars B450C were used.

Table 2. Parameters to characterize recycled and natural aggregates

Aggregate particle size (mm)	Water absorption (%)	Density (kg/m^3)	Fine content
0–2 (natural aggregate)	0.80	2562	f3
0–6 (natural aggregate)	1.31	2600	f3
4–10 (natural aggregate)	1.54	2673	f1.5
8–16 (natural aggregate)	1.06	2673	f1.5
4–16 (recycled aggregate)	4.48	2498	f4

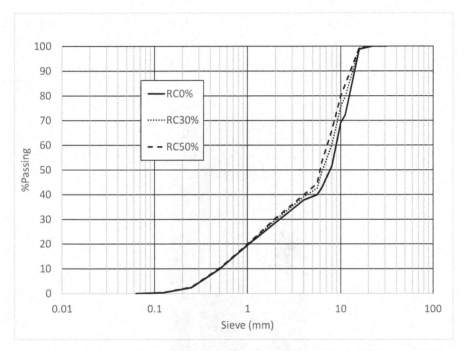

Fig. 4. Aggregate particle size distribution of concrete mixes RC0%, RC30% and RC50%

2.2 Testing Procedure

The test on each specimen was carried out by applying a horizontal load to the top of the reinforced concrete column connected to the plinth (Fig. 5). The horizontal load increases until the precast plinth-column system collapses, with a constant strain rate loading of 0.10 mm/sec.

The loading system can apply a horizontal force up to 500 kN, with maximum displacement at the top of the column up to 200 mm.

In all three specimens, a single crack at the base of the plinth was formed, when the collapse in the plinth-column system occurred, as shown in Fig. 6. In Table 4 the collapse force of the column and plinth systems is shown.

Table 3. Mechanical properties of concrete

Concrete mix design	$R_{c,28d}$ (MPa)	$R_{c,28d\ average}$ (MPa)	$f_{ct,}$ (MPa)	$f_{ct,average}$ (MPa)	E_c (MPa)
RC0%	37.5	37.87	3.55	3.44	28640
	38.2		3.41		
	37.9		3.35		
RC30%	37.1	38.10	3.53	3.48	28814
	39.1		3.49		
	38.1		3.43		
RC50%	37.8	34.97	3.30	3.13	24678
	33.7		2.96		
	33.4		3.13		

Fig. 5. Testing setup

The results show that the presence of coarse recycled aggregate in partial replacement to natural ones does not cause a reduction in the mechanical performance of the prefabricated plinth.

Fig. 6. Crack at the base of the plinths

Table 4. Collapse force of plinth-column systems

Specimen	Collapse force (kN)
Plinth RC0%-Column RC0%	98
Plinth RC30%-Column RC0%	102
Plinth RC50%-Column RC0%	100

3 Recycled Aggregates and Urban Planning

This case study concerns the use of recycled aggregates in the development and implementation of the coastal plans and municipal urban planning of three towns in southern Sardinia: Carloforte, Calasetta, Portoscuso. Nowadays, the municipal urban plan (PUC), the coastal plan (PUL), and the management plan of Nature 2000 Network (PdG) focus the attention on different aspects concerning the territory and the protection of the natural environment. An integrated approach to these planning strategies is essential to environmental, social, and economic sustainability. The analysis conducted aims to define a methodological approach to support decision-making processes in the development strategies on the use of recycled aggregates in coastal areas local planning. In this context, the strategic environmental assessment (SEA) represents an important methodological approach.

The methodological approach concerns two phases. The first phase regards the definition of a logical framework (LF), and analyses the relationships between the various coastal area plans. For each municipality, the following documents were considered: the Municipal Urban Plan, the coastal use plan, and the management plan of the Natura 2000 Network.

Based on future planned developments, in the second phase, the evaluation of recycled aggregates demand was estimated from the analysis of the LF, several actions to encourage the use of recycled aggregates also in coastal areas can be adopted: the expansion of the territory for new tourist complexes (Carloforte), the construction of pedestrian and cycle paths (Calasetta and Portoscuso) (Table 5).

Table 6 shows the applied methodology in this study. The Ministerial Decree of 17 January 2018 (Ministry of Infrastructure and Transport) defines the maximum percentage of recycled aggregates: 30% for concrete C30/37 and up to 80% for concrete with lower resistance. For the construction of road foundations, it is allowed to use 100% of RA.

Table 5. Elements underlying the assessment of the quantity of recycled aggregates in relation to new constructions and refurbishment

Elements for estimating the amount of AR for new buildings	Elements for estimating the quantities of AR for refurbishment
Each building reaches the maximum height allowed by the PUC Technical Implementation Standards	
The quantities of demolition waste are considered to be equal to the quantities of construction material (Morabito n.d.)	The quantity of concrete for maintenance work is considered equal to 50–100 kg/m^2 (Morabito, n.d.). The maintenance area is equal to 12% of the total existing surface of the buildings in zone A, B and C (Altamura, 2012)
In structural concrete, the percentage of recycled concrete aggregates (Compression resistance class C30 / 37) is a maximum of 30% (Technical Construction Standards D.M. 17.01.2018)	
Estimated quantity of AR: 0.7 m^3 for every m^3 of concrete	

The towns studied here, Calasetta, Carloforte, and Portoscuso, are three medium-sized towns located on the south-western coast of Sardinia (Fig. 7). All municipalities are characterized by the presence of one or more Natura 2000 sites.

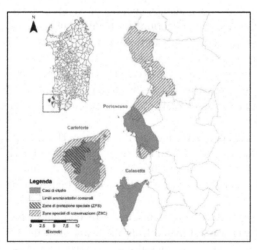

Fig. 7. Study area Source: elaborations on data available on the site of the Geoportal of the Sardinia Region

The planned actions in the three towns, according to the municipal plan, are as follows: the building of new tourist complexes in Carloforte; the construction of cycle tracks and pedestrian paths to connect the town center with the coastal areas in Calasetta; the construction of cycle tracks and pedestrian paths in Portoscuso. The analysis of planning systems indicates that recycled aggregates could use in different contexts, including coastal areas. The estimated quantities of recycled aggregates required for new constructions, refurbishments, cycle and pedestrian paths were 2, 0.1, and 0.5 t/m^2. In Table 6 are reported the estimated quantities of RA and C&DW that could be reused for new constructions, refurbishment, and road layers. According to the Ministerial Decree of 17 January 2018 NTC18, up to 30% by mass of replacement ratio of NA by RA can be used for concrete C30/37 strength class, this value can reach 80% when used for less resistant concrete, this value can reach 100%

Table 6. Estimated quantities of RA and recyclable C&DW

Town	Calasetta		Carloforte		Portoscuso	
RA	30%	80%	30%	80%	30%	80%
RA for new building (t)	8673	23127	15336	40897	18753	50008
RA for refurbishment (t)	152	404	342	911	486	1296
Town	Calasetta		Carloforte		Portoscuso	
RA	100%		100%		100%	
RA for road layers (t)	34198		167872		66989	
Town	Calasetta		Carloforte		Portoscuso	
RA total (t)	43022	57729	183550	209675	86228	118794
C&DW of concrete (t)	86044	115458	367100	419359	172456	236587

In this context, the evaluation suggested that up to 800000 t of concrete C&DW could be recycled.

4 Conclusions

The potential applications of including RCA in the production process of precast reinforced concrete elements is a good practice of circular economy, with several environmental and economic positive aspects. The tests conducted on the precast plinth including RCA, have shown that the presence of coarse recycled aggregate in partial replacement to natural ones does not cause a reduction in the mechanical performance of the prefabricated plinth.

The use of RCA will limit the exploitation of non-renewable natural resources, decrease the concrete debris disposed in landfills, by reusing them in the mix design. It will also reduce production and landfilling costs, due to the lower price of recycled aggregates if compared to natural ones and less amount of debris disposed.

The analysis conducted on the three towns, on the southwest coast of Sardinia Island, to explore the possibility of using RA in new construction projects (buildings and road layers for cycle and pedestrian paths) indicated that there are no impediments in using RA in coastal areas analyzing urban planning systems.

The final objective of this work is to strengthen the concept of sustainability in civil constructions which necessarily intends to provide an important contribution to the construction and demolition waste management plan for the Sardinia Island.

Funding Statement. Authors would like to acknowledge Sardegna Ricerche for the financial support of project: Materials for Sustainable Building and Infrastructure - Recycled Aggregates (MEISAR). POR FESR 2014/2020 - ASSE PRIORITARIO I "RICERCA SCIENTIFICA, SVILUPPO TECNOLOGICO E INNOVAZIONE.

The financial support of the Autonomous Region of Sardinia under Grant PO-FSE 2014–2020, CCI: 2014-IT05SFOP021, through the project "Retrofitting, Rehabilitation and Requalification of the Historical Cultural Architectural Heritage (R3-PAS)" is acknowledged by Flavio Stochino.

References

1. Italian Minister for the environment and protection of land and sea: DM 11/10/17 - Minimum environmental criteria for design services and works for the new construction, renovation and maintenance of public buildings (2017)
2. Kovler, K., Roussel, N.: Properties of fresh and hardened concrete. Cem. Concr. Res. **41**, 775–792 (2011)
3. Meyer, C.: The greening of the concrete industry. Cement Concr. Compos. **31**, 601–605 (2009)
4. Rao, A., Jha, K.N., Misra, S.: Use of aggregates from recycled construction and demolition waste in concrete. Resour. Conserv. Recycl. **50**, 71–81 (2007)
5. Pacheco, J., de Brito, J., Chastre, C., Evangelista, L.: Experimental investigation on the variability of the main mechanical properties of concrete produced with coarse recycled concrete aggregates. Constr. Build. Mater. **201**, 110–120 (2019)
6. Francesconi, L., Pani, L., Stochino, F.: Punching shear strength of reinforced recycled concrete slabs. Constr. Build. Mater. **127**, 248–263 (2016)
7. Koenders, E.A., Pepe, M., Martinelli, E.: Compressive strength and hydration processes of concrete with recycled aggregates. Cem. Concr. Res. **56**, 203–212 (2014)
8. Kou, S.C., Poon, C.S.: Effect of the quality of parent concrete on the properties of high performance recycled aggregate concrete. Constr. Build. Mater. **77**, 501–508 (2015)
9. Ajdukiewicz, A., Kliszczewicz, A.: Influence of recycled aggregates on mechanical properties of HS/HPC. Cement Concr. Compos. **24**, 269–279 (2002)
10. Etxeberria, M., Marı, A.R., Vazquez, E.: Recycled aggregate concrete as structural material. Mater. Struct. **40**, 529–541 (2007)
11. Rahal, K.N.: Mechanical properties of concrete with recycled coarse aggregate. Build. Environ. **42**(1), 407–415 (2007)
12. González-Fonteboa, B., Martínez-Abella, F.: Concretes with aggregates from demolition waste and silica fume. Materials and mechanical properties. Build. Environ. **43**(4), 429–437 (2008)
13. Pani, L., Francesconi, L., Rombi, J., Naitza, S., Balletto, G., Mei, G.: Recycled Aggregates, mechanical properties and environmental sustainability. Planning Nat. Ecosyst. Serv. INPUT Acad. **2019**, 431–442 (2019)

14. Pani, L., Francesconi, L., Rombi, J., Mistretta, F., Sassu, M., Stochino, F.: Effect of parent concrete on the performance of recycled aggregate concrete. Sustainability **12**(22), 1–17 (2020)
15. Pepe, M., Toledo Filho, R.D., Koenders, E.A., Martinelli, E.: Alternative processing procedures for recycled aggregates in structural concrete. Constr. Build. Mater. **69**, 124–132 (2014)
16. Stochino, F., Pani, L., Francesconi, L., Mistretta, F.: Cracking of reinforced recycled concrete slabs. Int. J. Struct. Glass Adv. Mater. Res. **1**(1), 3–9 (2017)
17. Tabsh, S.W., Abdelfatah, A.S.: Influence of recycled concrete aggregates on strength properties of concrete. Constr. Build. Mater. **23**, 1163–1167 (2009)
18. UNI EN 12620: ggregates for concrete (2008)
19. UNI 933–1: Tests for geometrical properties of aggregates. Part 1: Determination of particle size distribution - Sieving method (2012)
20. Italian Minister Ministry of Infrastructure and Transport: DM 17/01/18 – Technical standards for construction (2018)
21. UNI EN 12390–3: Testing hardened concrete. Part 3: Compressive strength of test specimens (2019)
22. UNI EN 12390–6: Tests on hardened concrete - Part 6: Splitting tensile strength of the specimens (2010)
23. UNI EN 12390–13: Test on hardened concrete - Part 13: Determination of the secant modulus of elasticity in compression (2013)
24. Xu, J.J., Chen, Z.P., Zhao, X.Y., Demartino, C., Ozbakkaloglu, T., Xue, J.Y.: Seismic performance of circular recycled aggregate concrete-filled steel tubular columns: FEM modelling and sensitivity analysis. Thin Walled Struct. **141**, 509–525 (2019)
25. Xu, J.J., Chen, Z.P., Ozbakkaloglu, T., Zhao, X.-Y., Demartino, C.: A critical assessment of the compressive behavior of reinforced recycled aggregate concrete columns. Eng. Struct. **161**, 161–175 (2018)
26. Xu, J.J., Chen, Z.P., Xiao, Y., Demartino, C., Wang, J.H.: Recycled aggregate concrete in FRP-confined columns: a review of experimental results. Compos. Struct. **174**, 277–291 (2017)
27. Pani, L., Rombi, J., Francesconi, L., Mereu, A.: Circular economy model of recycled aggregates for the construction sector of Sardinia Islan. Environ. Eng. Manag. J. **19**(10), 1847–1855 (2020)

Local Supply Chains and Circular Economy for Building Materials. The PLES Project in Sardinia

Giovanna Concu[✉], Maria Maddalena Achenza, Roberto Baccoli, Andrea Frattolillo,
Roberto Innamorati, Costantino Carlo Mastino, Riccardo Riu, and Monica Valdes

Department of Civil and Environmental Engineering and Architecture, University of Cagliari,
Via Marengo 3, 09123 Cagliari, Italy
gconcu@unica.it

Abstract. Sardinia is characterized by an economic and productive system of modest competitiveness. This connotation also distresses the construction sector, which is affected by historical problems related to insularity, employment difficulties, the lack of economic resources, as well as the contingent and more general economic-production crisis. This situation, associated with the high environmental impact connected to the construction industry, highlights the potential of innovative construction solutions based on the logic of the short supply chain, the circular economy, and the eco-balance. In that context the PLES (Local Products for Sustainable Buildings) project was carried out, with the aim of developing multilayer construction systems for walls and floors made of locally produced materials mainly of natural origin. This project, funded by the Sardinian public administration, was carried out through the collaboration between a research group and a cluster of companies operating in the Sardinian territory. This paper illustrates the objectives, activities and main results of the PLES project, which carried out a feasibility assessment of local supply chains start up for the production of building materials and eco-sustainable construction systems in Sardinia, highlighting both the critical issues and the positive repercussions.

Keywords: Building materials · Natural materials · Local supply chain · Energy efficiency · Eco-sustainable construction systems · Circular economy

1 Introduction

The construction sector is currently responsible on average for over 35% of the consumption of raw materials, soil, water, and energy and for over 30% of pollution and the production of waste. This situation requires a revision of the management models of the building stock, regarding both new and existing buildings. Focusing on the design and construction of new buildings, it should be emphasized that starting from 2021 all new buildings built in Italy will have to be "nearly Zero Energy Buildings" (nZEB) [1], namely buildings with almost zero energy needs [2–4]. This means significantly improving the energy performance of new buildings compared to the average of the

© Springer Nature Switzerland AG 2021
O. Gervasi et al. (Eds.): ICCSA 2021, LNCS 12958, pp. 44–58, 2021.
https://doi.org/10.1007/978-3-030-87016-4_4

national building stock [5]. In this context, the sustainability of building materials is of fundamental importance, and local supply chains take on a strategic role. In fact, the reduction of the environmental impact of a "green" building goes through the following factors:

- lower energy requirements than traditional buildings,
- lower water consumption compared to traditional buildings,
- lower environmental impact over the entire life cycle,
- best quality and indoor comfort.

These objectives can be achieved by means of the following strategies:

- increased use of natural ventilation,
- greater use of natural light and attention to passive solar gains,
- greater use of systems for low temperature heating and high temperature cooling, in other words systems that operate at a temperature close to that required with a low temperature difference,
- greater use of systems powered by renewable sources,
- greater use of *local and eco-sustainable materials.*

The resort to local short supply chains to produce building materials is particularly appropriate in contexts of isolated economies, such as those existing in island regions like Sardinia. Indeed, the situation of insularity increasingly encourages the implementation of self-sufficiency paths in the production and management of resources, to characterize the economy from the point of view of sustainability [6].

In this regard, it is worth underlining that the concept of sustainability involves both the environmental, the economic and the social aspects [7], therefore orienting the economy towards the track of sustainability suggests to implement solutions that enhance both the environmental, the economic and the social capitals.

The PLES project - Local Products for Sustainable Buildings - fits into this context. It is a project funded by the local authority Sardegna Ricerche [8], based on the synergy between the university and local companies for the achievement of a common goal. The PLES project fits into the general context of the bioeconomy and the circular economy, and in the specific context of sustainable construction. It is motivated by the need / opportunity to develop production processes based on the logic of short supply chain, circularity, and eco-balance, using eco-friendly, recyclable, locally available and energy-efficient construction materials. This need derives from considerations concerning various aspects, such as the need to renovate the construction sector in deep crisis, the condition of Sardinia's insularity, which requires self-sufficiency in terms of production and management of resources, the obligation to contain the impacts related to the construction sector.

This paper describes the PLES project in terms of objectives, activities and results achieved. The article is structured on 5 sections: after this introduction, Sect. 2 provides an overview of the project. Subsequently, Sect. 3 illustrates the main activities in which the project was divided, and Sect. 4 summarizes the results. Finally, Sect. 5 proposes some concluding remarks.

2 The PLES Project

The general objective of the PLES project, which also constitutes its scientific theme, was the development of constructive solutions for walls and floors consisting of multilayer packages that use sustainable materials, mainly of natural origin, and locally available. This objective was shared and pursued through the synergy between the research group and the companies belonging to the cluster supporting the project.

The project therefore had the objective of studying multilayered load-bearing elements including the insulating element, and which can be integrated with a finishing element capable of increasing the environmental acoustic comfort and adding aesthetic value to the panel. The multilayer package is made up as follows:

- structural elements:

  - Cross Laminated Timber (CLT) made of Sardinian Maritime Pine
  - masonry (clay bricks or concrete blocks)

- elements for thermal and acoustic insulation:

  - cork
  - sheep's wool
  - earth-based products

- finishing elements:

  - textile handicraft products
  - plasters of natural origin.

All the materials selected to make the multilayer packages are locally produced, and their choice was based on the following considerations.

The construction systems with CLT panels are having a rapid development throughout Europe thanks to their intrinsic advantages [9, 10]: naturalness, dimensional stability, the advanced degree of prefabrication at the production level, the rapidity of assembly, the remarkable properties of strength and stiffness. CLT elements are solid multi-layer load-bearing panels obtained by overlapping and gluing crossed layers of boards, which can be used both as walls and as floors. Recently, the first residential buildings with load-bearing structures in CLT were also built in Sardinia, however, using imported timber, in particular spruce from Austria or Germany, with a considerable increase in cost. A crucial point of the PLES project was the choice of using locally produced timber, namely Maritime Pine, contributing to the theme of sustainable development of zero-kilometer timber construction in Sardinia, using local resources. This in particular can enhance Sardinian forests, resulting in an increase in the forest area in order to guarantee the sustainability of the supply chain, with all the positive implications of environmental protection and ozone hole reduction, hydrogeological protection of a territory potentially at risk, and of development and economic impulse of traditionally depressed regional areas, as well as new life for the building market now in deep crisis [11, 12].

Cork, sheep's wool, earth, are also materials of natural origin, locally produced, and therefore consistent with the idea of biocompatibility and the production process in a short supply chain. These materials have interesting thermal and acoustic insulation characteristics - in particular the use of cork in construction is not new - however their systematic use is still penalized by the competition of materials manufactured on a large scale, which can therefore be placed on the market at a more competitive price. The definition of design criteria for the implementation of these materials in Sardinian timber-based walls or floors packages would give further impetus to the cork sector, to the emerging and innovative sectors of sheep's wool and earth as insulating materials, with the positive effects in terms of eco-sustainability and promotion in the employment and social sphere already highlighted for the Sardinian CLT panels.

The integration into the wall or floor construction systems of fine finishes, consisting of fine fabrics such as the traditional products of the island's textile craftsmanship, which can also bring a benefit in terms of noise reduction to the environment, expresses an innovative combination of traditional craftsmanship and technology, opening new scenarios in the field of design and technological research, with important repercussions in terms of development.

Alongside the wall and floor elements having the Sardinian CLT as a supporting structure, the study of the application of the insulating materials described above on traditional masonry elements (concrete and brick) was carried out too. Although these materials are obviously less sustainable than wood, this choice allows to better frame the performance of the timber-based packages in relation to the more traditional masonry elements, and to diversify the possibilities of using the innovative insulating materials.

The main activities in which the PLES project was articulated to achieve the intended objectives are illustrated in the next Sect. 3.

3   PLES Activities

The PLES project was developed through a series of activities:

1. Analysis of Production Processes;
2. Mechanical and Energetic Characterization of Materials;
3. Implementation of Models for Numerical Simulation;
4. Laboratory Tests on Manufactured Prototypes.

3.1   Analysis of Production Processes

The starting point of the project consisted in the analysis of the production processes related to the materials and construction systems considered. This analysis was conducted with reference to the Life Cycle Assessment (LCA) model [13] and made it possible to highlight the consumption of energy, the primary and secondary resources, and the emissions and production of non-recyclable waste. In detail, the production cycles of the following products were considered:

- Cross Laminated Timber panel made of Sardinian Maritime Pine (Fig. 1);

- clay bricks for masonry;
- concrete blocks for masonry;
- sheep's wool insulating element;
- raw earth insulating element;
- finishing based on natural plasters;
- finishing with textile handicraft products.

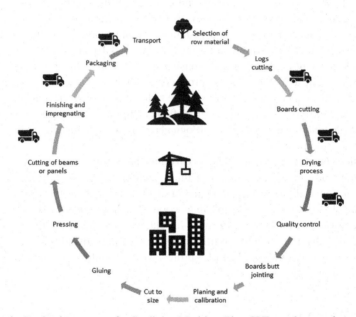

Fig. 1. Production process for Sardinian Maritime Pine CLT panels manufacturing.

The impacts were assessed in terms of both economic, environmental, and social sustainability, and the main aspects associated with the production and marketing of the individual products were highlighted. This phase allowed on the one hand to highlight the main critical issues associated with the various production processes and to indicate possible solutions, on the other hand to propose the development of new materials and/or production processes and the optimization of the already existing ones. Of relevance within the project is the analysis of the supply chain relating to the production of glued laminated timber elements based on Sardinian wood. This activity made it possible to identify the optimal methods for: i) selecting the areas for the supply of the wood resource, ii) selecting and cutting the plants, iii) processing the logs into boards, iv) drying the boards, and to point out the costs and criticalities of the process [11, 14].

3.2 Mechanical and Energetic Characterization of Materials

During the project, an intense activity of experimental tests was carried out on the basic materials and components of the stratigraphies. Specific tests were carried out for the physical-mechanical and thermoacoustic characterization of the products involved in the project and in general of similar products that the local companies intend to characterize, improve and / or promote.

The following tests were of paramount importance:

- tests for the characterization of Sardinian timber (Fig. 2),
- tests on various mix designs for lime-based plasters with natural and vegetable fibres such as wool, hemp, jute (Fig. 3),
- tests on panels in raw earth mixed with vegetable fibres such as hemp (Fig. 4).

Fig. 2. Non-destructive sonic testing on Sardinian Maritime Pine boards.

Fig. 3. Bending test (left) and compression test (right) on lime-plaster with natural fibres.

These products are completely innovative or handcrafted, therefore they are not equipped with technical data sheets that allow their marketing and use in construction. It is therefore necessary to acquire all the technical data useful for requesting the mandatory European certifications for placing them on the market.

In particular, the experimental tests have shown that Sardinian Maritime Pine is a medium-low quality material, especially compared to the woods of central Europe commonly used for the production of laminated timber, but its use in the form of CLT panels allows to obtain a final product with mechanical characteristics superior to those of the starting boards [15, 16].

Fig. 4. Compression test on raw hearth with hemp fibres.

3.3 Implementation of Models for Numerical Simulation

The project also involved the implementation of numerical models to simulate the mechanical and thermo-acoustic behavior of the multilayer packages and of the single constituent layers. This activity mainly consisted in the development and implementation, by means of calculation codes and commercial software, of numerical models for the simulation of the mechanical and thermo-acoustic performance, and the subsequent calibration according to the experimental results.

Particular attention was paid to modeling the mechanical behavior of the CLT panels (Fig. 5). This activity was carried out starting from the collection and study of the existing analytical models relating to the main mechanical characteristics of CLT, namely strengths and stiffnesses. These models were then compared with the experimental data resulting from the tests conducted on Sardinian Maritime Pine CLT elements. The comparison made it possible to adapt the existing models to the specific peculiarities of the local material, having quality generally lower than that of the Central European fir, the species on which most of the existing analytical models are calibrated.

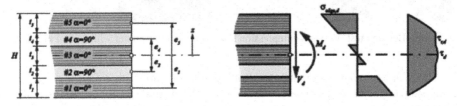

Fig. 5. 5-layer CLT panel subjected to bending action: stress distribution [17].

The simulation of the energetic and acoustic behavior of the building materials and components was based on experimental data relating to measurements of the thermal conductivity of the materials, of the permeability to water vapor and of the soundproofing and sound-absorbing power. Some data were measured with equipment that perform tests according to standardized international procedures, such as thermal conductivity, while other quantities, such as the sound absorption of some materials, were estimated based on measurements performed on-site. In some cases, moreover, to have all the data necessary to simulate the thermo-energetic and acoustic behavior of the prototypes, reference was made to technical standards databases or to scientific literature. Figures 6 and 7 show respectively a thermo-hygrometric simulation and an acoustic simulation of a stratigraphy.

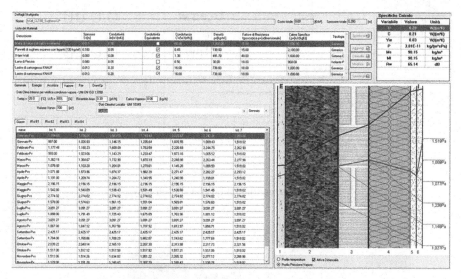

Fig. 6. Thermo-hygrometric simulation of a stratigraphy.

3.4 Laboratory Tests on Manufactured Prototypes

The last experimental activity carried out within the project involved the manufacturing of stratigraphy prototypes and the implementation of laboratory tests for the characterization of their mechanical and thermo-acoustic performance.

In particular, thermal and mechanical tests were carried out on Sardinian Maritime Pine CLT panels (Figs. 8 and 9) to obtain the main quantities, such as strength, stiffness and thermal conductivity, to define their performance, and acoustic tests on masonry (Fig. 10), CLT-based walls, and panels covered by handicraft fine fabric (Fig. 11) to define the soundproofing power of the stratigraphies.

The mechanical and energetic properties of the tested materials and construction systems were collected and implemented according to the procedures provided for compatibility with the BIM (Building Information Modeling) protocol [18]. Through this kind of coding, now indispensable for the advanced management of projects, a database has been created with the aim of promoting the marketing of the local products, and their use by designers and customers [19].

The main results achieved by the PLES project through the activities previously described are summarized in the next Sect. 4.

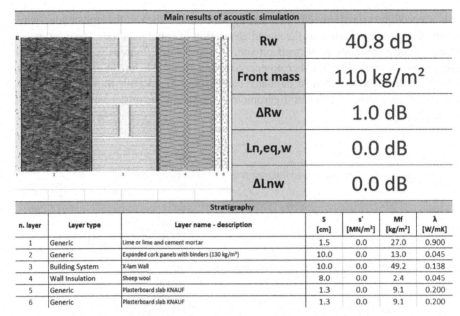

Main results of acoustic simulation		
	Rw	40.8 dB
	Front mass	110 kg/m²
	ΔRw	1.0 dB
	Ln,eq,w	0.0 dB
	ΔLnw	0.0 dB

Stratigraphy						
n. layer	Layer type	Layer name - description	S [cm]	s' [MN/m³]	Mf [kg/m²]	λ [W/mK]
1	Generic	Lime or lime and cement mortar	1.5	0.0	27.0	0.900
2	Generic	Expanded cork panels with binders (130 kg/m³)	10.0	0.0	13.0	0.045
3	Building System	X-lam Wall	10.0	0.0	49.2	0.138
4	Wall Insulation	Sheep wool	8.0	0.0	2.4	0.045
5	Generic	Plasterboard slab KNAUF	1.3	0.0	9.1	0.200
6	Generic	Plasterboard slab KNAUF	1.3	0.0	9.1	0.200

Fig. 7. Acoustic simulation of a stratigraphy.

Fig. 8. Conductivity measurements on CLT panels.

Fig. 9. Bending test on CLT panels.

Fig. 10. Acoustic measurements on clay-brick masonry.

Fig. 11. Acoustic measurements on textile panel.

4   PLES Results

The PLES project aimed to strengthen the Sardinian business system from a sustainable perspective through the enhancement of technologies and the implementation of innovative ideas and processes, in order to increase the competitiveness of regional companies in a global context through greater flows of technologies, skills, people. In this perspective, the main results achieved are the following:

- boost to the development of the Sardinian wood supply chain for structural use;
- support for the diversification of the production and destination of traditional materials such as sheep's wool, raw earth, cork;
- impulse to the development of the production sector of derivatives from vegetable fibres and of fabrics to be used in the construction sector;
- increased competitiveness and innovativeness of the artisan enterprises potentially interested;
- development of new production processes;
- optimization of existing production processes, also through the application of innovative tools and technologies.
  From a technical-practical point of view, the project has made it possible:
- to determine the mechanical performance of Sardinian Maritime Pine CLT panels and consequently to implement technical data sheets containing their mechanical properties, which can be used to encourage production and use of this innovative material (Fig. 12);

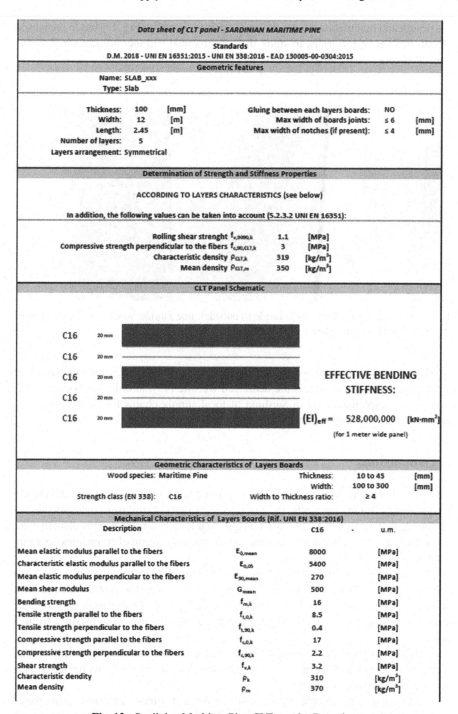

Fig. 12. Sardinian Maritime Pine CLT panel – Data sheet.

- to design and manufacture some prototypes of stratigraphy (Fig. 13) based on natural, local, innovative materials, to study their mechanical and thermo-acoustic behavior and to prepare the relative technical data sheets.

Fig. 13. Stratigraphy made of (from inside to outside): fine fabrics, wood panel, sheep's wool, 3-layer CLT, cork, natural plaster.

All the activities, contents, results and products of the PLES project have been implemented on a freely accessible dedicated website [19], in order to provide a solid basis for the implementation in Sardinia of local supply chains for the production of eco-sustainable building materials.

5   Conclusions

The PLES (Local Products for Sustainable Buildings) project was aimed at developing construction solutions for walls and floors consisting of multilayer packages that use sustainable materials, mainly of natural origin, and locally available. This objective was pursued through the synergy between the university and a group of companies operating in the Sardinian territory.

The project's activities demonstrated the structural-energetic effectiveness of the analysed stratigraphies, highlighting their suitability to meet the performance requirements for walls and floors, and pointing out the possibility of using high-performance, low environmental impact and locally produced construction systems in Sardinian building sector.

In addition, the project made it possible to evaluate the feasibility of implementing local supply chains in Sardinia to produce materials/building elements for sustainable construction and green building.

Of particular importance is the definition of the performance of load-bearing panels in Sardinian CLT, whose local production would allow the activation of a specific supply chain, with important positive effects in environmental, economic, and social terms.

The results of the PLES project can be considered as a basic platform on which to build effective and shared paths aimed at the implementation of these supply chains for sustainable building materials, with the involvement of all potentially interested parties in the Sardinian territory.

Acknowledgements. This study has been supported by POR FESR 2014/2020 - ASSE PRIOR-ITARIO I "RICERCA SCIENTIFICA, SVILUPPO TECNOLOGICO E INNOVAZIONE".

References

1. Directive 2010/31/ EU of the European Parliament
2. Kurnitski, J., et al.: How to define nearly net zero energy buildings nZEB. REHVA J. 6–12 (2012)
3. Wu, W., Harrison, M.S.: Residential net-zero energy buildings: Review and perspective. Renew. Sustain. Energy Rev. **142**, 110859 (2021)
4. Aelenei, L., et al.: Design issues for net zero-energy buildings. Open House Int. **38**(3), 7–14 (2013)
5. Gupta, A., Deshmukh, S.K.: Energy efficient construction materials. Key Eng. Mater. **678**, 35–49 (2016)
6. Clean energy for EU islands, https://ec.europa.eu/energy/topics/markets-and-consumers/clean-energy-eu-islands_en, last accessed 2021/06/18
7. Brundtland, G.H.: Our Common Future: Report of the World Commission on Environment and Development. UN-Dokument A/42/427, Geneva (1987)
8. Sardegna Ricerche, https://www.sardegnaricerche.it/en/, last accessed 2021/06/18
9. Brandner, R., Flatscher, G., Ringhofer, A., Schickhofer, G., Thiel, A.: Cross laminated timber (CLT): overview and development. Eur. J. Wood Wood Prod. **74**(3), 331–351 (2016). https://doi.org/10.1007/s00107-015-0999-5
10. Espinoza, O., Rodriguez Trujillo, V., Laguarda Mallo, M.F., Buehlmann, U.: Cross-laminated timber: status and research needs in Europe. BioResources **11**(1), 281–295 (2016)
11. Concu, G.: Sustainability of the timber supply chain on the island of sardinia. In: Gervasi, O., et al. (eds.) ICCSA 2020. LNCS, vol. 12255, pp. 353–367. Springer, Cham (2020). https://doi.org/10.1007/978-3-030-58820-5_27
12. Fragiacomo, M., Riu, R., Scotti, R.: Can structural timber foster short procurement chains within mediterranean forests? A research case in Sardinia. South-east Eur. For. **6**(1), 107–117 (2015)
13. Guinée, J.B., et al.: Life cycle assessment: past, present, and future. Environ. Sci. Technol. **45**(1), 90–96 (2011)
14. Concu, G.: Introductory Chapter: Timber and Sustainability in Construction. In: Concu, G. (eds) Timber Buildings and Sustainability, InTech (2019)
15. Concu, G.: Prediction of maritime pine boards modulus of elasticity by means of sonic testing on green timber. Appl. Sci. **11**(4), 1748 (2021)
16. Concu, G., De Nicolo, B., Fragiacomo, M., Trulli, N., Valdes, M.: Grading of maritime pine from Sardinia (Italy) for use in cross-laminated timber. Proc. Inst. Civil Eng. – Constr. Mater. **171**(1), 11–21 (2018). https://doi.org/10.1680/jcoma.16.00043
17. EN-1995:2008-06 Eurocode 5: Design of timber structures – Part 1-1: General – Common rules and rules for buildings. European Standard, European Committee for standardization

18. Mastino, C.C., Concu, G., Baccoli, R., Frattolillo, A., Di Bella, A.: Methods for acoustic classification in buildings: an example of application of bim procedures on wooden buildings. In: Proceedings of 48th International Congress and Exhibition on Noise Control Engineering, June 16–19, 2019, Madrid, Spain (2019)
19. The PLES project. https://sites.unica.it/ples/. Accessed 18 June 2021

Indulging in the 'Mediterranean Maritime World' – Diving Tourism in Insular Territories

Dionisia Koutsi[(✉)] and Anastasia Stratigea[iD]

Department of Geography and Regional Planning, School of Rural, Surveying and
Geoinformatics Engineering, National Technical University of Athens, Athens, Greece
koutsidionisia@mail.ntua.gr, stratige@central.ntua.gr

Abstract. Island regions in the Mediterranean have so far been highly attractive
tourism destinations due to their mild climate, relaxing atmosphere and the warm
Mediterranean spirit, culture and hospitality. However, the repercussions of the
prevailing polarized and mass tourism model are already noticeable in their bodies.
These, coupled with the predicted impacts of climate change (CC), can jeopardize
islands' socio-economic and environmental stability. In seeking to achieve sustainable and resilient developmental pathways, new more qualitative tourism options
need to be pursued, bridging valuable competencies of Mediterranean islands,
i.e. their natural/cultural wealth, both inland and underwater, with demanding,
authentic and experience-based tourism offers. Diving tourism represents a challenging, though yet not fully exploited, option in this respect and lies at the heart of
this work. More specifically, potential for diving tourism in Mediterranean islands
is explored by: sketching the policy context of the very essence of this tourism
form, i.e. protection of natural and cultural resources; displaying current successful examples in the Mediterranean and the Greek context; and featuring marine
spatial and other planning and policy concerns for releasing this islands' development potential and grasping opportunities of a rapidly escalating niche market in
a sustainable and resilient way.

Keywords: Island territories · Mediterranean region · Underwater natural and
cultural heritage · Diving tourism · Marine spatial planning

1 Introduction

Proximity of the Mediterranean coastal and island regions to the water element and their
strong connection with the maritime world as the 'vehicle' for commercial transactions
and intercultural exchange of their population has sculpted through time their social and
cultural wealth and attractiveness [1]. Such attributes are nowadays highly appreciated
by visitors, acknowledging also the mild climate, relaxing atmosphere and the warm
Mediterranean spirit, culture and hospitality these send out [2, 3].

Mediterranean islands are representative examples of such regions, being by far the
most highly appreciated world destinations [3]. In 2018 for example, Malta, Cyprus,
Crete and the Ionian Islands are falling into the top four European tourism destinations

© Springer Nature Switzerland AG 2021
O. Gervasi et al. (Eds.): ICCSA 2021, LNCS 12958, pp. 59–74, 2021.
https://doi.org/10.1007/978-3-030-87016-4_5

[4]. However, post-war developments of tourism sector in Mediterranean islands designate mainly a *mass and largely unsustainable polarized model* [5, 6], with severe repercussions in terms of seasonality, carrying capacity of ecosystems [7], and environmental burden, to name a few. Additionally, land sealing for massive tourist infrastructure deployment in coastal areas has led to the reduction of limited land, disruptions of coastal ecosystems, intense energy consumption as well as social and sectoral conflicts. This *polarized tourism model* in coastal areas – both in main land and especially island territories –, is currently highly *vulnerable* due to CC impacts, principally referring to heat and sea level rising as well as coastal erosion [8]. Realization of the significance of *CC impacts* on the socio-economic stability of, particularly, insular areas is crucial [8], placing at stake fishing and agriculture, but also coastal and maritime tourism as pillars of island economies [9]. Vulnerability of insular areas to CC is further worsened due to their limited capacity to design and implement efficient proactive policy measures. The currently ominous CC trends, however, call for urgent immediate (re)action and a reorientation from the mass to a more *sustainable, environmentally-friendly and responsible, resilient and all year round tourism model*, mainly featured by alternative tourism forms that are better adjusted to CC conditions, carrying capacity and competencies of such territories. This reorientation can also alleviate risks imposed by other external crises, e.g. COVID-19 pandemic, rendering mass tourism a restrictive travelling option [10] and unveiling the power of alternative forms for a dynamic post-pandemic tourism revival.

Maritime tourism, combined with *sea and coastal zone* soft recreational activities, is nowadays rapidly evolving [11]; and is recognized as a form of sustainable and resilient exploitation of natural and cultural, of land and maritime nature, capital. It is currently perceived as one of the most dynamic sea- and coastal-based sector for growth and job creation, in alignment with the European Blue Growth Strategy [12]. Of growing popularity is also a specific maritime tourism form, i.e. *diving tourism* (or scuba diving) [13, 14], deemed as a rapidly evolving niche market (over 27 million divers were certified from 1967 to 2018 [15]); and falling into the dominant trend for personalized, culture- and nature-based, sophisticated and authentic experiences [3, 16]. Diving tourism features a tailor-made and individualized form, primarily targeting elite, demanding, higher spending and all year-round tourist flows [17]; and addressing an environmentally-aware and keen on gathering new experiences in the spectacular maritime world community.

Diving destinations in Mediterranean islands offer a favorable environment, attributed to the unique wealth of *natural and cultural reserves*, such as coral reefs, protected species of flora and fauna as well as plenty of *Underwater Cultural Heritage* (UCH) sites. Diving in UCH sites in particular, especially in *historical wrecks*, has become extremely popular in recent times, presenting a chance to explore a peculiar, and largely unknown, part of the local, European or even global history, lying sunk at the bottom of the sea in harmony with surrounding extraordinary marine ecosystems [18]. UCH sites in the Mediterranean are, in many cases, linked to battlegrounds where historical martial events have occurred, witnessed through e.g. martial installations' sites, sunken ship and plane wrecks of World War (WW) I and II [1, 19]. Despite the rich WW I and especially WW II UCH evidence in the Mediterranean Sea however, the potential of *cultural diving tourism* is not yet fully exploited. This is, among others, mainly due to technical, legislative, governance, but also spatial delineation of these heritage sites, with the latter placing at stake vulnerable and valuable natural and cultural assets due to their exposure to human-induced pressures, e.g. overfishing, coastal zones' pollution to name a few [6].

Along these lines, the *goal* of this article is to open up the discourse as to the hidden underwater natural and cultural wealth of the Mediterranean region; and its exploitation for unfolding diving tourism potential and featuring alternative, sustainable and resilient, natural and cultural heritage-led and environmentally-friendly developmental pathways of Mediterranean islands. Towards this end, in Sect. 2, a review of current policy and legal considerations on the protection of marine natural and UCH resources – the decision environment – is carried out. Section 3 wanders in the Mediterranean by providing good practices of diving activity in coastal and insular areas. In Sect. 4, diving and UCH tourism potential in the Greek territory is sketched which, despite the distinguishable natural and cultural maritime resources, these remain unexploited mainly due to multiple legislative and planning barriers. Finally, in Sect. 5, certain (spatial) planning concerns for the integrated and sustainable diving tourism development in the Mediterranean Islands are articulated.

2 Protecting Marine Natural and Cultural Resources – An Issue of Glocal Relevance

A *healthy and wealthy* marine environment is a key driver for the sustainable development of island regions, while forming the ground for deploying *diving tourism activity.* It is linked to the sustainable management of natural and/or UCH resources of relevant sites, the protection and preservation of which is substantial for fulfilling expectations of both the demand – cultural and diving tourism community –, and the supply side – local entrepreneurship in relevant sites, targeting growth and employment objectives. However, the *multi-level and multi-sectoral* dimensions of both the natural and cultural (UCH) resources render their protection a *complex* but also, in many cases, *glocal* (global and local) *issue.* As such, it calls for policy guidelines that rest upon the international, European, national, regional and even the local level.

With regard to UCH, its precise definition as well as conditions for protection and sustainable exploitation is demarcated in the *2001 UNESCO Convention* [20] on the 'Protection of the Underwater Cultural Heritage', in accordance with the Law of the Sea [21]. In this Convention, UCH is defined as "*all traces of human existence having a cultural, historical or archaeological character which have been partially or totally under water, periodically or continuously, for at least 100 years*" [20, Article 1, p. 51]. As such are featured e.g. sunken vessels or aircraft or any part thereof, their cargo or other contents, together with their *archaeological and natural context.* Value of UCH is entrenched on social, historical, environmental, humanistic and cultural dimensions. When it comes to shipwrecks, however, value is decisively enriched by a series of events that occurred before, during and after its immersion, coupled with information regarding submersion period, last trip purpose, etc. [22]. The above factors, although crucial for shipwreck's value assessment, are not included in the UNESCO Convention, considering only *time* as a decisive UCH assessment criterion (sunk vessels > 100 years), excluding thus e.g. WW II shipwrecks; while its adoption by only 58 countries places at risk of loss a significant part of global UCH.

Sustainable exploitation of the *marine environment and related resources* is nowadays acquiring special attention at the *EU level* as well. Important milestones in this respect are the *Integrated Maritime Policy* (IMP) and *Blue Growth Strategy*, reflecting the will to open up the field of sustainable exploitation of European Seas to the benefit of growth and employment. Ambitious EU *goals* are mainly articulated in the:

- *Integrated Maritime Policy (IMP)* [23]: emphasizing the need for creating optimal conditions for the sustainable growth of maritime sectors and coastal regions; while ensuring achievement of the environmental objectives of EU.
- *Marine Strategy Framework Directive* [24]: aiming at the protection of the marine environment as a precious heritage; and motivating member states to deploy marine strategies and undertake action for its protection, preservation, and, where feasible, restoration.
- *Protocol on Integrated Coastal Zone Management* (ICZM) [25]: having at its heart the Mediterranean coastal zones, it features an inclusive approach for addressing problems emerging from high pressures exerted on the Mediterranean marine environment and coastal resources; and provides guidance towards a more sustainable development of these zones.
- *EU Biodiversity Strategy for 2020* [26]: predicting the design of measures to preserve vulnerable marine ecosystems (Action 14, p. 14) and the support of implementation of the Marine Strategy Framework Directive.
- *Blue Growth Strategy* [27]: focusing on the sustainable exploitation of marine resources as a driving force and a new source of economic prosperity. Maritime tourism is one of the five priority sectors of this strategy, targeting environmentally and culturally-friendly forms for serving local and regional development objectives.
- *Maritime Spatial Planning Directive (MSP)* [28]: representing the main IMP tool and a framework for properly handling available maritime space and resources. It aims at spatially balancing sectoral interests and achieving sustainable use of marine resources in line with the EU Sustainable Development Strategy. UCH protection and diving activity are parts of MSPs, same as Marine Protected Areas (MPA), with both serving eco-systems and diving sites' protection.
- *EU Biodiversity Strategy for 2030* [29]: predicting the preparation of national maritime spatial plans by member states in 2021. These cover all maritime sectors as well as area-based conservation and management; while they also address the protection of, among others, marine ecosystems.
- *European Strategy for more Growth and Jobs in Coastal and Maritime Tourism* [30]: promoting sustainable coastal and maritime tourism based on data collection, alternative tourism forms and stakeholders' engagement in MSP processes. It stresses the importance of (U)CH-based tourism and Underwater Archaeological Parks (UAPs) as pillars for sustainable tourism in coastal and island regions.

Review of the above key policy frameworks leads to the conclusion that while protection of *maritime natural and UCH sites* and their sustainable exploitation as *diving tourism spots* for serving local development and wealth is highlighted, no specific directions are provided at this level. Maritime tourism in general and diving tourism in natural and UCH sites in particular are supposed to be dealt with in relevant national, regional or even transnational MSP studies. However, the yet limited deployment of relevant strategic marine spatial plans and their specialization at lower spatial scales counteracts this providence. It has to be admitted though that MSP and ICZM definitely establish a more promising *maritime decision-making framework* for delineating diving tourism sites and tackling maritime sectoral competition as well as pressure exerted on them by other maritime activities (e.g. fishing, sea transportation).

3 'Diving' in the Mediterranean – Successful Examples of Natural and Cultural Underwater Sites

Mediterranean insular territories are endowed with spectacular underwater marine reserves. Additionally, as hosts of important civilizations and battlegrounds (e.g., WW I and II), they constitute significant UCH repositories, such as submerged cities and ancient ports, a large number of WW I and II UCH objects. The latter count over 15.000 wrecks [31]; and witness the dramatic repercussions of war events, but also ancient commercial shipping failures. Based on these assets, many Mediterranean islands form nowadays outstanding and some of the most visited *diving spots*, located in highly rated tourism destinations, like Portugal, Spain, Italy, France and Greece [32]. In most cases, these diving spots are featured as *diving parks* or MPAs, thus assuring documentation, protection and sustainable exploitation of local underwater assets. Few notable examples of these spots are presented in the following.

3.1 The Medes Islands in Spain

The Medes Islands, situated in the heart of the Costa Brava, Catalonia region, Spain, constitute one of the most visited and significant MPA in the western Mediterranean. MPA's sensitive ecosystem protection is pursued through the establishment of 0.39 km^2 (2%) of fully protected areas, 4.24 km^2 (21.8%) of partially protected areas and 14.85 km^2 (76.2%) of unprotected areas [33]. Although well known as a *natural reserve* (underwater corals, caves and plenty of flora and fauna species) (Fig. 1), it provides the chance for diving in the *Reggio Messina (115 m long)* in Medes Islands, the largest ship in Costa Brava, sunk deliberately in 1991 (Fig. 2); and *Avenire (47 m long)*, being sunk in a fierce storm near Cala Montgó cove in 1971 [34].

The official launch of the MPA is dated back to 1983. Protection status predicts prohibition of fishery and extraction of live marine species in a zone of 75 m around the islands. This status was extended in 1990, when the Marine Partial Nature Reserve was established, prohibiting all forms of fishing and harvesting of marine resource and the possession of fishing gear. Ten years later the reserve was transformed into a much larger *marine and terrestrial natural park*, allowing the integrated land and underwater management and protection of this area. Within the park and buffer zone, certain controlled traditional and recreational fishing activities are permitted. The extension was critical for improving MPA's environmental status, enabling integrated management and encouraging *nature-based responsible tourism.*

Fig. 1. The Dolphin Cave in Medes Islands, Source: [35]

Fig. 2. The Reggio Messina in Medes Islands, Source: [36]

The *number of diving visitors* in Medes Islands is defined in alignment to the restrictions of its protection status. An annual threshold, set by the Catalonia Government, predicts a maximum of 74,876 dives per year, allowing more divers to be part of the diving experience in the Medes Islands. Diving activity has a remarkable economic impact for the surrounding area, as showcased by the 10 million € revenue per year only for a small destination such as L'Estartit-Medes Islands [37].

3.2 Portofino Marine Protected Area in Genoa - Italy

In 1999, the Portofino MPA was established covering 3.74 km^2, both in land and underwater environment, and 13 km of coastline in the north-western coast of Italy in the Ligurian Sea [38]. The MPA was created in order for the underwater *cultural and natural landscapes* to be preserved and protected. It operates under a three-zoning plan, defining zone-specific regulations and restrictions. Human activities, including diving, fishing and anchoring are regulated and monitored. *Twenty authorized sites* can be found in the demarcated area (Fig. 3), featuring reefs, walls, the statue of the Crist of the Abyss and *16 shipwrecks* [39].

Portofino MPA is a *natural and cultural heritage diving area* attracting, in an annual basis, an average of 40,000 dives [38, 40]. Divers are wandering along coralliferous cliffs, a habitat of European interest and particularly vulnerable to mechanical damages. The most popular spots are the natural landscapes of the Carega Shoal (spot 11), the Althare Point (spot 17) and the Faro Cape (spot 21) [40]. Collection and uploading in a relevant website of diverse diving sites' information [location, depth, expertise required for each site, (e.g. Fig. 4), booking services etc.] for all 20 authorized sites is carried out by Portofino divers' community through *crowdsourcing* initiatives. Local population was against the establishment of the MPA, raising concerns as to its impacts on tourism flows and local revenues, emerging from limitations within the MPA's zones. However, and despite the reduced visitation in certain periods [38], MPA deployment has positively affected tourist flows and especially diving tourism [42], while keeping also track with a more sustainable and environmentally-friendly model and respective branding of the place.

3.3 Shipwreck Diving Destination in Malta

An outstanding example of *popular diving spots* in the Mediterranean is the island of Malta, a *wreck diving destination* with over 80 plane and ship wrecks at varying depths

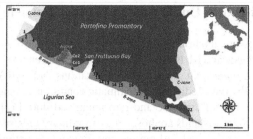
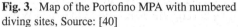

Fig. 3. Map of the Portofino MPA with numbered diving sites, Source: [40]

Fig. 4. MOHAWK DEER Wreck at the Portofino MPA, Source: [41]

around the coast, serving diversifying divers' experience levels. From the 2.77 million inbound tourists in 2019, approximately 6,5% have experienced diving activity (approx. 182,000 divers per year) [43], largely contributing to tourism attractiveness and local revenue. Preservation status and wreck diving in Malta have not so far been regulated. This entails risks as to the protection/preservation of UCH and raises safety issues for divers. A new regulation though is about to come in force soon, enforcing controlled access to a significant number of WW I and II underwater wrecks to Maltese and foreign divers. So far, about one-third of Malta's seabed has been thoroughly mapped, a process that started some 20 years ago and is expected to result in unimagined documentation [44].

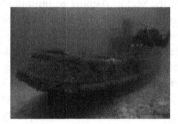

Fig. 5. The MV Xlendi, Cominoland, Karwela off Xatt l-Aħmar site in Malta, Source: [45]

Fig. 6. St. Michael wreck – Marsaskala, Source: [45]

Today Malta has established *7 conservation areas* around certain wrecks, already known as diving spots. Indicative examples are: MV Xlendi, Cominoland, Karwela off Xatt l-Aħmar (three particular diving spots in three different wrecks in close distance) (Fig. 5); Um el Faroud in Wied Iż-Żurrieq; Tug St. Michael (Fig. 6), Tug 10 in Marsaskala; Imperial Eagle off Qawra Point; Rożi, P29 off Ċirkewwa; Blenheim Bomber off Xrobb l-Għaġin; and Bristol Beaufighter off Exiles Point. Each region includes different, properly combined, natural and cultural assets, based on their proximity. For example, the Um el Faroud in Wied Iż-Żurrieq site refers to the Libyan oil tanker "MV Um El Faroud" and its transformation to an artificial reef.

4 Potential of Greece in Diving and Underwater Cultural Tourism

The inextricable link of Greece to the sea is uncurled along the 15.000 km of coastline, 40% of which are linked to its 9,837 islands and islets [46]. The Greek maritime environment is featured by unique *natural attributes*, e.g. coastline configurations, NATURA 2000 regions and wetlands. Additionally, the Mediterranean climatic conditions create natural landscapes that host a large variety of endemic and rare fauna and flora [47]. Apart from their exquisite *natural attributes*, islands are hosts of extraordinary *tangible and intangible cultural resources*, both in the land and marine environment. *Maritime UCH* is mainly the outcome of islands' strategic geopolitical position and role in WWs, location at the crossroad of sea trade routes, and the establishment of important civilizations back in the ancient times [3]. Based on the abundance/value of its natural and cultural underwater assets, Greece in general and *insular regions* in particular constitute ideal places for the development of *diving tourism*; and are already attracting the interest of diving community for gathering relative experiences in *ancient wrecks*, strongly connected with local mythology. This interest is expressed by the steadily increasing number of divers visiting Greece (increase by 42% in 2011–12 and 10% from 2012–13, counting about 230,000 divers in 2013) [48]. Despite this significant potential, diving tourism in natural and cultural diving spots in Greece has not yet attained the required attention and reached its potential.

Policy directions as to the spatial pattern of tourism development in Greece are provided by the Special Framework on Spatial Planning and Sustainable Development for Tourism (2009, as revised in 2013) [49], featuring strategic guidelines for the flourishing of the sector. Aiming to promote a more balanced and sustainable deployment of the sector, it places emphasis on alternative tourism forms, among which lie maritime tourism and more specifically *cruise, yachting and diving tourism*. The latter is promoted in already tourist developed but also developing areas; and roughly sketches territories that dispose particular marine natural and cultural assets, attractive to this niche market. Amendment of this framework in 2013 sustains this focus on alternative tourism forms, stressing also the high risks faced by coastal and island regions due to overtourism and impingement of their carrying capacity.

This policy framework, however, fell over predictions of the *legislative context*, placing, until recently, *significant obstacles* to diving activity by rendering accessibility of many potential diving sites totally prohibited. This reflected a steadily defensive attitude of the Ministry of Culture and the Ephorate of Underwater Antiquities against recreational diving. Banning accessibility served the goal of protecting submerged antiquities and cultural heritage in potential diving sites. In 2003, protection measures intensify, due to a Ministerial Decision characterizing shipwrecks and aircrafts, submerged in the Greek seas for over 50 years, as *cultural monuments*. Their protection is assured by a buffer zone of 300 m, within which diving was prohibited [6].

The concept of *diving parks*, as an important step for exploiting maritime natural and cultural assets, is firstly introduced in the Greek legislation in 2005, with the enactment of the Law 3409/2005 [50] for *recreational diving*, constituting a milestone for diving tourism in Greece and releasing diving activity, with a few exceptions, along almost the entire length of the country's coastline. Diving sites with significant archaeological value are defined as accessible UAPs, allowing respective activities under specific rules.

Such sites have already been nominated as *protected areas with cultural interest*. In 2014, the legislative framework has taken some further steps forward [51], by expanding diving parks in Natura 2000 MPAs, marine aquaculture, shipwrecks and Accessible Archaeological Sites, opening thus new chances for natural and cultural diving tourism in coastal and insular areas.

Following these developments, at present four UAPs are established in Greece, namely [52]: i) UAP at Methony Bay - Sapienza Island (Peloponnese), established in 2013, in which the ancient 'Granite Columns' and 'Roman Sarcophagi' shipwrecks are located; ii) UAP at Navarino Bay (Peloponnese), established in 2013, hosting the newer "Irene Serenade" shipwreck; iii) UAP at Pavlopetri (Lakonia), established in 2016, hosting the first seabed museum, where one of the most ancient sunken prehistoric settlements of the world lies (Fig. 7); and iv) the recent UAP at Alonissos and Northern Sporades established in 2020 (Fig. 8), hosting a classical shipwreck of the 5th century BC, which carried over 4.000 amphoras and was revealed in 1985 at a depth of 22–23 m.

Fig. 7. UAP at Pavlopetri Lakonia – Greece, Sunken Ancient City, Source: [53]

Fig. 8. UAP at Alonissos and Northern Sporades, Source: [54]

By getting insight into the above-mentioned UAPs, the importance of the Greek *underwater cultural assets* is unveiled, with reference to ancient but also more recent shipwrecks or archaeological remains of ancient cities. The ever-increasing interest for diving permissions in the Greek seas leads to intensified efforts for establishing more UAPs, by sustainably exploiting the shipwrecks in Kea island, promoting the diving sites of '*HMHS Britannic*', '*S/S Burdigala*' and '*Patris*' as well as the submerged city of Epidaurus; the yet unexploited site in Antikythera island; the *58 ancient shipwrecks* recently discovered in the neighborhood of Fournoi island, characterized as the *shipwreck capital of the world*; the Destroyer '*Queen Olga*' in Leros island, to name a few [55]. These, although the largest, and of high historical significance, shipwrecks in the Mediterranean Sea, remain unexplored, unexploited and, most importantly, *unprotected*.

Further improvements of the contemporary legislative framework include the incorporation, in 2018, of the European MSP Directive 2014/89/EC into the Greek legislation, broadening the *strategic marine spatial planning* context of the Greek policy, although the relevant strategic planning endeavor is not yet accomplished; and a recent law [56] placing *diving tourism* as a core activity along the Greek coastline. These are expected to alter the scenery of diving activity in Greece, giving prominence to its fabulous natural and cultural reserves as diving sites. Protected, previously inaccessible, diving spots are expected to raise divers' interest, abrogating seasonality drawbacks and creating multiplier effects in terms of quality of tourist flows as well as tourism entrepreneurship and new employment opportunities to the benefit of the local, regional but also national level.

5 Discussion – Open Issues

The importance attached to the protection and sustainable exploitation of maritime, natural and UCH resources as a means for local/regional development is nowadays highly acknowledged. Insular territories in the Mediterranean seem to be privileged in this respect due to the abundance of relevant resources, witnessing the long history and transactions taking place among their inhabitants. These resources can render Mediterranean insular territories globally attractive *diving tourism spots*, thus broadening their role/value in the tourist scene and their potential to become environmentally- and culturally-responsible, high class, all year-round tourist destinations. The above mentioned examples reveal that this potential is already partially captured; and is framed by the availability, type, narrative and value attached to these resources, as well as legislative context and related spatial tools. Thus the Spanish and Italian examples present cases where *MPA's* are established to protect these resources as well as monitor/control diving activity for serving sustainability objectives. Malta, despite lacking a fully regulatory regime for diving sites, seems to rate high as an outstanding example of popular diving spots, falling into the 7 declared *conservation areas*. Greece, despite endowed in natural and UCH resources, has quite recently taken steps to get into the diving tourism niche, though still lacking a compact national maritime spatial strategy as well as detailed spatial delineation/documentation of relevant resources.

Speaking from a (spatial) planning perspective, however, preservation and sustainable exploitation of maritime resources seems to be a rather *wicked planning and governance issue*, with multiple *spatial dimensions*. It also depicts important *challenges and open issues* that need to be properly handled, especially when one comes to UCH as the main focus of diving experience, *being mostly the case in the Greek coastal and marine environment*. Some critical thoughts on this topic are summarized in Fig. 9 and are shortly discussed in the following, presenting the need for a more *integrated and holistic approach* on the topic that stresses the multiple spatial, developmental, sectoral, societal, governance, etc. dimensions of the sustainable exploitation of maritime natural and cultural resources in Mediterranean islands for diving tourism.

At first, diving tourism, while grounded on the marine environment, is tightly interwoven with the coastal but also the land part of island communities; and should be perceived along the view of an *integrated approach* of land and maritime, natural and cultural islands' resources; and as part of the spatial, historical, economic, social, cultural etc. pathways through time of respective communities. This also brings to the forefront the need for *communities' engagement* in planning diving tourism products, realizing that underwater natural and especially cultural assets are most of the times closely linked to parts of the historical past of localities and touch upon social and ethical issues that need to be valued and sensitively dealt with. Additionally, narrative used for promoting cultural diving tourism has to respect memory and values of indigenous people and, furthermore, be enriched by them (historical facts, material, stories etc.), leading thus to a *community-based and value-driven* challenging narrative for establishing diving tourism activity in harmony with their territories and value systems.

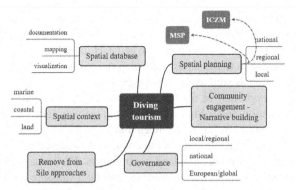

Fig. 9. Planning and governance concerns for diving tourism deployment in island regions

The *spatial context* relates also to the location identification of natural and especially cultural resources for demarcating potential diving sites. This holds true especially for UCH, a large number of which remains unknown; while lying in a rather difficult to access and manage environment – the marine one –, full of risks and unexpected challenges. Geolocating UCH (exact position, depth etc.), documenting (e.g. status, condition), identifying surrounding conditions and other natural assets, mapping and visualizing are necessary prerequisites for ensuring UCH sustainable and resilient exploitation, but also visitors' safety. Technology is a great ally in this respect. In fact, progress in *underwater technology* provides new potential towards the surveying, identification, navigation, excavation and meticulously documentation of UCH. Remarkable progress is also noticed in technologies that support wider communication of UCH objects to the public, e.g., Virtual Reality (VR) and the latest three-dimensional (3D) reconstruction techniques [57]. The integration of the above information into a *spatial database*, enriched with additional general but also specific content on the location and surrounding area, can form the basis for a more coherent and systematic endeavor to promote diving spots or networks of diving sites in the Mediterranean; while filling also the existing gap in the field and supporting *protection, preservation and monitoring* of submerged natural and cultural heritage from various risks ahead.

Marine Spatial Planning and *integrated coastal zone management*, as specific tools for regulating marine and terrestrial space and their interrelationships, are also critical issues as far as the *spatial context* is concerned. By following an *ecosystem-based app-roach*, MSP aims at matching maritime space to various uses, in a way that reduces conflicts and strengthens cross-sectoral cooperation and synergies' creation [58, 59]. MSP is thus crucial for demarcating specific diving tourism sites in harmony with the rest of maritime activities and assuring protection of underwater assets and safety of divers, while handling competition of maritime uses. Additionally, MSPs have to be in coordination with ICZM plans, predicting e.g. land-based infrastructures for diving tourism as well as other uses that have a competing counterpart in the marine environment and may contradict diving tourism activity. Strategic directions of MSP and ICZM need to be given at the national context, further detailed at the regional and local level, following a combined bottom-up and top-down approach. However, speaking of Greece, a strategic plan for managing maritime space and coastal zones does not yet exist, leading thus to fragmented efforts of locating marine or diving parks at the regional/local level. This becomes even more crucial in case of UCH, taking into account the lack of the necessary knowledge as to the status and preservation needs of UCH for its harmless and resilient exploitation as well as safe diving conditions.

The so far *'silo' approach* of natural and especially UCH handling, i.e. a monodisciplinary consideration and a kind of 'ownership' mostly taken by relevant scientific groups and professionals, has so far been a *barrier* for their interdisciplinary and integrated consideration, placing them in the context of sustainable local development for opening up new opportunities to island communities. Particularly in the context of Mediterranean island communities, this heritage can be a valuable resource for reaching sustainability objectives; while, at the same time, forming the ground for cultivating awareness and respect from both the local society and visitors. In case of UCH, for example, Greek experience demonstrates that 'silo' approaches, mainly due to the rather fragmented legislative framework, but also coupled with a well-rooted mindset of 'ownership' of submerged archaeological heritage by marine archaelogists and heritage scientists [60], has so far led to legal and bureaucratic deadlocks; and resignation from the potential of an important developmental pillar, especially for isolated and lagging behind insular communities.

Finally, speaking of the value of *UCH*, it is worth noting the saying of Ms. Nisha, UNESCO's Director and Representative to the Pacific States in the Side Event on 'Safeguarding Underwater Cultural Heritage for Sustainable Development', stating that *"UCH holds the history of the planet and human civilization that is now underwater"*. This statement features the *glocal nature of UCH*, reflecting its crosscutting value at various spatial scales and communities; and unveiling the glocal responsibility towards its protection. Same holds for *underwater natural heritage protection* as well. Risks affecting Mediterranean maritime natural and cultural heritage are further intensified under the CC era; and call for coordinated efforts at various spatial and decision-making levels. *Governance aspects* and shared action seem to be of particular importance for preserving the large number of UCH and the spectacular underwater seascapes and marine life in Mediterranean waters, both being at stake. Such a governance perspective places forward *opportunities* but also *barriers*; while addressing a *multitude of actors* in an effort to protect this legacy and carefully plan sustainable and resilient ways for sharing these common goods. In case of the Mediterranean and its abundant coastal and insular localities, successful *governance of this maritime heritage* can set the foundations for entrenching sustainable, human-centric, long term and qualitative sea-related future development paths, the way these Mediterranean communities are accustomed to go through centuries.

References

1. Koutsi, D., Stratigea, A.: Releasing cultural tourism potential of less-privileged island communities in the Mediterranean: an ICT-enabled, strategic and integrated participatory planning approach. In: Marques, R.P., Melo, A.I., Natario, M.M., Biscaia, R.B. (eds.) The Impact of Tourist Activities on Low-Density Territories: Evaluation Frameworks, Lessons, and Policy Recommendations. Springer Nature, Berlin (2020)

2. Baldacchino, G.: Island landscapes and European culture: an "island studies" perspective. J. Mar. Isl. Cult. **2**, 13–19 (2013). https://doi.org/10.1016/j.imic.2013.04.001
3. Koutsi, D., Stratigea, A.: Unburying hidden land and maritime cultural potential of small islands in the Mediterranean for tracking heritage-led local development paths. Heritage **2**(1), 938–966 (2019). https://doi.org/10.3390/heritage2010062
4. Eurostat: Eurostat regional yearbook 2020. Publications Office of the European Union, Luxemburg (2020). https://doi.org/10.2785/98733
5. Williams, A.: Mass tourism, culture and the historic city: theoretical perspectives. Riv. Sci. Tur. Ambient. Cult. Dirit. Econ. **1**, 9–29 (2010)
6. Tsilimigkas, G., Rempis, N.: Spatial planning framework, a challenge for marine tourism development: location of diving parks on Rhodes Island, Greece. Environ. Dev. Sustain. **23**, 1–26 (2021). https://doi.org/10.1007/s10668-021-01296-1
7. Sunlu, U.: Environmental impacts of tourism. In: Kocabulut, Ö., Yozukmaz, N., and Bertan, S. (eds.) Local Resources and Global Trades: Environments and Agriculture in the Mediterranean Region, pp. 263–270. CIHEAM, Bari (2003)
8. Arabadzhyan, A., Figini, P., García, C., González, M.M., Lam-González, Y.E., León, C.J.: Climate change, coastal tourism, and impact chains – a literature review. Current Issues Tourism **24**(16), 2233–2268 (2020). https://doi.org/10.1080/13683500.2020.1825351
9. Koutsi, D., Stratigea, A.: Integrated maritime policy and management of underwater cultural heritage. In: Defner, A., Skagianis, P., Rodakinias, P., Psatha, E. (Eds) 3rd National Conference of Urban and Regional Planning and Regional Development, pp. 565–577. University of Thessaly, Volos (2018) (In Greek)
10. Samarathunga, W., Gamage, D.: Alternative Tourism as an Alternate to Mass Tourism during the Post-COVID-19 Recovery Phase: the Case of Sri Lanka. Advance. Preprint, (2020). https://doi.org/10.31124/advance.12361301
11. Vázquez, R.M., García, J.M., De PValenciano, J.: Analysis and trends of global research on nautical, maritime and marine tourism. J. Marine Sci. Eng. **9**(1), 93 (2021). https://doi.org/10.3390/jmse9010093
12. European Union: Sustainable tourism in the Mediterranean (2012). https://cor.europa.eu/en/engage/studies/Documents/sustainable-tourism-mediterranean/sustainable-tourism-mediterranean.pdf. Accessed 27 Mar 2021
13. Daldeniz, B., Hampton, M.P.: Dive tourism and local communities: active participation or subject to impacts? Case studies from Malaysia. Int. J. Tour. Res. **15**(5), 507–520 (2012). https://doi.org/10.1002/jtr.1897
14. Mograbi, J., Rogerson, C.M.: Maximising the local pro-poor impacts of dive tourism: Sodwana Bay. South Africa. Urban Forum. **18**(2), 85–104 (2007). https://doi.org/10.1007/s12132-007-9002-9
15. PADI (Professional Association of Diving Instructors): Worldwide Corporate Statistics 2019. Data for 2013–2018 (2019). https://www.padi.com/sites/default/files/documents/2019-02/2019%20PADI%20Worldwide%20Statistics.pdf. Accessed 8 Mar 2021
16. Dwyer, L., Cooper, C., Edwards, D., Mistilis, N., Roman, C., Scott, N.: Megatrends Underpinning Tourism to 2020 Analysis of key drivers for change. CRC for Sustainable Tourism Pty Ltd (2008)
17. Jack, A.: Niche tourism within small island tourism economies: an analysis of scuba tourists in Bermuda. Master thesis. Arizona State University (2012)
18. Dimmock, K., Musa, G.: Scuba diving tourism system: a framework for collaborative management and sustainability. Mar. Policy. **54**, 52–58 (2015). https://doi.org/10.1016/j.marpol.2014.12.008
19. Kunwar, R.R., Karki, N.: A study of dark (disaster) tourism in reconstructed. Gaze J. Tour. Hosp. **11**(1), 140–180 (2020)

20. UNESCO: Convention on the protection of the underwater cultural heritage. In: General Conference of UNESCO. UNESCO, Paris (2001)
21. UNCLOS: United Nations convention on the law of the sea. United Nations, New York (1982)
22. Gibbs, M.: Cultural site formation processes in maritime archaeology: disaster response, salvage and Muckelroy 30 years on. Int. J. Naut. Archaeol. **35**(1), 4–19 (2006). https://doi.org/10.1111/j.1095-9270.2006.00088.x
23. COM(2007)575 final: 'An Integrated Maritime Policy for the European Union', Communication from the Commission to the European Parliament, the Council, the European Economic and Social Committee and the Committee of the Regions, Commission of the European Communities, Brussels, 10 Oct 2007
24. Directive 2008/56/EC: Establishing a framework for community action in the field of marine environmental policy – Marine Strategy Framework Directive. European Parliament and the Council of 17 June 2008, Official Journal of the European Union, L 164/19, 25 June 2008
25. Council Decision 2009/89/EC: On the signing, on behalf of the European Community, of the Protocol on Integrated Coastal Zone Management in the Mediterranean to the Convention for the Protection of the Marine Environment and the Coastal Region of the Mediterranean, Official Journal of the European Union, L 34/17, 4 Feb 2009
26. COM (2011) 244 final: 'Our life insurance, our natural capital: an EU biodiversity strategy to 2020', Communication from the Commission to the European Parliament, the Council, the European Economic and Social Committee and the Committee of the Regions, Commission of the European Communities, Brussels, 03 May 2011
27. COM (2012) 494 final: Blue Growth Opportunities for Marine and Maritime Sustainable Growth, Communication from the Commission to the European Parliament, the Council, the European Economic and Social Committee and the Committee of the Regions, European Commission, Brussels, 13 Sep 2012
28. Directive 2014/89/EU: Establishing a Framework for Maritime Spatial Planning. European Parliament and European Council. Off. J. Eur. Union, L257, 23 July 2014
29. COM (2020)380 final: 'EU Biodiversity Strategy for 2030- Bringing nature back into our lives', Communication from the Commission to the European Parliament, the Council, the European Economic and Social Committee and the Committee of the Regions, Commission of the European Communities, Brussels, 20 May 2020
30. SWD (2017)128 final: Report on the Blue Growth Strategy - Towards more Sustainable Growth and Jobs in the Blue Economy, European Commission, Brussels, 31 Mar 2017
31. Wreck.eu (2021). https://www.wrecksite.eu/. Accessed 14 Mar 2021
32. IYC (2018). https://iyc.com/10-top-dive-spots-mediterranean/. Accessed 15 Mar 2021
33. Vilas, D., et al.: The effects of marine protected areas on ecosystem recovery and fisheries using a comparative modelling approach. Aquat. Conserv. Mar. Freshw. Ecosyst. **30**(10), 1885–1901 (2020). https://doi.org/10.1002/aqc.3368
34. Torroella de Montgrí i l'Estartit Turisme: Medes Islands (2020). https://visitestartit.com/en/medes-islands/. Accessed 5 Mar 2021
35. Xtremesports.com. http://www.xtremespots.com/water-sports/scuba-diving/tunel-del-dofi-dolphins-cave-medes-islands-catalonia-spain/#!. Accessed 14 Mar 2021
36. El Rei Del Mar Diving Centre. https://www.elreidelmar.com/en/diving-spots. Accessed 14 Mar 2021
37. Palau-Saumell, R., Forgas-Coll, S., Sánchez-García, J., Prats, L.: Motivation and attachment to a diving destination: the case of Medes Islands (Catalonia, Spain). J. Vacat. Mark. **25**(3), 301–319 (2019)
38. Lucrezi, S., et al.: Scuba diving tourism systems and sustainability: Perceptions by the scuba diving industry in two Marine Protected Areas. Tour. Manag. **59**, 385–403 (2017). https://doi.org/10.1016/j.tourman.2016.09.004

39. Portofino   Divers.   https://portofinodivers.com/en/diving/portofino/marine-park.html. Accessed 8 Mar 2021
40. Betti, F., et al.: On the effects of recreational SCUBA diving on fragile benthic species: the Portofino MPA (NW Mediterranean Sea) case study. Ocean Coast. Manag. **182**, 104926 (2019). https://doi.org/10.1016/j.ocecoaman.2019.104926
41. Portofino Divers. https://portofinodivers.com/en/diving/wreck/mohawk-deer.html. Accessed 10 Mar 2021
42. Saayman, M., Saayman, A.: Are there economic benefits from marine protected areas? An analysis of scuba diver expenditure. Eur. J. Tour. Res. **19**, 23–39 (2018)
43. Bustelo, M.: Malta & Gozo: Breathtaking Places to Dive in the Mediterranean Sea (2020). https://blog.padi.com/2020/12/14/malta-gozo-breathtaking-places-to-dive-in-the-mediterranean-sea/. Accessed 21 Feb 2021
44. Depares, R.: Wreck diving to be regulated with new laws protecting underwater heritage (2019). https://timesofmalta.com/articles/view/wreck-diving-to-be-regulated-with-new-laws-protecting-underwater.702792. Accessed 6 Mar 2021
45. Malta Dives.com. https://maltadives.com/sites/mvcominoland-xattlahmar/en, https://maltadives.com/sites/stmichael-marsaskala/en. Accessed 14 Mar 2021
46. Beriatos, I., Papageorgiou, M. (eds.): Spatial and Environmental Planning: Development and Protection. University Publications of Thessaly, Volos (2013)
47. Piperis, S.: Greek Maritime Space—A Geographic Approach of its Dynamics with an Emphasis on Energy Sector. Master's thesis, School of Architecture, National Technical University of Athens (2017)
48. Reizidou, E.: Underwater Culture and Diving Tourism. Feasibility study. MOU, Ministry of Economy, Development and Tourism, Athens (2016)
49. Special Framework for Spatial Planning and Sustainable Development for Tourism and strategic environmental impact assessment. Official Government Gazette 1138/11–06–2009
50. Law 3409/2005: Recreational diving and other provisions. Official Government Gazette 273/4–11–2005
51. Law 4296/2014: Replacing article 13 of Law 3409/2005). Diving parks - organized diving Official Government Gazette 214 A/02–10–2014
52. BLUEMED: State-of-the-art analysis of Underwater Museums and Diving Parks. Deliverable 3.2.1, INTERREG Mediterranean, Programme co-financed by the European Regional Development Fund (2017)
53. Novo Scriptorium: Pavlopetri, Greece; a submerged prehistoric town. https://novoscriptorium.com/2019/07/17/pavlopetri-greece-the-oldest-known-submerged-town-in-the-world/. Accessed 27 Mar 2021
54. Greek Reporter: Underwater museum of peristera: the parthenon of shipwrecks. https://greekreporter.com/2021/05/31/diving-into-greeces-heritage-experience-of-a-lifetime-at-ancient-wreck/. Accessed 27 Mar 2021
55. Dionisia, K., Stratigea, A.: Leveraging underwater cultural heritage (UCH) potential for smart and sustainable development in Mediterranean islands. In: Gervasi, O., et al. (eds.) ICCSA 2020. LNCS, vol. 12255, pp. 237–252. Springer, Cham (2020). https://doi.org/10.1007/978-3-030-58820-5_19
56. Law 4688/2020: Special forms of tourism, provisions for tourism development and other provisions. Official Government Gazette 101/A/24–5–2020
57. Argyropoulos, V., Stratigea, A.: Sustainable management of underwater cultural heritage: the route from discovery to engagement — open issues in the mediterranean. Heritage **2**(2), 1588–1613 (2019). https://doi.org/10.3390/heritage2020098
58. Panagou, N., Kokkali, A., Stratigea, A.: Towards an integrated participatory marine/coastal and territorial spatial planning approach at the local level-planning tools and issues raised. Reg. Sci. Inq. **10**, 87–111 (2018)

59. Gómez-Ballesteros, M., et al.: Transboundary cooperation and mechanisms for maritime spatial planning implementation. SIMNORAT project. Marine Policy **127**, 104434 (2021). https://doi.org/10.1016/j.marpol.2021.104434

60. Nutley, D.M.: Look outwards, reach inwards, pass it on: the three tenures of underwater cultural heritage interpretation. In: Jameson, J.H., Scott-Ireton, D.A. (eds.) Out of the Blue: Public Interpretation of Maritime Cultural Resources, pp. 33–51. Springer US, Boston, MA (2007). https://doi.org/10.1007/978-0-387-47862-3_3

High-Resolution Spatial Data Analysis for Monitoring Urban Sprawl in Coastal Zones: A Case Study in Crete Island

Apostolos Lagarias$^{(\boxtimes)}$ and Anastasia Stratigea

Department of Geography and Regional Planning, School of Rural, Surveying and Geoinformatics Engineering, National Technical University of Athens (NTUA), Athens, Greece
lagarias@iacm.forth.gr, stratige@central.ntua.gr

Abstract. Urban sprawl heavily affects coastal areas worldwide, posing threats to the environment and resulting in unsustainable urban growth patterns. This is particularly true in the Mediterranean Region, where coastal and especially insular territories constitute distinct cases of fragile ecosystems, affected by long-lasting mass tourism development trends. This research proposes a methodology for monitoring urban sprawl in coastal areas. High-resolution data for built-up areas are used in this respect, provided by the Global Human Settlement Layer (GHSL). Spatial data are processed using GIS technology; and FRAGSTATS software is used to calculate spatial metrics that quantify density, clustering, geometrical complexity and dispersion of the built environment. The proposed methodology is applied to a case study in Crete, a remarkable example of Mediterranean island community, heavily affected by mass tourism development. Urban growth trends in the period 1975–2014 are explored in this respect; and urban sprawl patterns are analyzed at a disaggregated level along the northern coastal zone, using recent GHSL data based on Sentinel-2 images (period 2017–2018). Using a combination of principal component analysis and cluster analysis, different typologies are identified and zones mostly affected by urban sprawl are highlighted.

Keywords: Coastal zones · Urban sprawl · Spatial data · Spatial metrics · GIS · Mediterranean Region · Crete Island

1 Introduction

Coastal zones, i.e. the interface between the mainland and the sea, are places of remarkable natural and cultural richness and diversity, particularly vulnerable to natural and human pressures, which provide a wide variety of ecosystems' services [1]. Within these zones, a multitude of social, economic and environmental processes occur. Socio-economic processes in coastal zones, however, usually result in *spatial conflicts* and pose *pressure* on the natural (land and maritime) and human ecosystems.

© Springer Nature Switzerland AG 2021
O. Gervasi et al. (Eds.): ICCSA 2021, LNCS 12958, pp. 75–90, 2021.
https://doi.org/10.1007/978-3-030-87016-4_6

Coastal zones in the *Mediterranean Region* in particular, being important areas for human habitation and a range of economic activities through centuries, constitute exemplary cases of heavily affected territories in terms of urbanization processes that can be hardly assimilated by the coastal ecosystems. These processes are fueled by, among others, a *mass tourism development pattern*, which goes beyond capacity limits and threatens the sustainable use of coastal, land and maritime, resources. Deployment of infrastructure, artificial land expansion and the accelerated dispersion of built-up areas are key drivers of coastal urban sprawl processes, consuming vast amounts of land and placing relevant ecosystems at stake. As a result, urban sprawl in coastal areas has been recognized as an *unsustainable model of growth* [2], leading to biodiversity loss, pollution of soil and water deposits, overexploitation of natural land and maritime resources as well as land degradation, to name a few. In the European context, this pressure is expected to grow, taking into consideration the European strategy [3] for further exploiting coastal and maritime tourism opportunities, offered by the extraordinary naturally- and culturally-wealth and the great diversity of coastal regions. Coastal and maritime tourism is regarded as a major source of growth and jobs' creation, being listed as one of the five focus areas in the EU blue economy [4].

Islands provide a natural testing ground of urban spatial expansion within limited area [5]. Urban sprawl is a critical issue in coastal zones in Mediterranean island territories, perceived as distinct cases of fragile and vulnerable ecosystems, in many cases presenting a high degree of artificialization [6]. In such zones, disordered standalone urbanization and infrastructure development or combined with uncoordinated industrial, tourism-related, fishing and agricultural activities, guides currently the rapid degradation of coastal habitats/resources. *Vulnerability* of coastal ecosystems in general and *insular coastal ecosystems* in particular is predominantly attributed to their high environmental value, natural sites protected by international and European laws such as Natura 2000 network, including Sites of Community Importance (SCI), Special Protection Areas (SPA) etc. Coupled with the confined space, insular coastal zones usually dispose a rather limited *carrying capacity* [7]. Thus, a saturation point of coastal zones can be quickly reached, considering also that island territories constitute popular, mostly mass, leading tourism destinations, demonstrating summer peaks of tourist arrivals. Human activities, e.g. urbanization and tourism, have already a strong impact on many island coastal areas, while the state of these areas is expected to further deteriorate under the severe risks of Climate Change and environmental degradation [8], calling thus for urgent action. In doing so, the need to develop methodologies as well as increase technical capabilities and scientific knowledge for analyzing and monitoring *urban sprawl in coastal areas* and support more informed national and regional policies to unfold, becomes urgent.

Coastal urban sprawl is a *dynamic process*, and addressing its spatial and temporal dynamics is crucial for assessing the pressure on respective zones. To this end, detailed information is required for dealing with sustainable land management. However, a major drawback until recently was the lack of *high-resolution spatial data*, rendering the analysis and monitoring of urban sprawl in coastal zones a difficult task. As a result, comparative studies dealing with urban sprawl processes in coastal Mediterranean areas are sparse [9–12]; and are in most cases based on Corine Land Cover (CLC) data [13–16].

CLC data, however, while valuable in the exploration of land cover changes in agricultural and natural land cover categories, seems rather inappropriate for the analysis of urban sprawl in coastal zones due to the crude spatial resolution with the Minimum Mapping Unit (MMU) set to 25 ha. Additionally, since a large proportion of built-up areas are scattered within agricultural and semi-natural or natural areas, CLC data cannot really capture spatially-detailed processes of urban expansion.

Recently, a new generation of *high-resolution spatial data* has been developed, with the involvement of the European Environment Agency (EEA), the Copernicus Land Monitoring Service (CLMS), the Joint Research Center, etc. Based on the above advances and spatial data availability, the *focus* of the present work is on developing a methodology and using recent high-resolution data, specifically multi-temporal data for built-up areas, provided by the Global Human Settlement Layer (GHSL) [17], for indulging in the study of coastal urban sprawl phenomenon. More specifically, spatial data and spatial metrics are used to analyze patterns of coastal urban sprawl in Crete Island (Greece). In this respect, spatial metrics that quantify density, clustering, geometrical complexity and dispersion of the built environment, are explored at a disaggregated level. A new methodological framework is developed, involving the estimation of spatial metrics at a disaggregated/local level (tile analysis) combined by principal component analysis and cluster analysis. This is important, since urban sprawl usually results into complex and spatially differentiated patterns and by using high-resolution data typologies of urban sprawl can be accurately identified. Methodology is applied to a case study in Crete, a remarkable example of Mediterranean island, heavily burdened by mass tourism development. Research results provide a detailed mapping of urban sprawl patterns along the northern coastal zone, in order to support more informed planning and decision-making processes towards a currying capacity-oriented and sustainable coastal zone management.

The structure of the paper has as follows: in Sect. 2 the data and methodology are presented; in Sect. 3 the case study area is sketched and temporal growth trends are discussed; Sect. 4 includes the spatial metrics' estimation and the identification of different typologies; while finally Sect. 5 summarizes key conclusions of this research work.

2   Data and Methodology

Assessment of urban sprawl in the case study example of this work – Crete Island – is based on the GHSL *multi-temporal data* for built-up areas, processed by *Geospatial tools* and *GIS procedures* for quantifying built-up area expansion in the coastal zone. Multitemporal data for the period 1975–2014 are used to explore current trends; while high-resolution data (10m resolution), based on Sentinel-2 images for the period 2017–2018 (GHS-BUILT-S2), are used to analyze the structural and morphological attributes of urban sprawl patterns. *Spatial metrics* used in the proposed methodology can be defined as indicators, obtained from the analysis of thematic-categorical maps, which bring out the spatial component of the urban form and the dynamics of change and growth processes [18]. Estimations refer to the level of patches, defined as discrete areas that appear to be homogenous with respect to some characteristic, such as land use, habitat type, etc. Various examples of spatial metrics' application in urban landscape pattern analysis can be found in the literature [19–22].

The proposed methodology is applied to an island territory, namely Crete, a remarkable example of Mediterranean island, heavily burdened by mass tourism development. *Coastal urban sprawl patterns* are analyzed at a disaggregated level along the northern coastal zone, using recent GHSL data (period 2017–2018).

2.1 High-Resolution Spatial Data for Built-Up Areas

Recently, the availability of new sensors triggered the proliferation of moderate to high resolution (30–50 m) long time-series global datasets of human settlements [17]. As *high-resolution open spatial data* become available, enchased methodologies for the analysis and monitoring of urban sprawl in coastal zones can be developed. In this study, the following GHSL high-resolution data for built-up areas are used:

- GHS-BUILT: Multi-temporal classification of built-up presence as derived from Landsat image collections (1975, 1990, 2000, 2014) at 30 m spatial resolution. 7 categories are defined, namely $0 = $ no data, $1 = $ water surface, $2 = $ land no built-up in any epoch, $3 = $ built-up from 2000 to 2014 epochs, $4 = $ built-up from 1990 to 2000 epochs, $5 = $ built-up from 1975 to 1990 epochs, $6 = $ built-up up to 1975 epoch. Dataset is delivered as (8bit) VRT files, projected in the Pseudo Mercator (EPSG: 3857).
- GHS-BUILT-S2 R2020A: GHS built-up grid, derived from Sentinel-2 global image composite for reference year 2018, using Convolutional Neural Networks [18]. This dataset corresponds to a global map of built-up areas, expressed in terms of a probability grid at 10m spatial resolution. Built-up probability values are rescaled in the range 0–100 (0 for probability $ = 0$ and 100 for probability $ = 1$). Dataset is delivered as tiff raster files, while each tile inherits the projection of the UTM grid zone to which it belongs to.

To analyze trends of urban growth in the period 1975–2014 in the case study area, a density-gradient analysis was used, based on buffer zones from the coast. GHS-BUILT data were processed using the "Tabulate area" tool, provided in the ArcGIS Spatial Analyst. To analyze the built-up patterns for the period 2017–2018, GHS-BUILT-S2 R2020A data were used. A binary version of the raster was constructed by setting a threshold point to binarize the probabilistic output (built-up probability values) [23]. A cell is defined as "built-up" if raster value >20, while otherwise is defined as "non built-up".

2.2 Spatial Metrics

Spatial metrics are patch-based indicators that bring out the spatial component of the urban form and the dynamics of change and growth processes [18]. Such metrics have been developed under the framework of landscape ecology [24] for assessing density, geometry (shape) and dispersion of patches. Area/density/edge metrics, shape metrics, proximity metrics, contagion/diversity metrics, connectivity metrics, are usually distinguished. FRAGSTATS software [25], a public domain software (current version 4.2), is used to calculate a long list of spatial metrics. In this study, urban patches are defined as discrete built-up areas that are identified based on a binary raster grid. At this stage, only one class is defined, i.e. urban patches, representing built-up areas and featuring a developed/non-developed land dichotomy approach. The *spatial metrics* used in this study are:

- COV: the sum of the areas (in ha) of all patches expressed as percentage (%) of total landscape area.
- PD: Patch Density, estimated as the number of patches divided by the total landscape area.
- ED: Edge Density, estimated as total length (m) of patch edges, divided by total landscape area.
- MPS: Mean Patch Size, estimated as the mean area of patches.
- LPI: Largest Patch Index, estimated as the area of the largest patch divided by the total landscape area.
- SHAPE: An indicator that compares the actual perimeter of a patch to the minimum perimeter in the theoretical case of a simple geometrical shape.
- GYRATE: The mean distance (m) between each cell in the patch and the patch centroid. Gyrate is higher for large irregular/elongated patches.
- ENN: The mean Euclidean distance to the nearest neighboring patch, calculated as the shortest edge-to-edge distance.
- CONNECT: A measure of connection between patches, divided by the total number of possible connections among them. In this study, threshold distance is set to 100 m.
- PROX: A measure of proximity, estimated as the sum of patch area (m^2) divided by the nearest edge-to-edge distance squared (m^2) between the patch and the focal patch of all patches within a threshold distance (in this study set to 500 m) of the focal patch.

GHS-BUILT data are processed in *ArcGIS*, reclassified and exported as GeoTIFF grids that are used as input files in FRAGSTATS software. Uniform tiles with a side-length of 1 km are used to calculate spatial metrics at a spatially disaggregated/local level. FRAGSTATS results are exported as CSV (Comma-separated values) files; and are mapped in ArcGIS, by joining the raster file containing the tiles to the CSV file, based on a unique Tile_id Field. At a next step, and by using SPSS Statistics software, *Principal Component Analysis* (PCA) is used to combine the spatial metrics and reduce their number to a minimum set of explanatory factors. *Cluster analysis* is then applied, to explore different built environment typologies. PCA and cluster analysis have been widely used in urban morphology research [14, 26]. Using this method in the case study of Crete Island, zones mostly affected by urban sprawl can be identified, along the over 500 km coastline of the northern coastal zone.

3 Crete Island Case Study

3.1 Current State of the Study Region

Crete Island is marked by a multitude of cultural, historical and natural sites of great and supra-local importance. 53 Natura 2000 areas are hosted in this island, covering

3,710 square km (45% of total island area), along with 57 wildlife repositories and many important archaeological sites. Geomorphology is rough, with mountainous areas covering mainly the central and southern part, restraining urban development along the northern coast, where land is relatively flat. Crete has mild climate conditions, characterized as temperate to maritime in plain areas and mountainous in areas of higher elevation [27]. Major cities of the northern coast are Heraklion, Chania, Rethymno and Agios Nikolaos, while the town of Ierapetra is located in the southeast (Fig. 1). Total population is 591,772 inhabitants (Census 2011), increasing by 10% in the period 1991–2011, with most coastal communities gaining population, while inland communities displaying population decline trends. Agricultural land covers about 44% of total area, marginally increasing during the past decades. Olive groves cover 25.9% of the island, with olive oil being a main product of the primary sector. Forests cover only 3.5% of the island; however, transitional natural areas (mainly Natural grasslands and Sclerophyllous vegetation) cover a total of 45% and are decreasing by 21,000 ha since 1990. According to CLC data, artificial areas increased from 1.3% of total island area to 2.2% in 1990–2018. Discontinuous urban fabric, industrial/commercial areas as well as sport and leisure facilities are the most fast-growing land use categories in Cretan island.

Fig. 1. 3D view of Crete Island (northern coast), Source: Own elaboration

Crete is among the Greek islands where tourism has been developed in a very massive way since the 80's; and has been growing significantly since then, attracting yearly about 2 million foreign visitors [27]. Based on the mild climate conditions and the rich combination of natural and cultural attributes, tourist potential is high, with the tourism period spanning from April to October. Tourism facilities include 1,619 hotels with 96,367 bedrooms and a total of over 187,600 beds (in 2019). Airbnb platform has currently 18,000 registered rooms and houses/apartments, mostly concentrated along the northern coast and close to the major urban centers (Fig. 2). Direct employment in the tourism sector (hotels and restaurants) increased from 8% of total employment in 1991 to 15% in 2011. However, tourism-related employment also affects the constantly growing tertiary sector that contributes over 65% of total employment in Crete (Census 2011). During the period 1991–2011, employment in the primary sector was reduced from 30% to 13%, while remained relatively stable in the secondary sector (from 17% to 15% in the same period).

Fig. 2. Tourism facilities and Airbnb dispersion in Crete, Source: Own elaboration on Data from OpenStreetMap and InsideAirbnb Platform

In Crete, a *polarized pattern* of development is observed. The northern coast is actually overcrowded, hosting almost all major urban centers (except for Ierapetra), the major transportation infrastructure – VOAK highway (North Road Axis of Crete) –, the two major airports in Heraklion and Chania, and the major ports connecting Crete to mainland Greece. It also hosts the majority of tourism infrastructure, being the outcome of the domination of the 3S (Sea-Sun-Sand) mass tourism model since the '80s, with major tourism investments along the easily accessible sandy beaches of the northern coast. Furthermore, as a result of the mountainous geomorphology and inadequate transport infrastructure, the southern part of the island remains largely intact. In the northern coast, many areas have already exceeded own Tourism Carrying Capacity, a critical issue that needs to be addressed; while this part is confronted with environmental pressures due to coastal erosion threatening the coastline and, consequently, the current pattern of tourism development [28].

3.2   Coastal Urban Sprawl in the Island of Crete

Urban land expansion in Crete Island has been intense during the past decades, encroaching in a spontaneous and non-organized way, mainly along the northern coast. According to GHS multitemporal data elaboration, it is inferred that urban land has expanded by 23% as a total in Crete Island, corresponding to 4,120 ha of new built-up areas in the period 1975–2014. Rates of urban growth are higher in the Chania and Rethymno Prefectures (25% and 72% respectively); while in Heraklion Prefecture urban growth rate is estimated to 15% and in Lasithi Prefecture to 20%. The density gradient (Fig. 3) is flattened beyond a distance of 5th km from the coast, while in the immediate coastal zone (0–1 km) built-up areas are maximized. Therefore, the crucial coastal zone is perceived up to 5 km from the coast, followed by a hinterland zone. The 5 km coastal zone was used as the spatial basis for estimating spatial metrics at a disaggregated/local level. Distinctive examples of coastal areas, developed as resort towns in a sprawling way, are presented in Fig. 4.

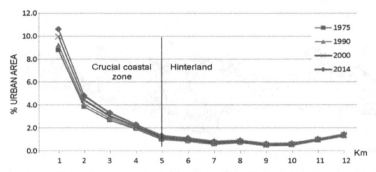

Fig. 3. Density gradient of built-up/urban areas along distance from the northern coast, Source: Own elaboration

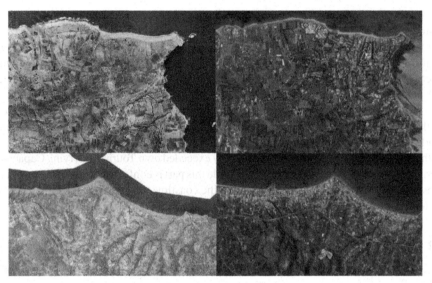

Fig. 4. Coastal development in the mass tourism resort areas of Hersonissos (up) and Platanias (down) (left side: 1945 aerophoto, obtained from http://gis.ktimanet.gr/ - right side: Google Earth 2020), Source: Own elaboration

4   Results

Based on the GHS-BUILT-S2 R2020A data for 2017–2018, the set of spatial metrics described in Sect. 2.2 was estimated in order for urban sprawl typologies in the study area to be analyzed. Patches were defined as "built-up areas", using a probability threshold equal to 20. Using a reclassification tool, all other areas in the analysis (non-built-up agricultural and natural land) were identified as "Background". The final dataset was masked, based on the 5 km zone along the northern coast, and rasterized at a spatial resolution of 10 m. Using the FRAGSTATS software, uniform tiles of 1X1km were applied, while a border rule was used so that only tiles with a maximum of 75% border/no data pixels to be processed. This choice was made in order to avoid estimations for tiles mainly outside the case study area or covered by sea. Based on these settings, 1469 valid tiles (with a least one patch inside) were processed, and spatial metrics were estimated at this disaggregated level. Maps showing the spatial distribution of selected metrics are presented in Fig. 5.

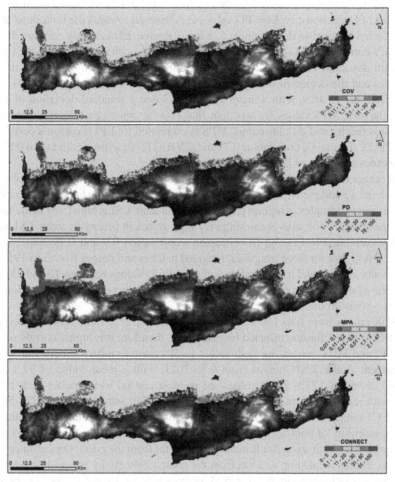

Fig. 5. Maps of selected metrics, distribution of values along the 1 km tiles, Source: Own elaboration.

Results demonstrate considerable differences in the spatial distribution of built-up areas along the northern coastal zone of Crete. COV ranges from 0 to 94, with a mean value of 5.7 and a standard deviation 12.4. High COV values in the range 31–94 are concentrated close to core urban areas, while COV values in the range 11–30 are associated with periurban cells and a few cells with intense tourism development. Most COV values are lower than 10, indicating very low density development along the coastal zone. COV is highly correlated to LPI (Pearson's correlation 0.95). This result is expected, since in very densely built-up cells a large continuous urban patch is usually formed.

PD ranges from 1 to 153, with a mean value of 23.9 and a standard deviation 24.3. High PD values (>50) spread are noticed in many parts of the northern coast, mainly around the major urban centers, but also in areas with immediate accessibility to the sea, e.g. Platanias-Colimbari zone in the west of Chania city and the Hersonissos-Malia area in the east of Heraklion city. Low PD values are observed towards the hinterland and in areas affected by tourism development to a lesser degree. ED is highly correlated to PD (Pearson's correlation 0.81) and ranges from 0.4 to 437, with a mean value of 51.5 and a standard deviation 72.2. MPS is an important metric as it directly measures the size of patches and the degree to which urban land is aggregated into larger clusters. MPS ranges from 0.1 to 46.9, with a mean value of 0.3 and a standard deviation of 11. In 97% of the tiles, MPS values are less than 1ha. This fact shows that development along the coast is patchy and discontinuous. MPS is correlated to: LPI (Pearson's correlation 0.66), PROX (Pearson's correlation 0.7) and GYRATE (Pearson's correlation 0.87), as those metrics are affected by the size of patches.

LSI ranges from 1 to 15.8, with a mean value of 4.8 and a standard deviation of 3. LSI is considered a good metric of urban sprawl, since it accounts for shape complexity and is maximized in complex, irregular patches of urban land. LSI is high (>5) in the largest part of the coastal zone, also presenting very high values in periurban areas. LSI metric is highly correlated to PD and ED (Pearson's correlation 0.9 and 0.79 respectively). GYRATE is higher for large irregular/elongated patches and ranges from 5 to 195, with a mean value of 12.4 and a standard deviation of 11.3. Values between 10 and 25 cover most parts of the northern coast, around major urban centers and tourism development zones as well as around a few inland settlements.

PROX ranges from 0 to 1506, with a mean value of 23.1 and a standard deviation 120. PROX is by definition affected by patch area, therefore it is highly correlated with COV, LPI and MPS, presenting high values (>50) close to urban centers and tourism development zones. ENN ranges from 0 to 1021, with a mean value of 92.9 and a standard deviation 123.5. ENN values are in most coastal tiles smaller than 100 m; while, with reference to the hinterland values, these fall into a range of 100–500 m. CONNECT ranges from 0 to 100 with a mean value of 16.4 and a standard deviation of 20.6. Connectivity of built-up areas at the local level (100 m) is higher in urban centers and in compactly built-up agricultural settlements far from the coast. On the other hand, in almost all tiles located up to 2 km from the coast, connectivity is very low (<20).

As many metrics are correlated, a PCA analysis was used to reduce the variables to a minimum set of factors. This will also ensure that collinearity is avoided, and synthetic indicators taking into account the main characteristics of the initial spatial metrics can be obtained. Varimax rotation with Kaiser Normalization has been used, while the KMO index (Kaiser–Meyer–Olkin) and communalities were estimated. A total of 3 factors were obtained (Table 1), with eigenvalues >1, accounting for 83.5% of the total variance of the initial variables. The indexes used for an evaluation of the PCA analysis show a good performance. KMO was estimated equal to 0.739, while communalities passed the test of 0.5 (all communalities >0.70). Bartlett's test of sphericity presents a small value of significance level (less than 0.05), therefore the hypothesis that correlation matrix is an identity matrix is rejected. In Factor 1 (F1) the COV, MPA, LPI, PROX, GYRATE metrics are loaded, in Factor 2 (F2) the LSI, PD, ED metrics and in Factor 3 (F3) the CONNECT and ENN metrics. F1 corresponds to Coverage and Aggregation of built-up areas, F2 to Patch/Edge Density, and F3 to Connectivity & Dispersion.

Table 1. PCA results (Rotated Component Matrix)

Metrics	Factors		
	F1	F2	F3
LPI	0.927	0.213	
PROX	0.910		
GYRATE	0.880		0.159
MPA	0.859	−0.114	0.122
COV	0.856	0.442	
LSI	0.107	0.945	
PD		0.939	
ED	0.463	0.826	
CONNECT	0.194	−0.324	0.753
ENN		−0.427	−0.735

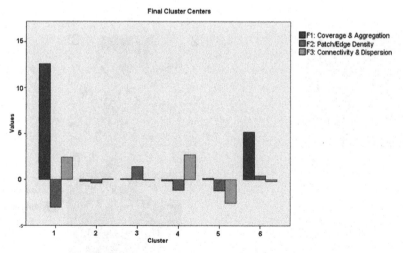

Fig. 6. Final cluster centers, Source: Own elaboration.

Using the PCA factors, *Cluster Analysis* was performed by the K-means method. Based on the Scree plot that shows the increase in homogeneity within each cluster with respect to the increase in the number of clusters, 6 clusters were selected as an optimal choice, since the slope of the curve is flattened at this point. Final cluster centers are presented in Fig. 6 and summary stats (mean values and standard deviation) for the spatial metrics per cluster are tabulated in Table 2. Typical built-up patterns per cluster are mapped in Fig. 7.

Table 2. Summary statistics for spatial metrics per cluster

Cluster		COV	PD	ED	MPS	LPI	LSI	GYRATE	ENN	PROX	CONNECT
1 N = 4	Mean	90.2	2.3	159	41.6	90.2	4.2	176.6	21	1157	91.7
	Std. D.	4.9	0.5	61.2	9.4	5.0	1.8	32.2	1,2	190	16.7
2 N = 911	Mean	1.4	13.7	19	0.1	0.6	3.6	10.3	81	2.5	14.5
	Std. D.	2.2	10.5	18.1	0.2	1.7	1.7	5.3	59	7.5	11.9
3 N = 369	Mean	13.9	58.9	140	0.3	6.6	9.0	14.9	40	30.3	8.9
	Std. D.	11.7	20.1	76.9	0.3	9.6	1.9	4.8	9	56.4	4.6
4 N = 72	Mean	0.6	4.2	6.8	0.1	0.5	2.1	12.0	41	3.0	89.8
	Std. D.	0.9	2.3	6.6	0.2	0.9	0.6	7.1	18	6.4	16.8
5 N = 92	Mean	0.2	3.0	2.8	0.1	0.1	1.7	8.4	480	0.0	0.6
	Std. D.	0.2	1.4	1.9	0.1	0.2	0.3	3.9	206	0.0	2.7
6 N = 21	Mean	73.1	14.4	247	6.2	70.5	6.5	48.0	27	741	32.6
	Std. D.	9.2	7.5	66.5	2.6	11.7	2.3	15.3	6	409	12.6
Total N = 1469	Mean	5.7	23.9	51.5	0.3	3.3	4.8	12.4	930	23.1	16.4
	Std. D.	12.4	24.3	72.2	2.3	11.0	3.0	11.3	1235	120.0	20.6

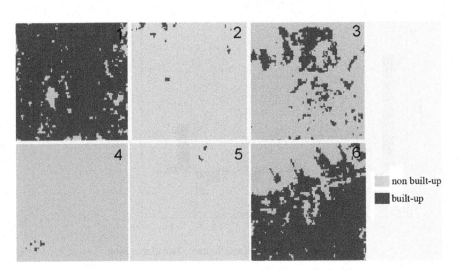

Fig. 7. Typical built-up patterns (per cluster), Source: Own elaboration.

The spatial distribution of clusters is presented in Fig. 8. Based on the spatial metrics estimated, Cluster 3 is considered as the main typology related to intense urban sprawl. Cluster 3 contains 359 tiles, located mainly in the immediate coastal zone and also concentrated in periurban zones around compactly built-up urban core areas. In Cluster 3 areas, PD and ED score the highest values (59 and 140 respectively). Edge complexity, as quantified by LSI, is very high; while MPS and LPI are relatively low. ENN presents an average of 400 m. Proximity between patches is relatively high (mean PROX = 30.3) but connectivity is very low (mean CONNECT = 8.9).

Fig. 8. Spatial distribution of clusters describing built-up typologies in the northern coast of Crete, Source: Own elaboration.

Cluster 1 and Cluster 6 are similar and include tiles with densely built-up urban and periurban areas. Cluster 2 includes 62% of total tiles, displaying transitional areas with relatively low built-up coverage and patch/edge density, but with high degree of dispersion (high ENN) and low connectivity (low CONNECT). These are in most cases agricultural and natural areas, presenting low-density scattered development; or transitional agricultural settlements, located in the hinterland zone and being marginally affected by tourism development and/or periurban processes. Clusters 4 and 5 include areas that are largely non-built and, yet, intact from urban sprawl processes.

5   Discussion and Conclusions

Conflicts between anthropogenic activity and the environment are exacerbating in Mediterranean coastal zones, implying an urgent need to control urban sprawl in such fragile environments. Monitoring coastal urban sprawl could provide the ground for awareness raising and better informing decision-making processes towards the sustainable development of Mediterranean Region as a whole. However, up to now, concrete methodologies for analyzing and monitoring urban sprawl have not been widely applied. In this study, such a methodology is proposed, processing high-resolution spatial data with GIS technology and using spatial metrics for analyzing coastal urban sprawl at a disaggregated level. In this respect, it steps forward previous aggregated level approaches [12, 22, 29].

In Greece, steps undertaken so far to regulate and sustainably manage coastal and maritime space are fragmented and are not integrated into a comprehensive policy framework [30]. This holds true for Crete Island as well, i.e. a remarkable example of Mediterranean insular territory, depicting unique natural and cultural attributes that are heavily affected by mass tourism and urbanization processes. The study of urban sprawl in the northern coastal zone of Crete shows that different typologies of built-up areas can be identified, locating zones mostly affected by urban sprawl. Results show that coastal urban sprawl is currently heavily affecting respective areas in Crete, with built-up areas expanding in a patchy and scattered way. Quantitative analysis, based on spatial metrics, reveals that 25% of land in the 5 km-width zone along the northern coast is classified as *intense urban sprawl area.* Another 62% of land is classified as transitional areas, with relatively low level of development but high degree of dispersion and low connectivity.

Temporal analysis of urban expansion in the period 1975–2014 shows that pressures on agricultural and natural land will continue; and will expand towards the hinterland zone in the immediate future. This can be attributed to pressures exerted by the mass tourism model. Furthermore, it is clear that tourism carrying capacity in specific zones along the northern coast has already been exceeded, causing severe degradation of Natura 2000 areas, wetlands, etc. [31]. Crete Region, lacking a more concrete spatial planning framework, is marked by a rather uncoordinated urban growth model. Recently the need for an alternative, sustainable tourism model has been underlined, rating high priorities relevant to the protection and preservation of the remarkable Cretan natural and cultural capital. Such values have sparked the Cretan Revised Regional Plan of 2017, in an effort to minimize intense land-consuming activities in coastal and environmentally-sensitive areas. Toward this end, this Plan sets as main spatial targets the change of the so far unsustainable growth model by restraining the expansion of built-up areas in agricultural and natural/forest land and shifting to a more environmentally-friendly tourism model, positively affecting quality of built environment in the largely saturated northern coast. Building restrictions in areas outside the regulated urban planning zones are thus encouraged, seeking to upgrade environmental quality and control spatial deployment of mass tourism; while a redirection towards alternative tourism forms in semi-mountainous inland areas is also pursued.

As possible future research, the proposed methodology could be applied to other coastal areas' examples for enchasing urban sprawl monitoring and reversing its negative effects in Mediterranean coastal zones.

Acknowledgements. The present research work is part of the postdoctoral research co-financed through the Greek State and EU (European Social Fund) accomplished under the framework of the Program "Workforce development, Education and continuing education", within the act "Financial assistance for Postdoc researchers – Cycle B", (MIS 5033021), led by IKY (State Scholarships Foundation of Greece).

Operational Programme
Human Resources Development,
Education and Lifelong Learning
Co-financed by Greece and the European Union

References

1. Lavalle, C., Gomes, C.R., Baranzelli, C., Batista e Silva, F.: Coastal Zones - Policy Alternatives Impacts on European Coastal Zones 2000–2050. Joint Research Center (JRC), European Union (EU) (2011)

2. EEA Report No 11/2016: Urban Sprawl in Europe. Joint EEA-FOEN Report. https://www.eea.europa.eu/publications/urban-sprawl-in-europe. Accessed 15 Apr 2021

3. COM (2014) 86 Final: A European Strategy for more Growth and Jobs in Coastal and Maritime Tourism. European Commission, Brussels (2014)

4. SWD (2017) 128 Final: Report on the Blue Growth Strategy - Towards more Sustainable Growth and Jobs in the Blue Economy. European Commission, Commission Staff Working Document, Brussels (2017)

5. Li, X., Lin, T., Zhang, G., Xiao, L., Zhao, Q., Cui, S.: Dynamic analysis of urban spatial expansion and its determinants in Xiamen Island. J. Geogr. Sci. **21**, 503–520 (2011). https://doi.org/10.1007/s11442-011-0860-7

6. Spilanis, I., Kizos, T., Vaitis, M., Koukourouvli, N.: Measuring the economic, social and environmental performance of European island regions: emerging issues for European and regional policy. Eur. Plan. Stud. **21**(12), 1998–2019 (2012). https://doi.org/10.1080/09654313.2012.722970

7. Ye, F., Park, J., Wang, F., Hu, X.: Analysis of early warning spatial and temporal differences of tourism carrying capacity in China's island cities. Sustainability **12**, 1328 (2020)

8. Giorgi, F., Lionello, P.: Climate change projections for the Mediterranean region. Global Planet. Change **63**, 90–104 (2008)

9. Cori, B.: Spatial dynamics of Mediterranean coastal regions. J. Coast. Conserv. **5**, 105–112 (1999)

10. Catalán, B., Saurí, D., Serra, P.: Urban sprawl in the Mediterranean? Patterns of growth and change in the Barcelona Metropolitan Region 1993–2000. Landscape Urban Plan. **85**(3–4), 174–184 (2008)

11. Romano, B., Zullo, F.: The urban transformation of Italy's adriatic coastal strip: fifty years of unsustainability. Land Use Policy **38**, 26–36 (2014)

12. Lagarias, A., Sayas, J.: Urban sprawl in the Mediterranean evidence from coastal medium-sized cities. Reg. Sci. Inquiry **10**(3), 815–832 (2018)

13. Colaninno, N., Cerda, J., Roca, J: Spatial Patterns of Land Use: Morphology and Demography in a Dynamic Evaluation of Urban Sprawl Phenomena along the Spanish Mediterranean Coast. ERSA Conference papers ERSA 11 776, European Regional Science Association (2011)

14. Bajocco, S., De Angelis, A., Perini, L., Ferrara, A., Salvati, L.: The impact of land use/land cover changes on land degradation dynamics: a Mediterranean case study. Environ. Manag. **49**, 980–989 (2012). https://doi.org/10.1007/s00267-012-9831-8

15. Salvati, L., Smiraglia, D., Bajocco, S., Munafò, M.: Land use changes in two mediterranean coastal regions: do urban areas matter? World Acad. Sci. Eng. Technol. Int. J. Environ. Ecol. Eng. **8**(9), 562–566 (2014)

16. Membrado, J.C., Huete, R., Mantecón, A.: Urban Sprawl and Northern European Residential Tourism in the Spanish Mediterranean Coast (2016). http://journals.openedition.org/viatourism/1426, https://doi.org/10.4000/viatourism.1426. Accessed 18 Mar 2021

17. Corbane, C., et al.: Automated global delineation of human settlements from 40 years of landsat satellite data archives. Big Earth Data **3**(2), 140–169 (2019)

18. Herold, M, Couclelis, H., Clarke, K.: The role of spatial metrics in the analysis and modeling of urban land use change. Comput. Environ. Urban Syst. **29**, 369–399 (2003)

19. Hepcan, C.C.: Quantifying landscape pattern and connectivity in a Mediterranean coastal settlement: the case of the Urla district, Turkey. Environ. Monit. Assess. **185**, 143–155 (2013)

20. Triantakonstantis, D., Stathakis, D.: Examining urban sprawl in Europe using spatial metrics. Geocarto Int. **30**(10), 1092–1112 (2015)

21. Reis, J.P., Silva, E.A.: Spatial metrics to study urban patterns in growing and shrinking cities. Urban Geogr. **37**(2), 246–271 (2016)

22. Prastacos, P., Lagarias, A., Chrysoulakis, N.: Using the Urban Atlas dataset for estimating spatial metrics. Methodology and application in urban areas of Greece. Cybergeo.: Eur. J. Geogr. Document 815 (2017). https://journals.openedition.org/cybergeo/28051. Accessed 15 Apr 2021
23. Corbane, C., et al.: Convolutional neural networks for global human settlements mapping from Sentinel-2 satellite imagery. Neural Comput. Appl. **33**, 6697–6720 (2021). https://doi.org/10.1007/s00521-020-05449-7
24. Pickett, S.T.A., et al.: Urban ecological systems: linking terrestrial ecological, physical, and socioeconomic components of metropolitan areas. Annu. Rev. Ecol. Syst. **32**, 127–157 (2001)
25. McGarigal, K., Cushman, S.A., Ene, E.: FRAGSTATS v4: Spatial Pattern Analysis Program for Categorical and Continuous Maps. Computer Software Program Produced by the Authors at the University of Massachusetts, Amherst (2002). http://www.umass.edu/landeco/research/fragstats/fragstats.html. Accessed 15 Apr 2021
26. Sémécurbe, F., Tannier, C., Roux, S.G.: Applying two fractal methods to characterise the local and global deviations from scale invariance of built patterns throughout mainland France. J. Geogr. Syst. **21**, 271–293 (2019). https://doi.org/10.1007/s10109-018-0286-1
27. Matzarakis, A., Nastos, P.: Analysis of tourism potential for Crete Island, Greece. Global NEST J. **13**(2), 141–149 (2011)
28. Alexandrakis, G., Manasakis, C., Poulos, S.E., Kampanis, N.A.: Valuating the effects of beach erosion to tourism revenue – a management perspective. Ocean Coast. Manag. **111**, 1–11 (2015)
29. Lagarias, A., Sayas, J.: Is there a common typology of urban sprawl in Mediterranean cities? A comparative analysis utilizing spatial metrics. J. Urban Reg. Econ. **4**, 813–850 (2019)
30. Tsilimigkas, G., Rempis, N.: Maritime spatial planning and spatial planning: synergy issues and incompatibilities – evidence from Crete island, Greece. Ocean Coast. Manag. **139**, 33–41 (2017)
31. National Tourism Organization (NTO) (In Greek): Study of Tourism Development of the Crete Region 2000–2006. Development Studies Company (2003). http://www.gnto.gov.gr/sites/default/files/files_basic_pages/meleti_B_fasi_kriti.pdf. Accessed 15 Apr 2021

Application of Anhydrous Calcium Sulphate in Cement Bound Granular Pavement Layers: Towards a Circular Economy Approach

James Rombi⊙, Mauro Coni(✉)⊙, Marco Olianas⊙, Marta Salis⊙, Silvia Portas⊙, and Antonio Scanu⊙

Department of Civil Environmental Engineering and Architecture, University of Cagliari, 09042 Cagliari, Italy
mconi@unica.it

Abstract. The reported research concerns about Anhydrous Calcium Sulphate (A.C.S.) potential applications in Cement Bound Granular Material (C.B.M.) pavement layers. A.C.S. is a secondary byproduct deriving from industrial production processes. This research aims to find the best C.B.M. mix, in terms of mechanical performances, in which A.C.S partially replaces Portland cement. A total of 5 different mixes were studied, with variable percentages of cement ranging between 1% and 3% and A.C.S. ranging between 0% and 4% . On each of the prepared specimens, compression strength and indirect tensile strength tests were performed. A trail pavement, under construction, based on the result of the laboratory tests, allows establishing the performances in working conditions.

The preliminary results are encouraging: good mechanical performances, if compared to traditional C.B.M. incorporating only Portland cement, can be observed when the overall binder content in the mix (given by the sum of cement and A.C.S. percentages) is kept in the range of 5%. There is a need to study new applications for byproducts to achieve sustainable development towards a circular economy strategy in the construction sector.

Keywords: Anhydrous Calcium Sulphate · Cement Bound Granular Material · Circular economy · By-product

1 Introduction

This paper focuses on using Anhydrous Calcium Sulphate (A.C.S.) in partial substitution of Portland cement as a binder in cement-treated base layers. In 2019, the annual cement production worldwide reached approximately 4.2 billion tons, producing around 1.4 billion tons of CO_2 per year, which is 8% of the total CO_2 emitted into the atmosphere [1, 2]. Half of this CO_2 derives from using fossil fuels to heat the kilns, and the other half is produced through the calcination of limestone [3].

The benefits of using A.C.S. instead of cement as a binder could be one way to reduce CO_2 production [4, 5]. A.C.S. is a byproduct for which energy and therefore CO_2 emissions has already been spent, and all potential applications can decrease the

© Springer Nature Switzerland AG 2021
O. Gervasi et al. (Eds.): ICCSA 2021, LNCS 12958, pp. 91–99, 2021.
https://doi.org/10.1007/978-3-030-87016-4_7

exploitation of non-renewable natural resources, used mainly in the construction industry, and limit the energy consumption and CO_2 emissions, representing an effective approach to reduce our environmental impact [6]. Furthermore, A.C.S. is obtained with lower temperatures than the calcinations of pozzolanic materials and Portland cement that are approximately 700–750 °C for A.C.S. and over 1400 °C for Portland's clinker [4, 5].

An important aspect linked to the combination of Portland cement and A.C.S. is the formation of Ettringite. This expansive compound needle-like shape interlocks among the Calcium silicate hydrate (C.S.H.) matrix contributing to improving the material's mechanical properties and providing good volume stability [7]. The expansive property of Ettringite can help to contrast the formation of the crack due to dry shrinkage of ordinary cement stabilized base materials [7, 8].

A.C.S. (CaSO4), also namely milled anhydrite, is obtained from the reaction of dried acid grade Fluorspar (CaF_2 97%) and Sulphuric Acid (H_2SO_4) during the production of Hydrogen Fluoride (H.F.) and consequent neutralization with lime, Eq. 1:

$$CaF_2 + H_2SO_4 \rightarrow 2HF + CaSO_4 \tag{1}$$

The milled anhydrite is a byproduct, and it represents a circular and constantly growing alternative compared to similar primary products. The A.C.S. used in this research derives from an industrial plant located in Sardinia (Italy) that is a worldwide leader in manufacturing and sales of inorganic fluorochemicals. Several production plants are located worldwide. The plant that has provided the A.C.S. has a potential average annual production of 240.000 t/year (Fig. 1.).

Fig. 1. Stockpiles of A.C.S.

In this research, four different mixes were prepared with several percentages by weight of Portland cement and A.C.S.: the idea is to replace the percentage of Portland cement with A.C.S. partially and also to introduce an additional percentage of

A.C.S. as a binder, reaching a total binder content of 5% and, achieving mechanical performances according to specifications. For comparison, a reference Cement Bound Granular Material (C.B.M.) mix was prepared without A.C.S.

C.B.M. usually contains less than 5% of cement mixed with granular aggregate and water [9] and, it is always mixed in a plant. The process works best if the granular material can be crushed rocks, natural gravel, or recycled aggregates, has a limited fines content and a low plasticity index [9]. Many tunneling projects are reusing the materials excavated from the galleries and, one of the applications is C.B.M. Granite byproducts obtained from tunneling works show good performances when used in C.B.M. mixes with low percentages of cement reaching 2% [10].

The aim is to obtain a mix design with the highest percentage of A.C.S. introduced in the mix, maintaining good performance in mechanical properties and respecting the environment. Reducing the amount of Portland cement in C.B.M. mixes could reduce CO_2 emissions in the atmosphere [4].

2 Materials and Methods

In this research, twenty-five cylindrical specimens (diameter 150 mm × 200 mm high) were cast, cured, and tested at seven days according to CNR 29/72 (Italian national center for research specifications). The materials used to prepare the mixes consisted of granular soil aggregate, Portland cement CEM IV/B 32.5 R, water, and A.C.S. in partial replacement of the binder. Table 1 and Table 2 technical sheets regarding chemical composition and Particle Size Distribution (PSD) of milled A.C.S. ($CaSO_4$) employed in this experimental study are reported.

Table 1. Chemical composition of milled A.C.S.

Parameter	Guaranteed value %	Typical value %
$CaSO_4$	min 93	97
SO_3	min 54	57
CaF_2	max 3	2
SiO_2	max 0.8	0.20
K_2O	max 0.2	0.01
MgO	max 0.5	0.10
Fe_2O_3	max 0.5	0.10
Al_2O_3	max 0.5	0.15
$Ca(OH)_2$	max 1	0.90
H_2O @ 110 °C	max 2	1
H_2O @ 110 °C	max 2	1
Ph	10	11

Table 2. Particle size distribution of milled ACS

PSD	Guaranteed value %	Typical value %	Analysis method
>0.425	max 5	2	Dry
>0.090	min 15–max 25	16	Sieve
<0.090	min 75–max 85	84	Analysis

According to UNI EN 932-1 (Italian organization for standardization) specifications for stockpiles, Granular soil aggregates samples were collected. Once in the laboratory, they were reduced according to UNI EN 932-2 specifications to perform further tests (Fig. 2.).

Fig. 2. Reduction of the granular sample UNI EN 932-2

According to UNI EN 933-1 specification and other tests, the pre-characterization phase continued conducting PSD tests focused on determining Atterberg limits following CNR-UNI 10014. After this phase was completed, PSD was compared with the aggregates grading requirements according to CNR 29/72.

Tests continued with determining the optimum water content and maximum dry density of the granular material, and, for this purpose, a modified Proctor test using UNI EN 13286-2 specifications was performed. Finally, specimens were cast (Fig. 3.), cured, and tested at seven days. Compression strength and indirect tensile strength tests were performed on the cylindrical specimens.

Fig. 3. Cylindrical specimens removed from the molds

3 Experimental Results

The results of PSD compared with the grading of soil-cement mixtures are reported in Fig. 4.

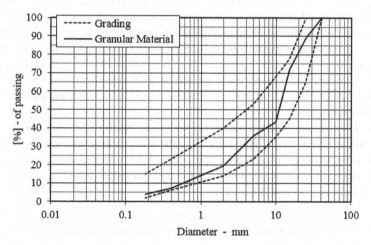

Fig. 4. Comparing PSD of granular material with aggregate grading used in C.B.M.

It is possible to see in the gr that the material is inside the grading. According to ASTM D3282-92, the material resulted in class A1-a. The tests performed on the granular soil material showed that it was non-plastic. Optimum water content and maximum dry density values obtained for the granular materials are reported in Fig. 5.

The chart shows that the value of optimum water content is 3.5% by weight on the aggregates.

After this first phase of the research was concluded, C.B.M. mixes were prepared. A total of 5 different mixes were studied, with variable percentages of cement and A.C.S. ranging between 1–3% and 0–4%, respectively. For each mix, five specimens

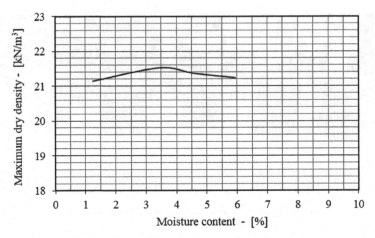

Fig. 5. A.A.S.H.T.O. values of granular soil material

were prepared, of which three were tested to determine compression strength and the remaining 2 for the indirect tensile strength test. Also, a reference C.B.M. mix with only Portland cement was cast and cured at seven days. The reference binder amount is 3% by weight of Portland cement that is 360 g of cement for each mix.

An important parameter to adapt depending on the amount of A.C.S. introduced in the mix is the water content: from the stoichiometric calculation, for every 100 g of A.C.S., the hydration reaction requires 25.4 g of water. It means that to maintain adequate workability, an increase in water content concerning the optimum from the Proctor test is necessary. Accordingly, the amount of water in each mix has been adjusted to take into account this.

Table 3 reports the binder's quantities per mixed batch (12 kg of aggregates), the mean values of unconfined compressive strength (U.C.S.), and indirect tensile strength (ITS) for each of the prepared set of specimens. Each mix proportion was named in terms of cement and A.C.S. percentage in the mix, preceded respectively by the letters P.C. (Portland Cement) and A.C.S.

Table 3. Binder quantities, UCS and ITS mean values

Notation	Portland cement g	ACS g	UCS MPa	ITS Mpa
PC3ACS0	360	0	5.54	0.28
PC3ACS2	360	240	6.79	0.40
PC2ACS1	240	120	4.03	0.22
PC2ACS3	240	360	5.75	0.46
PC1ACS4	120	480	4.30	0.52

PC3ACS0 represents the reference mix in which no A.C.S. was introduced.

The mean values of compressive strength alight good performances, especially for an overall binder content (given by the sum of cement and A.C.S. percentages) around 5%, if compared with the reference mix. The average compressive strength values performed on the samples (after seven days curing time) must be within the range of 2.5 and 4.5 MPa according to CNR 29/72. The standard also specifies that the construction manager can accept C.B.M. with compressive strength up to 7.5 MPa. It is essential to keep U.C.S. values reasonably below the upper limit to avoid brittle behaviors and consequently reflective cracking through the pavement layers until the surface during the infrastructure' service life period.

ITS values confirm the good performance alighted above; furthermore, it emphasizes the high strength generated by increasing the amount of A.C.S. while keeping a constant overall percentage of binder (5%). The PC1ACS4 mix has obtained the best result, with an ITS value almost doubled regarding the reference mix. This mix, the reduction of 66% in cement content, has been possible if compared with the reference mix, with a significant gain for the environment and the infrastructures' serviceability.

According to CNR 97/84, ITS must be greater than 0.25 MPa, so only the mix PC2ACS1 does not accomplish the standard requirements.

4 Conclusions and Further Developments

In this paper, the initial phase of the experimental campaign is reported to assess the mechanical properties of soil-cement mixes incorporating A.C.S. in partial replacement and CEM IV/B 32.5 R cement. A total of 25 cylindrical specimens were casted and tested: 4 mixes with A.C.S. and, for comparison, a reference C.B.M. without A.C.S. The following conclusions can be drawn from the results:

Analyzing the unconfined compressive strength, each mix accomplishes the standard requirements. Moreover, the use of A.C.S. combined with Portland cement, can provide adequate values of U.C.S., reducing the amount of cement in the mix.

ITS values confirm the excellent properties of the mixes that are more likely visible: the tests' outcomes show an enhancement in ITS values, increasing the amount of A.C.S. in the mix while keeping the overall binder content around 5%. Besides, each mix showed higher performance than the reference mix containing 3% of Portland cement.

Furthermore, the use of Portland cement and A.C.S. in the mix design, in a percentage by weight on the aggregates around 5%, provides several benefits as a binder in C.B.M. First, the possibility to lower the footprint of C.B.M. on the environment by reducing the amount of cement in the mix up to 66%, concerning the reference mix. Second, the noticeably improve the indirect tensile strength until a value almost doubled if compared to the reference mix, keeping the unconfined compressive strength within the standard's thresholds to avoid brittle behaviors.

Soon, a trail pavement will be built on the bases of the data obtained from the laboratory tests, in order to study the mechanical behavior in working conditions of the best designed C.B.M. mix. The road will be paved as a traditional infrastructure and used by heavy trucks and tested over time.

A 90 m long and 6 m wide embankment will be constructed, dividing the infrastructure into two sections paved as represented in Fig. 6, which differ only in the composition of the C.B.M. layer. In particular, the first section will have a reference C.B.M. layer without A.C.S. (PC3ACS0), whereas the second one will be constructed with a C.B.M. layer containing A.C.S. (the chosen mix is PC1ACS4).

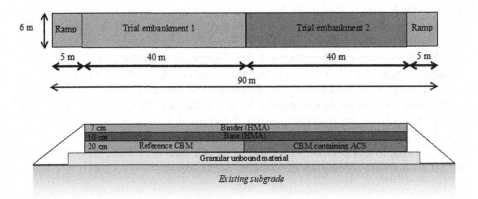

Fig. 6. Embankment's sections and layers' scheme

In situ tests will be performed to verify the potential applications and performances of A.C.S. in working conditions.

Acknowledgments. This study was supported and financed by the FLORSID within the project "Ricerca e sperimentazione sul sottoprodotto solfato di calcio nelle costruzioni e infrastrutture stradali".

Authors would like to thank in particular Dr. Luca Pala, Laboratory and R&D Director at Fluorsid S.p.a., for promoting and developing the project R.I.U.S.A. (Road Infrastructures by Using Synthetic Anhydrite),

Author Contributions:. Concept and methodology, J.R., M.C., M.O., and A.S.; experimental campaign and validation, J.R., M.O., and A.S.; analysis, M.O., J.R., A.S., and S.P.; writing, review and editing, J.R., M.S., A.S, S.P, MC and M.O.; project administration, M.C. and S.P. All authors have read and agreed to the published version of the manuscript.

References

1. Lehne, J., Preston, F.: Making Concrete Change, Innovation in Low-carbon Cement and Concrete. Chatham House, London (2018)
2. Andrew, R.M.: Global CO2 emissions from cement production. Earth Syst. Sci. Data **10**, 195–217 (2018)
3. Chen, I., Juenger, M.: Incorporation of waste materials into Portland cement clinker synthesized from natural raw materials. J. Mater. Sci. **44**, 2617–2627 (2009). https://doi.org/10.1007/s10853-009-3342-x

4. O'Rourke, B., et al.: Development of calcium sulfate–ggbs–Portland cement binders. Constr. Build. Mater. **23**, 340–346 (2009)
5. Gartner, E.: Industrially interesting approaches to "low-CO2" cements. Cem. Concr. Res. **34**, 1489–1498 (2004)
6. Shen, W., et al.: Investigation on the application of steel slag–fly ash–phosphogypsum solidified material as road base material. J. Hazard. Mater. **164**, 99–104 (2009)
7. Zhang, B., et al.: Slight-expansive road base course binder: properties, hydration and performance. Constr. Build. Mater. **150**, 626–633 (2017)
8. Li, J., et al.: Investigation on the preparation and performance of clinker-fly ash-gypsum road base course binder. Constr. Build. Mater. **212**, 39–48 (2019)
9. Xuan, D.X., et al.: Mechanical properties of cement-treated aggregate material – a review. Mater. Des. **33**, 496–502 (2012)
10. Rombi, J., et al.: The use of granite byproducts deriving from tunneling excavations for road construction purposes. In: 5th International conference on Sustainability of Road Infrastructures (2012)

Climate Change and Strategic Adaptation Planning in Mediterranean Insular Territories: Gathering Methodological Insights from Greek Experiences

Yiota Theodora[1] and Anastasia Stratigea[2(✉)]

[1] Department of Urban and Regional Planning, School of Architecture, National Technical
University of Athens, Athens, Greece
ptheodora@arch.ntua.gr
[2] Department of Geography and Regional Planning, School of Rural, Surveying and
Geoinformatics Engineering, National Technical University of Athens, Athens, Greece
stratige@central.ntua.gr

Abstract. In the 3rd Millennium, Climate Change (CC) constitutes a huge, multidimensional and largely impacting challenge for society as a whole, rating at the top of the global policy agenda. It is strongly associated with vulnerability of various types of regions and their capacity to cope with predicted but also largely unknown or not yet fully assessed CC repercussions. Insular territories, in this respect, despite their quite small contribution to CO_2 emissions, seem to be cruelly affected by CC impacts in the years to come. This holds especially true for Mediterranean insular territories, since Mediterranean as a whole constitutes a CC hot spot in the global scenery. Coping with the ominous CC impacts on the spatial capital and socio-economic structure of Mediterranean islands implies the deployment and implementation of comprehensive mitigation and proactive adaptation pathways. The latter is the focus of this paper, attempting to: highlight the contribution of contemporary planning approaches in support of proactive strategic planning for setting up CC adaptation plans; and critically comment on methodological aspects for CC adaptation and related deficits in case of two distinct Greek insular territories – Regions of Ionian and Northern Aegean islands – in order for more robust approaches to emerge to the benefit of addressing CC vulnerabilities in such fragile territorial systems.

Keywords: Climate Change (CC) · Spatial planning and Sustainable development · Mediterranean island territories · CC Adaptation planning · Strategic foresight · Governance

1 Introduction

'We are condemned to shape the future in order to survive' [1].

© Springer Nature Switzerland AG 2021
O. Gervasi et al. (Eds.): ICCSA 2021, LNCS 12958, pp. 100–115, 2021.
https://doi.org/10.1007/978-3-030-87016-4_8

Planning endeavours for informing policy making in seeking sustainability objectives in urban and regional contexts are carried out in a rapidly changing and largely unpredictable global decision environment. Among the key policy concerns in such an environment, *Climate Change* (CC) constitutes a *defining challenge*, the multidimensional and multilevel repercussions of which can assort CC to what in the planning terminology is grasped under the term *'wicked problems'* [2–5]. These are perceived as intractable ones due to the highly unknown or incomplete knowledge; their potential to influence ecological, social and economic realms across various spatial scales [6]; and their unstable or rapidly changing state/nature, to name a few; all exerting enormous pressure on the scientific and policy making communities, while testing their strength in proactive planning and risk/crisis management. Balint et al. [4] claim that confrontation of wicked planning problems is fraught with difficulties, mainly due to two types of *uncertainty*, namely the scientific uncertainty entailed in the solutions of these problems; and the uncertainty as to the way these solutions are grasped and accepted by the various societal and stakeholders' groups.

Notwithstanding the over than two decades intense discussions about CC in the global scene [7, 8] and the concrete directions for urgent action [7, 8], no quite tangible results have yet been reached by many national governments which, in many cases, have failed or fallen short to put in place a well-functioning *climate response and adaptation mechanism as well as related plans*. And although the latest articulated Paris Climate Agreement has been ratified by nearly every nation on earth (197 countries), its targets are not legally binding; hence there is no real obligation for countries to meet them or any sanctions when they fail to do so. Meanwhile, CC disastrous repercussions are intensifying, threatening the environment and its ecosystems and species, the human health and settlements as well as the economy.

Speaking of the spatial differentiation of CC repercussions, while CC is predicted to impact all types of regions, these impacts can, according to the IPCC [7], significantly differ, reflecting regions' diversifying vulnerability and adaptive capacity. In the same report, the high vulnerability of the *Mediterranean region* is highlighted – a region home to 500 million inhabitants, heating 20% faster than world average [8]. In fact, Mediterranean is confronted with multiple environmental stresses and systemic failures due to CC [9], which are expected to highly threaten stability of its natural and socioeconomic ecosystems, more than in any other sub-region of the world [7]. According to Plan Bleu [10], key sectors that are expected to be considerably affected by the CC impacts in the Mediterranean are agriculture and fishery, marked by a severe reduction of yields; tourism destinations, the attractiveness of which is expected to be beaten by heat waves and water resource scarcity; coastal areas and infrastructures, being at stake due to the action of waves, coastal storms, extreme weather events and the estimated sea level rise; human health as a result of discomfort to heat waves; and energy sector coping with increased consumption and water deficit for hydropower plants. Additionally, species composition, alien species' invasion, loss of biodiversity, land and sea degradation, debasement of forests due to heat waves and drought, fall among the prominent impacts of CC, affecting vulnerability of Mediterranean region [7].

In the light of the aforementioned threats, there is an urgent need for re-orienting planning endeavours, by shifting from reactive disaster response to a *proactive risk management* [11], which grasps spatial/sectoral intensity of CC impacts and develops adaptation plans as supplements of other developmental programs and policy pathways to sustainability and resilience. Of critical importance, in this respect, are *insular territories* as quite *fragile and vulnerable* areas in the Mediterranean [12, 13], in need of immediate adaptation to the risky CC incidents. The extremely strong pressures on the natural and cultural ecosystems of such regions, as a result of both the intensifying residential and tourist development trends and the often unregulated location of activities on land and at sea, alter the land- and seascape morphology, surpass carrying capacity of their territories and dramatically increase their vulnerability.

Thus at the heart of this article lie (Mediterranean) *island regions under CC risk*. More specifically, relevant CC adaptation planning efforts of two Greek island regions (NUTS2 level) – namely the Region of Ionian and the one of Northern Aegean – are explored. The *focus* of this work is on methodological aspects, critically examining steps of related adaptation plans and their deficits in order for more robust approaches to emerge when addressing CC vulnerabilities in such fragile insular territories. The work is structured as follows: Sect. 2 elaborates on planning considerations relevant to CC adaptation; in Sect. 3, CC adaptation strategy of Greece at the national/regional level is shortly presented; Sect. 4 gathers insight and critically comments methodological deficits of regional adaptation actions plans, carried out in the two insular case study regions; finally, in Sect. 5 some key conclusions are drawn.

2   CC Adaptation Planning - Methodological Considerations

Uncertainty and nonlinearity constitute key attributes when future development of socio-economic and spatial systems is concerned, being the outcome of both complex interactions taking place within these systems per se; and interactions between these systems and structures/processes operating in their external environment [14]. The dynamics of this environment are mainly driven by *key driving forces* of global reach, e.g. CC, globalization; with the trajectories of these forces featuring potential future images of this environment and, as a result, the ways this affects distinct spatial and socio-economic systems.

CC, as a key driver of change in the global decision environment, is currently a main and highly rated policy concern, rendering sustainability objectives of spatial and socio-economic systems at stake; and calling for *climate policy* reaction for sustaining resilience of such systems to escalating climate threats. Towards this end, capitalization on planning approaches, capable of capturing and properly handling peculiarities and uncertainties inherent in climate policy making can be of great help. Among them fall *governance*, *foresight* and related tools and studies as well as *strategic planning*, all three having at their core *participatory processes*, i.e. using participation as a bedrock in implementing relative planning endeavours. These approaches, as part of the planning arsenal in confronting with current challenges, are shortly described in the following, based on their high relevance to CC adaptation planning.

Governance is defined by Schmitter [15] as a participatory approach or a mechanism, capable of handling a broad range of *conflicting problems* across and within national, sub-national, and international levels as well as state and non-state actors [14]. It reflects the view that ability to handle critical societal challenges resides in actors, social networks, and institutions at multiple spatial layers [14]. Actors engaged in this approach – community groups, stakeholders, decision makers etc. – can bring on board valuable distributed knowledge and, through negotiations, reach a mutually satisfactory and binding decision outcome on a certain challenge; while also cooperate with each other for successfully implementing this decision. Governance is currently largely acknowledged as a means for undertaking *collective action* and effectively tackling evolving territories' *challenges and risks* – CC as well [16, 17]. This lies on its potential to establish horizontal and vertical, collaborative governmental schemes and wide societal coalitions for coping with such risks. Such schemes, among others, address: awareness raising and community empowerment to current societal challenges; collection of distributed knowledge for grasping policy options ahead; policy pathways and their prioritization in order for consensus to be built and their effective and efficient implementation to be ensured [18, 19]. As claimed by Lebel et al. [14], managing vulnerability and resilience of regions to CC and/or other challenges raises a number of key issues as to the: desired spatial system (re)configuration, portfolio of fields and sectors where capacity needs to be built/improved, ways the above decisions are made and implemented, to name a few; all raising issues of collective action and thus rendering governance a critical approach.

The term *"foresight"* is starkly defined by Coates [20: 1428) as *"an image, an insight, a picture, a concept about some future state or condition"*. More specifically, foresight is grasped as a forward-looking approach [21], capable of: exploring alternative future images, gaining important insights into the nature of change these imply, and thinking creatively about shaping desired future end states (Fig. 1). Foresight thus represents a tool for disentangling complexity and guiding, in decision-making processes, action upon a certain future [22]. Potential future images (e.g. scenarios) offer the chance to grasp future developments and incorporate them into the planning endeavour, thus properly featuring relevant (re)actions to emerging problems' solving. As such, they can feed today's policy decisions in order to properly manage forthcoming unpleasant developments or shape desired futures or even cope with emerging threats of potential risky futures, thus rendering these images a valuable ground knowledge for dealing with emerging climate crises. Foresight studies relate to a future thinking that is: *open-minded*, identifying and exploring key driving forces (e.g. CC, digital revolution, societal developments) that can affect world's change; *collective*, engaging stakeholders for gathering distributed knowledge and innovative insights on the ways such driving forces can affect societal, environmental, technological, sectoral, geographical etc. contexts in a medium- to long-term horizon; and *proactive*, being oriented to today's action in order for potential or emerging future challenges/risks to be properly handled. The value of longstanding *foresight tools* (e.g. scenarios, roadmapping, Delphi) in assessing CC evolution and related sectoral, regional, land and marine environment impacts is acknowledged [23, 24]. Such tools offer the chance to feature driving forces, megatrends, wildcards and other disrupting future conditions; and motivate today's robust policy decisions in order for future unenviable circumstances of the repercussions of such developments to be effectively and proactively handled. As such, foresight studies are prevalent in assessing evolution of CC and related impacts for preparing relevant adaptation plans.

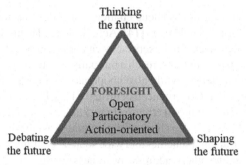

Fig. 1. Milestones of foresight, Source: [25]

Strategic (spatial) planning on the other hand, flourishing in Western countries during the '60s and '70s and witnessing a retreat during the '80s, has been reinstated in late '90s as a response to the need for more strategic approaches in confronting with *dilemmas* and making *intuitive judgments* in the current volatile decision circumstances [3, 26, 27]. For dealing with uncertainty and complexity, *strategic planning* falls into planners' arsenal as a *vision-driven* stepwise approach, viewing planning as a dynamic process of strategic choice; and being firmly oriented, in a structured and systematic way, towards the formulation of policy pathways that can reach this visionary end state [28]. In such a context, strategic planning seeks to identify (Fig. 2): a *desired end state* and *overarching goals* for a certain region/problem at hand; well-structured policy packages that can lead to this end state and are better adjusted to diversified external decision environments; and a proper set of indicators for steadily monitoring targets' achievements [28]. *Key components* of strategic planning are: i) The study of the *external environment* for sketching a distinct future image, within which decision-making at lower spatial scales is adjusted. ii) The study of the *internal environment,* i.e. gaining good insight into the study region/problem at hand, sketching the *current state* or "where we currently stand"; and the *desired future state* or "where we want to be in the future", expressed through a collaboratively defined *vision.* iii) The *policy paths* capable of linking current to visionary state. iv) The linkages of the internal and external environment, mostly grasped through a Strengths - Weaknesses - Opportunities and Threats (*SWOT) analysis* as an integral part of strategic planning exercises.

A critical issue for conducting strategic planning exercises is the exploration and preparation for a set of *plausible futures*, perceived as enablers for producing strategic planning outcomes that best fit in or adjust to them. A systematic exploration of such future states can be achieved by use of *foresight tools*, thus broadening potential of strategic planning endeavours to anticipate and strategically prepare for future changes [29]. Linking strategic planning with foresight tools, i.e. powering strategy deployment with a range of potential future states, establishes the concept of *strategic foresight*, i.e. *a scenario-based approach to strategic planning* [30]. As an innovative step forward, strategic foresight is capable of providing flexibility and openness in featuring strategic options in, among others, varying *climate crisis* circumstances [31]. Its value in CC adaptation studies lies on its potential to [31, 32]: broaden and enrich adaptation planning processes in coping with CC uncertainties; anticipate unexpected or highly risky future

CC circumstances (e.g. wildcards); stimulate creative thinking towards the exploration of and preparation for multiple CC future scenarios; and deeply delve into these scenarios for identifying robust policy options to cope with CC emergencies these scenarios may outline.

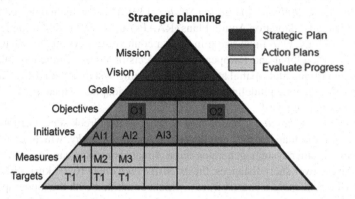

Fig. 2. Components of strategic planning, Source: [33]

Finally, *public participation (PP)* is a key pillar in confronting with CC. Its role has been early enough recognized by the United Nations Framework Convention on Climate Change [34: 17], which in Article 6 stresses participation potential in *"... addressing CC and its effects and developing adequate responses"*. The value of public participation in coping with CC was also recently confirmed by the Intergovernmental Panel on Climate Change Special Report on the impacts of global warming of 1.5 °C above pre-industrial levels, identifying PP in adaptation planning as a means to broaden *capacity* to cope with CC risks [35]. Since the beginning of the 3rd millennium, PP and its critical importance for *CC governance* has also been the subject of scientific discourse, resulting in a rich body of scholarly literature [36–38]. Public participation is actually perceived as an 'umbrella' term, enclosing various types of interaction forms among relevant actors (planners, decision makers, people, stakeholders, academia, etc.). It also serves a variety of goals, ranging from the pure provision of information for awareness raising to the gathering of insights out of a creative dialogue, debate and analysis as well as the adoption of participatory planning schemes towards co-deciding and co-designing CC policy pathways [5, 36, 38]. Furthermore, public participation seems to cross-cut a variety of spatial contexts, from the global to the very local one. However, it seems that a number of issues with regards to best practices, methodologies, enabling conditions etc. [37] for unfolding full potential of participatory approaches to climate governance and sketching efficient climate policy still need to be addressed.

3 Climate Change Adaptation Policy in Greece

Under the current severe CC circumstances, it is commonly acknowledged that featuring of comprehensive adaptation strategies at the national level, further scrutinized and implemented at subsequent spatial levels, is crucial as part of the global endeavour. Europe is an active global player in this respect and has taken the lead in climate neutrality initiatives by targeting to become the first carbon-neutral continent by 2050. Currently, however, only 15 EU member states have already adopted national climate laws and another 7 are preparing to do so. Greece is yet lacking a climate law, while has already set up a *CC National Adaptation Strategy* [39]. This has fuelled the, currently in progress, Regional Adaptation Action Plans (RAAPs) at NUTS2 level for implementing the national strategy. Questions rising in such a context are how this national strategy can, as part of the global and European, policy decision context: function, taking into account the environmental, spatial and sectoral planning system peculiarities; and allow flexibility so that general guidelines can be effectively adapted to local specificities and needs at lower spatial levels.

In setting up a *national CC adaptation strategy* in the Greek state, territorial peculiarities are of particular interest, namely: the *rough topography*, which, coupled with the prevailing weather system, generates acute climate contrasts, varying from Mediterranean to Alpine over short distances; the *extensive coastline* (16200 km) – 12 out of 13 regions of Greece dispose a coastal front – which, combined with the topography, gives rise to a variety of local micro-climatic conditions; the moderate to high *vulnerability* of coastal areas to the sea level rise, placing under pressure these highly productive, complex and vulnerable ecosystems that offer important ecosystem services and goods to communities; the large *number of islands*, with *insularity* drawbacks as well as diversification of islands' vulnerability and capacity to handle resilience and adaptation to CC issues being, in many cases, unbeatable barriers; and the, through centuries, growing interest in the development of *coastal urban fronts* – both in mainland and islands – with massive infrastructures of supralocal reach (e.g. transport, culture, leisure, tourism), being sited at a short distance from the sea.

3.1 CC Adaptation Strategy - The National Context

Seeking to develop the Greek CC adaptation strategy, a scientific venture, perceived as the first formal *"impulse"* of the CC debate in Greece, is conducted by the relevant Impacts Study Committee [40]. This is a principally *sector-oriented, multi- and interdisciplinary study of CC impacts and vulnerability assessments*, focusing on the macroeconomic cost of CC adaptation under the extreme scenario A2 of the IPCC scenarios. Emphasis is placed on the use of proper climate indicators and assessment methods to unveil potential CC impacts on the Greek territory. Their use has revealed that CC is expected to negatively impact all those production sectors (e.g. agriculture, fisheries, tourism), the performance and competitiveness of which depend mainly on the quality of land and biodiversity, water resource availability, mild climatic conditions and current sea level.

Especially *coastal regions*, both in mainland and islands, are extremely exposed to CC, with warming being considered to threaten the residential, tourist, forestry and agricultural use of land; and being further worsened by the intense urbanization and mass tourism activities, deployed in coastal ecosystems. Indeed, vulnerability of Greek coastal areas is high for the 32% of coastal areas and very high for the 58%, while only 10% demonstrate a moderate vulnerability to CC impacts [41]. At the same time, the rise in the average sea surface temperature is expected to affect professional *fishing* due to the decline in species' populations, with the majority of islands running the risk of losing up to 100% of their current catch. Changes are also foreseen in islands' *forests and wetlands*, with many of their valuable ecosystems being threatened by shrinkage or extinction. Furthermore, ominous are the *coastal zone* forecasts, designating a gradual shrink due to sea level rise. According to the EMEKA study [40], coastal landscapes but also existing recreational, cultural, tourist, technical etc. infrastructure are anticipated to alter or being lost in the long run. This is expected to further exacerbate due to the noticeable coastalization trends in Mediterranean coast; and gives rise to the issue of *resilience* and the need for immediate spatial redesign/reorganization of human activities/functions by transferring or modifying infrastructures/activities in affected coastal areas; and applying protection measures to minimize impact. In accomplishing these tasks, co-assessment of the *spatial dimension* of the CC adaptation process, by means of spatial data management and assessment/monitoring indicators, is required.

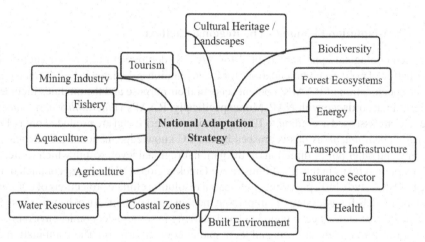

Fig. 3. Sectors addressed by NAS and related regional plans in Greece, Source: Adapted from [39] and [40]

Based on the above mentioned vulnerability assessment, identifying all types of spatial capital and socio-economic sectors threatened by CC in the Greek territory, the CC *National Adaptation Strategy* (NAS) was underpinned and announced in 2016. NAS, as a ten years strategic plan, demarcates the general *goals, principles and sectoral priorities* for an effective and developmental CC adaptation strategy (Fig. 3); and outlines relevant adaptation measures in Greece as a whole, in line with global and European concerns, as articulated by e.g. the UNFCCC [34] and the CC adaptation strategy of EU [42]. It establishes the ground for more informed science- and data-based adaptation policy making; while also articulates general adaptation measures with a special focus on the most vulnerable sectors and on mechanisms for assessing/monitoring their performance. In addition, it provides directions for the deployment of Regional Adaptation Action Plans (RAAPs); and targets raising of societal awareness with regard to CC risks and challenges ahead. Compatibility with other national policies, scientific soundness, public participation and consultation, social consensus and developmental perspective are NAS key attributes.

Taking into account that severity but also type of CC impacts vary among regions, and ability to cope with and adapt also differs across populations, economic sectors and regions, it seems plausible adaptation planning initiatives for strengthening resilience to extreme CC events to be undertaken at the *regional/local level*. In line with this view, NAS predicts detailed CC adaptation plans and articulation of respective policy measures at the regional level (NUTS2 level), by means of respective *RAAPs*. Each single RAAP will end up with a range of potential *adaptation measures*, addressing spatially- and sector-defined CC impacts of each single regional context; and informing or framing other spatial, sectoral/developmental plans at this specific level. RAAPs are to be delivered for each single region of the Greek territory, displaying a 7-years planning horizon (2020–2026) and being subject to revision in 2026. Although originally planned to be ready by the end of 2019, many are still in progress.

3.2 CC Adaptation Planning - The Regional Context

The methodological approach adopted for RAAPs' deployment in Greek regions and articulation of policy recommendations for CC adaptation is depicted in Fig. 4. Decisions on the specification of RAAPs' content sets out their purpose and the modules included therein, in accordance with NAP. More specifically, RAAPs *vulnerability assessments* as to CC are assessed according to IPCC emission scenarios and are grounded on: i) The *decision environment*, as this is grasped by the CC knowledge, national CC adaptation strategy and other policy directions at the national/regional level, within which strategic CC adaptation plans in the 13 administrative Greek regions (NUTS2) are conducted. ii) The EMEKA study [40], providing high spatial resolution climate projections of regional climatic models for assessing CC impacts at the regional level. iii) An exhaustive insight into the current state of each region at hand, delving into socio-economic, environmental, natural/cultural, etc. aspects and their spatial counterparts. iv) The combination of knowledge gathered in the previous steps, in order for indicator-based CC threats, in both sectoral and spatial contexts, to be identified; and assessments of CC impacts to be conducted. v) Deployment of the CC RAAP, featuring policy recommendations for priority sectors/areas in order to prevent, mitigate and remediate impacts, coupled with an estimation of the likely costs of measures and possible bodies in charge of their implementation. vi) RAAP validation for compliance and synergies' creation with other plans. vii) Assessment of targets' achievement by means of an indicator-based monitoring system. viii) A loose consultation process during the RAAP deployment; while prior to the implementation and monitoring stage, RAAP is opened to *public consultation* in order for stakeholders' views to be gathered and assessed and the final RAAP to emerge.

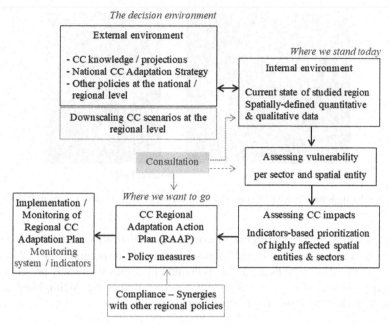

Fig. 4. Steps of the methodological approach for deploying RAAPs in Greece at the NUTS2 level. Source: Adapted from [43]

4 Critically Assessing Methodological Aspects of CC Regional Adaptation Plans – Case Study Insular Territories

This section attempts to critically comment on RAAPs' outcomes, produced by the implementation of the methodological steps of Sect. 3.2 in relevant insular case studies. The emphasis is on *methodological concerns/deficits* identified by the authors, which blur/impede ascertainment of concrete spatially- and sectoral-defined CC impacts and related policy recommendations in these highly vulnerable regions. Commenting on these deficits from a planning perspective can add value to future endeavours or even future revisions of these RAAPs.

4.1 The Case Studies

The Regions of Ionian and Northern Aegean islands (Fig. 5) are distinct insular territories due to the: particular geographical, spatial and socio-economic attributes as well as geopolitical significance (west and east insular border regions); climatic specificities; regional inequalities in terms of intra- and inter-linkages to other insular and mainland parts of the country; adequacy/quality of infrastructure (technical, social, productive); natural resource scarcity; limited size and scope of local economies; extended coastline (1056 km and 1311 km respectively), spread in a number of islands; intense coastalization pattern and degree of tourism seasonality; and habitation aspects of their islands. Of critical importance is also vulnerability addressed due to their insular nature and CC risks associated with their coastal compartments.

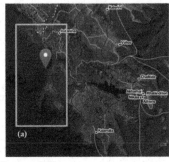 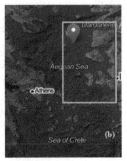

Source: [46]   Source: [47]

Fig. 5. Insular regions explored – (a) Ionian Islands [46] and (b) Northern Aegean Islands [47]

Key resources, forming the ground of work in this section, are the RAAPs of Northern Aegean (already finalized) [44] and Ionian Islands (still in progress) [45]. Although RAAPs of both island regions are at different maturity levels, their study presents great interest from a *methodological* and *spatial analysis* perspective, highlighting crucial issues to be addressed during their implementation.

4.2 Key Issues Emerging from RAAPs' Insights in Case Studies

Deep insight into RAAPs of the North Aegean and Ionian Islands unveils a range of *weaknesses* that are summarized as follows:

- *Generality of targets.* This is partly justified by the ambiguity of the overarching NAS objectives, preventing their further specialisation in RAAPs; and is a serious omission, confining RAAPs' value and affecting CC assessments as well as articulation of more concrete CC adaptation recommendations.
- *RAAPs' work is based on often out-dated data.* Main data sources for regional analysis are often drawn from previous regional developmental/spatial plans, most of which are, in the meantime, revised or under revision. Thus assessment of current state developments and updates, as part of RAAPs, is questioned.
- *Generality of proposed measures/actions.* While mitigation is a more global long term endeavour, adaptation seeks to entrench regions to a rather medium term towards unenviable CC repercussions. General description and the flaccid spatial and sectoral specialization confines RAAPs' usefulness in the studied regions.
- *Loose or non-existent interconnection between RAAPs and other spatial plans.* Although a number of spatial plans are explored, relevant linkages were generic, not really informing RAAPs or ensuring their compliance to these frameworks.
- *Limited orientation to social infrastructures in sectoral recommendations.* Adequacy/quality of social infrastructure, especially in education and health sectors, for building capacity and ensuring resilience of locales is largely missing. Their role is exceptional, especially in insular – isolated from mainland – contexts.
- *Insufficient consideration of the spatial dimension.* Peculiarities of regional contexts (e.g. coastal areas, built environment) are to large extent underestimated, simply

treated through the lens of general CC sectoral recommendations. Lack of a broader perspective of the spatial/functional linkages/dynamics both within and between islands at studied regions [48, 49] enfeebles CC vulnerability assessment, lacking the spatial dimension of socio-economic processes as well as the multiple and diverse pressures these exert on land and at sea. Lack of spatially-defined recommendations diminishes efficiency of RAAPs' CC adaptation measures.

- *Identification of "geographical areas" of reference with administrative ones* (regional/local government bodies). Emphasis on the administrative structure, regardless of climatic areas or spatio-functional specificities (e.g. siting of infrastructure), weakens management of intermunicipal/interregional climate adaptation issues. Redefining "geographical areas" by the use of e.g. climatic, geomorphological, functional attributes could broaden understanding of vulnerability of such areas.

Additionally to the aforementioned weaknesses and taking into account appropriate planning tools/approaches for mid- to long-term studies as a means for handling complex CC repercussions (see Sect. 2), the following concerns are noticed:

- Despite the very nature of a RAAP as a planning exercise, RAAPs studied in this work hardly reflect a *planners' rationale* in the sense of: technical linkages between stages of RAAPs approach and the way these are featured; use of outcomes of each single stage for enriching context of the rest ones; more spatial and developmental focus; and use of substantial participation schemes, all reflecting the lack of a planning expertise in the synthesis of the respective RAAPs' working groups.
- *Governance* in building up the studied RAAPs is *loose*, lacking vertical/horizontal interaction among all types of societal players. The latter are placed at a rather passive position, instead of actively engaging in all stages of RAAPs' deployment.
- The value of *public awareness raising and engagement* throughout the process of RAAPs has not been given relevant attention. The principles of public participation have not been adequately brought to RAAPs endeavours. Thus participatory processes lack a broad and substantial engagement and inclusiveness; and follow a rather RAAPs' legitimation approach. They are confined to information diffusion and collection of views of local and regional as well institutional decision makers through questionnaires (local/regionals administration, representatives of ministries, technical and commercial chambers etc.), largely ignoring community's perspective. RAAPs were mainly deployed by pure a team work of respective working groups, with the final product being opened for public e-consultation. Information on the way outcomes of these consultations have enriched RAAPs is not provided, a fact that is also indicative of the importance attached to the participatory processes in RAAPs and the benefits that can be reaped out of it.
- A *strategic view* of studied regions and a future *vision* to be reached is missing. This brings on board a certain inconsistency, namely while mean values of a range of CC-related indicators are calculated according to IPCC emission scenarios till 2100, vulnerability assessments take for granted the current state of the study regions, leaving behind their dynamics and goal-based future states, emerging by long term planning frameworks at the national and/or regional level.

5 Conclusions

Irrational use of natural resources through decades has changed the world's climate, making *tomorrow's climate a huge today's challenge*. Evidence of CC is already strong and indisputable; and calls for glocal (global-local) mitigation action but also adaptation response, both targeting long term sustainable futures and confining short- and mid-term damages of extreme and intense CC incidents. Such damages are currently fully grasped by a variety of glocal actors, setting forward efforts to prepare CC national and regional adaptation action plans. Planners and policy makers, in this respect, are in front of new challenging duties with regard to the: design of proper CC adaptation recommendations, enabling sustainability and resilience of local ecosystems; handling of imbalances of CC impacts; and entrenching of the most vulnerable regions, as the case of Mediterranean island territories.

Coping with challenges of CC impacts is a multi- and inter-disciplinary field of work. Planning discipline provides proper approaches for medium to long term studies and can thus constitute an *'umbrella' framework*, capable of: integrating the diversifying knowledge needed for recording, assessing and monitoring the evolution and impacts of CC; and linking this knowledge to decision-making, in alignment with local specificities and developmental prospects. Such an effort currently lies at the heart of the scientific and policy discourse. Against this backdrop, the assessment of the mid- and long-term effects of CC on the natural and built environment as well as on socio-economic activities acquires a new criticality for ensuring resilience and sustainable development of diversifying spatial contexts. This brings on board both predictive and preventive actions, being the outcome of collaborative processes at multiple layers and a broadened planning perspective, embracing environmental, spatial and sectoral dimensions as well as peculiarities of administration systems (centralized or decentralized). As such, CC adaptation plans cannot and should not be drawn up independently of spatial/sectoral policies linked to urban/regional development and the current institutional framework on environmental and spatial planning on the one hand; and the local conditions and needs on the other. Further on, vulnerability assessments have to be enriched and definitely be related to changes in the non-climate drivers of change, e.g., economic, social, governance, technological drivers.

Governments are currently deeply engaged in delivering national/regional adaptation plans as distinct CC initiatives that address, in a systematic way, CC preparedness. RAAPs, studied in this work, are part of the Greek nation's effort to entrench its regions against CC threats. Regions studied, i.e. Mediterranean insular territories, seem to be highly affected by CC repercussions in both their maritime as well as coastal and mainland parts; and respective RAAPs, apart from their focus on minimizing CC vulnerability, have additionally to be accomplished in consistency with goals of equity/cohesiveness of localities and their population; and as part of wider awareness and consensus building processes in these fragile though natural and cultural remarkable spatial contexts. Insights into RAAPs studied in this work, according to authors, seem to be *much more than before though less than needed* in such highly threatened Mediterranean insular complexes. Future research needs to focus on more robust CC adaptation approaches in fragile insular territories by strengthening linkages between the deployment of relevant plans and planning discipline's developments.

References

1. Beck, U.: World at Risk. Polity, Cambridge (2007)
2. Rittel, W.J.H., Webber, M.M.: Dilemmas in a general theory of planning. Policy Sci. **4**, 155–169 (1973)
3. Friend, J., Hickling, A.: Planning under Pressure: The Strategic Choice Approach, 3rd edn. Routledge, New York (2005).ISBN: 13 978-0750663731
4. Balint, J.P., Stewart, E.R., Desai, A., Walters, C.L.: Wicked Environmental Problems. Island Press, Washington, D.C. (2011).ISBN: 978-159-726-474-7
5. Stratigea, A.: Theory and Methods of Participatory Planning. Greek Academic Electronic Books, Athens (2015).ISBN: 978-960-603-241-7
6. Sprain, L.: Paradoxes of public participation in climate change governance. The Good Soc. **25**(1), 62–80 (2016). https://doi.org/10.5325/goodsociety.25.1.0062
7. IPCC: Climate Change 2014 - Impacts, Adaptation, and Vulnerability - Part B: Regional Aspects. Cambridge University Press (2014). ISBN 978-1-107-05816-3 Hardback
8. Mediterranean Experts on Climate and Environmental Change (MedECC): Risks Associated to Climate and Environmental Changes in the Mediterranean Region - A Preliminary Assessment by the MedECC Network Science-Policy Interface (2019). https://www.medecc.org/wp-content/uploads/2018/12/MedECC-Booklet_EN_WEB.pdf. Accessed 13 Mar 2021
9. Lionello, P., Platon, S., Rodo, X.: Preface: trends and climate change in the Mediterranean region. Global Planet. Change **63**, 87–89 (2008)
10. Plan Bleu: Study on Climate Change and Energy in the Mediterranean. Plan Bleu Regional Activity Center, Sophia Antipolis (2008). https://www.eib.org/attachments/country/climate_change_energy_mediterranean_en.pdf. Accessed 08 Apr 2021
11. Theodora, Y.: Natural hazards: key concerns for setting up an effective disaster management plan in Greece. Euro-Mediterr. J. Environ. Integr. **5**(2), 1–10 (2020). https://doi.org/10.1007/s41207-020-00174-y
12. Stratigea, A., Leka, A., Nicolaides, C.: Small and medium-sized cities and insular communities in the Mediterranean: coping with sustainability challenges in the smart city context. In: Stratigea, A., Kyriakides, E., Nicolaides, C. (eds.) Smart Cities in the Mediterranean: Coping with Sustainability Objectives in Small and Medium-sized Cities and Island Communities, pp. 3–29. Springer, Heidelberg (2017). https://doi.org/10.1007/978-3-319-54558-5_1 ISBN: 987-3-319-54557-8
13. Theodora, Y.: Cultural heritage as a means for local development in Mediterranean historic cities - the need for an urban policy. Heritage **3**(2), 152–175 (2020). https://doi.org/10.3390/heritage3020010
14. Lebel, L., et al.: Governance and the capacity to manage resilience in regional social-ecological systems. Ecol. Soc. 11(1), 19 (2006). http://www.ecologyandsociety.org/vol11/iss1/art19/. Accessed 19 Mar 2021
15. Schmitter, P.C.: Participation in governance arrangements: is there any reason to expect it will achieve "Sustainable and innovative policies in a multi-level context"? In: Grote, J.R., Gbikpi, B. (eds.) Participatory Governance, pp. 51–69. VS Verlag für Sozialwissenschaften, Wiesbaden (2002). https://doi.org/10.1007/978-3-663-11003-3_3, ISBN 978-3-8100-3237-9
16. Jordan, A.J., et al.: Emergence of polycentric climate governance and its future prospects. Nat. Clim. Chang. **5**, 977–982 (2015)
17. Bednar, D., Henstra, D., McBean, G.: The governance of climate change adaptation: are networks to blame for the implementation deficit? J. Environ. Policy Plann. **21**(6), 702–717 (2019). https://doi.org/10.1080/1523908X.2019.1670050
18. Rodriquez Bolivar, M.P.: Smart Technologies for Smart Governance—Transparency, Efficiency and Organizational Issues. Springer, Heidelberg (2018). https://doi.org/10.1007/978-3-319-58577-2ISBN: 978-3-319-58576-5

19. Marava, N., Alexopoulos, A., Stratigea, A.: Tracking paths to smart governance: the case of korydallos municipality. In: Stratigea, A., Kavroudakis, D. (eds.) Mediterranean Cities and Island Communities: Smart, Sustainable, Inclusive and Resilient, pp. 81–112. Springer, Cham (2019). https://doi.org/10.1007/978-3-319-99444-4_4 ISBN: 978-3-319-99443-7

20. Coates, J.F.: The future of foresight—A US perspective. Technol. Forecast. Soc. Chang. **77**(9), 1428–1437 (2010)

21. Amsteus, M.: The origin of foresight. World Futures: J. Global Educ. **68**(6), 390–405 (2012)

22. Schatzmann, J., Schafer, R., Eichelbaum, F.: Foresight 2.0 – definition, overview and evaluation. Eur. J. Futures Res. 15(15) (2013). https://doi.org/10.1007/s40309-01300015-4

23. De Franca Doria, M., Boyd, E., Tompkins, E., Neil Adger, W.: Using expert elicitation to define successful adaptation to climate change. Environ. Sci. Policy **12**(7), 810–819 (2009)

24. Cairns, G., Ahmed, I., Mullett, J., Wrigh, G.: Scenario method and stakeholder engagement: critical reflections on a climate change scenarios. Technol. Forecast. Soc. Chang. **80**, 1–10 (2013)

25. ForLearn platform: http://www.foresight-platform.eu/community/forlearn/. Accessed 19 Feb 2021

26. Salet, W., Faludi, A.: Three approaches to strategic planning. Revival Strateg. Spat. Plann. **155**, 172 (2000)

27. Albrechts, L., Healey, P., Kunzmann, K.: Strategic spatial planning and regional governance in Europe. J. Am. Plann. Assoc. **69**, 113–129 (2003)

28. Cornish, E. (ed.): Futuring: the Exploration of the Future. World Future Society, Chicago (2004).ISBN: 0-930242-57-2

29. Bengston, N.D., Kubik, H.G., Bishop, C.P.: Strengthening environmental foresight: potential contributions of futures research. Ecol. Soc. **17**(2), 10 (2012). https://doi.org/10.5751/ES-04794-170210

30. Roney, C.W.: Intersections of strategic planning and futures studies: methodological complementarities. J. Futures Stud. **15**(2), 71–100 (2010)

31. Onencan, A., Van De Walle, B., Enserink, B., Chelang, J., Kulei, F.: WeShareIt Game: Strategic foresight for climate-change induced disaster risk reduction. Procedia Eng. **159**, 307–315 (2016). https://doi.org/10.1016/j.proeng.2016.08.185

32. Fetzek, S., Mourad, B., Briggs, C., Lewis, K.: Why and How to Use Foresight Tools to Manage Climate Security Risks. Briefing Note, The Center for Climate and Security (2017)

33. Evans, M.: Workshop on Strategic Planning Model (2015). https://www.google.com/url?sa=t&rct=j&q=&esrc=s&source=web&cd=&ved=2ahUKEwitwsvx4oDwAhUdhP0HHeelA1gQFjABegQIBBAD&url=https%3A%2F%2Fexinfm.com%2Fworkshop_files%2Fstrategic_planning_model.ppt&usg=AOvVaw3j7C2-7wwKzhQ0iAP6ntXW. Accessed 22 Mar 2021

34. UNFCCC: United Nations Framework Convention for Climate Change (1992)

35. IPCC: Global Warming of 1.5 °C - An IPCC Special Report on the Impacts of Global Warming of 1.5 °C above Pre-industrial Levels and Related Global Greenhouse Gas Emission Pathways, in the Context of Strengthening the Global Response to the Threat of Climate Change, Sustainable Development, and Efforts to Eradicate Poverty. Geneva: IPCC (2018). https://www.ipcc.ch/sr15/. Accessed 16 Feb 2021

36. Few, R., Brown, K., Tompkins, E.L.: Public participation and climate change adaptation: avoiding the illusion of inclusion. Clim. Policy **7**(1), 46–59 (2007)

37. Jodoin, S., Duyck, S., Lofts, K.: Public participation and climate governance: an introduction. Rev. Eur. Commun. Int. Environ. Law **24**(2), 117–122 (2015). https://doi.org/10.1111/reel.12126

38. Hügel, S., Davis, R.A.: Public participation, engagement, and climate change adaptation: a review of the research literature. WIREs Clim. Change **11**, e645 (2020). https://doi.org/10.1002/wcc.645

39. National Adaptation Strategy (NAS): Ministry of Environment and Energy, Greece (2016)
40. EMEKA: Environmental, Economic, and Social Impacts of Climate Change in Greece, Climate Change Impacts Study Committee, Bank of Greece (in Greek) (2011)
41. Alexandrakis, G., Poulos, S., Petrakis, S., Collins, M.: The development of a Beach Vulnerability Index (BVI) for the assessment of erosion in the case of the North Cretan Coast (Aegean Sea). Hell. J. Geosci. **45**, 11–21 (2011)
42. COM216 final: An EU Strategy on Adaptation to Climate Change, Brussels, 16.4.2013 (2013)
43. Ministerial Decision 11258: Content of Regional Plans for CC Adaptation in alignment to Article 43 of Law 4414/2016 (A' 149). Government's Gazette No 873 of March 16 (2017)
44. Axon Envirogroup Ltd.: Regional Plan for Climate Change Adaptation. Region of Northern Aegean (2019)
45. Kougianos, J., et al.: Regional Plan for Climate Change Adaptation. Region of Ionian Islands (2019)
46. www.mapnall.com/el/Χάρτης-Περιφέρεια-Ιονίων-Νήσων_249099.html
47. www.mapnall.com/el/Χάρτης-Περιφέρεια-Βορείου-Αιγαίου_249078.html
48. Theodora, Y.: Aegean Sea - challenges and dilemmas in management and planning for local development in fragmented insular regions. Heritage **2**(3), 1762–1784 (2019). https://doi.org/10.3390/heritage2030108
49. Theodora, Y.: Tracing sustainable island complexes in response to insularity dilemmas _ methodological considerations. In: Gervasi, O., et al. (eds.) Computational Science and Its Applications – ICCSA 2020. LNCS, vol. 12255, pp. 278–293. Springer, Cham (2020). https://doi.org/10.1007/978-3-030-58820-5_22

International Workshop on Science, Technologies and Policies to Innovate Spatial Planning (STP4P 2021)

Strategic Guidelines to Increase the Resilience of Inland Areas: The Case of the Alta Val d'Agri (Basilicata-Italy)

Priscilla Sofia Dastoli$^{(\boxtimes)}$ and Piergiuseppe Pontrandolfi

University of Basilicata, DiCEM, CdS Architecture, Via Lanera, 20, 75100 Matera, Italy
`{priscilla.dastoli,piergiuseppe.pontrandolfi}@unibas.it`

Abstract. The following paper illustrates an integrated strategy proposal to increase the resilience of an internal area of Basilicata region. The strategy for this area moves on several pillars: on the one hand the need to network small municipalities to strengthen the inter-municipal system and cooperation practices, on the other hand, the need to develop an effective integration covering all the main systems in strategic design; finally, the duty to use consolidated and effective methodological tools, such as the Logical Framework Approach (LFA). The synthesis phase of the study was based on the construction of the Logframe matrix, where the conclusions of the analysis phase are summarized and the general objectives and specific objectives of the strategy, the actions to be undertaken, the products and the economic resources are indicated. Finally, the strategic actions have been specified in the map for each municipality in the case study area, to have a useful spatial framework supporting decision making and implementation phases.

Keywords: Inland area · Resilience · Local strategy

1 Introduction

In drafting an integrated strategy proposal to increase the resilience of an internal area, such as the Agri Valley, particular importance was attached to the analysis, interpretation and evaluation of the reference territorial context. Attention was paid to the integration of cognitive aspects from different sources, in order to identify resources and potential that can generate processes of recovery and resilience of the territory, in the desire to consolidate the relationship between knowledge and action [1].

The integrated strategy, which starts from a strategic vision of the territory, is the result of a set of intersectoral operations, strictly coherent and explicitly linked to each other, aimed at a common development objective and capable of creating an additional added value compared to individual disconnected operation. The same reasoning is what promotes the area as a strategic inter-municipal area [2], in which effective local development policies and an efficient organization of services can be favoured. The strengthening of inter-municipal systems and cooperation practices can lead the areas to

© Springer Nature Switzerland AG 2021
O. Gervasi et al. (Eds.): ICCSA 2021, LNCS 12958, pp. 119–130, 2021.
https://doi.org/10.1007/978-3-030-87016-4_9

develop a new strategic capacity in the construction of shared future scenarios and the identification of further development opportunities over a large area. In many contexts, the inter-municipal system has been indicated as the privileged place to develop and find common and more effective solutions. At the same time, there was an awareness of the need to create a real inter-municipal competence centre through which to intercept and internalize new professionals capable of supporting the processes of technological, but also social and economic innovation [3].

The effectiveness of the results and the quality of the interventions are the fundamental prerequisites of the strategy that needs to implement synergistic actions - between categories of economic, social and tourism operators, institutional levels, companies - both in terms of planning and implementation.

The territorial area of reference is the Alta Val d'Agri, upstream of the artificial dam of the Pertusillo dam which falls in the south-western quadrant of Basilicata. From an administrative point of view, this territory belongs entirely to the province of Potenza. The Alta Val d'Agri constitutes a particularly articulated territorial reality, since the considerable heritage of environmental, historical and cultural resources that characterize it is affected by numerous critical elements; among the most relevant problems are the abandonment of historic centres - which generates a widespread degradation of the architectural and landscape heritage - and issues related to social and economic factors, such as unemployment, population decline and the ageing of the same. The desire to increase the resilience of the territory is due to the awareness that the territorial system is in a phase of decline, with respect to its evolutionary cycle. Socio-ecological systems, of which territorial systems are second expression, tend to develop evolutionary cycles structured in four phases: use, conservation, release and reorganization that lead to the triggering of a new evolutionary cycle, composed of new system solutions [4]. The transition phase of the system - from decline to reorganization - requires high potential and high resilience. Therefore, in the face of a high potential, we intend to act to increase the resilience of the territorial system.

In recent decades, a critical element has been added, represented by the massive presence of oil extraction activities. In the collective imagination of the inhabitants of the valley, the presence of the deposit represented the engine of the recovery of a strong local economy and a reversal of the depopulation trend; however, about twenty years after the beginning of the exploitation of the oil resource, the hoped-for objectives have not yet been achieved. The industrial presence with such invasive characteristics is undoubtedly a foreign element in an inter-mountain valley dedicated above all to agriculture and animal husbandry, with an exceptional water resource that is constantly threatened. Therefore, for an integrated enhancement and sustainable development [5, 6] of the Alta Val d'Agri, which focuses on the existing cultural and architectural heritage and the naturalistic-environmental system as a driving force for recovery, the strategy indicates as a fundamental prerequisite that of a gradual decrease in extractions, in favour of RES devolpment [7–10].

The debate on the oil industry makes the case study a complex challenge that was intended to be addressed with a rational planning approach, based on three safeguard planning principles [11] that are considered to be the basis for implementing the proposal:

1. Efficient allocation of resources
2. Equity in the distribution of opportunities

3. Protection of non-renewable resources

The methodological approach of the research relies on a logical ordering procedure, in which general objectives, specific objectives, expected results, actions, indicators, means of verification, assumptions and inputs are compared through the implementation of the Logical Framework Approach (LFA) [11, 12]. The European Commission has adopted the LFA which is part of the integrated system of Project Cycle Management (PCM) [13]. It is a complex procedure that goes through the phases of interrogating the subjects actively involved (stakeholders) and arranging the basic needs, organized in the form of a hierarchical structure of problems (problem tree) to identify a program structure that links investments, actions and expected results. The construction of the Logical Framework is presented as a tool for the implementation and control of the design process and as a tool to aid in the evaluation of decisions. This program intends to develop an integrated procedure that sees the consequentiality between the contents of the participation tool and those of the program structure (Problems Tree and Objectives tree). The LFA is therefore a structured and logical approach to prioritize and determine the expected results of a strategic project.

2   The Territorial Context

Agri Valley falls in the south-western quadrant of Basilicata, between the Tyrrhenian and Ionian coasts; the name refers to the Agri river that has crossed the basin and originates from the western offshoots of *Serra di Calvello*, where the *Capo d'Agri* spring group is located. The Agri river basin has a very large area (1,686 sq km) and - from the point of view of morphotectonic evolution - it can be divided into three sectors, generally referred to as *Alta, Media* and *Bassa Val d'Agri*. This work intends to deepen the research on the area of the Alta Val d'Agri (see Fig. 1), upstream of the artificial limit of the Pertusillo dam which, from an administrative point of view, includes ten municipalities in the province of Potenza.

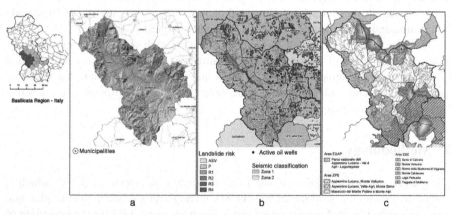

Fig. 1. The figure frames the Agri Valley in the Basilicata Region, underlining some aspects: the morphological characteristics (a), some natural and anthropic risks (b) and the strong naturalistic connotation of the area (c).

The field of study, due to the multiplicit of different environments that make possible the coexistence of a large number of plant and animal species, is almost entirely included in the perimeter of the *Appennino Lucano - Val d'Agri Lagonegrese* National Park, an area protected established in 2007.

Urban and rural settlement are complementary and contribute, together with the road network, to generally define the anthropic transformations in the landscape. The current urban settlement, and with it we refer to the smaller towns of the Alta Val d'Agri, is composed of a network of cores mostly located in the hills following a period of instability during the Middle Ages. The main road system is represented by the SS 585 (Strada di Fondovalle Agri) which, originating from the Atena Lucana motorway junction, crosses the valley and arrives on the Ionian Sea, connecting to the Ionian SS 106. Starting from this primary infrastructure, a system of roads classified of local interest is developed, which perform the function of connecting centres located on neighbouring slopes, connecting the individual centres to higher-level roads, allowing access to extra-urban areas and agricultural land.

The Alta Val d'Agri is characterized, from a demographic point of view, by the constant reduction of the resident population since the 1950s; currently, there are about 30,000 inhabitants.

The structure of the economic system of the study area shows a prevalence of agricultural enterprises (equal to about 32% of the total), of the trade sector (25%) and the tertiary sector (21%). The prevalence in the absolute value of the agricultural sector does not correspond to an employment structure consisting in terms of employees and employees of the companies. This denotes a system linked to individual and family businesses with a low level of industrialization of production processes. The fragmented agriculture is flanked by an industrial production system, which absorbs 29% of the employed and which balances employment in the more traditional sectors of construction (18%) and the tertiary sector (26%).

These parameters, updated to 2012, include the effects of the recent industrialization of the territory linked to the development of oil extraction. Trade, which is polarized in terms of supply in the urban centre of Villa d'Agri (Marsicovetere), maintains an important role even if the disproportion between the number of companies and employees/employees returns a fragmented picture with a marginal role of large-scale distribution and consequentlyt low levels of competitiveness [14].

The Agri valley is an area of Basilicata with a very high seismic risk, placing itself on the highest levels of regional danger because it is a tectonic depression bounded by faults in the Apennine direction and faults that interrupt the previous ones with an anti-Apennine trend. The seismicity of the valley is basically attributable to the active faults present in the area [15].

3 Methodology

The logical ordering procedure of the Logical Framework Approach (LFA), which is part of the Project Cycle Management (PCM), refers to the cyclical nature of planning and is organized in an Analysis phase and a Synthesis phase [16]. In the beginning of it provides for the organization and design of all activities, each context is different from the others and provides for a specific strategic plan. A second activity focuses on the assessment of the context, through an internal and external diagnosis, which is usually carried out through the SWOT analysis technique. In the third part, the most important decisions are made; in fact, the previous diagnosis makes it possible to define the strategic objectives as strong ideas to be placed at the base of the intervention plan and from which to infer the corresponding strategic lines that are intended to be adopted. In this phase, the techniques of the Problem tree and the Objective tree are prepared, to organize problems from causes to effects and objectives from means to ends. The last activity, which is part of the Synthesis phase, deals with the definition of the objectives for each strategic theme and the identification of the actions to be developed, in the management structure of the Logical Framework Matrix (LFM).

3.1 Context Evaluation

Through an analytical and support tool, for example, the SWOT (Strengths, Weaknesses, Opportunities, Threats) analysis, it is possible to detect all the spatial or social situations in which there is an incorrect use of resources, in the sense of the three principles of efficiency, equity and conservation of resources.

The use of this analysis, in the process of constructing intervention proposals and to encourage participation in the process of analysis, interpretation and evaluation of territorial phenomena [17–19], aims to systematically accompany the identification of problems and objectives. This practice has the strong logical limit of being a tautological tool in itself. That is, it repeats what is known from another source. This tool allows you to carry out control operations on multiple dimensions, precisely the dimensions of strengths, weaknesses, opportunities and threats.

The evaluation was made concerning topics of interest and, above all, to the various systems in which the territory under examination was considered:

– naturalistic-environmental system;
– tourism and historical, architectural and cultural heritage[20];
– settlement system and territorial armour;
– infrastructure system (see Fig. 2);
– economic system.

For each system, the strengths and weaknesses that characterize the present situation were first highlighted; subsequently, the analysis highlighted the opportunities and threats.

3.2 Problems and Objectives of the Alta Val d'Agri

At the basis of the strategic planning process is the identification of objectives, which are defined as the removal of problems which, in turn, are defined as everything that opposes the achievement of the objectives themselves.

In particular, the Problem Tree technique acquires the problems that have been reported or inferred, identifies the main problem and organizes all the problems, dividing them into problems that cause the main problem and problems that are effects of the

	S(STRENGTHS)	W(WEAKNESSES)	O(OPPORTUNITIES)	T(THREATS)
INFRATRUCTURAL SYSTEM	Presence of the S.S. 658 of the Agri valley floor of interregional interest which ensures accessibility to most of the inhabited centers and the productive areas of the valley, and connects the area to the west to the motorway network (SA-RC) to the east to the Ionian coastal area (SS 106).	Inadequacy of both local public transport and connection with the Ionian coast	The area is the subject of development programs and special financing that could affect the construction of connecting infrastructures with the Vallo di Diano	Marginalization of the territory with respect to road and railway infrastructures of national significance
	Presence of an extended secondary road network in good condition which also allows adequate accessibility to internal areas	Under-dimensioning of the Fondovalle dell'Agri road compared to the current flow of vehicles and vehicles	Use of public buildings at the busiest stops or exchanges to ensure a safe and adequate stop (services, waiting rooms, catering)	Cultural and commercial isolation due to poor accessibility
	Location of an airfield in the territory of Grumento	Absence of a railway line serving the area that reaches the Ionian coast	Modernization of existing road networks	
		Inadequate public transport for school commuting		
		Excessive distance from airports of international importance		

Fig. 2. SWOT analysis for the infrastructural system.

main problem. The same thing is done with the Objective Tree, which is to put the tree of problems in a positive way; it is necessary to express the problems in the form of an objective in which the main problem becomes the main objective, the problems-causes become the means to achieve the main objective and those that are the effects problems become the objectives that are to be achieved with the objective. For the different systems identified in the SWOT analysis, a Tree of Problems and a Tree of Objectives were respectively organized.

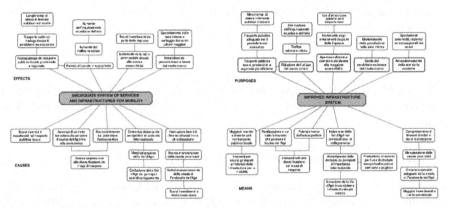

Fig. 3. The Problems tree (from causes to effects) and the Objectives tree (from means to ends) for the infrastructural system of the study area.

Figure 3 shows the organization of the Problem tree and the Objective tree for the infrastructural system, including traditional mobility and active mobility [21–23]. From the analysis of a branch of the Problem tree, it is observed that starting from the *"low incentive and investment in local public transport"*, for example, the effect *"of the high use of private vehicles"* is produced.

3.3 The Definition of the Strategy to Increase the Resilience of the Territory

The synthesis phase, therefore, continuing from the results that emerged from the analysis phase, develops the strategy into an operational program. In this phase, the actions to be taken, the resources available and to be found in relation to the objectives, the link between specific objectives and general objectives are defined in the Logframe matrix (or logical framework) [14].

From the organization of the Thematic Objective Trees - which present a general objective for each system considered - it was possible to identify and extrapolate eight specific objectives, they are:

1) Promote recovery strategies for public and private buildings for hospitality and tourist accommodation;
2) Risk mitigation at the urban and territorial scale;
3) Redevelopment of public areas and spaces in built-up areas, recovery and reuse of disused public buildings, restoration and reuse of buildings of historical and monumental value;
4) Rationalize and enhance services to individuals and businesses according to polycentric arts;
5) To improve the road infrastructures connecting the inhabited centres;
6) Improve the local public transport offer;
7) Develop productive chain activities to support tourism (agriculture and handicrafts);
8) Develop territorial marketing initiatives to promote the territory and slow tourism.

The strategy to be adopted concerns *"increasing the resilience of the territory of the Alta Val d'Agri"* and consists of two specific priority objectives: the mitigation of risks at the urban and territorial scale (OS2) and promotion of strategies for the recovery of public and private buildings for hospitality and tourist accommodation (OS1). The two objectives are closely related to the concept that the recovery of the properties must be aimed at the subsequent reuse of the same.

The synthesis phase is realized with the construction of the Logframe matrix - in which the conclusions of the analysis phase are summarized and the general objectives and specific objectives of the strategy, the actions to be undertaken, the products and the economic resources are thus indicated (Table 1).

Following the results of the Logframe matrix, the overall vision of the proposed strategy and the priority interventions are represented in two summary documents (see Figs. 4 and 5) for the entire area.

Table 1. The Logframe Matrix of the strategy in the Alta Val d'Agri

TERRITORY SECURITY AND ENHANCEMENT OF MINOR HISTORICAL CENTRES OF THE INLAND AREAS			
	Intervention logic		
General objective	Increase in the resilience of the territory of the Alta Val d'Agri: security and enhancement of historical centres		
Specific objectives	**OS 1 - Promote recovery strategies for public and private buildings for hospitality and tourist accommodation** **OS 2 - Risk mitigation at the urban and territorial scale**		
Products	1.1 Development of local economies linked to tourism 1.2 Revitalized historic fabrics 1.3 Increased safety and sustainability 1.4 Raise of the construction sector ----- omitted ----- 2.5 Consolidated and reusable buildings		
Actions	1.1.1 Incentives for tourism activities 1.1.2 Processes of innovation and reorganization of local activities 1.1.3 Public-private participation processes for the reuse of land plans 1.1.4 Training workshops involving specialized artisans, the elderly, young entrepreneurs to pass on local traditions 1.1.5 Promotion of experiential tourism through workshops in companies and / or in artisan shops 1.1.6 Promotion of services connected to naturalistic and cultural places located in public buildings, such as shelters and farmhouses 1.2.1 Reclamation strategies for unoccupied private buildings 1.2.2 Incentives and / or tax exemptions for those who reside in historic fabrics 1.2.3 Activation of services of collective utility 1.2.4 Development of marketing initiatives to promote smaller towns 1.3.1 Promote seismic adaptation and improvement interventions of the public building heritage ----- omitted ----- 2.5.3 Promote public / private participation in order to identify new uses that are compatible with the typological characteristics of the properties		
indicators	*Means of verification*		*Assumptions*
• n. di interventions • n. housing units recovered • m² sup. recovered	• Municipal Technical Office documents (UTC)		Gradual reduction of mining activities and definitive closure
• n. of interventions following studies • n. of urban planning instruments with actions for mitigate risks	• Municipal Technical Office documents (UTC)		
--- omitted---	---		
• n. consolidated buildings	• UTC		
Input	• Public and private financial resources; • Fund for the prevention of seismic risk (€169.709.059); • Agri Valley Operational Program > Axis 3 "Competitiveness" (€99.600.000) Specific goals: 3A.3.5, 3B.3.2, 3C.3.1, 3C.3.7, 3D.3.6 > Axis 4 " Energy and urban mobility " (€84.196.896) Specific goals: 4B.4.2, 4B.4.6 ---omitted--- > Axis 7 "Social inclusion" (€41.750.520) Specific goals: 9A.9.3, 9B.9.4		

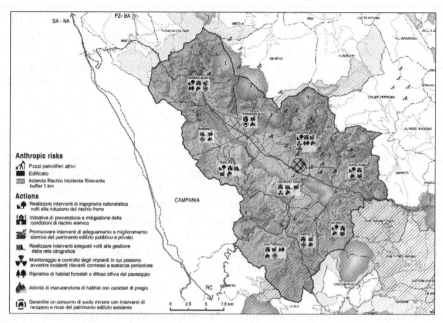

Fig. 4. The map shows the actions of the strategy for each municipality to increase the resilience of the entire area, in the theme of risk mitigation.

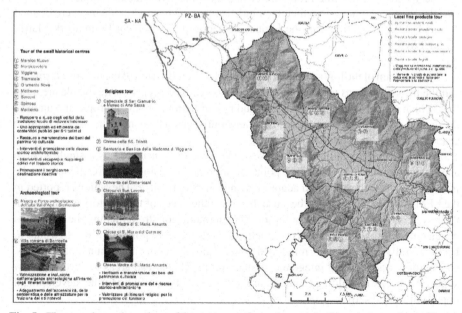

Fig. 5. The map shows the actions of the strategy to for each municipality to increase the resilience of the entire area, in the theme of enhancement of minor historical centres.

The first map (see Fig. 4) summarizes the actions for the territorial security and risk mitigation; the second map (see Fig. 5), focused on the recovery and tourist enhancement of the minor historic centres. These two graphical representations focus on only two aspects of the whole strategy. However, the concept that emerges strongly is that only by systematizing resources in an organized network between minor historic centres can resilience be increased.

4 Conclusions

The Alta Val D'Agri is experiencing a phase of decline, which emerges in particular in the population decrease, in the high rate of seniority and in the abandonment of housing, even of a certain historical value. However, it is also an area with considerable potential, both from a naturalistic and cultural point of view and in the production of local products.

The transition phase of the territorial system - from decline to reorganization - requires high potential and high resilience. Therefore, with high potential, action has been taken to increase the resilience of the territorial system through the proposal of an integrated strategy. This strategy retraced the main stages of the logical framework approach (LFA):

i.   the evaluation of the context, through an internal and external diagnosis, carried out with the SWOT analysis technique;
ii.   the definition of eight strategic objectives from which the main strategic line has been deduced, with the Problem tree and the Objectives tree technique;
iii. the Synthesis phase, in which the objectives for each strategic theme were defined and actions identified, in the logical structure of the Logical Framework Matrix (LFM).

Downstream of the logframe matrix results, the overall vision of the proposed strategy and the priority actions were represented in two synthesis maps for the whole area: the first, which concerns territorial security and risk mitigation, both anthropic and natural; the second, which focuses on the recovery and tourist enhancement of the smaller historic centres, as a starting point for the raise.

When all municipalities in the case study area are considered as a single system and have a common strategy that points to a common vision, their resilience can be increased, that is, the ability to adapt to change and reorganize. The actions reported in the LFM are clear and organic because they meet the needs of the territory and maintain their systemic character. They are also a starting point for strengthening the integrated management of planning and service activities - as the only possible way - to aspire to become a fully-function inter-municipal system. Strengthening inter-municipal systems, cooperation practices and integrated strategy proposal can lead areas to develop a new strategic capacity in building shared future scenarios and identifying further development opportunities [24–26].

References

1. Feludi, A.: Il nesso tra analisi e progetto: studio di un difficile rapporto. In: La Città e le sue scienze: la programmazione della città. Franco Angeli, Milano (1997)

2. Las Casas, G., Scorza, F., Murgante, B.: Conflicts and sustainable planning: peculiar instances coming from val d'agri structural inter-municipal plan. In: Papa, R., Fistola, R., Gargiulo, C. (eds.) Smart Planning: Sustainability and Mobility in the Age of Change. GET, pp. 163–178. Springer, Cham (2018). https://doi.org/10.1007/978-3-319-77682-8_10
3. Cardillo, G., Fusco, C., Mucci, M.N., Occhino, T., Picucci, A., Xilo, G.: Associazionismo e attuazione. I comuni alla prova della realizzazione della Strategia per le Aree Interne (2021)
4. Holling, C., Gunderson, L.H.: Resilience and adaptive cycles. In: Panarchy: Understanding Transformations in Human and Natural Systems, pp. 25–62 (2002)
5. Scorza, F., Grecu, V.: Assessing sustainability: research directions and relevant issues. In: Gervasi, O., et al. (eds.) Computational Science and Its Applications – ICCSA 2016. LNCS, vol. 9786, pp. 642–647. Springer, Cham (2016). https://doi.org/10.1007/978-3-319-42085-1_55
6. Dvarioniene, J., Grecu, V., Lai, S., Scorza, F.: Four perspectives of applied sustainability: research implications and possible integrations. In: Gervasi, O., et al. (eds.) Computational Science and Its Applications – ICCSA 2017. LNCS, vol. 10409, pp. 554–563. Springer, Cham (2017). https://doi.org/10.1007/978-3-319-62407-5_39
7. Saganeiti, L., Pilogallo, A., Faruolo, G., Scorza, F., Murgante, B.: Territorial fragmentation and renewable energy source plants: which relationship? Sustainability 12, 1828 (2020). https://doi.org/10.3390/SU12051828
8. Saganeiti, L., Pilogallo, A., Faruolo, G., Scorza, F., Murgante, B.: Energy landscape fragmentation: basilicata region (Italy) study case. In: Misra, S., et al. (eds.) Computational Science and Its Applications – ICCSA 2019, vol. 11621, pp. 692–700. Springer, Cham (2019). https://doi.org/10.1007/978-3-030-24302-9_50
9. Mazzariello, A., Pilogallo, A., Scorza, F., Murgante, B., Las Casas, G.: Carbon stock as an indicator for the estimation of anthropic pressure on territorial components. In: Gervasi, O., et al. (eds.) Computational Science and Its Applications – ICCSA 2018. LNCS, vol. 10964, pp. 697–711. Springer, Cham (2018). https://doi.org/10.1007/978-3-319-95174-4_53
10. Santopietro, L., Scorza, F.: The Italian experience of the covenant of mayors: a territorial evaluation. Sustainability 13, 1289 (2021). https://doi.org/10.3390/su13031289
11. Casas, G.L., Scorza, F.: Sustainable planning: a methodological toolkit. In: Gervasi, O., et al. (eds.) Computational Science and Its Applications – ICCSA 2016. LNCS, vol. 9786, pp. 627–635. Springer, Cham (2016). https://doi.org/10.1007/978-3-319-42085-1_53
12. Australian agency for international development: AusAid Guidelines (Draft) (2000)
13. Project Cycle Management. Manuale per la formazione, (2002) Strumenti Formez, Roma | Focus tematici. http://focus.formez.it/content/project-cycle-management-manuale-formazione-2002-strumenti-formez-roma. Accessed 08June 2021
14. Acierno, A., Las Casas, G.B., Pontrandolfi, P.: Non solo petrolio - fedOA. Federico II University Press, Naples (2019)
15. Priore, A.: Geologia e geomorfologia dell'alta Val d'Agri (Basilicata). In: Il territorio grumentino e la valle dell'Agri nell'antichità, Atti della Giornata di Studi, di Grumento Nova (PZ) Aprile 2009, pp. 11–19 (2010)
16. Las Casas, G., Sansone, A.: Un approccio rinnovato alla razionalità nel piano. In: Politiche e strumenti per il recupero urbano. Edicomedizioni, Monfalcone (GO) (2004)
17. Scorza, F., Casas, G.B.L., Murgante, B.: That's ReDO: ontologies and regional development planning. In: Murgante, B., et al. (eds.) Computational Science and Its Applications – ICCSA 2012. LNCS, vol. 7334, pp. 640–652. Springer, Heidelberg (2012). https://doi.org/10.1007/978-3-642-31075-1_48
18. Las Casas, G., Murgante, B., Scorza, F.: Regional local development strategies benefiting from open data and open tools and an outlook on the renewable energy sources contribution. In: Papa, R., Fistola, R. (eds.) Smart Energy in the Smart City. GET, pp. 275–290. Springer, Cham (2016). https://doi.org/10.1007/978-3-319-31157-9_14

19. Scorza, F., Casas, G.L., Murgante, B.: Overcoming interoperability weaknesses in e-government processes: organizing and sharing knowledge in regional development programs using ontologies. In: Lytras, M.D., Ordonez de Pablos, P., Ziderman, A., Roulstone, A., Maurer, H., Imber, J.B. (eds.) Organizational, Business, and Technological Aspects of the Knowledge Society. CCIS, vol. 112, pp. 243–253. Springer, Heidelberg (2010). https://doi.org/10.1007/978-3-642-16324-1_26

20. Pilogallo, A., Saganeiti, L., Scorza, F., Las Casas, G.: Tourism attractiveness: main components for a spacial appraisal of major destinations according with ecosystem services approach. In: Gervasi, O., et al. (eds.) Computational Science and Its Applications – ICCSA 2018. LNCS, vol. 10964, pp. 712–724. Springer, Cham (2018). https://doi.org/10.1007/978-3-319-95174-4_54

21. Fortunato, G., Scorza, F., Murgante, B.: Hybrid oriented sustainable urban development: a pattern of low-carbon access to schools in the city of Potenza. In: Gervasi, O., et al. (eds.) Computational Science and Its Applications. LNCS, vol. 12255, pp. 193–205. Springer, Cham (2020). https://doi.org/10.1007/978-3-030-58820-5_15

22. Scorza, F., Fortunato, G.: Cyclable cities: building feasible scenario through urban space-morphology assessment. J. Urban Plan. Dev. (2021). https://doi.org/10.1061/(ASCE)UP.1943-5444.0000713

23. Scorza, F., Fortunato, G., Carbone, R., Murgante, B., Pontrandolfi, P.: Increasing urban walkability through citizens' participation processes. Sustainability. 13, 5835 (2021). https://doi.org/10.3390/su13115835

24. Scorza, F., Saganeiti, L., Pilogallo, A., Murgante, B.: Ghost planning: the inefficiency of energy sector policies in a low population density region. Arch. DI Stud. URBANI E Reg. 34–55 (2020). https://doi.org/10.3280/ASUR2020-127-S1003

25. Las Casas, G., Scorza, F., Murgante, B.: Razionalità a-priori: una proposta verso una pianificazione antifragile. Sci. Reg. 18, 329–338 (2019). https://doi.org/10.14650/93656

26. Las Casas, G., Scorza, F., Murgante, B.: New urban agenda and open challenges for urban and regional planning. In: Calabrò, F., Della Spina, L., Bevilacqua, C. (eds.) New Metropolitan Perspectives. SIST, vol. 100, pp. 282–288. Springer, Cham (2019). https://doi.org/10.1007/978-3-319-92099-3_33

From the Recognition of the Identity Values to the Definition of Urban Regeneration Strategies. The Case of the Military Landscapes in Cagliari

Anna Maria Colavitti(✉) ⓘ, Alessio Floris ⓘ, Andrea Pirinu ⓘ, and Sergio Serra ⓘ

University of Cagliari, 09122 Cagliari, CA, Italy
amcolavt@unica.it

Abstract. The reuse of former military assets, or those in process of decommissioning, represents a topic of relevant interest for the scientific community, that involves different research fields, from restoration to urban planning. The issue is not limited to the design of a project of reuse and redevelopment for a specific area or building, but requires an integrated planning approach aimed at defining a framework of strategies for the regeneration of urban and territorial contexts, which are the result of socio-economic and settlement processes strongly affected by the historical military presence. In the territorial context of the Region of Sardinia, and in particular in the city of Cagliari, there is a wide range of military assets, which, due to the downsizing of the needs of national defence, is actually underutilized or dismissed. Even after ownership has been transferred to local authorities, former military assets are often in a state of long-term abandonment. Often located in the most strategic contexts with high environmental and landscape value, these areas have been excluded for decades from collective use and fruition, significantly affecting the development of the surrounding settlements. The military presence has in fact produced different outcomes, depending on the extent of military sites and the socio-economic context of reference. Often, they have carried out indirect actions that have led to opposing effects, sometimes positive, such as preserving environmental and natural resources or increasing job opportunities, or negative, such as irreversible landscape transformations or environmental pollution. Within an integrated land-use strategy for a sustainable growth of the community, the definition of new uses requires that public institutions follow a multi-objective decision-making process, which should include the active participation of all public and private actors. The paper focuses on the methods of analysis and representation of military urban landscapes, through a diachronic reconstruction of the settlement development and the recognition of the factors and conditions imposed by the military presence. In particular, we reflect on the need to preserve the identity of military landscapes in the definition of strategies for the regeneration of the settlement and territorial heritage but, at the same time, to offer new uses and facilities for the community, in order to increase the quality of urban life.

Keywords: Military landscape · Former military assets · Identity values

© Springer Nature Switzerland AG 2021
O. Gervasi et al. (Eds.): ICCSA 2021, LNCS 12958, pp. 131–144, 2021.
https://doi.org/10.1007/978-3-030-87016-4_10

1 Military Landscapes and Identity Values

Military heritage is the result of stratification of past ages and settlement dynamics that give it a historical value and a dimension of authenticity. Moreover, it often falls in areas of environmental and landscape value, representing a resource of collective interest.

In Italy there is growing attention to the military heritage, built since the Unification of Italy, at the same time as public buildings with different functions, supporting the organisation of the new state structure. Decentralised state administration facilities are often buildings of considerable architectural, landscape, symbolic and identity value, bearing witness to collective and individual memories. The disposed military heritage is characterised mainly by constructions realised between the two centuries, up to the 1930s, based on the reproduction in different territorial contexts of codified models and architectural languages and styles, also with the application of technological and organisational innovations in building production [1].

The extension of mandatory conscription to the entire country made it necessary to build new complexes to house the troops, often using convent and religious structures. The growth of European and Italian cities, generated by industrial development, overcame the confines of the ancient walls that marked the limit between urban and rural areas to follow new urban design methods, characterised by wide avenues for the circulation of motor vehicles and railway tracks along which new military settlements were located, as part of a system of main and minor strongholds, to give the national territory a homogeneous organisational structure. The barracks were often located outside the urban settlements contained by the city walls, both for hygienic and economic reasons, but still located nearby to avoid excluding soldiers from urban life.

In large cities, barracks and military settlements were used within the urban fabric to ensure public order. During the twenty years of Fascism, barracks were located around the perimeter of historical cities, along the now almost demolished walls, on the main communication and railway routes. In cities with military strongholds, such as Cagliari, entire military quarters were often built for strategic reasons.

During the Second World War, there was a need for additional space for military operations and exercises, with preference given to locations outside the cities to reduce the vulnerability of the urban fabric to air attacks. In the post-war period, there was a radical rethink of the distribution of barracks, with a reduction in the size of technical units and a greater distribution throughout the territory, although the existing structure of military property did not allow for complete renewal.

The locational, dimensional, functional, and architectural conditions of military settlements, which we still find in our cities today, are the result of the application of a series of codified technical and operational criteria for design and construction.

Although cities are organisms in continuous transformation and evolution, satellite imagery makes it easy to identify military installations in the urban fabric and in the territory, thanks to their typical and recognisable shape, highlighting the intrinsic value of the buildings and the significant potential for recovery. Often the barracks have remained unchanged over time, even when the surrounding context has been profoundly transformed by building development and infrastructural processes [2]. The buildings that make up the military areas (barracks, penitentiaries, arsenals, training areas, depots, fortresses and warehouses) take on particularly heterogeneous configurations, both because of their technical and highly specialised nature and because of their state of conservation and different levels of maintenance.

It is a heritage of public areas characterised by settlement forms, economic values, symbolic meanings, and evolutionary processes closely linked to the characteristics and history of the local contexts in which they are located.

Public ownership of the areas represents a new opportunity compared to the reuse of private brownfield sites, due to the high strategic potential to address relevant urban issues for land management, such as the reduction of land take by recovering the built environment and enhancing the system of open spaces and collective facilities.

At the same time, these perspectives are conditioned by the approach of the public administration, in particular the central state administration represented by the Ministry of Defense, which often follows different technical and financial logics and conveniences compared to the needs of local authorities whose task is to govern the territory.

The main aspect on which this work wants to focus is that most of the areas, structures and buildings, military sites that are returned to the community, incorporate a historical character, even if not monumental, and are the result of long processes of sedimentation, reuse and transformation of pre-existing structures, given their belonging to past historical eras.

Military settlements acquire a value linked to the nature of the places and are repositories of symbolic meanings rooted in local imagery that limit the possibilities of reuse, reconversion, possible demolition and replacement. Some military areas are nowadays incorporated and integrated into the consolidated fabric of the cities, which have been progressively built around the defensive structures. In other cases of more recent military areas, located outside the inhabited centres, they have lost their original function and their peripheral nature, to remain rather as extraneous areas to the urban fabrics that incorporate them, in the densest parts or at their margins. The paper analyses the impact of the military presence in the process of settlement development in the city of Cagliari, also through a critical reading of the urban evolution from the origins of the military stronghold to the progressive decommissioning of the unused public heritage.

The territory offers the possibility of a systematic application of the different methodologies of survey and representation currently in use, each of which brings different interpretations that contribute to the description of the characteristic signs of a palimpsest of considerable historical, cultural and landscape value.

The final reflections focus on the need to recognise and interpret the stratification of identity values of consolidated military landscapes in the elaboration of scenarios for the reuse of the heritage and urban and territorial regeneration.

2 The Case Study of the City of Cagliari

2.1 The Impact of Military Presence on Settlement Development

The events that have involved the city of Cagliari have inevitably influenced its development and defined its shape, produced by a process of systematic modification, mainly determined by contextual, historical and contemporary needs of a military nature. A large number of military garrisons and architectures, which fall both in the suburban area and in the consolidated settlement fabric, characterise the landscape of Cagliari, testifying to the important strategic role historically exercised by city, due to its favorable location in the Mediterranean [3].

The origin of this process can be traced back to the conquest of the hill of Castello by the Pisan army in 1214 and the consequent need for defence, which led to the construction of the city walls and the system of towers guarding the main entrances to the settlement [4].

The latter correspond to the 'Porta Maestra' or 'Porta dei Leoni' to the south-east, the 'Porta dell'Elefante' to the west, and the 'Porta di San Pancrazio' to the north, which still mark out the landscape of the city of Cagliari, delimiting the district of Castello and allowing a reading of the stratifications that contribute to defining its urban layout.

The strengthening of the city's fortifications gradually involved larger areas, due to the growth of further villages close to the walls, such as those of 'Stampace', 'Villanova' and 'Marina', originally known as 'La Pola', which were progressively incorporated within the defensive structure, with the construction of further garrisons [5].

The process of modification of the defensive structure and, consequently, of the morphology of the urban layout, proceeded uninterruptedly for centuries, due to the succession of new requirements arising from the changing geopolitical context, the recognition of the autonomy of the Kingdom of Sardinia and technological innovations. In the 18th century, the defensive system, by then outdated and oversized compared to actual needs, was subject to significant transformations and progressively destined to new functions.

In 1858, architect Gaetano Cima drew up the first urban development plan for the city of Cagliari, which was finally approved in 1861. Among the numerous interventions, only a small part of which was actually implemented, the plan provided for profound changes to the system of fortifications, but not their complete demolition, both for reasons related to their ownership, as they did not belong to the city, and for the recognition of their identity value, which did not prevent the achievement of the objectives set by the plan [6]. In 1866, with a Royal Decree, the city was officially removed from the list of military strongholds of the Kingdom, authorising the demolition of the defensive walls and active fortifications, sanctioning, in fact, the birth of what we can consider contemporary Cagliari [7]. From this moment onwards, there has been a sequence of operations aimed at integrating the historical defense system into the urban structure in functional terms, with the consequent allocation of its components to new uses, which have gradually been absorbed both in their physical dimension within the city and in their collective dimension, in recognition of the historical and identity value of these artifacts. The need to defend and protect the territory of Cagliari has involved not only the historical centre, but also coastal and peripheral areas in relation to the consolidated centre. Three areas can be identified with a strong presence of military facilities: the promontory of Calamosca and Sant'Elia, the hill of Monte Urpinu and the area of the former military airport of Elmas. In particular, the area of Sant'Elia and San Bartolomeo hills, originally called Is Mesas, and its extension towards the sea, now known as Calamosca, have been characterised by intense construction activity, exemplifying the different declinations assumed by the defensive system that have followed one another historically, due to their strategic location. The militarisation of these areas has historical roots, dating back to the Aragonese period, when, among others, the 'Torre del Poetto', 'Torre di Calamosca' and 'Torre del Prezzemolo' were built, while the origin of the 'Torre di Sant'Elia' could be traced back to the Pisan period [8, 9]. The dynamics of military infrastructures in these contexts increased further in relation to the new needs that emerged after the Unification of Italy and in particular in the period between the two world wars, for which it was necessary to provide additional garrisons, which were realised through the strengthening of the existing military heritage and the construction of new structures, proportionate to the new strategic needs and technological innovations introduced by the process of armaments development. In this sense, it is worth mentioning the 'Fortino di Sant'Elia' and the 'Fortino di Sant'Ignazio', whose construction dates back to the last decade of the eighteenth century, which, after being used to defend the hill and the Bay of Cagliari in general during the Savoy period, were gradually removed from their original function, to be reused, with substantial changes, during the Second World War [10]. In addition, the San Bartolomeo-Calamosca area was characterised by the construction of an articulated system of military facilities, due to additional locational needs arising from the emergency dictated by the world wars and the introduction of military mandatory conscription. In particular, many structures were built, such as the Mereu barracks, the Ederle barracks, the Cascino barracks and the Monfenera barracks, as well as support structures for military functions, such as the Logistics Park of the Navy, Campo Rossi and the firing range, and a series of depots, warehouses, batteries, stations and lodgings, which contributed to the formation of a true military ecosystem that still characterises the area nowadays. At the same time, two military areas were built in the Monte Urpinu area, which housed the fuel depots of the Air Force and Navy, including office buildings and accommodation. The consolidation of the military nature of these areas was favored by the Fascist regime's decision to grant full jurisdiction over military areas to the army, effectively excluding local authorities from the possibility of regulating their processes, a condition that persisted for a long time until the State law on the new regulation of military servitudes of 1976 [3]. Moreover, in this historical period, Cagliari's urban development was negatively conditioned by the lack of planning, despite the attempts attributable to the Plan of 1931, on the basis of which the master plan for the urban centre and its expansion areas was drawn up and approved in 1941, but never actually applied due to the bombing of the city in 1943. Following this event, the plan nevertheless constituted the basis for the elaboration of the Reconstruction Plan, drawn up in 1944 and approved in 1947, whose guidelines, although founded on the principles of the previous document, were mainly calibrated on the need to solve the emergency that had occurred, giving less importance to the regulation of the expansive growth of the city. The General Regulatory Plan (GRP) of 1962 by Mandolesi, definitively approved in 1965 and subsequently updated in 1977 and 1983, following the issuing of Regional Decree no. 2266/U (Floris Decree), overlooked the condition of constraint, dictated by military use, of large portions of Cagliari's territory. The urban planning tool focused mainly on the management of the city's transport system, failing to effectively regulate the expansive thrust produced by land rent and building speculation [7]. In addition, military areas are largely omitted from the plan documents, probably on the basis of recognised strategic and military secrecy requirements, or indicated as 'expansion areas' and 'green areas linked to public buildings', despite the fact that they had already been built for a long time. It cannot be ruled out that the plan itself considered the military function of some areas to be outdated and consequently assumed a new use for them, including them within the expansion areas. Following the intensification of the expansive dynamics, especially from the 1960s onwards, we have witnessed the formation of entire districts surrounding the areas occupied by military servitude, such as the districts of Sant'Elia, Sole, La Palma, Monte Urpinu and partly of the district of Poetto, which have been shaped by the presence of the military infrastructure.

The Region of Sardinia, as part of a consultation procedure with the Ministry of Defence, has completed a census of military areas and buildings in the territory [11]. As far as the city of Cagliari is concerned, the survey certified the presence of 50 military sites, covering a total of around 200 hectares, of which 70% is located in the area of Calamosca, Sant'Elia and Poetto.

All of these areas are currently undergoing an intensive process of disposal, due to a reduction in military requirements and the recognised importance of these areas, which requires them to be used for the benefit of the community.

2.2   Strategies for the Regeneration of the Military Landscape of Calamosca

The peculiarity of the Cagliari case study lies in the location of the military areas to be redeveloped, mostly concentrated on the Calamosca promontory, a landscape context characterised by territorial invariants and important environmental components, in a condition of perpetual mixture with the product of historical territorialisation processes due to defence requirements.

The buildings in this area are characterized by different types and legal status. Some of them have been in disuse for a long time, but are still owned by the Ministry of Defense, others have already been transferred to territorial authorities and are waiting for a new functional destination. Other assets, such as the former firing range of the Italian Army and the Fort of Sant'Ignazio, can potentially be disposed of because they are no longer useful for institutional purposes, and it is planned to transfer them to the Region, in accordance with the procedures provided for by the special regional statute. Other assets, such as the 'Campo Rossi' sports facility and the Ederle and Cascino barracks, will be disposed of following the implementation of specific programme agreements between the State and local authorities. In addition, there are a large number of assets that have been disused for a long time, for which it is hoped that they will be put to a new use in order to unlock their potential and counteract the progressive deterioration in which they are lying, which is not only a waste of resources but also a cost to the community. These areas, historically considered peripheral and isolated from the city context, which were characterised above all by the presence of agricultural and productive settlements, as well as by the presence of the military, were progressively reached by the development of the settlement of Cagliari and gradually incorporated into the urban fabric, although they remained mainly 'excluded' in functional terms, due to their military use. At the same time, the condition of constraint determined by the military use has also allowed, even if only in part, the containment of anthropic pressure on these contexts, which often fall in areas of landscape and environmental value, contributing to their preservation and protecting them from the process of urbanisation. The areas affected by military servitudes or adjacent to them are characterised by the presence of large areas with a medium-high level of naturalness, representing almost 40% of the military areas in the municipalities of Cagliari and Elmas. Despite these assumptions, the issue of regenerating disused or potentially disused military assets is not given due importance within urban and territorial development policies. Due to the strategic relevance of these areas at a metropolitan level, the local administrations of the vast area have initiated forms of inter-institutional collaboration during the joint drafting of the Inter-municipal Strategic Plan (ISP), through the activation of operational technical tables. The result of this coordination was the preparation of a strategic document that is structured according to actions aimed at rationalising and strengthening the system of services and urban welfare, through the relocation of military functions of the regional capital to peripheral areas of the metropolitan area, in order to make usable the supply of areas and buildings to accommodate services, equipment of collective interest and social housing [12]. It is necessary to consider that the municipal urban planning regulations, currently in a condition of uncertainty due to the lack of adaptation to the regional landscape tool, could represent an opportunity to express concrete strategies for the reutilization of the areas owned by the Ministry of Defense that are disused or for which conversion to civilian uses is planned. The current Municipal Urban Plan (MUP) identifies the homogeneous GM zones (areas for military equipment) and the GM* zone (areas for military equipment with a forecast of disposal) as areas for transformation and, in recognition of their urban relevance, indicates a series of provisions and standards in order to encourage their disposal and new use for civil and social uses, through implementation tools that favor the concert between the various bodies and stakeholders involved. In addition, specifically for the GM* areas included between the Poetto coast and the Su Siccu area, reuse scenarios and design solutions are defined, which foresee the urban redefinition and the reconversion of the use of buildings for integrated social housing and the establishment of a tourist accommodation center, as well as the strengthening of leisure facilities, entertainment and support to the Sant'Elia Urban Park. It is clear, therefore, the need for a further process of integration, after the one that has characterized the historical military infrastructure, which involves the military areas whose functions have persisted until contemporary times, in order to facilitate the reorganization territory and constitute a 'useful resource for the satisfaction of the needs expressed by local communities, which cannot ignore the historical, identity and collective values that can be recognized, because of the role that these areas have covered in the development of the settlement of the city of Cagliari.

In a favorable historical moment, coinciding with the launch of the Strategic Plan for the metropolitan area and the adaptation of the Municipal Urban Plan (MUP) to the Regional Landscape Plan (RLP), it is hoped that these addresses find concreteness in projects of reuse and re-functionalization that take into account the value of use of the assets and the characteristics of the historical, cultural and landscape context in which they are located.

2.3   Interpreting and Representing Landscape Transformations: The Sant'Elia Urban Park

The development of digital technologies and systems of survey and representation of the architecture and the territory contribute to the constitution of digital databases of high scientific value able to support the operative choices related to the ability of modification and conservation of places. In addition to the need for in-depth knowledge of the values and criticalities of a complex system, the ability to communicate the signs and forms that characterize the urban contexts, giving them a character of uniqueness that comes from the history of long term and then from the overlap of events that have redesigned the relationships between the physical and human components, acquires considerable importance. Expressing and sharing these signs becomes fundamental for the understanding and awareness of people who live in places because it favors the acquisition of a "new" consciousness, the first step for its protection and an essential contribution to preserving this memory.

Viollet Le Duc associates the relationship with architecture with the dialogue with nature as both can be subject to the same analysis and the same geometrical investigations [13]. If we accept this statement and use the operative guidelines suggested by the structuralism movement to define an operative methodology, "we can think of breaking down the landscape into its constituent parts to classify them and then recompose it to understand the relationships that link the different parts and each of them to the whole" [14]. Decomposing the landscape to understand it, reading the diversity (therefore the uniqueness), representing the signs that persist and define its forms and, in some ways, direct/condition the transformations linked to formal and informal action. This can be the contribution of the Sciences of representation within a multidisciplinary debate.

Drawing, within the process of study, becomes the crosscutting tool that can connect the different disciplines thanks to the ability to produce synthetic readings based on complex elaborations or because of direct perception of places. The reading, carried out in an approaching way, through a gradual path of careful attention, becomes the instrument able to find specific details, a "dominant" element and then to reach synthesis and summary drawings from the points recognizable only at the end of the journey, as real landmarks of urban perception. This path, carried out at different levels of reading to analyse and represent the marks of the urban landscape, enhances the perceptive component belonging to people who are involved and live the places. A direct understanding of the places requires a sliding scale and a full immersion in the landscape. It also needs a pedestrian role of the observer with a horizon line at a human level, characteristic of experiencing the city and is part of it [15]. The integrated application of different methodologies of survey and representation to the context of Cagliari, and in particular to the area of Calamosca and Sant'Elia, offers an output composed of images that enrich and complete, with a very subjective component, a cartographic knowledge. It currently can rely on aerial shots and aerial-photogrammetric representations that "give back an image conceived as a two dimensional idea [16]. It highlights the organization of the urban fabric and its relationship with the territory, in an overall view (Fig. 1), "an image far from the reality that perceives the human eye and the sensations that accompany the one who walks through the city" [17]. The maps and the zenithal views are indeed useful tools for a reading of the urban form, defined by the physical elements, recognizable as a predefined design difficult to refer to the perception.

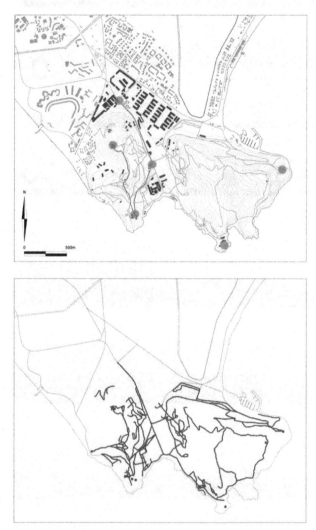

Fig. 1. Graphic elaboration on an aero-photogrammetric basis of the "military" SIGNS in the area of the Urban Park of Sant'Elia, constituted in particular by a dense network of paths with a strong naturalistic value that connect spaces (natural and artificial such as the former firing range created by the quarry activity) and "strongholds of urban perception", nodes of a path "on a human scale" and terraces on the landscape (drawings by Andrea Pirinu).

On the other hand, the views give back the visual image by fragments chosen, selected, and allowing immediate recognition of the places (Fig. 2). The images clearly express how the significant presence of military buildings has not compromised the strong "naturalness" of the place, which still preserves accessible spaces and wide views

Fig. 2. Re-elaboration on photographic basis. View from the sea approaching the coast and diachronic reading of the landscape transformations in the area of Calamosca (drawings by Andrea Pirinu, Giancarlo Sanna).

of the surrounding landscape. So the views, and more generally the drawings made in on the scene, integrate the information of the cartography in "a shift of scale that adds the third dimension to the architecture, leading back to the man also the greater human dimension" [16].

The urban landscape is composed of multiform images and dynamic relationships in which the boundary between description and interpretation of phenomena becomes elusive and no longer defined [18]. In this sense, the contribution of Drawing is realized with the definition of an image composed of a series of signs (Fig. 3) that captures different features, hidden glimpses, forgotten and rediscovered, historical views that can be reinterpreted, enhanced, and protected. The action of drawing with quick lines or reasoned synthesis, from a tool of registration, becomes a way of pre-vision design. To do this, however, it is necessary to overcome the "cultural derailment" [19] that derives from the current "primacy of accuracy over expressive clarity", reducing the considerable amount of information offered by digital databases and achieving representations that can communicate - even and especially to a wide audience - values and critical issues of a common heritage.

Fig. 3. Mosaic of graphic readings. Itinerary across the places, approach to the architecture and views towards the city and the landscape context (drawings by Andrea Pirinu).

3 Conclusions

The contemporary urban landscape is the result of the continuous transformations that have marked modern society and its dimension of multi-layered system requires specialized and integrated skills necessary for a careful analysis and management of the dynamics in action. The case study of the metropolitan city of Cagliari allows to reflect on the opportunities that emerge from the integration of the issue of former military sites in a framework of urban and territorial regeneration policies that take into account the identity value of these contexts, which were generally excluded from urban dynamics due to their original functions.

The military presence has driven long-lasting processes of territorialization that have generated settlement contexts characterized by a sum of material and immaterial values that can be recognized in the local collective consciousness.

The paper focuses on the role that this real estate asset, inherited from the military presence in the territory, could assume within a broad strategy for territorial regeneration, overcoming the approach to the recovery limited to the assignment of a new use destination to the existing built heritage.

The analysis of the evolution of the urban fabric, also through the representation of the different phases that have affected the urban development of the context in question, allows to chronologically reconstruct the origin of military sites and their gradual involvement within the urban dimension of Cagliari. The interpretation of the process of territorialization and urbanization underlines the cultural and identity components that qualify the military landscape and acquire greater relevance in the collective consciousness of the settled community.

Every strategy aimed at overcoming the situation of stasis in which disused military properties fall must necessarily consider the dynamics on which the development of these areas and their relationship with the existing city are based, but especially the consequences of their possible transformation, considering their role in the common memory [20].

The geographical location and typological characteristics of these areas are evidence of how the public administration, in the military form, has inspired processes of territorialization through the development of spaces that over time have certainly taken on a material connotation but, an aspect not to be overlooked, also of a symbolic nature [21].

The relationship between these areas and the reference context gives a dimension of authenticity to each urban and territorial context involved, characterized as a fundamental prerequisite for any regeneration goal.

To this regard, an analytical approach is necessary to reconfigure the relationships between these areas and the surrounding territory, which is the first step towards the introduction of new uses and functions of local interest, concerning the specific contexts. These conditions should be achieved through the cooperation of different stakeholders, both public and private, whose coordination can be facilitated by the drafting of planning tools that provide a certain and shared basis to regulate the satisfaction of the demands of the settled community [2]. Finally, the actions should combine economic profitability, recovery and virtuous reinterpretation of these heritages to redefine the structure and organization of certain parts of urban or territorial systems [1], calibrating the decision-making process, preparatory to the determination of new uses and functions, following the "memorial value" assigned to these areas, whose recognition takes on a collective and non-physical dimension [22].

References

1. Gastaldi, F., Camerin, F.: La rigenerazione urbana e i processi di dismissione del patrimonio immobiliare pubblico e militare in Italia. Territorio della Ricerca su Insediamenti e Ambiente **14**(8), 45–58 (2015)
2. Turri, F., Cappelletti, V., Zamperini, E.: Il recupero delle caserme: tutela del patrimonio e risorsa per la collettività. Territorio **46**, 72–84 (2008)
3. Perelli, C., Sistu, G.: Ammainare le bandiere? I beni militari e pianificazione urbana a Cagliari. Documenti geografici 1, 57–76 (2015). http://www.documentigeografici.it. Accessed 27 Apr 2021
4. Scano, D.: Forma Karalis, Gianni Trois Editore, Cagliari (1934)
5. Cossu, A.: Storia militare di Cagliari. Anatomia di una piazzaforte di prim'ordine (1217-1999), Valdes Editore, Cagliari (2001)
6. Principe, I.: Cagliari. In: Le città nella storia d'Italia, Laterza, Bari (1981)
7. Colavitti, A.M., Usai, N.: Cagliari, Alinea Editrice, Firenze (2007)
8. Bartolo, G., De Waelr, J., Tidu, A.: Il promontorio di Sant'Elia in Cagliari, Editrice S'Alvure, Oristano (2005)
9. Giannattasio, C., Grillo, S.M., Murru, S.: Il sistema di torri costiere in Sardegna (XVI–XVII sec.). Forma, materia, tecniche murarie, "L'Erma" of Bretschneider, Roma (2015)
10. Atzeni, C., Fiorino, D.R.: Sistemi fortificati piemontesi nel paesaggio costiero urbano di Cagliari: approcci interdisciplinari al progetto di restauro del rudere di Sant'Ignazio. Restauro Archeologico **25**(1), 74–99 (2017)
11. Region of Sardinia, Census of military sites (2006). https://www.regione.sardegna.it/j/v/2568? s=32660&v=2&c=3696&t=1. Accessed 27 Apr 2021
12. Colavitti, A.M., Serra, S., Usai, A.: Demanio militare e beni comuni: regolazione dei rapporti interistituzionali e coinvolgimento della società civile nei processi di valorizzazione della Regione Sardegna. In: Commons/Comune: geografie, luoghi, spazi, città. Società di studi geografici. Memorie geografiche, vol. 14, pp. 559–565 (2016)
13. Cianci, M.G.: La rappresentazione del paesaggio. Metodi, strumenti e procedure per l'analisi e la rappresentazione. Editore Alinea (2008)
14. Docci, M., Chiavoni, E.: Saper leggere l'architettura. Edizioni Laterza. Bari, Roma (2016)
15. Manganaro, M.: Interpretazioni di città., Note, appunti, ragionamenti per ampliare una ricerca. In: Questio XIII, pp. 23–24 (2011)
16. Rossi, M., Russo, M.: L'immagine della città: frammenti e percorsi nell'iconografia urbana. In: Iarossi M.P. (eds.) Ritratti di città in un interno. Bonomia University Press, Bologna (2014)
17. Báez Mezquita, J.M.: Il disegno dal vero nella documentazione della città. In: Questio XIV 25–26, pp. 7–18 (2012)
18. Chiavoni, E., Cianci, M.G., Colaceci, S.: Narration and representation of the urban landscape as a cultural and tourist resource. Rome and its lungoteveri (riverbanks) narration and representation of the urban landscape as a cultural and tourist resource. In: Agustín-Hernández, L., Sánchez, N.C., Mir, M.S. (eds.) XVIII Congreso Internacional de Expresión Gráfica Arquitectónica 2020, Zaragoza, p. 721 (2020)
19. Valerio, V.: La rappresentazione della montagna nel XIX secolo tra scienza e imitazione della natura. In: Dai Prà, E. (eds.) Approcci geo-storici e governo del territorio, Milano, p. 91 (2014)

20. Infussi, F., Merlini, C., Pasqui, G.: La dismissione delle aree militari: un'occasione per le politiche di rinnovo dei centri storici. In: Proceedings of XV SIU National Conference, Società Italiana degli Urbanisti. L'Urbanistica che cambia. Rischi e Valori. Pescara, 10–11 Maggio 2012. Planum. The Journal of Urbanism, vol. 25, Roma-Milano (2012)
21. Artioli, F.: Le aree militari nelle città italiane: patrimonio pubblico e rendita urbana nell'era dell'austerity e della crisi. Ital. J. Soc. Policy 1, 89–113 (2016)
22. Choay, F.: L'allegorie du patrimoine. Seuil, Paris (1992)

Applying Building Information Modeling to Road Pavements Management

Francesca Maltinti[1]($\boxtimes$) ⓘ, Luca Curreli[2] ⓘ, Emanuela Quaquero[1] ⓘ, Giulia Rubiu[1] ⓘ, and Mauro Coni[1] ⓘ

[1] Department of Civil and Environmental Engineering and Architecture (DICAAR), University of Cagliari, via Marengo 3, 09123 Cagliari, Italy
maltinti@unica.it
[2] Metassociati srl, Via Cesare Battisti, 1/b, 08015 Macomer (NU), Italy

Abstract. An efficient transport infrastructure system is essential for the social and economic development of a territory. It has become clear that the demographic increase and changes in the habits of the populations should be supported by a development of transport systems, often inadequate to the growing demand for mobility. Therefore, it was necessary to use technologies that would allow the design, management and monitoring of transport structures in an effective manner to ensure adequate levels of service and safety. In more recent times, this need has led to the development of new methodologies as Building Information Modeling (BIM), which is decisively influencing the construction sector, allowing for better results from an economic, management and performance point of view. The digitization of civil manufactures has changed the approach to design and in particular the use of BIM for infra-structures has led to changes of an instrumental nature in the processes related to all phases of design and construction.

This paper presents a new BIM procedure to support the management phases of a road infrastructure. It has been defined an informative model which can interface the three-dimensional model of a road pavement with a set of information related to monitoring activities.

Keywords: Building Information Modeling · Road pavement · Management

1 Introduction

Social and economic development of a territory is closely related to an efficient transport system. Over the years, it has become clear that the demographic increase and changes in the habits of the populations should be supported by a development of transport systems, often inadequate to the growing demand for mobility [1].

Civil structures, such as roads, bridges, dams, etc. are subjected to deterioration related to aging. Keeping track of their wear and performance conditions during exercise is essential to ensure adequate levels of comfort and safety [2]. Over time, an inadequate monitoring system entails high management costs and, in some cases, it could result in the loss of human lives. In the past and, unfortunately, even recently, tragic events have

© Springer Nature Switzerland AG 2021
O. Gervasi et al. (Eds.): ICCSA 2021, LNCS 12958, pp. 145–160, 2021.
https://doi.org/10.1007/978-3-030-87016-4_11

occurred, often due to the poor conditions of some components of the infrastructural works [3]. The way maintenance activities are conducted is one of the most critical aspects of management of civil works: often a manual approach is used to management information. This leads to a poor definition of the resources for life cycle management of constructions [4]. It is estimated that about 80% of the time during the Facility Management (FM) phases is used to reconstruct relevant information that is often dispersed during the pre-construction phases [5]. In this context Building Information Modeling (BIM) represents a key factor for the development of the information management process [6]. In the Architecture, Engineering and Construction (AEC) sector the adoption of BIM has resulted in significant savings during the early stages of the life cycle of a work due to the production of virtual models and an analytical approach [7]. Moreover, recent studies have shown great advantages even in the management phases [8, 9].

So far, BIM methodology has been applied mainly in the architectural and buildings construction fields where it has found considerable success, while in infrastructural one it is still at the beginning. However, widespread use of BIM in building construction has aroused growing interest also for Infrastructure - Building Information Modeling (I-BIM applications) [10–13]. Up to now, contributions in literature are still few. Some researchers have analyzed various possible uses of BIM in the infrastructural field, starting from Cho et al. [14] who propose a holistic BIM library concept to integrate geometry, property, and product information into a tunnel project or Yakubi [15] who highlights obstacles for applying BIM to civil infrastructure and requisite to promote it. More recently, Fabozzi et al. [16] test a procedure to implement geotechnical information into a BIM model for a benchmark case history of tunneling in the urban area of Naples.

Acampa et al. [17] present a case study where they apply the BIM oriented design method to the underground railway extension in the metropolitan area of Catania.

Dell'Acqua et al. [18] present an overview of BIM applied to railway projects and focus on the advantages of this methodology.

Guerra de Oliviera et al. [19] suggest possible improvements in the interoperability of maintenance data of the airport's runway of the Lamezia Terme International Airport with reference to the IFC Reference Processes.

Campisi et al. [20] give a great scientific contribution by defining a methodology to give key elements needed to design possible cycle path solutions by means the I-BIM technology.

Aritomi et al. [21] have devised a "road information model" with floor plans, profiles and cross sections based on parametric modeling of the geometry, Rebolj et al. [22] developed an updated version of the model. Lee and Kim [23] and Cho et al. [24] have developed an I-BIM methodology in the IFC format useful for geometry modeling and for archiving semantic information.

An interesting application of Heritage-BIM was proposed by Biancardo et al. [25] on an ancient road of Pompei.

In Asia and Americas, the largest number of I-BIM applications are detected, on the other hand, in Europe, Oceania and Africa, there is a lower attitude to the use of BIM in the infrastructural field [10].

On the other hand, in Italy, the Decree n.560 of 2017 makes the use of BIM method mandatory, starting from the largest tenders which often relate to infrastructures. Therefore, the need to apply BIM to infrastructures has now become urgent and important.

Use of BIM methodology facilitates design and management of a linear infrastructure because it allows to concentrate all aspects of the work in a single model, reducing possible errors and conflicts. This rationalization of processes brings benefits to public spending and increases the efficiency and profitability of the sector.

This paper presents a new BIM procedure to support the management phases of a road infrastructure. It has been defined an informative model which can interface the three-dimensional model of a road pavement with a set of information related to monitoring activities.

2 Case Study

The study concerned a section of the new SS 195, a very important infrastructure for improving the connection between the most important city and the south of Sardinia (Italy). During the construction process, the works were interrupted for a long time. In some areas, materials already installed were exposed to degradation action of atmospheric agents (see Fig. 1). A BIM model was created to support management of interventions of those road pavement sections where the criticalities were more evident.

Fig. 1. Territorial context of SS195 road and its materials degraded due to action of atmospheric agents.

2.1 BIM Model of the Road Pavement

A methodological approach was followed for the development of the model which led to the definition of different alternatives for achieving the set goal.

The modeling process was divided into four different macro phases. For each of these, sub-phases have been defined and specific actions and tools have been adopted. Weak interoperability between different tools and formats used was the major problems encountered (Fig. 2).

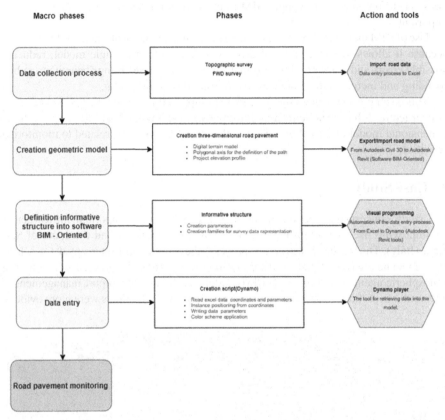

Fig. 2. Workflow.

The geometric model (see Fig. 3) was created using Autodesk's Civil3d software which follows a similar workflow of common road design softwares. The inputs for this phase were:

- Digital terrain model;
- Polygonal axis for creating horizontal alignment;
- Vertical alignment.

The design drawings in CAD format were the main source of the geometric data.

A topographical survey was carried out to reconstruct digital terrain model (DTM) and returned in.dwg format.

The software allows to read the geometric entities directly from Autocad elaborations. The points are parametric entities which made possible to use the information of the elevation. It was reported in the drawing by text form, by inserting it in the corresponding Z coordinate of each point.

The main axis of the project was then imported, this was read as a 2d polyline, which was used as the basis for the creation of the "path" object, a BIM object that dynamically interacts with the other elements of the model. It allowed to define the vertical alignment of the terrain and the road, which collects various information such as elevation in curves, project speed and type of road as reported in the Ministerial Decree No. 6792 of 05/11/2001.

The vertical alignment was obtained starting from the horizontal alignment and the DTM and was defined according to the choices made during the design phase.

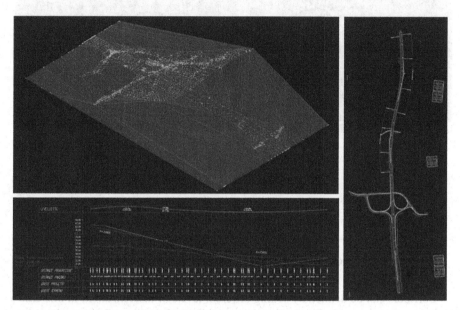

Fig. 3. The geometric model: DTM, horizontal alignment, vertical alignment.

The typical section of the road pavement has been defined starting from predefined schemes and then modified to adapt the model to the design choices. Each section is coded according to codes that allow to assign different geometric properties and create dynamic links with the entities of the project.

The changes in the model were made by using Subassembly Composer application, a visual programming environment that allows to visually compose complex components of type section and simulate their functioning with different values and target conditions. These components are imported into civil 3d in .pkt format.

The elements created so far are combined to create the three-dimensional model of the road pavement through the "corridor" object that manages the data, linking the various standard sections (applied to the different ranges of stations) to the base lines (horizontal alignment) and to the respective vertical alignment. In other words, it manages the connection of project-specific surface and alignment data with the content of components of type section. The object includes corridor body geometry, longitudinal feature lines, and embedded surfaces. A corridor allows to define and visualize components such as:

– feature lines which link points along point codes defined in components of type section;
– surfaces using link codes and feature lines.

During the elaboration of the corridor the interferences present along the route (hydraulic artifacts, intersections) were carefully considered. To obtain a result that could correctly represent the road solid object it was necessary to create different regions (Fig. 4).

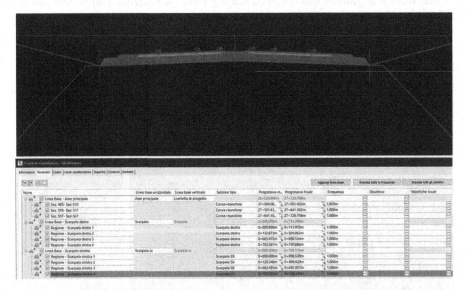

Fig. 4. Model of type section (top) and Corridor properties (down)

Corridors can be defined by setting different levels of discretization; in this case a step of 1m was chosen. In Fig. 5 a detail that highlights the coding relating to the points, connections and shapes described above is reported. The model created in this first phase was imported to Revit as a 3D solid.

Fig. 5. A detail that highlights the coding relating to the points, connections and shapes

2.2 The Information Model of the Road Pavement

BIM integrates the traditional 3D model of a building with all the information and properties about that building, such as design plans, product information, planning sequence and operations [26]. Therefore, the main aspect of this methodology is to produce an informative digital model that links geometric and alfa-numeric information to all the objects which compose the work. The structuring and management of a wide range of digital data and information about the status of the work creates the best conditions for conducting a "multicriteria" analysis that would allow the design and evaluation of different scenarios and intervention strategies, identifying the best combination that maximizes comprehensively the quality of the results.

In this case, the BIM authoring tool chosen for the development of the informative model was Revit by Autodesk. It is strongly oriented towards building modeling, but it allows to define very effectively data structures also in the infrastructural field. The dataset have to be able to 1) contain information relating to the type and characteristics of materials; 2) store the data relating to the surveys carried out on the pavement; 3) keep the history of the analysis and maintenance activities carried out during the operating phase.

Each element present within Revit is considered a Family. The family contains the geometric definition of the element and the parameters used for the information storage. Each instance of an element is defined and controlled by the family.

The parameters associated with different families of the project can be defined according to the discipline to which they belong. Although there are no specific sections relating to InfraBIM, it was possible to identify valid alternatives for grouping and defining the shared parameters for using in the infrastructural field.

Once the parameters have been defined, they are assigned to the families. To achieve the objective of this work, it was essential to find a field in the data set of families that contains the procedures and intervention times defined in the maintenance plan as required by Presidential Decree 207/2010 for each object of the model. Road pavement families were created from the solids generated in the previous stages. A family was created for each layer of the superstructure and the parameters relating to the characteristics of the materials used were assigned to each of them (see Fig. 6).

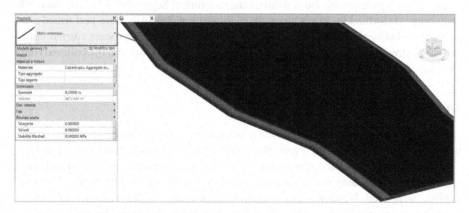

Fig. 6. Family of base layer and characteristics of material.

2.3 Pavement Monitoring via Falling Weight Deflectometer

A fundamental aspect for infrastructural monitoring is to be able to carry out checks quickly and accurately to be able to efficiently manage the resources to be allocated for maintenance work [27].

The falling weight deflectometer (FWD) is one of the most used non-destructive investigation tools in the world due to its precision and its operation that allows to simulate the loads to which roads are subject [28]. It is mounted on a trailer and towed by a vehicle specifically instrumented to monitor activities. Entire data collection process is controlled by an operator via a laptop [27]. The instrument records the temporary vertical deflection of the investigated surface by means of special sensors (geophones). The location of geophones respect to the center of fall of the mass allows to detect the deflection of the various points of the surface at a variable distance from the center of the load, thus allowing to evaluate a deflection basin. The analysis of the shape and characteristics of the deflection basin allows, through accurate back-calculation models, to determine the characteristics of the lower layers including the stiffness of the materials. Collected deflectometric data can be processed with different methods. They can be used to obtain indices, called Basin Index, which allow to obtain an initial indication of the conditions of the superstructure. Base Layer Index (BLI) provides information on the structural conditions of the base layer. Middle Layer Index (MLI) provides a high-level indication of the sub-base (foundation) layer, while Lower Layer Index (LLI) provides an indication of the condition of the sub-base layer [29].

The Fast FWD (FFWD), used for the survey, works in the same way of FWD but it allows investigations on the road pavement 5 times shorter than the original version. In the FFWD hydraulic systems for lifting the hammer mass have been replaced by an electric motor. Two investigation campaigns were carried out for the analysis of superstructure of SS n.195. During the first, on the morning of May 26th, 2020, a total of 456 beats were performed in 152 positions, 38 on each alignment. In each position 3 strokes were performed with load values between 800 kPa and 1400 kPa. The second investigation campaign was carried out on the morning of September 30th, 2020 and 108 beats were performed in 36 positions. In each position 3 strokes were performed with load values between 800 kPa and 1400 kPa. These measurements were carried out to verify the structural conditions of the base layer in cemented mix and the collected data were saved in a database.

2.4 Representation of the Survey Data

Since there were a large amount of data relating to the different layers of the pavement, it was necessary to search for a tool that would allow to represent them immediately.

A very simple geometric representation was selected, which could qualitatively provide information relating to the values detected by FFWD, by a color scheme. "Nested" families were used. Nesting a family consists in inserting it within another, in order to create a new one consisting of the union of the different geometries. A family that hosts another one is called the host family [30]. The families "Elastic modules" and "Basin Index" have been created. The families consist of cylinders: each of them represents a characteristic of the superstructure layer. For both families, a set of parameters has been defined. This set reports the value of the elastic modules and the value of BLI MLI and LLI; also text-type parameters have been defined to storage and manage qualitative information related to the structural conditions of the various layers.

2.5 Visual Programming for the Automation of the Data Entry Process

The FFWD survey data were collected in a spreadsheet in .xls format. The high amount of data and information to be connected to the BIM model would have made the process of manually compiling the schedules within Revit very long. Moreover, this process would have entailed a high probability of making mistakes and a considerable effort from a computational point of view. To solve this problem, it was decided to use the Dynamo software.

Dynamo is an open-source visual programming environment that allows construction users to process data, generate complex geometries and create automations without having to know a programming language [30]. Visual programming is an operating mode that does not involve the typing of a code list, but the connection and processing of graphic entities. The visual approach simplifies the development of applications by isolating the complexity of coding to the main users of Revit (architects, designers, engineers, companies, etc.). Nodes are the elementary entities in Dynamo, they are portions of programming code dedicated to carrying out specific operations which, combined, generate an algorithm. This process will produce a script capable of automating workflows, allowing, as in this case, direct input from an existing Excel file and the automatic compilation of parameter fields within Revit. The Dynamo work environment is accessible directly from Revit in the Manage>Visual programming section.

To reach the above target, a script has been defined in Dynamo (see Fig. 7).

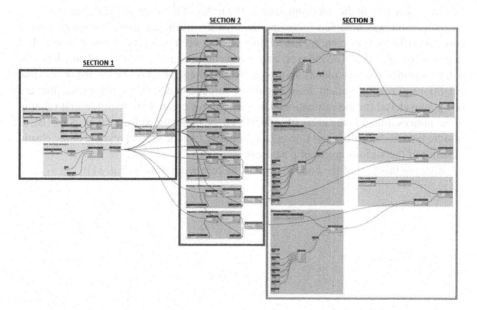

Fig. 7. Overall Dynamo script

It can be divided into three sections. The first (see Fig. 8), relating to the positioning of the instances on the model, reads the data from the spreadsheet and generates lists containing the coordinates of the points of the survey in the space at which various instances of the families that will contain the detected data are positioned.

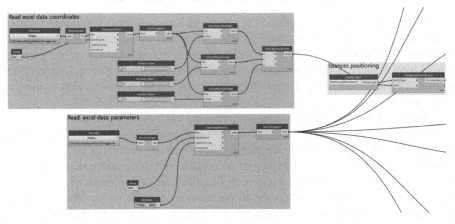

Fig. 8. The first part of Dynamo script

The second part of the script (see Fig. 9) reads the survey data from the spreadsheet and compiles the related parameters present in the families: the procedure for acquiring values is identical to the acquisition of coordinates.

Finally, the last part of the script (see Fig. 10) associates a color coding to the different families according to the data contained in the fields of the different parameters.

This result was obtained following the creation of dictionaries. Dictionaries are a very powerful tool for creating associative sets between two lists of equal length. The first is a list of "keys" (or indexes) and the second a set of "values" (or the data that will be returned for each index). In this case study, the keys represent the list of possible conditions of road pavement according to the value assumed by the parameters that are being considered for the evaluation. The dictionaries created are two: the first relating to the indices linked to the areas of influence of the deflections: Base layer index (BLI), Middle layer index (MLI) and Lower layer index (LLI); the second relating to the elastic modules of the various layers of pavement.

Running this part of the code generates the following results (Fig. 11):

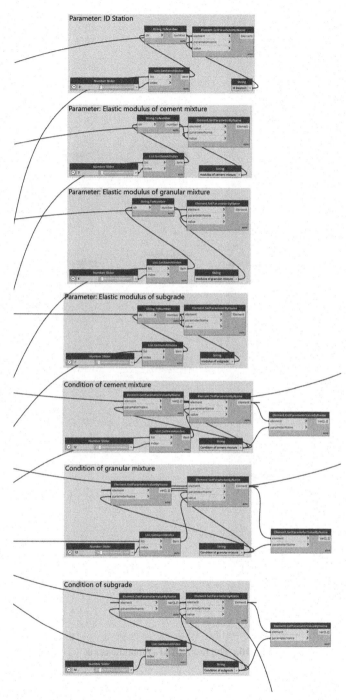

Fig. 9. The second part of Dynamo script

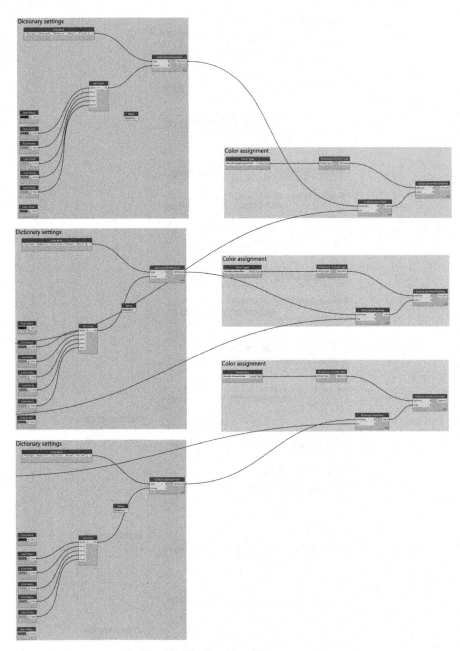

Fig. 10. The last part of Dynamo script

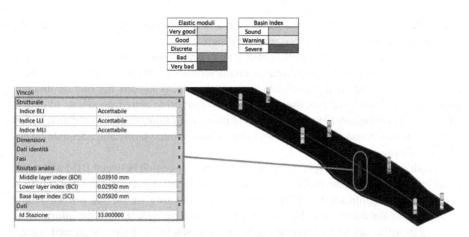

Fig. 11. Results of BIM application to represent road pavement performance.

3 Conclusion

In this work the Authors pursued the goal of defining BIM procedures that could be applied to road infrastructure sector. They tried to create a workflow that could support the management phase of a road infrastructure, with a view to exploiting the potential of integrated design. The methodological approach was structured according to the logic "definition of objectives - execution of alternatives - verification of the result", and led to the definition of practices that could be applied to any type of infrastructure, without, however, assuming that the alternative identified could be the best.

One of the aspects to which more attention was paid was to test the interoperability between the various applications used during the different phases of the work. Starting from the documentation provided by the construction company (Aleandri SPA), a great effort was made to transfer the project information from CAD formats to BIM software. The most important criticality found at the end of this phase is undoubtedly linked to the transfer formats of the documents. Although the direction in the field of BIM is to develop an open and neutral interchange format (IFC), this tool does not yet support BIM objects relating to the world of infrastructures. Moreover, during this work, shortcomings were found also for the transfer of simple geometries. The development of a tool that allows the sharing of data of an Infra-BIM model without redundancies or deficiencies seems to be still far away. However, the growing number of research activities promoted by Building Smart International as part of the new IFC standards dedicated to roads, bridges, urban and spatial planning, railways and airports, bodes well for a short time horizon.

Another important issue was the analysis of how the data deriving from infrastructure maintenance activities could be managed in an Infra-BIM model. From this point of view, the results obtained can be considered very satisfactory. The possibility of being able to define different parameters in the model to be able to dynamically associate a large amount of information makes BIM almost a necessity when it comes to infrastructural works; the visual programming tools, in fact, although not easy to use, make the data association processes a completely automatic step.

The model created in this work, although extremely simplified, allows to represent information relating to the performance characteristics of the pavement. A next step could be to associate the detected data with specific decay models in order to obtain a forecasting tool that, based on the results of the monitoring activities, allows to define which areas may be most exposed to critical issues over time, so that to obtain a better planning of maintenance interventions, savings in economic terms and adequate levels of safety during operation.

Another interesting perspective is related to the integration between BIM and territorial information systems (GIS). It is precisely in the infrastructural field that this link becomes more significant: the BIM model provides the information that is loaded onto a cartographic database. With this mechanism, a complete system of all the information deriving from the cartographic model and from the monitoring activities is created, which allows to manage maintenance activities in a highly defined and perfectly georeferenced environment.

Author Contributions. Conceptualization, all; methodology and formal analysis, Luca Curreli, Francesca Maltinti, Mauro Coni, Emanuela Quaquero, Giulia Rubiu; introduction and literary review Luca Curreli, Emanuela Quaquero, Giulia Rubiu; writing-original draft preparation, Luca Curreli, Francesca Maltinti; writing-review and editing Francesca Maltinti, Emanuela Quaquero, Giulia Rubiu; visualization, all. All authors have read and agreed to the published version of the manuscript.

References

1. Costin, A., Adibfar, A., Hu, H., Chen, S.S.: Building information modeling (BIM) for transportation infrastructure – literature review, applications, challenges, and recommendations. Autom. Constr. **2018**(94), 257–281 (2018). https://doi.org/10.1016/j.autcon.2018.07.001
2. Singh, P., Sadhu, A.: System identification-enhanced visualization tool for infrastructure monitoring and maintenance. Front. Built Environ. **6**, 76 (2020). https://doi.org/10.3389/fbuil.2020.00076
3. Mirza, S., Ali, M.S.: Infrastructure crisis - a proposed national infrastructure policy for Canada. Can. J. Civ. Eng. **2017**, 6 (2017). https://doi.org/10.1139/cjce-2016-0468
4. Heaton, J., Parlikad, A.K., Schooling, J.: Design and development of BIM models to support operations and maintenance. Comput. Ind. **111**, 172–186 (2019). https://doi.org/10.1016/j.compind.2019.08.001(2019)
5. Becerik-Gerber, B., Jazizadeh, F., Li, N., Calis, G.: Application areas and data requirements for BIM-enabled facilities management. J. Constr. Eng. Manag. **138**, 431–442 (2012). https://doi.org/10.1061/(ASCE)CO.1943-7862.0000433
6. Pärn, E.A., Edwards, D.J., Sing, M.C.P.: The building information modelling trajectory in facilities management: a review. Autom. Constr. **75**, 45–55 (2017). https://doi.org/10.1016/j.autcon.2016.12.003
7. Building Information Models (BIM): How It Has Changed FM. FMLink (2009)
8. Di Giuda, G.M., Maltese, S., Re Cecconi, F., Villa, V.: Il BIM per la gestione dei patrimoni immobiliari. Linee guida, livelli di dettaglio informativo grafico (LOD) e alfanumerico (LOI). Hoepli, (2017)

9. Di Giuda, G.M., Pellegrini, L., Schievano, M., Locatelli, M., Paleari, F.: BIM and post-occupancy evaluations for building management system: weaknesses and opportunities. In: Daniotti, B., Gianinetto, M., Della Torre, S. (eds.) Digital Transformation of the Design, Construction and Management Processes of the Built Environment. RD, pp. 319–327. Springer, Cham (2020). https://doi.org/10.1007/978-3-030-33570-0_29

10. Dell'Acqua, G.: BIM per Infrastrutture Lineari. Ingenio, Tekna Chen (2017)

11. Dell'Acqua, G.: Infrastructure-Building Information Modeling: Stato dell'Arte. Le Strade, Ottobre 2016. Casa Editrice la Fiaccola SRL (2016) http://www.lestradeweb.com/

12. Yabuki, N.: BIM and construction information modeling (CIM) in Japan. In: Proceedings of the International Conference on Computational Design in Engineering, Jeju, Korea, p. 325 (2012)

13. Japan Construction Information Technology Center, CIM Construction Information Modeling/Management, Japan

14. Cho, D., Cho, N.S., Cho, H., Kang, K.I.: Parametric modelling based approach for efficient quantity takeoff of NATM-tunnels. Gerontechnology 11(2), 70–75 (2012)

15. Yabuki, N.: Issues and implementation methods for BIM in the civil infrastructure domain. In: Teng, J.G. (ed) Proceedings of the 1st International Conference on Sustainable Urbanization (ICSU), Hong Kong, China (2010)

16. Fabozzi, S., Cipolletta, G., Capano, E., Asprone, D., Dell'Acqua, G., Bilotta, E.: BIM-FEM interoperability for the modelling of a traditional excavated tunnel, tunnels and underground cities: engineering and innovation meet archaeology, architecture and art. In: Proceedings of the WTC 2019 ITA-AITES World Tunnel Congress, pp. 785–794 (2019)

17. Acampa, G., Bona, N., Grasso, M., Ticali, D.: BIM: building information modeling for infrastructures. In: AIP Conference Proceedings, vol. 2040(1), p. 140008. AIP Publishing LLC (2018)

18. Dell'Acqua, G., De Oliveira, S.G., Biancardo, S.A.: Railway-BIM: analytical review, data standard and overall perspective. Ingegneria Ferroviaria 73(11), 901–923 (2018)

19. Guerra de Oliveira, S., Tibaut, A., Dell'Acqua, G.: Airport pavement management systems: an open BIM approach. In: Pasetto, M., Partl, M.N., Tebaldi, G. (eds.) ISAP APE 2019. LNCE, vol. 48, pp. 450–459. Springer, Cham (2020). https://doi.org/10.1007/978-3-030-29779-4_44

20. Campisi, T., Acampa, G., Marino, G., Tesoriere, G.: Cycling master plans in Italy: the I-BIM feasibility tool for cost and safety assessments. Sustainability 12(11), 4723 (2020)

21. Aritomi, K., Shibasaki, R., Yabuki, N.: The construction management cooperated with clients using a parametric information design method. In: Luo, Y. (ed.) CDVE 2005. LNCS, vol. 3675, pp. 157–165. Springer, Heidelberg (2005). https://doi.org/10.1007/11555223_18

22. Rebolj, D., Tibaut, A., Čuš-Babič, N., Magdič, A., Podbreznik, P.: Development and application of a road product model. Autom. Constr. 17(6), 719–728 (2008)

23. Lee, S.H., Kim, B.G.: IFC extension for road structures and digital modeling. Proc. Eng. 14, 1037–1042 (2011)

24. Cho, G.H., Song, J.K., Ju, K.B.: Analysis of road elements for the extension geometry part of IFC model schema. In: Proceedings of the First International Conference on Civil and Building Engineering Informatics (ICCBEI2013), Tokyo, Japan, pp. 457–460 (2013)

25. Biancardo, S.A., Russo, F., Veropalumbo, R., Vorobjovas, V., Dell'Acqua, G.: Modeling roman pavements using heritage-BIM: a case study in Pompeii. Balt. J. Road Bridge Eng. 15(3), 34–46 (2020)

26. Chen, Y.: Modeling and analysis methods of bridges and their effects on seismic responses: II—implementation. Comput. Struct. 59, 99–114 (1996). https://doi.org/10.1016/0045-7949(95)00226-X(1996)

27. Coni, M., Mistretta, F., Stochino, F., Rombi, J., Sassu, M., Puppio, M.L.: Fast falling weight deflectometer method for condition assessment of RC bridges. Appl. Sci. **11**, 1743 (2021). https://doi.org/10.3390/app11041743
28. Talvik, O., Aavik, A.: Use of FWD deflection basin parameters (SCI, BDI, BCI) for pavement condition assessment. Balt. J. Road Bridge Eng. **4**, 196–202 (2009). https://doi.org/10.3846/1822-427X.2009.4.196-202
29. Horak, E.: Surface moduli determined with the falling weight deflectometer used as benchmarking tool. In: Proceedings of the 26th Southern African Transport Conference (SATC 2007), South Africa, (2007). ISBN 1-920-01702-X, Document Transformation Technologies cc, Pretoria,
30. Pozzoli, S., Bonazza, M., Villa, S.W.: Autodesk Revit Architecture 2020. Guida Completa per la Progettazione BIM. Tecniche Nuove, Milano (2019). ISBN 978-88-481-4022-5

International Workshop on Sustainable Urban Energy Systems (SURENSYS 2021)

A Geographical Abacus of the Urban Building Heritage Based on Volunteered Geographic Information (VGI)

Stefano Pili[1(✉)], Giuseppe Desogus[2], Francesca Poggi[1], Caterina Frau[1], and Andrea Dessì[2]

[1] Sotacarbo SPA, Grande Miniera di Serbariu, 09013 Carbonia, Italy
stefano.pili@sotacarbo.it

[2] DICAAR – Department of Civil, Environmental Engineering and Architecture, University of Cagliari, Cagliari, Italy

Abstract. This paper describes the preliminary result of the research project "Urban Abacus of Building Energy performances (Abaco Urbano Energeticodegli Edifci – AUREE)" aimed at supporting the renovation and energy efficiency enhancement of urban building heritage financed by Ricerca Sistema Elettrico (MISE) program. The AUREE concept is a Web – GIS GeoBlog portal with some customized interfaces aimed to share the knowledge on urban building heritage and promote the participation of the stakeholders of the urban community. The methodological approach is specifically addressed to small and medium Mediterranean urban contexts that are characterized by a lack of baseline data. It is characterized by the implementation of a simple analytical Urban Building Energy Model (UBEM) based on spatial Open Data, typological study of the local building heritage and a web-based participative framework. After a touch on the theoretical context, the paper presents the general framework of the AUREE project and then focuses to the methodological approach for some participative interfaces. Via an experimentation on the city of Carbonia (Sardinia, IT), the paper presents an archetypes approach based on historical information that provides an exhaustive segmentation and classification of the urban building stock. They are the necessary basis for the UBEM and for the knowledge structure for the Geographical Abacus aimed to support homeowners on the early step of a building renovation decision.

Keywords: Building energy retrofit · UBEM · VGI · GIS

1 Introduction: Theoretical Context

Energy efficiency enhancement of urban areas is a major key point of the EU 2020 objectives in the new climate package for 2030 because the European building stock is responsible of about 40% of emissions. New buildings and new energy retrofitting technologies are characterised by high performances, but, due to the high presence of old and inefficient buildings and the growing of the consumption the average energy need value of the European building stock is still about 200 kWh/m^2 per year [1].

© Springer Nature Switzerland AG 2021
O. Gervasi et al. (Eds.): ICCSA 2021, LNCS 12958, pp. 163–173, 2021.
https://doi.org/10.1007/978-3-030-87016-4_12

Developing an urban strategy is considered essential to increase the efficiency of the building heritage because could channel the private investments and public financial resources on a holistic urban transformation design programs. But generally, the renovation of this huge and old building stock is only managed by the homeowners, supported by more or less effective national incentives that not consider the local building heritage peculiarity.

There are many literature exempla of guidelines or quality protocols about building heritage renovation and a lot of them focuses on energy efficiency enhancement [2, 3]. These are generally documents developed for a purely technical audience, that often, due to their intrinsic specificity, have difficulty in spreading even among operators in the construction industry and are almost unknown to non-technical citizens. The lack of shared knowledge between construction industry operators and non-technical actors about the building heritage is considered one of the main barriers in the recovery process [4].

In order to overcome these barriers, the development and testing of methodologies and supporting tools are becoming increasingly important. They include methodological procedures and technical tools aimed to link the perspective of the single building design process with the strategies at urban or neighbourhood scale and to promote the participation of all the local actors involved on the building stock renovation process. Thanks to the growing of geographic open data availability, examples of methodologies for supporting urban energy planning are increasingly numerous. Most of these are Urban Building Energy Modelling (UBEM) approaches [5] aimed to define the buildings stock energy needs and estimate the potential (theoretical, technical, and exploitable) of various efficiency technologies and/or design scenarios. In general, complex models could obtain more reliable results but require more data and onerous results analysis activities. Less complex models adopt several simplifying hypotheses, therefore they require fewer resources, and have usually more repeatable procedures. However, the uncertainty of the initial assumptions could, in this case, burden the results. One of the most used simplifying approaches is the "archetype", which involves a study of a representative sample of the heritage, in order to explicate some elements that characterize the energy need, and the use of appropriate methods (analytical, statistical, etc.) to extending the results of the sample to all similar buildings in the city. Some recent UBEM bottom – up approaches addressed to urban scale [6] adopt appropriate statistical calibration technique based on energy consumption data to improve the reliability of the results of the energy simulation. These tools focus on the energy demand estimation and, in order to limit the burden of the pre-processing activities, the physical input data on building heritage are highly typological. This approach could miss some important knowledge on architectonic characteristics and uses that are important to define reliable retrofitting hypothesis linked to local market. Moreover, although the spreading of smart metering systems, the energy consumption data generally are not easily available with a proper spatial and temporal details for all the cities contexts. The UBEM approach must be consistent to the tool purpose, to base data availability and economic and human resources, therefore the developments and testing of methodologies and new application that could be exported also on the more common urban planning practice is still an open field of research.

The aim of the AUREE Project (Urban Energy Abacus of Buildings) project is to develop and test a tool to support energy efficiency and renovation process of the building heritage based on a portal (Web - GIS, GeoBlog) which contains some specific interfaces aimed at sharing the knowledge of the building stock and promoting the participation of the local stakeholders.

Via the development of the Carbonia's case studio, the objective of this work is to develop and archetypal study, based on historical information, that provides an exhaustive segmentation and classification of the building stock. It will be the basis to create an interactive, spatial based and self updating Abacus of the building heritage. The descriptive approach of the heritage proper of the definition of construction guidelines is coupled with an easy urban energy model that could calculate the performances of more common building retrofitting scenarios also taking to account Volunteered Geographic information (VGI) provided by the stakeholders interactions trough the portal.

The paper presents first the general framework of the AUREE project that encompasses some layers about public building, residential heritage and others addressed to interact to local stakeholders. Then the peculiarities of the Carbonia's case study and the methodology for the archetypal segmentation are presented. The result section describes the structure of the Abacus interfaces and the relationship to the archetype definition and the participative based data. The methodology experimentation has been carried out on the city of Carbonia because it is a fascist's new town (1938) characterized by a rather homogeneous built heritage that is well documented on local urban planning tool and literature. At the end of the paper, the main critical aspects and the further step of the research project are pointed.

2   The AUREE General Framework

The methodology is mainly designed for small and medium-sized Italian cities and is based on information sources commonly available in the national territory such as: geographical OPEN data (regional GeoDB, ISTAT data,...), knowledge of the building heritage linked to local urban planning and thematic disciplinary references (technical regulations, scientific studies and gray literature,..). These data may be integrated with expeditious urban survey activities that are commonly implemented in the modern urban planning practices.

The methodology consists of an analysis and representation protocol of the building heritage on a geographical basis, combined with a tool for communication and involvement of local actors developed on the WEB GIS portal organized in three main sections that contain the information bases of the portal and some specific interfaces for interaction with local actors (see Fig. 1):

- Public buildings: it constitutes a support tool for energy management of the public buildings but also a tool for sharing the values of the public buildings heritage and to promote the transparency of energy uses;
- Residential heritage: contains the spatial representation of the energy performance of the building heritage and aims to directly involve the occupants in providing information on their home in order to have suggestions for specific retrofits in exchange;

– Geographical Abacus: collects and reorders knowledge on recurring elements of the building heritage on a GIS framework, favouring its dissemination among construction industry operators but also to a non-technical audience.

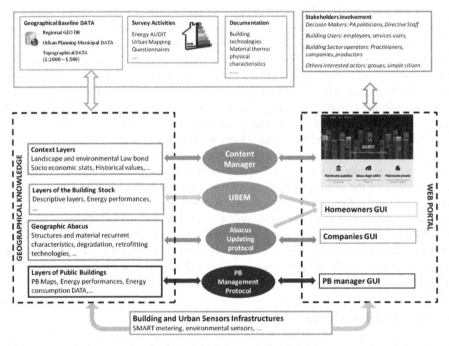

Fig. 1. AUREE general framework

In addition to these sections connected to specific interfaces, it is then possible to consider all the context layers, even if not directly linked to the aspects of energy efficiency, which can however influence the renovation potential (regulations, demography data,..). This is not a simple collection of regulatory constraints, it is an open set of themes that creates a shared background knowledge among decision makers and other stakeholders to direct towards the development of holistic approaches to urban planning.

In the case of public buildings, a protocol based on energy audit procedures and sensors monitoring is proposed. This approach aims to geographic representation and sharing of energy data and building values (transparency of Public energy uses), and at supporting the phases of project, construction, monitoring and management through BIM approaches.

For residential built heritage, an approach based on the study of building typologies and its recurring elements is proposed, coupled with the development of an Urban Building Energy Model (UBEM), useful for assessing the energy retrofit potential of the building heritage.

The abacus is a spatial database that contains the typological information of the recurring elements of the building heritage (structures, systems, usage profiles, and retrofit interventions) linked to the geographical reference element (the building footprint). It aims to support the project activities and the preliminary evaluation of various alternative of building renovations through the geographical representation of the most widespread architectures and the proposal of adequate technologies related to the local market.

The research purpose is therefore to define in detail the procedures and tools that connect the different thematic contents (public buildings layer, building heritage layer, geographical abacus, context layer, data collected by the sensors) to the representation and interaction with local actors through the portal (see Fig. 1).

This article focuses to the methodological approach developed for the Abacus of the residential building heritage with its relations with the participatory interfaces, leaving the description of the UBEM algorithms and of the other elements of the AUREE project to further publications.

3   Carbonia Case Study

Carbonia (about 27000 inh. ISTAT 2020) is a southern Sardinian (Italy) company town, founded starting from 1937 by fascist regime (see Fig. 2). It has a very peculiar building stock, mostly designed and built in a few decades, an emblem of 1930s industrial modernization in Sardinia.

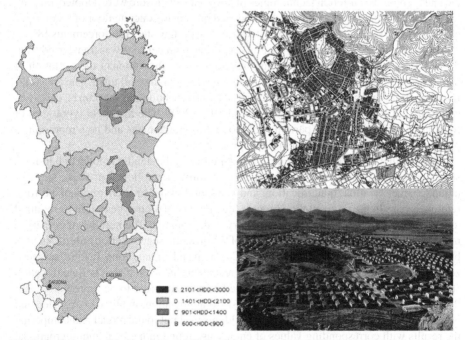

Fig. 2. Left: geographical position of Carbonia and climate classification of Sardinian territory. Right: current plan of Carbonia (up) and historical view of the foundation period (down).

The reasons for the foundation of Carbonia was the discovery of the massive coal deposits in Serbariu, and more upstream in the regime's desire to build an autarkic coal district able to answer the nationwide issue of energy sources. Before the discovery of Serbariu's mine, the only settlements present in the area were sporadic nucleuses of rural houses called "medau". Their construction probably dates back to the eighteenth century, when the occupation of Sardinia by the Duchy of Savoy favoured a repopulation of the countryside. One of the biggest aggregations of medau was precisely in Serbaiu [7].

The construction of the company town can be divided in two phases. The project of the first one provides for a population of 12,000 inhabitants, began in 1937 and concludes at the end of 1938. Shortly afterwards the inauguration, it started the construction of the second-phase project that was expected to welcome 50,000 residents and would have ended in the immediate post-war period. The outcome is a company town at the mouth of the mine, formed by the serial repetition of few building types, still inhabited nowadays.

In the first phase, a series of workers' lodging types was built. They consist mainly of two-storey four-family homes surrounded by a garden and designed in the forms of "autarkical rationalism", a sort of local version of the typical English cottage. In the second phase, on the other side, prevailed more intensive multi-storey buildings.

The peculiarity of the "autarkic project" emerges in the construction techniques. Masonries are always realized with local volcanic stone, called (inappropriately) trachyte, with only one example of reinforced concrete frame, in some of the buildings of the late typologies. Different technologies of horizontal enclosure were adopted, ranging from vaulted floors with cement bricks produced on site, to concrete floor of "Sap-type" or "Rex-type", both made of prefabricated beams with few steel reinforcements [8].

After the fall of fascist regime, the property of the built heritage was transferred from the coal company to the public building institutes. From that moment the evolution of the urban settlement reflects the one of every other Sardinian small town. The areas surrounding the company centre are characterized by private buildings that can be classified within the most common types of the period 1950–2000. The historical typologies of foundation period have been partially sold to the original tenants and now represents a problematic mixture of public and private property.

The peculiarity of Carbonia requires an adaptation of the standard model of buildings stocks energy classifications by archetypes. Generally, they follow four steps: segmentation, characterization, quantification, and validation of the final energy demand for a reference year. In the segmentation process, the number of archetype buildings required to represent the building stock of the country is determined. The number of archetype buildings is obtained from the combination of the different segmentation criteria, such as building type, construction year, main HVAC system and climate zone. In the characterization step, each archetype is described by its technical characteristics. The quantification step determines the distribution of archetype buildings in order to be representative of the building stock. To validate the building stock aggregation, the final energy demand is calculated using the defined archetype buildings as input to the model and comparing the results with corresponding values of energy use found in national and international statistics for a particular reference year [9] in case of a single urban centre the climate characterization is unique.

The choice of archetype for the segmentation phase can follow three criteria: the use of real buildings, the creation of example buildings and the creation of a synthetical average building. In the first, it is required the selection of a real existing building representing the most typical buildings in a specific category. The selection process is performed through a statistical analysis to find out the real building with characteristics like the mean geometrical and construction features of the statistical sample. In the second, it is necessary the creation of a virtual building which for each relevant parameter includes the most used material and systems based on expert inquiries and other sources of information. It is used in case of no statistical data are available. The third approach foresees the creation of a virtual building which for each relevant parameter includes the most used material and systems using basic statistical data. It is a statistical composite of the features found within a list of buildings in the stock [10]. The results of segmentation and classification of Carbonia's building stock are presented in the following section.

4   Results and Discussion

The case of Carbonia required a specific approach that is a synthesis of the previous ones. Due to its particular history, the age of the buildings is very characterizing. At the moment, only the residential buildings segmentation phase has been carried out. Three periods have been identified: pre foundation (1700–1937), foundation (1937–1950) and post foundation (1950–now). The choice of archetypization methodology differs by age of construction. In the first period only one type (medau) have been identified. It is an example building. Its features have been derived by historical studies [9]. The typization of buildings from the foundation period is quite peculiar. Each building is a model repeated numerous times. The models are real building types that not only represent the building stock but are the whole building stock themselves. Fifteen models have been identified. The studies conducted on the heritage to ensure its conservation are precious sources for its constructive features [10]. For the residual part of the urban stock, i.e. the post foundation, an example building methodology has been chosen. The most common post war types have been identified. They are semi-detached or isolated houses, detached houses, linear multi-storey, block multi-storey and tower multi-storey. For the definition of constructive features an experts based approach has been adopted. The proposed technologies have been verified with the limits imposed by Italian energy performance legislation, starting from 1976 (Fig. 3).

The representation of the energy characteristics of the residential built heritage is based on the study of building typologies and its recurring elements (Abacus) coupled with the development of an energy model at the urban scale (Urban Building Energy Modeling - UBEM), useful for preliminary evaluation the retrofit potential of the building stock. The Abacus and the Residential Heritage sections are strongly linked, in fact they are different representations of the same set of information based on: typological studies, UBEM results and data from participatory interfaces. Thanks to the processing capabilities typical of the GIS environment, an engineering UBEM has been set up which adopts an archetype approach capable of calculating the energy performance of each building on the basis of:

SEGMENT	AGE OF CONSTRUCTION	TYPE		FEATURES
Before foundation	<1937	Example building		From historical sources
Foundation	1937-1950	Real building		From original designs
After foundation	1950-2000	Example building		From expertise evaluations

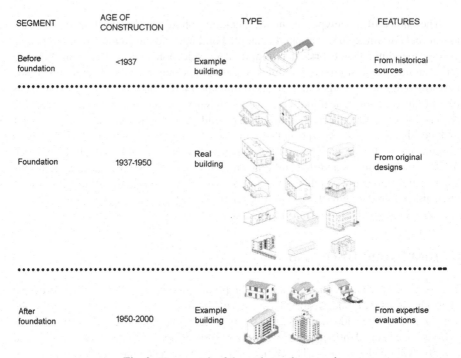

Fig. 3. Framework of the archetypal approach

- the geometries obtainable for each building from the topographic basis (dispersing surfaces, volumes,..);
- the typological characteristics of the building envelope and of the more common plant systems on the local context adopted to classify the entire residential heritage;
- a simplification of the calculation algorithms proposed by current technical standards (UNI TS 11300 series) [11].

In this way, thematic maps relating to the energy performance of the heritage are obtained, the occupants of the homes, after a profile registration, could use it to access a specific interface. The interface shows the information of the typological study and the preliminary results of UBEM, but asks the user to answer a questionnaire concerning some characteristics of his real estate unit and his profile of use (presence, time, comfort,..). These answers will be combined to UBEM results both to generate advice for specific energy retrofit actions and to modify the statistics that are the basis of the UBEM itself and the contents of the Abacus (for more detail on questionnaire see https://www.auree.it/).

As already mentioned, the Geographical Abacus is a spatial information database that collects and represents the knowledge on the recurring elements of the building heritage that are also at the basis of the development of UBEM, favouring its dissemination among operators in the sector and non-technical recipients, facilitating the link between market offer and demand. On this section the users can consult the map of building archetypes and learn through a structure organized by successive levels of knowledge detail (see Fig. 4): from the essential notions inherent to building efficiency and retrofit technologies up to the technical requirements addressed to a technical user. In other words, the disciplinary contents of the Abacus are similar to those of a technical and/or construction guideline, structured however as a spatial based multimedia hypertext that facilitates consultation. In fact, the information contents of the Abacus derive largely from typological knowledge approach carried out on the local context, but also integrate some UBEM results, and voluntary information deriving from the feedback from portal users. In order to fulfil the privacy regulatory framework, the complete answers of the questionnaire will be visible only to the user who completes it, only statistics by type and reprocessed representations by value classes will be included in the Abacus.

The first page, accessible to all users of the portal, presents a map of the study area where it is possible to select a building of interest, and access to a summary page dedicated to the archetype of the selected element (level 1). In the home, may also be present layers directly dedicated to the building elements (roof, wall,..) that allow you to go directly to level 2 of knowledge. Level 2, still mainly dedicated to non-technical users, acts as a hub to explore the various issues related to the efficiency of building. Some contents that are characterized by less variability in context of study, are directly linked to the typological studies (structures of the building envelope). For the others that show more variability (as: type of windows, plants, profile of uses,..) the interface report typological information improved with the statistics from the questionnaire for the selected archetype. From the thematic pages (level 2) it will then be possible to access to others interfaces (level 3) with more technical content such as in-depth information on retrofit technologies and typological efficiency scenarios, as well advice addressed to the occupants. From level 2 onwards, it will be possible to access a menu to contact local companies registered on the portal, linked to some specific services.The construction industry operators will be able to register on the portal by filling a profile form in a specific section where they can list the services offered and enter any local success stories in the use of innovative technologies or design approaches. If contacted by the owner, they will be able to access a summary sheet of the essential characteristics of the building and through the portal they will be able to develop a more in-depth knowledge of local services demand in order to better calibrate their offer.

The experimentation in a case study of excellence, that is so rich in information on the building heritage, will allow to define in detail the procedures and tools that connect the different thematic contents, to refine the representation aimed at interacting with local actors through the portal. The approach is developed for the theme of energy efficiency, however once the information structure and the communication tool will be tested, thanks to the modular structure of the GIS environment it will be possible to integrate on a spatial basis also other themes even not directly related to the original one in order to explore the theirs relationships.

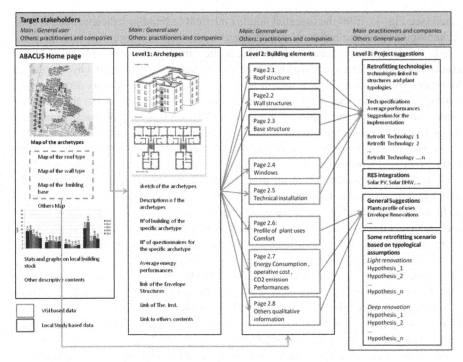

Fig. 4. Framework of the Abacus section

5   Conclusion and Further Research

The AUREE project is still in progress, but a partial version of portal is already available that contains a beta of the house occupant interface with the questionnaire (https://www.auree.it/). This paper shows how common available base date could define a local based archetype that could be used as a framework for the development of a web based sharing tool. During the next year, all the interfaces will be implemented and tested and the informative materials of the guidelines for the collection of assets will be loaded. In order to improve the effectiveness of the methodology, a key point will be the analysis of the flow of the VGI based data (quality, number, spatial distribution,…). The aspects that will have to be tested will mainly concern the following topics:

- appropriateness and effectiveness of the disciplinary contents integrated in the abacus;
- functionality of the interfaces of the Abacus and addressed to houses occupants;
- refinement of the procedures that link Abacus, UBEM and questionnaire.

Acknowledgment. The framework of the research is to be attributed to Pili S, the 1 and 2 paragraph has been wrote by Pili S., Poggi, F., and Frau C. Desogus G. and Dessi A. wrote the 3 paragraph, while par. 4 and 5 of has been wrote by the whole group. The resources for this publication has been given by the Sotacarbo SPA, within the "Research of Electric System" project funded by "Ministry of Economic Develop-ment" CUP: I34I19005780001.

References

1. https://www.odyssee-mure.eu/publications/br/energy-efficiency-trends-policies-buildings. pdf
2. De Santoli, L.: Guidelines on energy efficiency of cultural heritage. Energy Build. **86**, 534–540 (2015). https://doi.org/10.1016/j.enbuild.2014.10.050
3. MiBACT - Segreteria tecnica, Linee di indirizzo per il miglioramento dell'efficienza energetica nel patrimonio culturale, architettura, centri e nuclei storici ed urbani. http://www.benicu lturali.it/mibac/export/MiBAC/
4. Kranzl, L., ENTRANZE consortium: Final report of the policies to enforce the transition to nearly zero energy buildings in the EU-27 (ENTRANZE) founded by IEE (2014). http:// www.entranze.eu/pub/pub-policies
5. Ang, Y.Q., Berzolla, Z.M., Reinhart, C.F.: From concept to application: a review of use cases in urban building energy modelling. Appl. Energy **279**, 11573 (2020). https://doi.org/10.1016/ j.apenergy.2020.115738
6. Abbasabadi, N., Ashayeri, M.: Urban energy use modelling methods and tools: a review and an outlook. Build. Environ. **161**, 106–270 (2019). https://doi.org/10.1016/j.buildenv.2019. 106270
7. Sanna, A., Scanu, G.P.: Il Sulcis e l'Iglesiente: l'edilizia diffusa ei paesi. DEI, Roma (2008)
8. Sanna, A., Monni, G.: Recovery and Reuse of the Architectural and Urban Heritage of Carbonia, a 20th-Century Company Town. Materials for a Handbook. In: Toniolo, L., Boriani, M., Guidi, G. (eds.) Built Heritage: Monitoring Conservation Management. RD, pp. 55–67. Springer, Cham (2015). https://doi.org/10.1007/978-3-319-08533-3_5
9. Mata, É., Kalagasidis, A.S., Johnsson, F.: Building-stock aggregation through archetype buildings: France, Germany, Spain and the UK. Build. Environ. **81**, 270–282 (2014)
10. Monteiro, C.S., Cerezo, C., Pina, A., Ferrão, P.: A method for the generation of multi-detail building archetype definitions: application to the city of Lisbon. In: Proceedings of International Conference CISBAT 2015 Future Buildings and Districts Sustainability from Nano to Urban Scale, LESO-PB, EPFL (2015)
11. D.Lgs. 192/2005 (and s.m.s) and Italian Standard UNI/TS 11300 (2014). https://www.cti 2000.eu/la-uni-ts-11300/

International Workshop on Ports of the Future Smartness and Sustainability (SmartPorts 2021)

Fostering Ports Synergies by Centrality Measures: An Approach Based on Automated Identification Systems

Nadia Giuffrida[1](✉) (iD), Martina Fazio[2] (iD), Giuseppe Inturri[2] (iD),
and Matteo Ignaccolo[2] (iD)

[1] University College Dublin, Dublin, Ireland
nadia.giuffrida@ucd.ie
[2] University of Catania, Catania, Italy

Abstract. In recent decades, maritime transport is facing a continuous growth generating a rapid development of port infrastructures but also the need to adopt synergy policies between neighbouring ports in order to optimize spaces and resources. In this respect, the knowledge of the main maritime routes and traffic volumes for freight and passenger in each port is essential to establish hierarchies, intervention priorities and to evaluate infrastructure specializations in a planning perspective. In this study an approach based on Automatic Identification System (AIS) is used to build a mathematical model with trajectories vessels between ports, ships classification and traffic volumes, in order to frame a regional network of maritime trades. Network centrality indices are calculated to assess the spatial-temporal characteristics and structure of regional ports' network. The method is applied to the case study of ports located in Sicily, an Italian region characterized by the peculiarity of being an island with more than 1000 km of coasts and a strategic location in the centre of the Mediterranean Sea; both of these characteristics make it a breeding ground for port infrastructure development and terminal specialization.

Keywords: Ports centrality · Vessels tracking · Maritime transport network

1 Introduction

The recent episode of the blockade of the Suez Canal by an ultra-large container vessel has exposed the fragility of the global economy linked to maritime transport. In particular, this extraordinary event brought two considerations out at the spotlight: on the one hand the importance of maritime transport nodes, even when they are not final destinations of routes but only crossing spots; on the other hand, the importance of a system for monitoring the vessels movement in real time.

In this respect, ports can be considered as the main maritime transport nodes generating several negative impacts, not only in the seaside but also in the landside and in the surrounding urban areas. Understanding how to reduce such externalities by implementing policies which are sustainable both from an economic, social, and environmental point of view is crucial for ports development [1, 2]. Moreover, fostering synergies

© Springer Nature Switzerland AG 2021
O. Gervasi et al. (Eds.): ICCSA 2021, LNCS 12958, pp. 177–187, 2021.
https://doi.org/10.1007/978-3-030-87016-4_13

between ports and urban areas, by taking advantage of their coexistence, can play a key role for the sustainable development of cities [3, 4]. The analysis of port activities, indeed, can provide significant benefits not only to the single port, but also in a wider context of network planning. Understanding the importance of a port in the maritime transport network through its connections and the types of traffic can help decision-makers in establishing intervention priorities to ensure the efficiency of the infrastructure.

Based on this premise, this paper proposes an approach for analyzing the centrality of ports based on port calls detected by Automated Identification Systems (AIS) for maritime transport. The aim is to understand the importance of a port as a node within a maritime transport network, regardless of the amount of handled traffic, and to propose potential cooperation policies. The method will be applied to the case study of freight traffic in Sicilian ports (Italy) which are part of a Port System Authority.

2 State of the Art

Port networks can be compared to scale-free network [5], so it is possible to characterize them according to parameters related to the theory of complex networks [6]. In the analysis of a transport network through graph theory, centrality indexes can be used as accessibility measures since they allow to get the performance indicator and the level of connection of a node in a system (i.e. the ease to reach it) [7]. Methodologies based on the use of centrality indices provide an important support in transport planning to identify those nodes (airports, bus station, ports) that are strategically located in the transportation system and, therefore, to outline interventions for improving their efficiency [8, 9]. In the maritime sector, Ducruet et al. [10] propose a methodology to describe ports impacts by calculating centrality parameters; they compared the centrality indices with the traffic volume from official port statistics. Results of this study show that traditional data are not always able to accurately describe the characteristics of the network, demonstrating the importance to carry out centrality measures. Brandão et al. [11] analyse the properties and vulnerabilities of Brazilian ports through various centrality measurements (degree, eigenvector, flow betweenness centralities and layer centrality) considering a weighted network. By applying this methodology, the authors realized a ranking of ports in terms of centrality, and they inferred that the most impactful ports were private terminals.

AIS technology can be considered an aid to improve this type of port network analysis, allowing to gather a large amount of data of port calls in short time. The AIS technology aims at providing data related to vessels, such as identification, unit type, speed, position, trajectories, port calls and it is able to coverage the global fleet network in real-time. To transfer AIS data, ships are equipped with an AIS transponder integrated with a VHF (Very High Frequency) transceiver connected to a positioning system (e.g. GPS device). Moreover, there are also other electronic sensors such as a rate of turn indicator and a gyrocompass to acquire information related to the rate of turn and the geographical direction. Initially AIS data were used with the main purpose of reducing ship collisions phenomena and improving navigation safety, but now the fields of application are disparate [12]. There are several studies that addressed port issues by using AIS technology. Perez et al. [13] elaborated a spatial methodology which consists in the exploitation of AIS data to track vessels and then estimate vessel's emissions. Analogue study is that developed by Zhang et al. [14]. They provide a "bottom-up" activity-based model to infer vessel emission by integrating different type of database, not only from AIS, but also from port call registration and field investigation. He et al. [15] propose a data mining process for a more reliable managing of AIS data. After applying this procedure, authors recreated a safe navigation depth-reference map able to reflect the waterway depth and, therefore, to give information for safety navigation. Only a few recent studies propose the integration of AIS data and centrality measures. Wang et al. [16] provide an AIS data-driven approach to extract the global shipping network by taking into account only the container shipping network, using Gephi software. They considered three network levels (i.e. terminal, port and country), and for each level they calculated the number of nodes and links, average degree, network diameter, modularity, average clustering coefficient and the average path length. Sheng and Yin [17] elaborated a clustering algorithm able to calculate the degree centrality to extract shipping routes based on AIS data. Despite these works are focus on the concept of centrality, they did not take into account other specific measures that may be useful for the characterization of a port network, such as closeness, betweenness and eccentricity. The contribution of this work is to provide a methodology which also consider these measures, using AIS to evaluate centrality of ports in a regional network and analyse the potential synergies within port systems.

3 Materials and Methods

The approach is based on the following steps (Fig. 1):

1. A portion of data regarding port calls is acquired from the AIS (Sect. 3.1);
2. Data are manipulated to be uploaded in the network topology software (Sect. 3.2);
3. Centrality indexes evaluation is conducted within the software (Sect. 3.3).

AIS data
on vessels positioning

Port calls
Departures and arrivals

Centrality measures
Based on port calls

Fig. 1. A summary of the used approach

The three steps are described in detail in the following.

3.1 Online AIS Services

Several websites provide ship tracking using the AIS to display the location of the vessels and other information, such as route, speed and ship's type. Most of these service providers promise a "real-time" location, but actually the data displayed is always at least some minutes late; so websites are not a proper source to be used during navigation, but they are reliable for research purposes. Online AIS websites generally provides two main type of information: vessels positions and port calls (arrivals and departures). In this study we propose the use of port calls to characterize ports' centrality in a regional maritime transport network. The AIS service generally displays information related to name of the vessel, type of traffic, departure/arrival time for each port call (Fig. 2).

Expected	Arrivals	Departures	In Port			
Recent ship arrivals in Catania						
Arrival (LT)	Vessel		Built	GT	DWT	Size (m)
May 6, 13:00	EUROCARGO CATANIA Ro-Ro Cargo Ship		2011	29429	11320	193 x 26
May 6, 10:38	EUROCARGO PALERMO Ro-Ro Cargo Ship		2010	32839	10770	200 x 26
May 6, 07:39	EUROCARGO VENEZIA Ro-Ro Cargo Ship		2011	32841	10765	200 x 26
May 6, 06:50	ANNE Container Ship		2007	9981	11808	139 x 22

Fig. 2. Example of port calls shown on the free AIS provided VesselFinder for the port of Catania (https://www.vesselfinder.com/ports/ITCTA001)

3.2 Gephi Software

Once acquired, the data related to port calls are processed through a spreadsheet for the acquisition within the network software. The Gephi software (a free and Open Source software for visualization and exploration of graphs and networks) is used to visualize the topology of the maritime transport network and to calculate the centrality indices. The representation of the network on the software is carried out by means of tables relating to nodes and edges. Nodes table includes an identification number (ID) and a label; in the case of our network, nodes table includes also geographic coordinates of each port; the GeoLayout plugin in Gephi allows a geographical representation of the nodes in the Mercator system (Fig. 3). Edges table tells the software how the nodes are connected, including source node, target node and type of link (directed, undirected). The Gephi plugin Export-To-Earth allows to export the whole network in.kmz format and visualize it in a Geographic Information System (GIS).

3.3 Centrality Indexes

Gephi allows the computation of the following centrality indices: (i) Degree, In-Degree and Out-Degree; (ii) Closeness Centrality; (iii) Betweenness Centrality; (iv) Eccentricity.

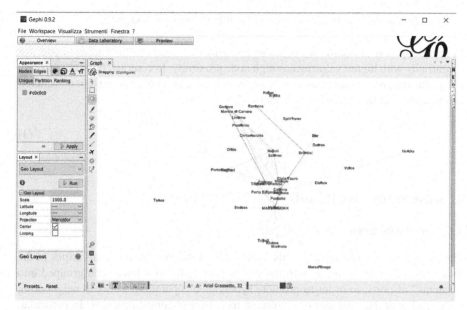

Fig. 3. Screenshot of the Gephi interface with a geocoded representation of ports network.

Degree, In-Degree and Out-Degree (k). Degree is a centrality measure that counts the number of links (L) incident upon a node (N). In the case of a directed network as the one of our study, one can talk about in-degree (the number of in-coming links) and out-degree (the number of out-going links). In the case of a port network, a high in-degree will mean that a port is a frequent destination of the other nodes in the network.

$$k = \frac{1}{N} \sum_{i=1}^{N} k_i = \frac{2L}{N}, \; i = 1, 2, \ldots, N \qquad (1)$$

Closeness Centrality (C_i). The Closeness of a node i is the average length of the shortest path between the node and all other nodes j in the graph (d_{ij}). The more central a node is, the closer it is to all other nodes. In our case, this shows the directness of links between the ports in the network.

$$C_i = \frac{N}{\sum_j d_{ij}} \qquad (2)$$

Betweenness Centrality (B_i). Betweenness centrality measures the number of times a node lies on the shortest path between other nodes. This highlights the propensity of a port to act as "bridge" (i.e. a stopping point) between origins and destinations.

$$B_i = \sum \frac{d(i)}{d} \qquad (3)$$

Where:

– d refers to the total number of shortest paths;

– $d(i)$ refers to the number of shortest paths that lie through node i.

Eccentricity (Ei). Eccentricity is the inverse of the distance to the furthest node. An eccentricity with higher value means high node proximity. In contrast, if the eccentricity is low, this means that there is at least one node that is located far. This could be considered as a measure of coverage of the port network.

$$E_i = \frac{1}{\max\{d_{ij}\}} \tag{4}$$

4 Case Study and Results

4.1 Territorial Framework

The approach has been applied to the case study of the Port System Authorities of the Sicily region, in Italy. Since 2016 the Italian port authorities have been grouped into "systems" of ports, in order to promote synergies of operations between neighboring nodes and with the final aim of increasing their overall competitiveness. In particular, three Port System Authorities are active in Sicily: Eastern Sicily System, including the ports of Augusta and Catania; Western Sicily System, including the ports of Palermo, Termini Imerese, Trapani and Porto Empedocle; Strait's System, including the Ports of Messina and Milazzo (in Sicily) and Villa San Giovanni and Reggio Calabria (located in Calabria, and which will not be taken into consideration in this study). The ports forming the different system authorities have very diverse vocations and trades and, consequently, it is easy to hope for synergies of operations.

The port of Catania is mainly a commercial port, in particular for Ro-Ro traffic; this is due to its central position with respect to the city of Catania and its metropolitan area (of about 1 million inhabitants), and its proximity to the main logistic areas of the large food distribution of eastern Sicily. The port of Augusta is part of the TEN-T Core European Network; it is an important industrial pole serving the Syracusan petrochemical center and it is also an important naval base of the Italian Navy; the port also includes an area dedicated to container and Ro-Ro traffic, which is currently undergoing infrastructural improvements.

The port of Palermo is mainly a passenger port, but which currently also hosts a significant traffic of containers for the Sicilian territory; it is also home to an important shipbuilding area managed by the Fincantieri company. In the recent regulatory plan of the port system, trade is foreseen to move to the port of Termini Imerese, in order to develop other areas in Palermo port for passenger and cruise transport. The port of Trapani is the primary maritime connections with the Egadi islands and Pantelleria, so it has a strong touristic vocation; historically, it is a reference port for trade with North African countries, and still maintains a trade route with Tunisia. The port of Porto Empedocle has historically been a hub for trade in salt and sulfur, and currently carries out mainly recreational activities.

The port of Messina is the first in Italy for passenger transport, with 10 million passengers per year before the pandemic. These figures are obviously due to the connection between Messina and the Calabrian ports of Villa San Giovanni and Reggio Calabria (also part of the Strait System Authority), which allow the connection of Sicily with the Italian peninsula. For these reasons Messina also records a high Ro-Ro traffic, but obviously to be considered only as in transit and not as origin or destination (which probably coincide with the cities of Catania or Palermo). As regards the port of Milazzo, there are two main types of traffic: passenger traffic connecting with the archipelago of the Aeolian Islands; freight traffic of liquid bulk, in particular hydrocarbons, due to a petroleum plant located in correspondence with the industrial port areas.

Table 1 shows the main freight statistics for the 2020 for all the ports of the case study.

Table 1. Statistics for the 2020 for the 8 ports (in tonns).

Port	Solid bulk	Liquid bulk	Ro-Ro	Container	Total freight	Passengers (cruise + ferry)
Catania	342.724	0	7.413.714	568.429	8.324.867	61.618
Augusta	1.042.452	22.987.553	0	0	24.030.005	0
Palermo	274.945	252.006	6.609.487	155.863	7.292.301	946.340
Trapani	33.234	0	82.699	144.749	260.682	816.624
P. Empedocle	323.242	0	25.902	0	349.144	40.113
T. Imerese	282.326	0	353.498	0	635.824	53.379
Milazzo	162.732	14.880.732	212.990	0	15.256.454	697.442
Messina	0	0	5.775.281	0	5.775.281	6.567.223

4.2 Data Acquisition

Data for port calls have been acquired manually from observations on an online provider of ship tracking services. Data have been collected for 2 weeks, from 23/07/2020 to 06/08/2020; the collected data were certainly influenced by the pandemic restrictions imposed by Italian government and for this reason it was decided to study only the port calls related to freight traffic. It was decided to exclude the traffic of liquid bulk from the analysis because the figures in the port of Augusta were not comparable to the ones in the other ports. Furthermore, the AIS did not record any port calls of exclusive freight traffic vessels in the selected period for the port of Messina (but mostly Ro-Pax), so this port was excluded from the analysis. Finally, after all the simplification, 7 ports and 3 traffic categories were taken into account.

All the port calls in which the Sicilian ports covered by the case study corresponded to an origin or a destination were taken into consideration. The entire route of each port call was included in the network, starting from the port of origin, and including also the intermediate stops.

4.3 Results

Figure 4 shows the whole network of connections of the Sicilian ports in GIS, exported from Gephi to.kmz format. The figure shows that the network includes (as well as several of the major Italian Thyrrenic ports) seaports located in Slovenia, Croatia, Montenegro, Albania, Greece, Malta, Turkey and North Africa, showing the relation between Sicilian Ports and the south and east of Mediterranean Sea. It is worth of notice that, even if it was not part of the case study, the Sicilian port of Pozzallo town is part of the network, mainly due to its role of intermediary connection with Maltese ports.

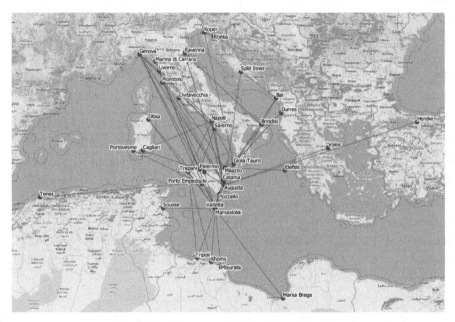

Fig. 4. Sicilian ports network in GIS after Gephi export.

Indexes have been evaluated for the global traffic and for 3 different traffic categories: Solid Bulk, Ro-Ro and Container. Table 2 shows results for all the traffic categories for the selected ports. Catania has the main centrality indexes when considering all the traffic categories. Augusta however has the main role of "stopping" port, with the highest betweenness for the selected period.

Table 3 shows results for the single traffic categories for each port. It must be highlighted that some calls were labelled as "General Cargo"; we decided not to use them in this representation, since it was not possible to trace back to the real traffic category (such vessels are often for mixed-use). Catania maintains its leadership also in the case of Ro-Ro traffic, showing also the highest amount of this traffic category in 2020. A different situation was recorded in the case of Container, where Trapani shows best centrality indexes, including betweenness. Augusta can be considered the only infrastructure with meaningful connections in the case of solid bulk.

Table 2. Global centrality indexes.

Port	Degree	In degree	Out degree	Eccentricity	Closeness	Betweenness
Catania	16.0	9.0	7.0	5.0	0.4	176.4
Augusta	13.0	8.0	5.0	5.0	0.4	202.8
Palermo	9.0	4.0	5.0	6.0	0.4	36.9
Trapani	6.0	4.0	2.0	5.0	0.4	72.0
Porto Empedocle	4.0	2.0	2.0	2.0	0.7	2.0
Milazzo	3.0	2.0	1.0	1.0	1.0	26.0
Termini Imerese	3.0	1.0	2.0	7.0	0.3	24.0

Table 3. Centrality indexes for differentiated traffic categories.

	Port	Degree	In degree	Out degree	Eccentricity	Closeness	Betweenness
Solid bulk	Augusta	6	4	2	1	1	8
	P. Empedocle	3	2	1	0	0	0
Container	Trapani	5	3	2	3	0.4	81
	Catania	4	3	1	9	0.2	34
	Palermo	2	1	1	6	0.2	49
	T. Imerese	2	1	1	1	1	0
Ro-Ro	Catania	11	6	5	2	0.7	27.2
	Palermo	6	3	3	3	0.5	1.7

4.4 Discussion: Policy Implications and Limitations

The analysis conducted, including the reasons for the exclusion of some traffic and ports, leads to the following considerations on the potential roles of Sicilian ports within their regional network:

– High degree centrality indices often correspond to high directness and coverage of the port in the network;
– There is a clear differentiation in the types of traffic handled in the port terminals which leads to a clear distinction of the indices for each traffic category;
– The Port System Authority of the Eastern Sicilian Sea could concentrate its activities on Ro-Ro traffic; in particular, in the search for synergy between the two ports, and given the available spaces, a share of the Ro-Ro traffic could be directed to the port of Augusta.

- The Port System Authority of the Western Sicilian Sea could concentrate its activities on increasing container traffic, in particular in the port of Trapani and taking advantage of the spaces available in the port of Termini Imerese.
- Ports of the System Authority of the Strait would keep their transit vocation to connect Sicily to the Italian peninsula
- The future of the industrial ports of Augusta and Milazzo must certainly be one of the key points in the planning of the respective port system authorities: the oil resources underlying their main activities will sooner or later run out and the recovery of the related port basins on which disused plants will gravitate.

Obviously, the results of these analyzes and related considerations suffer from some limitations of this study. First of all, the AIS data collected refer to the year 2020, with the beginning of the COVID-19 emergency: even if the reference period is one of the least impacted by the pandemic, one should consider that future trends will probably be significantly different from the traditional ones for maritime freight traffic. Furthermore, this analysis is restricted from a geographical point of view to the Sicily region, while the role of Sicilian ports is indisputably influenced by the surrounding ports; therefore, an analysis of the broader dynamics of the Mediterranean will be necessary in the future.

5   Conclusion

The purpose of the study is the characterization of the centrality of ports through the analysis of port calls automatically registered by AIS. Data acquisition using this innovative technological tool proves to be faster and more detailed than the traditional acquisition of statistics from port authorities. The calculation of centrality indices allows to analyse the importance of a port not only on the basis of the handled traffic, but also on its positioning as a node in the maritime transport network. This can help decision makers in the characterization of the specializations of a given port and its potential synergies with other nodes within a port system. From the application of the methodology to the case study of Sicilian ports, clear patterns of specialization emerged for the various ports and their related systems. The results suggest policies to promote further specialization of the ports towards the synergy of infrastructure operations in the Sicilian territory. The case study of this work is related to a local context, but future research could extend the application to the analysis of a port's centrality in the global maritime transport network.

Acknowledgements. The work has been partially financed by the project "THALASSA–Technology and materials for safe low consumption and low life cycle cost vessels and crafts" (unique project code CUP B46C18000720005) under the programme "PON Ricerca e Innovazione 2014–2020".

References

1. Ignaccolo, M., Inturri, G., Giuffrida, N., Torrisi, V.: A sustainable framework for the analysis of port systems. Eur. Trans. Int. J. Transp. Econ. Eng. Law (78), 7 (2020)

2. Giuffrida, N., Ignaccolo, M., Inturri, G., Torrisi, V.: Port-City shared areas to improve freight transport sustainability. In: International Conference on Computational Science and Its Applications pp. 67–82. Springer, Cham (2020)
3. Ignaccolo, M., Inturri, G., Cocuzza, E., Giuffrida, N., Torrisi, V.: Framework for the evaluation of the quality of pedestrian routes for the sustainability of port–city shared areas. In: WIT Transactions on the Built Environment, vol. 188, pp. 11–22 (2019)
4. Giuffrida, N., Cocuzza, E., Ignaccolo, M., Inturri, G.: A comprehensive index to evaluate non-motorized accessibility to port-cities. Int. J. Sustain. Dev. Planning 15(5), 743–749 (2020)
5. Barabási, A.L.: Scale-free networks: a decade and beyond. Science 325(5939), 412–413 (2009)
6. Laxe, F.G., Seoane, M.J.F., Montes, C.P.: Maritime degree, centrality and vulnerability: port hierarchies and emerging areas in containerized transport (2008–2010). J. Transp. Geogr. 24, 33–44 (2012)
7. Caprì, S., Ignaccolo, M., Inturri, G., Le Pira, M.: Green walking networks for climate change adaptation. Transp. Res. Part D: Transp. Environ. 45, 84–95 (2016)
8. Fleming, D.K., Hayuth, Y.: Spatial characteristics of transportation hubs: centrality and intermediacy. J. Transp. Geogr. 2(1), 3–18 (1994)
9. Jeon, J.W., Duru, O., Yeo, G.T.: Cruise port centrality and spatial patterns of cruise shipping in the Asian market. Marit. Policy Manag. 46(3), 257–276 (2019)
10. Ducruet, C., Lee, S.W., Ng, A.K.: Centrality and vulnerability in liner shipping networks: revisiting the Northeast Asian port hierarchy. Marit. Policy Manag. 37(1), 17–36 (2010)
11. Brandão, L.C., Del-Vecchio, R.R., Mello, J.C.C.B.S.D., Francisco, C.N.: Evaluating the importance of brazilian ports using graph centrality measures. Pesquisa Operacional, 40 (2020)
12. Yang, D., Wu, L., Wang, S., Jia, H., Li, K.X.: How big data enriches maritime research–a critical review of automatic identification system (AIS) data applications. Transp. Rev. 39(6), 755–773 (2019)
13. Perez, H.M., Chang, R., Billings, R., Kosub, T.L.: Automatic identification systems (AIS) data use in marine vessel emission estimation. In: 18th Annual International Emission Inventory Conference vol. 14, p.17 (2009)
14. Zhang, Y., Gu, J., Wang, W., Peng, Y., Wu, X., Feng, X.: Inland port vessel emissions inventory based on Ship Traffic Emission Assessment Model-Automatic Identification System. Adv. Mech. Eng. 9(7), 1687814017712878 (2017)
15. He, Z., Yang, F., Li, Z., Liu, K., Xiong, N.: Mining channel water depth information from IoT-based big automated identification system data for safe waterway navigation. IEEE Access 6, 75598–75608 (2018)
16. Wang, Z., Claramunt, C., Wang, Y.: Extracting global shipping networks from massive historical automatic identification system sensor data: a bottom-up approach. Sensors 19(15), 3363 (2019)
17. Sheng, P., Yin, J.: Extracting shipping route patterns by trajectory clustering model based on automatic identification system data. Sustainability 10(7), 2327 (2018)

Dimensioning of Container Terminals: Validation and Application Fields for a Stochastic Process

Vinicius Das Chagas[1], Maria Eugenia Lopez Lambas[2], Cristiano Marinacci[1], Stefano Ricci[1(✉)], and Luca Rizzetto[1]

[1] Department of Civil, Building and Environmental Engineering (DICEA), Sapienza Università di Roma, Via Eudossiana, 18, 00184 Roma, Italy
stefano.ricci@uniroma1.it

[2] Escuela de Ingenieros de Caminos, Universidad Politecnica de Madrid, Canales y Puertos, C/Profesor Aranguren S/N, 28040 Madrid, Spain

Abstract. The maritime terminals design process includes a series of strategic decision involving the engagement of relevant amount of resources. In fact, operating conditions near the maximum capacity generate congestion and the related negative consequences on capacity and regularity. The authors developed different methods and models capable to support some of these key decisions. These methods allow at selecting the most suitable parameters to describe terminals, to determine dimensional and equipment characteristics and to verify the production of the terminals. For all them, various extended investigations on operated port terminals for data acquisition and homogenization are available: surveys on operated terminals, sampling criteria to ensure quality of derived design parameters, analysis and correlations to provide design and operational elements. Past and present surveys cover a sampling of 40 European terminals for the setup of the method in 1985, a sampling of 93 terminals within 49 European ports in 2008 and a geographical extension to Latin America and the Carribean and an update of the method in 2021, specific object of the present paper.

Keywords: Ports · Terminals · Containers · Design · Operation

1 Introduction

Following the standardization of TEU containers in the 1960s, global container traffic increased significantly nowadays, which represents a quarter of maritime trade. Today, their handling is normally in two different typologies of ports: hubs and gateways. The maritime hubs are terminals, in which the main operations carried out are concentration and distribution by transhipment with final destinations outside the hinterland. Meanwhile, gateway ports, also known as import/export, carry out significant traffic volumes from and to powerful hinterland generating large loads. This type of port is usually located nearby industrial and consumer areas.

© Springer Nature Switzerland AG 2021
O. Gervasi et al. (Eds.): ICCSA 2021, LNCS 12958, pp. 188–197, 2021.
https://doi.org/10.1007/978-3-030-87016-4_14

According to [1], container terminals typically include their equipment and stacking facilities. However, from a logistical perspective, terminals only have two components: stocks and transport vehicles. Stocks' definition depends statically on their ability to store containers, while stowage or loading instructions are required dynamically to define the rules on how and where containers must be stored. The services of container terminals do not include routing and scheduling of ships, trains and trucks, while wage instructions exist in any case to define the location of the containers to be loaded. Two-dimensional or three-dimensional transport of containers include cranes and horizontal transport vehicles. Their logistical peculiarities include the assignment of tasks and the work sequences to perform, normally resulting in a range of alternative approaches and solutions [2].

In order to maximize the effectiveness of this process, robust and systematic methodological support is necessary. In this respect, the authors developed different methods and models [3] capable to support key decisions. In particular, stochastic methods, trained by the background data from operated terminals, largely demonstrated their ability to manage the preliminary dimensioning of container [4, 5] and bulk [6] terminals in ports. They are able to integrate dimensions and handiness of ships, terminal morphology, handling equipment, storage areas, etc., with the aim to support planning and design process as well as the operational management themselves.

These methods allow at selecting the most suitable parameters to describe the terminals, to determine their dimensional and equipment characteristics and to verify their production.

2   Background

The synthesis of structures and performances of terminals is within the three main clusters: Dimensional parameters (D), such as quay length, total stacking area, covered stacking area and uncovered stacking area; Equipment parameters (E), such as gantry cranes, other cranes, storage cranes and various loaders; Production parameters (P), such as: number of handled containers, TEU and container tonnage.

For all them, various extended investigations on operated port terminals for data acquisition and homogenization are available [4, 5] according to the methodological steps described below.

1) *Surveys on operated terminals* include: a) check of available database, b) enquiries to operators, c) direct measurements.
2) *Sampling criteria* to ensure quality of derived design parameters include: a) dimensional and geographical variety, b) randomness of terminals' selection, c) reliability of acquired data.
3) *Analysis and correlations* aimed at providing: Design elements, such as Dimensioning (D) and Equipment (E) parameters, from P parameters; Operational elements, such as Production (P) parameters, starting from D and E parameters.

The correlation of the parameters are by linear regressions, both within the same groups (D-D, E-E, P-P) and between various groups (D-E, D-P, E-P), qualified by the calculation of Pearson coefficients and the Student stochastic test.

Past and present surveys cover a sampling of 40 European terminals for the setup of the method in 1985 and a sampling of 93 terminals within 49 European ports for the update and the validation of the method in 2008.

3 Methodology

The present paper deals with a geographical extension of the model application to Latin America and the Carribean, as well as an update of the method.

The first step was the investigation on available public online database concerning the parameters required to proceed with the analysis by searching in public websites, such as *Marine Traffic*, *Fleetmon* and *Sea Rates* for general information about location of terminals at ports. The following step aimed at ministries, economic organizations and governmental websites. Lastly, after a careful selection of ports with container terminals, the research focus moves to the port authorities and terminal operators' themselves.

The following step was the preparation of a questionnaire for port authorities and terminal operators to gather the information not available or incomplete from the online sources. The questionnaire, developed in *Google Forms*, was in English, Portuguese and Spanish, covered 212 port authorities and terminal operators, though the rate of answers after the first round was not exceeding 3%. More rounds are anyway in plans. Nevertheless, the global data collection covered in Europe 208 terminals located in 34 countries and in Latin American and the Carribean 112 terminals located in 17 countries.

After the confirmation of the typology of terminal, containers only or multipurpose, the questions raised in the questionnaire concerns quay length, stacking areas (covered, uncovered and total), number of gantry cranes (STS, RTG, RMG), mobile harbor and storage cranes (straddle carriers, reach stackers, forklifts) and other loaders (semitrailers, tractors) as well as number of handled containers, TEU and tons.

The data analysis tackles the results of the survey, referred to 2019, by establishing a correlation between couples of parameters, measured by the Pearson correlation coefficient:

$$R = \frac{N \sum xy - (\sum x)(\sum y)}{\sqrt{\left[N \sum x^2 - (\sum x^2)\right]\left[N \sum y^2 - (\sum y)^2\right]}}$$

Where are:

- N = number of couples of scores;
- $\sum xy$ = sum of the products of paired scores;
- $\sum x$ = sum of x scores;
- $\sum y$ = sum of y scores;
- $\sum x^2$ = sum of squared x scores;
- $\sum y^2$ = sum of squared y scores.

The most direct relationships between the parameters corresponding to the shortest paths on the graph from any input to any output parameter is searchable using the Dijkstra algorithm [7].

Everything refer to three different scenarios: European terminals, Latin America and the Caribbean terminals, all terminals. The validation of the method bases on applications to test terminals not used for feeding the model.

4 Survey Results and Method Application

In Europe the largest amount of investigated terminals are from Belgium (10), Finland (10), France (16), Italy (20), Norway (20), Portugal (11), Spain (30), Sweden (14) and United Kingdom (18). Other terminals, ensuring better geographic coverage, are from Albania (1), Austria (2), Bulgaria (5), Croatia (2), Denmark (6), Estonia (3), Faroe Islands (2), Georgia (2), Germany (8), Gibraltar (1), Greece (3), Iceland (5), Ireland (4), Latvia (2), Lithuania (2), Malta (3), Moldova (1), Netherlands (9), Poland (5), Romania (1), Russia (7), Slovakia (1), Slovenia (1) and Ukraine (3).

In Latin America and the Caribbean the largest amount of terminals are from Argentina (18) and Brazil (36). Terminals from Bahamas (1), Chile (12), Colombia (7), Costa Rica (1), Dominican Republic (1), Ecuador (7), French Guyana (1), Guatemala (1), Guyana (1), Jamaica (1), Mexico (8), Panama (5), Paraguay (3), Peru (7), Surinam (1) and Uruguay (1) ensure a wide geographic coverage.

Despite the different sources investigated, the information is anyway not complete for all terminals. Table 1 shows the number of terminals with available data per parameter: the production parameters are the most difficult to find for the single terminals, meanwhile they are more frequently available globally at the port level.

Table 1. Number of available data per parameter

Dimension (D) parameters	Terminals with available data
1) Quay Length	240
2) Total Stacking Area	69
3) Covered Stacking Area	58
4) Uncovered Stacking Area	56
Equipment (E) parameters	Terminals with available data
5) Gantry Cranes	201
6) Other Cranes	104
7) Storage Cranes	155
8) Various Loaders	93
Traffic (T) parameters	Terminals with available data
9) Handled Containers	53
10) Handled TEU	111
11) Handled Tons	55

Intuitively, the greater is the number of couples of related parameters, the more reliable is the result. The matrix in Table 2 summarizes the number of couples of parameters. The minimum number of available data per couple of parameters (12) is enough to calculate correlations. Using a linear regressive method, the calculated correlation coefficients R populate Table 3, where the green color highlights the values of R > 0.55, also represented by the graph in the corner. Under this hypothesis, the dimensional parameter 3 (Covered Stacking Area) is not significantly correlated with any parameter, meanwhile the production parameter 11 (Handled Tons) is the most correlated with all others. The correlation coefficients are the first indicators of the robustness of the link between the parameters and, consequently, of the reliability of results achievable.

Table 2. Number of available data per couple of parameter

1										
2	64									
3	56	34								
4	55	35	34							
5	189	58	45	42						
6	93	34	29	32	79					
7	143	51	36	39	136	79				
8	87	37	25	26	89	50	89			
9	37	18	15	19	31	24	30	20		
10	78	35	25	30	60	42	56	37	53	
11	39	17	12	16	32	25	32	21	28	54
	1	2	3	4	5	6	7	8	9	10	11

Table 3. Linear regression correlation coefficients between parameters

1										
2	0.648									
3	0,108	0.312								
4	0.650	0.999	0.264							
5	0.569	0.375	-0.070	0.401						
6	0.139	0.119	0.238	-0.056	-0.005					
7	0.589	0.623	0.044	0.696	0.282	0.224				
8	0.493	0.576	0.238	0.535	0.656	0.111	0.396			
9	0.875	0.817	0.185	0.762	0.977	0.702	-0.182	0.203		
10	0.690	0.771	0.124	0.739	0.954	0.647	0.462	0.757	1.000	
11	0.829	0.824	0.438	0.738	0.986	0.023	0.329	0.641	1.000	0.999
	1	2	3	4	5	6	7	8	9	10	11

For a comparison synthetic comparison at a glance, Fig. 1 reports the corresponding matrices of correlation coefficients for the previous studies developed in 1985 [4] and 2008 [5].

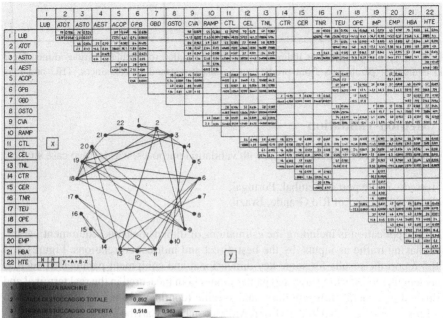

Fig. 1. Original correlation coefficients matrices from previous 1985 [4] and 2008 [5] studies

Indeed, the goals of the research is to link the parameters by direct or indirect correlations on a probabilistic basis: e.g., in the design phase, production parameters with dimensional and/or equipment parameters.

For this purpose, a shortest path search (by Dijkstra algorithm with length $= -|R|$ in the present application) identifies the most reliable direct or indirect link to the other parameters starting from the three production parameters: number of handled containers, TEU and tons (Fig. 2).

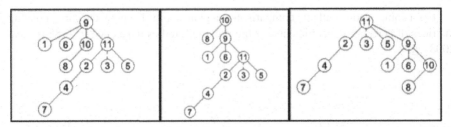

Fig. 2. Most reliable direct or indirect links (shortest paths) to calculate various dimensional and equipment parameters from production parameters (Handled containers, TEU and tons respectively)

5 Method Validation

The application of the methodology, with validation purposes, was for two case studies:

- Tersado, in the port of Setubal, Portugal;
- Tecon, in the port of Rio Grande, Brazil.

The application is including the estimations of dimensional and equipment parameters having traffic as inputs, by the best direct and indirect correlations. Figures 3, 4 and 5 report the results for some key dimensional and equipment parameters, such as quay length, total stacking area and gantry cranes both measured in the real terminal and estimated by general (full sampling) and specific (continental sampling) models, both for Tersado (Europe) and Tecon (Latin America and the Carribean).

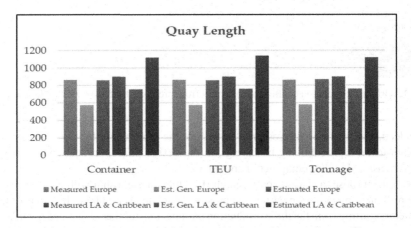

Fig. 3. Measured and estimated quay length [m] having as inputs various traffic parameters

In Tersado, the results obtained by the application of the general model for all input traffic parameters are quite reliable for equipment (about 5% deviations for gantry cranes), meanwhile by the Europe specific model the reliability increases relevantly for dimensional parameters (<10% deviations for length of quays and total stacking area).

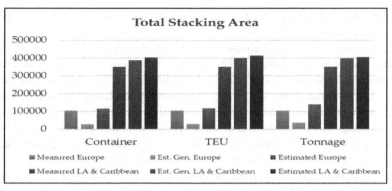

Fig. 4. Measured and estimated total stacking area [m^2] having as inputs various traffic parameters

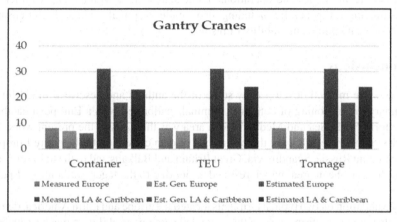

Fig. 5. Measured and estimated number of gantry cranes starting having as inputs various traffic parameters

In Tecon, the results obtained by the application of the general model for all input traffic parameters are quite reliable for dimensions (about 25% deviations for length of quays and total stocking areas), meanwhile by the Latin American and Carribean specific model the reliability increases for equipment parameters (about 35% deviations for gantry cranes).

In particular, for the length of quays the model is very well working for the European terminal (less than 5% deviation) when trained with the European database only, meanwhile for the Latin American terminal the model it is less reliable, anyway providing with good results (about 25% deviation) when trained with the General database. For the total stacking area, the results are very similar for the European Terminal and for the Latin American terminal, though with a better reached reliability (about 15% deviation). For the number of gantry cranes, the results are different for the European terminal, where the better results (about 15% deviation) are reached already by the model trained with the general database, and for the Latin America terminal, where the better results (about 35% deviation) are reached by the model trained with Latin American and the Caribbean database.

In all situations the model is almost unaffected by the selected container traffic input parameters (number of containers, TEU or tons). As a consolidated result of this validation, the model shows is ability to reach a reliability of less than 10% deviations in the European terminal and less of 30% deviations in the Latin American terminals. The difference could be due to the smaller dimension of the Latin American and Carribean sampling. Moreover, the use of more specific continental characterized model increases in both the case studies the reliability of the results, which is possibly due to the differences in traffic and terminal operational models across the Atlantic.

The results are generally different from those achieved in the previous researches carried out in 1985 and 2008, mainly for European terminals. The differences are mainly in the lower level correlation between parameters, which is largely in line with the evolution of technologies and operational models, as well as with the larger dimension of the sampling set, generally including also smaller terminals, which do not ensure a full homogeneity and comparability of results.

6 Conclusions

The regressive method developed by some of the authors and described in [3] for the preliminary dimensioning of container terminals calibrated with a European database, mainly form North Sea and Mediterranean area was the basis of the present work. The upgrades of this research were the extensions of data collection to the entire European area, including Russia, Scandinavia, Great Britain and Balkans and to the to Latin America and the Caribbean area, which resulted easier due to the lager availability of public data.

The validation on two typical terminals located in Europe and Latin America, demonstrated that model confirms, also in this extended version, its ability to reach a satisfying reliability, always less than 10% deviation in the European terminals and 30% deviation in the Latin American terminals. The difference could be due to the smaller dimension of the Latin American and Carribean sampling. Moreover, the use of more specific continental characterized model increases in both the case studies the reliability of the results, which is possibly due to the differences in traffic and terminal operational models across the Atlantic.

Main achievements are also the recommendations for future research developments and extensions (e.g. Asia and North America at first): segmentation of the terminals by size and technological advances, geographical areas, both to prevent that regional cultural or operational habits affect the global reliability of the results.

Moreover, the methodology is very open and extensible to other relevant parameters, such as environmental/energetic ones, presently under development, as well as to different typologies of terminals.

References

1. Steenken, D., Stefan, V., Robert, S.: Container terminal operation and operations research - A classification and literature review. OR Spectr. **26**, 3–49 (2004)

2. Gharehgozli, A., Zaerpour, N., Koster, R.D.: Container terminal layout design: transition and future. Marit. Econ. Logist. (2019). https://doi.org/10.1057/s41278-019-00131-9
3. Marinacci, C., Quattrini, A., Ricci, S.: Integrated design process of maritime terminals assisted by simulation models. 10th Int. Workshop Harbour, Marit. Multimodal Logistics Model. Simul., 1 190–201. (2008)
4. Florio, L., Malavasi, G.: Introduzione all'analisi strutturale degli impianti portuali di trasbordo container. Ingegneria Ferroviaria, 8, 454 (1985). (ISSN: 0020–0956)
5. Ricci, S., Marinacci, C.: Modelling support for maritime terminals planning and operation. Mar. Navig. Saf. Sea Transp., (2009). (ISBN: 978–041580479–0)
6. Lodewijks, G., Schott, D.L., Ottjes, J.A.: Modern dry bulk terminal design. Bulk Solids Handling **27**(6), 364–376 (2007)
7. Dijkstra, E.W.: A note on two problems in connexion with graphs. Numer. Math. **1**, 269–271 (1959)

Case Studies and Theoretical Approaches in Port Competition and Cooperation

Francesco Russo[ID] and Giuseppe Musolino[(✉)] [ID]

DIIES – Dipartimento di Ingegneria dell'Informazione, delle Infrastrutture e dell'Energia
Sostenibile - Università Mediterranea di Reggio Calabria, 89100 Reggio Calabria, Italy
{francesco.russo,giuseppe.musolino}@unirc.it

Abstract. Main factors change the international freight transport alimenting (and being alimented by) the increasing of globalization. In this scenario, the role of ports also changes. The single port cannot compete in the new global economic scenario. The port system arises from the alliance, or merge, of several ports to optimize the resources of the individual ports. The paper is articulated into two main parts. The first one presents the main theoretical approaches to explain how ports could respond to the new requirements imposed by gigantism, carriers' alliances and land-sea integration. The second one presents a critical analysis of some representative case studies of cooperation among ports, in order to aggregate the observed processes in some macro-classes. The work may be considered a first step of a research, able to open several directions to study the competition and cooperation process among ports with Transport System Models (TSMs). The use of TSMs could allow to extend the consolidated quantitative methods developed in the field of passengers' mobility and freight distribution on terrestrial transport networks to the field of maritime transport and ports.

Keywords: Ports · Maritime transport · Coopetition · Fourth-generation ports · Case studies

1 Introduction

In the last decades of the twentieth century, globalization has led to an increase in world trade never occurred before. In general, some areas of the world became production regions (e.g. Far East), while others became regions where intermediate and final consumption is concentrated (e.g. Europe).

Maritime transport represented the pillar through which globalization could be achieved, thanks to some phenomena that changed the global game: the naval gigantism and the alliances between shipping companies, on the sea side; and the improvement of hinterland accessibility, on the land side.

As far as concerns *alliances between shipping companies*, the market recently knew a strong acceleration. Focusing on the container segment, the consolidation started in the 1990' with the creation of the global alliances and it passed through different periods. In 1996, the first alliances between mid-sized and small carriers were born in order to

© Springer Nature Switzerland AG 2021
O. Gervasi et al. (Eds.): ICCSA 2021, LNCS 12958, pp. 198–212, 2021.
https://doi.org/10.1007/978-3-030-87016-4_15

extend their market coverage at global scale and to reduce the costs of larger vessels. The cooperation took the form of coordination of capacity. Since 2011 the availability of mega-ships was an entry barrier by many smaller carriers; therefore, they intensified cooperation with existing alliances. Until 2017, where only three global alliances exist consisting of three very large companies of about the same size [1]. The average market share of the three alliance was 92.3% in 2018, with a peak of 98.8% on the Asia-Europe route (see Table 1).

Table 1. Market share [%] of the main three container shipping alliances along the East-West routes. Year 2018. (% TEUs of capacity).

	2M Alliance(*) [%]	Ocean Alliance(#) [%]	The Alliance(§) [%]	Sum [%]	Other [%]	Total [%]
Trans-Pacific	17.5	42.2	27.0	86.7	13.3	100.0
Transatlantic	47.8	15.2	28.5	91.5	8.5	100.0
Asia-Europe	36.5	37.4	24.9	98.8	1.2	100.0
Average	33.9	31.6	26.8	92.3	7.6	100.0

(*) Maersk and Mediterranean Shipping Company; (#) Cosco, CMA, CGM and Evergreen; (§) ONE, Yang Ming and Hapag-Lloyd. (Source: [2]).

As far as concerns *naval gigantism*, the total world fleet accounted in 2019 for 2.20 billion dead-weight tons (dwt) of capacity (95,402 ships). Bulk carriers maintained the largest market share of vessels' capacity (38.2%). Oil tankers followed with 25.8%, and container ships have a share of 12.1%. Container ships are the ones that obtained the greatest increase from 2018 (+4.9%) (Table 2) [2].

Focusing on the container segment, containerships grew through several generations since the beginning of containerization [5], as showed in Table 3. The ships' dimensions were constrained by technical limits of Panama Canal, that was object of an infrastructural expansion in 2016.

The first generation of containerships was born with the birth of container technology in the mid-1950s. The early containerships were adapted from bulk vessels or tankers with capacity up to 800 TEUs and they were equipped with cranes on-board. They were followed by the cellular containerships since the end of 1960s which used the whole ship to stack containers and had no cranes on-board. During the 1980s the increasing success of container pushed for the construction of larger containerships, called Panamax and Panama max, with a capacity up to 4,500 TEUs.

The second generation of containerships, Post Panamax, aroused at the end of 1990s when the transport of a sufficient amount of cargo along a longer route (Africa circumnavigation) became profitable. Once the Panamax threshold was passed, containerships increased their capacities reaching 8,500 TEUs (Post Panamax I and II). By 2006, new Post Panamax containerships were built having a capacity between 11,000 and 15,000 TEUs. They were called Very Large Container Ships (VLCS) since they exceeded the limits of the expanded Panama Canal. An extension was the Ultra Large Container Ships (ULCS) above 18,000 TEUs in 2013, further expanded in 2017 above 21,000 TEUs.

Table 2. World fleet by principal vessel type, 2018–2019 (Thousand dead-weight tons and %).

Principal types	2018		2019		19/18
	d.w. tons x 1000	%	d.w. tons x 1000	%	%
Bulk carriers	818921	38,2	842438	38,2	2,9
Oil tankers	562035	26,2	567533	25,8	1,0
Container	253275	11,8	265668	12,1	4,9
Other types	218002	10,2	226854	10,3	4,1
Offshore	78269	3,7	80453	3,7	2,8
General cargo	73951	3,4	74000	3,4	0,1
Gas carriers	64407	3,0	69078	3,1	7,2
Chemical tankers	44457	2,1	46297	2,1	4,1
Ferries	6922	0,3	7097	0,3	2,5
Other/not avail.	23946	1,1	23929	1,1	− 0,1
Total	2144185	100,0	2203347	100,0	2,8

(Source: [2]).

The fourth generation of containerships, New-Panamax, or Neo-Panamax (NPX) was designed to fit exactly the limits of the expanded Panama Canal, opened in 2016. These ships have a capacity of about 12,500 TEU.

Next generation of container ships, the Malacca Max, could carry about 27,000–30,000 TEU, but they will not build until there are not sufficient volumes on the limited routes and ports they could serve.

As far as concerns *hinterland accessibility*, two (or more) ports, with the same (e.g. container) or with different functions and markets, might find convenient to jointly enhance hinterland access, rather than doing it in an independent or competitive way. This may be done by integrating their facilities in two different ways:

- with rail, road or fluvial gateways, or
- with a distripark, or a Special Economic Zone (SEZ).

In this context, ports gained strategic importance as they became crucial nodes in the global supply chain [3] and [4]. Ports were protagonists of epochal changes with respect to their vision and missions, modifying their historical attitude of mutual *competition* towards an attitude of progressive *cooperation*. It can be recalled the increasing cost for the port authority to dock depth following the ship depth [6].

The so-called *fourth-generation ports* were born ([7–9]). They are port systems, generally composed of two main ports, in which port operators and administrations cooperate by creating alliances on market segments, or by sharing infrastructures and

Table 3. Containerships' growth generations.

Generation	Year of constr	Name	TEUs		LOA$^{(\circ)}$
			Min	Max	[mt]
First	1956	Early Container	500	800	137
	1970	Fully Cellular	1000	2500	215
	1980	Panamax	3000	3400	250
	1985	Panamax max	3400	4500	290$^{(*)}$
Second	1988	Post Panamax I	4000	6000	300
	2000	Post Panamax II	6000	8500	340
Third	2006	VLCS	11000	15000	397
	2013	ULCS	18000	21000	400
Fourth	2014	New-Panamax	12500	366$^{(\$)}$	49$^{(\$)}$

$^{(\circ)}$ Length Over All; $^{(*)}$ technical limits of Panama Canal before the expansion in 2016, ($) technical limits of Panama Canal after the expansion in 2016. (Source: [5]).

services for customers, or by integrating different production segments. The aim is to increase the utilities of different stakeholders reducing the investments. The cooperative-competitive behaviour of fourth-generation ports can be called *coopetition*.

The remaining part of the paper is articulated as follows. Section 2 presents the background theory of port coopetition, introducing a theoretical equilibrium model of competition-cooperation, based on the topological-behavioral paradigm of Transportation System Models (TSMs). Section 3 reports some case studies regarding port cooperation, selected from the literature. The last section reports the conclusions and the research perspectives.

2   Theoretical Approaches on Port Coopetition

The port industry has undergone a process of rationalization during the last years of the twentieth century. UNCTAD introduced the definition of fourth generation of port [7], in order to describe this process that considers common operators and administrations. The first works on the theme of passage from strong competitions to (weak) new form of cooperation are published in last two decades.

The behaviour of many port operators was investigated in [10] by observing that, in the era of the global economy, a port no longer enjoys a natural monopoly, as it did in the past. It is therefore necessary to initiate forms of competition and cooperation between ports to provide services that fit the strategies of shipping companies. On this basis, a new strategic option is proposed known as coopetition, the combination of competition and cooperation, for the port industry, analysing a case of coopetition between the container ports of Hong Kong and southern China.

The general problem posed in [7] of the relationship between competition and cooperation between ports, was investigated using game theory. The ports of Shanghai and Ningbo are analyzed by means of game theory in [11]. In the paper, the most advanced strategies of cooperation are investigated, for example, bleak strategy, punitive strategy, face-to-face strategy.

In the following years several works have addressed the issue of coopetition with game theory, among others it can be recalled. The ports of the Yangtze River Delta are analyzed in [12]. The problems of coopetition between ports are formalized in [13], in which each individual port makes investment decisions, anticipating protective anticipating the congestion problems that the overall system has. In a subsequent work [14], a bi-level approach to improve the resilience of the overall port network is presented.

From what emerges from the literature there are no works that address the issue of coopetition between ports using the Transport System Models (TSMs). A further research was carried out using search engines freely accessible on the web via keywords, which led to the same result.

TSMs simulate a transport system through a process, in which transport supply and travel demand interact. The three main elements of the TSM are therefore: the transport supply model, the travel demand model and the supply-demand interaction model.

The transport supply model must represent the utilities for users deriving from the use of transport infrastructures and services. The approach used is the topological model, given by a network model, with links, nodes and cost functions (e.g. time-flow relationship).

The travel demand model simulates user choices based on the performance of infrastructure and services. Travel demand models can be behavioural or non-behavioural. In the behavioural approach [15], demand models can be stochastic or deterministic according to whether the (dis) utility associated with each user's choice is a random variable; or a deterministic variable.

The supply-demand interaction model allows simulating the interaction between the user's choices and the performance of the infrastructure and the service. The model uses the topological-behavioural paradigm. The demand-supply interaction models can be classified into ([16, 17]): static and dynamic, according to whether they allow to simulate a transport system in stationary or evolving conditions due to travel demand peaks or temporary changes in supply capacity. Static models can be divided into: free-flowing models, such as Network Loading (NL), and models based on an equilibrium approach, such as User Equilibrium (UE) and System Optimum (SO) ([18, 19]).

The class of models based on the equilibrium approach is the one of interest for the solution of the coopetition problem. The idea is to extend the TSMs from the consolidated field of passengers' mobility and freight distribution on terrestrial transport networks to a different field: the one of maritime ports. This is a distinctive feature from the existing published studies.

UE and SO equilibrium models rely on different behavioural assumptions.

- UE model simulates the behaviour of a carrier, who choices a port among the available set of ports, in order to minimize his individual cost. *There is a competition attitude between ports.*

- SO model simulates the behaviour of a carrier, who choices the port among the available set of ports, in order to minimize the total cost (of all carriers). *There is a cooperation attitude among ports.* The SO costs and flows correspond to objectives that a port system manager generally pursues.

3 Port Systems Coopetition: The Fourth-Generation Port

The last two decades were characterized by the behaviour of closer ports to cooperate, other than the traditional behaviour to compete [20]. As reported in the introduction, three were drivers of the cooperation process.

- The alliances between shipping companies reduced the bargaining power of port authorities and made ports vulnerable in relation to the requests of deeper channels and berths, and of higher capacity of container terminals [21].
- The naval gigantism together with hub-and-spoke shipping services determined pressure on ports to invest in the development of sea-side material facilities. But, not all the ports can sustain this competitive game, which requires relevant amount of funds and which risks to replicate similar investments in ports located in proximity [22].
- Some ports in proximity find more convenient to jointly enhance hinterland access and to develop shared port centric logistics systems, rather than acting in an autonomous way.

In each port, different specific background factors and measures (e.g. planned investments in physical infrastructures, management, in human resources and organisation by the individual port authorities) could be identified to respond to above drivers. They could have generated some increase in traffic demand for the individual ports irrespective of the cooperation initiatives.

The forms of cooperation among ports are different. They may be classified from a very general point of view according to the following experimental criteria:

- cooperation in the ports' governance (Sect. 3.1), merging the previous authorities;
- cooperation among ports on multiple market segments (Sect. 3.2);
- cooperation on one market segment (e.g. container) (Sect. 3.3)
- cooperation based on a supply infrastructural project (Sect. 3.4).

The following paragraphs report four case studies regarding port cooperation, selected from the literature according to the above classification. Even if several case studies may be recalled for each criterion of cooperation, the paper presents the most exemplificative ones.

3.1 Cooperation in the Ports' Governance: The Italian Ports Merger

Italy is the only country which proposed the "port system" concept at national scale in 2015 [23].

Before the reform, Italy had 24 Port Authorities and Italian commercial ports handled 483,8 [tons x 10^6] of freight, composed by liquid bulk, with 182,3 [tons x 10^6] and 37,7% of share; container, with 114,7 [tons x 10^6] and 23,7% of share; and ro-ro with 93,9 [tons x 10^6] and 19,4% of share [24].

The Italian Port and Logistics Strategic Plan [23] proposed as final objective to obtain larger port systems than the previous ones respected to each region interested. The attention was focused to have a sort of one-to-one port system and administrative region, where in each port system there is one port core (see Table 4), as defined by EU (see [25, 25]).

Table 4. Authority port systems in Italy.

Name	Ports
Mar Ligure Occidentale	Genova(*), Savona, Vado and Prà
Mar Ligure Orientale	La Spezia(*), Marina di Carrara
Mar Tirreno Settentrionale	Livorno(*), Capraia, Piombino, Portoferraio, Rio Marina, Cavo
Mar Tirreno Centro Settentrionale	Civitavecchia, Fiumicino, Gaeta
Mar Tirreno Centrale	Napoli(*), Salerno, Castellammare di Stabia
Gioia Tauro e della Calabria	Gioia Tauro(*), Corigliano Calabro, Crotone, Palmi
Stretto (di Messina)	Messina, Milazzo, Tremestieri, Reggio Calabria, Villa S. Giovanni
Mare di Sardegna	Cagliari(*), Foxi-Sarroch, Olbia, Porto Torres, Golfo Aranci, Oristano, Portoscuso-Portovesme, S. Teresa di Gallura
Mare di Sicilia Occidentale	Palermo(*), Termini Imerese, Porto Empedocle, Trapani
Mare di Sicilia Orientale	Augusta(*), Catania
Mare Ionio	Taranto(*)
Mare Adriatico Meridionale	Bari(*), Brindisi, Manfredonia, Barletta, Monopoli
Mare Adriatico Centrale	Ancona(*), Falconara Marittima, Pescara, Pesaro, San Benedetto del Tronto, Ortona
Mare Adriatico Centro-Settentrionale	Ravenna(*)
Mare Adriatico Settentrionale	Venezia(*), Chioggia
Mare Adriatico Orientale	Trieste(*), Monfalcone

(*) core port.

The attempt of the reform was to insert historical ports, as Genova and Naples, in a larger context as a port system. The port of Genova with the ports of Savona, Vado and Prà, are structured in the "Autorità di Sistema Portuale del Mar Ligure Occidentale".

The port of Naples with the ports of Salerno and Castellammare di Stabia, are structured in the "Autorità di Sistema Portuale del Mar Tirreno Centrale".

In two cases the port system was designed to be larger than regional administrative borders: in the North Adriatic range and in the South Tyrrhenian range.

The first proposal of the North Adriatic port authority defined a port system composed of ports belonging to four Regions: Trieste (Friuli), Venezia (Veneto), Ravenna (Emilia), Ancona (Marche). However, the final version of the national law, instead of one system, proposed four ports authorities reproducing the status-quo. For what concerns the South Tyrrhenian range, the "Autorità di Sistema Portuale del Mar Tirreno Meridionale" unified all the ports of Calabria Region, leaded by port of Gioia Tauro, with the ports of Messina and Milazzo in Sicily. Today, this port system has been subdivided into two sub-systems, the "Autorità di Sistema Portuale dello Stretto", including the Sicilian ports of Messina and Milazzo and the Calabrian ports of Reggio Calabria and Villa S. Giovanni, and the "Autorità di Sistema Portuale di Gioia Tauro e della Calabria", including Gioia Tauro and the remaining Calabrian ports. It can be noted the slimming evolution from the original proposal, determined by local policy.

It is still too early to observe tangible effects of cooperation among the ports, involved in each "port system", given the reduced amount of time since the national reform took place.

3.2   Cooperation on Multiple Market Segments

The ports of Copenhagen and Malmö lie in the Oresund Strait between Sweden and Denmark. Copenhagen is the capital of Denmark. Malmö is the third city of Sweden. In 2005 the Oresund Bridge, the "fixed link" between Sweden and Denmark, was opened enhancing the integration and the centrality on the region, and favouring the settlement of clusters of internationally oriented industries.

The cooperation between the two ports started in 2001, leading to a new subject called Copenhagen Malmö Port (CMP) [26]. This process led to the first case of bi-national port in Europe.

The following key factors encouraged the cooperation process: the risk that the Oresund Bridge would lead to a loss of traffic among the two countries (ferry and container); the better utilization of resources (labour, land, capital) and of infrastructures (capacity); the creation of scale economies in management and administration, and of synergies in investments; the creation of a new single player in the market visible by customers. The negotiation lasted some years, and it reached success because it was supported by the CEOs of both ports and from the political and societal community, driven by the aim to increase the integration of Oresund Region.

3.3   Cooperation on a Market Segment

3.3.1   Seattle and Tacoma (USA)

The ports of Seattle and Tacoma are located in the Puget Sound Region, along the Pacific North-West Cost of North America. Tacoma has a population of about 860,000 and has historically been industrially based. Seattle has a population of over 2.1 million and has emerged as a new technology centre and tourist destination.

The two ports have competed against each other for decades [26] [21]. However, in 2015, they took the decision to set a long-term cooperation by forming the North-West Seaport Alliance; in order to compete in the container market with new ports along the West Coast, and with ports on the East Coast accessible from Asia through the expanded Panama Canal. Because of the differences in the scope and size of the two ports, and due to political and institutional reasons, the container business was the only asset "assigned" to the Alliance, even because it was of similar entity between the two ports.

After a long negotiation, the decision of the two ports to cooperate was accelerated after the Grand Alliance decision to relocate from the Port of Seattle to the Port of Tacoma. This decision helped both private and public stakeholders to become aware about the local problems determined by the competition between the two ports. The common accepted opinion was to give up the doing nothing option [28]).

According to the business plan elaborated in 2014 for the ten-years lasting period of the alliance [21], the ex-ante estimation was to pass from 3.4 million of TEUs in 2014 to 3.85 million of TEUs in 2019 until reaching 6.0 million of TEUs in 2026; and from 34,000 jobs in 2014 to 48,500 jobs in 2026, The ex-post analysis shows that the number of the containers handled were 3.77 million of TEUs in 2019 and the number of jobs were 36,800 in 2017.

3.3.2 Kobe and Osaka (Japan)

In Japan large port complexes have played a role of critical importance to the economic as well as urban development of these bay areas. They have developed not only marine terminals for domestic and international shipping, but also spaces for industrial and urban activities through extensive land reclamation in the bays [29]. The Osaka Bay area has long been the centre of the country: politically, economically, and culturally. Today it has a population of about 20 million and roughly 17% of the nation's GDP.

In 2015, the ports of Kobe and Osaka handled cargos for 97 and 74 million tons, respectively. Kobe is more international trade oriented than Osaka with the share of international trade being 53% for Kobe and 47% for Osaka. As for foreign trade containers, Kobe and Osaka respectively handled 2.1 million and 2.0 million TEU, for a total of 4.1 million TEU. The total international container throughput of Japan was 17.3 million TEU in 2015.

In 2014, under a new national port policy, the ports of Kobe and Osaka jointly established a port management company, the Kobe-Osaka International Port Corporation (KOIP), to merge their container terminal business. It is not the merger of the two port authorities, but that of their container terminal business, retaining the mother port authorities running separately as before [22].

The objectives of KOIP were: (1) effectively develop terminals without duplication, (2) respond more flexibly to market needs and changes, (3) strengthen bargaining powers to shipping lines, and (4) provide more choices of port services with shippers.

The company leases terminal infrastructures from their respective owners, the national government, city governments and the two LCTCs. KOIP is a product of compromise between retaining the autonomy of the two cities and promoting the collaborative management of their container terminals.

3.3.3 Ningbo and Zhoushan (China)

The "one port-one city" policy in China in the last decades of the XX century generated the development of similar port development projects, even within the same province, causing inter-port competition to capture cargo within the same hinterland. The slow-down of China's economic growth accelerated the port cooperation process in order to optimize resources allocation and to meet clients' requirements.

Ningbo and Zhoushan ports are two adjacent ports in Zhejiang Province (China). They are located in the same area, use the same channel and anchorage, and share the same hinterland. However, each port had independent policies and planning objectives, construction, operation and management structures. In 2006 the Chinese Ministry of Transport launched the regional port integration programme between Ningbo Port and Zhoushan Port.

Before the integration in 2005, Ningbo port handled 5.21 million of TEUs and Zhoushan port only 54.9 thousand of TEUs. After 10-year of integration, the total throughput of Ningbo-Zhoushan port reached 26.5 million of TEUs in 2017. The coop-eration on the container market segment boosted the growth of container handled in the two ports.

The growth of container throughput was registered also in other Chinese ports, but it was not of the entity Ningbo-Zhoushan one. Shanghai Port, that shares a common inland market with Ningbo-Zhoushan port, passed from 18.08 million of TEUs in 2005 to 40.18 million of TEUs in 2017. The integration process of the two ports contributed very significantly to the fast-growing container throughput of Ningbo-Zhoushan port, if compared with the ports increase without port integration, whether in the same economic region or not [30]. The other contribute was due to the economic growth at the Yangtze River Delta in last decade.

The main ports of Pearl River Delta (Guangzou, Shenzen, Hong Kong) are working to verify different ways of cooperation, starting from the cooperation between Shenzen and Guangzou [31].

3.4 Cooperation on a Supply Infrastructural Project

3.4.1 Los Angeles and Long Beach

The ports of Los Angeles and Long Beach are located directly adjacent to each other within San Pedro Bay, California [32]. Since their founding over a century ago, the Ports of Los Angeles and Long Beach have been subject to numerous merger proposals. However, their reciprocal attitude was substantially competitive until the beginning of the 80s' [27]. In those years an authority between the ports was created, in order to finance and develop an intermodal railyard to manage the hinterland congestion. Later, in 1989, the ports used the same mechanism of the authority, to finance, develop and operate a second regional railroad project, known as the Alameda Corridor Project. These projects represent the highest degree of governance integration undertaken by the two ports. In the latest decades, further projects on material and immaterial infrastructures were planned and implemented to consolidate the cooperation process of the two ports.

The growth of container throughput was constant and continuous during the last four decades of cooperation of the two ports. As far as concerns the container segment, the number of handled container in the two ports passed from 1,13 million of TEUs, with 56% (0,63 million of TEUs) of market share of Los Angeles and 44% (0,51 MTEUs) of Long Beach in 1980, to 16,9 million of TEUs in 2017, with similar market shares. The cooperation based on a supply infrastructural project created the conditions for an increment of handled freight in the two ports.

3.5 Lesson Learned

The critical analysis of the four experimental typologies highlights that different levels of cooperation among ports exist. The cooperation may be defined as a continuum from a maximum level, that is the merger, to a minimum one, that is the alliance on specific projects, as Fig. 1 shows (see [28, 33, 34]).

The merger conveys the decisions of the individual partners (e.g. authorities) into a new institutional subject (e.g. one new authority), that defines and pursues new and coherent goals. The description of the reform of the Italian port system in 2015, reported in Sect. 4.1, is an exemplificative case of merger process among port authorities.

The alliance allows the individual partners (e.g. authorities) to keep their own independency in order to pursue common objectives. The alliance has a limited period before becoming extinct.

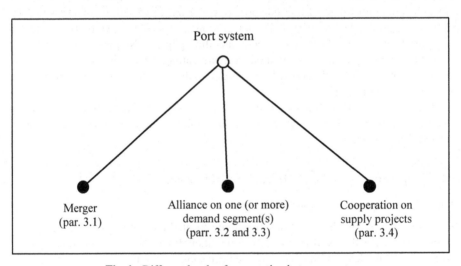

Fig. 1. Different levels of cooperation between ports.

Three functional types of alliance may be identified [22].

- *The cooperation in multiple market segments provides for the maintenance of strategic authority in each of the ports, and the sharing of management for the shared economic sectors.* The description of the pioneering cooperation between the two ports of Copenhagen and Malmö, belonging to different states, is representative of this type of cooperation.

- *The alliance on one market segment is particularly widespread for the container sector in which the three processes (gigantism, alliances, sea-land integration) have the greatest impact.* The three case studies of Seattle and Tacoma (USA), Kobe and Osaka (Japan), and Ningbo and Zhoushan (China), are representative of this type of alliance as their cooperation was carried out by sharing the container market segment. The opening of a discussion table between Shanghai and Ningbo-Zhoushan, which could produce the largest container port system in the world, is an example of the prospects that this type of alliance offers.
- *The cooperation on a single infrastructure project is the weakest form of alliance. In this case neither the policy nor the management are shared. The collaboration is only on the creation of an infrastructure of common interest for the two ports.* The case study of Los Angeles and Long Beach (USA), who started to cooperate on the base of a common infrastructural project, belongs to this type of alliance.

According to this approach, the definition of fourth-generation port [7], that considers common operators and administrations, may be actualized by considering two main categories of cooperation (see [27, 30]):

- vertical cooperation of ports.
- horizontal cooperation among the ports.

In the two cases the term cooperation holds. While the cooperation between shipping lines has been popular since several years and co-exists with competition; the attitude to cooperate between ports in proximity, or inside a territorial system, was carried out by port authorities, and in general by public bodies. Their general strategy may be deployed by means of two elements. The first one allows ports, belonging to a territorial system, to have cooperative interactions in order to increase the competitiveness of the whole territorial system (or of the port) while simultaneously improving the performances of individual ports [34] and [35]. The second one supports the inclusive port development of the economy participating to the development of the port related area [37].

4 Conclusions

The problem of merger and of alliance between the ports is a crucial issue of the current evolution of maritime transport. Due to carrier alliances and to increasing dimension of ships, some ports operate according to new patterns, moving from the historical and well-known competition attitude towards a cooperation one.

This process could be observed in some important nodes of transport and logistics of world trade scenario: from Europe, to USA, Japan and China. The issues of this change could allow to understanding the future evolution of the international port network.

The main conclusions that can be drawn concern two main elements. The first concerns the possibility of using the basic equations of Transportation System Models (TSMs) to explain how port systems respond to the major changes that have occurred in the maritime transport sector (gigantism, alliances, land-sea integration). The second group of conclusions concerns the possibility of aggregating the real observed cases in some representative macro-cases of coopetition between ports, in order to be able to study the resulting systems with TSM methods.

The work may be considered as a step of the research because it opens several directions to study the maritime system with TSMs. The core equations of TSMs could allow to extend the consolidated quantitative methods developed in the field of passengers' mobility and freight distribution on terrestrial transport networks to the field of maritime transport and ports. The use of the TSM makes it possible to compare in the same formal context the different conditions in which the various ports that are part of the alliance can operate, without the need to use different formal environments for the various conditions of coopetition that may arise.

The proposed approach is particularly useful for policy makers because it allows to study the system in the various phases, evaluating, for each one, the costs for the users and therefore the effectiveness. The approach is also useful for technicians because it allows to integrate the port node in the simulation models of the overall transport system (sea and land), thus allowing to arrive at a single overall model.

References

1. International Transport Forum, The impact of alliances in container shipping. Case-Specific Policy Analysis Reports. OECD-ITF (2018)
2. UNCTAD: Review of maritime transport (2019)
3. Musolino, G., Chilà, G.: Structural factors for a third-generation port: Planning general logistics interventions in Gioia Tauro. WIT Transactions on the Built Environment, vol. 204, WIT Press (2021). ISSN 1743–3509
4. Russo, F., Panuccio, P., Rindone, C.: Structural factors for a third-generation port: Between hinterland regeneration and smart town in Gioia Tauro. WIT Transactions on the Built Environment, vol. 204, WIT Press (2021). ISSN 1743-3509
5. Rodrigue, J.P.: The Geography of Transport Systems, Fifth Editions. Routledge, New York (2020)
6. Tchang, G.S.: The impact of ship size on ports' nautical costs. Marit. Policy Manage. **47**(1), 27–42 (2020)
7. UNCTAD: Fourth-generation Port: technical note. Ports newsletter n. 19, UNCTAD Secretariat (1999)
8. Paixao, A.C., Marlow, P.B.: Fourth generation ports: a question of agility? Int. J. Phys. Distrib. Logistics. Manag. **33**(4), 355–376 (2003)
9. Russo, F., Musolino, G.: Quantitative characteristics for port generations: the Italian case study. Int. J. Transp Dev. Integr. **4**(2), 103–112 (2020)
10. Song, D.W.: Port co-opetition in concept and practice. Marit. Policy Manage. **30**(1), 29–44 (2003)
11. Xian-jing, Z.: Analysis of game theory for coopetition of ports. Logistics Engineering and Management, en.cnki.com.cn (2009)
12. Shao, Y.: Analysis on the game of co-opetition of ports in the China Yangtze Delta-Taking Shanghai port and Ningbo-Zhoushan port as an example. J. Korean Navig. Port Res. **36**, 123–129 (2012)
13. Asadabadi, A., Miller-Hooks, E.: Co-opetition in enhancing global port network resiliency: a multi-leader, common-follower game theoretic approach. Transp. Res. Part B: Methodological. **108**, 281–298 (2018)

14. Asadabadi, A., Miller-Hooks, E.: Maritime port network resiliency and reliability through co-opetition. Transp. Res. Part E: Logistics Transp. Rev. **137**, 101916 (2020) Pergamon
15. Ben-Akiva, M., Lerman, S.R.: Discrete Choice Analysis. MIT Press, Theory and Application to Travel Demand (2020)
16. Cascetta, E.: Transportation Systems Analysis. Models and Applications. Springer-Verlag, New York (2009). https://doi.org/10.1007/978-0-387-75857-2
17. Cantarella G.E., Watling D., de Luca S., Di Pace R.: Dynamics and Stochasticity in Transportation Systems, Tools for Transportation Network Modelling, 1st Edition. Elsevier (2019)
18. Cantarella, G.E., Cascetta, E.: Dynamic processes and equilibrium in transportation networks. Transp. Sci. **29**, 305–329 (1995)
19. Wardrop, J.G.: Some theoretical aspects of road traffic research, In: Proceedings of Institution of Civil Engineers, Part II, pp. 325–378 (1952).
20. Martín-Alcalde, E., Sergi, S., Ng, A.K.Y.: Port-focal logistics and the evolution of port regions in a globalized world. In: Tae-Woo, L.P., Cullinane, K. (eds.) Dynamic Shipping and Port Development in the Globalized Economy: Emerging Trends in Ports, vol. 2, pp. 102–127. Palmgrave, Mcmillan (2016)
21. Yoshitani, T.: PNW seaport alliance: stakeholder's benefits of port cooperation . Res. Transp. Bus. Manage. **26**, 14–17 (2018)
22. Inoue, S.: Realities and challenges of port alliance in Japan-Ports of Kobe and Osaka. Res. Transp. Bus. Manage. **26**, 45–55 (2018)
23. MIT: Piano Strategico nazionale della portualità e della logistica. Final report, Italian Ministry of Infrastructures and Transport, Rome (2015)
24. Censis: V Rapporto sull'economia del mare. Cluster marittimo e sviluppo in Italia. Federazione del Mare (2016)
25. European Parliament and Council: Union guidelines for the development of the trans-European transport network, Regulation (EU) n. 1315/2013 of 11 December 2013 (2013a)
26. European Parliament and Council: Establishing the Connecting Europe Facility, Regulation (EU) n. 1316/2013 of 11 December 2013 (2013b)
27. de Langen, P.W., Nijdam, M.H.: A best practice in cross-border port cooperation: cohopenagen malmo port. In: Notteboom, T., Ducruet, C., de Langen, P. (eds.) Ports in Proximity Competition and Coordination, pp. 163–174. Ashgate, England (2009)
28. Heaver, T., Meersman, H., Van De Voorde, E.: Co-operation and competition in international container transport: strategies for ports. Marit. Policy Manage. **28**(3), 293–305 (2010)
29. The NorthWest Seaport Alliance: Marine Cargo, economic impact analysis. Port of Tacoma and Port of Seattle.
30. Shinohara, M.: Port competition paradigms and Japanese port clusters. In: Notteboom, T., Ducruet, C., de Langen, P. (eds.) Ports in Proximity Competition and Coordination, pp. 237–246. Ashgate, England (2009)
31. Dong, G., Zheng, S., Lee, P.T.: The effects of regional port integration: the case of Ningbo-Zhousan port. Transp. Res. Part E: Logistics Transp. Rev. **120**, 1–15 (2018)
32. Wang, K., Ng, A.K.Y., Lam, J.S.L., Fu, X.: Cooperation or competition? Factors and conditions affecting regional port governance in South China, Marit. Econ. Logistics **14**, 386–408 (2012)
33. Knatz, G.: Port mergers: why not Los Angeles and Long Beach? Res. Transp Bus. Manag. **26**, 26–33 (2018)
34. Slack, B., Gouvernal, E., Debrie, J.: Proximity and Port governance. In: Notteboom, T., Ducruet, C., de Langen, P., (eds.) Ports in Proximity Competition and Coordination, pp. 75–86. Ashgate, England (2009)

35. Lee, P.T.-W., Cullinane, K.: Dynamic shipping and port development in the globalized economy: Emerging Trends in Ports, vol. 2, pp. 1–10. Palmgrave, Mcmillan (2016). https://doi.org/10.1057/9781137514233
36. Russo, F., Musolino, G.: The role of emerging ICT in the ports: Increasing utilities according to shared decisions. Front. Future Trans. **2**(722812), (2021). https://doi.org/10.3389/ffutr.2021.722812
37. Kavirathna, C.A., Kawasaki, T., Hanaoka, S.: Intra-port coopetition under different combinations of terminal ownership. Transp. Res. Part E: Logistics Transp. Rev. **128**, 32–148 (2019)
38. Jansen, M., van Tulder, R., Afrianto, R.: Exploring the conditions for inclusive port development: the case of Indonesia. Marit. Policy Manage. **45**(7), 924–943 (2018)

Greening the Last Mile in Port Cities: Environmental Benefits of Switching from Road to Railway for the Port of Naples

Stefano de Luca⬭, Chiara Fiori(⊠)⬭, Lucas Joel Cistenas, and Pasquale Argento

DICIV – Department of Civil Engineering, University of Salerno, 84084 Fisciano (SA), Italy
cfiori@unisa.it

Abstract. The aim of this study is to assess the CO2eq impact due to the shift of the container transport from road (trucks) to rail (electric trains). This specific case study involves the Port of Naples, in the South of Italy. In particular, different scenarios were identified in which mixed solutions for road and rail freight transport could replace the current scenario (freight transport by road only). The results show that, for the same amount of TEU handled, rail transport allows a 50% reduction in global CO2eq emissions (Well-To-Wheels) compared to road transport.

Keywords: Port · Energy consumption · Urban real driving cycles · Well-To-Wheels analysis

1 Introduction

Last mile connections are a critical issue of any port system and may significantly affect the efficiency and the environmental sustainability of the entire logistic process, especially in urban contexts. In the maritime sector, last mile is assuming an increasing role and it is attracting important investments from the European Union.

Currently, the last mile of many urban ports is mainly supplied by road transport, with not negligible effects on the environment, on the urban congestion, on road safety and the quality of life of the involved urban communities.

Indeed, it is well known, in fact, that road transport (cars, trucks, buses and vehicles) is responsible for almost three quarters of total CO2 emissions in the transport sector [1] and that the European Union (EU) has set the goal of achieving low-emission mobility by 2050 and zero-emission mobility in the long term.

In such a context, as also clearly specified by the EU in the White Paper for Transport [2], one of the main objectives is to "Optimize the effectiveness of multimodal logistics chains, by increasing the use of more energy-efficient modes of transport". To this end, the EU has set the following objectives and intervention strategies:

© Springer Nature Switzerland AG 2021
O. Gervasi et al. (Eds.): ICCSA 2021, LNCS 12958, pp. 213–222, 2021.
https://doi.org/10.1007/978-3-030-87016-4_16

i.   Shift 30% of road freight transport to other modes on journeys over 300 km by 2030. In 2050, this share should increase up to the 50% thanks to efficient and environmentally friendly freight corridors. Adequate infrastructures will have to be introduced to achieve this target.

ii. Complete the European high-speed rail network by 2050. Triple the existing high-speed rail network by 2030 and maintain a solid connection among Member States.

iii. Make a multi-modal TEN-T 'core network' fully operational across the EU by 2030 and a high quality and capacity network with a range of related information services by 2050.

iv. Ensure by 2050 that all major seaports are sufficiently connected to the rail freight system and, where possible, to inland waterways.

To this aim, acting on the ports last mile is becoming a priority in Transport Planning of port communities that have the core port located in densely populated contexts.

This is the context of a project of the Central Tyrrhenian Sea Port System Authority (AdSPMTC), which envisages the construction of a freight rail yard inside the port area equipped with 5 pick-up and delivery tracks with 750 m electrically driven trains and a capacity per train of 50 TEU.

The present study aims at assessing the changes of CO2eq emitted in the considered study area, City of Naples, for containerized freight transport in the new configuration.

In particular, different scenarios have been identified in which mixed solutions for road and rail freight transport could replace the current scenario (freight transport by road only).

The rest of the paper is organized as follows: in Sect. 2 the case study and the different scenarios analyzed are reported; the methodology is reported in Sect. 3; Results and Conclusions end the paper.

2   Case Study

The scenario analyzed includes a possible future development of the Levante Terminal and the construction of a rail link between the Port of Naples and the Naples San Giovanni Barra Station. The project envisages a new railway terminal to serve the Port of Naples, guaranteeing the presence of an arrivals and departures segment of length of 750 m. The considered solution envisages a junction at the station of Napoli S. Giovanni Barra which is connected to the port by a new arrivals and departures (A/D) bundle.

The object of the analysis is, therefore, the city of Naples on which the port of Naples directly impacts through the flows of incoming and outgoing road freight demand. In particular, the attention was focused on the road arteries accessing/exiting to/from the Port of Naples. The routes considered for the evaluation of the energy consumption are one for road transport (see Fig. 1 - Input: AB, Green line $\cong$ 4 km; Output: BA, Yellow line $\cong$ 2 km) and one for rail transport (see Fig. 1 - Input/Output: CD/DC, Red line $\cong$ 3 km). The total length of entry/exit from the port for the two cases, road and rail, is about 6 km so that comparisons can be made in the two modes of transport on similar distances.

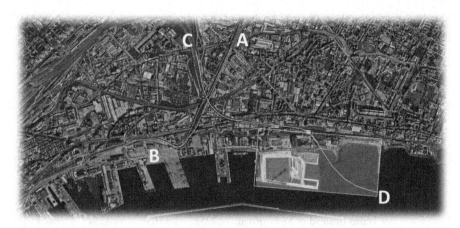

Fig. 1. Distance travelled by road and rail freight vehicles to and from the Port of Naples from the entrance of the city and to/from suburban areas.

With respect to the operational context described above, 4 scenarios have been implemented.

1. Scenario 0: represents the current state or Do-Nothing Scenario in which all goods enter/exit the Port by road.
2. Scenario 1: identified as "Realistic-Regional" which foresees a purely regional catchment area and, therefore, only Import freight flows interested in rail services. It is also assumed that the maximum freight flow on rail is 75,000 TEU (current annual limit with respect to the number of trains that can be handled).
3. Scenario 2: identified as "National", which foresees both Import and Export demand interested in rail services. It is foreseen, therefore, that rail freight transport is also shared in the Export phase. The maximum permissible freight flows are always the same.
4. Scenario 3: Assumes a higher number of trains per day that can be operated on the line. An increase from 5 to 9 trains per day is foreseen and therefore demand flows up to a maximum of 135,000 TEU per year by rail.

Finally, the analyses have been carried out by assuming a 50% split between Import and Export (Statistical Bulletin 2018 - AdSPMTC) and assuming two growth scenarios: the first involving a movement of 600,000 TEU (Statistical Bulletin 2018 - AdSPMTC) and the second with an increase in the transport of goods of 40% (1 million TEU).

In Table 1 a detail of the four Scenarios is reported.

Table 1. Scenarios for the preliminary analysis of environmental impacts in the new AdSPMTC project hypothesis for container freight transport in the port of Naples.

Scenarios	50% Import & 50% Export		600k TEU		1000k TEU	
			Export	Import	Export	Import
0	Do-Nothing	Road	300k	300k	500k	500k
		Rail	*0*	*0*	*0*	*0*
1	Realistic-Regional	Road	300k	225k	500k	425k
		Rail	*0*	*75k*	*0*	*75k*
2	National	Road	225k	225k	425k	425k
		Rail	*75k*	*75k*	*75k*	*75k*
3	9 Trains (instead of 5)	Road	225k	165k	425k	365k
		Rail	*75k*	*135k*	*75k*	*135k*

3 Methodology

The approach used in the analysis is the Well-To-Wheels (WTW) one. This consists of two sub-analyses:

- a Tank-To-Wheels TTW (from the tank to the wheels) analysis which considers the in-use consumption and emissions of the vehicle,
- a Well-To-Tank WTT (from well to tank) analysis which takes into account the extraction, conversion and transport processes of the energy carrier used.

For the estimation of consumption and emissions in use in road freight transport (TTW analysis), microscopic models known from the literature were adopted in which specific fuel consumption is calculated as a function of speed profile over time [3–5]. The adopted polynomial relation is the following:

$$SFC\left[\frac{l}{km}\right] = a \cdot v^2(t) + b \cdot v(t) + c \tag{1}$$

In particular, the values of parameters a, b and c are given in [3] for a large truck and the specific consumption as a function of speed has a trend as shown in Fig. 2.

These models have been subsequently applied to real urban cycles in the city of Naples for a realistic estimation of the consumption considering the driving behaviour in a real urban environment. Indeed, the consumption evaluated on real urban driving cycles, for conventional vehicles, has different values from an average consumption value assumed constant and referred to a fixed speed for the whole route considered. Especially in urban areas for conventional vehicles the consumption is higher because, in the case of microscopic analysis, a driving dynamic is considered, which is influenced by the actual traffic conditions, the driving style of the driver and the characteristics of the route (e.g. gradients). The speed profile in the real case is therefore characterised by

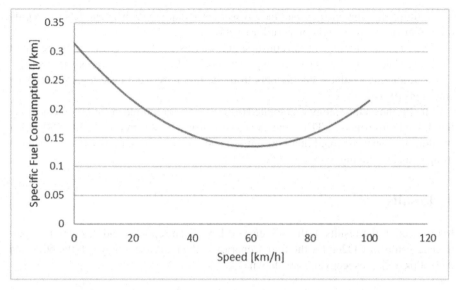

Fig. 2. Specific fuel consumption trend as a function of speed.

frequent start & stop phenomena with acceleration and deceleration phases which are not considered when estimating the consumption of a vehicle on a route based only on an average consumption referring to a specific constant speed value [4–7].

Figure 3 shows an example of an urban cycle in the city of Naples.

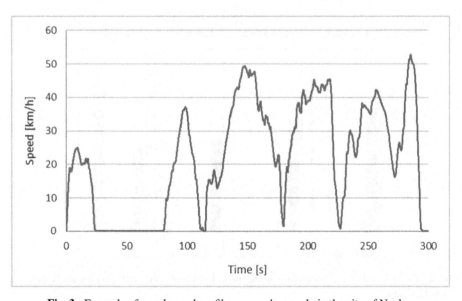

Fig. 3. Example of a real speed profile on an urban cycle in the city of Naples.

Additionally, specific payload factors were also applied to these models to account for the impact of the weight on board the vehicle.

The TTW calculation of train consumption was instead based on data from the report "Railway Handbook, Energy Consumption and CO2 Emissions" for goods trains [8].

Additionally, available coefficients from the literature were used to estimate WTT emissions [9, 10].

Finally, the methodology was applied to the scenarios reported in Table 1 by assuming for all scenarios trucks (1 TEU) and electrically driven goods trains (750 m of 50 TEU). In addition, it was assumed that both Import and Export freight transport is carried out using vehicles moving with a load factor of 1.

4   Results

In this section the results in the 4 Scenarios have been reported and discussed. In particular, results of CO2eq for the four scenarios in the two cases analyzed: the 600k and the 1000k TEU, respectively, are shown.

4.1   Scenarios Comparison: Well-To-Wheels Analysis – 600k TEU Case

Figure 4 shows the results of the tonnes of CO2eq, in the Tank-To-Wheels (TTW) and Well-To-Tank (WTT) analysis, produced in the 4 scenarios considered in the case of a yearly movement of 600k TEU.

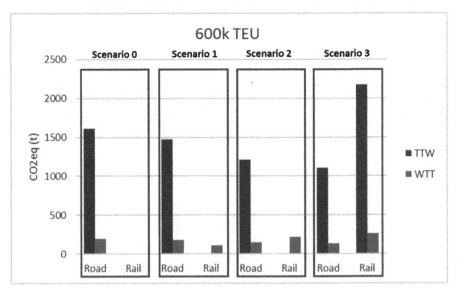

Fig. 4. Comparison of the 4 scenarios in the Tank-To-Wheels and Well-To-Tank analysis in the 600k TEU case.

Figure 5 shows the results of the tonnes of CO2eq, in the Well-To-Wheels (WTW) analysis, produced in the 4 scenarios considered in the case of a yearly movement of 600k TEU.

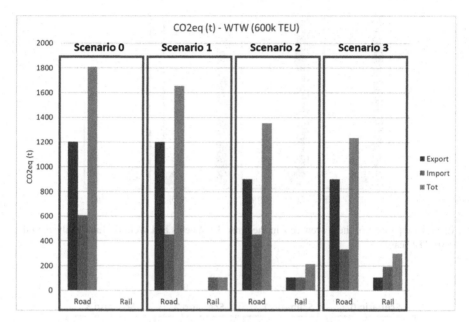

Fig. 5. Comparison of the 4 scenarios in the Well-To-Wheels analysis in the 600k TEU case.

Comparing Scenario 1, 2 and 3 with the do-nothing scenario (Scenario 0) results show that in Scenario 1, shifting 75k TEU of freight from road to rail a reduction of the 8.4% of CO2eq (WTW) emissions in the road mode and a 6% increase in the rail mode are observed.

In Scenario 2, 150k TEU are shifted to rail mode causing a 25% reduction in emissions from road mode and an 11.9% increase in emissions associated with rail mode.

Finally, in Scenario 3, the shift of 210k TEU to rail mode produces a 31.7% reduction in emissions associated with road transport and a 16.7% increase in emissions associated with rail transport.

4.2 Scenarios Comparison: Well-To-Wheels Analysis – 1000k TEU Case

Figure 6 shows the results of the tonnes of CO2eq, in the Tank-To-Wheels (TTW) and Well-To-Tank (WTT) analysis, produced in the 4 scenarios considered in the case of a yearly movement of 1000k TEU.

Figure 7 shows the results of the tonnes of CO2eq, in the WTW analysis, emitted in the 4 scenarios considered in the case of an annual movement of 1000k TEU, thus assuming an increase in freight transport of 40%.

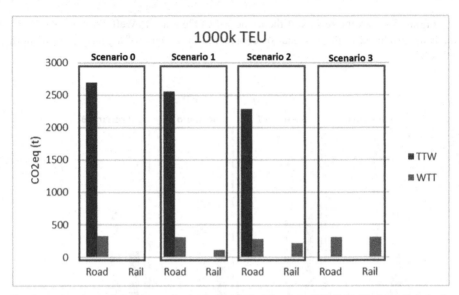

Fig. 6. Comparison of the 4 scenarios in the Tank-To-Wheels and Well-To-Tank analysis in the 1000k TEU case.

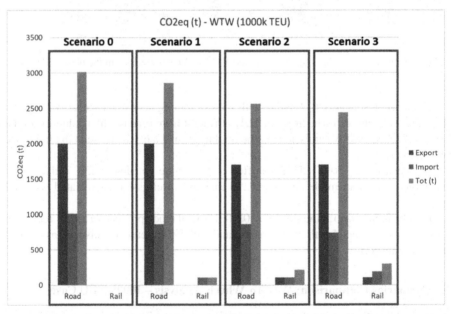

Fig. 7. Comparison of the 4 scenarios in the Well-To-Wheels analysis in the 1000k TEU case.

Also, for the 1000k TEU case, a comparison among Scenario 1, 2 and 3 with the do-nothing scenario (Scenario 0) is reported. Results highlight that in Scenario 1, shifting 75k TEU of freight transport from road to rail results in a 5% reduction in CO2eq (WTW) emissions in the road mode and a 3.5% increase in the rail mode.

In Scenario 2, 150k TEU are shifted to rail mode causing a 15% reduction in emissions from road mode and a 7.1% increase in emissions associated with rail mode.

Finally, in Scenario 3, the shift of 210k TEU to rail mode results in a 19% reduction in emissions associated with road transport and a 10% increase in emissions associated with rail transport.

4.3 Scenarios Comparison: Summary

The analysis shows that for the same number of TEU handled, rail transport allows a reduction in global CO2eq emissions (Well-To-Wheels) of 50% compared to road transport.

It is also noted that the limit of 75k TEU in the proposed configuration for rail transport produces a limited reduction in global emissions because the modal shift to rail is limited compared to the total volume of goods to be handled. Specifically, in the 1000k TEU scenarios the percentage reduction compared to the do-nothing scenario is smaller (−1.5% to −9%) than for the 600k TEU scenarios (−2.4% to −15%) (see Table 2).

Finally, the increasing of the capacity of rail transport from 75k TEU to 135k TEU (from 5 to 9 trains) reduces the overall impact by 15% and 9% in comparison with the do-nothing scenario, for the 600k and 1000k TEU cases respectively (see Table 2).

Table 2. Comparison of the 4 scenarios in the WTW analysis in the 600k and 1000k TEU cases.

Scenarios		600k TEU CO2eq (t)		1000k TEU CO2eq (t)	
0	Do-nothing	1807		3012	
1	Realistic-Regional	1763	−2.4%	2968	−1.5%
2	National	1571	−13.1%	2775	−7.9%
3	9 Trains (instead of 5)	1535	−15%	2740	−9%

5   Conclusion

Aim of the present study is to assess the CO2eq impact due to the shift of the container transport from road (trucks) to rail (electric trains). This case study focused on the Port of Naples, in the South of Italy. Different scenarios were identified in which mixed solutions for road and rail freight transport could replace the current scenario (freight transport by road only). Specifically, Scenario 0 is the Do-nothing scenario in which all goods enter/exit the Port by road; Scenario 1 named "Realistic-Regional" foresees a purely regional catchment area and, therefore, only Import freight flows interested in rail services. It is also assumed that the maximum freight flow on rail is 75,000 TEU (current annual limit with respect to the number of trains that can be handled); Scenario 2, identified as "National", foresees both Import and Export demand interested in rail services. It is foreseen, therefore, that rail freight transport is also shared in the Export phase; Scenario 3 assumes a higher number of trains per day that can be operated on the line. An increase from 5 to 9 trains per day is foreseen and therefore demand flows up to a maximum of 135,000 TEU per year by rail.

Additionally, the analyses have been carried out by assuming a 50% split between Import and Export (Statistical Bulletin 2018 - AdSPMTC) and assuming two growth scenarios: the first involving a movement of 600,000 TEU (Statistical Bulletin 2018 - AdSPMTC) and the second with an increase in the transport of goods of 40% (1 million TEU).

The analysis shows that for the same number of TEU handled, rail transport allows a reduction in global CO2eq emissions (Well-To-Wheels) of 50% compared to road transport.

It is important to highlight that the limit of 75k TEU in the proposed configuration for rail transport produces a limited reduction in global emissions because the modal shift to rail is limited compared to the total volume of goods to be handled.

Acknowledgements. Research in this paper has been funded by the Italian program PON AIM – Attraction and International Mobility, Linea 1 (AIM1877579–3-CUPD44I18000220006) and the funding have been provided by the Italian Ministry of the Education, University and Research (MIUR), Italy. Additionally, authors wish to thank University of Salerno for financial support under local grants 2019 - ORSA192341 and 2020 - ORSA205224.

References

1. IEA - International energy agency: Tracking Transport (2019)
2. EC. White paper: Roadmap to a single European transport area, towards a competitive and resource efficient transport system. COM (2011)
3. Huboyo, H.S., Handayani, W., Samadikun, B.P.: Potential air pollutant emission from private vehicles based on vehicle route. IOP conference series. Earth Environ. Sci. **70**, 012013 (2017)
4. Santiangeli, A., Fiori, C., Zuccari, F., Dell'Era, A., Orecchini, F., D'Orazio, A.: Experimental analysis of the auxiliaries consumption in the energy balance of a pre-series plug-in hybrid-electric vehicle. Energy. Procedia **45**, 779–788 (2014)
5. Orecchini, F., Santiangeli, A., Fiori, C.: Analisi energetica di un veicolo ibrido plug-in in un ciclo reale urbano (2012)
6. Fiori, C., Ahn, K., Rakha, H.: Power-based electric vehicle energy consumption model: model development and validation. Appl. Energy. **168**, 257–268 (2016)
7. Fiori, C., et al.: The effect of electrified mobility on the relationship between traffic conditions and energy consumption. Transp. Res. Part Transp. Environ. **67**, 275–290 (2019)
8. UIC IEA: Railway Handbook, Energy Consumption and CO2 Emissions (2017)
9. CEI-CIVES: Confronto delle emissioni di gas climalteranti di diverse tecnologie veicolari (2010)
10. ISPRA: Fattori di emissione atmosferica di CO2 e altri gas a effetto serra nel settore elettrico (2017)

How to Create a Cross-border Port Community by Networking Ports with Each Other: The Experimentation of the EasyLog System

Patrizia Serra[1]([✉]) [ID], Gianfranco Fancello[1] [ID], Riccardo Bozzo[2], and Andrea Zoratti[3]

[1] DICAAR – Department of Civil and Environmental Engineering and Architecture,
University of Cagliari, 09123 Cagliari, Italy
pserra@unica.it
[2] University of Genova, Genova, Italy
[3] Genova, Italy

Abstract. This paper describes the real-world experimentation of an innovative ICT (Information and Communication Technology) integrated system, the so-called EasyLog system, which enables the exchange of operational information in an orderly and secure way between five Tyrrhenian ports. The proposed system, dedicated to ro-ro transport, is highly innovative as it allows a set of ports to exchange operational information in a simple and secure way, also adapting the necessary technological equipment of the gate to the different local needs. The experimentation demonstrated the efficiency of the system in the exchange of embarkation/disembarkation lists between the ports concerned, demonstrating its suitability to share essential information for the purpose of optimizing port operations. The developed system can overcome the barriers that typically hinder the development of ICT solutions shared between ports through a structure that guarantees the autonomy of the individual local systems while ensuring their interconnection through the so-called EasyLog Connector. The lean automation of port gates using smart glasses for augmented reality represents another element of innovation, allowing easy and flexible automation even in poorly digitized ports, or where economic or operational constraints make traditional gate automation complex.

Keywords: Smart ports · ICT · Port innovation · Virtual gate automation · Smart glasses for augmented reality · Ro-ro tracking

1 Introduction

Digital-based technologies, in particular Information Technologies (IT) and Information Systems (IS), facilitating communication and decision-making processes, are widely recognized as a key factor for the efficiency of logistics systems and intermodal chains [1, 2]. Around two-thirds of logistic managers declare themselves aware of the need to revamp their business model to survive in the digital age [3].

© Springer Nature Switzerland AG 2021
O. Gervasi et al. (Eds.): ICCSA 2021, LNCS 12958, pp. 223–239, 2021.
https://doi.org/10.1007/978-3-030-87016-4_17

Particularly, in the port community, IT and IS are believed to facilitate monitoring and decision making and to enhance the acquisition and distribution of information, as well as efficiency and security in operations [4–7].

The port community can be defined as an intelligent community, where the port node is a point of convergence of a multiplicity of actors, actions, and information. Cooperation and information sharing through digitization, as well as high-quality information, are recognized to be crucial for the efficiency and safety of port operations [8, 9]. It is also worth noting that digitization is becoming more and more popular also to compensate for the lack of physical port infrastructures through the development of intangible infrastructures [10], thus overcoming the natural physical boundary of port systems by emphasizing booking, prevention, and forecasting activities.

An increasing number of ports have now independently initiated technological and digital upgrading [11], but mainly in the container sector. As for ports and terminals dedicated to rolling traffic, also called ro-ro ports, the levels of digitization are generally low, although several best practices are available. Extensive use of traditional methods of document exchange and manual management of the entire gate-in/gate-out procedure is still predominant in many ro-ro ports, as well as random or non-optimized management of parking areas. Likewise, automated control systems for the duration of the port stay are rare and so are computerized archives of port accesses, with important limits related to security issues. Although several independent port-related digitization processes can be found, they are mostly adopted within larger ports and transport companies. More importantly, digital integration between the various ports and operators is still lacking, albeit necessary to embrace a more holistic vision of the transport chain [12].

Traditionally, ports exchange a couple of institutional data with each other but tend not to exchange operational data, which instead would be essential for better management of port activities. For example, in the field of ro-ro transport, the possibility to know in advance from the port of origin the list of oncoming ro-ro units would allow better planning and management of port activities, areas and equipment, with consequent greater efficiency of logistics operations. Similarly, the advance knowledge of ro-ro vehicles arriving for boarding from the road would allow optimizing not only the control and acceptance operations at port gates but also a better planning of yard areas.

This paper describes the real-world experimentation of a newly developed integrated IT system, the so-called EasyLog system, for the optimized and secure management of gate operations and the secure exchange of information in and between five Tyrrhenian ports with different levels of digitization. This work represents the continuation of a previous paper [13] that described the operational context of the implementation of the EasyLog system and the functional requirements underlying its development.

The proposed integrated IT system, dedicated to ro-ro transport, represents an element of absolute innovation of its kind as, for the first time, it allows a set of ports to exchange operational information in a simple and secure way, also adapting the necessary technological gate equipment to the different local needs. Using a logistic metaphor, the port nodes of the EasyLog system can be assimilated to control points of a transport chain where the ro-ro cargo unit is read and the information transferred to the next node, so that it can prepare itself to welcome the oncoming cargo in the best possible way. The EasyLog system can allow coordinating the maritime connections between its ports with the implicitly expected result of improving cross-border mobility and encouraging the development of intermodality in the area.

The framework of the paper is as follows. Section 2 briefly describes the path of modernization of ports over the decades and the positioning of the EasyLog system. Section 3 describes the developed ICT integrated system, and its structure and functionalities. Section 4 introduces the test area. Section 5 describes the experimentation while Sect. 6 discusses its results. Finally, Sect. 7 concludes.

2   The Path of Digital Innovation of Ports over the Decades

Starting from the 1960s and until the 1980s, ports were mainly defined as industrial, as they were mostly a direct extension of the mining or manufacturing industry. In order for ports to become an integral part of the supply chain and a fundamental cog in not only industrial but also distribution activities, it is necessary to wait until the 1990s, when the growth of international markets and containerization, the relocation of production, and the development of emerging markets produced the lengthening of logistics chains and imposed the need for common standards and cooperation between the different actors involved.

Since the 1980s, the modernization of seaports has been shaped by digital innovation through three main stages of transformation [10]:

- first stage (1980s): transformation into paperless procedures (development of the first EDI-based port community system, development of maritime industry-specific UN/EDIFACT message standards, etc.)
- second stage (1990s–2000s): transformation into automated procedures (application of automatic identification systems AIS, introduction of radio-frequency identification for terminal operations, etc.). Mainly static information, lack of data exchanged in real time
- third stage (2010s–onwards): transformation into digital procedures to improve responsiveness and decision making and to support the ongoing interaction and connection between the actors involved (Internet of Things, big data, blockchain, artificial intelligence, digital twin, sensors, mobile technologies, cloud computing, machine learning, etc.). An ever-increasing number of ports are implementing Port Community Systems (PCS) to enable the targeted and secure exchange of information and increase cooperation within the port community.

Now, as supply chains become increasingly integrated and connected, the connectivity of stakeholders should be ensured not only within the single port community but also between the various nodes of the transport network [11]. The main obstacle to achieving this goal is no longer technological but rather linked to the resistance that some operators pose in changing the paradigm to their working approach: from a single activity approach to a process approach, from an individual approach to a system approach.

Several challenges have so far characterized and slowed down the development of shared digital solutions in the port community. Different levels of digital maturity between actors, missing standards, lack of systemic vision, the reluctance of operators to share information are some of the main obstacles which hinder the adoption of shared technological solutions in the port area [14, 15].

The innovative IT system presented in this paper tries to overcome the barriers above through the development of an integrated modular system that ensures the independence and autonomy of local systems while ensuring their simple interconnection through a shared information exchange protocol.

3   The EasyLog System

The conceptual structure underlying the EasyLog system originated from the need to share between ports of departure and destination some sets of information relating to goods moving on rolling stock. The driving idea was to design an IT system that could become a sort of standard model of communication between ports, aimed primarily at the rolling stock sector but open to use in other scenarios.

The basic functionalities of the system were developed to ensure the following requirements:

- interoperability with any ICT system already in use in the port
- data exchange capacity between ports equipped with different ICT systems (PCS, TOS – Terminal Operating Systems, ICT systems of shipping companies, etc.)
- future opening to additional ports
- use of open and extensible standards
- infrastructure not based on centralized supports, such as central servers or databases, to be maintained by third parties.

In line with these requirements, the EasyLog system is designed according to a modular and scalable structure in which each port independently manages its own local module. The main innovation lies in the concept of the EasyLog Connector. The latter is defined centrally to constitute the heart of the exchange system and is intended as a set of rules for data exchange, formatting, and availability of the data. The data are collected and processed in the local systems and subsequently transferred to the Connector for their analysis and distribution to the various actors (Fig. 1).

The Connector overcomes the need for a central server for data storage and allows ports to communicate with each other using a common language between the ports of origin and destination. The Connector is based on:

- resilience to input (different possibilities of data input depending on the available hardware environment)
- asynchronous connection for data exchange in "pull" mode (the data made available by the person who generates them are taken from the person who receives them)
- data exchange in the form of XML files with defined formatting schemes (XSD), universally readable

- remote access data repository via FTP protocol by the EasyLog user concerned.

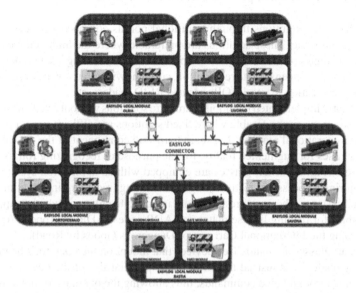

Fig. 1. Modular scheme of the EasyLog system. Source: EasyLog project

Each node independently provides both the software part relating to the interface of its local system with the EasyLog Connector, and the master data configuration of the other EasyLog nodes with which it is connected. This avoids centralized management of personal data and allows to independently manage the possible addition of new ports.

3.1   The Hardware and Software Components of the EasyLog Local Modules

The EasyLog local module combines hardware and software components installed at the various nodes that make up the EasyLog network. Such components include:

- hardware for reading vehicle license plates and other information of interest installed at the port gate
- dialogue software between the hardware and the information system
- Optical Character Recognition (OCR) software for automated license plate recognition
- software for processing and managing the data entered into the system
- hardware environment (computer, server) for the processing and management software
- hardware and software internet connection service for data exchange with other EasyLog nodes.

Depending on the local situation (purchase cost, budget availability, availability of physical spaces, integration with current procedures, local needs, importance attributed to any other data of interest on the security side - attendance detection, access authorizations, time slot booking checks or operational process), the EasyLog system allows to implement the automation of port gates with different levels of automation:

1. Fixed hardware solutions through traditional portals equipped with cameras, illuminators, bars, etc. These solutions are preferable where the high volumes handled justify the high cost of set-up and maintenance. The access gates can be equipped with cameras for license plate recognition, columns with intercom, cameras for driver identity verification, barcode, QRcode and RFID readers, etc.
2. Virtual gates implemented by mobile hardware solutions without fixed infrastructure. These solutions are preferable where fixed solutions are difficult to set up, both for cost and operational reasons. The main hardware component of the virtual gate are smart glasses for augmented reality, for the purpose of recognizing rolling stock in port areas (Fig. 2). Smart glasses are equipped with an application system capable of acquiring, processing, historicizing, transmitting, receiving information from/to external systems. They capture and record images and videos on which to apply OCR algorithms for reading license plates and ADR codes (ADR - European Agreement concerning the International Carriage of Dangerous Goods by Road).
The smart glasses are hands-free devices that mount on the operator's head and are robustly made for industrial use. One of the peculiarities of the device is that it is controlled through voice commands, thus allowing the operator to move freely and use the necessary tools and equipment, even while on the move. In this way the operator can maintain full awareness of the situation and maximum productivity. The smart glasses are equipped with an articulated arm that allows the operator to adapt them to his/her preferential eye. The viewer displays some applications that the operator can use for the recognition of vehicle and ADR license plates. They are also equipped with a satellite localization system, and wireless/mobile connectivity to allow communication to the back-end service.

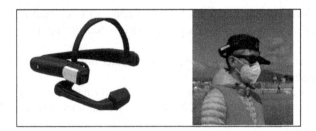

Fig. 2. Smart glasses device used in the virtual gate. Source: EasyLog project

The software component of the virtual gate includes two application modules: a software component on the smart glasses, and a back-office software component for user management, manual data input, data query/control, and data transmission/reception via the EasyLog Connector. The data collected and processed by the software component of the smart glasses are exchanged with the back-office component where they are processed and then transmitted to the EasyLog Connector.

The back-office software component is a web application and consists of the following macro functions:

- management of the truck announcement process
- creation of the loading lists based on the forecast of arrival
- import of cargo lists of incoming ships through the EasyLog Connector
- sending the loading lists of departing ships via the EasyLog Connector
- management of gate-in/gate-out activities of rolling stock
- management of embarkation/disembarkation activities of ro-ro ships
- management of the records of road haulers and terminal operators.

By managing the process of creating the loading/unloading lists, it will be possible to describe the list of ro-ro units expected to embark or disembark from the ship.

System users in the back-office component are profiled according to the following setting:

- operational users who introduce remote input via web interface (such as the registered haulier who enters/integrates data relating to his transport)
- supervisor users who perform data management and can intervene to modify/integrate data already written in the system
- administrator users for profile management, system configuration and parameterization.

3.2 Minimum Dataset and Information Acquisition

The minimum set of data necessary for the basic functionality of the EasyLog system consists of the following information:

- place of detection
- license plate (nationality + actual license plate)
- date and time of passage.

From an IT point of view, this set of information constitutes the unique key to identify an EasyLog data. The data can be acquired in different ways for each node, possibly even in several places within the same node, for example:

- gate in/gate out
- embarkation/disembarkation of the ship.

To this minimum dataset, the system allows to associate, even later, further information of interest such as vehicle length, damage detection, any ADR codes, etc.

Depending on the availability of information, three possible cases for data transfer are defined:

1. STANDARD CASE: the minimum dataset is known. The input information contains the minimum dataset and, in particular, the destination of the goods and therefore the destination node concerned. Once the input from the detection system (smart glasses, camera, etc.) has been acquired, the information relating to the node of destination is entered and a file is generated only for it.
2. BROADCAST CASE: the destination is unknown. Not being able to generate a unique identification flow for a single recipient node, a broadcast file associated with a minimum set of information is generated which remains in an "open" state and which is made available to all connected EasyLog nodes. When the destination is known, all files will be deleted except that of the destination node.
3. SPECIAL CASE: adding information. The system allows to update or integrate the information even after sending the data file to the destination node. In this case, a data transmission file will be prepared from the origin node containing the previous and additional data relating to the plate together with the "update" command.

Figure 3 illustrates the information flow considering the three cases.

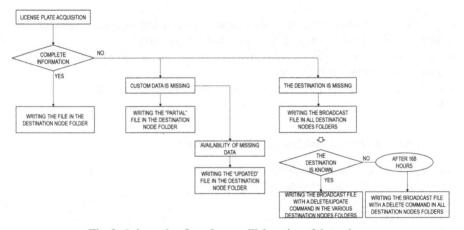

Fig. 3. Information flow. Source: Elaboration of the authors.

4   The Experimentation Area

The geographic context of intervention concerned five Tyrrhenian ports: Bastia, in France, and Livorno, Olbia, Portoferraio and Savona, in Italy. The five ports showed very different levels of automation and digitization. Some of them were already equipped with well-structured PCSs and terminal operating systems, such as Livorno and Bastia, whereas others lacked any IT managing system for rolling cargo, such as Portoferraio, Olbia, and Savona.

The choice of the specific configuration of the EasyLog local system was dictated by local needs, depending on the availability of physical spaces, integration with current operating procedures, and the economy of operation and installation. The hard configuration was chosen for the ports of Bastia and Livorno while the virtual automation for the ports of Olbia, Portoferraio and Savona (Fig. 4).

For a description of the state of fact and the technological needs identified in the five ports, the interested reader can refer to [13].

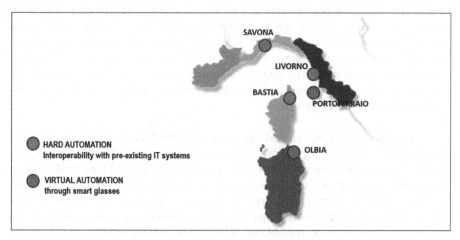

Fig. 4. EasyLog local modules. Source: EasyLog project

5   The Experimentation

The experimentation of the EasyLog integrated IT system was carried out in May 2021 in order to assess:

- the effectiveness of the system functionalities (advance notification of units arriving by sea at the port of destination, management of the records of road haulers and terminal operators, truck announcement)
- the effectiveness of the system to exchange data between the ports in the network using the EasyLog Connector
- the effectiveness of the innovative virtual gates operated through smart glasses to effectively manage gate-in/gate-out operations and boarding/disembarkation operations
- the interoperability of the EasyLog system with any IT systems (including any automated gates) already in place in the port.

It should be noted that license plate reading activities are typically carried out under controlled conditions with fixed cameras, with ad hoc optics and lighting. Given the innovative nature of the virtual gate operated through smart glasses and the lack of previous experience regarding its degree of accuracy, and also considering the variable nature of the scanning conditions that characterize its operations, the experimentation also had to evaluate the aspects of accuracy and reliability of the system in order to introduce any corrections that would allow to optimize its performance.

The experimentation was carried out in two phases:

- Phase 1: virtual testing. A preliminary trial was performed in a laboratory environment by simulating the five port nodes, and related data acquisition and sharing
- Phase 2: real-world testing. A field trial was performed in situ at the five port nodes with the involvements of real port operators and transporters. The field trials were carried out in a first phase under standard conditions and in a second phase by operating in critical conditions through stress tests. In particular, two days of severe bad weather in the port of Olbia made it possible to test the operation of the smart glasses device even in critical environmental conditions characterized by pouring rain, gusts of wind and significantly reduced brightness.

The experimentation was carried out considering the four maritime corridors displayed in Fig. 5. Considering the maritime corridors in the experimentation was fundamental to allow the complete traceability of the information and logistic flow along the entire maritime corridor that connects the port of origin with the port of destination. The trial covered the entire process from the moment the haulier books access to port x to embark a semi-trailer destined for port y, until the moment the same semi-trailer is unloaded at port y and made available for collection by another hauler.

The users involved in the testing of the system were trucking companies, terminal operators and the port authorities involved, at different levels, in the activities of gate-in/gate-out, loading/unloading and delivery/collection of ro-ro units in the port:

- shippers reserve their ship voyages
- trucking companies announce the delivery and/or withdrawal of their semi-trailers
- terminal operators manage gate-in/gate-out and loading/unloading activities
- port security operators manage gate-in/gate-out at port gates.

By way of example, this paper describes the information flow that characterized the testing of the EasyLog system along the Olbia-Livorno maritime corridor. This corridor constitutes an interesting case example for experimentation purposes as it connects two ports that are very different from the point of view of digitization.

On one side of the corridor is the port of Livorno. Livorno is a terminalized multipurpose port with a high level of automation. It is already equipped with an advanced PCS, the so-called TPCS - Tuscan Port Community System, which facilitates the exchange of information between the multiple operators operating within the port (terminal operators, port authorities, customs agencies, forwarders, etc.), and with a port monitoring system, the so-called Monica - Monitoring and Control Application, which integrates a multiplicity of information sources deriving from applications or sensor nodes, to provide a series of value-added services to the port community.

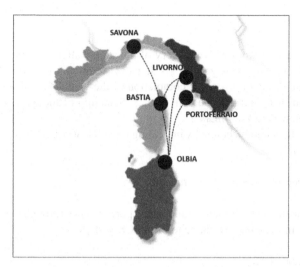

Fig. 5. Maritime corridors tested. Source: EasyLog project

The implementation of the EasyLog system at the port of Livorno concerned its connection with the other EasyLog nodes through the Connector, and the digitization of a series of services previously digitized only for containers such as the arrival notice at the terminal and the registration of transit, embarkation and disembarkation for rolling goods, also allowing the optimization of related yard operations.

The experimentation at the port of Livorno involved the terminal LTM and its gate, named Galvani Gate, which is automated through a physical portal equipped with OCR cameras, and managed through its Gate Transit Security (GTS) system.

On the other side of the corridor is the port of Olbia. Olbia is not currently equipped with any telematic support for the management of the physical and information flows relating to Ro-Ro traffic, and access to its port area is manned by terminal staff. The implementation of the EasyLog system at the port of Olbia introduced gate automation through the creation of a mobile gate operated by smart glasses and the development of a back-office app that enables various functions: truck announcement, ship announcement, management of loading and disembarkation list, connection with the other EasyLog nodes through the Connector.

Below is a schematic description of the activities and actors involved in the testing of the system functions in the two ports of Livorno and Olbia.

Port of Livorno - Arrival of the semi-trailer by road and boarding on the ship to Olbia

Forwarder:

– Using the "Truck booking" form of the TPCS, enters the booking to embark a semi-trailer at the LTM terminal with destination Olbia and engages the trucking company to deliver the unit.

Hauler:

- Reserves the port slot for the delivery of the semi-trailer by completing the truck announcement using a wizard in six steps (1. terminal selection, 2. selection of the estimated time of arrival, 3. completion of the vehicle and driver information, 4. selection of the units to be delivered, 5. Selection of the units to be picked, 6. Confirmation of the summary).
- Completes the announcement by indicating the truck and the driver who will deliver the semi-trailer.

Gate Transit Security system - Galvani Gate:

- Records the transit of the semi-trailer at the port entrance through the OCR cameras.
- Makes the information available to the TPCS system.

Terminal operator - LTM:

- Gate-in the semi-trailer by verifying data, driver, and port of destination.
- Proceeds to board the semi-trailer.
- Declares the completion of boarding and departure of the ship on the TPCS.

EASYLOG Connector:

- Sends the cargo list of the incoming ship to the port of Olbia using the EasyLog Connector.

Port of Olbia - Arrival of the ro-ro unit by ship and departure by road

EASYLOG Connector:

- receives from the port of Livorno the loading list of the ship(s) arriving in Livorno from Olbia.

Back-office operator:

- makes available the forecast disembarkation list sent by the port of Livorno by displaying it on the smart glasses (the forecast disembarkation list coincides with the embarkation list of the port of Livorno)

Port operators:

- using smart glasses, the operator in the apron opens the disembarkation operations on the ship arrived from Livorno.
- using smart glasses, verify the received disembarkation list and confirm the ro-ro units actually disembarked.

Back-office operator:

- at the end of disembarkation operations, makes available the final disembarkation list of semi-trailers now available for withdrawal.

Hauler:

- using the "Truck announcement" service, announces its arrival at the port to collect the semi-trailer arrived by ship from Livorno.
- completes the announcement by indicating the tractor and driver who will collect the unit.

Back-office application:

- makes available the list of oncoming trucks for withdrawal.

Port security:

- using smart glasses, verifies and accepts the tractor for the withdrawal of the semi-trailer.
- using smart glasses, records the transit of the semi-trailer as it exits the port gate.
- declares the gate-out of the semi-trailer.
- as the trucks arrive in port, views the list of ro-ro units left in the yard and ready for withdrawal.

6 Experimentation Results

The EasyLog Connector was found to be effective in the exchange of embarkation/disembarkation lists between the port of origin and destination, proving adequate for the sharing of essential information for the purpose of optimizing port operations.

The experimentation has generally given encouraging results as regards the potential deriving from the use of smart glasses in the management of port operations. Some minor operational problems emerged related to the novelty of the product, which in any case did not compromise its good functioning and were indeed useful to introduce some precautions in use.

In the management of gate-in/gate-out operations at port gates and embarkation/disembarkation in the port apron, the smart glasses device has proved effective for capturing and recognizing the number plates of stationary and moving vehicles up to an average speed of 30 km/h (although peaks close to 50 km/h have been recorded). As for the perspective angle, the smart-glasses device managed to capture and recognize the license plate correctly, even with perspective angles of 40°. During boarding or disembarking operations, it was observed that when the operator is positioned sideways to the loading ramp of the ship, the license plates of the vehicles can be tilted in many ways with respect to the camera of the smart glasses. This aspect made it necessary to perform a calibration of the device before starting the plate detection operations to improve the reliability of the recognition (the plate is still read but with a lower "confidence" of the result compared to the case of the calibrated smart glasses).

The device was also tested in various lighting conditions and during a thunderstorm. In both cases, the performance of the device did not undergo significant variations as the environmental conditions changed. Image acquisitions were made with stationary vehicles in a range from 25 to 7800 lx. In particular, the system correctly recognized the number plates of all vehicles both during the tests carried out just before sunset (average number of lux in the environment = 1200) and during sunset (average number of lux in the environment = 25). In case of rain, there was a range of variation between 100 and 700 lx. Similarly, the microphone for voice control was able to acquire voice commands without major problems, despite the noisy background that typically characterizes port activities. The only voice problem encountered was in the case of strong gusts of wind whose hiss made it difficult for smart glasses to recognize voice commands, a condition that was aggravated by the use of an FFP2[1] mask for COVID19 protection by the operator. This problem was solved by adopting a simple additional microphone (a mobile phone earphone) connected via a standard 3.5 mm jack audio cable to the device and placing the microphone inside the FFP2 mask.

Two terminal operators, three maritime companies and three port authorities took part in the experimentation. The involvement in the trial of the safety and security staff of the ports allowed moving and operating safely in the port area during the experimentation activity. At the end of the experimentation, the operators who took part in the trial were asked to express an opinion on the device tested and its functionalities. All the operators interviewed expressed a positive opinion on the potential use of the device in the port area. As for the usability of the smart-glasses device, it lived up to expectations. The operators found the device light in wearing and comfortable thanks to its articulated arm that can be adapted to the different needs of a field operator. During the trial, the operators were able to choose in front of which eye to place the display, the height and the distance of the display, and to rotate the display to move it away from the visual field when not used.

6.1 Limitations of the Research

The experimentation conducted was primarily aimed at testing the functioning of the proposed ICT system for the purposes of its operational feasibility. Although from a qualitative point of view the experimentation gave encouraging results regarding the validity of the proposed solution and its applicability to the operational port context, the limited number of tests carried out so far does not allow to provide a quantitative statistical evaluation of the reliability of the system. To this end, a broader experimental campaign is being planned, which envisages the direct involvement of at least three ports. The new experimental campaign will also provide for the recognition of foreign license plates and container codes and will evaluate the reliability of the system from a statistical-quantitative perspective through the assessment of various performance indicators (rate

---

[1] Personal protective equipment that prevents the user from inhaling aerosols, vapors and gases that are dangerous to health. It guarantees a minimum filtration of 94% and internal penetration of no more than 8%.

of correct recognition of license plates, reduction of the recognition rate in case of bad weather, correct recognition rate according to the transit speed of the vehicles at the gate, license plate reading speed according to the operator's position with respect to the vehicle, etc.).

7 Conclusions and Future Prospects

This study has described the experience of the EasyLog project, which designed, developed and tested an innovative ICT integrated system that enables the exchange of operational information in an orderly and secure way between five ports in the Tyrrhenian area. The developed system has three strong elements of innovation:

- differently from the existing ICT port systems developed as autonomous and closed systems, it can enable the interconnection of different ports, thus allowing the secure and orderly exchange of information, and improving efficiency, reliability and security in operations along the maritime transport chain
- it can overcome the barriers that typically hinder the development of shared ICT solutions among ports (a.o., different digital maturity levels, missing standards, lack of willingness to share data, etc.) through a structure that guarantees the autonomy of individual local systems while guaranteeing their interconnection through the so-called EasyLog Connector
- it can allow easy and flexible automation even in ports poorly digitized, or where economic or operational constraints make traditional gate automation complex, by introducing the innovative virtual gate created using smart glasses.

The proposed ICT integrated port system together with its Connector and virtual gates were tested in the five ports and along four maritime corridors to verify their functionality.

The Connector proved to be effective in the exchange of embarkation/disembarkation lists between the port of origin and destination, proving to be adequate for the sharing of essential information for the purpose of optimizing port operations. The experimentation gave encouraging results as regards the potential deriving from the use of smart glasses in the management of port operations. Some minor operational problems emerged related to the novelty of the product, which in any case did not compromise its good functioning and were useful for introducing some precautions in use. Given the challenging conditions of use and the experimental nature of the proposed system, the proposed solution turned out to be a good compromise between the following characteristics: usability, simplicity of operational flows, speed in completing scanning activities, and response times of user feedback.

Although a wider experimental campaign is necessary for the statistical-quantitative evaluation of the reliability of the system, the experimentation has confirmed the operational potential of the developed system and its applicability to the port context. The positive results of the experimentation pave the way for the future implementation of the system with the expansion of its scope of application. The enlargement of the EasyLog network with the inclusion of other nodes such as interports, backport logistics areas, distribution centres, etc., could guarantee real traceability of all the salient moments of the movement of a rolling vehicle, allowing an approach to optimize the entire logistics chain, and no longer only the maritime branch.

Acknowledgements. This research is based upon the EASYLOG Project funded under the Interreg IT-FR Maritime Program 2014–2020 (The EasyLog project website is available at http://int erreg-maritime.eu/web/EasyLog). The authors would like to thank all the partners and subjects who took part in the project. A special thanks goes to Alexio Picco, Simone Siria and Matteo Tebaldi of the CIRCLE Group, Matteo Apollonio and Massimo Bagozzi of the DBA Group, and Giuseppe Scapellato and Dino Dentone of DATACH, who contributed to the development of the EasyLog system and implemented its local modules in the ports of Olbia, Livorno, Portoferraio, and Savona.

References

1. Belfkih, A., Duvallet, C., Sadeg, B.: The internet of things for smart ports: application to the Port of Le Havre. In: International Conference on Intelligent Platform for Smart Port - IPaSPort 2017 (2017)
2. Fernández, P., et al.: SmartPort - a platform for sensor data monitoring in a seaport based on FIWARE. Sensors **16**(3), 417 (2016)
3. https://www.forbes.com/sites/insights-penske/2018/09/04/the-4-forces-transforming-logist ics-supply-chain-and-transportation-today/?sh=3cbdcef6b752
4. Fancello, G., Serra, P., Schintu, A., Zoratti, A.: Performance evaluation of a tracking system for intermodal traffic: an experimentation in the Tyrrhenian area. Eur. Transp. (2020, in press)
5. Baron, M.L., Mathieu, H.: PCS interoperability in Europe: a market for PCS operators? Int. J. Logist. Manag. **24**(1), 117–129 (2013)
6. Van Baalen, P., Zuidwijk, R., Van Nunen, J.: Port inter-organizational information systems: capabilities to service global supply chains. Found. Trends Technol. Inf. Oper. Manag. **2**(2–3), 81–241 (2009)
7. Posti, A., Hakkinen, J., Tapaninen, U.: Promoting information exchange with a port community system–case Finland. Int. Supply Chain Manag. Collab. Pract. **4**, 455–473 (2011)
8. Carlan, V., Sys, C., Vanelslander, T.: How port community systems can contribute to port competitiveness: developing a cost–benefit framework. Res. Transp. Bus. Manag. **19**, 51–64 (2016)
9. Zhao, W., Goodchild, A.V.: The impact of truck arrival information on container terminal rehandling. Transp. Res. Part E Logist. Transp. Rev. **46**(3), 327–343 (2010)
10. Heilig, L., Schwarze, S., Voß, S.: An analysis of digital transformation in the history and future of modern ports. In: Proceedings of the 50th Hawaii International Conference on System Sciences (HICSS). IEEE (2017)
11. Jović, M., Kavran, N., Aksentijević, S., Tijan, E.: The transition of Croatian seaports into smart ports. In: 42nd International Convention on Information and Communication Technology, Electronics and Microelectronics – MIPRO, pp. 1386–1390. IEEE (2019)
12. Riedl, J., Delenclos, F.X., Rasmussen, A.: To Get Smart, Ports Go Digital. The Boston Consulting Group (2018). https://www.bcg.com/it-it/publications/2018/to-get-smart-ports-go-digital.aspx. Accessed Apr 2021
13. Serra, P., Fancello, G.: Use of ICT for more efficient port operations: the experience of the EASYLOG project. In: Gervasi, O., et al. (eds.) ICCSA 2020. LNCS, vol. 12255, pp. 3–14. Springer, Cham (2020). https://doi.org/10.1007/978-3-030-58820-5_1

14. Heilig, L., Voß, S.: Information systems in seaports: a categorization and overview. Inf. Technol. Manag. **18**(3), 179–201 (2016). https://doi.org/10.1007/s10799-016-0269-1
15. Yang, Y., Zhong, M., Yao, H., Yu, F., Fu, X., Postolache, O.: Internet of things for smart ports: technologies and challenges. IEEE Instrum. Meas. Mag. **21**(1), 34–43 (2018)

Can the Blockchain Facilitate the Development of an Interport Community?

Patrizia Serra[1]([⊠]) [ID], Gianfranco Fancello[1] [ID], Roberto Tonelli[2] [ID],
and Lodovica Marchesi[2] [ID]

[1] DICAAR – Department of Civil and Environmental Engineering and Architecture,
University of Cagliari, 09123 Cagliari, Italy
pserra@unica.it
[2] DMI – Department of Mathematics and Computer Science, University of Cagliari,
09123 Cagliari, Italy

Abstract. Seaports are part of a complex and information-intensive maritime supply chain that includes a set of organizations and operators who need to exchange a large amount of information and data with each other. As supply chains become increasingly integrated and connected, the connectivity of stakeholders must be ensured not only within individual ports but also between ports. This paper explores the application prospects and practical implications of the application of Blockchain technology for the establishment of an interport community within which different ports organized as a network can exchange information and data in a secure and effective way. With the support of SWOT (Strengths, Weaknesses, Opportunities, Threats) analysis, this paper addresses several research questions concerning the practical impacts, benefits, pros and cons, economic and technical barriers related to the implementation of Blockchain technology to support the creation of an interport community.

Keywords: Blockchain · Port 4.0 · Inter-port connectivity · Smart port

1 Introduction

In the framework of the 4.0 revolution, digital transformation is of utmost importance for port and maritime logistics. Particularly, as crucial nodes in supply chains, seaports are required to constantly innovate and evolve in order to keep up with technological changes and remain competitive. Since the 1980s, the modernization of seaports has been shaped by digital innovation through three main stages of transformation:

- first stage (1980s): transformation into paperless procedures (development of the first EDI-based port community system, development of maritime industry-specific UN/EDIFACT message standards, etc.)
- second stage (1990s–2000s): transformation into automated procedures (application of automatic identification systems AIS, introduction of radio-frequency identification for port operations, etc.)

O. Gervasi et al. (Eds.): ICCSA 2021, LNCS 12958, pp. 240–251, 2021.
https://doi.org/10.1007/978-3-030-87016-4_18

- third stage (2010s–onwards): transformation into digital procedures to improve responsiveness and decision making (sensors, mobile technologies, cloud computing, machine learning, etc.), and to support the ongoing interaction and connection between the actors involved.

Now, as supply chains become increasingly integrated and connected, it is essential to ensure the connectivity of stakeholders not only within the single port but also between the various nodes of the transport network [1, 2]. In particular, seaports are part of a complex and information-intensive maritime supply chain that includes a set of organizations and operators that are connected and distributed [3]. However, several challenges have so far characterized and slowed down the development of shared digital solutions in the port community: different levels of digital maturity between actors, missing standards, reluctance of operators to participate and share information, etc. [4]. The recently much debated Blockchain technology could offer interesting opportunities in this regard and is believed to have a huge impact on the future of the digitization of port and maritime logistics [5].

Blockchain is defined as a digital ledger, decentralized and distributed, shared and agreed on a peer-to-peer network, where transactions are recorded and added in chronological order with the aim of creating permanent and tamper-proof records [6]. Whatever the sector of application, Blockchain technology allows for more secure tracking of all types of transactions (money transactions, data transactions, information transactions, etc.), reducing delays, additional costs and human errors [7]. Blockchain is designed to achieve decentralization, real-time peer-to-peer operation, anonymity, transparency, irreversibility and integrity in a widely applicable manner [8]. In the context of shipping, Blockchain technology is potentially a solution to the problem of distrust among players, as it does not rely on commercial third parties, but on a network of peers [9]. It is also believed to have the potential to positively affect maritime processes [10] and accelerate the physical flow of goods [11].

The growing interest towards Blockchain technology in the shipping sector is also evidenced by the development of the related scientific literature. In order to have an overview of the quantitative impact (in terms of number of published works) the topic of Blockchain in the maritime sector is having on the scientific literature, in early December 2020 a preliminary keyword search was carried out using the Scopus database. The search identified 61 studies (including only journal articles and conference proceedings), all published starting from 2017, which contained the following terms in the title, abstract or keywords: Blockchain + shipping, Blockchain + maritime, Blockchain + port(s). Most of these studies seem to focus primarily on the main trends and challenges, technical aspects, general opportunities and impacts related to state-of-the-art technologies, while the practical implications of adopting Blockchain solutions for specific port processes, as well as the actual repercussions for the different actors, seem to need further investigation, also considering that the technology is still new and immature [12, 13]. In fact, some trials and Blockchain pilot projects are already available in the maritime industry. However, most of them are linked to autonomous initiatives of industrial operators or single ports. For example, Maersk and IBM have decided to jointly build their own Blockchain solution to reduce the cost of global shipping by eliminating inefficiencies resulting from paper-based processes [14] while the ports of Rotterdam and Antwerp are developing their own Blockchains. In this regard, it should be emphasized that as long as Blockchain exists only in individual ports or in small groups of operators, its benefits will not be fully explored and exploited. In fact, in increasingly connected and integrated markets, the new era of digitization concerns not only the port's ability to become smart, but above all the ability to do so by connecting to larger networks.

In light of the above, this study intends to add to the existing literature by exploring the application prospects and practical implications of Blockchain technology for the construction of an interport community within which different ports organized as a network can exchange information and data in a secure and effective way.

2   Case Study

The idea for this exploratory study was born in the framework of a previous research project, the so-called EasyLog project, which designed and implemented an ICT system for the exchange and sharing of operational data between five ro-ro ports in the upper Tyrrhenian Sea [1]. The EasyLog system was designed according to a modular structure in which each port had its own customized local module for managing gate-in gate-out operations, and the five local modules communicated with each other using a shared set of rules for data exchange, formatting and availability. The EasyLog system allowed the exchange of data both within the port (between haulers, port authorities, and terminal operators) and between the five ports of the network. Despite the important innovation introduced by the EasyLog system, it did not include all the parties involved in the process (for example, shipping companies), it concerned only a limited number of operational information related to gate operations but no sensitive data, its process phases were not systematically linked between the stakeholders, thus leaving some room for improvements that Blockchain technology can potentially achieve. Figure 1 illustrates a simplified flow diagram relating to the diverse activities, and related information flows and operators involved, that could potentially benefit from the use of Blockchain for the purpose of creating an interport community between port "x" and port "y".

With the support of SWOT (Strengths, Weaknesses, Opportunities and Threats) analysis, this paper analyzes the application prospects to exploit the advantages of Blockchain to facilitate the secure exchange of information between the ports and the parties involved in an interport logistics chain.

3   Research Questions

It should be emphasized that, to the best of the authors' knowledge, no available studies have been found that explore the practical implications and impacts of the application of Blockchain technology for the establishment of an interport community.

This exploratory study tries to provide insights on the topic by addressing the following research questions:

- Can Blockchain facilitate the development of an integrated port community?

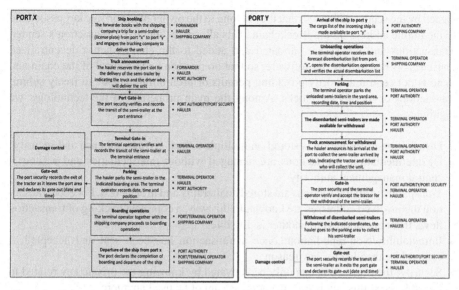

Fig. 1. Procedural and informative workflow in a ro-ro interport logistics chain. Source: elaboration of the authors

- Which logistic activities in an interport community would be most impacted by Blockchain and in which way?
- What parties involved in a port community would benefit the most from Blockchain?
- What are the pros and cons of introducing Blockchain in a port community?

4 Blockchain and Smart Contracts

In order to better understand why Blockchain technology and Smart Contracts can be helpful for port logistics and transportation we first recall a few basic notions and properties to grasp insights on how to use them for the establishment of an interport community avoiding to deeply dive into unessential details for this work.

The Blockchain is a distributed, shared database whose past history is unalterable. It is open to anyone who wants to contribute by installing the management software and a copy of it on their computer (thus becoming a node of the network). It is equipped with mechanisms to reach consensus among all nodes on the information to be stored, so that no one can take control of it, not even generating a mass of fictitious nodes. The security of the Blockchain technology is such that, even if only one copy of the Blockchain remained, from this copy it could be restarted by reconstructing all past operations. Furthermore, if one were to alter the past history of such a single copy, this would still require a prohibitive number of calculations. Basically, Blockchain can be thought of as an automatic, non-centralized, inexpensive, and secure way to gain trust.

Transaction and all the related information are cryptographically signed and packed into temporally ordered blocks which are all cryptographically linked to the previous one by means of hashing to create an inalterable chain of information. Transactions are signed by the sender address so that they belong to the owner of the private key associated to the public address on the Blockchain. This allows to "identify" transaction's sender. Transactions and blocks are validated and added to the chain when a decentralized consensus is reached by the software, so that no one can be in control of the chain and there is not central authority providing permits or prohibiting anyone to freely submit transactions or to validate blocks. Among the main properties of the technology, we highlight:

- Distribution: information is stored on multiple nodes, giving resilience and security
- Disintermediation: transactions are managed without intermediaries and without a central management authority
- Transparency: all transactions are stored unalterably and in clear text. For each transaction the involved addresses are known. In this way, a complete tracking of transaction flows from one address to another is possible
- Immutability/Non-repudiation: once a transaction has been sent and accepted, it cannot be cancelled for any reason
- Security: the transaction can only be activated by knowing the private key related to the address. If this key is lost, the address cannot be used anymore
- "Notarial" storage: it is possible to use special transactions to store information on the Blockchain. This information (usually limited to a few tens of Bytes per transaction) is used to certify the existence and integrity of a document, or set of documents, at a certain date
- Programmability: complex actions can be programmed and executed by on chain software called Smart Contracts (SC), which are also fully verifiable and can be activated by multiple parties involved (with their respective private keys). Ethereum is the currency that offers the most features

Another fundamental property of the Blockchain is that it can be the infrastructure for running Smart Contracts. Smart Contracts are automated contracts, in which participants prove their identity and approval of the contract with their private key. According to [15] a Smart Contract is a computerized protocol for executing transactions, which executes the terms of a contract.

The general objectives of a Smart Contract are to satisfy the usual contractual conditions (such as payment terms, rights, confidentiality, and even enforcement), to minimize both deliberate and accidental exceptions, and to minimize the need for trusted intermediaries. A Smart Contract is basically a program, which runs on a secure medium (trusted) and is itself secure. It takes digital signatures of participants, and other information, from secure sources as input. In output, it transfers cryptocurrency amounts, can activate other contracts, record information or connect to external systems. Smart Contracts also often have a user interface that emulates the jargon and logic of contract clauses.

Since the execution of a software program is deterministic and immutable, with the same input and program status, the code can be considered a contract. Once the contractual clauses are correctly inserted in the code of a Smart Contract, and this is accepted by the contractors, the effects are no longer linked to their will or the action of intermediaries.

Obviously, the code must have no errors, must be executed correctly and must not be modified; the inputs to the code must come from safe and identified sources; the code outputs must achieve the desired effects. In other words, there must be a mechanism that guarantees the trust that the contractors place in the smart contract. This is granted by the Blockchain, which provides all the aforementioned guarantees without the need for a central authority. The introduction of Ethereum in 2015 led to a Blockchain and a low-level language, along with various high-level and effectively usable languages (e.g., Solidity and Yul), to extensively code and execute Turing-complete Smart Contracts [16].

With respect to the application of such technology to port logistic and shipping it is now clear that the Blockchain can contribute to the digital innovation in a number of ways, from granting transparency and unforgeability of records to data security and trust, to the automation of many operations and checks by means of Smart Contracts execution, to managing authorizations and permits for different actors by mean of Blockchain addresses and the related private keys.

Another immediate advantage provided by the technology is supply chain flows tracking with respect to physical, financial and logical information flows. In the next section we discuss all these and other aspects of the application of Blockchain technology for the establishment of an interport community by means of a detailed SWOT analysis.

5 SWOT Analysis

It should be emphasized that, to the best of the authors' knowledge, no available studies have been found that explore the practical implications of Blockchain technologies for what concerns strengths, weaknesses, opportunities and threats in managing port logistics and in particular for the case of an interport community. In the following, we present a SWOT analysis for this specific case examining how the Blockchain can be used to concretely contribute to enhance port logistics. Table 1 identifies the main features

Table 1. SWOT analysis of Blockchain technology

Strengths	Weaknesses
• Trust	• Governance
• Security	• Scalability
• Transparency	• Adoption
• Tamper proof	• Redundancy
• Identity management	• Compliancy to GDPR
Opportunities	**Threats**
• Traceability	• Privacy
• Disintermediation	• Legal aspects and normative
• Cost reduction	• Connection to out-of-chain
• Supply chain flow	data
management	
• Coordination	

contributing to the four dimensions of the SWOT analysis. The individual aspects are then discussed in the following paragraphs.

5.1 Strengths

Trust: In ports it is important that companies in the supply chain can trust each other to share information and increase efficiency in shared processes. A major obstacle to data sharing is that a leakage in sensitive information can affect companies' business. Managing the information flow of shared data with the Blockchain on the contrary can provide a trusted and unforgeable corpus of data records that can help in clearly identify responsibilities and sources of damages, delays, misconducts, errors and other aspects.

Security: Records stored into Blockchain blocks are secure since a double encryption mechanism is in place [17]. First, transactions are validated by means of private keys that make extensive use of cryptography. Thus, transactions cannot be altered and are secure. Second, each block is cryptographically chained to the previous one so that any attempt of records manipulation in a block is mirrored in changes in all the following blocks, so that after the addition of some block at the end of the chain data can be considered secured.

Transparency: Shipping companies typically keep their data reserved and secret in order to keep a competitive advantage over their competitors. On the other hand, port logistics can benefit from data sharing for planning in advance, for monitoring and coordinating operations and so on. Recording data on the Blockchain directly provides transparency and renders information directly and immediately available to authorized actors [17]. This is especially useful when the information needs to be updated and quickly broadcast to all the actors. With Blockchain solutions, data is shared in real-time, and payment can be made and confirmed almost instantly.

Tamper Proof: Transparency is also provided by the tamper proof of Blockchain data. In fact, once data are loaded into the blocks they cannot be manipulated or altered in any way. All the actors involved in port logistic will benefit from this certainty of information not only in real time but also for what concerns historical data for retrospective analysis for process improvement.

Identity Management: Given that all writing operations on Blockchain are managed through Blockchain addresses which can operate only using the associated private keyword all operations can directly be reconducted to the address' owners providing a transparent a built-in mechanism for managing identities. Furthermore, Smart Contracts can be written so that only specific addresses are allowed to perform specific operations providing a built-in secure mechanism for managing permits and authorizations.

5.2 Weaknesses

Governance: The missing of a central authority can be an advantage but also a problem. In some cases, in fact there is the need for organizing some governance at different levels.

In port logistic, once multiple participants are connected, questions will arise about the governance of the system, how and who is authorized to access the data (accessibility), and who owns the data (ownership) shared in the Blockchain. Furthermore, in the case of a private Blockchain solution, there is the question of who is the neutral party in charge of setting the network rules and granting access authorization.

Scalability: Blockchain technology suffers from scalability and performance problems: all nodes in the chain have to process all transactions and this may present a problem with large-scale and especially global implementations [8]. In a large interport community the number of actors and operation involved can be cumbersome and peaks of activities in short time (e.g. load or download of a ferry carrier) can become critical. The adoption of the correct Blockchain solution must take into account this problematic so that the proper transaction rates and throughputs must be assured to match logistic needs.

Adoption: The adoption of Blockchain technology can be difficult due to technical and functional aspects. Implementing Blockchain technology on a very large scale would require a great deal of computing power. Currently, only a few larger companies seem to be experimenting with Blockchain. Eventually, they will create a platform that SMEs could also connect to. SMEs, however, may be reluctant to participate in the platforms of these large players. Also, because different companies' databases may use different standards or languages to store data, interaction may prove difficult. Addressing this would require resources and time to align databases or invest in a shared language for the Blockchain.

Redundancy: Blockchain provides a redundant distributed ledger replicated on all the nodes. If this is an advantage for what concerns security, transparency and trust, it can be seen as a waste of resources which could be leveraged to other purposes. This may become particularly problematic when storage and computational power are critical resources for the actors involved.

Compliance to GDPR: In the framework of EU GDPR (General Data Protection Regulation) all sensitive data pertaining to private citizens or companies must be treated according to a strict regulation. In particular, citizens and companies have the right to be forgotten, so that upon a specific request all organization keeping citizens' or companies' data must remove them from their public databases. In the case of Blockchain all data recorded on the ledger cannot be removed or canceled anymore. This means that a specific strategy must be adopted from the very beginning to decide and plan what data must be recorded on-chain and what data must be kept off-chain.

5.3 Opportunities

Traceability: The Blockchain natively stores record in a temporally ordered sequence of valid transactions so that all operations related to port logistic can immediately be tracked, like load or unload of tracks and containers into shipments and other physical movements. But also, other events, like business agreements, buy and sell, signing of insurance contracts, can be easily included into the Blockchain tracking system, strongly reducing monitoring and auditing costs [17].

Disintermediation and Cost Reduction: Currently many of the port logistic transactions are carried out by e-mail or telephone calls, there are several intermediaries involved, with consequent increases in costs and possible human errors. As for the Blockchain and the smart contracts, these promise an increase in efficiency, a reduction in brokerage costs and greater neutrality in the regulation of contracts. In fact, since all the relevant events of a supply chain are recorded in a certain and immutable way, all the notified parties can immediately plan the consequent actions, including any payments [18].

Supply Chain Flow Management: The Blockchain is the ideal technology for supply chain management, where the supply can be physical or simply information flow [18]. Instead of exchanging documentation, the stakeholders involved in the process are given permission to access the blocks where the data is stored. This leads to the creation of unique and shared information that can be accessed in real-time and with lower transaction costs. The process can be further accelerated by involving stakeholders external to the process (banks and insurance companies). The database can be further enhanced by using Internet of Things (IoT) devices and connecting them as Blockchain nodes. Furthermore, by connecting smart devices, it is also possible to fully automate the process.

Coordination: Currently, each freight operator has its own management platform and data set, with limited interconnection capacities. Operators operate with a limited view of the situation and of the impact of each element on the overall performance of the supply chain. Container supply chain information is dispersed. With Blockchain, transport operators can securely share their information with their trading partners through a reliable, multi-layered data access architecture. This would foster interoperability, efficiency and productivity. Furthermore, different Blockchain networks could interact with each other around the world [18].

5.4 Threats

Privacy: User privacy could be reduced because all nodes contain a complete copy of the ledger and there is no central authority to contact in the event of an obvious security breach [8]. One of the solutions is a platform that will combine a Blockchain, repurposed as an access control moderator, with an off-chain storage solution [19]. Users will not have to trust third parties and are always aware of the data that is collected about them and how it is used. Furthermore, the Blockchain recognizes users as owners of their personal data.

Legal Aspects and Normative: Currently there is a lack in the normative and regulation for what concerns the role of Blockchain technology as distributed ledger and on the legal recognition of Smart Contracts. This lack creates insecurity, because some aspects of smart contract technology could be adopted by the logistics market, only to be upregulated, or even to be considered illegal [20].

Connection to Out-of-Chain Data: When dealing with massive documents, due to space constraints or costs, the typical pattern is to store them off-chain and to upload on-chain only their hashes and a pointer or reference to the external storage location. This does not grant that the external storage has the same properties the Blockchain has, and eventually the external storage can be dismissed over time. In this case only the metadata related to the documents can be retrieved but not the documents themselves. When planning to use off-chain storage this aspect must be considered [21].

6 Answer to Research Questions and Conclusions

Based on the considerations made, it can be said that Blockchain has considerable potential to facilitate the development of an integrated interport community as it can increase trust between the parties, it can provide a facilitated communication platform, and it allows to guarantee the identities of the involved parties and their will to send the transaction. The logistic activities that can be most affected by the Blockchain seem to be those relating to the notarization of contractual documents and passageways to the gates, including photographs and documents relating to the state of vehicles and goods for any insurance purposes. In addition, the management of access authorizations to the system in all ports with a single system and in a decentralized way, the guarantee of the origin of documents, and the sharing and secure transmission of information and notifications of events between the port actors, while preserving privacy and data ownership, can significantly benefit from the Blockchain. All the players may benefit from the use of the Blockchain in support of intermodal traffic, from the for-profit enterprises, such as freight forwarders, terminal operators, shipping companies, haulers, to the port authorities. The former can think of reducing direct costs and increasing efficiency, thanks to a greater automation, the reduction of intermediaries and delays, but also of reducing indirect costs, such as legal ones, thanks to the decrease in disputes guaranteed by Blockchain certification and smart contracts. The latter can also have advantages in terms of reducing costs and having greater guarantees that laws and regulations are respected. The pros of introducing Blockchain to a cross-border port community have been clearly listed in the previous sections. As for the cons, there are probably no negative consequences related to the introduction of a technology that increases the transparency of operations, the trust of the parties, the automation of many activities, the security and confidentiality of data transfers. The only reasons, not all justifiable, why one party could negatively view the introduction of the Blockchain in a cross-border port community may include the need to bear the costs of technological adoption and transition, low propensity to increase transparency, little trust against a new technology, possible privacy or scalability issues or system governance issues.

Acknowledgements. This research was supported by the EasyLog project (Interreg IT-FR Maritime Program 2014–2020).

References

1. Serra, P., Fancello, G.: Use of ICT for more efficient port operations: the experience of the EasyLog project. In: Gervasi, O., et al. (eds.) ICCSA 2020. LNCS, vol. 12255, pp. 3–14. Springer, Cham (2020). https://doi.org/10.1007/978-3-030-58820-5_1
2. Jović, M., Kavran, N., Aksentijević, S., Tijan, E.: The transition of Croatian seaports into smart ports. In: 42nd International Convention on Information and Communication Technology, Electronics and Microelectronics – MIPRO, pp. 1386–1390. IEEE (2019)
3. Stopford, M.: Maritime Economics, 3rd edn. Routledge, London (2017)
4. Heilig, L., Schwarze, S., Voß, S.: An analysis of digital transformation in the history and future of modern ports. In: Proceedings of the 50th Hawaii International Conference on System Sciences (2017)
5. Weernink, M.O., van den Engh, W., Francisconi, M., Thorborg, F.: The blockchain potential for port logistics (2017). https://smart-port.nl/wp-content/uploads/2017/10/White-Paper-Blockchain.pdf
6. Treiblmaier, H.: Toward more rigorous blockchain research: recommendations for writing blockchain case studies. In: Treiblmaier, H., Clohessy, T. (eds.) Blockchain and Distributed Ledger Technology Use Cases. PI, pp. 1–31. Springer, Cham (2020). https://doi.org/10.1007/978-3-030-44337-5_1
7. Jović, M., Filipović, M., Tijan, E., Jardas, M.: A review of blockchain technology implementation in shipping industry. Pomorstvo 33(2), 140–148 (2019)
8. Tijan, E., Aksentijević, S., Ivanić, K., Jardas, M.: Blockchain technology implementation in logistics. Sustainability 11(4), 1185 (2019)
9. Jabbar, K., Bjørn, P.: Infrastructural grind: introducing blockchain technology in the shipping domain. In: Proceedings of the 2018 ACM Conference on Supporting Groupwork, pp. 297–308 (2018)
10. Gausdal, A.H., Czachorowski, K.V., Solesvik, M.Z.: Applying blockchain technology: evidence from Norwegian companies. Sustainability 10(6), 1985 (2018)
11. Lindman, J., Tuunainen, V.K., Rossi, M.: Opportunities and risks of blockchain technologies–a research agenda. In: Proceedings of the 50th Hawaii International Conference on System Sciences (2017)
12. Dutta, P., Choi, T.M., Somani, S., Butala, R.: Blockchain technology in supply chain operations: applications, challenges and research opportunities. Transp. Res. Part E Logist. Transp. Rev. 142, 102067 (2020)
13. Bavassano, G., Ferrari, C., Tei, A.: Blockchain: how shipping industry is dealing with the ultimate technological leap. Res. Transp. Bus. Manag. 100428 (2020)
14. IBM: TradeLens: how IBM and Maersk are sharing blockchain to build a global trade platform – THINK blog (2018). https://www.ibm.com/blogs/think/2018/11/tradelens-how-ibm-and-maersk-are-sharing-Blockchain-to-build-a-global-trade-platform/
15. Nakamoto, S.: Bitcoin: a peer-to-peer electronic cash system (2008). https://bitcoin.org/bitcoin.pdf. Accessed June 2021
16. Wood, G.: Ethereum: a secure decentralised generalised transactionledger (2014). (updated version). https://ethereum.github.io/yellowpaper/paper.pdf. Accessed June 2021
17. Ahmad, R., Hasan, H., Jayaraman, R., Salah, K., Omar, M.: Blockchain applications and architectures for port operations and logistics management. Res. Trasp. Bus. Manag. 100620 (2021)
18. Irannezhad, E.: The architectural design requirements of a blockchain-based port community system. Logistics 4, 30 (2020)

19. Laurent, M., Kaaniche, N., Le, C., Vander Plaetse, M.: A blockchain-based access control scheme. In: SECRYPT 2018: 15th International Conference on Security and Cryptography, July 2018, Porto, Portugal, pp. 168–176 (2018). https://doi.org/10.5200/0006855601680176. hal-01864317
20. Gatteschi, V., Lamberti, F., Demartini, C., Pranteda, C., Santamaria, V.: Blockchain and smart contracts for insurance: is the technology mature enough? MDPI: Future Internet **10**(6), 8–13 (2019). https://doi.org/10.3390/fi10020020
21. Marchesi, L., Marchesi, M., Destefanis, G., Barabino, G., Tigano, D.: Design patterns for gas optimization in ethereum. In: Proceedings of the IEEE International Workshop on Blockchain Oriented Software Engineering (2020)

Cartography and Security. Port Security: Trends and Perspectives

Giuseppe Borruso[1]([⊠]), Ginevra Balletto[2], Alessandra Milesi[2], and Mara Ladu[2]

[1] DEAMS - Department of Economics, Business, Mathematics and Statistics Sciences "Bruno de Finetti", University of Trieste, 34127 Trieste, Italy
giuseppe.borruso@deams.units.it
[2] DICAAR - Department of Civil and Environmental Engineering and Architecture, University of Cagliari, 09100 Cagliari, Italy
balletto@unica.it

Abstract. Safety and security represent central elements of policies at local, national and international levels. They are recalled particularly to-date in light of issues related to major threats as terrorism and, recently health-related events as global pandemics and epidemics. These two concepts are particularly relevant and become central in choices dealing with social and economical aspects. With a particular focus on Geographical Information Technologies and the Information and Communication Technologies (ICT), the paper hereby presented focuses on cartographic and geographic aspects on security, particularly related to the port areas and to the relations these have with the rest of the transport systems and cities with which, at least in more mature economies, they share spaces and issues. Starting from more general considerations that links cartography and security, in the present work we examine the topic by means of recent research projects dealing with the Port of Trieste and the perspectives related to security.

Keywords: Port security · Smart ports · ICT · Trieste

1 Introduction

Cartography and security represent a combination that can dates back to the beginning of the history of cartography and geographical representations. From the very beginning, maps, charts and all the tools related to geographical representation, as well as the processing and analysis of geographical data - then, especially in the most current period of development and expansion of Information and Communication Technologies - have had a strong link with security in the broadest sense.

Cartography was always related to issues of security, protection and military control. In particular, geodetic cartography was born and facilitates the determination of borders, the correct positioning of natural and anthropogenic elements on the ground, effectively supporting the armed forces of the various countries [1–4]. Knowledge of a state's own territory, as well as that of others, of potential adversaries or enemies, becomes both a tactical and strategic element of survival or dominion by a state - or an alliance between states [5, 6].

© Springer Nature Switzerland AG 2021
O. Gervasi et al. (Eds.): ICCSA 2021, LNCS 12958, pp. 252–261, 2021.
https://doi.org/10.1007/978-3-030-87016-4_19

In particular, the basic topographic cartography is made, for a good part of the modern period, by military institutes - the British Ordnance Survey and the Italian Military Geographical Institute are just two of the examples in which the military and the presence of terms attributable to these are verifiable [1, 2].

The most recent period is undoubtedly the one in which the technological impact was disruptive and decisive, in relation to the spread of geographic information technologies [7–10]. Modern smartphones, a technological tool for information and communication within everyone's reach, represent a concentration of technology [11], available until a few decades ago only to selected categories of users and professionals, often characterized by very high levels of secrecy.

Furthermore, we can say that the high-speed Internet connection, our real-time positioning via smartphone equipped with GPS, access to navigable geographic databases and satellite images, functions now considered basic in common mobile phone applications, all have a military origin from the beginning linked to security.

In fact, these applications are largely the offspring of the Cold War: the Internet network - originally DARPA-Net - was designed to connect research centers and military bases by land with redundancy systems in communications, in the event of multiple nuclear attacks on US soil. GPS was conceived (https://www.nasa.gov/directorates/heo/scan/communications/policy/GPS_History.html; https://www.gps.gov/systems/gps/modernization/sa/) as a way to identify - today we would say geolocalize - in a precise manner the submarines capable of launching ICBM missiles (Intercontinental Ballistic Missiles). Geographic data, and satellite images in particular, used in spy satellites in the acquisition of data relating to the opponent's or enemy's terrain, through remote acquisition technologies, mainly from satellite - but today with a return to air vehicles, thanks, above all, to drones.

The end of the 90s and the beginning of the 2000s probably represent the turning point: from the cartographic and Geo-informatic side we witnessed the flourishing of most applications in the field of software, data architecture and publishing in the cartographic field and geo-informatics [9]. To-date we are witnessing an unprecedented integration of the geographic information substrate with that of other sciences and applications: hard sciences, but also human sciences, including social ones, often with reference to issues such as urban security and analysis. Geolocalized criminal events for their prevention and mitigation towards an increase in security [12].

On the operational side, the continuous increase in data transmission speed on the Internet, the gradual declassification of historical satellite images, together with the development of private producers of high-resolution satellite images, simplify the use of data and content, including geographical ones. A major boost was given during the Clinton-Gore administration in the United States.

A major boost was given during the Clinton-Gore administration in the United States. In the course of 2000, the decision to 'turn off' the SA (Selective Availability) from the GPS signal must be attributed to this administration, thus significantly increasing the accuracy of positioning and navigation even for civilian uses, and therefore not limiting it to military ones.

In the same administration, the then Vice President Al Gore [13] launched the idea of the 'Digital Earth'. This was a virtual, geo-referenced environment in which anyone, from children to adults, can navigate, explore and learn about the Earth, through a virtual globe [8], recalling a whole series of information and news, and a possible meeting place for onlookers, scientists, looking for solutions to technological and social problems.

Consideration on the use of charts and maps as real information weapons - or disinformation - as they have often been used to convey certain messages, would deserve a separate chapter and an in-depth study, implicitly or explicitly linked to the security of a country or a given context [5, 6].

More recently, with reference to the Covid-19 outbreak, the issues related to health and the quest for tackling human life has put many expectations and doubts at the same time on the geo-technologies as means for identifying hotspots of disease spreading and in helping tracking and tracing of cases for containing diffusion.

The rest of the paper is organized as it follows. In Sect. 2, the city-port relationships are analysed, in terms of the characteristics joining these two spatial areas. Section 3 tackles the case study of the project SECNET, with particular reference to its geographical aspects and the implications on security. Concluding remarks in Sect. 4 summarize the main findings and open issues still to be tackled.

2   City-Port: Relationships, Flows and Security

The relationship between city and port is complex due to important and interesting challenges in terms of safety (movement of people and goods), both on the sea-side and long connections (extra regional and national), and in the city and operation [14, 15].

An important consideration concerns the port location and the development of cities. In a period in which navigation took place mainly by sail, the geographical position in the shelter became important, combined with that including still and mobile waters (streams, such as rivers or streams), useful for washing and cleaning the basins [16].

This was useful to avoid water stagnation, and therefore the dilution of possible pollutants and the reduction of the formation of concretions of algae and other living organisms on the keel of the boats. Port locations linked to internal water systems were therefore privileged, for reasons related to cleaning and purification given by mobile water as well as, in subsequent phases, thanks to the potential, in some contexts, of the internal navigability of water courses, which therefore performed a dual role (of decontamination of the waters of the basin and of internal connection) [17].

The same idea is valid for industrial production, often located in the close proximity of ports. Where there is industry, there is a need for a receptor basin, and, always, for a system, a network of rivers or dilution streams. The development of canal ports, just remember the best known in Europe, in the North Sea, such as Hamburg and Rotterdam, can therefore be linked to these logics [18].

The following and recent evolutions of transport have changed the logic: the railway - subsequently the road and today, again the railway - has led the port systems to settle on deeply different logics and arrangements as regards the permeability of crossing and relations between territories [19, 20].

The more mature economies, in the oldest industrialized countries, have often had the key to commercial and industrial success in ports. During the early stages of a port's development the relationship between infrastructure - and related activities - and the city is very close, and the city and port almost overlap in spatial location [21].

With the evolution of ports, first looking for more numerous docks and larger warehouses, then above all for piers and open spaces for positioning and handling goods, the relationship between port and city becomes less strong, nonetheless relevant in terms of induced traffic and congestion, but also in terms of the economic spillovers. Major European ports today - i.e., Rotterdam, Hamburg, etc. - are located far from the most historical and active part of the city, in areas where goods can be moved and stored, transferring them to the final markets, thanks to a strong integration with different modes of transport (Fig. 1).

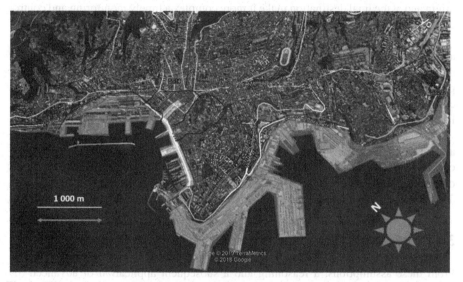

Fig. 1. The city and port of Trieste (Italy). Highlighted, in the left centre of the image the earlier port areas (yellow). On the left, part of the 'Old Port' (in pale blue, now to be converted to light port operations), on the right, the 'New Port' with container, multipurpose and oil terminals, shunting areas included. Red lines indicate the early city - port expansions. (Color figure online)

The city and its port, in fact, in most cases do not become the final destination of the goods that are moved there, but increasingly as a place of transit and modal exchange, towards destinations - and, in the case of gateway ports, maritime, in the case of the hub ports - further away, in a process of evolution of the relations between them from setting, through expansion, to specialization [26] That becomes important particularly with the transformation of port functions to serve vast hinterlands with destinations deep into it.

In this sense, the relationship becomes above all one of coexistence of proximity, however, the network or the separation wall between the two areas, when located in proximity to each other, which actually divide two worlds that travel at different speeds and with different relationships. The case is different in which, instead of goods, passengers are considered [22].

In this case, the link with the city is stronger. Both for cruise transport and for ferries, the urban locations of the ports are preferable: often associated with the "image" of the city, due to the scenic impact of arriving in the city's central part, instead of docking at an anonymous commercial pier, and for the same connection with the passenger transport system (rail, car, bus, etc.) [23].

Here the permeability is stronger, as it is the coexistence between urban and port functions. Users of passenger transport services also become users of the city, either in the form of tourists - and therefore of urban functions - or as users of part of the same transport and support infrastructures for port operations aimed at passenger transport.

From the point of view of safety, the consequences are of various type: the goods follow the logic of long networks, where therefore the traceability and controls at the origin and at the final destination make it more complex a timely monitoring and control of what actually transits, more than stationing in port facilities [24].

Different, and in some respects more delicate, given its urban implications, the characters and implications of passenger transport. If cruise transport has operating modes directly borrowed from air transport, and therefore with a series of access controls for people and goods on cruise ships which in fact limits connections with the surrounding environment to points of well monitored access, in the case of passenger transport by ferry the issue becomes more complex.

Here the main pressures with urban environments are formed in a short time frame, and the continuous movement of people and vehicles makes it difficult to control precisely. A common consideration that can be developed is that the spaces involved in port operations, both relating to goods and passengers, require precise territorial references, and therefore increasingly precise and punctual cartographic and geographical supports.

3   Port Security. The Case of the SECNET - GIS Project

From these assumptions, a reasoning and a subsequent application of advanced 3D visualization and modeling systems and 360° images were developed to support port security. The Italy - Slovenia project called SECNET (https://www.ita-slo.eu/it/secnet) saw the participation of various subjects linked to the issue of cross-border security, with particular reference to IT, involving, among others, the three ports of the North Adriatic (Venice, Trieste and Koper), in addition to two universities (Trieste and Koper) [25]. The main objective of SECNET was to strengthen the institutional capacity of the ports of the Program Area (North Adriatic Port: Venice, Trieste and Koper), as well as to create the basis for a coordinated and permanent governance of port security at cross-border level. This can be done thanks to innovative ICT tools, jointly developing plans for long-term actions and strategies, increasing coordination and cooperation between ports to strengthen their security and competitiveness. From the identification of weaknesses present in the port security of the partner realities, concrete pilot actions were defined and implemented for the application of ICT in the field of perimeter surveillance and cyber-security of the systems, which allowed to standardize port security measures, such as to consolidate the safety and competitiveness of these ports of the Program Area.

The University of Trieste had the task of drafting various documents, such as the survey on best practices in the field of port security; the cross-border action plan on port security, including the final text of a memorandum of understanding by the various ports involved on common and shared commitments in terms of security. In addition to this, understanding the importance of the geographical and territorial component, has led to strengthening the GIS component by supporting the harmonization of data related to the port facilities, these including the development plans of the area. Although not initially considered within the project itself, the research unit considered relevant keeping the geographical databases and assets homogeneous in order to provide a solid and viable backbone for the geolocalized solutions tested and to host further evolutions (Fig. 2).

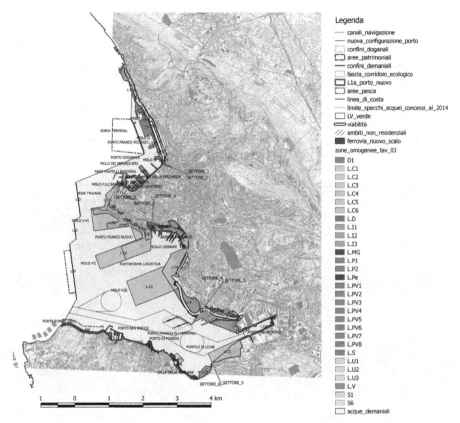

Fig. 2. Port urban plan of Trieste Harbour (source: GIS elaboration from Trieste port authority data) https://www.porto.trieste.it/

In collaboration with Tosolini Productions, it was possible to develop some geolocalized 360° images, which can be integrated with virtual and augmented reality systems. These are the Logistics Platform, located in the southern part of the Port of Trieste (Fig. 3, pin marker 1) and the newly established Free zone, named FreeEste, located in a rear port area (Fig. 3, pin marker 2).

The places chosen are particularly significant: the Logistics Platform (operational from 22 April 2021) and the Free Zone (operational from January 2019), which led to a reorganization of the accesses for security reasons. Figures 4 and 5 illustrate the platform developed to combine the 360° view (on the left of the image) and the geographical location (on the right of the image, represented by the spherical photo icon).

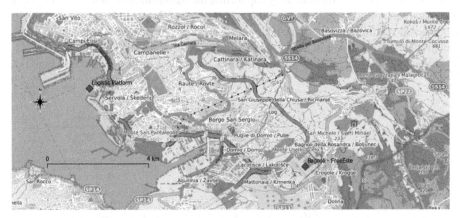

Fig. 3. Positions of the two points of 360° photos acquisition in port and port-related areas: the new logistic platform (left) and the free port - inland terminal FreeEste.

Fig. 4. 360° views at logistic platform (Port of Trieste) https://seekbeak.com/v/vYD1GPOozby

Such applications represent a demonstration of the potentials given by these tools to implement monitoring systems for a situation awareness of facilities. Also, the possibility of linking this kind of imagery with other hyper textual tools (images, video, link to other applications) can help in integrating information from different sources, guaranteeing situational awareness of an area, other than allowing to create and present scenarios for simulating different cases.

Future and further evolutions of the system will imply a test of the integration of such systems into security systems and geographical databases, experimenting also the possibility to implement real time monitoring systems.

Fig. 5. 360° views at FreeEste (Trieste free zone) https://seekbeak.com/v/KV6zareVjeZ

4 Concluding Remarks

Security and cartography are united by a strong bond. Security has a link with the territory, similarly with cartography, meaning both the traditional and the most modern forms of representation. In fact, cartography represents probably the most important tool for visualization, understanding, acquisition of awareness and planning of actions aimed at reducing risks and unexpected events. Today, the main challenges concerning security have to do more and more with globalization, based on increasingly frequent movements of people and goods. The nodes of these flows are therefore the most sensitive places, and therefore often the most vulnerable, in which it is necessary to intervene to increase aspects related to safety, including health [27].

Furthermore, these places host most economic activities of different use and purpose [28]. Among these nodes, the ports (together with the airports) are the places where the commitment is directed the most. Systems based on ICT - Information and Communication Technology - are increasingly developed to increase security, both the more traditional and the IT type. In this sense, the most interesting prospects seem to be those in which different systems are integrated with each other, multiplying the effect of the technologies involved. The experimentation developed as part of SECNET - GIS research goes in this direction: combining a relatively traditional geographical information base with a series of applications aimed at improving visualization and understanding aspects, such as the use of 360° images and VR/AR tools (virtual and augmented reality). These, in the present phase developed for demonstration purposes, can in subsequent applications find development in dynamic systems, able to connect data and information in large and updated images of a sensitive territorial area.

References

1. Traversi, C.: Tecnica cartografica. Istituto Geografico Militare, Firenze (1968)

2. Cuccoli, L., Torresani, S.: Introduzione alla cartografia e alle rappresentazioni grafiche. CLUEB, Bologna (1985)
3. Robinson, A.H., Morrison, J.L., Muehrcke, P.C., Kimerling, A.J., Guptil, S.C.: Elements of Catrography, 6th edn. Wiley, New York (1995)
4. Dorling, D., Fairbairn, D.: Mapping. Ways of Representing the World. Longman, Harlow (1999)
5. Boria, E.: Cartografia e potere. Utet, Torino (2007)
6. Boria, E.: Carte come armi. Edizioni Nuova Cultura, Torino (2012)
7. Favretto, A.: I mappamondi virtuali. Uno strumento per la didattica della Geografia e della Cartografia. Patron, Bologna (2009)
8. Favretto, A.: Cartografia nelle nuvole. Patron, Bologna (2016)
9. Borruso, G.: Cartografia e Informazione Geografica "2.0 e oltre", Webmapping, WebGIS. Un'introduzione, Bollettino dell'Associazione Italiana di Cartografia, **147**, 7–15 (2013)
10. Pesaresi, C.: Applicazioni GIS. Principi metodologici e linee di ricerca. Esercitazioni ed esemplificazioni guida. UTET, Torino (2017)
11. DiBiase, D.: Personal communication, The Geospatial Revolution, Episode One, Penn State University, min. 2:10 (2015)
12. Ratcliffe, J., Chainey, S.: GIS and Crime Mapping. Wiley, Chichester (2005)
13. Gore, A.: The digital earth: understanding our Planet in the 21st Century. OpenGIS Consortium (OGC), portal.opengeospatial.org (1998)
14. Daamen, T.A., Vries, I.: Governing the European port–city interface: institutional impacts on spatial projects between city and port. J. Transp. Geogr. **27**, 4–13 (2013)
15. Schubert, D.: Spatial restructuring of port cities: periods from inclusion to fragmentation and re-integration of city and port in Hamburg. In: Carpenter, A., Lozano, R. (eds.) European port cities in transition. SS, pp. 109–126. Springer, Cham (2020). https://doi.org/10.1007/978-3-030-36464-9_7
16. Aiosa, S.: Dall'archeologia alla contemporaneità. Brevi storie di ponti e di porti. In I ponti ei porti tra metafora e realtà, pp. 19–48. Palermo University Press (2020)
17. Biga, M.G.: Porti del Mediterraneo orientale in epoca preclassica: i dati testuali. Segni, Immagini e Storia dei centri costieri euro-mediterranei **4**, 17 (2019)
18. Hein, C.M., Rutte, R.J., van Mil, Y.B.C.: North sea crossings: historical geo-spatial mapping as a tool to understand the local development of port cities in a global context. In: The Urbanisation of the Sea: From Concepts and Analysis to Design, pp. 33–44. NAi Publishers (2020)
19. Wang, J., Jiao, J., Ma, L.: An organizational model and border port hinterlands for the China-Europe railway express. J. Geog. Sci. **28**(9), 1275–1287 (2018). https://doi.org/10.1007/s11 442-018-1525-6
20. Liu, P., Wang, C., Xie, J., Mu, D., Lim, M.K.: Towards green port-hinterland transportation: coordinating railway and road infrastructure in Shandong Province, China. Transp. Res. Part D Transp. Environ. **94**, 102806 (2021)
21. Monios, J., Bergqvist, R., Woxenius, J.: Port-centric cities: the role of freight distribution in defining the port-city relationship. J. Transp. Geogr. **66**, 53–64 (2018)
22. Zhao, Q., Xu, H., Wall, R.S., Stavropoulos, S.: Building a bridge between port and city: improving the urban competitiveness of port cities. J. Transp. Geogr. **59**, 120–133 (2017)
23. Sun, L., Li, K.Y., Luo, M.F., Hu, C.B., Deng, Y.J.: Cooperative compensation mechanism under the balance of 'Cruise-Port-City' benefits of cruise ports. In: International Forum on Shipping, Ports and Airports (IFSPA) 2019, Hong Kong Polytechnic University, September 2019
24. Gallo, A., Accorsi, R., Goh, A., Hsiao, H., Manzini, R.: A traceability-support system to control safety and sustainability indicators in food distribution. Food Contr. **124**, 107866 (2021)

25. https://www.ita-slo.eu/en/secnet
26. Rodrigue, J.P., Comtois, C., Slack, B.: The Geography of Transport Systems, 4th edn. Routledge, New York (2017)
27. Murgante, B., Borruso, G., Balletto, G., Castiglia, P., Dettori, M.: Why Italy first? Health, geographical and planning aspects of the COVID-19 outbreak. Sustainability. **12**(12), 5064 (2020). https://doi.org/10.3390/su12125064
28. Vallega, A.: Geografia delle strategie marittime. Dal mondo dei mercanti alla società transindustriale. Mursia, Milano (1997)

Towards Edge Computing Based Monitoring for Smart Ports

Vladimir V. Shakhov[1,2(✉)] [iD] and Anastasia N. Yurgenson[2]

[1] Novosibirsk State Technical University, Novosibirsk 630073, Russia
shaxov@corp.nstu.ru
[2] Institute of Computational Mathematics and Mathematical Geophysics,
Novosibirsk 630090, Russia
{shakhov,nastya}@rav.sscc.ru
http://www.nstu.ru, https://icmmg.nsc.ru

Abstract. The development of smart ports requires the use of modern innovative digital solutions based on the latest advances in information and communication technologies. The Internet of Things opens the way for the creation of efficient technologies for smart ports. Smart sensors are a key element of the port's digital infrastructure. For example, wireless sensor networks that detect or predict pipeline leaks and inform port operators can prevent catastrophic environmental disaster and huge economic losses. The paradigm of Edge computing, where data is processed close to its source, alleviates the problem of transferring and storing huge amounts of sensing data. Smart sensors can analyze data, make decisions and transmit results to port operators in a compact form. Thus, the problem is to optimize the transmission of the computed solution, taking into account the trade-off between cost and reliability. In this paper, we focus on this issue.

Keywords: Wireless sensor networks · Edge computing · Infrastructure monitoring

1 Introduction

The development of smart ports requires the use of modern innovative digital solutions based on the latest advances in information and communication technologies. Lack of accurate and timely information about the health of the port infrastructure results in many errors, severe delays and redundant labor-intensive work. Further, a decrease in the capacity of an individual transport hub can drastically affect the global supply chains. Seaports handle 80% of the world trade [1]. In the port, the interests of the transport, industrial and civil sectors are closely intertwined, giving rise to multifaceted problems of ensuring the reliability, productivity and profitability of logistics services. The Internet of Things (IoT) opens the way for the creation of technologies for smart ports that can effectively solve the following tasks: maintain an ever-growing foreign trade turnover and service associated traffic flows, reduce potentially harmful impacts on the environment and public health, prevent anthropogenic disasters, increase resilience to natural disasters, and support the efficient resource consumption [2].

O. Gervasi et al. (Eds.): ICCSA 2021, LNCS 12958, pp. 262–271, 2021.
https://doi.org/10.1007/978-3-030-87016-4_20

Smart sensors are a key element of the port's digital infrastructure. These sensors are mounted on container yards, cranes, roads, pipelines and can transmit real-time data about working conditions of docks and other infrastructure. Smart sensors can reduce the need for regular inspections and provide data that helps owners plan preventive maintenance more effectively. The cost of many sensor systems for structural health monitoring can be included in the cost of the structures themselves. This can lead to a quick return on investment in countries with high labor costs. The handling equipment of any transport hub must operate at maximum efficiency and be properly maintained. A wireless sensor networks can ensure that connected handling equipment is servicing the increasing volume of cargo shipments in real time. Smart sensors installed in container terminals collect information about the location of cargo and equipment, the status of operations and energy consumption. The information system analyzes information in real time and transmits it to terminal personnel to identify bottlenecks and initiate appropriate actions. In this way, operating costs can be significantly reduced by reducing equipment downtime and minimizing energy consumption.

Seaports must meet certain safety standards. The smart sensors can be used for motion-based intrusion detection and pattern recognition, and then the sensors, using network technology, alert security personnel of potential threats. Sensor networks help address security concerns in ports by providing safe operating procedures. For example, sensor networks can alert vehicle drivers to stay within the track. Similar systems can maintain the correct alignment of the cranes during loading and unloading etc.

An important component of the seaport infrastructure is pipelines for the transportation of liquid cargo, including crude oil, oil products, chemicals and industrial gases. For example, the port of Rotterdam has an extensive network of more than 1,500 km of pipelines [3]. Also, extensive pipeline networks connect ports and industrial clusters. Intelligent sensor networks that detect or predict pipeline leaks can prevent catastrophic environmental disaster and huge economic losses [4].

In recent articles, researchers have noted the following topical challenges that wireless sensor networks face in smart ports [5]. Network nodes share and retransmit huge amounts of data and information in real time. Therefore, the problem of energy consumption requires attention. Next, the port environment is unfavorable for wireless communication. The signal can be shielded, reflected, and scattered. This results in data packets corruption and degraded network performance.

The paradigm of Edge computing, where data is processed close to its source, alleviates the problem of transferring and storing huge amounts of data. Smart sensors can analyze data, make decisions and transmit results to port operators in a compact form. Thus, the problem is to optimize the transmission of the computed solution, taking into account the trade-off between cost and reliability. In this paper, we focus on this issue.

The remainder of this paper is organized as follows. Section 2 provides related works. Section 3 formulates a system model, problem statements and provides the corresponding mathematical results. The performance analysis of these results is provided in Sect. 4. Conclusions are drawn in Sect. 5.

2 Related Works

There is a lack of publications regarding smart port monitoring systems. Usually, to improve the efficiency of the port operations, investigators develop simulation or analytical models using some averaged historical data or not using data at all [6–8].

In [9], the authors noted that an intelligent information system can improve the visibility, reliability and safety of a marine terminal, and cited the example of the port of Marseille, where the doublet of Neptune and Ci5 improved the quality of service for the flow of goods. However, as also noted, an intelligent information system required constant exchange of data and information between ports. Smart sensors must collect and transmit huge amounts of data such as geolocation, sea depth, wind speed, humidity, temperature, vibration, pressure, shock, etc.

The use of intelligent monitoring systems in the port shows great potential. Indeed, one of the most important and serious problems of modern cities is air pollution. Experts from the World Health Organization and the United Nations are expressing serious concern about this. A promising way to address this challenge is to use networks of smart sensors [10]. The maritime ports make a significant contribution to the pollution of the urban atmosphere. For example, the port's contribution to Shanghai's air pollution is about 30% only for the major air pollutants (SO_2, NO_x and $PM_{2.5}$) and the Port of Hamburg produces about 28% of the NO_x emissions of the entire city [11]. In addition, it is noted that quantitative data on emissions from ports can only give an approximate picture of reality. The assessment of the corresponding contribution to pollution can be based on indirect information such as data from a similar port or subjective opinions of experts. Also, due to imperfect equipment, the data collected may be incomplete or inaccurate. There are precedents for port terminal emissions studies based on confidential and inaccurate data [12]. Next, aggregated anonymized data collected in a traditional way can be useful for obtaining environmental certifications. However, detailed data are needed to adequately control emissions and make effective decisions to reduce air pollution. Intelligent monitoring systems allow emissions to be assigned to specific sources or categories of emissions, such as ocean vessels, vehicles, handling equipment etc.

Currently, various political and social groups are actively discussing the danger of greenhouse gases, taking measures to reduce emissions of air pollutants, and lobbying for appropriate decisions at the intergovernmental level. This problem is in the focus of attention of the media and the public. There is growing interest in air quality issues and increased public support for action to reduce emissions. Given the intensity of maritime trade, we can expect an increasing demand for comprehensive and high quality air emission inventory tools. As a consequence, it can be predicted that port organizations will actively develop, implement and improve air emission inventory processes [13].

Let us remark that monitoring is also needed for other emissions such as sewage, noise emissions etc. Edge computing based monitoring for smart ports enables efficient monitoring of different emissions, detection of pollution sources and the introduction of environmentally friendly technologies such as vacuum mooring systems to reduce engine run time. It also opens up opportunities for optimizing the port operation in order to effectively improve the environmental situation. The lack of research on information systems for smart ports comes as a particular surprise [14].

The information systems for smart ports have been briefly described in [15]. In the recent survey [5] author claim that modern information systems for smart ports have to be deployed to manage, monitor, and store massive amounts of various data. And hence, application of Edge computing for the smart port tasks is an attractive open research challenge.

3 Models

Assume, smart sensors treat data (e.g. using a lightweight machine learning algorithm [16]) and get decision, which has to be delivered to port operators through a binary wireless communication channel. The sensor report is a message of N bits. Let the probability of an error of a single bit is p. If a redundant noise-correcting code is used, then the code is capable of correcting up to k errors. For example, if we use a double error-correcting Hamming code then $k = 2$. Therefore, the link transmission of a message is successful if

$$n_e \leq k$$

where n_e is the number of errors in the message. The transmission of bits is assumed to be independent. The designation h is used for the distance between the sensor and the sink in the term of hops (i.e. h hops). The topology of subnetwork sensor-sink is a simple chain.

Let us calculate the probability of successful message transmission. We use the property of Bernoulli trials, i.e.

$$F(x) = \begin{cases} 0, & x < 0 \\ 1 - p, & 0 \leq x < 1 \\ 1, & x \geq 1 \end{cases}$$

where $F(x)$ is CDF of the random variable as follows: the number of errors in a single bit (0 or 1). Let us consider an elementary event when there are exactly j errors in a message containing N bits. It follows from the properties of independent random variables that the probability of this event is

$$p^j(1 - p)^{N-j}$$

Noting that the number of ways of taking j bits from N possibilities is described by the corresponding binomial coefficient C_N^j,

$$C_N^j = \frac{N!}{j!(N - j)!}$$

Thus, we have got the binomial distribution

$$P(n_e = j) = \frac{N!}{j!(N - j)!}p^j(1 - p)^{N-j}, \quad j \in \mathbb{N}_{[0;N]}$$

and next

$$P(n_e \le k) = \sum_{j=0}^{k} C_N^j p^j (1-p)^{N-j}$$

This is the probability of one link successful transmission. Now, there are two possible situations:

- An intermedia node transmits the message and only a sink restore the message.
- The message is corrected (if it is necessary) in each intermedia node.

Without loss of generality, we pass the case of message recovery after an even number of errors in the same bit. In the first case 1 bit of the message is correctly transmitted with the probability p^h. Therefore, the probability of final success in this case is as follows:

$$P_1 = \sum_{j=0}^{k} C_N^j q^j (1-q)^{N-j}$$

where

$$q = 1 - (1-p)^h$$

In the second case

$$P_2 = \left(\sum_{j=0}^{k} C_N^j p^j (1-p)^{N-j} \right)^h$$

In the case of heterogeneous error probability these formulas are modified as follows

$$P_1 = \sum_{j=0}^{k} C_N^j \left(1 - \prod_{i=1}^{h} (1-p_i) \right)^j \left(\prod_{i=1}^{h} (1-p_i) \right)^{N-j}$$

and

$$P_2 = \prod_{i=1}^{h} \sum_{j=0}^{k} C_N^j p_i^j (1-p_i)^{N-j}$$

where p_i, $i \in [1, h]$ is the 1-bit error probability in the i-th link.

To improve packet delivering reliability multiple stock can be used [17]. It is reasonable to assume that the sinks are located at the boundaries of the chain formed by the sensors, and the transmission is carried out in both directions. Cognitive radio technologies can be used to prevent interference and spectrum cost problems in highly dynamic environments [18–20]. The formulas for reliable transmission become as follows:

$$P_1 = \sum_{j=0}^{k} C_N^j (1-(1-p)^h)^j (1-p)^{h(N-j)}$$

$$+ \sum_{j=0}^{k} C_N^j \left(1 - (1-p)^{L-h}\right)^j (1-p)^{(L-h)(N-j)}$$

$$- \sum_{j=0}^{k} C_N^j \left(1 - (1-p)^{h}\right)^j (1-p)^{h(N-j)}$$

$$* \sum_{j=0}^{k} C_N^j \left(1 - (1-p)^{L-h}\right)^j (1-p)^{(L-h)(N-j)}$$

and

$$P_2 = \left(\sum_{j=0}^{k} C_N^j p^j (1-p)^{N-j}\right)^h + \left(\sum_{j=0}^{k} C_N^j p^j (1-p)^{N-j}\right)^{L-h} - \left(\sum_{j=0}^{k} C_N^j p^j (1-p)^{N-j}\right)^L$$

where L is the length of the chain. By combining the options of recovering messages in intermediate nodes and one/two sinks, we get four strategies for delivering the resulting message. The formulas can be easily generalized for star topologies.

4   Performance Analysis

It is clear that the second approach to transmit the message with decision is more reliable than the first approach, i.e.

$$P_1 < P_2 \ \forall N, k, h$$

However, the price for this is the energy consumption for packet recovering relay nodes.

It needs to remark, that in the case of single sink and $h = 1$ the message is recovering once, so we cannot to say about the choice of strategies.

For the case of two sinks, the lowest reliability corresponds to a node equal to the distance from both sinks. If L is odd, then there are two such sensors. The value of this reliability is as follows:

$$P_{min} = 2 \left(\sum_{j=0}^{k} C_N^j p^j (1-p)^{N-j}\right)^{L/2} - \left(\sum_{j=0}^{k} C_N^j p^j (1-p)^{N-j}\right)^L$$

Increasing the packet length, we improve the transmission reliability. However, starting from a certain value p, this length becomes unimportant. This proposition is demonstrated in Figs. 1, 2 and 3.

Here, the message length ranges from 5 to 21 bits, and the probability of error in one bit ranges from 0.01 to 0.5. The threshold for the number of errors is assumed to be as follows:

$$k = \left\lfloor \frac{N}{2} \right\rfloor$$

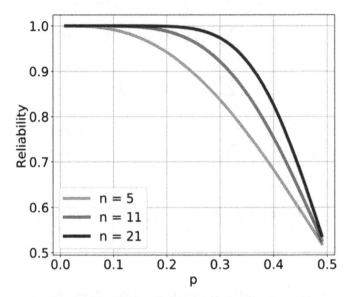

Fig. 1. The effect of one-bit error probability, $h = 1$.

There is a single sink. The option of message recovering in intermedia nodes has been applied. If the probability of an error in one bit is large enough ($p > 0.5$), the reliability is practically independent of the message length. This situation is typical for jamming attacks. Also, if p is small enough ($p < 0.1$) then it is reasonable to use short messages and thus save the energy of network nodes.

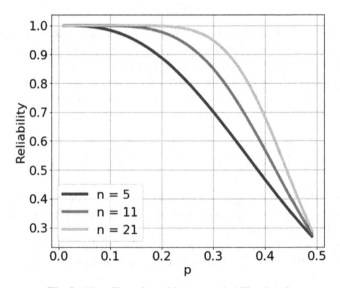

Fig. 2. The effect of one-bit error probability, $h = 2$.

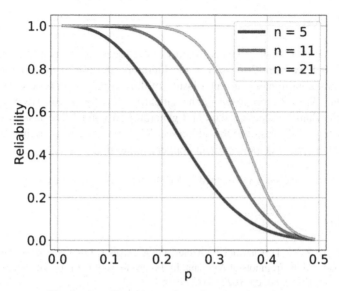

Fig. 3. The effect of one-bit error probability, $h = 8$.

The reliability drastically decreases with increasing the sensor-to-sink distance.

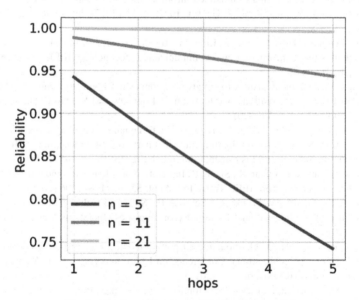

Fig. 4. Number of hops vs packet length, $p = 0.2$.

Also, it needs to remark that the packet size prevails over sensor-to-sink distance while maintaining transmission reliability. It is shown in Fig. 4. We can achieve a significant improvement in delivery reliability by increasing the message length.

5   Conclusion

While the benefits of smart systems for cost-effectiveness, security and environmental safety of ports have been discussed in the literature, the use of the Edge computing concept in this area remains an open issue. In this work, we propose to partially fill the noted gap. We have proposed mathematical models for a scenario when a smart sensor independently processes data and generates an output. The task is reduced to reliable delivery of the result to the addressee. We looked at several delivery scenarios and analyzed the parameters that affect delivery reliability.

Funding. The reported study was funded by RFBR and NSFC, project number 21-57-53001.

References

1. Millefiori, L., Zissis, D., Cazzanti, L., Arcieri, G.: A distributed approach to estimating sea port operational regions from lots of AIS data. In: Proceedings of IEEE International Conference on Big Data (Big Data), pp. 1627–1632 (2016)
2. Molavi, A., Shi, J., Wu, Y., Lim, G.J.: Enabling smart ports through the integration of microgrids: a two-stage stochastic programming approach. Appl. Energy **258**, 114022 (2020)
3. Hein, C.: Oil spaces: the global petroleumscape in the Rotterdam/The Hague area. J. Urban Hist. **44**(5), 887–929 (2018)
4. Gómez, C., Green, D.: Small unmanned airborne systems to support oil and gas pipeline monitoring and mapping. Arab. J. Geosci. **10**(9), 1–17 (2017). https://doi.org/10.1007/s12 517-017-2989-x
5. Yau, K., Peng, S., Qadir, J., Low, Y., Ling, M.: Towards smart port infrastructures: enhancing port activities using information and communications technology. IEEE Access **8**, 83387–83404 (2020)
6. Lakhmas, K., Sedqui, P.: Toward a smart port congestion optimizing model. In: Proceedings of IEEE 13th International Colloquium of Logistics and Supply Chain Management (LOGISTIQUA), pp. 1–5 (2020)
7. Huang, X., Wang, J., Xu, Y., Zhu, Y., Tang, T., Xu, F.: Dynamic modeling and analysis of wave compensation system based on floating crane in smart port. In: Proceedings of International Symposium in Sensing and Instrumentation in IoT Era (ISSI), pp. 1–5 (2018)
8. Rolan, A., Manteca, P., Oktar, R., Siano, P.: Integration of cold ironing and renewable sources in the Barcelona smart port. IEEE Trans. Ind. Appl. **55**(6), 7198–7206 (2019)
9. Douaioui, K., Fri, M., Mabrouki, C., Semma, E.: Smart port: design and perspectives. In: Proceedings of 4th International Conference on Logistics Operations Management (GOL), pp. 1–6 (2018)
10. Shakhov, V., Sokolova, O.: On modeling air pollution detection with internet of vehicles. In: Proceedings of 15th International Conference on Ubiquitous Information Management and Communication (IMCOM), pp. 1–3 (2021)
11. Cammin, P., Yu, J., Heilig, L., Voß, S.: Monitoring of air emissions in maritime ports. Transp. Res. Part D Transp. Environ. **87**, 102479 (2020)
12. Martínez-Moya, J., Vazquez-Paja, B., Gimenez Maldonado, J.A.: Energy efficiency and CO_2 emissions of port container terminal equipment: evidence from the Port of Valencia. Energy Policy **131**, 312–319 (2019)
13. Zis, T.: Green ports. In: Psaraftis, H.N. (ed.) Sustainable Shipping, pp. 407–432. Springer, Cham (2019). https://doi.org/10.1007/978-3-030-04330-8_12

14. Tichavska, M., Tovar, B., Gritsenko, D., Johansson, L., Jalkanen, J.P.: Air emissions from ships in port: does regulation make a difference? Transp. Policy **75**, 128–140 (2019)
15. Heilig, L., Voß, S.: Information systems in seaports: a categorization and overview. Inf. Technol. Manag. **18**(3), 179–201 (2016)
16. Jan, S., Ahmed, S., Shakhov, V.V., Koo, I.: Toward a lightweight intrusion detection system for the internet of things. IEEE Access **7**, 42450–42471 (2019)
17. Migov, D., Shakhov, V.: Reliability of ad hoc networks with imperfect nodes. In: Jonsson, M., Vinel, A., Bellalta, B., Belyaev, E. (eds.) MACOM 2014. LNCS, vol. 8715, pp. 49–58. Springer, Cham (2014). https://doi.org/10.1007/978-3-319-10262-7_5
18. Ozger, M., Alagoz, F., Akan, O.: Clustering in multi-channel cognitive radio ad hoc and sensor networks. IEEE Commun. Mag. **56**(4), 156–162 (2018)
19. Shakhov, V., Koo, I.: An efficient clustering protocol for cognitive radio sensor networks. Electronics **10**, 84 (2021)
20. Tsiropoulos, G., Dobre, O., Ahmed, M., Baddour, K.: Radio resource allocation techniques for efficient spectrum access in cognitive radio networks. IEEE Commun. Surv. Tutor. **18**(1), 824–847 (2016)

International Workshop on Smart Tourism (SmartTourism 2021)

Ancient Mining Paths and Slow Tourism. Assessments and Challenges in Sardinia (Italy)

Ginevra Balletto[1]([⊠]), Giuseppe Borruso[2], Alessandra Milesi[1], Mara Ladu[1], and Luigi Mundula[1]

[1] DICAAR - Department of Civil and Environmental Engineering and Architecture, University of Cagliari, 09100 Cagliari, Italy
{balletto,mara.ladu,luigimundula}@unica.it

[2] DEAMS - Department of Economics, Business, Mathematics and Statistics Sciences "Bruno de Finetti", University of Trieste, 34127 Trieste, Italy
giuseppe.borruso@deams.units.it

Abstract. Slow tourism is a sustainable way of traveling: it is not based on the consumption of resources and at the same time is linked to the discovery of local places and traditions. This kind of tourism, which favors a harmonious and responsible development of the territory, is spreading more and more in Italy as a form that best responds to the new restrictions and needs related to the health emergency. More precisely, paths have become one of the most successful and appreciated declinations of slow tourism. A comprehensive strategy has been defined by the Region of Sardinia aimed at diversifying the tourist offer where the paths are becoming an integral part of the island's tourism product portfolio, together with other types of tourism related to culture, sport, food, nature. Within this scenario, this paper investigates the role of the paths in the tourist development of the Sardinia Region. It takes the Sulcis Iglesiente area as a research area. Here, the establishment of the Santa Barbara Mining Path (SBP), in a sensitive area marked by intense mining activity, offers the opportunity to set up an initial assessment of the effects of these initiatives in terms of enhancing the landscape and developing the communities settled. The authors analyze and highlight some of the principles potentially replicable to implement a structured walkability strategy at the regional level. Within this framework, the authors define a methodology to compare, by specific index proposal, the new concepts of SBPs with the first SBP realized in Sardinia.

Keywords: Slow tourism · Mining path · Sustainable tourism · Geomineral Park

1 Introduction

Italy has a very ancient tourist tradition thanks to the variety of its landscapes [1] and the rich historical, artistic and natural heritage of global significance [2, 3], confirming itself as the nation that holds the largest number of sites included by UNESCO in the list of world heritage sites (55) [4]. According to the Bank of Italy estimates, the tourism sector in Italy generated just over 5% of the national GDP and over 6% of the employed

© Springer Nature Switzerland AG 2021
O. Gervasi et al. (Eds.): ICCSA 2021, LNCS 12958, pp. 275–287, 2021.
https://doi.org/10.1007/978-3-030-87016-4_21

in 2019, which is equivalent to a higher economic impact than that recorded in France and Germany [5].

Although in the last twenty years the tourism sector has experienced exponential growth on a global scale, the health emergency marked a sharp break in that trend that seemed destined to increase in the coming years. In fact, the Covid-19 pandemic has hit the whole world, putting all economic sectors in crisis. In this context, the tourism sector is among the most vulnerable, being affected both in terms of supply and demand [6]: on the one hand, the restrictions imposed on free movement within national and international borders have reduced the number of bookings; on the other hand, the entire sector also had to change the consolidated standards to adapt to the particular contingent moment which altered the lifestyles in everyday life as well as the ways of traveling, forcing us to keep certain distances. In this sense, sustainable tourism, in its declination of slow tourism, is the most responsive to new needs [7]. The 2017 has been defined as the International Year of Sustainable Tourism by the UN, which recognized its specific role in pursuing inclusive economic growth in balance with the environment. In Italy too, after the national year of the paths (2016), of the villages (2017) and of Italian food (2018), 2019 has been declared the year of slow tourism [8], understood as that form of experiential tourism, innovative and sustainable capable of enhancing the territory in all its diversity as it makes movement, even more than halfway, an integral part of the journey [9]. Even the ways of crossing and using the places are the most diverse. They include cultural and natural itineraries, religious and spiritual paths, journeys on horseback and aboard historic trains up to the cycle paths, a significant expression of the changes that are affecting the tourism industry at European level in a sporting, healthy and sustainable way [10]. Within this scenario, the paths are enjoying great success in Italy, becoming one of the main symbols of slow tourism. In fact, in 2017 the MiBACT established the Digital Atlas of the Paths of Italy [11] to support the process of enhancement and promotion of a series of contexts that have been little known up to now, especially in the internal areas of the country. The clear approach adopted at national level to promote new ways of managing and using the territory is the basis of the Strategic Tourism Plan 2017–2022, which identifies sustainability, innovation and accessibility/permeability of territories as transversal principles [12, 13]. These same principles guide government strategies and policies on a regional scale, where the concept of slow tourism finds its precise expression.

On the basis of the considerations set out so far, this contribution investigates the role of slow tourism, in particular of the walks, in defining the policies for the tourism development of the Sardinia Region and takes the territory of Sulcis-Iglesiente as a research area, where the recent establishment of the Santa Barbara Path - Mining Route in a sensitive area marked by intense mining activity, offers the opportunity to set up an initial assessment of the effects of these initiatives in terms of enhancement of the landscape and of development of the local community.

The conception of the mining landscape and the surrounding heritage as an element to be valued originated with the establishment of the GeoMining Historical Environmental Park of Sardinia (Geomineral Park). It was formally established in 2001 after a work begun many years earlier with the aim of safeguarding and enhancing the tangible and intangible values in 8 specific areas of the Region, consisting of the geological context, the mining engineering heritage of industrial archeology, the traditions and knowledge of the local community.

After an initial assessment of the geomineral contexts and their enhancement, the authors analyze the principles and potentially replicable elements and demonstrate how this first experience is proving to be a best practice for starting a structured planning of walkability at the regional level, also involving other territorial contexts that they choose to promote forms of slow tourism starting from the enhancement of the local environmental, historical and cultural resource.

The present study is organized into the following parts:

- Material (Sect. 2), which focuses on the origins and characteristics of the Santa Barbara Path and the new proposals;
- Methodology to compare the new proposals with Santa Barbara path by index proposal (Sect. 3);
- Case study, where the authors apply the methodology (Sect. 4)
- Study results and conclusions (Sect. 5).

2   Material: The *'Best Practice'* of Mining Path of Santa Barbara (Sardinia, Italy)

The economy of Sardinia, for a long time, has been characterized by an intense mining activity that has bequeathed a landscape of abandoned sites and industrial archeology which, in recent decades, has been at the center of a series of policies and projects aimed at its progressive enhancement. A first action was the establishment, in 2001, of the Geomineral Historic and Environmental park of Sardinia (Geomineral Park), as a tool to protect and safeguard all the tangible and intangible heritage made up of the geological context, the technical-scientific heritage and mining engineering, the heritage of industrial archeology, from the documentary heritage of works and from culture, traditions and knowledge. It extends to the regional level, including the main territorial areas affected by extractive activities. In fact, it is divided into 8 areas covering 81 Municipalities of Sardinia, for a total area of approximately 3800 km^2 [14].

In the wake of this awareness, in Sulcis Iglesiente, a historic region of south-western Sardinia, interesting bottom-up initiatives have been created for the protection and enhancement of the territory. First the birth of the Pozzo Sella Onlus Association in 2001 with the aim of contributing to the development of the Geomineral Park and to which we owe the creation of the Santa Barbara Path, then the establishment, in 2016, of the Foundation called "Cammino Minerario di Santa Barbara", with the task of implementing, promoting and managing the path [15–20].

These are projects in response to the economic crisis and the abandonment of the territory. As a matter of fact, the area of Sulcis Iglesiente has been for millennia interested in a complex mining activity, such as to be considered the main extractive basin not only of the Island but of the whole Mediterranean. This territory was the most important district for national and international mining due to its large production of lead and zinc. The crisis in the mining sector and the subsequent closure of the mines in the 1990s left a rich heritage of industrial archeology and infrastructure, as well as a unique landscape.

01_SBP - SW Sulcis - Iglesiente - Arburese- Guspinese

The Santa Barbara Path [21] retraces the ancient mining routes of the Sulcis Iglesiente - Guspinese, developing as a ring for a length of about 500 km, divided into 30 arches of 16 km each.

It is accessible on foot, by bicycle or by horse and its altitude spans from zero at the sea level to an altitude of 900 m. The 30 stages of the route have been defined on the basis of the following parameters: length in km, difficulty traveling and availability of accommodation facilities. The landscape of the path is characterized by a complex geological heritage and industrial archeology - mineral deposits, excavations and mine dumps and buildings - from an important ancient archeological heritage - domus de nuraghi, sacred wells, etc. - and significant heritage natural (beaches, cliffs, lagoons, etc.). All these elements highlight the vastity of mining operations carried out in the main mining places of the district, such as the great mines of Monteponi, San Giovanni and Masua, and their related processing plants and handling systems, as the historical Laveria Lamarmora and Porto Flavia plants.

Along the route there is also a significant number of points of historical-cultural and naturalistic interest, reception and refreshment activities.

Thanks to its particular features, the Santa Barbara Path has been included in the regional register of historical-religious paths of Sardinia since 2013. Subsequently, in 2017 the Ministry of Cultural Heritage and Activities and Tourism has included it in the first 'Atlas of the Paths of Italy'.

In recent years, the projects have been conceived as a model to other local initiatives.

After the positive experience of the of Santa Barbara Path (01_SBP) of the Sulcis Iglesiente and in the light of the growing interest developed in it, the Pozzo Sella Onlus Association has launched an intense activity aimed at verifying the existence of favorable conditions for the construction of new walks in other island contexts characterized by a similar historical, cultural, environmental and religious heritage inherited from the mining activity developed in Sardinia. These studies have led to the development of the proposal for the establishment of three other itineraries dedicated to the patron saint of miners in order to enhance the former paths linked to mining present in other areas of Sardinia (Fig. 1):

- 02_SBP in the north-west, in the Nurra area
- 03_SBP in the central south in the territories of Ogliastra, Barbagia di Seulo and Sarcidano
- 04_SBP in the south east in the Sarrabus Gerrei area.

02_SBP - NW Nurra

The project of the "Mineral Santa Barbara Path of the North-West" retraces the ancient mining routes of the Nurra - historical region in the North-Western of Sardinia - developing as a ring for a length of about 500 km, involving 7 Municipalities: Sassari (37% of the total length of the itinerary), Alghero (35%), Porto Torres (10%), Olmedo (8%), Putifigari (8%) and Uri (2%). The current definition of the project aimed at making known and enhancing the great historical, cultural, environmental, geological, landscape and

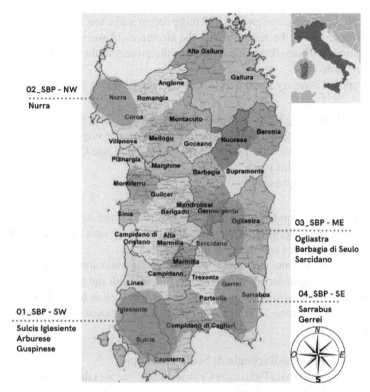

Fig. 1. Location of mining paths of Santa Barbara, Sardinia, Italy (01–04 SBP)

religious heritage linked to the past mining activity and to the other human events that characterize the territory.

The basic conditions that led to conceive and propose the construction of the new Path can be summarized as follows:

- the presence, in the Nurra, of disused mining sites that can be traced back to the Phoenician, Punic and Roman periods, playing an important role in mining production with particular reference to the metal sector;
- the presence, in the former mining sites themselves, of churches and religious buildings dedicated to the patroness of miners, whose veneration is still practiced today with celebrations and processions in the former mines of Olmedo, Argentiera and Canaglia, and of the Orthodox church dedicated to Santa Barbara in historic center of Alghero;
- the coincidence of long stretches of the Santa Barbara Path with some historical routes of the local pilgrimage, such as the one traveled by the faithful from the town of Putifigari to the Sanctuary of N.S. of Valverde in the municipality of Alghero.

These elements reinforce the meaning and the spirituality of the Path. More specifically, it is possible to affirm that the significant heritage present in the territory of Nurra, together with the presence of ancient and more recent paths that allow to reach the mining sites widespread in the territory with the structures of worship dedicated to Santa Barbara, can be considered the true matrix for the project of the Santa Barbara Mining Path of the North-West.

The proposed itinerary has the following characteristics:

- Length: 204 km along a circular route that starts and ends at the Olmedo mine;
- Stages/days of walking: 11 with an average of 19 km per stage;
- Altimeters from 0 (beaches of Alghero) to 406 m asl Monte Capparone;
- 60% of the route on dirt roads;
- 70% already easily accessible;

Stages and stopping points coinciding with the abandoned mines to be regenerated (Olmedo, Calabona, Argentiera, Canaglia) and with other sites equipped with existing accommodation facilities and/or to be implemented.

The hypothesized route will also allow to reach the main archaeological sites of the territory, the most significant geological emergencies with the relative paleontological peculiarities and the most significant hills of the territory such as Monte Timidone (360 m asl) and Monte Capparone (406 m asl) from which it is possible to admire the Nurra Landscape.

03_SBP - ME Ogliastra-Barbagia di Seulo-Sarcidano

The "Mineral Santa Barbara Path of the Central-South" retraces the ancient mining routes of the Ogliastra Barbagia di Seulo Sarcidano - historical region in the Central South Sardinia - developing as a ring for a length of about 60 km, involving 5 Municipalities: Mandas, Seui, Seulo, Gadoni and Laconi.

Some critical issues in terms of walkability and tourist use, essentially due to the morphological characteristics of the site, the location of the itinerary and the linearity of the existing path, are offset by numerous favorable aspects to the realization of the Path: the presence of ancient paths in the area that can be redeveloped and reused; the possibility of overcoming morphological barriers through the construction of low-impact infrastructures; the possibility of creating a ring route with the integration of other route, including the historic green train; the new life for the Funtana Raminosa mine as a museum and the redevelopment of the industrial archeology structures of the San Sebastiano-Corongiu anthracite mine.

The proposed itinerary has the following characteristics:

- Total length: 175 km (of which 110 in the green train) along a ring route that starts and arrives at Mandas station;
- Stages/days of walking: No. 4 with an average length of 16 km per stage, to which the first and last leg of the itinerary to be covered with the green train must be added;
- Altimeters: from 345 (course of the Flumendosa) to 1100 m asl (in the municipality of Seui);
- 60% of the route with the green train;
- 35% on paths and dirt roads that are already easily accessible;

- 5% on asphalted roads and/or paving in built-up areas;

Stages and stopping points coinciding with the inhabited centers directly involved (Mandas, Seui, Seulo, Santa Sofia and Laconi), where an adequate accommodation system exists and can be implemented. In the "Funtana Ramiosa mine" it is possible to host pilgrims/hikers in the old miners' homes and in the former mine's guesthouse.

04_SBP - SE Sarrabus - Gerrei
The idea of establishing a new itinerary called "Mineral Santa Barbara Path of the "South-Est" arises from the presence in the Sarrabus Gerrei area of numerous disused mining companies that have played an important role in the past mining production and from the presence in the same mining sites of churches and religious buildings dedicated to the patroness of miners as evidence of the ancient veneration for Santa Barbara, still practiced today with celebrations and processions in various municipalities in the area. Furthermore, the presence of ancient and recent paths that allow you to walk to the disused mining sites and the connected places of worship dedicated to Santa Barbara, represents the real opportunity for the realization of the new itinerary. The idea is that of a circular route with the following characteristics:

- length: 235 km along a circular route that starts and arrives from the inhabited center of the municipality of Sinnai;
- Stages/days of walking: n. 10/13 with an average length of 23/18 km per stage, to be defined according to the accommodation facilities or stopping points that can be created in the stages that exceed 30 km in length; (from Villasalto to San Vito, from San Vito to Sardinia Outdoors and from Sardinia Outdoors to Burcei);
- Altimeters from 804 (Sa Cotte and Baccas in the municipality of Donori) to 13 m asl (inhabited center of S. Vito);
- 75% on paths, mule tracks and dirt roads;
- 25% on asphalted and/or paved roads in built-up areas;
- Stages and stopping points coinciding with the inhabited centers crossed (Sinnai, Donori, Silius, Goni, Ballao, Armungia, Villasalto, San Vito and Burcei), while the possibility of creating adequate accommodation facilities and/or stopping points in the structures must be verified abandoned mines starting from the village of Monte Narba.

The itinerary, to be covered on foot, will allow you to reach geosites of considerable importance (fossiliferous geosite with graptolites of Peinconi north of the town of Goni, the course of the Rio Ollastu etc.) which, thanks also to the archaeological and mineralogical heritage put in evidence from the past mining activity, allows to tell the evolution of the earth's crust in the last 350 million years and archaeological sites (archaeological park of Pranu Mutteddu in Goni, sacred well of Funtana Coberta in Ballao, urban nuraghe of Armungia, castle of Orguglioso in Silius etc.) which testify to the presence of man in the territory in the last 5,500 years.

3   A Comparative Methodology: An Index Proposal

The following methodology aims to compare the recently proposed Santa Barbara paths, here named 02, 03 and 04 SBP, with the first realized Santa Barbara path, here named 01_SBP. In particular, considering that 01_SBP represents a 'best practice' [7, 22] in terms of export and replication of the mining path model, a specific replication method based on a composite index was developed, referring to the inclusion of community and environment (ICE Index). In particular, the methodology allows to evaluate how the recent proposals of the new three paths (02–04 SBP) are in line with the Guidelines for the development of the Territorial Tourist Product, Santa Barbara Mining Trail [23], with particular reference to the following factors: *prevention*, through the enhancement of oriented projects to anticipate social and environmental problems; *promotion*, through community-environment policies based on well-being and quality of life; *participation*, through an active and responsible role in terms of the community and the environment; *partnerships*, with network forms for shared planning and joint management of initiatives. In this sense, the main factors of inclusion (community-environment), such as belonging to the Geomining park (an area with strong characterizations in terms of enhancement of the mine landscape; number of municipal administrations involved, local reference population, incidence of natural-original mine paths, ...) constitute the first indicators on which the ICE index is based. The ICE index aims to compare proposals and to support decisions for the advancement of their design. The conceptual model of the method is shown below. It will be subject to future application on a larger number of indicators that can be extrapolated from a database built by the authors in previous research [19] and by the Foundation of the Santa Barbara path itself [21], (Fig. 2).

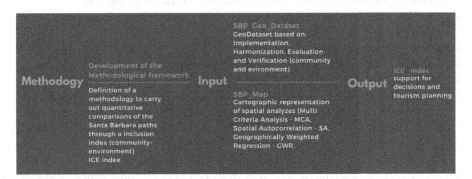

Fig. 2. Methodological framework

In particular, the ICE index can be represented as follow:

$$\text{ICE Index} = \frac{\sum_{i=1}^{n} i * Wi}{\sum_{i=1}^{n} Wi}$$

where i = incidence factor of community-environment inclusion factors (divided into *prevention, promotion, participation, partnerships*). The definition of specific weights, which also derive from 'Guidelines for the development of the Territorial Tourist Product, Santa Barbara Mining Route' [see note 2], is particularly important in the computation of the different indexes. ICE index must then be divided by maximum Ice index in order to obtain ICE index relating to the group for which the comparison is to be made.

4   Case Study. Methodology Application to the Mining Paths of Santa Barbara in Sardinia (01–04 SBP)

The process of enhancing the real estate assets inherited from the previous mining activity and of redevelopment of the landscape shaped by human actions took place in the past according to the approach aimed at the creation of museums in the sites. The mining landscape, with its buildings and areas, created for functional purposes and, often, without any stylistic pretense, become museums of themselves, according to an approach widespread in large part of national and international disused mining sites which, however, has not given great results. A new approach was adopted on the occasion of the establishment of the Santa Barbara path which, through the enhancement of the existing routes, which connect the various disused mining sites, determines the transition from the concept of node (museum) to the concept of network (landscape). The objective of this contribution is to define criteria for the comparative analysis of the Santa Barbara Path in the Sulcis Iglesiente area with the three new paths being defined in other historical regions of Sardinia, in order to highlight the determining factors for the project's success. A first analysis allowed to compare the four paths obtaining the following summary scheme (Fig. 3):

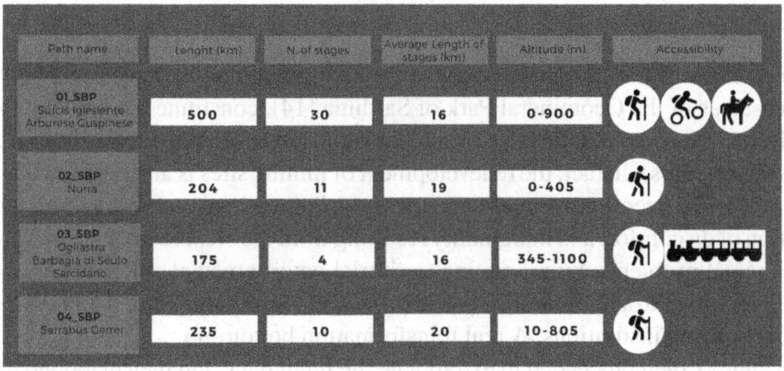

Fig. 3. Synthesis scheme of mining paths 01–04 Santa Barbara Path (SBP), Sardinia.

Furthermore, since the four paths analyzed fall within the Geomineral Park (Fig. 4), it was considered appropriate to evaluate for each one the incidence in terms of territorial area concerned and number of municipalities crossed within the same Park, the population and number of municipalities involved, as well as the percentage incidence of original and/or rural routes.

In this sense, the numerous strategies, which later became actions on the territory (tangible - museums, environmental laboratories - and intangible - training and

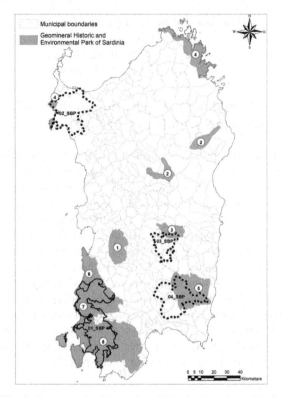

Fig. 4. Framework of the paths within the Geomineral Park.

awareness-raising) for the enhancement of the disused mining heritage promoted in the eight sub-areas of the Geomineral Park of Sardinia [14], constitute the preconditions of the Paths in terms of community-environment inclusion (prevention, promotion, participation, partnerships). In fact, the redevelopment of mining sites is an operation that is not only aimed at the recovery of landscape contexts, but at a real reconversion in terms of prevention of discomfort and marginality resulting from the closure of mines with related environmental problems, by promoting territorial-environmental emergencies and collective creativity, through the active participation of communities and partnerships with public and private institutions. A real transformation bottom-up.

The authors then proceeded to extrapolate the input data, and then elaborate the ICE index referring to the 'best practice' (01_SBP). It should be noted that $w_i = 1/n$, where n = number of incidence factors (i), in accordance with the Statute of the Foundation of the Path of Santa Barbara and with the first outcomes of the Strategic Plan of the homonymous route. In the summary scheme (Fig. 5) the inputs and outputs are reported. The first results that emerged are discussed in Sect. 5.

Path name	N. Municipalities sub area of the Geo-mining park	N. Municipalities crossed by the path	Municipalities areas crossed (sq km)	N inhabitants of the municipalities crossed	% of original or natural paths	Network elements	ICE idex
01_SBP Sulcis Iglesiente Arburese Guspinese	39	26	2 416	153 076	75%	Abandoned mining area Mining villages Country churches Archeological sites Geological sites Mine landscapes	1
02_SBP Nurra	5	6	1 020	197 387	60%		0.55
03_SBP Ogliastra Barbagia di Seulo Sarcidano	4	5	420	6 623	35%		0.22
04_SBP Sarrabus Gerrei	11	9	874	29 184	75%		0.41
Total	59	46	4730	386 270			

Fig. 5. Framework - input data and output data

5 Results and Conclusion

The three proposals of Ways 02, 03 and 04 SBP constitute a first territorial application of replication with adaptation of the 'best practice' 01 SBP. In this sense, the evaluation of the ICE index (Fig. 5) allows us to highlight how the three proposals still differ considerably from the reference case, in particular 03_SBP.

In fact, the few municipalities and the small size of the communities involved determine an ICE index about half lower than that of the reference case (01_SBP).

In light of this assessment, in the design phase of the three paths (02–04 SBP) it will be necessary to build solid networks of active participation of communities and institutions also outside the system, in order to achieve similar conditions with respect to the reference case. In addition, even the incidence of the originality of the route - very low in 03 SBP - can be recovered through a slow multimodal mobility system.

In other words, the exportability of the best practice, at the moment, does not occur in absolute terms for the following reasons: the proposed routes insist in marginal portions compared to the sub-areas of the Geomineral Park, and therefore do not benefit from the related direct and the limited number of municipalities involved does not facilitate network actions. In fact, at the basis of the success of the paths, in addition to material actions, the ability to network between institutions and communities plays a strategic role, able to favor the transition from anticommons (mining activities) to commons (museum, cultural tourism activities), through semicommons (temporary cultural and tourist use) [24].

The next phases of the research will be aimed at defining further elements of incidence (i) to support the evaluation of the ICE (Inclusion of Community and Environment) index, organized by macro-categories (prevention, promotion, participation, partnerships) for which the weights will be determined in accordance with the three-year update of the Strategic Plan of the Foundation Mining Path of Santa Barbara.

This work is part of the activities of the scientific committee of the 'Foundation Mining Path of Santa Barbara' (prof G. Balletto, Prof R. Paci, Prof I. Meloni, University of Cagliari).

References

1. Lanzani, A.: I paesaggi italiani, vol. 21. Meltemi Editore srl (2003)
2. Casini, L.: Un patrimonio culturale senza frontiere? Aedon **2**, 1–3 (2018)
3. Pettenati, G.: I paesaggi culturali Unesco in Italia. FrancoAngeli (2019)
4. http://www.unesco.it/it/ItaliaNellUnesco/Detail/188
5. Petrella, A., et al.: Questioni di Economia e finanza. Turismo in Italia. Numeri e potenziale di sviluppo, no. 505. Banca d'Italia, Roma (2019). https://www.bancaditalia.it/pubblicazioni/qef/2019-0505/QEF_505_19.pdf
6. UNWTO: COVID-19: Putting People First. UNWTO, 14 April 2020. https://www.unwto.org/tourism-covid-19
7. Balletto, G., Milesi, A., Ladu, M., Borruso, G.: A dashboard for supporting slow tourism in green infrastructures. a methodological proposal in Sardinia (Italy). Sustainability **12**(9), 3579 (2020)
8. https://www.beniculturali.it/mibac/export/MiBAC/sito-MiBAC/Contenuti/MibacUnif/Comunicati/visualizza_asset.html_611361093.html
9. Costa, S., Coles, R., Boultwood, A.: Landscape experience and the speed of walking. Landsc. Flux 124–128 (2015)
10. ENIT: Il mercato del cicloturismo in Europa. Politiche, andamenti e prospettive, A cura della Direzione Centrale Programmazione e Comunicazione (2015)
11. Portale. www.camminiditalia.it
12. MiBACT: Piano Strategico di Sviluppo per il Turismo 2017–2022. MiBACT, Roma (2016). https://www.beniculturali.it/mibac/multimedia/MiBAC/documents/1481892223634_PST_2017_IT.pdf
13. Presenza, A., Formato, R.: Management della destinazione turistica: attori, strategie e indicatori di performance. FrancoAngeli (2018)
14. Parco Geominerario Web Site. http://www.parcogeominerario.eu/. Accessed 15 Sept 2019
15. Balletto, G., Milesi, A., Ladu, M., Borruso G.: Le reti per la reinvenzione del passato. Il caso del Cammino di Santa Barbara (Sardegna, Italia). In: Proceedings of the 23rd IPSAPA/ISPALEM International Scientific Conference Napoli, Italy, 4–5 July 2019, pp. 179–191 (2019). ISBN 978-88-942329-5-0
16. Balletto, G., Milesi, A., Mundula, L., Borruso, G.: Wave, walk and bike tourism. The case of Sulcis (Sardinia-Italy). In: Gargiulo, C., Zoppi, C. (eds.) Planning, Nature and Ecosystem Services, pp. 881–892. FedOAPress, Naples (2019)
17. Ladu, M., Milesi, A., Borruso, G., Balletto, G.: Turismo lento nel Sulcis Iglesiente. Mappe di comunità per le sfide dello sviluppo turistico locale. In: Atti della XXIII Conferenza Nazionale ASITA, 12–14 novembre 2019, Trieste, pp: 595–602 (2019). ISBN 978-88-941232-5-8
18. Balletto, G., Milesi, A., Battino, S., Borruso, G., Mundula, L.: Slow tourism and smart community. The case of Sulcis - Iglesiente (Sardinia - Italy). In: Misra, S., et al. (eds.) ICCSA 2019. LNCS, vol. 11624, pp. 184–199. Springer, Cham (2019). ISBN 978-3-030-24310-4. https://doi.org/10.1007/978-3-030-24311-1_13
19. Balletto, G., Milesi, A., Ladu, M., Borruso, G.: A dashboard for supporting slow tourism in green infrastructures. A methodological proposal in Sardinia (Italy). Sustainability **12**(9), 3579 (2020). https://doi.org/10.3390/su12093579
20. Ladu, M., Balletto, G., Milesi, A., Borruso, G.: Il ruolo delle tecnologie digitali nella promozione del turismo lento in Sardegna (Italia). Una proposta per il Cammino di Santa Barbara. In: AA. VV., Atti della XXIII Conferenza Nazionale SIU, Torino 17–18 Giugno 2021 - Piani e politiche per una nuova accessibilità, vol. 08, pp. 80–89. Planum Publisher e Società Italiana degli Urbanisti, Roma Milano (2021). ISBN 978-88-99237-35-6. https://doi.org/10.53143/PLM.C.821

21. Cammino Minerario di Santa Barbara Web Site. https://www.camminominerariodisantabarb
ara.org/. Accessed 15 Sept 2019
22. Il sole24ore Web Site. https://www.ilsole24ore.com/art/santa-barbara-primo-posto-top-10-
cammini-d-italia-ACdqaT9
23. Fondazione Cammino di Santa Barbara: Il cammino minerario di Santa Barbara linee guida
per lo sviluppo del prodotto turistico territoriale (2018). https://www.camminominerariodisan
tabarbara.org/wp-content/uploads/2020/02/CMSB_Linee-Guida.pdf. Accessed 11 May 2020
24. Balletto, G., Milesi, A., Fenu, N., Borruso, G., Mundula, L.: Military training areas as
semicommons: the territorial valorization of Quirra (Sardinia) from easements to ecosystem
services. Sustainability **12**(2), 622 (2020)

Sustainability, Tourism and Digitalization. The City Smart Approach in Las Palmas de Gran Canaria (Canary Islands)

Ainhoa Amaro García[1] and Silvia Battino[2]([⊠])

[1] University of Las Palmas de Gran Canaria, Canary Islands,
35017 Las Palmas de Gran Canaria, Spain
[2] DiSea - University of Sassari, 07100 Sassari, Sardinia, Italy
sbattino@uniss.it

Abstract. To achieve the environmental and socio-economic sustainability goals set by the 2030 Agenda, tourist destinations, particularly those that have already reached maturity, have taken steps to change their development model in the short and long term. In this context, the smartness approach can help local governments to implement smart growth projects to improve, even in a sustainable way, the use of places by tourists and, also, to optimize the residents' quality of life.

This is even more true in this historical moment characterized by the covid-19 health emergency which imposed compliance with various rules, one of which is social distancing. Thus, it is fundamental that the territories are transformed into smart spaces where the innovative aspect is the basis for efficiently offering resources and services.

Starting from these considerations, the aim of the paper is to highlight the role of Information and Communication Technologies (ICT) on the island of Gran Canaria (Canary Islands). The Island and in particular the city of Las Palmas de Gran Canaria have been working for a long time to promote knowledge and valorization of the territory through greater use of new technologies and applications, for example, for smartphones and tablets. The city, to meet the "new" demands of the post-covid era, has refined, and activated new tools to enhance the tourism experience.

Keywords: Smart tourism · Sustainability · Innovation · Las Palmas de Gran Canaria

1 Introduction

The Year 2020 will be remembered as the year of the most important health, economic and social crisis of modern times[1]. The Covid-19 pandemic brought the world system to its knees and the tourism sector was one of the economic sectors most affected. The

---

[1] The study was supported by the "Fondo di Ateneo per la Ricerca 2020" (University of Sassari). This paper is the result of the joint work of the authors. In particular: Sects. 1, 2, 3 and 4 have been written by Silvia Battino and Sects. 5 and 6 by Ainhoa Amaro García.

© Springer Nature Switzerland AG 2021
O. Gervasi et al. (Eds.): ICCSA 2021, LNCS 12958, pp. 288–301, 2021.
https://doi.org/10.1007/978-3-030-87016-4_22

travel world has been put on "stand-by" due to health restrictions that have affected each country. According to data from the World Tourism Organization in 2020 [1] international arrivals have decreased by 74% compared to the previous year due to social distancing, restrictions, and general insecurity, which means on the one hand discourage departures, but on the other motivate and transform the needs of future tourist demand. There are several studies [2–5] which show that there is a need to travel in search of regenerative and rebalancing activities in contact with nature. Therefore, vacations are characterized by sustainability and alternative experiences to know and learn the identity aspects of the host destination. In this context there are different realities that move with more determination and efficiency to offer "new and alternative" forms of tourism that can meet both the needs of future tourists and the facilities to achieve the Agenda 2030 sustainable goals.

The constant search for tools that can improve the level of sustainability has inevitably led the many tourism realities make a real transition to an intelligent model in where technological innovations play the main role in the organization of structured and efficient spaces. These new ways of innovations are linked and interactive spaces that help to be able to compete in a highly globalized sector such as tourism [6].

The need to create "cohesive" spaces starts when the smart concept is applied to different spaces. In particular, the requirement to make spaces more accessible and integrated, starts in urban contexts, where the role of Information Communication Technologies (ICTs) has been key to activate different projects of development and sustainable growth. We talk about Smart Cities as intelligent places whose main purpose is not only to improve the quality of life of its dwellers but also on the environment, transport, governance, and social life. In other words, tourism must benefit from the positive effects of innovation [7–10].

The smartness approach has not limited to the urban sphere but has also affected other realities such as Smart Villages, Smart Tourism Destinations (STDs) and Smart Islands [11–15]. In these spaces, the tourism sector deserves more attention for smart responses to be found to also satisfy the needs of tourists and to organize a structured offer of resources and services [16, 17].

The concept of "smart tourism" is therefore now an integral part of the "new" travel experience: apps for smartphones and tablets, social networks, and blogs, specifically dedicated to transport bookings, accommodations, and other commodities and services. These tools motivate the modern tourist to experience the places of the vacation independently [11, 18, 19].

2 Objectives and Methodology

The purpose of this paper is to understand the importance of the use of new technologies and how they can help tourist destinations to design new resources and services for tourism, in order to improve the competitiveness and image of the territories. The first part of the work begins with a short review of the literature on the concept of smartness, starting from urban contexts. The second part is, instead, dedicated to the case study of Gran Canaria, an important island of the Canary Islands, and specifically of the capital city of Las Palmas de Gran Canaria, which has been carrying out innovative initiatives and projects to improve its tourist areas for the longest time.

3 Related Works

There are several negatives perceived and endured by residents due to an excessive tourist presence [20]. This phenomenon is particularly felt in urban areas and, specifically, in those cities that serve as tourist hubs whose attractiveness takes on national and international characteristics. Hence the emergence of smart city paradigm´s as a solution to overcome the above dichotomy and to ensure that both tourists and dwellers can together benefit from the same urban spaces [10]. In fact, the evolution of information technology and telecommunications has allowed the administration of multiple information related to different places and to assure, contemporarily, the attractiveness of their tourist elements. In this way, the cultural needs of an ever increasing number of travelers are better satisfied, driven to move in an experiential and not exclusively recreational perspective, where, thanks to the computer-mediated reality, perception can be followed by reflection to ensure that the experience itself is remembered in time. In this sense, in this perspective it should be interpreted the 2018 biannual project of the European Commission "European Capital of Smart Tourism - ECoST" with which the EU wanted to reward European cities that were committed with admirable ideas and practices to become smart tourist destinations. Accessibility, sustainability, digitization and integral use of their cultural heritage and creative capacities were to be the operational commitments of these capitals [21, 22].

Digital technologies are constantly and rapidly evolving, hence the need to activate punctual and constant monitoring to acquire useful information to measure the level and quality of digitization of tourism places: first and foremost, of the most complex and heterogeneous urban functionality destinations, to keep their attractiveness high in terms of competitiveness and efficiency [23]. Thus, smart cities become prescriptive examples for current urban spaces, and it is no coincidence that the indicators of their smartness level, which are highlighted on four basic guidelines (sustainability, resilience, accessibility, and inclusivity), need careful checks related to their efficacy to better support the sustainability goal under the European Strategy 2020 [24, 25]. In this sense if urban smartness is high, the more city users (permanent and temporary) will enter symbiosis with the city. Using, analyzing, and organizing what is shared on social media (from tweeter to facebook) as a measure of the urban sensing becomes a real means to meet the needs of residents and visitors: this geo-referenced information allows the construction of dynamic maps to describe and synthesize the use of the city. Those who use the city, including visitors, are not only consumers of information, but also, they are become producers of the same information and contribute (consciously or unconsciously) to the development of the Internet of Things and to the evolutionary transition from the "smart city" to the "sentient city". Specifically, mobile devices together with ITC and the network contribute significantly to improve the position and the possibility of displacement of tourists and to enhance urban resources: smart map, sensing location and augmented reality stand out for these purposes [26–28].

In the instance of island territories, the resources invested in information technology are significant because as a tourist destination, and not only that, but they also had to compete at an international level and propose, at the same time, models of sustainable living for both guests and hosts [29]. In the European context, this smart approach leads to consider islands as exemplary places: laboratories where innovative projects can be tested [30, 31]. Among all of them, we would like to mention the European Project Smart Islands that since 2015 involves several island realities such as the island of Majorca in Spain, Yeu in France, Favignana in Italy, Kythnos in Greece, Saaremaa in Estonia, and Samsø in Denmark that have committed to adopt smart solutions to improve development and growth also in a touristic perspective [32].

The enhancement of digitized facilities and infrastructures has been found to be useful and strategic, even with the spread of COVID-19 for the aforementioned spread of the use of the same, and to overcome the obligation of "stay at home" in favor of a "staycation" thanks to the proliferation and consequent spread of offline cultural activities and the creation of intelligent tourism products that are realized in "augmented reality" (AR) and "virtual reality" (VR) [10]. Consequently, e-tourism, in view of the damage caused to the tourism industry by the current pandemic, seems to have to represent itself the challenge existing between current models and to evaluate critically its ontological and gnoseological conceptions through a transformative study related to its own temporality, reflexivity, equity, transparency, multiplicity and creativity [33]. New challenges, therefore, require the search for a juxtaposition of short to medium term, and long-term perspectives in tourism governance.

The COVID-19 pandemic and its consequent impact on mobility (contraction and/or optimization), not least in terms of tourism [34], has certainly led to a growing awareness of the importance of digital use within the limits of the presence of digital divide situations both in its cognitive and infrastructural dimensions. Cities, those that are already smart, are likely to obtain from this pandemic situation significant improvements in their cyberspace in terms of sustainability and attractiveness [35].

4 The Territorial Context

The island of Gran Canaria is one of seven islands - El Hierro, La Palma, La Gomera, Tenerife, Fuerteventura, Lanzarote and six islets as Alegranza, Graciosa (with Ley 1/2018 reforming the Estatuto de Autonomía de Canarias the status of this *islote* was changed to *isla*), Montaña Clara, Roque del Este, Roque del Oeste, and Lobos - that compose the Canary Islands Archipelago (Autonomous Community of Spain) [36–39]. Gran Canaria's population is 851,231 in 2019 [40], which is distributed among 21 municipalities. Of these, the most populated are Las Palmas de Gran Canaria with 377,650 inhabitants, Telde with 102,005 inh. and Santa Lucia de Tirajana with 53,542 inh. Las Palmas de Gran Canaria was founded in 1478 and it is also the capital of the Island located on the north-eastern coast. In addition to being one of the most populated urban realities of the Island and the Archipelago, it also occupies the ninth place in the ranking of the Mainland with a population density of 3,755 inh./km^2. Due to the warm climate, the favorable geographical position of the archipelago, the wide range of beaches and the peculiar morphology of the territory, the image of the island is mainly linked to the combination of sun and sea and consequently its tourist offer has been structured to meet the needs of sun&beach tourists. The territory also offers other attractions related to nature and culture that allow the local government to diversify the product "leisure" and activate interesting strategies of local sustainable development [41–45]. The tourists who visited Gran Canaria in 2019 were 4,189,013 and most of them, mainly from Northern European countries, preferred accommodation in hotels (74.6%).

The tourists' motivation for spending their vacations on the island is mainly linked to relaxation (59.3%), and the activities carried out include hours spent on the beach (71.6%), in the swimming pool (56.5%), walking (67.0%) or visiting by themselves the numerous attractions of the island (42.5%). However, it is interesting to note that almost all travelers (92.4%) make use of internet connection (personal or free wifi) to consult thematic maps (60.3%) and information on the destination (43.9%), share images and videos (53.9%), download applications of tourist interest (6.5%) [46].

In this island tourism landscape, Las Palmas de Gran Canaria is the main urban destination and there were 442,845 tourists who chose to stay overnight in the city (2019) for an average presence of 3.19 days [47]. The urban space is also visited annually by a regular flow of cruise passengers (723,655 in 2019) [48]. These tourists move around attracted by the many urban resources: from Las Canteras beach to Santa Catalina Park, from Casa de Colón to Mercado de Vegueta for example.

Since a long time, the Cabildo de Gran Canaria has focused its attention on the drawing up of strategies for the tourist development of the territory to make the Island a leading smart tourist destination in the world. The "Estrategia Integral de Turismo de Gran Canaria (EITGC)" is therefore the current strategic document that aims to combine different aspects: the tourism product management and its promotion, the sustainable development, the public policies, and competitiveness. To ensure that the territory can aspire to the title of smart destination, all actors must be involved in the creation of innovative networks capable of boosting sustainable and competitive tourism [49].

As it has underlined before, the pandemic has caused a huge impact on Gran Canaria due to its dependence of tourism as a main source of income. However, this new situation has been used as an opportunity to diversify the traditional model into a technological destination. Apart from the structural initiatives that Gran Canaria has made from 2016–2020, the administration has decided to take advantage of this new pandemic scenery through the project "SMARTDEST" that improves intelligence of space collaboration with the implementation of Information Technology Solution and Communications to involve an Intelligent Tourist Destination [50]. This project is divided into various initiatives to be carried out within, among others objectives, transform Gran Canaria into a Smart Tourist Destinations (DTI), understanding DTI as an innovative tourist destination, consolidated on an technological infrastructure cutting-edge, which guarantees the sustainable development of the tourist territory, accessible to all and facilitates the integration of the visitor with the environment and their experience in the destination, while improving the quality of life of the residents.

Consequently, one of the main positive impacts that this new initiative has on the territory is that the numbers of national and international workers who want to work remotely from the island is considerably increasing. Gran Canaria offers them the opportunity to share projects and then plan activities that would like to do after work, offering the possibility to combine work with pleasure.

5   The Smart Tourism Projects in the Island's Urban Space: Las Palmas de Gran Canaria

Over the years, a common strategic framework has been consolidated for the incorporation of ICT to the management of the Spanish territory. In this sense, both public administrations and private providers of technological products and services have contributed to the development of this framework, some of them though the policies implementation for the integration of ICT in society, and others, proposing technological solutions that make this possible. In 2000, the summit held by the European Union, based on the Lisbon Strategy, established the line of work of an Information Society for all as one of the conditions to make the European common market the most competitive and dynamic economy in the world. After ten years, the European Union approves the 2010 Program and creates the Advance Plan aimed at the intensive use of ICTs for the improvement of competitiveness and productivity, the promotion of social and regional equality and the improvement of the well-being and quality of life of citizens. In refers to these European projects we mention the "Civitas Destinations" project on sustainable mobility solutions are sought and integrated for the needs of both residents and tourists. The project includes from 2016 the island capital the city of Las Palmas de Gran Canaria together with five other cities as Funchal (Madeira, Portugal), Limassol (Cyprus), La Valetta (Malta), Elba Island (Italy) and Rethymno (Crete, Greece) [51]. However, the municipality of Las Palmas de Gran Canaria had already started actively working to make the city more tech-friendly before 2016 with the "Plan Estratégico de Nuevas Tecnologías y Telecomunicaciones 2012–2014" giving rise to 44 smart projects. Through its line of work LPA_Smart City promotes the use of ICTs in 5 scenarios: a. Mobility, b. Urban services, c. E-Government, d. Tourism and e. Teleworking [52, 53].

a. Mobility
In this context we have to take into account two applications: the LPA Park and LPA Accessible (see Fig. 1). The first is an application for IOS and Android smartphones. It is unique in the Canary Islands due to its characteristics, and it makes easier to obtain the Regulated Parking ticket without having to go to the nearest parking meter or use coins or cash. Since its creation, in September 2013, and until April 2014, more than 100,000 parking operations were managed with the LPA Park application. The second one (LPA accessible) is a mobile application that contains a repository of black spots (not accessible) and white spots (accessible) of Las Palmas de Gran Canaria, in buildings, streets, roads and urban facilities of the capital. It allows you to view possible architectural barriers and receive special alerts, being able to filter into different categories. This tool allows you to automatically send alerts and incidents to family members, users, or the Local Police itself, to report the location if the person suffers an incident or needs assistance. At the same time, it allows building with this information a database owned by the City Council of Las Palmas de Gran Canaria to improve the accessibility of the city.
Another digital initiative we want to mention is one that promotes better accessibility of rururban spaces as well. The City Council of Las Palmas de Gran Canaria promotes public access to broadband Internet in rural areas of the capital through its Wimax network, while expanding its Wi-Fi network, which already has more than 20 areas in

Fig. 1. APPs OF Las Palmas de Gran Canaria. Source: Ayuntamiento de Las Palmas de Gran Canaria, 2010.

the city (see Fig. 2). With this improvement in areas such as Las Mesas and in urban spaces such as Avenida Mesa y López, the aim is to facilitate the use of information technologies both for citizens and tourists and for companies in the municipality. Wifi access is free under the terms set by the National Markets and Competition Commission (CNMC) and is available as a payment method for higher bandwidths.

b. Urban services

In relation to urban services, the LPA Avisa is a service and information tool on the city's facilities, put into operation in February 2013, which allows citizens to report incidents and breakdowns in the capital of Gran Canaria. It is available for devices with IOS and Android operating systems and has undergone different updates. It allows you to photograph the incident and report it to a municipal technician, georeferenced it, add comments to complete a previously reported fault or problem, view the history of notices and, finally, show the degree of satisfaction with the resolution of the incident.

c. E-Government

Through comprehensive tax management, promoted by the Treasury and Heritage Area, all tax and collection procedures raised by the citizen are attended to in a personalized way, in an average period of less than four days. The implanted system also allows a statistical control of the waiting times in which each citizen is attended, allowing to speed up and improve the response almost immediately. Another example is the *Certificados de Residencia* digitalized. The modification of the travel conditions for the Canarias residents, based on the requirement of the Ministry of Development to have the certificate in each of their trips by plane to benefit from the discount on the ticket, triggered the development, by the Las Palmas de Gran Canaria City Council, of a pioneering system for obtaining these certificates online. The implementation took place in September

Fig. 2. Wi-fi city points in Las Palmas de Gran Canaria. *Source*: Ayuntamiento de Las Palmas de Gran Canaria, 2010.

2012, and since then, the number of electronic certificates issued has grown to reach 90% of the total documents issued. Then we want to mention the *Cita Previa* the prior appointment system that allows the City Council to adapt its offer of attention services to the real needs of citizens, while reducing waiting times significantly, until reaching the initially planned objective of not exceeding 10 min at any time of the day.

d. Tourism

The new demands of an increasingly independent and connected tourist before, during and after their vacation has pushed the local government to find efficient solutions to improve mobility and access to the destination for the tourist population as well. In the city of Las Palmas, data is being collected on where and how tourists move to have more information about the areas most visited. There are several useful applications for tourists and the local community to enjoy the city, including LPA Visit and Smart Beach. The first tool contains all the tourist information of the city. The application, available for both iOS (Apple Store) and Android (Google Play,) devices allows offline access to all the contents of the Las Palmas de Gran Canaria tourist portal www.lpavisit.com, with the novelty that they can be consulted without it being essential for the tourist to have a data connection. LPA Visit contains information of interest about all the historical sites of the capital, gastronomic references, accommodation, cultural offer, and the municipal agenda, among other contents, which will be available in a first version in both English and Spanish.

The second tool, instead, aims to quantify the number of people who make use of the surroundings of city's beaches - Playa de Las Canteras, Las Alcaravaneras, La Laja - to assess its environmental, resource and economic impact (see Fig. 3). Also develop a system of indicators to support decision-making in the efficient management of beach infrastructures and the dimensioning of public services intended to serve beach users. It is also intended to be able to predict, in an intelligent way, the allocation of resources according to non-seasonal variables (temperature, events, arrival of cruise ships, etc.). This action, to be carried out on Playa de Las Canteras, involves both a sensorization infrastructure and a technological architecture that allows incorporating new sensors into the software and managing the deployed ones, the development of predictive models and the creation of a management scorecard.

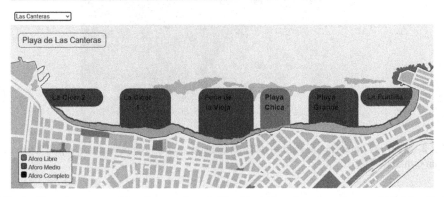

Fig. 3. Capacity status of Las Canteras beach. The Gran Canaria palms. Source: LPA-Mar (last accessed 2021/04/27).

e. Teleworking

In a bid to mitigate the economic fallout of the coronavirus pandemic, the regional government is investing €500,000 in a campaign to lure Spanish and international home-workers to the archipelago for long-term stays. The Ministry of Tourism, Industry and Commerce of the Government of the Canary Islands has designed an action plan that seeks to attract the remote workers in the international market. With many working remotely at the wake of Covid-19 crisis, such travelers have emerged as an important segment in the tourism industry of the Canary Islands (see Fig. 4).

The plan to attract this category of tourists incorporates a series of actions taking advantage of the current situation where teleworking is a trend. In addition, during the first week of November, a few events will be held on the Islands. This is the "Repeople" meeting, the most important event on teleworking in Europe that will take place in Gran Canaria. The event will also coincide with the presence of members of "WIFI Tribe", the world's leading community in coworking and coiling who have chosen Gran Canaria to telecommute for a season (see Fig. 5).

Fig. 4. Teleworking official Gran Canaria website. Source: Nomadcity (last accessed 2021/04/29).

The Canary Islands has the lowest incidence rate in Spain – its 14-day cumulative number of coronavirus cases per 100,000 inhabitants stands at 37, compared to the national average of 236. The region's tourism industry, which has been devastated by the pandemic, was expecting to rebound in time for its winter high season, but these hopes have been dashed by the second home lockdown in England ordered by the government of British Prime Minister Boris Johnson as well as the spike in coronavirus cases in Germany.

In fact, the administration has created an official website to describe the opportunities to telework from Canaria to attract national and international citizens who are teleworking with lockdown in their countries.

Fig. 5. Section "work from Gran Canaria" of the teleworking official Gran Canaria website. Source: Nomadcity. (last accessed 2021/04/29).

6 Conclusions

The Canary Islands has been characterized from its origins for being a tourist destination of sun and beach. However, some Canarias cities, aware of the advantages offered by the diversification of the tourism industry, have known how to take precedence over market flows and rethink their situation in the face of new tourism practices. Faced with this new scenario, the ICT's have served as support for the transformation process of the capital as a smart destination.

Las Palmas de Gran Canaria is a clear example of having established itself as a full member of the Spanish Network of Smart Cities (RECI) whose main objective is to exchange experiences and work together to develop a sustainable management model and improve the quality of life of citizens.

A smart city is, in general terms, a city that applies technology and innovation to make both its infrastructures and its services more interactive and efficient, as well as so that citizens and visitors can be more aware of them. The road that a city must travel to become a smart city is long, full of small advances that bring it closer to its citizens; a path that is never completed but that makes the city grow with each step. The Smart City Plan for Las Palmas de Gran Canaria demonstrates this situation and involves a substantial reform of the stimulus policies and helps the deployment of smart cities and islands maintained up to now by operating in four areas of action: mobility, urban services, tourism, electronic governance, and teleworking.

This is even more valid at this time of global health emergency. To overcome this crisis, smart tourist cities are looking for measures and strategies for a new tourism cycle. Las Palmas de Gran Canaria draws a roadmap that addresses the post-COVID-19 situation quickly and efficiently through the monitoring of searches carried out on the Internet about the capital and about flight, hotel, or restaurant reservations for define the real interest that exists to travel to the city; as well as the capacity of the places most visited by tourists and residents in order to check their availability.

The aims of these initiatives are to observe, analyze and report in real time the dynamics of search and reservations on the Internet as a working tool to decide the different activation strategies of the urban destination. And, in addition, offer the citizen and/or visitor information about the physical safety distance from public spaces and the possibility to combine work with pleasure.

The two most representative cases are on the one hand, the virtual three-color traffic light located on the tourist beaches of the capital; These will indicate to users if the capacity on the sand is low, medium, or high, and in this way, bathers can know which beaches have more space before accessing them. On the other hand, the change of the accommodation in Las Palmas de Gran Canaria from a tourist accommodation to a teleworking space.

References

1. World Tourism Organization (UNWTO): COVID-19 and Tourism. 2020: A Year in Review. UNTWO (2021). https://webunwto.s3.eu-west-1.amazonaws.com/s3fs-public/2020-12/2020_Year_in_Review_0.pdf. Accessed 21 Mar 2021

2. Everingham, P., Chassagne, N.: Post COVID-19 ecological and social reset: moving away from capitalist growth models towards tourism as Buen Vivir. Tour. Geogr. **22**(3), 555–566 (2020)
3. Fletcher, R., Murray Mas, I., Blazquez-Salom, M., Blanco-Romero, A.: Tourism, degrowth, and the COVID-19 Crisis. Polit. Ecol. Netw. (2020). https://politicalecologynetwork.org/2020/03/24/tourism-degrowth-and-the-covid-19-crisis/. Accessed 15 Apr 2021
4. Ioannides, D., Gyimòthy, S.: The COVID-19 crisis as an opportunity for escaping the unsustainable global tourism path. Tour. Geogr. **22**(3), 624–632 (2020)
5. Sharma, D.G., Thomas, A., Paul, J.: Reviving tourism industry post-COVID.19: a resilience-based framework. Tour. Manag. Perspect. **37**, 1–10 (2021). Article no. 100786
6. Battino, S., Lampreu, S.: La Regione Sardegna ed il Turismo 4.0 per lo sviluppo e la promozione del territorio. ANNALI DEL TURISMO - Edizioni Geoprogress **VII**, 57–76 (2018)
7. Giffinger, R., Fertner, C., Kramar, H., Kalasek, R., Pichler-Milanović, N.Y., Meijers, E.: Smart Cities: Ranking of European Medium-Sized Cities. Vienna University of Technology Vienna, Austria: Centre of Regional Science (SRF) (2007)
8. Murgante, B., Borruso, G.: Cities and smartness: a critical analysis of opportunities and risks. In: Murgante, B., et al. (eds.) ICCSA 2013. LNCS, vol. 7973, pp. 630–642. Springer, Heidelberg (2013). https://doi.org/10.1007/978-3-642-39646-5_46
9. Komninos, N., Pallot, M., Shaffers, H.: Spacial issue on smart cities and the future internet Europe. J. Knowl. Econ. **4**(2), 119–134 (2013)
10. Lee, P., Hunter, W.C., Chung, N.: Smart tourism city: developments and transformations. Sustainability **12**(3958), 1–15 (2020)
11. Buhalis, D., Amaranggana, A.: Smart tourism destinations. In: Xiang, Z., Tussyadiah, I. (eds.) Information and Communication Technologies in Tourism 2014, pp. 553–564. Springer, Cham (2013). https://doi.org/10.1007/978-3-319-03973-2_40
12. Li, Y., Hu, C., Huang, C., Duan, L.: The concept of smart tourism in the context of tourism information services. Tour. Manag. **58**, 293–300 (2017)
13. Guzal-Dec, D., Zwolinska-Ligaj, M.: The social field of smart villages concept: the case of peripheral region—Lublin province in Poland. In: Proceedings of the 2018 International Conference Economic Science for Rural Development, Jelgava, Latvia, vol. 49, pp. 296–306 (2018)
14. Matos, A., Pinto, B., Barros, F., Martins, S., Martins, J., Au-Yong-Oliveira, M.: Smart cities and smart tourism: what future do they bring? In: Rocha, Á., Adeli, H., Reis, L.P., Costanzo, S. (eds.) WorldCIST'19 2019. AISC, vol. 932, pp. 358–370. Springer, Cham (2019). https://doi.org/10.1007/978-3-030-16187-3_35
15. Um, T., Chung, N.: Does smart tourism technology matter? Lessons from three smart tourism cities in South Korea. Asia Pac. J. Tour. Res. 1–19 (2019)
16. Calle, J., García, M., García, F.: Las ciudades Patrimonio de la Humanidad ante el paradigma Smart. Actas del Seminario Internacional Destinos Turísticos Inteligentes: nuevos horizontesen la investigación y gestión del turismo, 7–37 (2017)
17. Jovicic, D.Z.: From the traditional understanding of tourism destination to the smart tourism destination. Curr. Issue Tour. **22**(3), 276–282 (2018)
18. Flemming, S.: The geographies of social networks and innovation in tourism. Tour. Geogr. **9**(1), 22–48 (2017)
19. Battino, S., Lampreu, S.: The role of the sharing economy for a sustainable and innovative development of rural areas: a case study in Sardinia (Italy). Sustainability **11**(3004), 1–20 (2019)
20. Dodds, R., Butler, R.W. (eds.): Overtourism: Issues, Realities and Solutions. De Gruyter, Berlin/Boston (2019)

21. The European Commission Project "European Capital of Smart Tourism - ECoST". https://www.interregeurope.eu/policylearning/good-practices/item/3801/european-capital-of-smart-tourism-initiative-including-category-on-cultural-heritage-and-creativity/
22. Ivona, A.: European urban regeneration through intelligent applications, central European. J. Geogr. Sustain. Dev. **2**(2), 15–23 (2020)
23. Camerada, M.V.: Innovazione digitale e destinazioni turistiche intelligenti. Il Protocollo SMAS. In: Sechi Nuvole, M. (eds.) Antropizzazione, turismo e innovazione tecnologica. Un approccio multiscalare per l'analisi dello sviluppo sostenibile e intelligente del territorio. AGEI – Geotema, Anno XXII, pp. 104–118 (2018)
24. Auci, S., Mundula, L.: La misura delle smart cities e gli obiettivi della strategia EU 2020: una riflessione critica. In: Lazzeroni, M., Morazzoni, M., Paradiso, M. (eds.) Nuove geografie dell'innovazione e dell'informazione. Dinamiche, trasformazioni, rappresentazioni, Geotema, pp. 59, 57–69. (2019)
25. D'Acunto, A., Mena, M., Polimanti, F., Zoppis, F.: Smart City Index – Sostenibilità. EY Advisory S.p.A, Milano (2020)
26. Thrift, N.: The 'sentient' city and what it may portend. Big Data Soc. **1**(1), 1–21 (2014)
27. Mangano, S., Ugolini, G.M.: Nuove tecnologie e smart map per un turismo urbano e una mobilità intelligente. Bollettino A.I.C. **160**, 8–21 (2017)
28. Carbone, L.: Versioni e visioni della e-narrazione dell'urban sensing. In: Lazzeroni, M., Morazzoni, M., Paradiso, M. (eds.) Nuove geografie dell'innovazione e dell'informazione, vol. 59, pp. 70–77. Dinamiche, trasformazioni, rappresentazioni. Geotema (2019)
29. Cohen, B.: What Exactly is a Smart City (2012). https://www.fastcompany.com/1680538/what-exactly-is-a-smart-city
30. Herrera Priano, F., López Armas, R., Fajardo Guerra, C.: A model for the smart development of island territories. In: Proceedings of the 17th International Digital Governement Research Conference on Digital Government Research, pp. 465–474. ACM, Shangai (2016)
31. Avelar, S.: Island tourism: keep it smart and sustainable—an exploratory approach. In: Kavoura, A., Kefallonitis, E., Giovanis, A. (eds.) Strategic Innovative Marketing and Tourism. SPBE, pp. 703–709. Springer, Cham (2019). https://doi.org/10.1007/978-3-030-12453-3_81
32. European Project Smart Islands. https://www.eesc.europa.eu/. Accessed 03 Apr 2021
33. Gretzel, U., et al.: E tourism beyond COVID 19: a call for transformative research. Inf. Technol. Tour. **22**, 187–203 (2020)
34. Simancas Cruz, M., Hernández Martín, R., Padrón Fumero, N. (eds.) Turismo pos-COVID-19. Reflexiones, retos y oportunidades, Cátedra de Turismo CajaCanarias-Ashotel de la Universidad de La Laguna, La Laguna (2020)
35. Kunzmann, K.R.: Smart cities after Covid-19: ten narratives. disP – Plann. Rev. **56**(2), 20–31 (2020)
36. Donato, C.: Le Canarie e "l'industria" turistica. Osservazioni su di uno spazio che ripensa il proprio sviluppo attraverso strategie ecosostenibili. Edizioni Goliardiche, Trieste (2001)
37. Hernandez Hernandez, P.: Natura y cultura de las Islas Canarias. Tafor Publicaciones, La Laguna (Tenerife) (2003)
38. Battino, S.: Ecoturismo nell'isola di Lanzarote. In: Donato, C. (ed.) Turismo rurale, agriturismo ed ecoturismo quali esperienze di un percorso sostenibile. EUT, Trieste (2007)
39. Armas Castilla, N.: Comentarios sobre la insularidad de La Graciosa en el Nuevo Estatuto de Autonomía de Canarias. Anales de la Facultad de Derecho – Universidad de La Laguna, **36**, 85–93 (2019)
40. ISTAC – Instituto Canario de Estadistica: Cifras Oficiales de Población. Series anuales. Municipios 2000–2020 (2021). http://www.gobiernodecanarias.org/istac/temas_estadisticos/demografia/poblacion/cifraspadronales/E30245A.html

41. Gonzáles Morales, A., Hernández Luis, J.Á.: Turismo y Reservas de la Biosfera: el caso de Canarias orientales. In: Book of Proceedings – International Conference on Tourism & Management Studies, vol. 1, pp. 947–959. Algarve (2011)

42. López Galán, E., Cabrera Guillén, D.: Plan Estratégico Turístico del Norte de Gran Canaria (2011)

43. Battino, S.: Lungo le rutas del vino alla scoperta del paesaggio vitivinicolo di Lanzarote nelle Isole Fortunate. Bollettino dell'AIC **156**, 102–114 (2016)

44. Dóniz-Páez, J., Quintero Alonso, C.: Propuesta de rutas de geoturismo urbano en Icod de Los Vinos. Cuadernos Geográficos **55**(2), 320–343 (2016)

45. Hernández Luis, J.Á., Gonzáles Morales, A., Hernández Torre, S.S., Ramón Ojeda, A.Á.: El impact del turismo de masas en las islas Canarias en el context de las Reservas Mundiales de la Biosfera. Cuadernos de Turismo **40**, 363–387 (2017)

46. Promotur: Profile of tourist visiting Gran Canaria (2019). https://turismodeislascanarias.com/en/research/profile-tourist-visiting-gran-canaria-2019/

47. Ayuntamento de Las Palmas de Gran Canaria: Situación Del Sector Turístico Las Palmas de Gran Canaria Año (2019). https://lpavisit.com/es/observatorio-turistico

48. Gobierno de España: Estadísticas tráfico portuario. http://www.puertos.es/en-us

49. Gran Canaria – Patronato de Turismo: Estrategia Integral de Turismo de Gran Canaria 2017–2020. https://www.grancanaria.com/turismo/es/area-profesional/promocion-turistica/plan-estrategico

50. Gran Canaria Patronato de Turismo: Proyecto Smartdest – Destino Turístico Inteligente. https://www.grancanaria.com/turismo/es/area-profesional/promocion-turistica/smartdest/

51. Civitas Destinations Project. https://civitas.eu/destinations. Accessed 17 Apr 2021

52. Ayuntamiento de Las Palmas de Gran Canaria: Plan Estratégico de Nuevas Tecnologías y Telecomunicaciones 2012–2014. https://www.laspalmasgc.es/export/sites/laspalmasgc/.galleries/documentos-innovacion/pe.pdf

53. Ayuntamiento de Las Palmas de Gran Canaria: LPA INTELIGENCIA AZUL - 2016 – 2019. https://www.laspalmasgc.es/es/areas-tematicas/innovacion/lpa-inteligencia-azul/

International Workshop on Space Syntax for Cities in Theory and Practice (Syntax_City 2021)

A Literature Review on the Assessment of Vitality and Its Theoretical Framework. Emerging Perspectives for Geodesign in the Urban Context

Alfonso Annunziata and Chiara Garau[✉]

Department of Civil and Environmental Engineering and Architecture, University of Cagliari, 09129 Cagliari, Italy
cgarau@unica.it

Abstract. Vitality and Urbanity, as conditions for economic vibrancy and social diversity, are central objectives of policies for urban sustainable development. Vitality and urbanity are herein defined as distinctive urban qualities emerging from the combination of diverse practices, integrated into urban form and influencing the sense of place. The proposed study investigates the components of urban form that influence urbanity and vitality. A broad literature review on the formalization and operationalization of the concepts of urbanity and vitality is presented. The comparative analysis of selected articles investigates five aspects: i) conceptualization of urbanity and vitality; ii) identification of factors impacting urbanity and vitality; iii) definition of indicators and protocols; iv) co-relations among urban form factors and levels of vitality and urbanity and v) relevance and impact of investigated methodologies on planning processes. This study aims to define the theoretical foundation of a methodology that utilizes space syntax and spatial analysis techniques to address three issues related to sustainable urban development: clear representation of conditions of urbanity, understanding of criticalities and formulation of policies and strategies for reinforcing vibrant urban spaces. The proposed theoretical framework thus contributes to the application of the Geodesign paradigm to the urban realm by supporting the essential understanding of the spatial culture of a place.

Keywords: Vitality · Urbanity · Morphology · Space syntax · Geodesign

1 Introduction

Urban areas are emerging as the place where different global phenomena concur, including concentration and increase of population, social and spatial injustice, environmental

---

This paper is the result of the joint work of the authors. 'Abstract' 'Methodology', 'Results' and 'Definition of key aspects' were written jointly by the authors. Alfonso Annunziata wrote the 'Introduction' and 'Concepts and methods'. Chiara Garau wrote the 'Discussion' and 'Conclusions'.

O. Gervasi et al. (Eds.): ICCSA 2021, LNCS 12958, pp. 305–322, 2021.
https://doi.org/10.1007/978-3-030-87016-4_23

issues as well as economic development and the production of cultural, social, scientific and institutional innovation. The role of urban governance and spatial planning in addressing the potential of the built environment to impact quality of life, sustainability, inclusion, and cultural and social diversity, emerges as a central question. Within this perspective, the issues of urbanity, vibrancy and urban vitality are central.

Vitality and vibrancy refer, in fact, to a fundamental urban quality resulting from the plurality of activities. Urbanity, on the other hand, concerns a quality distinctive of urban condition resulting from a specific combination of functions, amenities, practices, cultural constructs, social and emotional interactions, integrated into urban form and determining the sense of place. A consolidated tradition in urban studies, [1–6] investigates the spatial and functional components of the built environment that affect urban quality, while recognizing the relevance of vitality and urbanity as a central objective of urban planning. Within this perspective, urban morphology, as the study of the structural attributes of urban form and of its generative processes, emerges as the privileged dimension for investigating the relation between the spatial, physical, functional aspects of the urban realm and urbanity and vitality. More precisely, building on the Conzenian morphological tradition [7], urban form is conceptualized as the product of three components: i) the system of open spaces and, in particular of spaces of movement; ii) the system of plots and of buildings arranged on plots; iii) patterns of land-use. Space-syntax and Geo spatial theories and techniques have, in the recent years, fostered the establishment of conceptual apparatuses and methodologies aimed at individuating and describing components of urban form and at developing a common and essential morphological understanding of urbanity and vitality and of their determinants [8, 9]. Consequently, this article presents a comprehensive literature review on the formalization and operationalization of urbanity and vitality.

The literature review investigates articles indexed in the Scopus and Web of Science database and is articulated on four stages: i) definition of queries containing the terms urbanity, vitality, urban morphology; ii) selection of a set of articles related to the categories of urban studies; iii) comparative analysis of the most relevant articles. The comparative analysis focuses on four aspects: i) conceptualization of urbanity and vitality; ii) identification of dimensions of urban form; iii) definition of factors of urban form impacting vitality, protocols and indicators for quantitative analysis of urban form; iv) output and results of the case study analysis, including co-relation among factors of urban form and measured levels of vitality and urbanity, or categorization and evaluation of urban spaces; and v) relevance and impact of metrics of urbanity and vitality on planning processes.

The aim of the literature review is to propose a theoretical framework instrumental to the development of a replicable methodology, based on open data, for the assessment of morphological factors conducive to the urbanity and vitality of public spaces across metropolitan areas, the understanding of criticalities and the formulation of policies and strategies for reinforcing meaningful and vibrant urban spaces. This theoretical framework represents a relevant contribution to the application of geodesign perspective to urbanized territories. Geodesign, in fact, is a data informed paradigm that utilizes spatial information to structure place-shaping processes [10, 11]. Hence, its effectiveness in orienting design solutions and planning strategies in the urban context could be improved via the utilization of spatial analysis and space syntax techniques for understanding the spatial culture of a metropolitan region, and the relation between the configuration of spatial structures and patterns of collective practices determining urbanity and vitality.

The article is structured on five sections: After the introduction, notions of vitality, urbanity and urban form are presented. Then, in Sect. 3, the methodology and the case study are presented. In Sects. 4 and 5 the results from the literature review are presented and discussed. Finally, the Conclusions in Sect. 6, summarise the findings of the study and illustrates hypotheses for the future development of the research.

2   Concepts and Methods

The notions of urbanity, vitality and vibrancy are rooted in the essential aspect of the city as the place where propinquity fosters the encounter with the difference, transfer of knowledge, contamination of cultures and traditions, determining the production of identities, subjects, ideas and practices [12]. The role of the city is, thus, the promotion of contacts, emulation, transaction among individuals, groups and classes. The city is the stage-set where the drama of social life unfolds, in the continuous alternating of spectators and actors [13]. The notions of vitality, vibrancy and urbanity capture this aspect, summarising the specific qualities of the urban realm, and more precisely of competitive, resilient, prosperous urban environments.

A first issue emerging form studies on urban morphology concerns the terminological inconsistencies. More precisely, the terms vitality, vibrancy and urbanity are not synonym: urbanity can be defined as the quality of vital urban places, yet these concepts are not equal. Building on Montgomery [14], urbanity is the distinctive quality of the urban condition, and a central attribute of good urban places, hence of places revealing a unique sense of place. In this regard, urbanity is a peculiar condition determined by urban form, social and interpersonal relations, multiplicity of practices mediated by specific cultural constructs. The sociological perspective on urbanity underlines its situational nature, and its influence on socio-political relations and everyday life [15]. Hence, urbanity is herein defined as a condition resulting from a specific configuration of practices and socio-political interactions incorporated into urban form and influencing the sense of place. The latter, in fact, embodies a cultural, cognitive and emotional dimension and can be defined as the complex of beliefs, emotions, and meanings, symbols and qualities that an individual or a group ascribes to a region or space [16–18]. As a consequence, vitality – as the capacity of the built environment to facilitate social practices and economic activities [19, 20] - and vibrancy – as the potential of a place to respond to basic human needs and social public demands, creating a liveable environment [21] - emerge as pre-conditions of urbanity and of sense of place. Vitality and vibrancy are, as a result, central objectives of urban sustainable development. Vibrancy, in particular, engenders positive emotional experiences, stimulates creativity and produces resilience and prosperity. Moreover, a vital and liveable environment incorporates opportunities for multiple and varied social contacts, enabling the formation of interpersonal ties conducive to trust, co-operation, solidarity and empathy [5, 20, 22–24]. These ordinary virtues, in turn, are a central condition for the co-existence of different needs, identities, customs in the contemporary city [25, 26].

Moreover, Vibrancy and vitality are associated to active street life and diversity of uses - sustained by adequate levels of demand and, thus, by population density - and influence the image of a place [6]. Diversity, density, active street life and imageability are, in turn, influenced by urban form [5, 6]. The principle of Soft environmental determinism implies, in fact, that the structure of a space orients human activities by determining specific patterns of affordances. For instance, the conditions of spatial and functional proximity refer to the potential of spaces to generate specific patterns of co-presence and determine the frequency of encounters and social contacts conducive to the creation and activation of a community [25].

Urban form entails the structural and functional properties of the built environment, including the configuration of the system of public open spaces, the conformation of plots and of buildings located on plots and the distribution of land uses. In particular, the configuration of the system of open spaces refers to the set of topological relations among streets and square, that interdepend in the overall urban structure. Configurational attributes of the built environment influence the patterns of natural movement, co-presence, and co-awareness across the urban space. Co-presence refers to the simultaneous presence, within a space, of people that may not know each other; co-awareness refers to a group of people who use and share a space and are aware of one another. These two patterns are the raw material for the creation of a community. Furthermore, patterns of natural movement are observed to affect the distribution of economic activity and of land uses [27] thus influencing the formation and location of vibrant and vital cores and engendering the multi-scale structure of pervasive centrality across the urban space [3, 23, 28–31].

The formalization of urban morphology in terms of specific variables, and their relevance in influencing urban vitality and vibrancy are described in the subsequent sections.

3 Methodology

This study investigates the existing literature on urban morphology and vitality, to identify which aspects of the functional, configurational and compositional dimensions of the built environment are most relevant in terms of their influence on the vibrancy and liveability of the urban realm. This study is thus articulated on five steps: i) selection of a sub-set of relevant articles; ii) construction of a matrix for the analysis of existing studies; iii) comparative analysis of articles selected in stage i; iv) identification of aspects of urban morphology influencing urban vitality and v) measurement of their relevance within the sub-set of the articles analysed; More precisely, articles are retrieved from the Google Scholar database via a query containing the terms "urban morphology", "vitality" OR "vibrancy" OR "urbanity". Relevant articles are selected according to three criteria: pertinence to the discipline of urban and regional studies; publication on Open Access journals or storage on open platforms; and period of publication included in the time-span 2016–2021. Google Scholar and Open Access journals and platforms are privileged because they represent optimal solutions for accessing and communicating research findings, thus increasing the potential of research on the urban realm to impact planning processes and urban policies. The matrix is articulated on eight criteria, including definition of the urban condition investigated, aspects of urban form considered, definition of the unit of analysis, definition of independent and dependent variables, results, and relevance and impacts of findings. Lastly, a set of independent variables, related to central environmental determinants of vitality is identified; the centrality of the selected variables is then evaluated via four indicators: Relevance (REL), defined as the ratio of article considering the i-th variable over the total number of articles selected; Frequency of positive co-relations (FPOS), defined as the ratio of studies observing a positive co-relation between the i-th variable and urban vitality, over the total number of articles considering the i-th variable; Frequency of negative co-relations (FNEG); and net normalized influence (NET), defined as the product of relevance and the difference between frequency of positive co-relations and frequency of negative co-relations (see Table 2). This methodology thus encompasses a replicable, time-saving procedure for the comparative analysis of research publications, for the identification of pertinent and relevant variables and of recurrent co-relations among independent and dependent variables. The aim of the comparative analysis discussed in the subsequent sections is, thus, to identify components of urban form and properties of the urban landscape that influence vitality.

4   Results

The comparative analysis focuses on a sub-set of 21 relevant articles. Google Scholar returns 6770 entries to the query ((“urban form” OR “urban morphology”) AND (“vitality” OR “vibrancy”)). The Web of Science database identifies 28 articles. Studies on the impact of urban form components on urban vitality are pre-eminently associated to the Categories “Urban studies” (11 articles), “Environmental studies” (11 articles) and “Green Sustainable Science and Society” (7 articles). The sum of citations is equal to 201; the average number of citations per item is 7.18, determining an H-index of 7. These values and the positive trend in the total number of citations per year underline two aspects; the increasing relevance of studies on urban form and vitality in the disciplinary areas of urban and environmental studies, and the need for further studies, aimed at operationalizing the relation among components of the built environment and urban vitality. The analysis of the theoretical framework of the articles reveals the centrality of the studies conducted by Jacobs [5], Montgomery [14], Gehl [2, 7] whose findings define the foundation of contemporary research on urban morphology and on its significance as a pre-condition for sustainable, vibrant urban spaces. The selected articles focus on vitality (0.67), vibrancy (0.14), and urbanity (0.10). Yet a clear distinction among these terms does not emerge: they converge on the notion of the potential of the urban realm to induce lively social and economic activities. The concepts of vitality, vibrancy and urbanity are frequently associated with the conditions of liveability, variety, diversity and sustainability [20, 32–34]; in particular vitality, vibrancy and urbanity emerge as a central aspect of urban sustainable development, and as a distinctive condition of multi-functional, varied, urban environments. In particular, Jacobs' conceptualization of diversity as a condition for vitality emerges as a central aspect [5, 35, 36]. Moreover, urban form is conceptualized as the product of distinct structures. In particular, building on Conzen's findings [7], urban form comprises three dimensions: the spatial structure of spaces for movement, the built fabric, constituted by the system of plots and buildings, and the land use pattern. These dimensions encompass the categories defined by Jacobs as aspects of diversity: Connectivity, operationalized in terms of block size and border vacuums, typological variety of buildings, density, diversity of primary and secondary uses [5, 35, 36].

Table 1. Results of the comparative content analysis for the most relevant selected articles

Title	Urban condition investigated	Unit of analysis	Independent variables
Jacobs-Crisioni et al. [37]	Patterns of activities	Regular grid unit	Population Density (DPOP); Density of POIs (DPOI); Distance from tourist squares (TS); Condition of districts (Advantaged vs Disadvantaged) (AD)
Ye and Van Nes [9]	Urban vitality	Modules of a 150 × 150 m grid	Integration (IN); Building Density (FAR); Diversity of Uses (DVLU)
Ye et al. [8]	Urbanity	Grid/block	Choice (CH) Building Density (FAR); Proportion of Built Area (GSI); Vertical Dimension (H); Diversity of uses (DVLU)
Delclòs-Alió and Miralles-Guasch [36]	Urban vitality	Modules of a 100 × 100 m grid	Population Density (DPOP); Housing Density (HD); Building Density (FAR); Diversity of Uses (DVLU); Block Size (BLS); Road Section (SW); Diversity of Buildings Age (DAB); Proximity to transport nodes (DTRN); Distance from border vacuums (DBV)

(*continued*)

Table 1. (*continued*)

Title	Urban condition investigated	Unit of analysis	Independent variables
Ye et al. [19]	Vitality	Block	Building Density (FAR); Proportion of Built Area (GSI); Vertical Dimension (H); Diversity of uses (DVLU)
Zeng et al. [38]	Urban vitality	Sub-district	Population Density (DPOP); Road Density (RDI); Building density (FAR); Density of POIs (DPOI); Diversity of Uses (DVLU)
Lu et al. [39]	Urban vitality	District	Population Density (DPOP); Local Tax income (LTI); Area (S); Compactness (RCI); Proximity to transport nodes (DTRN); Diversity of Uses (DVLU); Floor rea ratio (FAR); Proportion of Built Area (GSI); Road Density (RDI); POI Density (DPOI)
Lu et al. [40]	Vibrancy/vitality	Sub-district	Population Density (DPOP); Price Levels (HPL); Density of Roads (RDI); Proximity to transport nodes (DTRN); Building Density (FAR); Proportion of Built Area (GSI); Diversity of Uses (DVLU); Shape indicator (RCI); Landscape Qual ind (GCI)

(*continued*)

Table 1. (*continued*)

Title	Urban condition investigated	Unit of analysis	Independent variables
Meng and Xing [33]	Urban Vibrancy	Block	Density of POIs (DPOI); Building Density (FAR); Landscape Shape Index of buildings; Average vertical dimension (H); Perc of non-built A; Road Density (RDI)
Sulis et al. [41]	Urban vitality	Spatial Units based on 400 m buffer around stations	Diversity (DV); Intensity (I); Variability (V); Consistency (C); Integration (IN); POI Density (DPOI)
Tang et al. [21]	Urban vibrancy	District	Road Integration (IN); Road Choice (CH); Diversity of Uses (DVLU); Density of residence (DPOP); Density of traffic (TRD); Density of POIs (DPOI); Distance to city center; Distance to airport (DTRN)
Yue et al. [34]	Vitality	Sub-district	Diversity of buildings age (DAB); Block size; Road junction; Road length (BLS); Diversity of uses (DVLU) Population density (DPOP); Density and diversity of POI (DPOI) (DVLU); Road density (RDI); Proximity to transport nodes (DTRN); Border Vacuum distance (BVD)

(*continued*)

Table 1. (*continued*)

Title	Urban condition investigated	Unit of analysis	Independent variables
Zhang et al. [42]	Urban vitality	Block	Proximity to transport nodes (DTRN); Road Density (RDI); Block Size (BLS); Vertical Dimension (H); Diversity of Uses (DVLU); Building Density (FAR); Price Level (HPL)
Zumelzu and Barrientos-Trinanes [20]	Urban vitality	District	Front Size (BLS); Proportion of Built Area (GSI); Diversity of uses (DVLU); Population Density (DPOP)
Fuentes et al. [35]	Urban vitality	Modules of a 100 × 100 m grid	Population Density (DPOP); Housing Density (HD); Building Density (FAR); Diversity of Uses (DVLU); Block Size (BLS); Road Section (SW); Diversity of Buildings Age (DAB); Proximity to transport nodes (DTRN); Distance from border vacuums (DBV)
Kim [43]	Urban vitality	Sub-district	Street Density (RDI); Block Size (BLS); Proximity to transport nodes (DTRN); Building Entrance Distance (BED); Building Density (FAR); Open space Ratio (OSR); Diversity of Uses (DVLU)

(*continued*)

Table 1. (*continued*)

Title	Urban condition investigated	Unit of analysis	Independent variables
Li et al. [24]	Urban vibrancy	District	Density of Roads (RDI); Integration-Choice (IN*CH); Building Density (FAR); Proportion of Built Area (GSI); Diversity of buildings age (DAB); Diversity of uses (DVLU) POI Density (DPOI); Proximity to transport nodes (DTRN)
Liu et al. [32]	Urban vitality	Regular grid unit	POI Density (DPOI); Diversity of uses (DVLU); Building density (FAR); Road Access (RA); House price level (HPL); Salary level (SL); Job richness (JR); Business popularity (BP)
Niklas et al. [44]	Urbanity	District	Proximity to transport nodes (DTRN); Proportion of Built area (GSI); Industrial A ratio; Population density (DPOP); POI Density (DPOI)
Zhong et al. [45]	Living convenience	Building	Daily Accessible Area; Proximity to transport nodes (DTRN); Density and diversity of POI (DPOI); Diversity of uses (DVLU)

(*continued*)

Table 1. (*continued*)

Title	Urban condition investigated	Unit of analysis	Independent variables
Yue et al. [46]	Urban vitality	Sub-district	Diversity of Uses (DVLU); Block Size (BLS); Diversity of Buildings Age (DAB); Population Density (DPOP); POI Density (DPOI); Ratio of Residential Area (RRES); Road Density (RDI); Border Vacuum Distance (BVD); Proximity to transport nodes (DTRN)

4.1 Definition of Key Aspects

A relevant methodological issue concerns the definition of the unit of analysis. Studies on urban form and vitality focus on the metropolitan scale, and consider as unit of analysis parcels of the built environment ranging from the block to the district scale (see Table 1). In particular, the module of a regular grid super-imposed to the urban fabric emerges as the most frequent utilised unit of analysis (29%). The percentage of studies utilising a subdivision of the urban layout in parcels at the sub-district and district level is equal, in both cases, to 24%. In four cases (19%) the unit of analysis is constituted by the urban block. Lastly, 14 variables are identified as significant factors influencing urban vitality: Closeness Centrality (IN), Betweenness Centrality (CH), Density of Points of interest (DPOI), Diversity of Uses (DVLU), buildings density/floor area ratio (FAR), Proportion of built area (GSI), number of floors or vertical dimension of buildings (H), population Density (DPOP), Block size (BLS), Road density (RDI), Proximity to transport nodes (DTRN), Border Vacuum distance (BVD), Price levels (HPL), and Diversity of buildings age (DAB) (see Table 1). More precisely, border vacuum refers to negative impacts on intensity of pedestrian activities determined in surrounding areas by artificial impermeable borders, constituted by major infrastructures or mono-functional, segregated groups of buildings. Closeness centrality, operationalized in terms of the a-dimensional variable integration, refers to the distance of any space from all other spaces in the same spatial structure; betweenness centrality, operationalised in terms of the a-dimensional variable choice, refers to the probability that a specific space is comprised in the shortest path from any space to all other spaces in the same spatial structure [3, 23, 28, 47, 48]. Consequently, integration and choice capture two fundamental components of the impact of urban layout configuration on accessibility and on patterns of activity: these components are, respectively, the to-movement potential of a space, hence its relevance as a destination, and the through-movement potential of a space, hence its significance as a transit space.

Table 2. Relevance of properties of urban form on vitality and vibrancy determined measuring Relevance (REL), Frequency of positive co-relations in literature (FPOS), Frequency of negative co-relations in Literature (FNEG), net influence (NI) and Net normalized influence (NET)

Variable	N	REL	FPOS	FNEG	NI	NET
HPL (Price Level)	3.00	0.14	0.67	0.00	0.67	0.10
IN (Closeness Centrality)	3.00	0.14	0.67	0.00	0.67	0.10
BVD (Border Vacuum distance)	4.00	0.19	1.00	0.00	1.00	0.19
CH (Betweenness Centrality)	4.00	0.19	0.50	0.00	0.50	0.10
H (Vertical dimension)	4.00	0.19	0.50	0.25	0.25	0.05
DAB (Diversity of Build. age)	5.00	0.24	0.80	0.00	0.80	0.19
BLS (Block Size)	8.00	0.38	0.00	0.75	-0.75	-0.29
GSI (Ratio of built area)	9.00	0.43	0.56	0.11	0.44	0.19
RDI (Road Density)	9.00	0.43	0.44	0.00	0.44	0.19
DTRN (Proximity to Transport nodes)	11.00	0.52	1.00	0.00	1.00	0.52
DPOP (Population Density)	11.00	0.52	0.82	0.09	0.73	0.38
DPOI (Density of POIs)	12.00	0.57	0.83	0.00	0.83	0.48
FAR (Building Density)	13.00	0.62	0.69	0.08	0.62	0.38
DVLU (Diversity of Uses)	19.00	0.90	0.95	0.00	0.95	0.86

Despite their significance, the relevance of Integration and Choice as explanatory/independent variables in studies on urban vitality, is modest and equal to 0.14 and 0.19, respectively, and the frequency of positive co-relations on vitality is equal to 0.67 for Integration and 0.50 for Choice, determining a Net Influence equal to 0.10 for both variables (see Table 2). Diversity of primary and secondary uses and of points of interests, measured via Shannon's Entropy index, emerges as the most relevant independent variable (see Table 2). Relevance is equal to 0.90, the frequency of positive co-relations is equal to 0.95, determining a net normalized influence of 0.86. Diversity of uses emerges, thus, as the most significant condition of the built environment associated to urban vitality. Density of POIs, and proximity of transportation nodes also emerge as factors of the urban structure relevant in terms of impact on vitality and vibrancy. Relevance is equal to 0.57 and to 0.52 respectively, Frequency of positive co-relations to 0.83 and 1.00 and the net normalized influence on vitality is equal to 0.48 and 0.52 respectively. Building Density, measured via the Floor Area Ratio indicator, and Population density, are listed as distinct variables, despite expressing concentration of population, considered as a factor influencing opportunities for social contacts. Yet, as observed by Jacobs, conceptualization of concentration in terms of population density could engender an ambiguous representation of conditions of congestion that determine negative impacts on vibrancy and vitality. Relevance of Building density and Population Density is equal to 0.62 and 0.52, the Frequency of positive co-relations to 0.69 and 0.82 respectively and the Net normalized influence is equal to 0.38 for both variables. A relevant factor, engendering a negative influence on vitality is Block size: the relevance is equal to 0.38, its frequency of negative co-relations is equal to 0.75, determining a net normalized influence equal to −0.29. Lastly, a modest significance as a condition for vitality is observed for factors Ratio of built area (NET = 0.19); Road density (NET = 0.19), Border vacuum distance (NET = 0.19), Diversity of Buildings age (0.19), Price levels (=0.10) and vertical dimension of buildings (NET = 0.05) (see Table 2). The results presented in this section, and their implications in terms of perspectives for operationalising the relation among built environment components and vitality, are comprehensively analysed and discussed in the subsequent section.

5 Discussion

Results presented in the previous section encompass a set of implications for the development of an analytical method for assessing urban form in terms of its influence on urbanity and vitality. A first observation concerns the terminological ambiguity in the definition of the dependent variable. Vitality, vibrancy and urbanity can not be considered as synonym. Urbanity refers, in fact, to a condition resulting from a specific configuration of practices and socio-political interactions incorporated into urban form and influencing the sense of place. On the other hand, vitality and vibrancy respectively denote the capacity of the built environment to facilitate social practices and economic activities and the potential of a place to respond to basic human needs and social public demands. As a consequence, the concept of Urban Intensity is herein introduced to denote the potential of the built environment to promote utilitarian, recreational and social activities, fostering inter-personal contacts and meaningful human-environment transactions, conducive to sociability and sense of place. A second consideration concerns the impact of data availability, comprehensiveness, consistency and accuracy on the validity, representativeness, replicability and relevance of indicators formulated to objectively and quantitatively describe built environment and its influence on human practices [23]. A further issue concerns the definition of the unit of analysis. The selection of blocks or block-groups as the object of study is consistent with the organization of urban governance processes. Blocks and blocks groups are considered, in fact, as independent spatial units which can encompass diverse functions. Consequently, they emerge as elementary components of the urban landscape, and as the primary object of design, development, planning and management actions [42]. Yet, the selection of regular grid cells as the unit of analysis implies the homogeneity of the spatial elements investigated. In this case, the dimension of the cell unit should not be so modest to separate plots and buildings related variables from public space configurational variables, nor so ample to reduce the resolution- and the relevance - of the description of the urban landscape [8, 9, 36]. With regard to the components of urban form that influence vitality, results underline the validity of Jacobs' observations concerning the quantity, plurality and variety of functions and of primary and secondary uses, as a central condition for producing social and economic vitality. A further relevant aspect of built environment is the transport dimension of accessibility: both the density or proximity of transportation nodes, and the porosity and permeability of the urban layout emerge as significant conditions for vitality. Yet, existing studies tend to focus on connectivity, as the configurational property of the urban layout that primarily affects accessibility. Connectivity, operationalized in terms of Block Size or Road Intersection Distance and Road density, emerges as the second most relevant factor (REL = 0.76), determining a net normalized influence, obtained aggregating indicators calculated for Block Size and Road Density, equal to 0.48.

As a consequence, a relevant gap in the existing literature concerns the comprehensive consideration of the influence of urban layout configuration on patterns of movement, and, more precisely, the operationalization of centrality. Space syntax theories underline, in fact, the relevance of the configurational properties of betweenness centrality and closeness centrality, described in quantitative terms by the indicators Choice and Integration, as extrinsic factors that affect patterns of natural movement, co-presence and co-awareness, safety and consequently, the distribution of economic activities and the formation of local centres [3, 27, 28, 49].

Consequently, an analytic method for assessing urban intensity, should encompass indicators representative of configurational properties of the system of public open spaces, including betweenness and closeness centrality and connectivity, distribution of transit nodes, concentration of population, spatial arrangement of plots, and land uses patterns, operationalized in terms of density and diversity of functions. Moreover, the development of quantitative methods combining spatial analysis and space syntax techniques is instrumental in the application of the geodesign paradigm to the urban context. Geodesign is defined, in fact, as a set of concepts and methods for using geographic knowledge to inform design and planning processes. It emerges as a perspective central to supporting smart and sustainable urban development. Consequently, its effective application to the urban context requires the establishment of techniques for the quantitative analysis of urban landscape aimed at assisting in the comprehensive understanding of the spatial culture embodied in urban morphology.

6 Conclusions

This article presents a Literature review on Urban morphology and on its influence on urbanity, vitality and vibrancy. The objective is to define a theoretical framework for operationalizing the relation between urban morphology components and vitality. The study focuses, primarily, on four issues. First, the terminological ambiguity, engendered by the utilization of the terms vitality, vibrancy and urbanity. The second issue concerns the definition of the optimal unit of analysis, as a pre-condition for a relevant, representative and precise quantitative description of urban morphology. The third issue concerns the identification of relevant dimensions of urban morphology. The last aspect is the identification of properties of the built environment related to vitality, vibrancy and urbanity, of representative indicators, the evaluation of their relevance across the literature, and of their significance as independent variables.

The relevance of this study lies in three aspects: firstly, the introduction of the concept of urban intensity, to denote the potential of the urban landscape to promote pedestrian activities, social contacts and meaningful experiences of urban spaces, conducive to sense of place and involving the dimensions of subjectivity and sociability. Secondly, the identification of properties of the built environment, including diversity of land uses, density of points of interest, proximity to transportation nodes, concentration of population, connectivity, centrality, emerging as significant conditions of intensity and urbanity. Lastly, this study underlines a major gap in existing literature, consisting in the marginal consideration of effects of urban space configuration on patterns of movement and activity. In particular, the topological properties of closeness centrality and betweenness centrality are limitedly considered, despite research in space syntax theory has demonstrated their influence on natural movement, co-presence, co-awareness and on the formation of centres of economic activity. Findings from this study represent the first stage of a research aimed at developing a methodological framework for the quantitative analysis of urban morphology in terms of its effect on vibrancy, intensity and urbanity. The development of quantitative methods analysis is instrumental to the introduction of the geo-design paradigm into the context of urban planning and urban governance. Geo-design, as a conceptualization of design as an iterative process based on geo-spatial information, impact simulation and stakeholders inputs, emerges as a set of notions and methods facilitating holistic planning and design processes and assisting smart and sustainable urban development [50]. Yet, as observed by Ye et al. [8] the absence of analytic methods for adequately understanding urban form limits the effectiveness of current geo-design methods in supporting urban design. As a consequence, the future development of this research will focus on the definition of a set of indicators and of a model for operationalizing properties and factors of urban form that affect urban intensity. The objective is, thus, the development of a method for the quantitative analysis of urban morphology aimed at supporting urban planning by measuring the potential of the built environment to foster the intensification of individual and group practices, and by individuating fragile areas and emergent urban landscape criticalities.

Acknowledgments. This study was supported by the project "Space Syntax and Multicriteria Analysis for the Measurement of Walkability in the Build Environment", founded by the programme "Bando 2019 Mobilità Giovani Ricercatori (MGR)", financed by the Autonomous Region of Sardinia (under the Regional Law of 7 August 2007, n. 7 "Promotion of Scientific Research and Technological Innovation in Sardinia"). This study was also supported by the MIUR) through the project "WEAKI TRANSIT: WEAK-demand areas Innovative TRANsport Shared services for Italian Towns (Project protocol: 20174ARRHT_004; CUP Code: F74I19001290001), financed with the PRIN 2017 (Research Projects of National Relevance) programme. We authorize the MIUR to reproduce and distribute reprints for Governmental purposes, notwithstanding any copyright notations thereon. Any opinions, findings and conclusions or recommendations expressed in this material are those of the authors, and do not necessarily reflect the views of the MIUR.

This study was also supported by the project 'Investigating the relationships between knowledge-building and design and decision-making in spatial planning with geodesign', founded by the Foundation of Sardinia and Autonomous Region of Sardinia (Fondazione di Sardegna – Convenzione triennale tra la Fondazione di Sardegna e gli Atenei Sardi Regione Sardegna 2018).

References

1. Carmona, M.: Place value: place quality and its impact on health, social, economic and environmental outcomes. J. Urban Des. **24**, 1–48 (2019). https://doi.org/10.1080/13574809. 2018.1472523

2. Gehl, J.: Life Between Buildings: Using Public Space. Island Press, Washington, D.C. (2011)
3. Hillier, B.: Space is the machine: a configurational theory of architecture. Space Syntax, University College of London, London, United Kingdom (2007)
4. Whyte, W.H.: The social life of small urban spaces (1980)
5. Jacobs, J.: The Death and Life of Great American Cities. Vintage, New York (2016)
6. Lynch, K.: The Image of the City. MIT Press, Cambridge (1960)
7. Conzen, M.R.G.: Alnwick, Northumberland: A Study in Town-Plan Analysis. Transactions and Papers (Institute of British Geographers), pp. iii–122 (1960). https://doi.org/10.2307/621094
8. Ye, Y., Yeh, A., Zhuang, Y., van Nes, A., Liu, J.: "Form Syntax" as a contribution to geodesign: a morphological tool for urbanity-making in urban design. URBAN DESIGN Int. 22, 73–90 (2017). https://doi.org/10.1057/s41289-016-0035-3
9. Ye, Y., Van Nes, A.: Quantitative tools in urban morphology: combining space syntax, spacematrix and mixed-use index in a GIS framework. Urban Morphol. 18, 97–118 (2014)
10. Foster, K.: Geodesign parsed: placing it within the rubric of recognized design theories. Landsc. Urban Plan. 156, 92–100 (2016). https://doi.org/10.1016/j.landurbplan.2016.06.017
11. Steinitz, C.: A Framework for Geodesign: Changing Geography by Design. Esri, Redlands (2012)
12. Secchi, B.: La città dei ricchi e la città dei poveri. Gius. Laterza & Figli Spa (2013)
13. Mumford, L.: What is a city. Archit. Rec. 82, 59–62 (1937)
14. Montgomery, J.: Making a city: urbanity, vitality and urban design. 3, 93–116 (1998). https://doi.org/10.1080/13574809808724418
15. Boudreau, J.-A.: Reflections on urbanity as an object of study and a critical epistemology. In: Critical Urban Studies: New Directions, p. 55 (2010)
16. Garau, C., Annunziata, A., Yamu, C.: The multi-method tool 'PAST' for evaluating cultural routes in historical cities: evidence from Cagliari, Italy. Sustainability 12 (2020). https://doi.org/10.3390/su12145513
17. McCunn, L.J., Gifford, R.: Spatial navigation and place imageability in sense of place. Cities 74, 208–218 (2018). https://doi.org/10.1016/j.cities.2017.12.006
18. Shamai, S.: Sense of place: an empirical measurement. Geoforum 22, 347–358 (1991). https://doi.org/10.1016/0016-7185(91)90017-K
19. Ye, Y., Li, D., Liu, X.: How block density and typology affect urban vitality: an exploratory analysis in Shenzhen, China 39, 631–652 (2018). https://doi.org/10.1080/02723638.2017.1381536
20. Zumelzu, A., Barrientos-Trinanes, M.: Analysis of the effects of urban form on neighborhood vitality: five cases in Valdivia, Southern Chile. J. Hous. Built Environ. 34(3), 897–925 (2019). https://doi.org/10.1007/s10901-019-09694-8
21. Tang, L., et al.: Exploring the influence of urban form on urban vibrancy in Shenzhen based on mobile phone data. Sustainability 10 (2018). https://doi.org/10.3390/su10124565
22. Annunziata, A.: Spazi urbani praticabili. FrancoAngeli (2020)
23. Garau, C., Annunziata, A., Yamu, C.: A walkability assessment tool coupling multi-criteria analysis and space syntax: the case study of Iglesias, Italy. Eur. Plan. Stud. 1–23 (2020). https://doi.org/10.1080/09654313.2020.1761947
24. Li, S., Wu, C., Lin, Y., Li, Z., Du, Q.: Urban morphology promotes urban vibrancy from the spatiotemporal and synergetic perspectives: a case study using multisource data in Shenzhen, China. Sustainability 12 (2020). https://doi.org/10.3390/su12124829
25. Chan, J.: Urban Ethics in the Anthropocene The Moral Dimensions of Six Emerging Conditions in Contemporary Urbanism. Palgrave Macmillan, London (2019)
26. Connolly, J.J.T.: From Jacobs to the just city: a foundation for challenging the green planning orthodoxy. Cities 91, 64–70 (2019). https://doi.org/10.1016/j.cities.2018.05.011

27. Hillier, B., Penn, A., Hanson, J., Grajewski, T., Xu, J.: Natural movement: or, configuration and attraction in urban pedestrian movement. Environ. Plann. B Plann. Des. **20**, 29–66 (1993). https://doi.org/10.1068/b200029

28. Yamu, C., Van Nes, A.: an integrated modeling approach combining multifractal urban planning with a space syntax perspective. Urban Sci. **1** (2017). https://doi.org/10.3390/urbansci1040037

29. Hidayati, I., Yamu, C., Tan, W.: The emergence of mobility inequality in greater jakarta, indonesia: a socio-spatial analysis of path dependencies in transport-land use policies. Sustainability. **11**, 5115 (2019)

30. Hillier, B., Burdett, R., Peponis, J., Penn, A.: Creating life: or, does architecture determine anything? Archit. Comport./Archit. Behav. **3**, 233–250 (1986)

31. Yamu, C.: It is simply complex(ity). disP – Plan. Rev. **50**, 43–53 (2014). https://doi.org/10.1080/02513625.2014.1007662

32. Liu, S., Zhang, L., Long, Y., Long, Y., Xu, M.: A new urban vitality analysis and evaluation framework based on human activity modeling using multi-source big data. ISPRS Int. J. Geo-Inf. **9** (2020). https://doi.org/10.3390/ijgi9110617

33. Meng, Y., Xing, H.: Exploring the relationship between landscape characteristics and urban vibrancy: a case study using morphology and review data. Cities **95**, 102389 (2019). https://doi.org/10.1016/j.cities.2019.102389

34. Yue, W., Chen, Y., Zhang, Q., Liu, Y.: Spatial explicit assessment of urban vitality using multi-source data: a case of Shanghai, China. Sustainability **11** (2019). https://doi.org/10.3390/su11030638

35. Fuentes, L., Miralles-Guasch, C., Truffello, R., Delclòs-Alió, X., Flores, M., Rodríguez, S.: Santiago de Chile through the Eyes of Jane Jacobs. Analysis of the conditions for urban vitality in a Latin American Metropolis. Land **9** (2020). https://doi.org/10.3390/land9120498

36. Delclòs-Alió, X., Miralles-Guasch, C.: Looking at Barcelona through Jane Jacobs's eyes: mapping the basic conditions for urban vitality in a Mediterranean conurbation. Land Use Policy **75**, 505–517 (2018). https://doi.org/10.1016/j.landusepol.2018.04.026

37. Jacobs-Crisioni, C., Rietveld, P., Koomen, E., Tranos, E.: Evaluating the impact of land-use density and mix on spatiotemporal urban activity patterns: an exploratory study using mobile phone data. Environ. Plan. A **46**, 2769–2785 (2014). https://doi.org/10.1068/a130309p

38. Zeng, C., Song, Y., He, Q., Shen, F.: Spatially explicit assessment on urban vitality: case studies in Chicago and Wuhan. Sustain. Urban Areas **40**, 296–306 (2018). https://doi.org/10.1016/j.scs.2018.04.021

39. Lu, S., Huang, Y., Shi, C., Yang, X.: Exploring the associations between urban form and neighborhood vibrancy: a case study of Chengdu, China. ISPRS Int. J. Geo-Inf. **8** (2019). https://doi.org/10.3390/ijgi8040165

40. Lu, S., Shi, C., Yang, X.: Impacts of built environment on urban vitality: regression analyses of Beijing and Chengdu, China. Int. J. Environ. Res. Public Health **16** (2019). https://doi.org/10.3390/ijerph16234592

41. Sulis, P., Manley, E., Zhong, C., Batty, M.: Using mobility data as proxy for measuring urban vitality. J. Spat. Inf. Sci. **2018**, 137–162 (2018)

42. Zhang, A., Xia, C., Chu, J., Lin, J., Li, W., Wu, J.: Portraying urban landscape: a quantitative analysis system applied in fifteen metropolises in China. Sustain. Urban Areas **46**, 101396 (2019). https://doi.org/10.1016/j.scs.2018.12.024

43. Kim, S.: Urban vitality, urban form, and land use: their relations within a geographical boundary for walkers. Sustainability **12** (2020). https://doi.org/10.3390/su122410633

44. Niklas, U., von Behren, S., Soylu, T., Kopp, J., Chlond, B., Vortisch, P.: Spatial factor—using a random forest classification model to measure an internationally comparable urbanity index. Urban Sci. **4** (2020). https://doi.org/10.3390/urbansci4030036

45. Zhong, T., Lü, G., Zhong, X., Tang, H., Ye, Y.: Measuring human-scale living convenience through multi-sourced urban data and a geodesign approach: buildings as analytical units. Sustainability **12** (2020). https://doi.org/10.3390/su12114712

46. Yue, W., Chen, Y., Thy, P.T.M., Fan, P., Liu, Y., Zhang, W.: Identifying urban vitality in metropolitan areas of developing countries from a comparative perspective: Ho Chi Minh City versus Shanghai. Sustain. Urban Areas **65**, 102609 (2021). https://doi.org/10.1016/j.scs.2020.102609

47. Yamu, C., van Nes, A., Garau, C.: Bill Hillier's legacy: space syntax—a synopsis of basic concepts, measures, and empirical application. Sustainability **13**, 1–25 (2021)

48. Garau, C., Annunziata, A.: Supporting children's independent activities in smart and playable public places. Sustainability **12**, 8352 (2020)

49. Vaughan, L.: The spatial syntax of urban segregation. Prog. Plan. **67**, 205–294 (2007). https://doi.org/10.1016/j.progress.2007.03.001

50. Caglioni, M., Campagna, M.: Geodesign for collaborative spatial planning: three case studies at different scales. In: Garbolino, E., Voiron-Canicio, C. (eds.) Ecosystem and Territorial Resilience, pp. 323–345. Elsevier (2021). Chapter 12. https://doi.org/10.1016/B978-0-12-818215-4.00012-2

Measuring the Degree of Permeability of the Main Route Network with Angular Step Depth Analyses

Akkelies van Nes[1,2(✉)]

[1] Department of Civil Engineering, Western Norway University of Applied Science, Postbox 7030, 5020 Bergen, Norway
avn@hvl.no
[2] Department of Urbanism, Faculty of Architecture, TU-Delft, Julianalaan 134, 2628BL Delft, The Netherlands
a.vannes@tudelft.nl

Abstract. In this contribution a new space syntax analyses method is presented for analysing the degree of permeability in the main route network of towns and cities. First, a presentation is given on the methodological development of the various approaches taken until the present day. Then, a description is given on how this new analysis method can be used to conduct a permeability analyses of a main route network using the DepthmapX software. Finally, this method is applied to 25 different cities around the globe. As it turns out, the method presents an objective way in which to identify the foreground network in built environments, and to measure the degree of permeability or connectivity to the background network.

Keywords: Main route network · Permeability · Foreground network · Background network · Methodological development · Space Syntax

1 Introduction

The main or primary route network in towns and cities function as the spatial armature of the built environment. These routes connect across neighbourhoods and they are vital links between the surrounding suburbs and urban centres [1]. In many ways, the main route network contributes to wayfinding in large metropolitan areas, connecting suburbs with city centres and neighbourhoods with one another. Moreover, they tend to have a fractal structure, where the main route network operates at the highest level as the overall fractal structure model [2].

There are two issues regarding the of conduction spatial analyses of main route networks. The first issue is about how to identify the network objectively. Often they can be easily identified on maps for some cities, whereas for others it becomes a rather subjective matter [3]. Therefore, throughout the years, the various angular analyses methods developed in Space Syntax since 2001 has contributed to this. The first attempts were done by Turner [4] and Dalton [5] in 2001. Refinements in calculations formulas

© Springer Nature Switzerland AG 2021
O. Gervasi et al. (Eds.): ICCSA 2021, LNCS 12958, pp. 323–336, 2021.
https://doi.org/10.1007/978-3-030-87016-4_24

and software improvements were done in 2005 [6, 7]. Later on, the focus on identifying the main route network was done in 2009 [3] and 2012 [8]. This network is not used to identify the through movement potentials in urban areas [8].

The second issue related to the main route network is about measuring or calculating the degree of accessibility and permeability between a neighbourhood and the network. The first attempt was used in a research project on residential burglary and space [9, 10]. Later on, the method was refined in a research project on deprived neighbourhoods in the Netherlands [11].

Applying the identification of the main route network together with degrees of permeability to their vicinity provides information on the spatial properties of the foreground network and how it is connected to the background network of various types of built environments. The purpose of this contribution is to give an objective methodological description on how to process these methods, and to show some examples of different kinds of built environments where this method is applied.

2 Methodological Development Until Present Day

The classic Space Syntax analyses with topological distance (the total number of direction changes) is a powerful tool to measure to-movement potentials. As research has shown, most people frequent streets and most shops locate along these streets with the highest spatial integration values [12–14]. Registrations of pedestrian and traffic flow data could quantitatively be correlated with the various integration values. However, the number of pedestrians and cars registered along a primary route system and the main shopping streets appears to have proportionally higher values than the spatial integration values of an axial analysis [15].

The first attempt was to apply the integration gradient method [15], based on the calculations of the local integration [16]. These calculations gave indications of the main route network and better correlations with the pedestrian flow data than the global and local axial integration analyses. Since then, some researchers drew the main route network in metropolitan areas by hand [17]. Here the main route network is named 'the middle-scale network' and the method is named 'the flat city model' [18]. This approach has been criticized to lack objectivity and predictability [3]. However, some discoveries were made regarding how these routes were connected to ost-war and pre-war neighbourhoods. As it turned out, the main routes tend to go *through* post-war neighbourhoods, whereas they tend to go *around* post-war neighbourhoods.

Figure 1 shows an example of tracking the main routes for Amsterdam, where they are drawn manually and coloured in black. All streets directly connected to the main routes are coloured in dark grey, whereas the remaining streets are coloured in light grey. The degree of permeability to the neighbourhood can vary, because at that time there were no objective methods for identifying or calculating the main route network.

After the millennium, new attempts were made by adding angular weighting on the spatial relationship between the axes. Alasdair Turner developed some formulas to add angular weighting into the spatial integration analyses of the axial maps [4]. Nick Dalton made a test software, named Meanda, where the formula was applied to the axial map [5]. In 2005, the calculations were improved by breaking up the axial maps into segments.

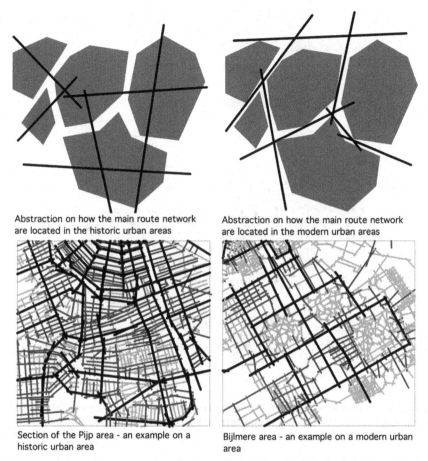

Abstraction on how the main route network
are located in the historic urban areas

Abstraction on how the main route network
are located in the modern urban areas

Section of the Pijp area - an example on a
historic urban area

Bijlmere area - an example on a modern urban
area

Fig. 1. Abstractions on how main routes are located in traditional and modern urban areas (top) and manual registrations of the main route network with one step analyses of two areas in Amsterdam (bottom).

The segment length and a refined method of the angular weighting between segments were added into the earlier versions of the Depthmap software [6]. As the application of this method show, the main route network could now be identified through the angular total depth analyses method.

Some experiments with the total angular depth analyses using various topological radii were made by the author in 2009 for identifying the main route network [3]. However, these methods were replaced with the development of the angular choice analyses in 2012. These new calculation methods, developed by Bill Hiller, Tao Yang, and Alasdair Turner consisted of normalizing the results from the spatial calculations [8]. The authors tested out the calculations on 50 different cities around the globe. The normalised angular choice calculations (NACH) turned out to be useful to identify the main route network, and hence to show the through movement potentials in built environments.

Fig. 2. How to calculate step depth from the main routes (top) and the analyses of the step depth from main routes with the dispersal of burglaries in the Dutch town of Gouda (bottom)

The next step is to reveal the development of various approaches in which to measure the degree of permeability or accessibility from the main route network to the local street network. The calculations of the angular total depth and angular choice were used as a basis for identifying the main route network in a research project of space and crime in the two Dutch towns of Alkmaar and Gouda. Here we wanted to test out how the location of intruded homes was related to the number of direction changes from the main route network. When the main route network was identified, the number of direction changes for every street was counted manually and put into an excel file. When aggregating all the various spatial data with one another and spatial data with the burglary data in SPSS, the following was found. All spatial data on a macro and micro scale and the dispersal of burglaries were dependent on the number of direction changes from the main route network [9, 10]. The higher number of directional changes from the main route network, the higher risk of a burglary. Likewise, the higher number of direction changes from the main route network, the more building entrances are turned away from streets. Figure 2 shows the number of directional changes from the main route network and the dispersal of burglaries for a neighbourhood in Gouda.

In the first years, the step depth from the main routes were done manually. It can be a time-consuming task. Therefore, in 2013 the angular step depth from the main route network could easily be applied with the DepthmapX software. In a research project on space and social security we had to analyse 43 problem neighbourhoods. These neighbourhoods were located in 25 different cities. The position of these problem neighbourhoods in relation to the whole town or city needed to be taken into consideration [11]. At that time, experiments with DepthmapX was carried out to explore the angular choice calculations. It turned out that 90% of the problem neighbourhoods lacked permeability from the main route network [11].

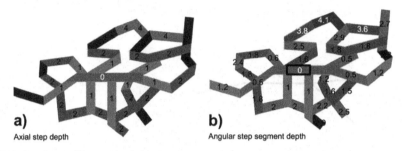

Fig. 3. The principle of axial a) and angular choice step depth b). (Color figure online)

Before explaining how the method is carried out, an explanation on the basics of angular analyses is needed. Figure 3 shows the principles on how axial a) and angular step depth b) is carried out from the axis and segment on level 0. For the topological step depth analyses from the axial map, each directional change has a value like 1. For example, changing direction three times from the red axis has a value of 3. The angle between the axes is not taken into account in the first image (a). In the angular step depth analyses from the segment in the second image (b) the angular weighting between the segments is take into account. The segments with a low degree of angular deviation from the red segment will receive a low value and will be like a continuous route. Segments with a sharp angular deviation have high values.

According to Hillier, a city consists of a very high number of short lines and a very low number of long lines. Often these long lines are connected to other long lines with a low number of angular deviation [7]. The angular choice analysis is thus able to highlight the continuous main route network in Depthmap X. This creates a starting point to easily calculate the degree of permeability of the main route network to the various neighbourhoods.

Figure 4 shows the angular weighting used in DepthmapX in image a. Image b shows a shallow angle of incidence, which most main routes tend to follow. Image c shows a sharp angle of incidence, which are mostly found on local streets. The basis of calculating angular relationships is the formula for calculating angular mean depth of a segment in relation to all other segments, is shown in image d. As can be seen in the j-graph (below right), the segments that have a shallow angle of incidence tend to demonstrate low values. In this way, segment A, B and C tend to be a part of the main route network due to the low degree of angular deviation.

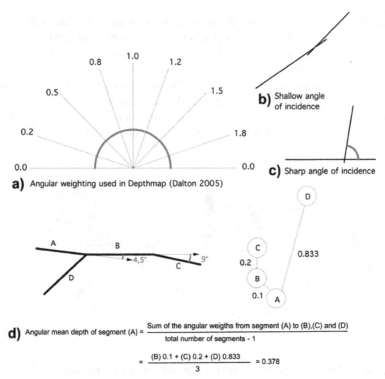

Fig. 4. The angular weighting used in Depthmap a), and examples on a shallow b) and a sharp c) angle of incidence. The calculation of angular mean depth of segment A is shown in image d) with a j-graph.

As world-wide research has shown since 2012, it is clear that the main route network is highlighted through the angular choice value analyses. The next step is to describe how to calculate the degree of permeability from this main route network to the local streets of the various neighbourhoods.

The following steps are taken in DepthmapX software. First, run the angular choice analyses with radius 'n' or a high radius. Then open up the scatterplot. Make sure that the X and the Y axis have the same values, thus that it is the choice values with radius 'n' on each axis in the scatterplot. Then a straight diagonal line is shown in the scatterplot. Mark all the dots that are not dark blue. Then open up the processed map. Most of the main routes are now marked in yellow. Then you press the step depth button. Even though not all main routes are marked, those with a shallow angular deviation receive values close to 0 in the angular step depth analyses. Remember to rename the column from 'angular step depth' to 'angular step depth main routes'. A separate column is now made in the table. To make the map more visible, go to colour range and manually invert it so that the main routes are red, and the streets with around 90 degrees from the main routes have a green/blue colour.

In the following section, examples from the findings are shown.

3   Analysis of 25 Different Cities

First, the angular step depth analysis map of a few of the 25 cities will be shown and discussed. At the end, the various mean values from the whole city, the historic city centre or downtown area, and a modern area/neighbourhood will be presented from all 25 cases.

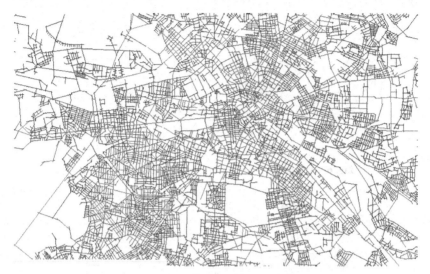

Fig. 5. Angular step depth from main routes in Berlin

The first case presented is Berlin, a typical European city with old and new areas. Figure 5 shows an angular step depth analysis from the main route network of Berlin. In the historical areas, the main route network is well embedded in the neighbourhoods. The post-War neighbourhoods are poorly accessible from this network. This pattern can be seen in most cities. Examples on this are Amsterdam, Auckland, Curacao, Oslo, Prague, Rome, Rotterdam, and Shenzhen.

The next step is to test the angular step depth from main routes in cities with a strict orthogonal street structure. Barcelona present one example, shown in Fig. 6. As can be seen from the figure, the neighbourhoods in the Cerda grid are well connected to the main routes. The remaining streets are poorly connected to the main route network.

Another atypical city is Venice, shown in Fig. 7. At first sight this city might look like a labyrinth, however, the main routes are clearly visible in the angular choice analyses. However, the degree of permeability to the surrounding neighbourhoods are rather low.

In a city located within a hilly landscape, several side streets tend to have sharp angles. Figure 8 shows the case of the Norwegian city of Bergen. The city is squeezed between seven mountains. However, the main routes are still highlighted in the choice analyses, and the permeability from the main routes to local streets to pre-War neighbourhoods are much higher than in the post-War neighbourhoods.

To test out the role of hills, Fig. 9 shows an angular step depth analysis from the main routes of the Chilean city Valparaiso. The city is located along the coast of Chile in

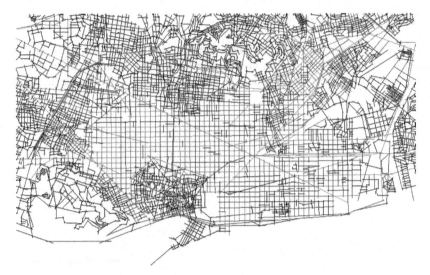

Fig. 6. Angular step depth from main routes in Barcelona

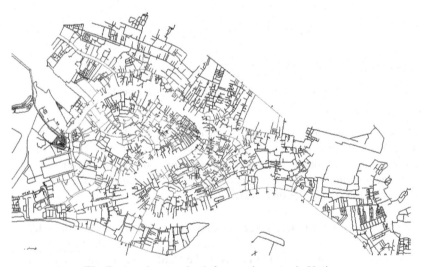

Fig. 7. Angular step depth from main routes in Venice

a hilly landscape. Most informal settlements are located on these hills. The two centres are highlighted in the analyses (coloured in red), whereas the informal settlements are poorly connected to the main route network. The centres are located in less hilly areas and have an orthogonal street structure.

Seemingly informal areas tend to be poorly connected to the main route network. Bangkok, shown in Fig. 10, represents a case in Asia. Here all the informal areas have low degree of accessibility from the main route network.

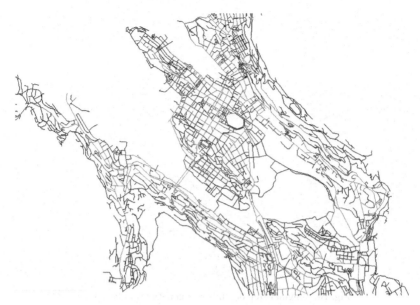

Fig. 8. Angular step depth from main routes in Bergen

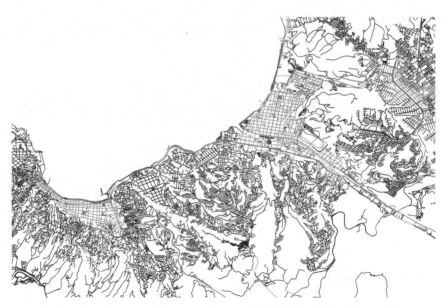

Fig. 9. Angular step depth from main routes in Valparaíso (Color figure online)

Figure 11 shows an angular step depth analysis from the main route network in the Jordanian city of Amman. Amman is a typical Arabic city with a labyrinth-like street network. However, the main route network is clearly visible. The residential areas are very segregated and have low degree of permeability to the main route network.

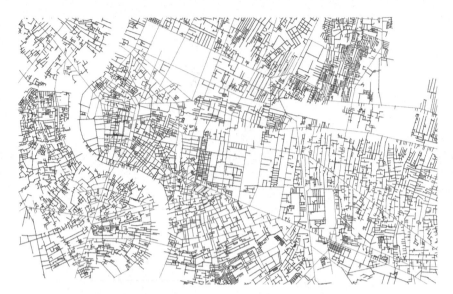

Fig. 10. Angular step depth from main routes in Bangkok

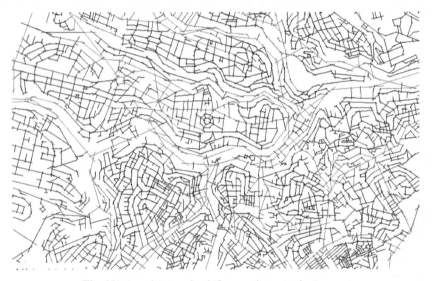

Fig. 11. Angular step depth from main routes in Amman

Often Persian and Arab built environments have a segregated background network in comparison with other cities. This becomes visible when analysing the angular step depth from the main route network. Examples on this is Banda Ace, Cairo, and Kumasi.

How is it then, in a city with an extreme orthogonal street structure? Figure 12 shows an angular step depth analysis from the main routes in Manhattan in New York. Event

Fig. 12. Angular step depth from main routes in Manhattan, New York

through it looks like that every street is poorly connected to the main route network, we need to reveal the numerical values of the segments.

The next step is to reveal then numerical data for 25 different cities around the globe. The first column shows the mean values from the angular step depth analyses taken from the main routes for the whole city. Then the mean values for a selection of streets from a historical area or city centre, and one modern area is taken for each city.

Table 1 shows all the mean depth values from the main routes for all cases. All the lowest values are coloured in red and the highest value are coloured in blue. Regarding whole cities, values close to 1 means that the foreground network is well connected to the background network. Values higher than 3 means that the background network is poorly accessible from the main route network. Thus, there is a higher degree of permeability in the foreground network towards the background network.

As can be seen from the table, cities with strict orthogonal street pattern have high levels of permeability between the foreground and the background network. Examples of this are Manhattan, Buenos Aires, Vienna, and Barcelona. Conversely, cities that have low permeability to their main routes are Cairo, Kumasi, Kyoto, Prague, Valparaíso, and Venice Santa Lucia. Often these cities have a labyrinth-like background network. Even though Kyoto seems to have a strict orthogonal street pattern in its city centre, the surrounding suburbs possess a segregated street network due to their location in the surrounding hills.

The middle column shows the mean values for the various historic city centres of all 25 cities. Here, most cities score much lower mean values than the whole city, except Manhattan. Here, the downtown area has a less strict orthogonal street pattern than the uptown areas around central park, which affects the mean values of the angular step depth numbers.

Table 1. Mean values for the angular step depth analyses taken from the main route network of 25 cities.

Name city	Whole city	City centre	New area
Amsterdam	2,2478	1,5825	2,4923
Amman	2,02188	1,93251	2,20938
Annaba	2,05184	0,801747	1,96466
Auckland	2,85923	1,66449	2,59099
Banda Aceh	2,18964	1,20436	1,89563
Bangkok	2,33625	1,50212	1,62153
Barcelona	1,69178	0,705555	1,73358
Beijing	2,47926	1,44686	1,73106
Bergen	2,65356	1,68042	2,2245
Berlin	2,2159	1,16706	2,27712
Biskra	2,18677	1,48748	1,87917
Buenos Aires	1,60948	1,75528	1,12891
Cairo	3,08287	2,37121	2,32297
Curacao	2,24119	1,58604	3,24073
Iowa City	2,79248	2,15661	1,38503
Kumasi	3,90077	2,08806	4,12918
Kyoto	3,36705	1,06573	1,854
Manhattan	1,04709	1,16277	0,855865
Oslo	2,55071	1,15036	2,14669
Prague	3,44805	1,54576	2,16
Rotterdam	2,79008	1,29618	1,88321
Rome	2,49263	1,76955	1,90366
Shenzhen	2,15641	1,34339	1,88282
Valparaíso	14,0341	2,43736	6,64219
Venice	3,23003	1,42988	5,21389
Vienna	1,33824	0,775668	1,31193

The left column shows the values from the newer areas or city centres of all 25 towns. The areas scoring 3 and higher have very low degree of permeability of their main routes. Often informal settlements or segregated modern housing areas with gated communities, contribute to poor levels of permeability. In, the city is located in a hilly landscape and has several informal areas scattered around the hills. The city centre, located in the flat areas, has an orthogonal street grid with high degree of permeability. However, the surrounding neighbourhoods are poorly accessible from the main routes.

4 Conclusions and Discussion

The experiment with 25 different cities has proven that it is possible to measure the degree of permeability between the foreground and background network. The findings of the investigated cities from various cultures shows the following.

Arab cities tend to have lower degree of permeability between the foreground and background network. Even though cities like Cairo and Banda Ace tend to have historic central areas with European planning influences, the overall spatial layout shown that these cities have a highly segregated background network in comparison with other cities. It is related to various cultural contexts [19].

Cities with orthogonal grids tend to have a high degree of permeability between the foreground and the background network. However, this is not always the case. Beijing and Iowa City demonstrate that these urban areas have a highly integrated foreground network, but are poorly connected to an orthogonal background network. Conversely, cities that do not have an orthogonal street pattern can still have high level of permeability between the main routes and the surrounding neighbourhoods. Vienna has a dense network of primary routes with an extremely high degree of permeability to the various surrounding neighbourhoods. Vienna even scores better than the downtown area of Manhattan.

Hills and slopes can influence the degree of permeability of the main route network towards the background network. However, this must be seen together with the cultural context. The hilly city of Bergen still has an average permeability between the main routes and the various local neighbourhoods. In the case of Valparaíso, issues of poverty, in combination with a hilly landscape contributes to the extreme low levels of permeability between main routes and low-income neighbourhoods.

What is the usefulness of this method? First of all, it is now possible to quantify the relationship between the foreground and background network of cities. In 2016 Hillier attempted to build a theory or understanding on the generic function of cities [19]. Hillier's concept of the foreground network explains the location of micro economic activities, whereas his concept of the background network provides understandings on the relationship between culture and space [20].

The next step is to apply this method to various socio-economic data, such as crime data, public transport accessibility, the degree of functional mixing, degree of building density, the location pattern of shops, property, and rental prices, socio-economic data on inhabitants, registrations of gender differences in public spaces, sexual harassment data, perception of safety, registrations of social, optional, and necessary activities, etc. Systematic empirical testing of this method contributes to creating further operational spatial analyses tools for evaluating planning and urban design proposals, creating a spatial diagnosis of poorly functioning neighbourhoods, and for option testing in urban renewal projects.

Acknowledgements. The author is grateful to all students throughout the years and colleagues that have provided a set of axial maps for testing out the method.

References

1. van Nes A., Yamu, C.: Introduction to Space Syntax in Urban Studies, Springer Nature, Berlin (2021). https://doi.org/10.1007/978-3-030-59140-3
2. Yamu, C., van Nes, A.: An integrated modeling approach. combining multifractal urban planning with a space syntax perspective, Urban Sci. 1, 37 (2017)
3. van Nes, A.: Analysing larger metropolitan areas. On identification criteria for middle scale networks. In: Proceedings Space Syntax, 7th International Symposium. KTH, Stockholm (2009)
4. Turner, A.: Angular analysis. In: Proceedings Space Syntax, 3rd International Symposium. Georgia Tech, Atlanta (2001)
5. Dalton, N.: Fractional configurational analysis and the solution to the Manhattan problem. In: Proceedings Space Syntax, 3rd international symposium, Georgia Tech, Atlanta (2001).
6. Hillier, B., Iida, S.: Network effects and psychological effects: a theory of urban movement, In Proceedings Space Syntax, 5th International Symposium, Techne Press, TU-Delft, Delft (2005)
7. Hillier, B., Turner, A., Yang, T., Park, H.-T.: Metric and topo-geometric properties of urban street networks. In: Proceedings Space Syntax, 6th International Symposium. Istanbul Technical University, Istanbul (2007)
8. Hillier, B., Yang, T., Turner, A.: Normalising least angle choice in Depthmap and how it opens up a new perspective on the global and local analysis of city space. J. Space Syntax 3(2), 155–193 (2012)
9. López, M., van Nes, A.: Space and crime in Dutch built environments. Macro and micro spatial conditions for residential burglaries and thefts from cars. In: Proceedings Space Syntax, 6th International Symposium. Istanbul Technical University, Istanbul (2007)
10. van Nes, A., López, M.: Macro and micro scale spatial variables and the distribution of residential burglaries and thefts from cars: an investigation of space and crime in the Dutch cities of Alkmaar and Gouda. J. Space Syntax 1(2), 296–314 (2010)
11. van Nes, A., López, M.: Spatial-socio classification of deprived neighbourhoods in the Netherlands. In: Proceedings Space Syntax, 9th International Symposium. Sejong University, Seoul (2013)
12. Hillier, B., Penn, A., Hanson, J., Grajewski, T., Xu, J.: Natural movement: or, configuration and attraction in urban pedestrian movement. Environ. Plan. B 20, 29–66 (1993)
13. Penn, A., Hillier, B., Banister, D., Xu, J.: Configurational modelling of urban movement network. Environ. Plan. B: Plan. Des. 25, 59–84 (1998)
14. van Nes, A.: The impact of the ring roads on the location pattern of shops in town and city centres. A space syntax approach. Sustainability 13(6) (2021, forthcomming)
15. Read, S.; Space syntax and the Dutch city – the supergrid. In: Proceedings Space Syntax, 1st International Symposium. UCL, London (1997)
16. Yamu, C., van Nes, A., Garau, C.: Bill Hillier's legacy: space syntax – a synopsis of basic concepts, measures, and empirical application. Sustainability 13(6), 3394 (2021)
17. Bruyns, G., van Nes, A., Pinila, C., Rocco, R., Roseman, J.: The Fifth City, International Forum on Urbanism (IFoU). TU-Delft, Delft (2007)
18. Read, S.: Flat city; a space syntax derived urban movement network model. In: Proceedings Space Syntax, 5th International Symposium. Techne Press, TU-Delft, Delft (2005)
19. Hillier, B.: What are cities for? And how does it relate to their spatial form? J. Space Syntax 6(2), 199–212 (2016)
20. van Nes, A.: What is the explanatory power of space syntax theory? In: Proceedings Space Syntax, 11th International Symposium. University of Lisbon, Lisbon (2017)

International Workshop on Theoretical and Computational Chemistry and Its Applications (TCCMA 2021)

A Computational Analysis of the Reaction of Atomic Oxygen O(^{3}P) with Acrylonitrile

Luca Mancini[1]($^{(\boxtimes)}$) (ID) and Emília Valença Ferreira de Aragão[1,2] (ID)

[1] Dipartimento di Chimica, Biologia e Biotecnologie,
Università degli Studi di Perugia, 06123 Perugia, Italy
{luca.mancini2,emilia.dearagao}@studenti.unipg.it
[2] Master-Tec SrL, Via Sicilia 41, 06128 Perugia, Italy
emilia.dearagao@master-tec.it

Abstract. The work is focused on the characterization of a long-range interacting complex in the reaction between atomic oxygen, in its ground state O(^{3}P) and acrylonitrile CH$_2$CHCN, also known as vinyl cyanide or cyano ethylene, through electronic structure calculations. Different ab initio methods have been used in order to understand which functional provides a better description of the long-range interaction. The results of the work suggest that B2PLYPD3 gives the best description of the long-range interaction, while CAM-B3LYP represents the best compromise between chemical accuracy and computational cost.

Keywords: Ab initio calculations · Astrochemistry · Combustion chemistry

1 Introduction

The reaction between atomic oxygen, in its ground electronic state O(^{3}P) and acrylonitrile can be of great interest in several fields, such as astrochemistry and combustion chemistry.

The study of planets and moons which share similarities with primitive Earth is fundamental to understand the evolution of the prebiotic chemistry in our planet, since the appearance of life has drastically changed the characteristics of Earth. One of the best candidates for this purpose is Titan, Saturn's largest moon as well as one of the few moons of the Solar System, which possess a thick atmosphere.

The presence of acrylonitrile in Titan's atmosphere has been inferred by the detection of ionic species using Cassini mass spectrometer [1,2] and later confirmed in 2017 by the first spectroscopic detection of the molecule by ALMA (Atacama Large Millimeter/submillimeter Array) [3]. The reaction with atomic oxygen can be a destruction route of acrylonitrile, even though oxygenated species in the atmosphere of Titan are not abundant [4–6]. This process can be at play also in the Interstellar Medium, also known with the acronym ISM.

© Springer Nature Switzerland AG 2021
O. Gervasi et al. (Eds.): ICCSA 2021, LNCS 12958, pp. 339–350, 2021.
https://doi.org/10.1007/978-3-030-87016-4_25

The first detection of acrylonitrile goes back to 1975 towards the SgrB2 molecular cloud [7]. This represents the first detected molecule containing a carbon-carbon double bond. Since the first detection, the presence of acrylonitrile has been revealed in a wide variety of environments, such as the TMC-1 dark cloud where, in 1983, four rotational transitions at 3 cm and 1.5 cm were observed for the first time [8]. An analysis of the excitation of several rotational transitions has been performed, in 1999, towards the SgrB2(N) hot molecular core [9], while later in 2008 the CH_2CHCN molecule has been detected in the C-rich star IRC +10216 [10]. The analysis of the relatively high rotational temperature brought the authors to the conclusion that this species is excited in the circumstellar envelope by radiative pumping to excited vibrational states. Later in 2014 A. Lopez-Sepulcre et al. reported a new laboratory characterization in the 19–1983 GHz range, together with new astronomical detection between 80 and 280 GHz of acrylonitrile in its ground and vibrationally excited states with the IRAM-30m facilities [11]. A new analysis of the L1154 prestellar core has been carried out in 2019, where several N-containing species have been detected for the first time [12]. The inventory of the aforementioned molecules includes small and simple species such ah CN and NCCN, together with more complex species like CH_3CN, CH_2CN, HCCNC and CH_2CHCN. A detailed chemical network has been built involving all the nitrogen bearing species detected in order to understand the isocyanogen formation in the ISM. Moreover, the reactions of $O(^3P)$ with these substrates play a key role in combustion science and atmospheric chemistry [13–18], considering the ease with which this species is formed and the high reactivity. The presence of nitrogen atoms in several fuels or biomass combustion [19] makes it interesting to investigate the reaction of oxygen atoms with these substrates.

In the present work we performed a theoretical study of the first step of the reaction of acrylonitrile with atomic oxygen, focusing our interest on the analysis of different theoretical methods which can be used for the identification of a van der Waals adduct in the entrance channel.

The presence of a van der Waals adduct can affect the chemical reactivity of bimolecular reactions as it was already found in several systems [20–24].

The title reaction has been already investigated theoretically by J. Sun et al. [25] who performed an exploration of the triplet potential energy surface. An experimental characterization has been performed by H. P. Upadhyay et al. [26] in a flow discharge tube using the $O(^3P)$ chemiluminescence titration method. More generally it is reasonable to think that the formation of a van der Waals adduct is one of the first stages of most of the reactions. The long-range interaction in the formed complex can lead to molecular geometries that can promote or hinder the evolution of the reaction. As a consequence the formation of a van der Waals complex can strongly affect the rate constants. Unfortunately the identification of the aforementioned complexes appears to be difficult with mostly used ab initio methods. In the following sections a comparison between the results obtained at different levels of theory is presented. In particular the analysis started with a benchmark work in order to compare different methods, see next sections for more details, while the last part of the work is focused on the comparison between two particular level of theory: B3LYP and CAM-B3LYP.

2   Methods

The investigation of the title system has been performed adopting a computational strategy which has been successfully used in several cases [27–36]. In particular electronic structure calculations have been performed for the reactants and for the long-range complex on the overall triplet Potential Energy Surface (PES). In all calculations, the geometries of the stationary points were treated with two different methods: one for optimization and another to obtain more accurate energy values. Geometry optimizations were performed in order to benchmark several methods: density functional theory (DFT), with the BHandHLYP functional [37,38]; the Becke-3-parameter exchange and Lee-Yang- Parr correlation (B3LYP) [39,40] combined or not with Grimme's D3BJ [41,42] dispersion (B3LYPD3); Coulomb Attenuating Method (CAM-B3LYP) [43]; double-hybrid DFT method B2PLYP [44] combined or not with Grimme's D3BJ dispersion (B2PLYPD3) and the long-range corrected functional ωB97X [45] also with the inclusion of both Grimme's D2 and D3 dispersion model (ωB97XD; ωB97XD3) [46–48]. In particular the aforementioned functional, named CAM-B3LYP (Coulomb Attenuating Method-B3LYP) represents a new hybrid exchange-correlation functional with improved long-range properties with respect to the B3LYP [43]. In detail, the electron repulsion operator $\frac{1}{r_{12}}$, which was already divided into short-range and long-range parts by Tsuneda and collaborators [49] as follows:

$$\frac{1}{r_{12}} = \frac{1 - erf(\mu r_{12})}{r_{12}} + \frac{erf(\mu r_{12})}{r_{12}}$$ (1)

is now implemented using two parameters α and β:

$$\frac{1}{r_{12}} = \frac{1 - [\alpha + \beta * erf(\mu r_{12})]}{r_{12}} + \frac{\alpha + \beta * erf(\mu r_{12})}{r_{12}}$$ (2)

where $0 \leq \alpha + \beta \leq 1$ together with $0 \leq \alpha \leq 1$ and $0 \leq \beta \leq 1$.

All the above mentioned methods have been used in conjunction with the correlation consistent valence polarized basis set aug-cc-pVTZ [50]. The same level of theory used for geometry optimization was used to perform a vibrational frequency analysis in order to assign the nature of each identified stationary point (i.e. minimum if all the frequencies are real and saddle point if there is one, and only one, imaginary frequency). Then for each stationary point for all the employed methods, a more accurate energy value was computed at coupled cluster level, including single and double excitations as well as perturbative estimate of connected triples (CCSD(T)) [51–53]. Finally, energies obtained from every method were corrected to 0 K by adding the zero-point energy correction derived from the frequency calculations.

All the calculations were performed using the Gaussian09 software [54], while the analysis of the vibrational frequencies was done using Avogadro [55].

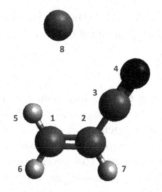

Fig. 1. Geometry of the long-range identified complex

Table 1. Bond distances, in Å, obtained at the different level of theory

Dist./ Funct	B3LY P	B3LY P-D3	CAM-B3LY P	B2PLY P	B2PL YP-D3	ωB97 X	ωB97 XD	ωB97X D3	BHand HLYP
C_1-H_5	1.081	1.081	1.080	1.079	1.079	1.082	1.081	1.082	1.073
C_1-H_6	1.080	1.081	1.080	1.079	1.079	1.081	1.081	1.081	1.073
C_1-C_2	1.331	1.331	1.324	1.334	1.334	1.325	1.327	1.326	1.320
C_2-H_7	1.083	1.083	1.081	1.081	1.081	1.082	1.082	1.082	1.074
C_2-C_3	1.426	1.426	1.428	1.428	1.428	1.435	1.430	1.435	1.425
C_3-N_4	1.154	1.154	1.146	1.161	1.161	1.149	1.149	1.149	1.139
O_8-C_1	3.643	3.444	3.584	3.634	3.573	3.462	3.601	3.399	3.633
O_8-C_2	3.758	3.590	3.735	3.830	3.764	3.615	3.834	3.566	3.860
O_8-C_3	2.996	2.883	3.001	3.131	3.069	2.893	3.171	2.867	3.193
O_8-N_4	2.794	2.787	2.848	2.995	2.954	2.771	3.066	2.775	3.077
O_8-H_5	2.853	2.647	2.773	2.793	2.738	2.655	2.740	2.588	2.778

3   Results and Discussion

The data obtained from electronic structure calculations clearly show the formation of a long-range complex as the first step of the reaction between $O(^3P)$ and
acrylonitrile. The process appears to be exothermic at all the previously cited
levels of theory. The structure of the complex shows the interaction of the oxygen
atom with the double bond between C_1 and C_2 of the CH_2CHCN molecule. In
Table 1 are reported the bond distances, expressed in angstroms, obtained at the
different levels of theory. The geometry of the complex with all the atom labels is
reported in Fig. 1. A comparison between the values of bond distances obtained
with the different theoretical methods can bring to the conclusion that there are
no significant differences in the values of the distances related to covalent bonds,

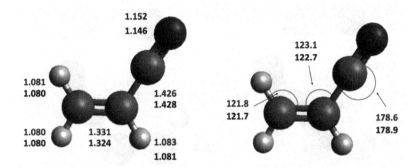

Fig. 2. Bond lengths (Å) and angles for the reactant at the B3LYP/aug-cc-pVTZ (blue) and CAM- B3LYP/aug-cc-pVTZ (green) level of theory. (Color figure online)

Table 2. Energies obtained at the different level of theory, with respect to the reactant energy asymptote.

Method	$E_{REL(Method)}$	$E_{REL(CCSD(T))}$
	kJ mol⁻¹	kJ mol⁻¹
B3LYP	-3.0	-5.1
B3LYP-D3	-8.0	-4.3
CAM-B3LYP	-4.3	-5.3
B2PLYP	-0.9	-5.7
B2PLYP-D3	-2.4	-5.5
ωB97X	-7.6	-4.1
ωB97XD	-4.0	-5.7
ωB97XD3	-11.1	-3.8
BHandHLYP	-3.0	-5.9

such as C-C, C-H and C-N, how can be seen also from the comparison of the structure of the reactant in Fig. 2. Nevertheless some discrepancies can be noted in the description of the long-range interaction. In particular it is possible to notice some differences in the interaction distance O_8-C_5 between B3LYP and CAM-B3LYP functionals. As expected, the use of CAM-B3LYP with respect to B3LYP allows us to obtain results more in line with other functionals which include the dispersion effects, such as B2PLYPD3 and ωB97XD3. In order to have a better comprehension of the differences between the methods it is possible to compare the energies obtained from the various calculations.

In Table 2 the energies obtained at the different levels of theory are reported. In particular the first column reports the electronic energies computed at the defined level of theory (in kJ mol⁻¹), while in the last column are reported the values obtained by the CCSD(T) calculations starting from the geometry optimized at the lower level of theory. The values are corrected at 0 K including the zero point correction obtained from the harmonic vibrational calculations

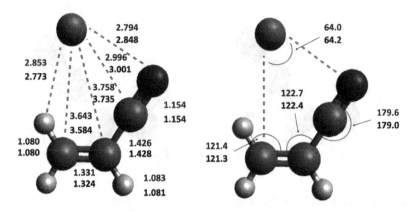

Fig. 3. Bond lengths (Å) and angles for the vdW adduct at the B3LYP/aug-cc-pVTZ (blue) and CAM-B3LYP/aug-cc-pVTZ (green) level of theory. (Color figure online)

performed at the same level of theory used for the geometry optimization. The analysis of the values of energy reported in Table 2 shows no significant differences in the values of the CCSD(T) corrected energy, which is usually considered in the construction of the potential energy surface. In particular we can notice that most of the time the difference is lower than $5 \, \text{kJ mol}^{-1}$, which is considered to be the uncertainty associated to accurate calculations.

Since no significant differences can be noticed between the employed methods we decided to focus our attention on the comparison between the B3LYP method and CAM-B3LYP, which is presented as an improvement of the B3LYP in order to include the long-range interaction. In Figs. 2 and 3 a comparison of the bond distances (in Å) and angles (in °) between the two methods is reported for the reactant (vinyl cyanide) and for the complex respectively. The results of the B3LYP/aug-cc-pVTZ analysis are shown in blue while the values derived from the CAM-B3LYP/aug-cc-pVTZ calculations are displayed in green.

As previously mentioned the main differences can be appreciated in the description of the long-range O-C interaction with deviations lower than 0.1 Å for the bond distances and of a maximum of 0.6° for the angles. The analysis of the harmonic vibrational frequencies, reported in Table 3, shows small differences between the two levels of theory. In particular it can be important to compare the first two rows (named a and b) related to the O_8-H_5 and O_8-N_4 intermolecular stretching. The c-m values reported in Table 3 are related to the intramolecular bonding, while the n-r values are related to the intramolecular stretching. These differences lead to a small variation on the zero-point correction which is equal to $134.1 \, \text{kJ mol}^{-1}$ at B3LYP/aug-cc-pVTZ and $135.7 \, \text{kJ}$ mol^{-1} at CAM-B3LYP/aug-cc-pVTZ level of theory.

Table 3. Harmonic vibrational frequencies (cm^{-1}) of the vdW adduct obtained at the B3LYP/aug-cc-pVTZ and CAM-B3LYP/aug-cc-pVTZ level of theory.

	B3LYP	CAM-B3LYP
a	54.1	62.9
b	75.3	74.8
c	43.6	42.3
d	237.2	242.4
e	354.5	360.2
f	585.9	592.6
g	713.1	725.3
h	882.7	890.3
i	1005.3	1019.4
j	1008.8	1033.0
k	1113.1	1122.4
l	1324.1	1333.9
m	1448.5	1456.9
n	1672.3	1712.2
o	2319.8	2386.6
p	3155.7	3175.6
q	3171.6	3202.0
R	3248.8	3269.4

A last comparison between the two methods, together with the B2PLYPD3 method, can be performed considering the first steps of the reaction, shown in Fig. 4. The reaction starts with a barrierless formation of the previously described complex, MIN1, followed by the formation of the minimum MIN2 in which we can notice the formation of a chemical bond between C_1 and O, through a small barrier, represented by TS1. No particular differences can be noticed in the values of energy obtained at CCSD(T)/aug-cc-pVTZ level considering the geometries optimized at B3LYP level (in blue) and at CAM-B3LYP (in green) level of theory. A last comparison can be done between two other methods, such as CAM-B3LYP and B2PLYPD3. As can be seen in Fig. 4, some small discrepancies are present between the two methods. Nevertheless all the aforementioned differences are smaller then the uncertainty of accurate calculations.

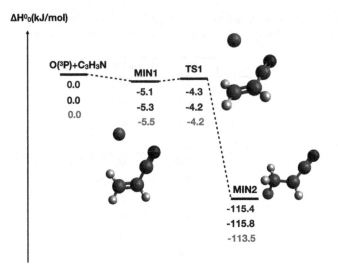

Fig. 4. Schematic representation of the potential energy surface for the first steps of the attack of the $O(^3P)$ atom to the acrylonitrile molecule. Energies are computed at CCSD(T)/aug-cc-pVTZ level with zero-point corrections at B3LYP/aug-cc-pVTZ (blue), CAM-B3LYP/aug-cc-pVTZ (green) and B2PLYPD3/aug-cc-pVTZ (orange) levels of theory. (Color figure online)

4   Conclusions

In the present work we performed a benchmark analysis of the first step of the reaction between atomic oxygen $O(^3P)$ and acrylonitrile (CH_2CHCN) using different theoretical methods: DFT (with BHandHLYP, B3LYP and B3LYPD3 functional), double-hybrid DFT (with B2PLYP and B2PLYPD3 functionals) and the long-range corrected functional ωB97X, ωB97XD and ωB97XD3. As far as optimized geometries for stationary points are concerned, all the methods seem to provide similar results. In particular, the B3LYP functional appears to be a good compromise between accuracy and computational cost for the characterization of minima. The analysis of the long-range interaction can be performed also using the CAM-B3LYP functional, which provides better estimate of the interactions than the B3LYP functional but needs lower computational resources than the B2PLYPD3 functional. The best choice for the estimate of the energies appears to be the use of correlated methods like CCSD(T). A more general conclusion can be presented concerning the first steps of the reaction mechanism, which appears to be in agreement with the previous determination by J. Sun et al. [25]. In particular the oxygen atom starts to interact with the electron density of multiple bonds in the molecule to form an exothermic addition intermediate. The comparison with B3LYP and CAM-B3LYP functionals suggests the possibility to use a combined strategy for the analysis of the Potential Energy Surfaces which will allow us to locate the long-range complexes at CAM-B3LYP level to be included in the reaction pathways.

Acknowledgements. This project has received funding from the European Union's Horizon 2020 research and innovation programme under the Marie Skłodowska-Curie grant agreement No 811312 for the project "Astro-Chemical Origins" (ACO). This work was supported by the Italian Space Agency (ASI) BANDO ASI DC-VUM-2017-034 CONTRATTO DI FINANZIAMENTO ASI N. 2019-3 U.O, "Vita nello spazio - Origine, presenza, persistenza della vita nello spazio, dalle molecole agli estremofili". The authors acknowledge the Dipartimento di Ingegneria Civile e Ambientale of the University of Perugia for allocated computing time within the project "Dipartimenti di Eccellenza 2018–2022".

References

1. Vuitton, V., Yelle, R., McEwan, M.: Ion chemistry and n-containing molecules in Titan's upper atmosphere. Icarus **191**(2), 722–742 (2007)
2. Cui, J., et al.: Analysis of Titan's neutral upper atmosphere from Cassini ion neutral mass spectrometer measurements. Icarus **200**(2), 581–615 (2009)
3. Palmer, M.Y., et al.: Alma detection and astrobiological potential of vinyl cyanide on Titan. Sci. Adv. **3**(7), e1700022 (2017)
4. Feuchtgruber, H., et al.: Oxygen in the stratospheres of the giant planets and Titan. In: The Universe as Seen by ISO, vol. 427, p. 133 (1999)
5. Teanby, N., et al.: The origin of Titan's external oxygen: further constraints from ALMA upper limits on CS and CH2NH. Astron. J. **155**(6), 251 (2018)
6. Hörst, S.M., Vuitton, V., Yelle, R.V.: Origin of oxygen species in Titan's atmosphere. J. Geophys. Res. Planets **113**(E10), 1–14 (2008)
7. Gardner, F., Winnewisser, G.: The detection of interstellar vinyl cyanide/acrylonitrile. Astrophys. J. **195**, L127–L130 (1975)
8. Matthews, H.E., Sears, T.J.: The detection of vinyl cyanide in TMC-1. Astrophys. J. **272**, 149–153 (1983)
9. Nummelin, A., Bergman, P.: Vibrationally excited vinyl cyanide in SGR B2(N). Astron. Astrophys. **341**, L59–L62 (1999)
10. Agúndez, M., Fonfría, J.P., Cernicharo, J., Pardo, J., Guélin, M.: Detection of circumstellar CH2CHCN, CH2CN, CH3CCH, and H2CS. Astron. Astrophys. **479**(2), 493–501 (2008)
11. López, A., et al.: Laboratory characterization and astrophysical detection of vibrationally excited states of vinyl cyanide in Orion-KL. Astron. Astrophys. **572**, A44 (2014)
12. Vastel, C., Loison, J.C., Wakelam, V., Lefloch, B.: Isocyanogen formation in the cold interstellar medium. Astron. Astrophys. **625**, A91 (2019)
13. Cavallotti, C., et al.: Relevance of the channel leading to formaldehyde + triplet ethylidene in the $O(^3P)+$ propene reaction under combustion conditions. J. Phys. Chem. Lett. **5**(23), 4213–4218 (2014)
14. Balucani, N., Leonori, F., Casavecchia, P.: Crossed molecular beam studies of bimolecular reactions of relevance in combustion. Energy **43**(1), 47–54 (2012)
15. Cavallotti, C., et al.: Theoretical study of the extent of intersystem crossing in the $O(^3P)$ + C6H6 reaction with experimental validation. J. Phys. Chem. Lett. **11**(22), 9621–9628 (2020)
16. Leonori, F., Occhiogrosso, A., Balucani, N., Bucci, A., Petrucci, R., Casavecchia, P.: Crossed molecular beam dynamics studies of the $O(^3P)$ + allene reaction: primary products, branching ratios, and dominant role of intersystem crossing. J. Phys. Chem. Lett. **3**(1), 75–80 (2012)

17. Balucani, N., Leonori, F., Casavecchia, P., Fu, B., Bowman, J.M.: Crossed molecular beams and quasiclassical trajectory surface hopping studies of the multichannel nonadiabatic $O(^3P)$ + ethylene reaction at high collision energy. J. Phys. Chem. A **119**(50), 12498–12511 (2015)

18. Fu, B., et al.: Experimental and theoretical studies of the $O(^3P)$ + C2H4 reaction dynamics: collision energy dependence of branching ratios and extent of intersystem crossing. J. Chem. Phys. **137**(22), 22A532 (2012)

19. Simoneit, B.R., Rushdi, A., Bin Abas, M., Didyk, B.: Alkyl amides and nitriles as novel tracers for biomass burning. Environ. Sci. Technol. **37**(1), 16–21 (2003)

20. Skouteris, D., Manolopoulos, D.E., Bian, W., Werner, H.J., Lai, L.H., Liu, K.: van der Waals interactions in the CL + HD reaction. Science **286**(5445), 1713–1716 (1999)

21. Balucani, N., et al.: The dynamics of the prototype abstraction reaction $Cl(^2P3/2,1/2)$ + H2: a comparison of crossed molecular beam experiments with exact quantum scattering calculations on coupled ab initio potential energy surfaces. Phys. Chem. Chem. Phys. **6**(21), 5007–5017 (2004)

22. Skouteris, D., et al.: Experimental and theoretical differential cross sections for the reactions Cl+H2/D2. J. Chem. Phys. **114**(24), 10662–10672 (2001)

23. Heard, D.E.: Rapid acceleration of hydrogen atom abstraction reactions of OH at very low temperatures through weakly bound complexes and tunneling. Acc. Chem. Res. **51**(11), 2620–2627 (2018)

24. Recio, P., et al.: Efficient intersystem crossing from weakly bound pre-reactive complex avoids the entrance barrier of bimolecular reactions. Nat. Chem. (submitted)

25. Sun, J., et al.: Theoretical investigation on atmospheric reaction of atomic $O(^3P)$ with acrylonitrile. Comput. Theor. Chem. **1052**, 17–25 (2015)

26. Upadhyaya, H.P., et al.: Reaction kinetics of $O(^3P)$ with acrylonitrile and crotononitrile. Chem. Phys. Lett. **274**(4), 383–389 (1997)

27. Falcinelli, S., Rosi, M., Cavalli, S., Pirani, F., Vecchiocattivi, F.: Stereoselectivity in autoionization reactions of hydrogenated molecules by metastable noble gas atoms: the role of electronic couplings. Chem. Eur. J. **22**(35), 12518–12526 (2016)

28. Leonori, F., et al.: Crossed-beam and theoretical studies of the $S(^1D)$ + C_2H_2 reaction. J. Phys. Chem. A **113**(16), 4330–4339 (2009)

29. Bartolomei, M., et al.: The intermolecular potential in NO-N$_2$ and (NO-N$_2$)$^+$ systems: implications for the neutralization of ionic molecular aggregates. Phys. Chem. Chem. Phys. **10**(39), 5993–6001 (2008)

30. de Petris, G., Cartoni, A., Rosi, M., Barone, V., Puzzarini, C., Troiani, A.: The proton affinity and gas-phase basicity of sulfur dioxide. ChemPhysChem **12**(1), 112–115 (2011)

31. Leonori, F., et al.: Observation of organosulfur products (thiovinoxy, thioketene and thioformyl) in crossed-beam experiments and low temperature rate coefficients for the reaction $S(^1D)$ + C_2H_4. Phys. Chem. Chem. Phys. **11**(23), 4701–4706 (2009)

32. de Petris, G., Rosi, M., Troiani, A.: SSOH and HSSO radicals: an experimental and theoretical study of $[S_2OH]^{0/+/-}$ species. J. Phys. Chem. A **111**(28), 6526–6533 (2007)

33. Rosi, M., Falcinelli, S., Balucani, N., Casavecchia, P., Leonori, F., Skouteris, D.: Theoretical study of reactions relevant for atmospheric models of Titan: interaction of excited nitrogen atoms with small hydrocarbons. In: Murgante, B., et al. (eds.) ICCSA 2012. LNCS, vol. 7333, pp. 331–344. Springer, Heidelberg (2012). https://doi.org/10.1007/978-3-642-31125-3_26

34. Berteloite, C., et al.: Low temperature kinetics, crossed beam dynamics and theoretical studies of the reaction $S(^1D) + CH_4$ and low temperature kinetics of $S(^1D)$ + C_2H_2. Phys. Chem. Chem. Phys. **13**(18), 8485–8501 (2011)
35. Rosi, M., Falcinelli, S., Balucani, N., Casavecchia, P., Skouteris, D.: A theoretical study of formation routes and dimerization of methanimine and implications for the aerosols formation in the upper atmosphere of Titan. In: Murgante, B., et al. (eds.) ICCSA 2013. LNCS, vol. 7971, pp. 47–56. Springer, Heidelberg (2013). https://doi.org/10.1007/978-3-642-39637-3_4
36. Sleiman, C., El Dib, G., Rosi, M., Skouteris, D., Balucani, N., Canosa, A.: Low temperature kinetics and theoretical studies of the reaction $CN + CH_3NH_2$: a potential source of cyanamide and methyl cyanamide in the interstellar medium. Phys. Chem. Chem. Phys. **20**(8), 5478–5489 (2018)
37. Becke, A.D.: A new mixing of Hartree-Fock and local density-functional theories. J. Chem. Phys. **98**(2), 1372–1377 (1993)
38. Lee, C., Yang, W., Parr, R.G.: Development of the Colle-Salvetti correlation-energy formula into a functional of the electron density. Phys. Rev. B **37**(2), 785 (1988)
39. Becke, A.D.: Density functional thermochemistry. III. The role of exact exchange. J. Chem. Phys. **98**(7), 5648–5652 (1993). https://doi.org/10.1063/1.464913
40. Stephens, P.J., Devlin, F.J., Chabalowski, C.F., Frisch, M.J.: *Ab initio* calculation of vibrational absorption and circular dichroism spectra using density functional force fields. J. Phys. Chem. **98**(45), 11623–11627 (1994)
41. Grimme, S., Ehrlich, S., Goerigk, L.: Effect of the damping function in dispersion corrected density functional theory. J. Comput. Chem. **32**(7), 1456–1465 (2011)
42. Goerigk, L., Grimme, S.: Efficient and accurate double-hybrid-meta-GGA density functionals-evaluation with the extended GMTKN30 database for general main group thermochemistry, kinetics, and noncovalent interactions. J. Chem. Theory Comput. **7**(2), 291–309 (2011)
43. Yanai, T., Tew, D.P., Handy, N.C.: A new hybrid exchange-correlation functional using the Coulomb-attenuating method (CAM-B3LYP). Chem. Phys. Lett. **393**(1–3), 51–57 (2004)
44. Grimme, S.: Semiempirical hybrid density functional with perturbative second-order correlation. J. Chem. Phys. **124**(3), 034108 (2006)
45. Chai, J.D., Head-Gordon, M.: Systematic optimization of long-range corrected hybrid density functionals. J. Chem. Phys. **128**(8), 084106 (2008)
46. Chai, J.D., Head-Gordon, M.: Long-range corrected hybrid density functionals with damped atom-atom dispersion corrections. Phys. Chem. Chem. Phys. **10**(44), 6615–6620 (2008)
47. Lin, Y.S., Li, G.D., Mao, S.P., Chai, J.D.: Long-range corrected hybrid density functionals with improved dispersion corrections. J. Chem. Theory Comput. **9**(1), 263–272 (2013)
48. Goerigk, L., Hansen, A., Bauer, C., Ehrlich, S., Najibi, A., Grimme, S.: A look at the density functional theory zoo with the advanced GMTKN55 database for general main group thermochemistry, kinetics and noncovalent interactions. Phys. Chem. Chem. Phys. **19**(48), 32184–32215 (2017)
49. Tawada, Y., Tsuneda, T., Yanagisawa, S., Yanai, T., Hirao, K.: A long-range-corrected time-dependent density functional theory. J. Chem. Phys. **120**(18), 8425–8433 (2004)
50. Dunning, T.H., Jr.: Gaussian basis sets for use in correlated molecular calculations. I. The atoms boron through neon and hydrogen. J. Chem. Phys. **90**(2), 1007–1023 (1989)

51. Bartlett, R.J.: Many-body perturbation theory and coupled cluster theory for electron correlation in molecules. Annu. Rev. Phys. Chem. **32**(1), 359–401 (1981)
52. Raghavachari, K., Trucks, G.W., Pople, J.A., Head-Gordon, M.: A fifth-order perturbation comparison of electron correlation theories. Chem. Phys. Lett. **157**(6), 479–483 (1989)
53. Olsen, J., Jørgensen, P., Koch, H., Balkova, A., Bartlett, R.J.: Full configuration-interaction and state of the art correlation calculations on water in a valence double-zeta basis with polarization functions. J. Chem. Phys. **104**(20), 8007–8015 (1996)
54. Frisch, M., et al.: Gaussian 09, Revision A. 02, 2009, Gaussian. Inc., Wallingford CT (2009)
55. Hanwell, M.D., Curtis, D.E., Lonie, D.C., Vandermeersch, T., Zurek, E., Hutchison, G.R.: Avogadro: an advanced semantic chemical editor, visualization, and analysis platform. J. Cheminform. **4**(1), 1–17 (2012)

A Minimal Model of Potential Energy Surface for the CO_2 – CO System

Concetta Caglioti[1,2] (ID), Maria Noelia Faginas Lago[1] (ID), Andrea Lombardi[1] (ID),
and Federico Palazzetti[1(✉)] (ID)

[1] Dipartimento di Chimica, Biologia e Biotecnologie – Università degli Studi di Perugia,
Perugia, Italy
federico.palazzetti@unipg.it

[2] Dipartimento di Medicina e Chirurgia - Università degli Studi di Perugia, Perugia, Italy

Abstract. Analytical models of potential energy surfaces are desirable for applications to classical and quantum molecular dynamics simulations, as well as calculation of spectroscopic properties. Here, we present a minimal model based on the expansion in spherical harmonics of the interaction potential between CO_2 and CO molecules, both assumed as rigid rotors. This approach consists in determining a minimal number of energy points related to representative mutual orientations of the molecules (configurations) by *ab initio* calculations. The spherical harmonics expansion represents an exact transformation of these quantum chemical input data. The model permits interpolation and possible implementation of sets of input data at a higher level of theory.

Keywords: van der Waals clusters · Intermolecular interactions · Planetary atmospheres · Spherical harmonics expansion

1 Introduction

The CO_2 – CO system has a remarkable importance in many areas, that span from the environmental and industrial chemistry to the chemistry of terrestrial and other planetary atmospheres [1]. These molecules are interconverted in the Boudouard reaction, where CO disproportionates to give C and CO_2. This reaction has been traditionally studied because of its environmental and industrial implications [2], while more recently it attracted interest in physics of plasmas, where the reaction is induced by high vibrational excitation [3]. The van der Waals cluster CO_2 – CO was initially characterized by rotational and vibrational spectroscopy [4], where a T-shaped configuration (CO and CO_2 are perpendicularly oriented) was observed, while theoretical investigations on this weakly bound complex was performed by using molecular mechanics for cluster modeling [5]. The dimer was investigated in argon matrices, to study conformational dynamics [6, 7], and afterwards theoretically characterized by Symmetry Adapted Perturbation Theory [8]. Molecular beam electric resonance spectroscopy was then employed to measure the dipole moment [9]. More recently, *ab initio* methods were employed to calculate the vibrational spectrum of various van der Waals complexes, including CO_2 – CO.

© Springer Nature Switzerland AG 2021
O. Gervasi et al. (Eds.): ICCSA 2021, LNCS 12958, pp. 351–362, 2021.
https://doi.org/10.1007/978-3-030-87016-4_26

The most recent experimental study, performed by infrared spectroscopy, reported the existence of a new T-shaped isomer [10]. In 2019, a four-dimensional potential energy surface obtained by CCSD(T)-F12 method calculated on more than 30,000 energy points, employing 147 expansion terms, revealed dynamical features of this complex, such as the minima and the related saddle points and the temperature dependence of the second virial coefficient [11].

In this article, we consider the case of the CO_2 – CO system, where both molecules are treated as rigid rotors and represent the potential energy surface in the analytical form, suitable for classical and quantum treatment of collisional processes, as well as for the calculation of spectroscopical properties. The potential energy surface is expanded into a series of nine spherical harmonics. This method has been extensively used to represent the potential interaction of van der Waals complexes formed by four and five bodies [12, 13]. Previously, expansion of the intermolecular potential in spherical (and hyperspherical) harmonics has been employed to represent non reacting systems of molecular pairs: rigid diatomic molecules of increasing complexity such as O_2-O_2 [14], N_2-N_2 [15], H_2-H_2 [16], N_2-O_2 [17], N_2-NO [18] and more recently CO – CO and the general case CO – HF [19]; five-body systems containing water H_2O – H_2 [20], H_2O – N_2 and H_2O – O_2 [21], H_2O – HF [22]; hydrogen peroxide [23, 24] and hydrogen persulfide [25, 26], where the torsion motion is not hindered.

Here, we have calculated a minimal number of points, 243 points, of the potential energy surface corresponding to significant configurations, whose choice and number relies on symmetry properties of the system. These configurations are the input data of the potential expansion. Since CO_2 and CO belong to the group symmetries $D_{\infty h}$ and $D_{\infty v}$, respectively, this system is similar to N_2 – NO [18] and the potential energy surface is properly described by at least nine significant configurations, while for the simpler O_2 – O_2 system, five significant configurations were enough for a comprehensive description of the potential interaction. The potential energy surface depends on four coordinates: a radial and three angular coordinates. The radial coordinate is the distance between the center-of-mass of the interacting molecules, that for CO_2 corresponds to the C atom. The expansion is given in terms of spherical harmonics, which depend on the angular coordinates. Their choice depends on the dimension and on the symmetry properties of the system and the number corresponds to the number of significant configurations. The expansion moments are function of the radial coordinate and are determined by solving a system of linear equations, where the known vector is the energy of the significant configurations. This approach represents an exact transformation, permitting interpolation among the energy points as requested by dynamical applications [27]. For each of the nine configurations, 27 single energy points have been calculated at the MP2 level of theory, employing the aug-cc-pVQZ basis set.

The article is structured as follows: in Sect. 2, we give a description of the coordinates frame, of the significant configurations and of quantum mechanical calculations; in Sect. 3, we report the interaction potential expanded in spherical harmonics; in Sect. 4, the results are discussed; in Sect. 5, the conclusions end the paper.

2 Potential Energy Surface

2.1 Coordinates

The potential energy surface of CO_2 – CO depends on a radial and three angular coordinates. In Fig. 1, we report the system embedded in the *xyz* Cartesian reference frame, where the origin of the axes corresponds to the center-of-mass of the system. The radial coordinate r is the distance that separates the centers-of-mass of the molecules; θ_a, $0 \leq \theta_a, \leq \pi$ is the angle given by the intersection between the vector $\mathbf{r}$ that joins the centers-of-mass of the two molecules and the O – C – O bond in CO_2, while θ_b, $0 \leq \theta_b$, $\leq \pi$ is the angle given by the intersection between the vector $\mathbf{r}$ and the C – O bond in CO; finally, the dihedral angle ϕ, $0 \leq \phi < 2\pi$, is defined as the intersection between the semiplanes passing through the axes of the two molecules and the origin of the Cartesian axes.

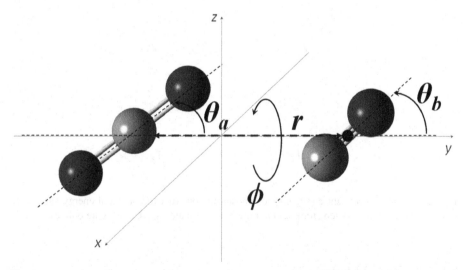

Fig. 1. The radial, r, and the angular, θ_a, θ_b, and ϕ, coordinates for the CO_2 - CO system (in red the oxygen atoms and in grey the carbon atoms). (Color figure online)

2.2 Configurations

The choice of the significant configurations relies on considerations upon geometry and symmetry properties of the system. A proper choice of these configurations would permit to represent uniformly the potential energy surface, although with a small number of terms, within the considered distance range. The significant configurations for CO_2 - CO (Fig. 2) are identified by capital letters: L, H, X, Z and T. The L configurations are characterized by a linear mutual orientation of the molecular axes, with $\theta_a = 0$, while θ_b is 0 in the configuration corresponding to the carbon of CO in the closest position to CO_2, L_1, and π in the opposite case, L_2. In the H configuration the molecular axes are parallel, thus $\theta_a = \theta_b = \pi/2$, and $\phi = 0$. The X configuration is characterized by the dihedral angle $\phi = \pi/2$; both the angles θ_a and θ_b are also $\pi/2$. The Z_1 configuration presents a parallel orientation of the molecular axes, with $\theta_a = \theta_b = \pi/4$ and $\phi = 0$. The configuration Z_2 is characterized by $\theta_a = \pi/4$, $\theta_b = 3\pi/4$ and $\phi = 0$. Finally, in the T configurations the molecular axes are perpendicular, more precisely in T_1, $\theta_a = \pi/2$ and $\theta_b = 0$, in T_2 $\theta_a = \pi/2$, $\theta_b = 0$ and $\phi = 0$; in T_3 $\theta_a = \pi/2$, $\theta_b = 0$ and $\phi = \pi$.

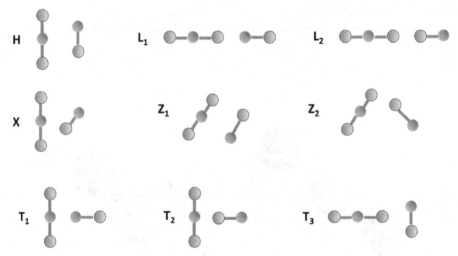

Fig. 2. The nine significant configurations chosen to construct the potential energy surface of CO_2 - CO (in red the oxygen atoms and in grey the carbon atoms). (Color figure online)

2.3 *Ab initio* Calculations

Ab initio calculations have been performed by the Gaussian09 software package [28]. The geometries have been optimized by MP2/aug-cc-pVTZ, obtaining the following geometries: in CO, the bond length is 1.14 Å, while in CO_2 the bond length is 1.17 Å and the bond angle is 180.0°. We have calculated about 250 energy points, corresponding to 27 radial grid points between 2.0 and 8.0 Å for each of the nine significant configurations at the MP2 level of theory with aug-cc-pVQZ basis set. For each configuration, we have estimated the Basis Set Superposition Error by counterpoise correction for the smallest value of the distance, 2.8 Å.

3 Spherical Harmonics Expansion of the Intermolecular Potential

The interaction potential is given by the expansion of a series of spherical harmonics $\mathcal{Y}_{L_1 L_2}^{L0}(\theta_1, \theta_2, \phi)$ and their expansion terms $v_{L_1 L_2 L}(r)$:

$$V(r; \theta_1, \theta_2, \phi) = \Sigma_{L_1 L_2 L}\, v_{L_1 L_2 L}(r)\, \mathcal{Y}_{L_1 L_2}^{L0}(\theta_1, \theta_2, \phi) \tag{1}$$

L_1 and L_2 are non-negative integer numbers and represent the order of the spherical harmonics, while L is a combination of L_1 and L_2 and is given by $|L_1 - L_2| \leq L \leq L_1 + L_2$. The spherical harmonic $\mathcal{Y}_{L_1 L_2}^{L0}(\theta_1, \theta_2, \phi)$ is decomposed into two spherical harmonics $\mathcal{Y}_{L_1}^m(\theta_1, \phi_1)$ and $\mathcal{Y}_{L_2}^{-m}(\theta_2, \phi_2)$, where m is an integer number $-\min(L_1, L_2) \leq m \leq \min(L_1, L_2)$. The interaction potential is thus written as a product of the two spherical harmonics:

$$V(r; \alpha, \theta_1, \theta_2, \phi) = \Sigma_i\, w_i(\alpha) \Sigma_{L_1 L_2 L} \begin{pmatrix} L_1 & L_2 & L \\ m & -m & 0 \end{pmatrix} v_{L_1 L_2 L}(r)\, \mathcal{Y}_{L_1}^m(\theta_1, 0)\, \mathcal{Y}_{L_2}^{-m}(\theta_2, \phi) \tag{2}$$

Here, the 2×3 matrix within parenthesis is a 3-j symbol. The angular coordinates ϕ_1 and ϕ_2 are both dihedral angles, referred respectively to CO_2 and CO. The dihedral angle ϕ is the difference between ϕ_1 and ϕ_2. Thus, the spherical harmonics are written as $\mathcal{Y}_{L_1}^m(\theta_1, \phi)$ and $\mathcal{Y}_{L_2}^{-m}(\theta_2, 0)$.

The choice of the spherical harmonics of this expansion relies upon the symmetry characteristics of the system. The set of spherical harmonics is formed by only even values for L_1 and both even and odd values for L_2. Thus, the interaction potential for this system is given by

$$\begin{aligned}
V_{CO_2 - CO}(r; \theta_1, \theta_2, \phi) &= v_{000}(r) + \sqrt{3}v_{011}(r)\cos\theta_2 + \frac{\sqrt{5}}{4}v_{022}(r)(1 + \\
&3\cos(2\theta_2)) + \frac{\sqrt{5}}{4}v_{202}(r)(1 + 3\cos(2\theta_1)) - \frac{1}{2}\sqrt{\frac{3}{2}}v_{211}(r)[(1 + \\
&3\cos(2\theta_1))\cos\theta_2 + 3\cos\phi\,\sin(2\theta_1)\sin\theta_2] + \frac{3}{2}v_{213}(R)\left[\frac{1}{2}(1 + \right. \\
&3\cos(2\theta_1))\cos\theta_2 - \cos\phi\,\sin(2\theta_1)\sin\theta_2\left.\right] + \frac{\sqrt{5}}{4}v_{220}(R)\left[\frac{1}{4}(1 + 3\cos(2\theta_1))(1 + \right. \\
&3\cos(2\theta_2)) + 3\cos\phi\,\sin(2\theta_1)\sin(2\theta_2) + \frac{3}{4}\cos(2\phi)(\cos(2\theta_1) - 1)(\cos(2\theta_2) - \\
&1)\left.\right] - \frac{5}{4\sqrt{14}}v_{222}(r)\left[\frac{1}{2}(1 + 3\cos(2\theta_1))(1 + 3\cos(2\theta_2)) + \right. \\
&3\cos\phi\,\sin(2\theta_1)\sin(2\theta_2) - \frac{3}{2}\cos(2\phi)(\cos(2\theta_1) - 1)(\cos(2\theta_2) - 1)\left.\right] + \\
&3\sqrt{\frac{5}{14}}v_{224}(r)\left[\frac{1}{8}(1 + 3\cos(2\theta_1))(1 + 3\cos(2\theta_2)) - \cos\phi\,\sin(2\theta_1)\sin(2\theta_2) + \right. \\
&\frac{1}{16}\cos(2\phi)(\cos(2\theta_1) - 1)(\cos(2\theta_2) - 1)\left.\right]
\end{aligned} \tag{3}$$

The expansion moments $v_{L_1 L_2 L}(r)$ are given as a linear combination of the energy points of the significant configurations as a function of the distance:

$$v_{000}(r) = \frac{1}{18}\left(4V_H(r) + V_{L_1}(r) + V_{L_2}(r) + 2V_{T_1}(r) + 2V_{T_2}(r) + 4V_{T_3}(r) + 4V_X(r)\right) \tag{4}$$

$$v_{011}(r) = \frac{V_{L_1}(r) - V_{L_2}(r) + 2V_{T_1}(r) - 2V_{T_2}(r)}{6\sqrt{3}} \tag{5}$$

$$v_{022}(r) = \frac{-2V_H(r) + V_{L_1}(r) + V_{L_2}(r) + 2V_{T_1}(r) + 2V_{T_2}(r) - 2V_{T_3}(r) - 2V_X(r)}{9\sqrt{5}} \tag{6}$$

$$v_{202}(r) = -\frac{2V_H(r) - V_{L_1}(r) - V_{L_2}(r) + V_{T_1}(r) + V_{T_2}(r) - 4V_{T_3}(r) + 2V_X(r)}{9\sqrt{5}} \tag{7}$$

$$v_{211}(r) = \frac{1}{30\sqrt{6}} \left(6\sqrt{2}V_H(r) + (-4 + 3\sqrt{2})V_{L_1}(r) + (4 + 3\sqrt{2})V_{L_2}(r) + \right.$$
$$\left. (4 + 3\sqrt{2})V_{T_1}(r) + (-4 + 3\sqrt{2})V_{T_2}(r) + 6\sqrt{2}V_{T_3}(r) - 12\sqrt{2}V_{Z_1}(r) - 12\sqrt{2}V_{Z_2}(r) \right) \tag{8}$$

$$v_{213}(r) = \frac{1}{15\sqrt{2}} \left(2V_H(r) + (1 + \sqrt{2})V_{L_1}(r) + (1 - \sqrt{2})V_{L_2}(r) + (1 - \sqrt{2})V_{T_1}(r) + \right.$$
$$\left. (1 + \sqrt{2})V_{T_2}(r) + 2V_{T_3}(r) - 4V_{Z_1}(r) - 4V_{Z_2}(r) \right) \tag{9}$$

$$v_{220}(r) = \frac{1}{45}\sqrt{\frac{2}{5}} \left(7\sqrt{2}V_H(r) + (-3 + \sqrt{2})V_{L_1}(r) + (3 + \sqrt{2})V_{L_2}(r) - \right.$$
$$\left. (3 + \sqrt{2})V_{T_1}(r) + (3 - \sqrt{2})V_{T_2}(r) - 2\sqrt{2}V_{T_3}(r) - 5\sqrt{2}V_X(r) + 6\sqrt{2}V_{Z_1}(r) - 6\sqrt{2}V_{Z_2}(r) \right) \tag{10}$$

$$v_{222}(r) = \frac{1}{45\sqrt{14}} \left(20V_H(r) + (-4 + 3\sqrt{2})V_{L_1}(r) - (4 + 3\sqrt{2})V_{L_2}(r) + \right.$$
$$\left. (4 + 3\sqrt{2})V_{T_1}(r) + (4 - 3\sqrt{2})V_{T_2}(r) + 8V_{T_3}(r) - 28V_X(r) - 12V_{Z_1}(r) + 12V_{Z_2}(r) \right) \tag{11}$$

$$v_{224}(r) = \frac{2}{15}\sqrt{\frac{2}{35}} \left(2V_H(r) + (1 + \sqrt{2})V_{L_1}(r) + (1 - \sqrt{2})V_{L_2}(r) + (1 + \sqrt{2})V_{T_1}(r) - \right.$$
$$\left. (1 + \sqrt{2})V_{T_2}(r) - 2V_{T_3}(r) - 4V_{Z_1}(r) + 4V_{Z_2}(r) \right) \tag{12}$$

The binding energy of the CO_2 - CO van der Waals cluster is given by the difference between the energy of the complex and the energies of the isolate molecules:

$$Ebinding = E_{CO_2\text{-}CO} - (E_{CO_2} + E_{CO}) \tag{13}$$

In Table 1, we report the BSSE estimation by counterpoise correction of the energies of the complex for each configuration at 2.8 Å. The BSSE is in average 3.33 kJ/mol; it is more pronounced in the L configurations, where the collinear orientation determines a very small distance between the O of CO_2 and one of the two atoms of CO.

4   Results and Discussions

In Fig. 3, we report the potential energy profiles of the configurations H and X. Both configurations present a minimum at *ca.* 3.4 Å; X is more attractive, the potential is about 2.5 kJ/mol, while the potential well of H is *ca.* 1.5 kJ/mol.

Table 1. The Basis Set Superposition Error, in kJ/mol, estimated for the nine significant configurations.

Configuration	BSSE (kJ/mol)
H	0.94
L1	10.42
L2	8.12
T1	2.12
T2	1.53
T3	0.74
X	0.90
Z1	2.21
Z2	3.02

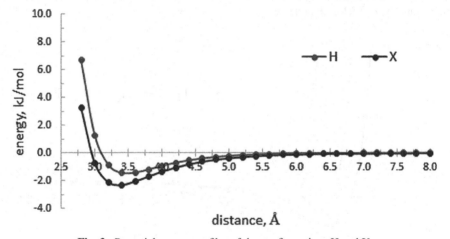

Fig. 3. Potential energy profiles of the configurations H and X.

In Fig. 4, we show the cuts of the potential energy surface related to L_1 and L_2. In these two collinearly oriented molecules, L_1 is more stable than L_2. This latter presents in fact a repulsive potential, while the first one shows a minimum at *ca.* 4.8 Å, with a potential well of about 1 kJ/mol.

In Fig. 5, the perpendicularly oriented configurations T_1, T_2 and T_3 are reported. The configuration T_1 is the most stable among the set of significant configurations we have considered, it coincides with the dimer observed experimentally by Legon *et al.* [4], the distance between the C atom of the CO and the C atom of CO_2 is *ca.* 3.1 Å, about 0.1 Å shorter than the complex found experimentally. The equilibrium distance of T_1 is located at *ca.* 3.9 Å and the depth of the well is about 6 kJ/mol, 1 kJ/mol more attractive than that obtained by Badri *et al.* [11], employing the best basis set at the CCSD(T) level of theory. The configuration T_2 presents a minimum at 3.7 Å, where the energy is about

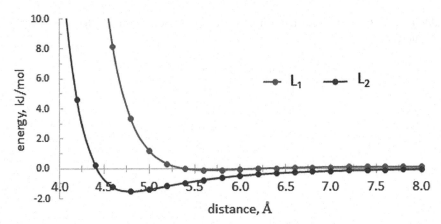

Fig. 4. Potential energy profiles of the configurations L_1 and L_2.

4 kJ/mol. The configuration T_3 is the least stable of these set of configurations, with a minimum of *ca.* 3 kJ/mol, at 4.4 Å.

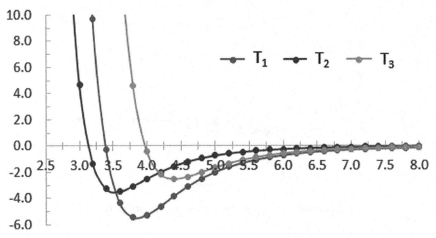

Fig. 5. Potential energy profiles of the configurations T_1, T_2 and T_3.

In Fig. 6, we finally report the potential energy profiles of the Z configurations. The configuration Z_1 presents a minimum of about 3.0 kJ/mol at 4.0 Å. The configuration Z_2 is less attractive then Z_1, having a minimum of *ca.* 1.0 kJ/mol.

In Fig. 7, we report the isotropic component of the potential, given by averaging the contributions to the interaction potential according to Eq. 4. The minimum is about 1 kJ/mol at 4.6 Å. Finally, in Fig. 8 we show the anisotropic components of the potential that correspond to the expansion terms as a function of the distance.

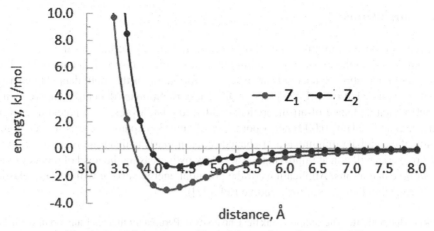

Fig. 6. Potential energy profiles of the configurations Z_1 and Z_2.

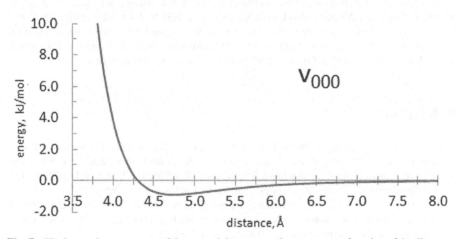

Fig. 7. The isotropic component of the potential energy surface, v_{000}, as a function of the distance.

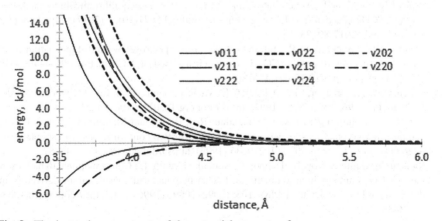

Fig. 8. The isotropic components of the potential energy surface, v_{011}, v_{022}, v_{200}, v_{211}, v_{213}, v_{220}, v_{222}, v_{224}, as a function of the distance.

5   Conclusions

We have proposed a minimal model of the potential energy surface for the $CO_2 - CO$ system, based on the expansion of a limited number, nine, of spherical harmonics. The interaction potential expansion is an exact transformation of the input data, 243 energy points calculated at the MP2/aug-cc-pVQZ. These preliminary data are compared with experimental and state-of-art theoretical results; this latter presents a potential energy surface calculated on 30,000 energy points, involving 134 expansion terms. The configuration of the global minimum is a "T-shaped" one, similarly to that found experimentally. Future works will aim at improving the accuracy by increasing the level of theory of the *ab initio* calculations. Applications of the potential energy surface will concern elastic scattering simulations (see for example Ref. [27]).

Acknowledgement. The authors thank the University of Perugia for financial support through the AMIS project ("Dipartimenti di Eccellenza-2018-2022"). AL acknowledges the Dipartimento di Chimica, Biologia e Biotecnologie for funding under the "Fondo Ricerca di Base 2019" program and the Italian Space Agency (ASI) Life in Space project (ASI N. 2019-3-U.0). NFL thanks the Dipartimento di Chimica, Biologia e Biotecnologie for funding under the "Fondo Ricerca di Base 2020" program. The authors also thank the OU Supercomputing Center for Education & Research (OSCER) at the University of Oklahoma (OU) for the allocated computing time.

References

1. Lombardi, A., Laganà, A., Pirani, F., Palazzetti, F., Lago, N.F.: Carbon Oxides in Gas Flows and Earth and Planetary Atmospheres: State-to-State Simulations of Energy Transfer and Dissociation Reactions. In: Murgante, B., et al. (eds.) ICCSA 2013. LNCS, vol. 7972, pp. 17–31. Springer, Heidelberg (2013). https://doi.org/10.1007/978-3-642-39643-4_2
2. Pramhaas, V., et al.: Interplay between CO disproportionation and oxidation: on the origin of the CO reaction onset on atomic layer deposition-grown Pt/ZrO_2 model catalysts. ACS Catal. **11**, 208–214 (2021). https://doi.org/10.1021/acscatal.0c03974
3. Barreto, P.R.P., et al.: Gas phase Boudouard reactions involving singlet–singlet and singlet–triplet CO vibrationally excited states: implications for the non-equilibrium vibrational kinetics of CO/CO2 plasmas. The European Physical Journal D **71**(10), 1 (2017). https://doi.org/10.1140/epjd/e2017-80103-1
4. Legon, A.C., Suckley, A.P.: Infrared diode-laser spectroscopy and Fourier-transform microwave spectroscopy of the (CO_2, CO) dimer in a pulsed jet. J. Chem. Phys. **91**, 4440–4447 (1989). https://doi.org/10.1063/1.456780
5. Parish, C.A., Augspurger, J.D., Dykstra, C.E.: Weakly bound complexes of carbon monoxide. J. Chem. Phys. **96**, 2069–2079 (1992). https://doi.org/10.1021/j100184a011
6. Raducu, V., Dahoo, J.R., Brosset, P., Gauthier-Roy, B., Abouaf-Marguin, L.: The CO: CO_2 complex in argon matrices: experimental evidence for two conformations with spontaneous interconversion. J. Chem. Phys. **102**, 9235 (1995). https://doi.org/10.1063/1.468873
7. Raducu, V., Gauthier-Roy, B., Dahoo, R., Abouaf-Marguin, L.: Conformational dynamics of the CO: CO_2 complex in argon matrices. I. Thermodynamical considerations derived from the observed kinetics. J. Chem. Phys. **105**, 10092–10096 (1996). doi: https://doi.org/10.1063/1.472838

8. Langlet, J., et al.: Modelling of some structural and vibrational properties of CO: CO_2 complexes in gas phase and embedded in solid argon. J. Mol. Struct. **489**, 145–159 (1999). https://doi.org/10.1016/S0022-2860(98)00911-9

9. Muenther, J.S., Bhattacharjee, J.S.: The electric dipole moment of the CO_2 – CO van der Waals Complex. J. Mol Spectr. **190**, 290–293 (1998). https://doi.org/10.1006/jmsp.1998.7601

10. Sheybani-Deloui, S., Barclay, A.J., Michaelian, K.H., McKellar, A.R.W., Moazzen-Ahmadi, N.: Communication: spectroscopic observation of the O-bonded T-shaped isomer of the CO-CO_2 dimer and two of its intermolecular frequencies. J. Chem. Phys. **143**, 121101 (2015). https://doi.org/10.1063/1.4932043

11. Badri, A., Shirkov, L., Jaidane, N.E., Hochlaf, M.: Explicitly correlated potential energy surface of the CO_2–CO van der Waals dimer and applications. Phys. Chem. Chem. Phys. **21**, 15871 (2019). https://doi.org/10.1039/c9cp02657f

12. Palazzetti, F., Munusamy, E., Lombardi, A., Grossi, G., Aquilanti, V.: Spherical and hyperspherical representation of potential energy surfaces for intermolecular interactions. Int. J. Quant. Chem. **111**, 318–332 (2011). https://doi.org/10.1002/qua.22688

13. Van der Avoird, A., Wormer, P.E.S., Szalevicz, R.: From Intermolecular potentials to the spectra of van der Waals molecules, and vice versa. Chem. Rev. **94**, 1931 (1994). https://doi.org/10.1021/cr00031a009

14. Aquilanti, V., Bartolomei, M., Cappelletti, D., Carmona-Novillo, E., Pirani, F.: The N2–N2 system: an experimental potential energy surface and calculated rotovibrational levels of the molecular nitrogen dimer. J. Chem- Phys. **117**, 615 (2002). https://doi.org/10.1063/1.1482696

15. Aquilanti, V., et al.: Molecular beam scattering of aligned oxygen molecules. The nature of the bond in the O_2-O_2 dimer. J. Am. Chem. Soc. **121**, 10794 (1999). doi: https://doi.org/10.1021/ja9917215

16. Barreto, P.R.P., Cruz, A.C.P.S., Euclides, H.O., Albernaz, A.F., Correa, E.: Spherical harmonics representation of the potential energy surface for the $H_2 \cdots H_2$ van der Waals complex. J. Mol. Model. **26**(10), 1–8 (2020). https://doi.org/10.1007/s00894-020-04537-8

17. Aquilanti, V., Bartolomei, M., Carmona-Novillo, E., Pirani, F.: The asymmetric dimer N2–O2: characterization of the potential energy surface and quantum mechanical calculation of rotovibrational levels. J. Chem. Phys. **118**, 2214 (2003). https://doi.org/10.1063/1.1533015

18. Bartolomei, M., et al.: The intermolecular potential in NO–N2 and (NO–N2)+ systems: implications for the neutralization of ionic molecular aggregates. Phys. Chem. Chem. Phys. **10**, 5993–6001 (2008). https://doi.org/10.1039/B808200F

19. Barreto, P.R.P., et al.: The spherical-harmonics representation for the interaction between diatomic molecules: the general case and applications to COCO and COHF. J. Mol. Spectr. **337**, 163–177 (2017). https://doi.org/10.1016/j.jms.2017.05.009

20. Barreto, P.R.P., Ribas, V.W., Palazzetti, F.: Potential energy surface for the H2O–H2 system. J. Phys. Chem. A **113**, 15047–15054 (2009). https://doi.org/10.1021/jp9051819

21. Barreto, P.R.B., et al.: Potential energy surfaces for interactions of H$_2$O with H$_2$, N$_2$ and O$_2$: a hyperspherical harmonics representation, and a minimal model for the H$_2$O–rare-gas-atom systems. Comp. Theor. Chem. **990**, 53–61 (2012). https://doi.org/10.1016/j.comptc.2011.12.024

22. Caglioti, C., Palazzetti, F.: Potential energy surfaces for water interacting with diatomic heteronuclear molecules: H$_2$O – HF as a case study. Chem. Phys. Lett. **776**, 138692 (2021). https://doi.org/10.1016/j.cplett.2021.138692

23. Barreto, P.R.P., Vilela, A.F.A., Lombardi, A., Maciel, G.S., Palazzetti, F., Aquilanti, V.: The hydrogen peroxide−rare gas systems: quantum chemical calculations and hyperspherical harmonic representation of the potential energy surface for atom−floppy molecule interactions. J. Phys. Chem. A **111**, 12754–12762 (2007). https://doi.org/10.1021/jp076268v

24. Barreto, P.R.P., Albernaz, A.F., Palazzetti, F., Lombardi, A., Grossi, G., Aquilanti, V.: Hyper-spherical representation of potential energy surfaces: intermolecular interactions in tetra-atomic and penta-atomic systems. Phys. Scr. **84**, 028111 (2011). https://doi.org/10.1088/0031-8949/84/02/028111

25. Maciel, G.S., Barreto, P.R.P., Palazzetti, F., Lombardi, A., Aquilanti, V.: A quantum chemical study of H_2S_2: Intramolecular torsional mode and intermolecular interactions with rare gases. J. Chem. Phys. **129**, 164302 (2008). https://doi.org/10.1063/1.2994732

26. Barreto, P.R.P., Albernaz, A.F., Palazzetti, F.: Potential energy surfaces for van der Waals complexes of rare gases with H_2S and H_2S_2: extension to xenon interactions and hyperspherical harmonics representation. Int. J. Quant. Chem. **112**, 834–847 (2012). https://doi.org/10.1002/qua.23073

27. Lombardi, A., Palazzetti, F., Maciel, G.S., Aquilanti, V., Sevryuk, M.B.: Simulation of oriented collision dynamics of simple chiral molecules. Int. J. Quant. Chem. **111**, 1651–1658 (2010). https://doi.org/10.1002/qua.22816

28. Gaussian 09, et al.: Gaussian, Inc., Wallingford CT (2016)

Classification of Biomolecules
by Invariant Shape Coordinates
and Deformation Indexes

Lombardi Andrea[1,2(✉)] and Noelia Faginas-Lago[1,2]

[1] Dipartimento di Chimica, Biologia e Biotecnologie,
Università di Perugia, Perugia, Italy
andrea.lombardi@unipg.it, noelia.faginaslago@unipg.it
http://www.chm.unipg.it/gruppi?q=node/48
[2] Master-tec s.r.l., Via Sicilia 41, 06128 Perugia, Italy

Abstract. In this paper we consider to approach the issue of the classification of protein structures by assigning them, in a unique way, sets of invariant parameters. To such purpose we suggest the use of shape parameters and deformation indexes derived from "symmetric" hyperspherical coordinates, as introduced by us in previous works. We give a resume of the theoretical background of coordinate and parameter derivation, followed by an application of the method to some representative protein structures.

Keywords: Protein structure classification · Hyperspherical coordinates · Invariant shape coordinates

1 Introduction

The classification of structures of proteins is a longstanding issue, mainly motivated by the need for comparison and recognition of them in connection to folding process. The use of appropriate invariant parameters, uniquely associated to a given molecular geometry, can in principle induce a kind of structure classification, leading to emergence of patterns and regularities. A comprehensive statistics of such parameters could also be a test for the quality of the experimental measured and theoretically predicted structures. The recent increased use of computational approaches based on machine learning and neural networks, oriented to the search for hidden patterns and regularities, further motivates renewed efforts in such direction [1].

Convenient sets of invariant parameters can be derived from the hyperspherical approach to molecular dynamics, traditionally adopted for quantum reactive scattering calculations. Quantum hyperspherical dynamics relies on the definition of sets of hyperspherical functions [2–4] for three and four-body collisions (see e.g. [5–10]), which in turn depend in the symmetry properties of the particular angular coordinate set adopted. The Hamiltonian in so called "symmetric" hyperspherical coordinates is invariant with respect to the possible product

© Springer Nature Switzerland AG 2021
O. Gervasi et al. (Eds.): ICCSA 2021, LNCS 12958, pp. 363–374, 2021.
https://doi.org/10.1007/978-3-030-87016-4_27

arrangements, as in multi-channel processes, and for such reason is largely preferable with respect to other approaches. The same hyperspherical basis functions, due to their symmetry properties, can be combined in finite sums to represent the intermolecular and intramolecular interactions [11–38].

In spite of the original application to few-atom systems, hyperspherical coordinates can be derived for any number of atoms and used for molecular dynamics simulations of large molecules based on classical mechanics (see e.g. [39]).

Unlike Cartesian coordinates, the hyperspherical ones partition the degrees of freedom into shape coordinates, ordinary rotations and kinematic rotations angles [7,40–44]. A kinetic energy term corresponds to each such variable sets and can be evaluated in the classical mechanics framework as a function of hyperangular momenta. The hyperspherical Hamilton function, is remisicent of the quantum hyperspherical Hamiltonian operator (differing for some purely quantum extra-terms). Integration of Hamilton's equations in Cartesian coordinates can be still retained with hyperspherical coordinates since a procedure based on matrix transformations of the set of position vectors has been developed, which allows for the evaluation of the energy terms appearing in the Hyperspherical Hamilton function as a function of time [7,41].

The global shape of the system in the three-dimensional physical space is invariant under the action of both ordinary and kinematic rotations. As a consequence shape coordinates must be themselves invariant with respect to both kinds of rotations, as shown in previous works [40,45–50].

Exactly for such invariance property of shape hyperspherical coordinates, we consider them suitable as shape parameters for the classification of local structures of biomolecules.

The paper is organized as follows. In Sect. 2 the basic theory of hyperspherical coordinates and the derivation of shape coordinates and deformation indexes are reported. Applications to two examples of protein structures is illustrated in Sect. 3. Section 4 contains conclusions and perspectives.

2   Methodology

The hyperspherical coordinates are defined, for an N-particle system, starting from the corresponding set of $N-1$ Jacobi vectors $\mathbf{Q}_\alpha$, where $\alpha = 1, \cdots, N-1$. These can be obtained as a combinations of the position vectors of the N particles in the center of mass reference frame, denoted as $\mathbf{r}_\alpha$ [40]. In practice, the construction of Jacobi vectors proceeds as follows: take the vector which connects particles 1 and 2, then the one connecting the center of mass of the pair to the third particle, and so on, up to the $(N-1)$th vector, which connects the center of mass of the first $N-1$ particles to the Nth particle. The coefficients of the combination depends on the particle masses, see Sect. 2.1 for details. The generalization of the radius coordinate of the spherical system to the N particle case leads to the hyperradius ρ, which is the modulus of a vector of dimension $3N-3$, spanning the configuration space of the system. The Cartesian components of the hyperradial vector are just the Jacobi vector components. The transformation linking the Jacobi vector components with the hyperradius and $3N - 4$ "hyperangles", defines the hyperspherical coordinates. There are in principle many alternative choices for the a angular variables, the one leading to the so called "symmetric" hyperspherical representation is the most convenient for us. The symmetric hyperspherical coordinates are generated by a matrix transformation known as *singular value decomposition*, applied to the position matrix containing column-wise the Cartesian vector of the particle system. The details of such transformation are described in the following section.

2.1   Hyperspherical Coordinates for Many Particle Systems

The *singular value decomposition* [51] is a matrix decomposition theorem that can be applied to any given set of N vectors arranged column-wise to form a 3 x N position matrix, and it is precisely the tool allowing for a general definition of hyperspherical coordinates.

Let us suppose we have a collection of $N \geq 2$ particles with masses $m_1, \cdots, m_N$ and positions identified by a set of radii vectors in the center of mass reference frame, $\mathbf{r_1}, \cdots, \mathbf{r_N}$. Mass *scaled* radii vectors, $\mathbf{q}_\alpha = (m_\alpha/M)^{1/2}\mathbf{r}_\alpha$ $(1 \leq \alpha \leq N)$, can be simply obtained, with $M = \sum_\alpha^N m_\alpha$ is the total mass of the system.

The $3 \times N$ position matrix is denoted by Z and contains, column-wise, the components of the mass scaled vectors:

$$Z = \begin{pmatrix} q_{1,1} & q_{1,2} & \cdots & q_{1,N} \\ q_{2,1} & q_{2,2} & \cdots & q_{2,N} \\ q_{3,1} & q_{3,2} & \cdots & q_{3,N} \end{pmatrix}. \tag{1}$$

The action of an orthogonal matrix R^t (transpose of a matrix $R \in O(3)$) on the position matrix Z by left-multiplication generates rotations in the three-dimensional physical space. An orthogonal matrix $K \in O(N)$ acting in the position matrix by right-multiplication, instead rotates the coordinate frame in the so called *kinematic space* [6,41], $Z' = ZK$.

Some of the allowed K matrices have the following form:

$$K = \begin{pmatrix} k_{1,1} & k_{1,2} & \cdots & (m_1/M)^{1/2} \\ k_{2,1} & k_{2,2} & \cdots & (m_2/M)^{1/2} \\ \cdots & \cdots & \cdots & \cdots \\ k_{N,1} & k_{N,2} & \cdots & (m_N/M)^{1/2} \end{pmatrix} \tag{2}$$

and its application to the Z matrix generates a subset of all the possible Cartesian frames. The last column of such Z matrices are identically zero, due to the separation of center of mass motion, so the number of degrees of freedom is reduced to $3N - 3$. The matrix Z with one less column is called *reduced position matrix*.

The sets of $(N - 1)$ Jacobi and related vectors invariably generate reduced matrices.

The Jacobi vectors can be generated in many different ways, as linear combinations of the N Cartesian particle position vectors, and always the coefficients of the combination are function of the particle masses [52,53]. The different vector sets are close to the different particle coupling schemes, the asymptotic (reactive) channels of the system; properly defined kinematic rotations smoothly connect them.

The *singular value decomposition* when applied to the $3 \times n$ position matrix Z (where $n = N$ or $n = N - 1$) gives a product of three matrices:

$$Z = R \Xi K^t \tag{3}$$

where $R \in O(3)$ and $K \in O(n)$ are 3×3 and $3 \times n$ orthogonal matrices, respectively. The elements of the $3 \times n$ matrix Ξ are zeroes, with the possible exception of the diagonal entries, $\Xi_{11} = \xi_1, \Xi_{22} = \xi_2, \Xi_{33} = \xi_3$, which are subjected to the inequality $\xi_1 \geq \xi_2 \geq \xi_3 \geq 0$.

The values ξ_i, $(i = 1, 2, 3)$ are called the *singular values* of the matrix Z and are uniquely determined, although the factors R and K in Eq. 3 are not. If $N \leq 3$ and Z is the full $3 \times N$ position matrix, then the smallest singular value ξ_3 is necessarily zero. The singular values are connected to the hyperradius as follows [40,41]:

$$\xi_1^2 + \xi_2^2 + \xi_3^2 = \rho^2. \tag{4}$$

The ξ's are invariant under both ordinary rotations in the three-dimensional physical space and kinematic rotations [6,7,41,54]. The invariance makes the ξ useful set of parameters for molecular dynamics [40,55–58] and in the study of the minimum energy structures of N-particle systems.

In the special case $n = N - 1 = 3$, the matrix Z represents four particles or four center systems and the two matrices R and K cannot be chosen to be *special orthogonal* ($R \in SO(3)$ and $K \in SO(n)$), but have to be orthogonal matrices ($O(3)$). In this case it can be seen that if the determinant of Z is lower than zero, its sign depends on the sign of the product of the ξ's, and so one has $\xi_3 \leq 0$. This fact is directly connected to the mirror image and chirality sign of the system [45,59,60].

2.2   Invariant Deformation Indexes

The singular values (ξ_1, ξ_2, ξ_3), besides being invariant under kinematic and ordinary rotations [61], are related to the moments of inertia of the system:

$$\frac{I_1}{M} = \xi_2^2 + \xi_3^2$$
$$\frac{I_2}{M} = \xi_1^2 + \xi_3^2 \tag{5}$$
$$\frac{I_3}{M} = \xi_1^2 + \xi_2^2$$

where I_1, I_2 and I_3 are the moments of inertia in the principal axis reference frame. Consequently, they can be thought of as representative of the mass distribution with respect to the principal axis frame and will be referred to as shape coordinates. From Eq. 4 one obtains:

$$I_1 + I_2 + I_3 = 2M\rho^2. \tag{6}$$

The values of the ξ's determine whether the system is an asymmetric, symmetric or a spherical rotor. Spherical top configurations are those for which $\xi_1 = \xi_2 = \xi_3$, prolate tops those for which $\xi_3 = \xi_2 < \xi_1$, while oblate tops occur when $\xi_1 = \xi_2 > \xi_3$.

The ξ's can be represented in terms of the hyperradius and two angles θ and ϕ as follows:

$$\xi_1 = \rho \sin \theta \cos \phi$$
$$\xi_2 = \rho \sin \theta \sin \phi \tag{7}$$
$$\xi_2 = \rho \cos \theta$$

Parameters measuring the deviation from the spherical top shapes, can be introduced by two following *deformation indexes* [40]:

$$\xi_+ = \frac{\xi_2^2 - \xi_3^2}{\rho^2}, \quad \xi_+ \geq 0 \tag{8}$$

which is zero for prolate top configurations, and

$$\xi_- = \frac{\xi_2^2 - \xi_1^2}{\rho^2}, \quad \xi_- \leq 0 \tag{9}$$

which is zero for oblate top configurations. By definition, when both indexes are zero, one has a spherical rotor.

3 Invariant and Deformation Index Distribution for Protein Structures

Given a certain molecular structure, the procedure illustrated in Sects. 2.1 and 2.2 allows to uniquely assign to that a set of values of the ξ's and deformation indexes. These can be used for the classification of global structures of large molecular systems, looking for patterns and regularities.

As an example of application, we consider a plot of protein structures in the shape coordinate space and in the subspace of deformation indexes, as defined in the previous sections. In a previous work, a similar study was applied to Lennard-Jones clusters and chiral molecules [43,48]. The calculation of the indexes requires the values of the invariant ξ's for each protein structure. There is no need to perform the complete singular value decomposition, since it can be seen that following relation comes from Eq. 3:

$$ZZ^t = R\Xi\Xi^t R^t \tag{10}$$

where the product $\Xi\Xi^t$ is a 3×3 square diagonal matrix, whose entries are the squares of the ξ's. The diagonal entries are just the eigenvalues of the product matrix ZZ^t, which can be obtained from the position matrix. Using the Cartesian components of the mass scaled atomic position vectors (see Sect. 2.1), one has to calculate the ZZ^t matrix and diagonalize by a numerical procedure or by resorting to Cardano's formula for the third degree characteristic equation [40].

Here we analyze 3 protein structures randomly chosen from the Protein Data Bank [62], these are identified as 1A0N, 1A03 and 1A23 in the database. The extracted Cartesian coordinates are the starting point to build up the product matrix of Eq. 10 and generate the ξ values and the deformation indexes of Eqs. 8 and 9 for each structure. In this case, we analysed separately the ξ's and the deformation indexes for three representative amino acids, Glycine (GLY), Proline (PRO) and Alanine (ALA), considering their local structures as they occur in the protein chain (also repeatedly), as resulting from the [62] database. In Figs. 1 and 2, the deformation indexes ξ_+ and ξ_- are represented in a 2-dimensional plot for the 1A0N and 1A23 structures respectively, defining the average index subspace to which the amino acid structure belongs. The allowed deformation values draw a clear shaped region in the index space for the three target amino acids.

In Fig. 3 the values of the individual shape coordinates ξ_1, ξ_2 are shown as they distribute in two-dimensional plots, for the three amino acids above, as obtained from the structure 1A03. It can be seen from the above figures

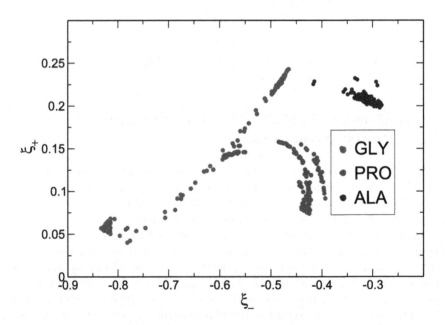

Fig. 1. Two-dimensional plot of the ξ_+ and ξ_+ invariant deformation indexes, for the GLY, PRO and ALA amino acid configuration, as obtained from the protein structure identified as 1a0n in the database [62]

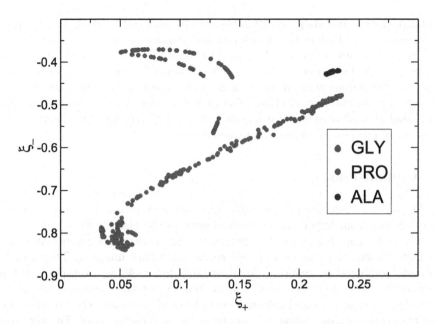

Fig. 2. Two-dimensional plot of the ξ_+ and ξ_+ invariant deformation indexes, for the GLY, PRO and ALA amino acid configuration, as obtained from the protein structure identified as 1a23 in the database [62]

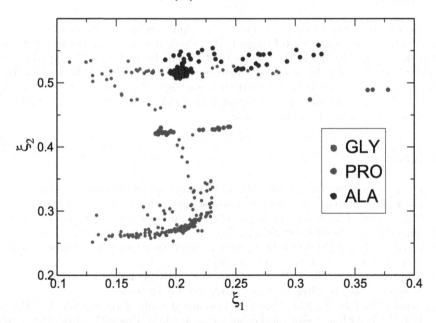

Fig. 3. Two-dimensional plots of the ξ_i, $i = 1, 2, 3$ invariant shape coordinates, for the GLY, PRO and ALA amino acid configurations as occurring in the structure identified as 1A03 in the database [62].

that parameters and shape coordinates are not uniformly distributed but tend to localize in a subset of the coordinate and parameter spaces. Assuming that the set of structure so far analysed could be considered as representative of all proteins, could be indeed an image of the "allowed" regions in the parameter space for the aforementioned three amino acids, a sort of footprint characteristic of such units in the protein chains. Confirmation and extension to other amino acid residues and to structural motifs will require systematic application to a large set of protein structures from the database.

4 Conclusions

In this paper we suggested the possible application of invariant structure parameters derived from hyperspherical coordinates to the classification problem for protein molecular structures. The parameters are three shape coordinates, and we have shown that can be assigned to any structure uniquely. They can be properly combined to generate deformation indexes. As an example, a set of protein structures has been analysed, limited to just three amino acids, using both shape coordinates and deformation indexes, determining their distribution and the corresponding "allowed" regions in the parameter space. Further steps will be the application to larger numbers of structures and to all the basic amino acids present in the protein chains, as well as extension to other biomolecules such as DNA.

Acknowledgments. Thanks are due to the Dipartimento di Chimica, Biologia e Biotecnologie dell'Università di Perugia (FRB, Fondo per la Ricerca di Base 2019 and 2020) and to the MIUR and the University of Perugia for the financial support of the AMIS project through the program "Dipartimenti di Eccellenza". A. L. acknowledges financial support from MIUR PRIN 2015 (contract 2015F59J3R_002). A.L. thanks the OU Supercomputing Center for Education & Research (OSCER) at the University of Oklahoma, for allocated computing time.

References

1. Perri, D., Simonetti, M., Lombardi, A., Faginas-Lago, N., Gervasi, O.: Binary classification of proteins by a machine learning approach. In: Gervasi, O., et al. (eds.) ICCSA 2020. LNCS, vol. 12255, pp. 549–558. Springer, Cham (2020). https://doi.org/10.1007/978-3-030-58820-5_41
2. Zhao, B., Guo, H.: State-to-state quantum reactive scattering in four-atom systems. WIREs Comput. Mol. Sci. **7**, e1301 (2017)
3. Skouteris, D., Castillo, J., Manolopoulos, D.E.: ABC: a quantum reactive scattering program. Comput. Phys. Commun. **133**, 128–135 (2000)
4. Lepetit, B., Launay, J.M.: Quantum-mechanical study of the reaction $He + H_2^+ \rightarrow HeH^+ + H$ with hyperspherical coordinates. J. Chem. Phys. **95**, 5159–5168 (1991)
5. Aquilanti, V., Beddoni, A., Cavalli, S., Lombardi, A., Littlejohn, R.: Collective hyperspherical coordinates for polyatomic molecules and clusters. Mol. Phys. **98**(21), 1763–1770 (2000)

6. Aquilanti, V., Beddoni, A., Lombardi, A., Littlejohn, R.: Hyperspherical harmonics for polyatomic systems: basis set for kinematic rotations. Int. J. Quantum Chem. **89**(4), 277–291 (2002)
7. Aquilanti, V., Lombardi, A., Littlejohn, R.: Hyperspherical harmonics for polyatomic systems: basis set for collective motions. Theoret. Chem. Acc. **111**(2–6), 400–406 (2004)
8. Kuppermann, A.: Quantum reaction dynamics and hyperspherical harmonics. Isr. J. Chem. **43**, 229 (2003)
9. De Fazio, D., Cavalli, S., Aquilanti, V.: Benchmark quantum mechanical calculations of vibrationally resolved cross sections and rate constants on ab initio potential energy surfaces for the F + HD reaction: comparisons with experiments. J. Phys. Chem. A **120**, 5288–5299 (2016)
10. Aquilanti, V., Cavalli, S.: The quantum-mechanical Hamiltonian for tetraatomic systems insymmetric hyperspherical coordinates. J. Chem. Soc. Faraday Trans. **93**, 801–809 (1997)
11. Barreto, P.R.P., Vilela, A.F.A., Lombardi, A., Maciel, G.S., Palazzetti, F., Aquilanti, V.: The hydrogen peroxide-rare gas systems: quantum chemical calculations and hyperspherical harmonic representation of the potential energy surface for atom–floppy molecule interactions. J. Phys. Chem. A **111**(49), 12754–12762 (2007)
12. Lombardi, A., Laganà, A., Pirani, F., Palazzetti, F., Lago, N.F.: Carbon oxides in gas flows and earth and planetary atmospheres: state-to-state simulations of energy transfer and dissociation reactions. In: Murgante, B., et al. (eds.) ICCSA 2013. LNCS, vol. 7972, pp. 17–31. Springer, Heidelberg (2013). https://doi.org/10.1007/978-3-642-39643-4_2
13. Lago, N.F., Albertí, M., Laganà, A., Lombardi, A.: Water $(H_2O)_m$ or benzene $(C_6H_6)_n$ aggregates to solvate the K^+? In: Murgante, B., et al. (eds.) ICCSA 2013. LNCS, vol. 7971, pp. 1–15. Springer, Heidelberg (2013). https://doi.org/10.1007/978-3-642-39637-3_1
14. Faginas-Lago, N., Albertí, M., Costantini, A., Laganá, A., Lombardi, A., Pacifici, L.: An innovative synergistic grid approach to the computational study of protein aggregation mechanisms. J. Mol. Model. **20**(7), 2226 (2014)
15. Faginas-Lago, N., Yeni, D., Huarte, F., Alcamì, M., Martin, F.: Adsorption of hydrogen molecules on carbon nanotubes using quantum chemistry and molecular dynamics. J. Phys. Chem. A **120**, 6451–6458 (2016)
16. Faginas-Lago, N., Lombardi, A., Albertí, M., Grossi, G.: Accurate analytic intermolecular potential for the simulation of Na^+ and K^+ ion hydration in liquid water. J. Mol. Liq. **204**, 192–197 (2015)
17. Albertí, M., Faginas Lago, N.: Competitive solvation of K^+ by C_6H_6 and H_2O in the K^+-$(C_6h_6)_n$-$(H_2O)_m$ (n = 1–4; m = 1–6) aggregates. Eur. Phys. J. D **67**, 73 (2013)
18. Albertí, M., Faginas Lago, N.: Ion size influence on the Ar solvation shells of M^+-C_6F_6 clusters (m = na, k, rb, cs). J. Phys. Chem. A **116**, 3094–3102 (2012)
19. Albertí, M., Faginas Lago, N., Pirani, F.: Ar solvation shells in K^+-HFBz: from cluster rearrangement to solvation dynamics. J. Phys. Chem. A **115**, 10871–10879 (2011)
20. Lago, N.F., Albertí, M., Laganà, A., Lombardi, A., Pacifici, L., Costantini, A.: The molecular stirrer catalytic effect in methane ice formation. In: Murgante, B., et al. (eds.) ICCSA 2014. LNCS, vol. 8579, pp. 585–600. Springer, Cham (2014). https://doi.org/10.1007/978-3-319-09144-0_40

21. Faginas-Lago, N., Huarte Larrañaga, F., Albertí, M.: On the suitability of the ILJ function to match different formulations of the electrostatic potential for water-water interactions. Eur. Phys. J. D **55**(1), 75 (2009)
22. Bartolomei, M., Pirani, F., Laganà, A., Lombardi, A.: A full dimensional grid empowered simulation of the $CO_2 + CO_2$ processes. J. Comput. Chem. **33**, 1806 (2012)
23. Lombardi, A., Lago, N.F., Laganà, A., Pirani, F., Falcinelli, S.: A bond-bond portable approach to intermolecular interactions: simulations for N-methylacetamide and carbon dioxide dimers. In: Murgante, B., et al. (eds.) ICCSA 2012. LNCS, vol. 7333, pp. 387–400. Springer, Heidelberg (2012). https://doi.org/10.1007/978-3-642-31125-3_30
24. Albertí, M., Faginas-Lago, N., Laganà, A., Pirani, F.: A portable intermolecular potential for molecular dynamics studies of NMA-NMA and NMA-H_2O aggregates. Phys. Chem. Chem. Phys. **13**(18), 8422–8432 (2011)
25. Albertí, M., Faginas-Lago, N., Pirani, F.: Benzene water interaction: from gaseous dimers to solvated aggregates. Chem. Phys. **399**, 232 (2012)
26. Falcinelli, S., et al.: Modeling the intermolecular interactions and characterization of the dynamics of collisional autoionization processes. In: Murgante, B., et al. (eds.) ICCSA 2013. LNCS, vol. 7971, pp. 69–83. Springer, Heidelberg (2013). https://doi.org/10.1007/978-3-642-39637-3_6
27. Lombardi, A., Faginas-Lago, N., Pacifici, L., Costantini, A.: Modeling of energy transfer from vibrationally excited CO_2 molecules: cross sections and probabilities for kinetic modeling of atmospheres, flows, and plasmas. J. Phys. Chem. A **117**(45), 11430–11440 (2013)
28. Lombardi, A., Pirani, F., Laganà, A., Bartolomei, M.: Energy transfer dynamics and kinetics of elementary processes (promoted) by gas-phase CO_2-N_2 collisions: selectivity control by the anisotropy of the interaction. J. Comput. Chem. **37**, 1463–1475 (2016)
29. Pacifici, L., Verdicchio, M., Faginas-Lago, N., Lombardi, A., Costantini, A.: A high-level ab initio study of the N2 + N2 reaction channel. J. Comput. Chem. **34**(31), 2668–2676 (2013)
30. Lombardi, A., Faginas-Lago, N., Pacifici, L., Grossi, G.: Energy transfer upon collision of selectively excited CO_2 molecules: state-to-state cross sections and probabilities for modeling of atmospheres and gaseous flows. J. Chem. Phys. **143**, 034307 (2015)
31. Celiberto, R., et al.: Atomic and molecular data for spacecraft re-entry plasmas. Plasma Sources Sci. Technol. **25**(3), 033004 (2016)
32. Faginas-Lago, N., Lombardi, A., Albertí, M.: Aqueous n-methylacetamide: new analytic potentials and a molecular dynamics study. J. Mol. Liq. **224**, 792–800 (2016)
33. Palazzetti, F., Munusamy, E., Lombardi, A., Grossi, G., Aquilanti, V.: Spherical and hyperspherical representation of potential energy surfaces for intermolecular interactions. Int. J. Quantum Chem. **111**(2), 318–332 (2011)
34. Lombardi, A., Palazzetti, F.: A comparison of interatomic potentials for rare gas nanoaggregates. J. Mol. Struct. (Thoechem) **852**(1–3), 22–29 (2008)
35. Barreto, P.R., Albernaz, A.F., Palazzetti, F., Lombardi, A., Grossi, G., Aquilanti, V.: Hyperspherical representation of potential energy surfaces: intermolecular interactions in tetra-atomic and penta-atomic systems. Phys. Scr. **84**(2), 028111 (2011)

36. Barreto, P.R., et al.: Potential energy surfaces for interactions of H_2O with H_2, N_2 and O_2: a hyperspherical harmonics representation, and a minimal model for the H_2O-rare-gas-atom systems. Comput. Theor. Chem. **990**, 53–61 (2012)

37. Lombardi, A., Pirani, F., Bartolomei, M., Coletti, C., Laganà, A.: A full dimensional potential energy function and the calculation of the state-specific properties of the CO+ N_2 inelastic processes within an Open Molecular Science Cloud perspective. Front. Chem. **7**, 309 (2019)

38. Faginas Lago, N., Lombardi, A., Vekeman, J., Rosi, M., et al.: Molecular dynamics of CH_4/N_2 mixtures on a flexible graphene layer: adsorption and selectivity case study. Front. Chem. **7**, 386 (2019)

39. Nakamura, M., et al.: Dynamical, spectroscopic and computational imaging of bond breaking in photodissociation: roaming and role of conical intersections. Faraday Discuss. **177**, 77–98 (2015)

40. Aquilanti, V., Lombardi, A., Yurtsever, E.: Global view of classical clusters: the hyperspherical approach to structure and dynamics. Phys. Chem. Chem. Phys. **4**(20), 5040–5051 (2002)

41. Sevryuk, M.B., Lombardi, A., Aquilanti, V.: Hyperangular momenta and energy partitions in multidimensional many-particle classical mechanics: the invariance approach to cluster dynamics. Phys. Rev. A **72**(3), 033201 (2005)

42. Castro Palacio, J., Velazquez Abad, L., Lombardi, A., Aquilanti, V., Rubayo Soneira, J.: Normal and hyperspherical mode analysis of NO-doped Kr crystals upon Rydberg excitation of the impurity. J. Chem. Phys. **126**(17), 174701 (2007)

43. Lombardi, A., Palazzetti, F., Aquilanti, V.: Molecular dynamics of chiral molecules in hyperspherical coordinates. In: Misra, S., et al. (eds.) ICCSA 2019. LNCS, vol. 11624, pp. 413–427. Springer, Cham (2019). https://doi.org/10.1007/978-3-030-24311-1_30

44. Lombardi, A., Palazzetti, F., Sevryuk, M.B.: Hyperspherical coordinates and energy partitions for reactive processes and clusters. In: AIP Conference Proceedings, vol. 2186, p. 030014. AIP Publishing LLC (2019)

45. Lombardi, A., Palazzetti, F.: Chirality in molecular collision dynamics. J. Phys.: Condens. Matter **30**(6), 063003 (2018)

46. Lombardi, A., Palazzetti, F., Peroncelli, L., Grossi, G., Aquilanti, V., Sevryuk, M.: Few-body quantum and many-body classical hyperspherical approaches to reactions and to cluster dynamics. Theoret. Chem. Acc. **117**(5–6), 709–721 (2007)

47. Aquilanti, V., Grossi, G., Lombardi, A., Maciel, G.S., Palazzetti, F.: Aligned molecular collisions and a stereodynamical mechanism for selective chirality. Rend. Fis. Acc. Lincei **22**, 125–135 (2011)

48. Lombardi, A., Faginas-Lago, N., Aquilanti, V.: The invariance approach to structure and dynamics: classical hyperspherical coordinates. In: Misra, S., et al. (eds.) ICCSA 2019. LNCS, vol. 11624, pp. 428–438. Springer, Cham (2019). https://doi.org/10.1007/978-3-030-24311-1_31

49. Caglioti, C., Dos Santos, R.F., Lombardi, A., Palazzetti, F., Aquilanti, V.: Screens displaying structural properties of aminoacids in polypeptide chains: alanine as a case study. In: Misra, S., et al. (eds.) ICCSA 2019. LNCS, vol. 11624, pp. 439–449. Springer, Cham (2019). https://doi.org/10.1007/978-3-030-24311-1_32

50. Caglioti, C., Ferreira, R.d.S., Palazzetti, F., Lombardi, A., Aquilanti, V.: Screen representation of structural properties of alanine in polypeptide chains. In: AIP Conference Proceedings, vol. 2186, p. 030015. AIP Publishing LLC (2019)

51. Horn, R.A., Johnson, C.R.: Matrix Analysis, 2nd edn. University Press, Cambridge (1990)

52. Gatti, F., Lung, C.: Vector parametrization of the n-atom problem in quantum mechanics. I. Jacobi vectors. J. Chem. Phys. **108**, 8804–8820 (1998)
53. Aquilanti, V., Lombardi, A., Yurtsever, E.: Global view of classical clusters: the hyperspherical approach to structure and dynamics. Phys. Chem. Chem. Phys. **4**, 5040–5051 (2002)
54. Aquilanti, V., Lombardi, A., Sevryuk, M.B.: Phase-space invariants for aggregates of particles: hyperangular momenta and partitions of the classical kinetic energy. J. Chem. Phys. **121**, 5579 (2004)
55. Aquilanti, V., Carmona Novillo, E., Garcia, E., Lombardi, A., Sevryuk, M.B., Yurtsever, E.: Invariant energy partitions in chemical reactions and cluster dynamics simulations. Comput. Mat. Sci. **35**, 187–191 (2006)
56. Aquilanti, V., Lombardi, A., Sevryuk, M.B., Yurtsever, E.: Phase-space invariants as indicators of the critical behavior of nanoaggregates. Phys. Rev. Lett. **93**, 113402 (2004)
57. Calvo, F., Gadea, X., Lombardi, A., Aquilanti, V.: Isomerization dynamics and thermodynamics of ionic argon clusters. J. Chem. Phys. **125**, 114307 (2006)
58. Lombardi, A., Aquilanti, V., Yurtsever, E., Sevryuk, M.B.: Specific heats of clusters near a phase transition: energy partitions among internal modes. Chem. Phys. Lett. **30**, 424–428 (2006)
59. Lombardi, A., Maciel, G.S., Palazzetti, F., Grossi, G., Aquilanti, V.: Alignment and chirality in gaseous flows. J. Vacuum Soc. Jpn. **53**(11), 645–653 (2010)
60. Palazzetti, F., et al.: Aligned molecules: chirality discrimination in photodissociation and in molecular dynamics. Rendiconti Lincei **24**(3), 299–308 (2013)
61. Littlejohn, R.G., Mitchell, A., Aquilanti, V.: Quantum dynamics of kinematic invariants in tetra-and polyatomic systems. Phys. Chem. Chem. Phys. **1**, 1259–1264 (1999)
62. Berman, H., et al.: The protein data bank. Nucleic Acid Res. **28**, 235–242 (2000)

Numerical Simulation of the Reactive Transport at Pore Scale in 3D

Vadim Lisitsa[1]($\boxtimes$) ⓘ, Tatyana Khachkova[1], Dmitry Prokhorov[1], Yaroslav Bazaikin[1], and Yongfei Yang[2,3]

[1] Sobolev Institute of Mathematics SB RAS, 4 Koptug Avenue, Novosibirsk 630090, Russia
lisitsavv@ipgg.sbras.ru
[2] Key Laboratory of Unconventional Oil and Gas Development (China University of Petroleum (East China)), Ministry of Education, Qingdao 266580, People's Republic of China
[3] Research Center of Multiphase Flow in Porous Media, School of Petroleum Engineering, China University of Petroleum (East China), Qingdao 266580, People's Republic of China

Abstract. The paper presents a finite-difference algorithm for reactive transport simulation at the pore scale in 3D. We simulate the matrix dissolution and crystal precipitation due to heterogeneous reactions, acquired at the fluid-solid interface. The fluid flow and the reactive transport are computed using finite difference method on a regular rectangular mesh, whereas the immersed boundary conditions are applied to account for irregular interface geometry. The time-evolving pore-to-matrix surface is defined implicitly by the level-set method. The algorithm is implemented using Graphic Processor Units.

Keywords: Pore-scale · Reactive transport · Level-set · Immersed boundaries

1 Introduction

There are numerous application of the reactive transport simulation, such as enhanced oil recovery [7], CO_2 sequestration in carbonate formations [17], bio-cementation [5], salt precipitation [3], and injection of non-condensable gases into geothermal fields [11]. At the pore scale, the main mechanism causing changes in the pore space geometry and morphology is the heterogeneous reactions at the fluid-solid interface. These reactions may lead to matrix dissolution or minerals precipitation. Changes in the pore space and rock matrix structure at the pore scale affect the macroscopic properties of the rocks, including porosity, hydraulic permeability [2,15], mechanical compliance [13], electric resistivity [12] and others.

The research was supported by the Russian Science Foundation grant no. 21-71-20003.

O. Gervasi et al. (Eds.): ICCSA 2021, LNCS 12958, pp. 375–387, 2021.
https://doi.org/10.1007/978-3-030-87016-4_28

Nowadays, predictive reactive transport simulations are used to estimate the effect of chemically active fluid filtration at the reservoir scale in application to CO_2 sequestration geothermal fields exploration and others [23]. At the reservoir scale, permeability, diffusion coefficient, reaction rates, and species concentrations are defined inside the grid cells and connected to the porosity be some empirical relations. These relations came from the lab [13] or using analytical averaging techniques for relatively simple structures [4]. In the lab, it is generally troublesome to reproduce the reservoir conditions (pressure, temperature, etc.). Moreover, the experiments are time-consuming, and they can be conducted only once for a single sample. The analytical averaging applies to relatively simple models, such as a periodical, and they are hard to extend to real rocks or porous materials structure. Thus, numerical simulation is the most attractive option because it combines lab experiments' flexibility with theoretical investigations' accuracy. Moreover, it is possible to vary input parameters such as inlet pressure of flow rate, reactions rates, etc., and estimate their effect on the macroscopic parameters used in the reactive transport models at the reservoir scale; see [23] for a review.

Transport at the pore-scale fluid flow has to be simulated directly by solving Stokes or Navier-Stokes equation. Then the solution of the convection-diffusion equation provides the distribution of the active components. Finally, the evolution of the fluid-solid interface has to be simulated [18]. The main difference in the known approaches to simulate reactive transport at the pore scale is the interface treatment. The simplest approach is to use the same regular mesh to approximate Stokes and convection diffusion equation and to define a formal parameter such as mass or volumetric fraction of the solid phase in the "boundary" cells. After that additional equations are introduced to estimate changes of the introduced parameter due to chemical reactions [10,26]. This approach is easy to implement, however it requires the additional equation are based on a number of empirical relations. Among the methods based on the direct representation of the interface and heterogeneous reactions, it is worth mentioning the front-tracing, level-set, and phase-field methods. In the front-tracking method, the interface is represented explicitly and then combined with the finite-volumes and truncated-cell approach to simulate fluid flow and reactant transport [18]. However, this approach is hard to implement in domains with complex topology and geometry, which is always the case for porous materials. Implicit representation of the interface used in the level-set [19], and phase-field [25] methods, where the interface is the zero-level of an arbitrary function. This representation simplifies the treatment of the interface evolution, including the topology changes. Moreover, the last two methods are implemented on the regular rectangular meshes in combination with the immersed boundary method [20,22] for the level-set, or the diffused interface approach for the phase-field.

In this research, we developed the level-set based algorithm for the reactive transport simulation at the pore scale. We state the problem and formulate the mathematical model in Sect. 2. In Sect. 3 we provide numerical algorithms to solve Stocks, equation, convection-diffusion equation, and level-set evolution and redistancing. We illustrate applicability of the algorithm to simulation of the pore space geometry changes in a carbonate rock due to chemical dissolution in Sect. 4.

2 Statement of the Problem

We assume that the interface moves with the slowest rate to simulate reactive transport at the pore scale. Thus, this rate defines the time scale of the problem in general. The fluid flow rate is also low, and it stabilizes instantly when pore space geometry changes slightly. Thus, the problem can be split into three stages: solution of Stokes equation to define the flow in the pore space, solution of the convection-diffusion equation to simulate the chemical species propagation, and correction of the pore space geometry due to dissolution.

We consider the problem stated in $D \subseteq R^3$. The domain is bounded. Assume, that $D = D_p(t) \cup D_m(t)$, where $D_p(t)$ and $D_m(t)$ correspond to pore space and the rock matrix, respectively. Subdomains $D_p(t)$ and $D_m(t)$ are time-dependent and nonintersecting. We define the domain boundary as $\partial D = S_{outlet} \cup S_{inlet} \cup S_{nf}$, where S_{outlet} and S_{inlet} are the outlet and inlet surfaces, S_{nf} correspond to all other boundaries where the no-flow boundary condition will be used. We also introduce the pore-to-matrix interface as $\bar{D}_p(t) \cap \bar{D}_m(t) = S(t)$. A sketch of the model is presented in Fig. 1.

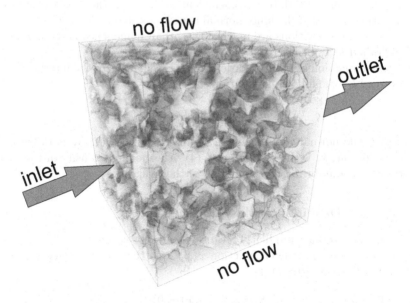

Fig. 1. A sketch of the computational domain. The matrix of the material is blue, the pore space is green. (Color figure online)

The fluid flow is simulated in the pore space $D_p(t)$ by solving steady-state Stokes equation:

$$\mu\nabla^2 \boldsymbol{u} - \nabla p = 0,$$
$$\nabla \cdot \boldsymbol{u} = 0. \tag{1}$$

with boundary conditions

$$u(\boldsymbol{x}) = 0, \qquad \boldsymbol{x} \in S(t) \cup S_{nf},$$
$$p(\boldsymbol{x}) = p_{bc}(\boldsymbol{x}), \ \boldsymbol{x} \in S_{inlet} \cup S_{outlet}, \tag{2}$$

where p is the fluid pressure, $\boldsymbol{u} = (u_1, u_2, u_3)^T \in R^3$ is the velocity vector, μ is the dynamic viscosity of the fluid, $p_{bc}(\boldsymbol{x})$ are the values of the pressure at the opposite boundaries S_{inlet} and S_{outlet}, the spatial coordinates are defined by the vector $\boldsymbol{x} = (x_1, x_2, x_3)^T$.

Propagation of the reactant in $D_p(t)$ satisfies the convection-diffusion equation:

$$\frac{\partial C}{\partial t} + \nabla \cdot (\boldsymbol{u}C - D\nabla C) = 0, \tag{3}$$

with boundary conditions:

$$D\frac{\partial C}{\partial n} = k_r(C - C_s), \ \boldsymbol{x} \in S(t),$$
$$C = C_{in}, \qquad\qquad \boldsymbol{x} \in S_{inlet}, \tag{4}$$
$$\frac{\partial C}{\partial n} = 0, \qquad\qquad \boldsymbol{x} \in S_{outlet} \cup S_{nf}.$$

In these notations, the diffusion coefficient is D, C is the active component concentration, vector of the inner normal is $\boldsymbol{n}$, k_r is the reaction rate. We assume the heterogeneous reactions are much slower, than homogeneous ones. Thus, we omit right-had sides in Eq. (3).

Chemical reaction of the first-order causes the changes in the interface, which are governed by the following equation:

$$v_n(\boldsymbol{x}, t) = \frac{K_c k_r}{\rho}(C - C_s), \ \boldsymbol{x} \in S(t), \tag{5}$$

where v_n is the normal component of the interface velocity, K_c is the stoichiometric coefficient, k_r is the reaction rate (4), ρ is the mass density of the matrix mineral, C_s is equilibrium concentration of the reactant.

2.1   Implicit Definition of the Interface

To define the interface implicitly we use the level-set method [19]. It means, that we introduce an artificial function $\varphi(\boldsymbol{x}, t)$, so that the interface $S(t)$ is the zero-level of function $\varphi(\boldsymbol{x}, t)$; i.e.

$$S(t) = \{\boldsymbol{x} | \varphi(\boldsymbol{x}) = 0\}.$$

Consequently, we define subdomains D_p and D_m as

$$D_p(\boldsymbol{x}, t) = \{\boldsymbol{x} | \varphi(x, t) > 0\}, \ D_m(\boldsymbol{x}, t) = \{\boldsymbol{x} | \varphi(x, t) < 0\}.$$

Typically, the level-set function is the signed-distance from the interface. Thus, $\|\nabla_x \varphi(\boldsymbol{x}, t)\| = 1$, and

$$\boldsymbol{n} = \nabla_x \varphi(\boldsymbol{x}, t).$$

The interface evolution Eq. (5) can be extended to the level-set function as follows [8, 19]:

$$\begin{aligned} \frac{\partial \varphi(\boldsymbol{x}, t)}{\partial t} + v_n(\boldsymbol{x}, t) &= 0, \\ \varphi(\boldsymbol{x}, 0) &= \varphi_0, \end{aligned} \tag{6}$$

where v_n is the normal velocity, as defined by Eq. (5).

3   Finite-Difference Approximation

To solve Eqs. (1), (3), and (6) numerically, we suggest applying the finite-differences. In particular, the staggered-grid schemes will be used. Introduce a regular rectangular grid with the grid cells $C_{i,j,k} = [h_1(i - 1/2), h_1(i + 1/2)] \times [h_2(j - 1/2), h_2(j + 1/2)] \times [h_3(k - 1/2), h_3(k + 1/2)]$ and define the pressure, concentration, and the level-set function in the centers of the cells $p_{i,j,k} = p(ih_1, jh_2, kh_3)$, $C_{i,j,k}^n = C(ih_1, jh_2, kh_3 n\tau)$, and $\varphi_{i,j,k}^n = \varphi(ih_1, jh_2, kh_3, n\tau)$, velocity components are placed at the corresponding faces $(u_1)_{i+1/2,j,k} = u_1((i+1/2)h_1, jh_2, kh_3)$, $(u_2)_{i,j+1/2,k} = u_2(ih_1, (j+1/2)h_2, kh_3)$, $(u_3)_{i,j,k+1/2} = u_3(ih_1, jh_2, (k + 1/2)h_3)$. In these notations h_1, h_2, and h_3 are the grid steps in space, τ is the grid step in time.

3.1   Approximation of Stokes Equation

We use the second-order accurate finite-difference scheme to approximate Eq. 1:

$$\begin{aligned} \mu L[u_1]_{i+1/2,j,k} - D_1^c[p]_{i+1/2,j,k} &= 0, & \text{if } \varphi_{i+1/2,j,k} &> 0, \\ \mu L[u_2]_{i,j+1/2,k} - D_2^c[p]_{i,j+1/2} &= 0, & \text{if } \varphi_{i,j+1/2,k} &> 0, \\ \mu L[u_3]_{i,j,k+1/2} - D_3^c[p]_{i,j,k+1/2} &= 0, & \text{if } \varphi_{i,j,k+1/2} &> 0, \\ D_1^c[u_1]_{i,j,k} + D_2^c[u_2]_{i,j,k} + D_3^c[u_3]_{i,j,k} &= 0, & \text{if } \varphi_{i,j,k} &> 0, \end{aligned} \tag{7}$$

where

$$L[f]_{I,J,K} = D_1^2[f]_{I,J,K} + D_2^2[f]_{I,J,K} + D_3^2[f]_{I,J,K} \tag{8}$$

$$D_1^2[f]_{I,J,K} = \frac{f_{I+1,J,K} - 2f_{I,J,K} + f_{I,J,K}}{h_1^2} = \left. \frac{\partial^2 f}{\partial x_1^2} \right|_{I,J,K} + O(h_1^2), \tag{9}$$

$$D_1^c[f]_{I,J,K} = \frac{f_{I+1/1,J,K} - f_{I,J-1/2,K}}{h_1} = \left. \frac{\partial f}{\partial x_1} \right|_{I,J,K} + O(h_1^2). \tag{10}$$

Indices I, J, and K can be integer or fractional, but i, j, and k are integers only. The operators approximating derivatives with respect to the other spatial direction can be obtained by the permutations of the role of spatial indices. Note, that the projection-type methods to solve Stokes equation are based on the solution of the Poisson equation to correct the pressure. This equation is stated with Neumann boundary conditions at the interface Γ and appropriate boundary conditions at the inlet and outlet boundary. Thus the problem is equivalent to numerical simulation of electric current in pore space, and can be efficiently solved with Krylov-type methods with suitable preconditioner [12].

The level-set function defines the interface which is not aligned to the grid lines, thus immersed boundary conditions (IBC) are required to treat the boundary conditions properly [9,14,16]. The idea of the IBC is to extrapolate the solution to the points belonged to $D_m(t)$ which are close to the interface and required for the computation. After that the solution can be computed using (7) in all points inside the domain $D_p(t)$.

3.2   Approximation of the Convection-Diffusion Equation

To approximate Eq. (3) We use the first-order accurate scheme:

$$\frac{C_{i,j,k}^{n+1}-C_{i,j,k}^n}{\tau} + D_1^1[u_1C]_{i,j,k}^n + D_2^1[u_2C]_{i,j,k}^n + D_3^1[u_3C]_{i,j,k}^n - DL[C]_{i,j,k}^n = 0,$$
$$\varphi_{i,j,k} > 0,$$
(11)

where

$$D_1^1[u_1C]_{i,j,k}^n = \frac{F_{i+1/2,j,k}-F_{i_1-1/2,j,k}}{h},$$
$$F_{i+1/2,j,k} = \begin{cases} (u_1)_{i+1/2,j,k}C_{i+1,j,k}, & (u_1)_{i+1/2,j,k} < 0 \\ (u_1)_{i+1/2,j,k}C_{i,j,k}, & (u_1)_{i+1/2,j,k} > 0 \end{cases}$$
(12)

Operators, approximating the derivatives to the other spatial direction, can be obtained using the spatial indices' permutation. Operator $D[f]_{I,J,K}$ is introduced above in Eq. (8).

Similar to the Stokes equation approximation, we use the IBC to account for the Robin boundary condition at the interface $S(t)$. Detailed discussion of IBC construction for the Robin boundary conditions in reactive transport is presented in [15].

3.3   Interface Evolution

Evolution of the interface satisfy Eq. (6), which can be solved by finite differences:

$$\frac{\varphi_{i,j,k}^{n+1}-\varphi_{i,j,k}^n}{\tau} = -(v_n)_{i,j,k}^n,$$
(13)

where $(v_n)_{i,j,k}^n$ is the velocity of the surface.

Function $\phi(x), t$ is defined in the entire domain D, and the Eq. (6) is also should be satisfied in D. However, its the right-hand side (function $v_n(x)$) is defined only at the interface S, thus, it needs to be prolongated elsewhere. It can be done, by assuming $v_n(x)$ is constant along the normal direction to S. Thus, v_n is the steady-state solution of the following equation:

$$\frac{\partial q}{\partial t} + sign(\varphi)\left(\frac{\nabla\varphi}{|\nabla\varphi|}\cdot\nabla q\right) = 0,$$
$$q(x,0) = \tilde{v}_n(x,t_0),$$
(14)

where $\tilde{v}_n$ are the initial conditions, that is the velocity at the interface.

Following [6] we approximate gradient of φ with central-difference scheme, and apply the upwind scheme to compute the spatial derivatives of q. The solution of (14) is only required inside a strip $D_s = \{ \boldsymbol{x} : |\varphi(\boldsymbol{x})| \leq 2\sqrt{h_1^2 + h_2^2 + h_3^2} \}$. This means, that the solution can be obtained in as few as 3–5 iterations. Also, a redistancing procedure is needed to keep the φ being a signed distance [24].

4   Numerical Experiments

4.1   Validation Against Lab Data

To illustrate the algorithm's applicability to the realistic models, we considered the CT-scans of an aquifer in the Middle East carbonate samples presented in [2]. Four different samples were studied in [2] subjected to CO_2 saturation with the further dissolution of the carbonate matrix. The samples' difference was in the original pore space structure and the flow rate used for the saturation. Ten CT-scans were acquired during the saturation process for each sample to follow the pore space evolution. The CT-scans are provided in [1]. We considered the sample called AH from the set. We subtract a subvolume of 200^3 voxels to simulate the reactive transport in the carbonate. The CT-scans resolution was $5.2 \ \mu m$ per voxel; thus, the considered subsamples' size was about one mm^3.

We consider the solid matrix and the fluid properties according to [2]. The core matrix is calcite with mass density $\rho = 2710$ kg/m^3, and stoichiometric coefficient of the reaction equals to one; i.e., $K = 1$. The fluid is the reservoir water under the assumption that changes in the reactant concentration do not affect the fluid's physical properties. Thus we fix the dynamic viscosity $\mu = 0.00028$ Pa·s. The diffusion coefficient was equal to $7.5 \cdot 10^{-9}$ m^2/s, reaction rate $k_r = 0.08$ m/s, and the pressure drop was $4\,$Pa. The active component is the cation H^+ with equilibrium concentration corresponding to $pH = 7$, whereas acidity at the inlet was $pH = 3$ following laboratory experiments presented in [13].

In Fig. 2 we provide the pore space and the flow stream-lines at three different time instants. It is noticeable that the main flow path is formed, causing the wormhole creation. To illustrate the influence of the pore space changes on the rock's hydro-dynamical properties, we provide the plots of the porosity, permeability, and tortuosity as functions of model time (Fig. 3). Both porosity and permeability increase in time, but relatively low porosity increase leads to the substantial increase of permeability due to the wormholes formation. At the same time, tortuosity decreases slightly because the preferred flow path preexisted in the original model (the top picture in Fig. 2). The cross-plots of permeability in dependence on porosity and tortuosity in dependence on porosity are provided in Fig. (4), showing a rapid increase of the permeability when porosity increases. These results are in the agreement with lab measurements provided in [2].

Fig. 2. Pore space representation (left) and stream-lines (right) at different time instants (0, 500, 1000 s.) for the simulation of carbonate dissolution.

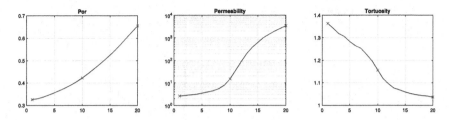

Fig. 3. Dependence of the porosity (left), permeability (middle), and trotuosity (right) on the model time. Red markers correspond to instants from Fig. 2. (Color figure online)

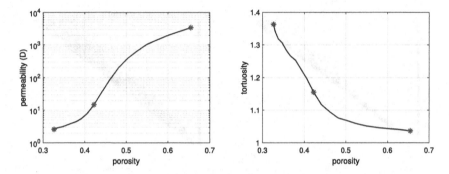

Fig. 4. Cross-plots of permeability in dependence on porosity (left) and tortuosity in dependence on porosity (right). Red markers correspond to instants from Fig. 2. (Color figure online)

4.2 Analysis of the Topology Changes Due to Chemical Matrix Dissolution

In the previous experiment we illustrated that the reaction rate k_{chem}, diffusion coefficient D, flow rate defined by the pressure drop dP, and initial species concentration defined by pH strongly affect the changes in the geometry and topology of the pore space, as well as permeability of the rock sample. To study these effects we performed a series of simulations varying the parameters as follows: $k_{chem} \in \{10^{-3}, 10^{-2}, 10^{-1}, 10^{0}\}$, $D \in \{10^{-9}, 10^{-8}, 10^{-7}\}$, $dP \in \{0.5, 1, 2\}$, $pH \in \{3, 4, 5\}$. As the pore space model we considered the same CT-scan as before. We simulated reactive transport up to 1000 s of the model time, fixing the level-sets every 10 s. Thus, we get a series of 100 pore space geometries for each simulations. Also, we estimated the changes in the permeability, hydraulic tortuosity, and formation factors at the same time instants. Later, using the saved level-sets we estimated the porosity and specific surface of the pore space as function of time. Moreover, we compute the persistence diagrams for one-dimensional Betti number, that is the topological parameters of the pore space indicating the number of independent cycles (channels) [21]. We assume that the changes in pore space topology may characterize the evolution of the hydraulic permeability of the sample. Similar to what was done in 2D case in [15], we intro-

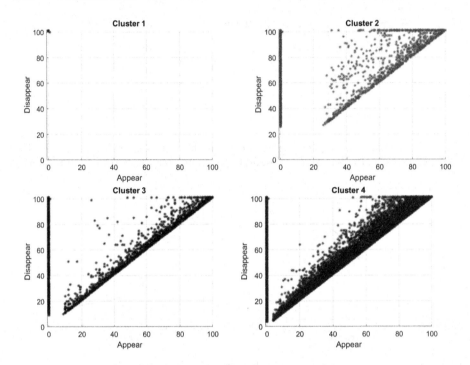

Fig. 5. Persistence diagrams for Betti 1 number of the pore space topology. Horizontal axis indicate the instant when a new component appears. Vertical one represents the instant when a component disappears.

duced the formal measure in the space of the persistence diagrams and applied K-means clustering procedure to separate different scenarios of pore space topology evolution. We stable got four different clusters, with persistence diagrams for mean element in each cluster presented in Fig. 5. According to the diagrams the models from the first cluster remain unchanged, because all connectivity components exist up to the very last instant. The topology of the samples from the three clusters evolved significantly, with the intensity of the pore space changes increases with the cluster number. This assumption is also confirmed by the porosity and permeability changes (Fig. 6). Both porosity and permeability of the models from the blue cluster grow rapidly, whereas they remain constant for the models from the green cluster. Finally, we considered how the separation into clusters related to the input parameters. In Fig. 7 we provide the correspondence between the input parameters dP, D, k_{chem} and the clustering with respect to persistence diagrams, where the positions of the points correspond to the coordinates in the space of the input parameters, and the colors correspond to the different clusters. Note, that the dominating parameter is the reaction rate. Moreover if the reaction rate is low, the results are independent of dP, D; indeed no reaction accrues in this case. However, if the reaction takes

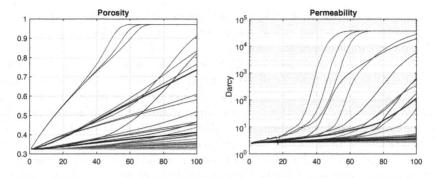

Fig. 6. Evolution of the porosity (left) and permeability (right). Different colors correspond to different clusters. (Color figure online)

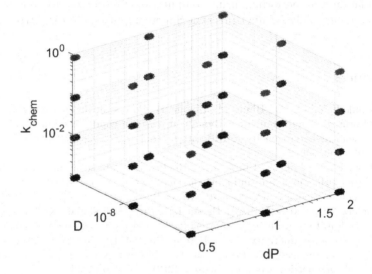

Fig. 7. Correspondence between the input parameters dP, D, k_{chem} and the clustering with respect to persistence diagrams. The positions of the points correspond to the coordinates in the space of the input parameters, and the colors correspond to the different clusters. (Color figure online)

place ($k_{chem} > 10^{-2}$) the changes in the pore space topology are affected by the diffusion, rather than the flow rate.

5   Conclusions

We presented an algorithm for numerical simulation of reactive transport at the pore scale in 3D. The algorithm is based on the combination of the level-set method to handle evolution of the pore-to-matrix interface with finite differences to simulate fluid flow and reactive transport. Implementation of the algorithm is oriented on the use of GPUs; i.e., all numerical simulations are performed using GPUs. In the current research we presented the results computed using a single-GPU implementation which allows us simulating reactive transport in models of the size of up to 300^3 voxels. However, the algorithm is easy to extend to multi-GPU architecture. To illustrate applicability of the algorithm to a realistic problems we simulated CO_2 injection to a carbonate sample. Moreover, we performed a series of simulations varying input parameters such as reaction rate, flow rate and the diffusion coefficient and studied their effect on the pore space topology changes. In particular, we suggested a new methodology to quantify the changes in the topology based on the persistence diagrams for one dimensional Betti numbers. The use of the bottleneck metric in the space of the persistence diagrams allowed us to apply clustering techniques, to distinguish different scenarios of core matrix dissolution.

Simulation were performed using computational resources of Peter the Great Saint-Petersburg Polytechnic University Supercomputing Center (https://www.spbstu.ru/).

References

1. Al-Khulaifi, Y., Lin, Q., Blunt, M., Bijeljic, B.: Pore-scale dissolution by CO_2 saturated brine in a multi-mineral carbonate at reservoir conditions: impact of physical and chemical heterogeneity (2019). https://doi.org/10.5285/52b08e7f-9fba-40a1-b0b5-dda9a3c83be2
2. Al-Khulaifi, Y., Lin, Q., Blunt, M.J., Bijeljic, B.: Pore-scale dissolution by CO_2 saturated brine in a multimineral carbonate at reservoir conditions: impact of physical and chemical heterogeneity. Water Resour. Res. **55**(4), 3171–3193 (2019)
3. Alizadeh, A.H., Akbarabadi, M., Barsotti, E., Piri, M., Fishman, N., Nagarajan, N.: Salt precipitation in ultratight porous media and its impact on pore connectivity and hydraulic conductivity. Water Resour. Res. **54**(4), 2768–2780 (2018)
4. Costa, T.B., Kennedy, K., Peszynska, M.: Hybrid three-scale model for evolving pore-scale geometries. Comput. Geosci. **22**(3), 925–950 (2018)
5. Dadda, A., et al.: Characterization of microstructural and physical properties changes in biocemented sand using 3D x-ray microtomography. Acta Geotech. **12**(5), 955–970 (2017). https://doi.org/10.1007/s11440-017-0578-5
6. Fedkiw, R.P., Aslam, T., Merriman, B., Osher, S.: A non-oscillatory Eulerian approach to interfaces in multimaterial flows (the ghost fluid method). J. Comput. Phys. **152**(2), 457–492 (1999)
7. Ghommem, M., Zhao, W., Dyer, S., Qiu, X., Brady, D.: Carbonate acidizing: modeling, analysis, and characterization of wormhole formation and propagation. J. Petrol. Sci. Eng. **131**, 18–33 (2015)
8. Gibou, F., Fedkiw, R., Osher, S.: A review of level-set methods and some recent applications. J. Comput. Phys. **353**, 82–109 (2018)
9. Johansen, H., Colella, P.: A cartesian grid embedded boundary method for Poisson's equation on irregular domains. J. Comput. Phys. **147**(1), 60–85 (1998)
10. Kang, Q., Chen, L., Valocchi, A.J., Viswanathan, H.S.: Pore-scale study of dissolution-induced changes in permeability and porosity of porous media. J. Hydrol. **517**, 1049–1055 (2014)

11. Kaya, E., Zarrouk, S.J.: Reinjection of greenhouse gases into geothermal reservoirs. Int. J. Greenhouse Gas Control **67**, 111–129 (2017)
12. Khachkova, T., Lisitsa, V., Reshetova, G., Tcheverda, V.: GPU-based algorithm for evaluating the electrical resistivity of digital rocks. Comput. Math. Appl. **82**, 200–211 (2021)
13. Lebedev, M., Zhang, Y., Sarmadivaleh, M., Barifcani, A., Al-Khdheeawi, E., Iglauer, S.: Carbon geosequestration in limestone: pore-scale dissolution and geomechanical weakening. Int. J. Greenhouse Gas Control **66**, 106–119 (2017)
14. Li, X., Huang, H., Meakin, P.: Level set simulation of coupled advection-diffusion and pore structure evolution due to mineral precipitation in porous media. Water Resour. Res. **44**(12), W12407 (2008)
15. Lisitsa, V., Bazaikin, Y., Khachkova, T.: Computational topology-based characterization of pore space changes due to chemical dissolution of rocks. Appl. Math. Model. **88**, 21–37 (2020). https://doi.org/10.1016/j.apm.2020.06.037
16. Luo, K., Zhuang, Z., Fan, J., Haugen, N.E.L.: A ghost-cell immersed boundary method for simulations of heat transfer in compressible flows under different boundary conditions. Int. J. Heat Mass Transf. **92**, 708–717 (2016)
17. Miller, K., Vanorio, T., Keehm, Y.: Evolution of permeability and microstructure of tight carbonates due to numerical simulation of calcite dissolution. J. Geophys. Res.: Solid Earth **122**(6), 4460–4474 (2017)
18. Molins, S., et al.: Pore-scale controls on calcite dissolution rates from flow-through laboratory and numerical experiments. Environ. Sci. Technol. **48**(13), 7453–7460 (2014)
19. Osher, S., Fedkiw, R.P.: Level set methods: an overview and some recent results. J. Comput. Phys. **169**(2), 463–502 (2001)
20. Peskin, C.S.: Flow patterns around heart valves: a numerical method. J. Comput. Phys. **10**, 252–271 (1972)
21. Prokhorov, D., Lisitsa, V., Bazaikin, Y.: Digital image reduction for the analysis of topological changes in the pore space of rock matrix. Comput. Geotech. **136**, 104171 (2021)
22. Sotiropoulos, F., Yang, X.: Immersed boundary methods for simulating fluid-structure interaction. Prog. Aerosp. Sci. **65**, 1–21 (2014)
23. Steefel, C.I., et al.: Reactive transport codes for subsurface environmental simulation. Comput. Geosci. **19**(3), 445–478 (2015)
24. Sussman, M., Fatemi, E.: An efficient, interface-preserving level set redistancing algorithm and its application to interfacial incompressible fluid flow. SIAM J. Sci. Comput. **20**(4), 1165–1191 (1999)
25. Xu, Z., Meakin, P.: Phase-field modeling of solute precipitation and dissolution. J. Chem. Phys. **129**(1), 014705 (2008)
26. Yoon, H., Valocchi, A.J., Werth, C.J., Dewers, T.: Pore-scale simulation of mixing-induced calcium carbonate precipitation and dissolution in a microfluidic pore network. Water Resour. Res. **48**(2), W02524 (2012)

A New Method for Binary Classification of Proteins with Machine Learning

Damiano Perri[1,3]([⊠]) [ID], Marco Simonetti[1,3] [ID], Andrea Lombardi[2] [ID],
Noelia Faginas-Lago[2] [ID], and Osvaldo Gervasi[3] [ID]

[1] Department of Mathematics and Computer Science, University of Florence,
Florence, Italy
damiano.perri@unifi.it
[2] Department of Chemistry, Biology and Biotechnology, University of Perugia,
Perugia, Italy
[3] Department of Mathematics and Computer Science, University of Perugia,
Perugia, Italy

Abstract. In this work we set out to find a method to classify protein structures using a Deep Learning methodology. Our Artificial Intelligence has been trained to recognize complex biomolecule structures extrapolated from the Protein Data Bank (PDB) database and reprocessed as images; for this purpose various tests have been conducted with pre-trained Convolutional Neural Networks, such as InceptionResNetV2 or InceptionV3, in order to extract significant features from these images and correctly classify the molecule. A comparative analysis of the performances of the various networks will therefore be produced.

Keywords: Machine Learning · Computational chemistry · Protein Data Bank · Convolutional Neural Network · Image processing · Orthogonal axonometry

1 Introduction

The classification of the geometric structures of proteins and the individuation of possible simple criteria to base their discrimination are complex tasks and a longstanding issue in chemical sciences. To investigate the relationships between structure and activity and for a satisfactory theoretical understanding of the protein folding process, the ability to assess the "correctness" and similarity of possible spatial arrangements of such macromolecules is a prerequisite.

The recent increased practicability of computational approaches based on Deep Learning and Neural Networks further motivates renewed efforts in such direction, since it permits one to resort to approaches based on the search for hidden patterns and regularities across large set of experimentally resolved protein structures.

In a recent paper [1], we developed an approach to the basic problem of classifying as "real" a protein given its amino acid sequence, using a Deep Learning

© Springer Nature Switzerland AG 2021
O. Gervasi et al. (Eds.): ICCSA 2021, LNCS 12958, pp. 388–397, 2021.
https://doi.org/10.1007/978-3-030-87016-4_29

approach, based upon a Convolutional Neural Network (CNN) trained on a large set of data.

In the present paper, which is intended as a continuation of such previous work, a Convolutional Neural Network is again aimed at classifying as "true" or "false" a given structure, but the CNN has been developed after new significant improvements to the original approach for the recognition of the geometric structures. The idea was not to lose valuable spatial information regarding the shape of the protein to be examined, so we moved beyond the molecule model as a simple sequence of amino acids, to get to a more effective and realistic description preserving spatial information. To this purpose we exploited the well known suitability of Convolutional Neural Networks for image analysis, where they are particularly appreciated in the recognition of images and their characteristics, both on two-dimensional or three-dimensional objects, through the extraction of particular features from images so that different kind of objects, like people or things, can be correctly classified.

In this article we illustrate our approach to the problem using a two-dimensional representation based on 2D Convolutional Neural Networks, where any given protein is mapped into a two-dimensional grid of coloured pixels and then processed by the CNN in order to extract the relevant features and the characteristic properties to carry out the protein classification. In order to train the neural network, similarly to the previous work, the set of protein structures was obtained from the Protein Data Bank (PDB) [2] an open access repository containing data about proteins and nucleic acids' structures.

The paper is organized as follows. In Sect. 2 we briefly point out some key points about data extraction for protein classification. Section 3 illustrates the characteristics of our CNN, reports details about data extraction and processing. Preliminary applications, for training and validation, are also reported. Conclusions and perspectives are in Sect. 4.

2 Strategies for Classification of Complex Molecular Structures

For some years now, the use of Machine Learning techniques has rapidly become more and more pervasive in the world of Biology [3,4] and Chemistry [5–8], especially in the field of classification of macro-molecules that are generally found in the modeling of protein and bio-molecular structures [9]. The identification and correct assignment of the protein attribute to a generic bio-molecule is of considerable importance both for the purposes of genomic mapping and for the preparation of new and more specific groups of drugs [10–12].

Various methodologies are continuously suggested that take into consideration different aspects [13], such as chemical-physical properties [14] or geometric structure [15,16], to reach the goal. In the first case, two different approaches are possible:

1. attention is focused on a chemical-physical feature of interest and the bio-molecules are labelled, also using a deep learning or SVM (Support Vector Machine) technique to obtain an accurate and automated classifier;
2. an n-dimensional vector with the descriptors of the chemical-physical properties to be examined is produced with an attached class label [17].

Several studies have confirmed that the combination of protein characteristics is preferable in order to obtain better predictive information than the use of single protein characteristics [18].

In the second case, the spatial arrangement of the various amino acid chains is evaluated for classification, both with SVM [19] and Machine Learning/Deep Learning [20,21] techniques. Today, convolutional neural networks are widely used in image analysis. They allow the extraction of features thanks to which object recognition or image classification can be performed [22–24]. Our research fits into this last channel with the aim of testing a way to correctly classify protein groups. Most of the work in this area has mainly focused on the study of the sequence and position of amino acids in the protein chain (primary or secondary sequence); our research has tried to maintain the information related to the sequences, simultaneously capturing all the geometric characteristics using 2D axonometric maps.

3   Methodology: The Architecture of the System

The system is a classic binary classifier whose task is to correctly subdivide the biomolecules given in input as "protein" or "non-protein". The data relating to the molecules to be examined are passed to the neural network as two-dimensional image processing, which faithfully reconstructs the geometric structure of the molecule itself.

3.1   Data Extraction and Processing

In order to validate our methodology, we have extracted from the PDB a sufficient number of records useful to effectively train the network; after several tests, it was found that good results were obtained with a number of samples around 3,000 units. This allowed us to select a group of proteins (equal to 2,911 molecules, with 16,924,350 amino acids) with the best images of their structure and focus our attention on the results. The whole process, from data extraction to image evaluation by the neural network, was performed in Python3, with the help of well-known libraries useful for scientific computing and data processing, such as Numpy and Pandas.

The various steps required for the generation and management of the dataset are listed below:

1) Data extraction in XML format from the PDB database, identification of the necessary information we wish to keep and its subsequent transformation into a single object managed by the Pandas library (Fig. 1)

	id	Cartn_x	Cartn_y	Cartn_z	auth_comp_id	amin_code	group_PDB	type_symbol	file
0	1	44.080	-3.124	8.654	MET	8421504	ATOM	N	190l.txt
1	2	43.646	-1.771	8.714	MET	8421504	ATOM	C	190l.txt
2	3	42.260	-1.784	9.335	MET	8421504	ATOM	C	190l.txt
3	4	41.490	-2.712	9.135	MET	8421504	ATOM	O	190l.txt
4	5	43.668	-1.224	7.269	MET	8421504	ATOM	C	190l.txt
...	...	...	...	...	...	...	...	...	...
16924345	2309	4.709	50.805	38.087	GLY	65535	ATOM	O	9abp.txt
16924346	2310	2.795	50.913	36.873	LYS	8421376	ATOM	N	9abp.txt
16924347	2311	2.496	52.321	37.153	LYS	8421376	ATOM	C	9abp.txt
16924348	2312	1.126	52.680	36.577	LYS	8421376	ATOM	C	9abp.txt
16924349	2313	0.882	52.522	35.363	LYS	8421376	ATOM	O	9abp.txt

16924350 rows × 9 columns

Fig. 1. Information extracted: spatial position, name and colour code of amino acids

2) Data cleaning, with the elimination of any duplicate records, possibly generated by the two different methods of measuring the crystal lattice structure for the molecule
3) Association of a unique RGB color code to each amino acid present in proteins (e.g. Alanine 128, Glycine 65280, Lysine 8421376), in order to visualize the structure of the molecule as an image, on which every single amino acid is coloured in a different way

Fig. 2. Orthogonal axonometry

• Visualization of the molecule according to a multiview orthographic axonometric map with orthogonal projections on three planes (horizontal plane, vertical plane and lateral/profile plane - an example of this type of axonometry is shown in Fig. 2), in order to split and project the whole 3D image on a flat surface, without losing the isometricity and symmetries on the x, y and z components for the individual amino acids. From the analysis of the coordinates of all the amino acids present in the dataset, it was possible through an appropriate translation for the origin of the Cartesian reference system and an integer mapping for the numerical values of the coordinates themselves to represent each single protein in the domain $D = [0, 3200]^3 \subset \mathbb{N}^3$; this allowed us to refer to each point (x, y, z) belonging to the cube D as a 3-indices tuple for the tensor with dimensions $3200 \times 3200 \times 3200$, capable of containing the entire biomolecule

- Each image has been processed to fit within the 299×299 pixel dimensions, necessary as input dimensions for a 2D convolutional neural network; in order to avoid distorting the original axonometric proportions, the figures have been carefully cut out at the edges and in the central areas, to reduce unnecessary black padding.

Therefore, for each single protein, the various amino acids were projected, as colored dots, on the three main planes: in Fig. 3 four images obtained with our method for four different proteins are shown.

4) Generation of false samples, necessary for the learning of the neural network. It was decided to proceed starting from the original images; for the single amino acids belonging to each protein we applied a mutation probability, established at the beginning of the process (in our case experimental tests made us lean towards a fixed value of 5%), which induced a colour change on the coloured points representing the amino acid: 2911 images of false proteins were thus produced. In Fig. 4 a portion of a true protein is reproduced (above) with its false analogue (below): it is possible to notice the differences due to the mutation process (pixel that occupies the same position in the two figures, but has different colors).

3.2 Training and Validation

The performances of two neural networks were analyzed: InceptionV3 and InceptionResNetV2. These networks were trained through the **transfer learning** technique which allowed us to obtain high accuracy values with a reduced number of learning epochs.

Transfer learning is the process by which a neural network learn a new task through knowledge's transfer a related task previously learned. Using transfer learning, the weight values of the convolutional layers are imported (they are generally used for feature extraction and already present as initial parameters of the network itself), and only the final layers of the neural network that are generally used for classification are trained [25, 26]. Both networks are pre-trained on ImageNet which is an image dataset used for object recognition consisting of 14 million photographs.

The model used for the InceptionV3 neural network is shown in the Table 1, while the model used for the InceptionResNetV2 neural network is shown in the Table 2.

Table 1. InceptionV3 model

Layer (type)	Output Shape	Param #
inception_v3	(None, 8, 8, 2048)	21802784
flatten (Flatten)	(None, 131072)	0
dense (Dense)	(None, 64)	8388672
dense_1 (Dense)	(None, 64)	4160
dense_2 (Dense)	(None, 1)	65
Total Params:		30,195,681
Trainable Params:		30,161,249

Table 2. InceptionResNetV2 model

Layer (type)	Output Shape	Param #
inception_resnet_v2	(None, 8, 8, 1536)	54336736
flatten (Flatten)	(None, 98304)	0
dense (Dense)	(None, 64)	6291520
dense_1 (Dense)	(None, 64)	4160
dense_2 (Dense)	(None, 1)	65
Total Params:		60,632,481
Trainable Params:		60,571,937

The results of the training are summarized in the Table 3, where it can be seen that the InceptionV3 network has a higher accuracy's percentage in recognizing false proteins from true ones compared to the results obtained by InceptionResNetV2. The Confusion Matrices [27] of the two models indicate that they are both able to classify proteins with good results, also we believe that a correct parameters' modulation, through the realization of ad-hoc models, can further increase the degree of accuracy. The matrices are shown in Fig. 5.

Table 3. Final results

	InceptionV3	InceptionResNetV2
Accuracy Train Set	99.06%	98.36%
Accuracy Test Set	94.57%	92.14%
Model Size	461 MB	465 MB

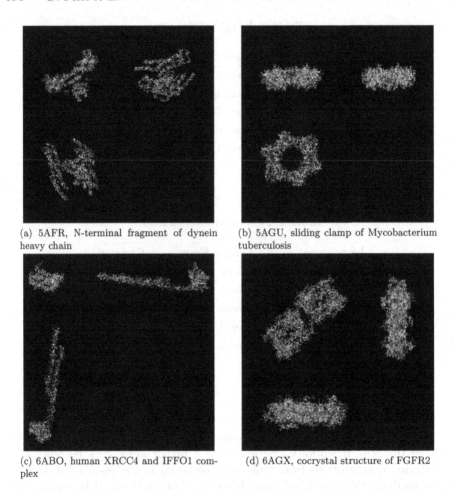

(a) 5AFR, N-terminal fragment of dynein heavy chain

(b) 5AGU, sliding clamp of Mycobacterium tuberculosis

(c) 6ABO, human XRCC4 and IFFO1 complex

(d) 6AGX, cocrystal structure of FGFR2

Fig. 3. Images of 4 proteins obtained with our representation method

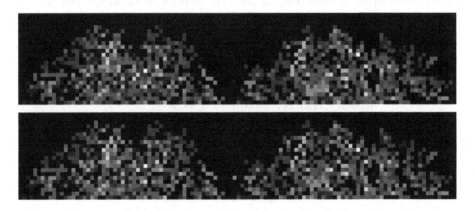

Fig. 4. Differences between the same portion of a real molecule (above) and its false analogue (below)

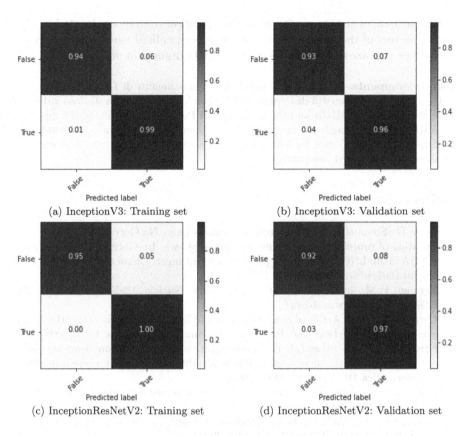

(a) InceptionV3: Training set

(b) InceptionV3: Validation set

(c) InceptionResNetV2: Training set

(d) InceptionResNetV2: Validation set

Fig. 5. Confusion matrices

4   Conclusions and Future Works

In this work we presented an improved Convolutional Neural Network for the classification of protein structure. Preliminary results appear encouraging, showing that the methodology used for the representation of the protein geometry, based on a 2D projected image associated to each molecule, retains most of the spatial information and is suitable for recognition. Also, the computational performances seems quite good, being calculations extremely fast as we provide the neural network with an image for each molecule.

However, considerations on the general nature of the CNNs used lead us to think that specifically designed neural networks could significantly improve the results, or even outperform them. A further research path worth being followed is to train the neural network using a greater number of samples, to better analyze the link between the samples' structural complexity and the classification capacity of the neural network itself. We believe that even better performance might be achieved if we developed a neural network customised for the graphical representation we proposed. Our representation is in fact very particular and within our images the areas with a high information content are located in very specific sectors of the images. Furthermore, a personalised neural network could also reduce the size in MegaBytes of the model obtained in output.

Acknowledgments. AL and NFL thank the Dipartimento di Chimica, Biologia e Biotecnologie dell'Università di Perugia (FRB, Fondo per la Ricerca di Base 2019 and 2020) and the Italian MIUR and the University of Perugia for the financial support of the AMIS project through the program "Dipartimenti di Eccellenza". AL thanks the OU Supercomputing Center for Education & Research (OSCER) at the University of Oklahoma, for allocated computing time.

References

1. Perri, D., Simonetti, M., Lombardi, A., Faginas-Lago, N., Gervasi, O.: Binary classification of proteins by a machine learning approach. In: Gervasi, O., et al. (eds.) ICCSA 2020. LNCS, vol. 12255, pp. 549–558. Springer, Cham (2020). https://doi.org/10.1007/978-3-030-58820-5_41

2. Berman, H.M., et al.: The protein data bank. Nucleic Acids Res. **28**, 235–242 (2000). http://www.rcsb.org/

3. Cartwright, H.M.: Artificial neural networks in biology and chemistry—the evolution of a new analytical tool. In: Artificial Neural Networks, pp. 1–13 (2008)

4. Krishnan, V.G., Westhead, D.R.: A comparative study of machine-learning methods to predict the effects of single nucleotide poly- morphisms on protein function. Bioinformatics **19**(17), 2199–2209 (2003)

5. Dral, P.O.: Quantum chemistry in the age of machine learning. J. Phys. Chem. Lett. **11**(6), 2336–2347 (2020)

6. Goldman, B.B., Walters, W.P.: Machine learning in computational chemistry. Annu. Rep. Comput. Chem. **2**, 127–140 (2006)

7. Panteleev, J., Gao, H., Jia, L.: Recent applications of machine learning in medicinal chemistry. Bioorg. Med. Chem. Lett. **28**(17), 2807–2815 (2018)

8. Mater, A.C., Coote, M.L.: Deep learning in chemistry. J. Chem. Inf. Model. **59**(6), 2545–2559 (2019)

9. Bakhtiarizadeh, M.R., Moradi-Shahrbabak, M., Ebrahimi, M., Ebrahimie, E.: Neural network and SVM classifiers accurately predict lipid binding proteins, irrespective of sequence homology. J. Theoret. Biol. **356**, 213–222 (2014)

10. Ou-Yang, S., Jun-yan, L., Kong, X., Liang, Z., Luo, C., Jiang, H.: Computational drug discovery. Acta Pharmacologica Sinica **33**(9), 1131–1140 (2012)

11. Sliwoski, G., Kothiwale, S., Meiler, J., Lowe, E.W.: Computational methods in drug discovery. Pharmacol. Rev. **66**(1), 334–395 (2014)

12. Jamali, A.A., Ferdousi, R., Razzaghi, S., Li, J., Safdari, R., Ebrahimie, E.: Drug-Miner: comparative analysis of machine learning algorithms for prediction of potential druggable proteins. Drug Discovery Today **21**(5), 718–724 (2016)

13. Rishi Das Roy and Debasis Dash: Selection of relevant features from amino acids enables development of robust classifiers. Amino Acids **46**(5), 1343–1351 (2014). https://doi.org/10.1007/s00726-014-1697-z

14. Taniguchi, M.: Combination of single-molecule electrical measurements and machine learning for the identification of single biomolecules. ACS Omega **5**(2), 959–964 (2020)

15. Brandt, S., Sittel, F., Ernst, M., Stock, G.: Machine learning of biomolecular reaction coordinates. J. Phys. Chem. Lett. **9**(9), 2144–2150 (2018)
16. Cang, Z., Mu, L., Wei, G.-W.: Representability of algebraic topology for biomolecules in machine learning based scoring and virtual screening. PLoS Comput. Biol. **14**(1), e1005929 (2018)
17. Michael Gromiha, M., Ahmad, S., Suwa, M.: Neural network based prediction of protein structure and function: comparison with other machine learning methods. In: 2008 IEEE International Joint Conference on Neural Networks (IEEE World Congress on Computational Intelligence), pp. 1739–1744. IEEE (2008)
18. Ong, S.A.K., Lin, H.H., Chen, Y.Z., Li, Z.R., Cao, Z.: Efficacy of different protein descriptors in predicting protein functional families. BMC Bioinform. **8**(1), 1–14 (2007)
19. Cai, C.Z., Han, L.Y., Ji, Z.L., Chen, X., Chen, Y.Z.: SVM-Prot: web-based support vector machine software for functional classification of a protein from its primary sequence. Nucleic Acids Res. **31**(13), 3692–3697 (2003)
20. Cui, J., et al.: Advances in exploration of machine learning methods for predicting functional class and interaction profiles of proteins and peptides irrespective of sequence homology. Curr. Bioinform. **2**(2), 95–112 (2007)
21. Ding, C.H.Q., Dubchak, I.: Multi-class protein fold recognition using support vector machines and neural networks. Bioinformatics **17**(4), 349–358 (2001)
22. Perri, D., Sylos Labini, P., Gervasi, O., Tasso, S., Vella, F.: Towards a learning-based performance modeling for accelerating deep neural networks. In: Misra, S., et al. (eds.) ICCSA 2019. LNCS, vol. 11619, pp. 665–676. Springer, Cham (2019). https://doi.org/10.1007/978-3-030-24289-3_49 ISBN 978-3- 030-24289-3
23. Biondi, G., Franzoni, V., Gervasi, O., Perri, D.: An approach for improving automatic mouth emotion recognition. In: Misra, S., et al. (eds.) ICCSA 2019. LNCS, vol. 11619, pp. 649–664. Springer, Cham (2019). https://doi.org/10.1007/978-3-030-24289-3_48 ISBN 978-3-030-24289-3
24. Labini, P.S., et al.: On the anatomy of predictive models for accelerating GPU convolution kernels and beyond. ACM Trans. Archit. Code Optim. **18**(1) (2021). https://doi.org/10.1145/3434402, ISSN 1544-3566
25. Franzoni, V., Biondi, G., Perri, D., Gervasi, O.: Enhancing mouth-based emotion recognition using transfer learning. Sensors **20**(18) (2020). https://doi.org/10.3390/s20185222, https://www.mdpi.com/1424-8220/20/18/5222, ISSN 1424-8220
26. Benedetti, P., Perri, D., Simonetti, M., Gervasi, O., Reali, G., Femminella, M.: Skin cancer classification using inception network and transfer learning. In: Gervasi, O., et al. (eds.) ICCSA 2020. LNCS, vol. 12249, pp. 536–545. Springer, Cham (2020). https://doi.org/10.1007/978-3-030-58799-4_39
27. Visa, S., Ramsay, B., Ralescu, A.L., Van Der Knaap, E.: Confusion matrix-based feature selection. MAICS **710**, 120–127 (2011)

Multilayered Modelling of the Metallation of Biological Targets

Iogann Tolbatov[1](✉) ⓘ, Alessandro Marrone[2] ⓘ, Roberto Paciotti[2] ⓘ,
Nazzareno Re[2] ⓘ, and Cecilia Coletti[2] ⓘ

[1] Institut de Chimie Moleculaire de l'Université de Bourgogne (ICMUB), Université de
Bourgogne Franche-Comté (UBFC), Avenue Alain Savary 9, Dijon, France
iogann.tolbatov@u-bourgogne.fr
[2] Dipartimento di Farmacia, Università "G d'Annunzio" di Chieti-Pescara, via dei Vestini 31,
Chieti, Italy

Abstract. The unique property of metals – the remarkable ability to modulate the electronic structure of both metal center and bound ligands – is the reason for their omnipresence in enzymes and in metal-coordinating biological factors. Modern metallodrug chemistry began with the serendipitous unveiling of the antitumour properties of cisplatin, followed by an avalanche of synthesized novel metallodrugs. The metallation of biological targets has then become a new paradigm in the field of bioinorganic chemistry, and a plethora of computational approaches have been developed and utilized to ease the detailed comprehension of its mechnisms with a focus on medical applications. Studies of the electronic structure of metallodrugs and of the coordination of metal elements with biomolecular ligands, as well as an accurate description of both thermodynamics and kinetics of reactions with biomolecules, are crucial for development of novel metallodrugs with improved therapeutic profiles. Here, we provide an account of the application of multilayered computational schemes developed in our group for the study of processes leading and/or culminating with the metallation of biomolecules, the key step in the mechanism of action of metallodrugs.

1 Introduction

The essential role of metals in biological systems demonstrates the exceptional adaptability of coordinative bond, which causes reciprocal adjustment in the electronic structure of both the metal center and its ligands, thus allowing enzymes and/or metal-coordinating biological factors to be players in a very fine chemistry. The same reasons motivate the interest for metal-based drugs or metallodrugs in which the peculiar interaction between the metal and the biological targets may lead and modulate the therapeutical benefit.

Since the serendipitous finding [1] of cisplatin with its still wide employment in the anticancer therapy [2], a growing interest has been focused on the identification of novel metallodrugs, leading to a vast body of literature data. One of the most appealing aspects of cisplatin pharmacodynamics is represented by its capability of binding at DNA nucleobases: the Pt(II) center of cisplatin is mostly coordinated at two consecutive

© Springer Nature Switzerland AG 2021
O. Gervasi et al. (Eds.): ICCSA 2021, LNCS 12958, pp. 398–412, 2021.
https://doi.org/10.1007/978-3-030-87016-4_30

intrastrand GG or AG nucleobases [3] in the major groove of the DNA duplex, and causing a specific structural aberration capable of inducing apoptosis [4].

The metallation of biological targets has thus become a new paradigm in the domain of bioinorganic chemistry, and many endeavours have been devoted to achieve a comprehensive understanding of how this process could be therapeutically exploited [5].

The match between the multifacet chemistry disclosed by metal compounds with the extreme complexity of biological systems makes the comprehension of the metallation process a particularly challenging task even in the in vitro context. Again, the cisplatin example has taught to us that, despite metallation eventuates in the coordination of a metal center to a specific biological target, this process is the result of an intricate sequence of chemical events that are triggered when the metallodrug starts to interact with the components of the biological medium: the cisplatin aquation equilibrium taking place in the cytoplasm has been recognized as responsible of its activation [6].

The studies of electronic structure and metal coordination for metallodrugs and biomolecules, as well as an in-depth characterization of both thermodynamics and kinetics of the involved reactions, are of utmost importance at the initial stages of investigations and are followed by the quantum mechanical (QM) methods which target the particular bioinorganic systems.

Based on a consolidated expertise in the bioinorganic computational chemistry [7, 8], several computational strategies were designed and adopted by our research group to include a QM description of the structure and/or reactivity of metallodrugs, most of them implying the combination and/or hybridization of different level of theories.

In this report, we provide for an account of applications of multilayered computational approaches for the investigation of the processes leading and/or culminating with the metallation of biomolecules implicated in the mechanism of action of metallodrugs (Fig. 1). The word "multilayered" will be used herein with a twofold meaning, but with a unique address (Fig. 2). On one hand, a multilayered representation of the whole system, generally made of the metallodrug, the bulk, and the biological target, may support the extraction of reduced models: for example, the activation processes taking place before the contact between the metallodrug Pt-bispidine (vide infra) with its target – in the bulk layer – as well as the reaction of the aquo forms of Pt-bispidine with guanine sites – in the target layer – may be both investigated by means of QM methods (Fig. 2a). On the other hand, the term "multilayered" can also be used to indicate the treatment of different portion of the system with different level of theories, thus, referring to a "layering" of the introspection accuracy: for example, the use of QM/MM approaches allowing to investigate the reaction within a metallodrug with its binding site at QM level of theory, while describing the remaining portions of the system within an empirical force field (Fig. 2b).

In either cases the multilayered approach is used to treat the most chemically relevant portion of the system at high level of theory, thus allowing to study the thermodynamics and kinetics of the processes involved in the metallation of biological targets.

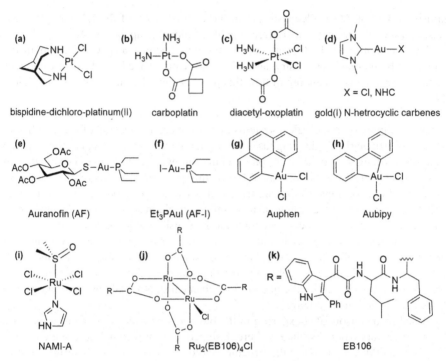

Fig. 1. The Pt, Au, and Ru-based metallodrugs described in the present report.

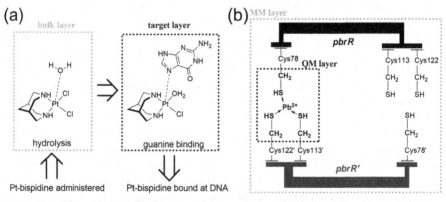

Fig. 2. Rendition of the twofold meaning of the word "multilayer". (a) The administered metallodrug Pt-bispidine undergoes to hydrolytic activation, a process occurring in the bulk layer. Afterwards, the aquo forms of Pt-bispidine react with guanine sites at DNA, a process occurring in the target layer. (b) The description of the coordinative bonds between a lead ion and the cysteine triad formed by a pbrR dimer requires a high-level of theory, hence the Pb^{2+} ion and the side chains of Cys78, Cys113', and Cys122' are included in the QM layer. On the other hand, the lasting protein environment, exerting an electrostatic and steric influence on the lead binding, can be described by an empirical force field, hence included in the MM layer.

2 Pt(II) and Pt(IV) Metallodrugs

A body of evidence has definitely ascertained the crucial role played by aquation in the mode of action of cisplatin [9, 10], and helped the elucidation of the structure-activity relationships affecting the cisplatin-like Pt(II) anticancer complexes and the possibility of its targeted release through different supports [11, 12]. In recent studies, it was found that cisplatin and its iodide analogue cis-[PtI$_2$(NH$_3$)$_2$] display remarkable dissimilarities in their reactivity with the model proteins cytochrome c and lysozyme [13–15]. In order to unveil the molecular rationale for such comportment, a computational DFT approach was utilized for the investigation of the reactions of cis-[PtCl$_2$(NH$_3$)$_2$] and cis-[PtI$_2$(NH$_3$)$_2$] with molecular models (Ls) of the aminoacid sidechains – cysteine, methionine, histidine [14], a procedure which was found to give relevant insights on the reaction mechanism of cisplatin even in a solvent-free environment [16, 17]. It was concluded that the reaction of such Pt(II) complexes with sulfur-containing amino acids leads to a prompt loss of their halide ligands, which is followed by the loss of ammonia by the resultant cis-[Pt(L)$_2$(NH$_3$)$_2$] complexes in reaction with a ligand excess. On the other hand, the reaction of cis-[PtCl$_2$(NH$_3$)$_2$] and cis-[PtI$_2$(NH$_3$)$_2$] with imidazole results into the loss of their halide ligands. Nevertheless, the formed cis-[PtL$_2$(NH$_3$)$_2$] complex does not release ammonia in reaction with imidazole in excess. The differences in reactivity of these two platinum complexes with small models of amino acid side chains correspond well to their behavior observed in reactions with model proteins. This allowed to conclude that the role played by protein itself is crucial in activating the anomalous reactivity of the cis-[PtI$_2$(NH$_3$)$_2$] and in determining the formed protein adducts.

Bispidine is an anticancer drug with propitious qualities, such as minor side effects, ability to overcome inherent or acquired resistance, improved DNA targeting, and a simplified drug administration [18] (Fig. 1a). In order to shed light upon its reactivity and mode of action, we carried out a DFT study [19] focusing on the analysis of the first and second aquation steps as well as of the ensuing reactions with guanine, the primary objective of the platinum-based antitumor compounds. Consistently with the experimental data, calculations indicate that the bispidine is substantially less reactive with water molecules compared to cisplatin, its kinetic constant being fivefold smaller than the corresponding value for cisplatin [20]. Nevertheless, it was shown that the aquated complexes demonstrate an exceptional reactivity with guanine with the activation free energies proximate to those for the analogous aquated complexes of cisplatin, 20.8 vs 20.4 kcal mol^{-1} and 21.3 vs 20.9 kcal mol^{-1}, for the binding of the mono- and diaqua complex of the bispidine, respectively [19] (Fig. 2a).

Nowadays, carboplatin is the anticancer drug that is used ubiquitously, since it causes less side effects than cisplatin [21] (Fig. 1b). The scaffold of carbolatin resembles much cisplatin with the two attached stable cis ammino ligands, however, carbolatin possesses a dicarboxylate chelate ring instead of two labile chloro ligands of cisplatin. Both metallodrugs operate in the analogous way, indeed, carboplatin was found to form the Pt(NH$_3$)$_2$$^{2+}$-DNA adducts in vivo [22]. However, the bidentate malonate ring is less labile than chloride ions, causing the lesser reactivity of carboplatin than cisplatin. For the purpose of studying the mode of action of carboplatin, we carried out an ab initio study on the mechanism of carboplatin activation by chloride ions in different pH conditions [23], demonstrating that in neutral conditions, or in weak acidic conditions characteristic for the hypoxic tumor milieu, the process is unlikely to take place at physiological temperature, an indication that is not involved in the mechanism of carboplatin activation. Stronger nucleophiles than chloride are needed to activate carboplatin.

Carbonate, an omnipresent species in biological systems, existing in considerable concentration (24 mM) in blood plasma, was thus considered to play a possible role in carboplatin activation mechanism. A computational study was carried out with a focus on the initial steps of the process, consisting of the detachment of one arm of the malonato chelating ring of carboplatin accompanied by the decarboxylation, yielding cis-[Pt(CBDCA-O)(OH)(NH$_3$)$_2$]$^-$ [24]. We considered both carbonate and bicarbonate ions as attacking species, since they are both present in the carbonate buffer at physiological pH. The ring opening by the carbonate ion has the reaction free energy and activation enthalpy values lower (by ca. 2.4–4.8 kcal mol^{-1} at various levels of theory) than the corresponding reaction with bicarbonate, thus proving that the carboplatin activation should be ascribed to the carbonate ion, consistently with existing experimental data [25]. As in the case of chloride ions, the effect of the environment acidity was taken into consideration and indicated that carboplatin activation occurs via the protonation of the carbonate to a bicarbonate complex, which is subsequently decarboxylated to the ultimate hydroxo complex. The rate-determining step of the entire process is the opening of the ring, immediately followed by the protonation to the corresponding bicarbonate complex. After a facile decarboxylation by means of a mechanism of bicarbonate rotation, a hydroxo-coordinated bicarbonate intermediate is produced, which promptly undergoes the final CO$_2$ dissociation (activation enthalpy and free energy below 4.8 kcal mol^{-1}). The whole process, is exoergic with a rather low free energy of activation (less than 28.7 kcal mol^{-1}) suggesting that the reaction with carbonate might be a feasible and plausible pathway for the activation of carboplatin in the biological milieu [24].

An auspicious approach to circumvent one of the main disadvantages of cisplatin, i.e. its severe side effects [26], is the use of six-coordinate Pt(IV) complexes which can act as prodrugs after their permeation into the target cell, where they are reduced by glutathione or ascorbate, to the active four-coordinate square planar Pt(II) analogues which, in turn, form the adduct with the final DNA target [27]. The main side effects of Pt(II) complexes, early hydrolysis and subsequent binding to proteins of plasma, are impeded due to substantial inertness of low spin d^6 Pt(IV) complexes, a feature which might even enable an oral administration of the drug. The Pt(IV) to Pt(II) reduction occurs simultaneously to the detachment of two axial ligands and, being the key step for the drug activation, was thoroughly studied by electrochemical and chemical approaches [28]. Cyclic voltammetry was comprehensively utilized to investigate the reduction–oxidation process in Pt(IV) antitumor complexes, and only a single irreversible reduction event was demonstrated for this irreversible reduction instead of the standard redox potential for the Pt(IV)/Pt(II) couple. An insight on the two-electron reduction mechanism of the [Pt^{IV}(NH$_3$)$_2$(CH$_3$COO)$_2$Cl$_2$] complex was recently obtained from a theoretical DFT study [29] (Fig. 1c). It disentangled the stepwise mechanism consisting of the initial one-electron reduction of the [Pt^{IV}(NH$_3$)$_2$(CH$_3$COO)$_2$Cl$_2$] complex, producing the hexacoordinated platinum(III) [Pt^{III}(NH$_3$)$_2$(CH$_3$COO)$_2$Cl$_2$]$^-$ intermediate and the detached acetate, with an activation free energy of 6.46 kcal mol^{-1}. On the contrary, the formed pentacoordinated [Pt^{III}(NH$_3$)$_2$(CH$_3$COO)Cl$_2$] species is reduced by the second electron by means of a barrierless concerted process to the eventual $[Pt^{II}(NH_3)_2(CH_3COO)_2]$ derivative.

3   Au(I) and Au(III) Metallodrugs

Gold(I) N–heterocyclic carbenes (NHC) [Au(I)(NHC)R], in which R can be either an anionic or a neutral ligand, e.g. Cl^-, PH_3, or NHC, are ubiquitously used in medicinal chemistry [30] as anti-arthritic, antibacterial, and anticancer agents [31, 32] (Fig. 1d). Nevertheless, comprehensive understanding of the reaction mechanism of these gold carbene compounds with amino acids and fragments of proteins linger predominantly unrevealed. In a recent investigation [33], the reactivity of [Au(I)(NHC)Cl] with various nucleophiles was evaluated, including water, N-terminal of any amino acid, as well as the side chains of cysteine, selenocysteine, methionine, histidine, arginine, lysine. The computed results demonstrate that the substitution of chloride by the examined residues is slightly exergonic. It was found that the hydration of the [Au(I)(NHC)Cl] complex happens relatively fast with the free energy of activation of 23.0 kcal mol^{-1}. Nevertheless such barrier is considerably higher than the barriers for the amino acid side chains, implying that [Au(I)(NHC)Cl] complexes interact with their biomolecular targets before being hydrolyzed. The smallest barriers were computed for cysteine and selenocysteine, thus substantiating the predominant binding of [Au(I)(NHC)]$^+$ to the cysteine and selenocysteine residues of thioredoxin in agreement with experimental data [34]. Low barriers were also computed for the nitrogen-based nucleophile sites: arginine, lysine, and N-terminal amine (16–19 kcal mol^{-1}). This indicates that there is only a weak differentiation in reactivity between S/Se and N-based nucleophile sites. As a consequence, when no cystein and selenocysteine residues are available or when they are buried in the protein, the [Au(I)(NHC)]$^+$ moiety could also bind to N-based sites, suggesting that accessibility on the protein surface might play a relevant role on the binding preference of such compounds.

Recently, it was experimentally shown that the biscarbene Au(I)-NHC complexes $[(Me_2Im)_2Au]^+$ activate the cell apoptosis mechanism by thioredoxin reductase (TrxR) inhibition. During this process they consecutively release two NHC ligands in a two-step reaction, forming a $[Au(Cys)_2]$ complex [30]. A DFT study focused on characterization of the first steps of the mechanism of action of these anticancer complexes was carried out, addressing the substitution of carbene ligand by capped cysteine and selenocysteine which modeled the side chains of respective protein residues [35]. Numerous reaction mechanisms were investigated, including those involving the protonation of the detached carbene, as well as both neutral and deprotonated forms of cysteine and selenocysteine, i.e. the examined nucleophiles in the reaction of ligand exchange on the metal center. Results indicate that the reaction can only happen with anionic thiolate or selenothiolate, together with a concomitant transfer of proton to the detached carbene from the acidic constituent of the buffer. The availability of a buffer is indeed necessary in experiments in physiological conditions, so that experimental and theoretical results converge and indicate the importance of the biological environment for such reactions to take place. The substitution of carbene is a marginally exergonic process with fairly low barriers of 21.3 kcal mol^{-1} and 19.6 kcal mol^{-1}, respectively, for capped cysteine and selenocysteine, consistently with the available kinetic experimental results for free amino acids [36].

Auranofin (AF) is the gold-based metallodrug for the therapy of rheumatoid arthritis [37]; and it is being currently reevaluated as antibacterial, antiviral, antifungal, and antiparasitic agent [38] (Fig. 1e). Its iodide analogue Au(PEt₃)I, in which iodide substitutes the thiosugar, is efficacious in vitro against ovarian and colorectal cancer due to its increased cytotoxicity [39] (Fig. 1f). Reactivity of AF and AF-I complexes with selected aminoacids and protein fragments were recently investigated in a joint experimental and theoretical study [40]. It was demonstrated that the aquation of AF and AF-I is thermodynamically reprobated, hence both complexes interact with the biomolecules, loosing either thiosugar or iodide, respectively. DFT calculations for the ligand exchange reactions of AF and AF-I with the models of side chains of Cys, Sec, Met, and His displayed the thermodynamical and kinetic unfavorability of substitution of either thiosugar or iodide. It was demonstrated that only anionic cysteine and selenocysteine interact with these Au-based metallodrugs, exhibiting the barriers for substitution of iodide as being substantially lower than the corresponding values for thiosugar [40].

The bipyridyl gold(III) complexes [Au(phen)Cl₂]Cl phen = phenantroline and [Au(bpy)Cl₂]PF₆ bpy = bipyridine, named auphen and aubipy, respectively, have been extensively investigated due to their capability of selectively blocking the aquaglyceroporin AQP-3 [41], the latter channel protein being recognized to be involved in the tumorigenesis [42] (Fig. 1g). Aiming to attain a detailed understanding of the Aubipy binding and its effects on the performance of AQP3, the classical MD simulations were employed for the studies of the structures of non-covalent and covalent Aubipy–AQP3 adducts [43] (Fig. 1h). Substantial structural and functional changes in AQP3, caused by the attachment of the gold-containing fragment, were discovered through the simulation of unbound, non-covalently and covalently bound adducts. Peculiarly, the extracellular pores of both the non-covalently and covalently bound complexes experience changes in size and shape decreasing the flux of water molecules. This finding is confirmed by examination of the channel radius and water density along the transmembrane, and by evaluating the flux of water in the monomer of AQP3 bound to gold. Indeed, the water permeability is prevented by the binding of the gold complex causing a contraction of the pore at the extracellular boundary due to conformational rearrangement produced by the metal complex. These results are of an utmost value for the design of novel Au(III) complexes for the selective inhibition of AQP3, for instance, permitting the determination of aromatic ligands with asymmetric substitution arrangement in the two pyridil rings that might additionally stabilize the coordinative adduct. Moreover, the increase of binding of the Au(III) complex binding can be obtained by optimizing the hydrophobic and π-stacking interactions. Meticulous refinement of the interactions between the metallacycle and pore may augment the selectivity of the compound for inhibition of AQP3 juxtaposed to other isoforms of aquaglyceroporin [43].

The mechanism of inhibition of AQP3 by Au(III) complexes with phenanthroline (phen) ligands was clarified at the molecular level in a recent study via a combination of biophysical techniques and advanced computational methods [44]. A set of novel Au(III)-based complexes with phen ligands was synthesized, and their stability in water solution was studied together with their antitumoral properties in vitro. Their capability to inhibit the permeation of glycerol via AQP3 was studied by stopped-flow spectroscopy, by which it was found that several complexes possess AQP3 inhibition properties surpassing the cytotoxicity of benchmark compounds Aubipy and Auphen [44]. It was shown that the dichloro form of the studied Auphen-like complexes is stable under physiological conditions whereas Aubipy is found mostly in the chloro hydroxo form [43]. This contrasting speciation principally influences the noncoordinative interaction with AQP3. Indeed, both Auphen and its 5-chloro derivative bind at the side of extracellular pore analogously to Aubipy, yet they reach dissimilar residues and obtain a different orientation. Auphen-like complexes protrude the metal atom toward the side chain of the gold binding site Cys40, at a reduced distance in comparison to Aubipy, thus indicating that these complexes are able to access their final coordinative site more efficiently. These conclusions agree with the better inhibition of glycerol permeation by Auphen than by Aubipy. Moreover, it was indicated that the coordinative adducts formed between Auphen and AQP3 have a structural correspondance with those formed by Aubipy, they produce conformational rearrangements of the protein, which ultimately result in pore closure and the inhibition of AQP3. These results form a crucial foundation for the future conception of gold-based inhibitors which attack selectively different AQP isoforms [44].

4 Ru(II) and Ru(III) Anticancer Drugs

Several Ru(II) and Ru(III) complexes with nitrogen or aromatic ligands were studied for their remarkable in vitro antitumor activity and their preferential localization in tumor tissues [45, 46]. Despite the body of data testifying the anticancer potential of ruthenium complexes, a full atomistic understanding of their mode of action remains elusive, thus, feeding the interest in the modelling of their binding at biological targets.

The thermodynamics of the binding of $[Ru(NH_3)_5]^{2+}$ and $[Ru(NH_3)_5]^{3+}$ at DNA nucleobases and peptides has been computationally studied to assess the affinity of Ru(II) and Ru(III) monofunctional scaffolds toward possible biological targets [47]. In particular, the computed enthalpies and free energies for the bond dissociation show that the Ru(II) complexes, in analogy with cisplatin, disclose a high affinity for the N7 of guanine, although either histidine or sulfur-containing residues, cysteine and methionine, are also favorite binding sites, though to a lesser extent. A different profile of binding affinity was computed for Ru(III) complexes characterized by their stronger coordination to the dimethyl-phosphate anion $[(MeO)_2PO_2]^-$, a model of the phosphodiester backbone of the DNA double helix. This outcome markedly differentiates Ru(III) from Ru(II), whose binding at the phosphate moiety has been estimated to be labile in solution, and highlights the preferential targeting of Ru(III) complexes for the DNA backbone or anionic protein groups. The weak antitumor activity of Ru(III) species, observed experimentally, seems to be corroborated by the computational data, and, in accordance, postulates the Ru(III) → Ru(II) reduction as the crucial activating step.

Bifunctional complexes such as $[Ru(NH_3)_4Cl_2]$, $[Ru(NH_3)_4(H_2O)_2]^{2+}$, [cis-[cis-RuCl_2(azpy)_2], and $RuCl_2(bpy)_2$] were evaluated in terms of their affinity toward DNA or protein sites. The presence of a chloro or aquo ligand was found to only marginally affect the enthalpy of dissociation and free energy in solution of the bond between Ru(II) and guanine, whereas the arylazopyridine or polypyridyl ligands induced only a slight diminishing of these affinity parameters.

Among the most promising ruthenium anticancer drugs [48], the New Anti-tumor Metastasis Inhibitor (NAMI-A) has been investigated in details to provide a complete mechanistic insight of its activation via aquation by using DFT methods [49] (Fig. 1i). In the study three water molecules were included explicitly to improve the Poisson-Boltzmann (PB) implicit solvation energies and better represent the water assistance to the chloro-aquo ligand exchange. The calculations show that the aquation of the considered Ru(III) octahedral complex passes via a 7-coordinated transition state. The values for the activation free energies of the first and second aquation steps of 24.8 and 30.5 kcal·mol^{-1}, correspond well with the experimental evidence indicating that the first aquation of this complex is kinetically controlled while the second aquation is much slower.

Recently, a DFT study was performed with the aim to disentangle the anomalous stability of a ruthenium complex [Ru$_2$(EB106)$_4$Cl] (Fig. 1j), where EB106 is the antitumor drug (2-phenylindol-3-yl)glyoxyl-L-leucine-L-phenylalanine), which was synthesized in order to conjoin the antitumoral effects of EB106 and the therapeutic capabilities of the ruthenium mixed valence (II, III) core, thus being designed for the transport of diverse cytotoxic agents [50] (Fig. 1k). Surprisingly, [Ru$_2$(EB106)$_4$Cl] displayed a complete absence of reactivity toward protein targets, being utterly non-cytotoxic. The DFT study and the analysis of the solvent-accessible and van der Waals surfaces allowed to conclude that for the paddle-wheel shaped complexes of ruthenium, the selection of ligand is pivotal and its structural features are to be taken into account over the plain availability of the carboxylic group crucial for the attachment to the Ru$_2$(II,III) core. Certainly, the multidrug delivery systems improve their therapeutic properties. However, the ligand structure may exert a pronounced influence on the entire chemical profile, damaging the activation of drug, i.e. the release of ligand and eventually the medicinal effects. This investigation indicates that the chemical properties of the ligand designed for the coordination to the di-rithenium core should be carefully evaluated when a prodrug is conceived. Ideally, the reactivity should not be disrupted by the usage of ligands with a proper steric hindrance. Moreover, it can be concluded that the increase of the ligands occupancy may cause a diminished or even absent reactivity. That is why computational methods are quintessential for the decision on the appropriateness of the selected ligand as they help in the prediction of the bimetallic center reactivity and provide the mechanistic comprehension of its mode of action, which is of utmost importance for considering its therapeutic application. Remarkably, the careful evaluation of this balance has significant benefits in optimization of drug transport to its biomolecular target and of the intended pharmaceutical effects. Additionally, it is possible to accurately modulate the stability of the designed complexes by coordinating them to the Ru$_2$ core, thus circumventing undesirable side-reactivity and ameliorating the medication [50].

5 Metal Cations Targeting Proteins: *golB, pbrR*

It is long known that Au(I) cations display antibacterial properties [51], by displacing essential metals, thus obtruding with the correct metabolism, obstructing the redox equilibrium and damaging the cell membrane, causing the death of cell [52]. This leads several bacterial species to evolve their protein systems controlling the concentration of intracellular gold ion [53]. For example, Au-specific transcriptional regulators of *merR*-type developed by bacteria such as *Cupriavidus metallidurans* and *Salmonella enterica* and spot gold ions and regulate the production of specific resistance factors [54]. One of these proteins, *golB*, possessing an exceptional selectivity for Au(I) ions was studied recently, and the X-ray structures of its apo and Au(I)-bound forms were reported [55], whereas its exceptional affinity toward Au(I) cations was studied computationally [56]. Molecular dynamic simulations allowed the sampling of the conformations of apo protein, which are favorable for the sequestration of Au(I) into the Cys-XX-Cys motif. Subsequently, the assessment of the structural features determining the Au(I) chelation was obtained by the usage of QM/MM calculations on metal-bound structures of golB, and the most probable protonation state for gold binding motif was determined. Consistently with experimental data, it was concluded that the Au(I) affinity of *golB* is regulated by changes of protein conformations, which influence the Cys10–Cys13 distance, thus serving as a molecular switch between the states responsible for the Au(I) sequestration or release in reaction to exterior stimuli. Interestingly it was noted that the structure of protein around the metal binding motif accomodates for the protonation state of Au(I)-*golB* with one cysteine being neutral and the other one deprotonated, consequently augmenting the selectivity for binding of Au(I) over other metal cations [56].

Industrialization increases the contamination of the ecosphere by lead (Pb) which, accretes in the ecosystem and causes the poisoning of food chain [57]. The studies of various mechanisms allowing bacteria to preserving homeostasis in conditions of the lead excess [58] is of utmost importance for the conception of new approaches for the isolation of Pb and its ensuing removal from polluted milieu. A unique protein which grants the resistance toward lead was found in *Cupriavidus metallidurans*, and it is the sole known metalloprotein in nature with a specific selectivity toward Pb(II), which permits the binding of Pb(II) with a thousandfold affinity as compared to other heavy metals [59]. Recently, the X-ray structures of apo and Pb(II)-bound *pbrR*, a Pb-responsive protein responsible of the modulation of the *pbr* operon in bacteria [60] were reported [61], and the binding of the cation Pb(II) at pbrR was studied computationally [62] (Fig. 2b). It was shown that the tris-cysteine motif formed by two helices of two packed *pbrR* monomers yields the conformations liable for the Pb(II) sequestration. Moreover, the most probable protonation state for the lead binding motif was defined by QM/MM computations, and its structural properties responsible for Pb(II) complexation were determined. Additionally, it was demonstrated that the binding affinity for Pb(II) is augmented by the formation of the thiol–thiolate–thiolate protonation state in Pb(II)-*pbrR*, which is prompted by the protein structure around the metal binding motif. Consistently with experimental results, *pbrR* switches on the Pb(II) sequestration/release-prone states, by changing the protonation states of Cys78' and Cys122 aa well as the distance between those residues in response to variation of pH of its environment [62]. Moreover, the coordination of Pb(II) in the metal-binding motif of *pbrR* was investigated by the usage of topological schemes based on cationic dummy atoms and the classical molecular dynamics simulations [63], underlining again the crucial role of a tri-cysteine motif for the emergence of the selectivity toward the Pb(II) cation.

Summary

The extraordinary capability of metals to coordinate with various biomolecular targets presents them as an inestimable supply of active molecules in the field of medicinal chemistry. Due to the availability of the metal center, their properties cannot be facilely imitated by organic molecules, thus resulting in metal-based complexes being a separate class of medicinally applicable compounds with respect to organic drugs. Therefore, the optimization of the strategies of the computational modelling of their interaction with biomolecules is of utmost importance, in order to have the possibility to fine-tune their therapeutic and medicinal properties.

In this short review, we discussed the strategies developed in our group for multilayered modelling of the metallation of biological targets, which, being usually the parts of proteins and DNA, are too computationally expensive to be studied with a single approach due to their sheer size of up to several thousands atoms. That is why the usage of multilayered approaches is essential. The most chemically relevant portion of the system is done at the highest level of theory, thus allowing to study the thermodynamics and kinetics of the processes involved in the metallation of biological targets. On the other hand, the effects of the surrounding areas are taken into account by the use of an empirical force field.

Even with the permanent development of computational resources, the separation of studied systems into the zones treated with an increased accuracy and the greater regions, the effect of which is taken into account with the employment of a less precise yet better scalable methodology, will continue to be the modus opernadi of choice in this field.

References

1. Rosenberg, B., Van Camp, L., Krigas, T.: Inhibition of cell division in escherichia coli by electrolysis products from a platinum electrode. Nature **205**(4972), 698–699 (1965). https://doi.org/10.1038/205698a0
2. Ghosh, S.: Cisplatin: The first metal based anticancer drug. Bioorg. Chem. **88**, 102925 (2019). https://doi.org/10.1016/j.bioorg.2019.102925
3. Jamieson, E.R., Lippard, S.J.: Structure, recognition, and processing of cisplatin−DNA adducts. Chem. Rev. **99**(9), 2467–2498 (1999). https://doi.org/10.1021/cr980421n
4. Zamble, D.B., Mikata, Y., Eng, C.H., Sandman, K.E., Lippard, S.J.: Testis-specific HMG-domain protein alters the responses of cells to cisplatin. J. Inorg. Biochem. **91**(3), 451–462 (2002). https://doi.org/10.1016/S0162-0134(02)00472-5
5. Mjos, K.D., Orvig, C.: Metallodrugs in medicinal inorganic chemistry. Chem. Rev. **114**(8), 4540–4563 (2014). https://doi.org/10.1021/cr400460s
6. Lippert, B.: Impact of cisplatin on the recent development of Pt coordination chemistry: a case study. Coord. Chem. Rev. **182**(1), 263–295 (1999). https://doi.org/10.1016/S0010-8545(98)00192-1
7. Paciotti, R., Tolbatov, I., Graziani, V., Marrone, A., Re, N., Coletti, C.: Insights on the activity of platinum-based anticancer complexes through computational methods. In: AIP Conference Proceedings, vol. 2040, p. 020019:1–4. AIP Publishing LLC (2018). doi: https://doi.org/10.1063/1.5079061

8. Paciotti, R., Tolbatov, I., Marrone, A., Storchi, L., Re, N., Coletti, C.: Computational investigations of bioinorganic complexes: The case of calcium, gold and platinum ions. In: AIP Conference Proceedings, vol. 2186, issue 1, p. 030011:1–4. AIP Publishing LLC (2019). doi: https://doi.org/10.1063/1.5137922

9. De Petris, A., et al.: Vibrational signatures of the naked aqua complexes from platinum(II) anticancer drugs. J. Phys. Chem. Lett. **4**, 3631–3635 (2013). https://doi.org/10.1021/jz4 01959s

10. Corinti, D., et al.: Hydrolysis of cis- and transplatin: structure and reactivity of the aqua complexes in a solvent free environment. RSC Adv. **7**, 15877–15884 (2017). https://doi.org/ 10.1039/C7RA01182B

11. Cuevas-Flores, M.D.R., Garcia-Revilla, M.A., Bartolomei, M.: Noncovalent interactions between cisplatin and graphene prototypes. J. Comp. Chem. **39**, 71–80 (2018). https://doi. org/10.1002/jcc.24920

12. Cuevas-Flores, M.R., Bartolomei, M., García-Revilla, M.A., Coletti, C.: Interaction and reactivity of cisplatin physisorbed on graphene oxide nano-prototypes. Nanomaterials **10**, 1074 (2020). https://doi.org/10.3390/nano10061074

13. Messori, L., Marzo, T., Gabbiani, C., Valdes, A.A., Quiroga, A.G., Merlino, A.: Peculiar features in the crystal structure of the adduct formed between cis-PtI2(NH3)2 and hen egg white lysozyme. Inorg. Chem. **52**(24), 13827–13829 (2013). https://doi.org/10.1021/ic402611m

14. Tolbatov, I., et al.: Reactions of cisplatin and cis-[PtI2(NH3)2] with molecular models of relevant protein sidechains: a comparative analysis. J. Inorg. Biochem. **209**, 111096 (2020). https://doi.org/10.1016/j.jinorgbio.2020.111096

15. Parro, T., et al.: The second generation of iodido complexes: trans-[PtI2(amine)(amine′)] bearing different aliphatic amines. J. Inorg. Biochem. **127**, 182–187 (2013). https://doi.org/ 10.1016/j.jinorgbio.2013.04.010

16. Paciotti, R., et al.: Cisplatin and transplatin interaction with methionine: bonding motifs assayed by vibrational spectroscopy in the isolated ionic complexes. Phys. Chem. Chem. Phys. **19**, 26697–26707 (2017). https://doi.org/10.1039/C7CP05203K

17. Corinti, D., et al.: Cisplatin primary complex with l-histidine target revealed by IR multiple photon dissociation (IRMPD) spectroscopy. ChemPhysChem **18**, 318–325 (2017). https:// doi.org/10.1002/cphc.201601172

18. Tomassoli, I., Gündisch, D.: Bispidine as a privileged scaffold. Curr. Top. Med. Chem. **16**(11), 1314–1342 (2016)

19. Graziani, V., Coletti, C., Marrone, A., Re, N.: Activation and reactivity of a bispidine analogue of cisplatin: A theoretical investigation. J. Phys. Chem. A **120**(27), 5175–5186 (2016). https:// doi.org/10.1021/acs.jpca.6b00844

20. Cui, H., Goddard, R., Pörschke, K.R., Hamacher, A., Kassack, M.U.: Bispidine analogues of cisplatin, carboplatin, and oxaliplatin. Synthesis, structures, and cytotoxicity. Inorg. Chem. **53**(7), 3371–3384 (2014). doi: https://doi.org/10.1021/ic402737f

21. Ho, G.Y., Woodward, N., Coward, J.I.: Cisplatin versus carboplatin: comparative review of therapeutic management in solid malignancies. Crit. Rev. Oncol. Hematol. **102**, 37–46 (2016). https://doi.org/10.1016/j.critrevonc.2016.03.014

22. Boulikas, T., Vougiouka, M.: Cisplatin and platinum drugs at the molecular level. Oncol. Rep. **10**(6), 1663–1682 (2003). https://doi.org/10.3892/or.10.6.1663

23. Ciancetta, A., Coletti, C., Marrone, A., Re, N.: Activation of carboplatin by chloride ions: a theoretical investigation. Theor. Chem. Acc. **129**(6), 757–769 (2011). https://doi.org/10. 1007/s00214-011-0933-9

24. Ciancetta, A., Coletti, C., Marrone, A., Re, N.: Activation of carboplatin by carbonate: a theoretical investigation. Dalton Trans. **41**(41), 12960–12969 (2012). https://doi.org/10.1039/ C2DT30556A

25. Di Pasqua, A.J., Goodisman, J., Dabrowiak, J.C.: Understanding how the platinum anticancer drug carboplatin works: from the bottle to the cell. Inorganica Chim. Acta **389**, 29–35 (2012). https://doi.org/10.1016/j.ica.2012.01.028

26. Aldossary, S.A.: Review on pharmacology of cisplatin: clinical use, toxicity and mechanism of resistance of cisplatin. Biomed. Pharmacol. J. **12**(1), 7–15 (2019). https://doi.org/10.13005/bpj/1608

27. Yimit, A., Adebali, O., Sancar, A., Jiang, Y.: Differential damage and repair of DNA-adducts induced by anti-cancer drug cisplatin across mouse organs. Nature Comm. **10**(1), 1–11 (2019). https://doi.org/10.1038/s41467-019-08290-2

28. Wexselblatt, E., Gibson, D.: What do we know about the reduction of Pt (IV) pro-drugs? J. Inorg. Biochem. **117**, 220–229 (2012). https://doi.org/10.1016/j.jinorgbio.2012.06.013

29. Tolbatov, I., Coletti, C., Marrone, A., Re, N.: Insight into the electrochemical reduction mechanism of Pt (IV) anticancer complexes. Inorg. Chem. **57**(6), 3411–3419 (2018). https://doi.org/10.1021/acs.inorgchem.8b00177

30. Schmidt, C., et al.: A gold (I) biscarbene complex with improved activity as a TrxR inhibitor and cytotoxic drug: comparative studies with different gold metallodrugs. Metallomics **11**(3), 533–545 (2019). https://doi.org/10.1039/c8mt00306h

31. Liu, W., Gust, R.: Metal N-heterocyclic carbene complexes as potential antitumor metallo-drugs. Chem. Soc. Rev. **42**(2), 755–773 (2013). https://doi.org/10.1039/C2CS35314H

32. Graham, G.G., Champion, G.D., Ziegler, J.B.: The cellular metabolism and effects of gold complexes. Met. Based Drugs **1**(5–6), 395–404 (1994)

33. Tolbatov, I., Coletti, C., Marrone, A., Re, N.: Reactivity of gold (I) monocarbene complexes with protein targets: a theoretical study. Int. J. Mol. Sci. **20**(4), 820 (2019). https://doi.org/10.3390/ijms20040820

34. Pratesi, A., et al.: Insights on the mechanism of thioredoxin reductase inhibition by gold N-heterocyclic carbene compounds using the synthetic linear selenocysteine containing C-terminal peptide hTrxR (488–499): an ESI-MS investigation. J. Inorg. Biochem. **136**, 161–169 (2014). https://doi.org/10.1016/j.jinorgbio.2014.01.009

35. Tolbatov, I., Coletti, C., Marrone, A., Re, N.: Insight into the substitution mechanism of antitumor Au (I) N-heterocyclic carbene complexes by cysteine and selenocysteine. Inorg. Chem. **59**(5), 3312–3320 (2020). https://doi.org/10.1021/acs.inorgchem.0c00106

36. Hickey, J.L., Ruhayel, R.A., Barnard, P.J., Baker, M.V., Berners-Price, S.J., Filipovska, A.: Mitochondria-targeted chemotherapeutics: the rational design of gold (I) N-heterocyclic car-bene complexes that are selectively toxic to cancer cells and target protein selenols in prefer-ence to thiols. J. Am. Chem. Soc. **130**(38), 12570–12571 (2008). https://doi.org/10.1021/ja804027j

37. Zhang, X., et al.: Repurposing of auranofin: thioredoxin reductase remains a primary target of the drug. Biochimie **162**, 46–54 (2019). https://doi.org/10.1016/j.biochi.2019.03.015

38. Madeira, J.M., Gibson, D.L., Kean, W.F., Klegeris, A.: The biological activity of auranofin: implications for novel treatment of diseases. Inflammopharmacology **20**(6), 297–306 (2012). https://doi.org/10.1007/s10787-012-0149-1

39. Marzo, T., et al.: Replacement of the thiosugar of auranofin with iodide enhances the anticancer potency in a mouse model of ovarian cancer. ACS Med. Chem. Lett. **10**(4), 656–660 (2019). https://doi.org/10.1021/acsmedchemlett.9b00007

40. Tolbatov, I., et al.: Mechanistic insights into the anticancer properties of the auranofin analog Au(PEt3)I: a theoretical and experimental study. Front. Chem. **8**, 812 (2020). https://doi.org/10.3389/fchem.2020.00812

41. Casini, A., et al.: Chemistry, antiproliferative properties, tumor selectivity, and molecular mechanisms of novel gold(III) compounds for cancer treatment: a systematic study. J. Biol. Inorg. Chem. **14**, 1139–1149 (2009). https://doi.org/10.1007/s00775-009-0558-9

42. Hara-Chikuma, M., Verkman, A.S.: Prevention of skin tumorigenesis and impairment of epidermal cell proliferation by targeted aquaporin-3 gene disruption. Mol. Cell Biol. **28**, 326–332 (2008). https://doi.org/10.1128/MCB.01482-07

43. Graziani, V., Marrone, A., Re, N., Coletti, C., Platts, J.A., Casini, A.: A multilevel theoretical study to disclose the binding mechanisms of gold (III) bipyridyl compounds as selective aquaglyceroporin inhibitors. Chem. Eur. J. **23**(55), 13802–13813 (2017). https://doi.org/10.1002/chem.201703092

44. Wenzel, M.N., et al.: Insights into the mechanisms of aquaporin-3 inhibition by gold (III) complexes: the importance of non-coordinative adduct formation. Inorg. Chem. **58**(3), 2140–2148 (2019). https://doi.org/10.1021/acs.inorgchem.8b03233

45. Clarke, M.J.: Ruthenium metallopharmaceuticals. Coord. Chem. Rev. **232**, 69–93 (2002). https://doi.org/10.1016/S0010-8545(02)00025-5

46. Ang, W.H., Dyson, P.J.: Classical and non-classical ruthenium-based anticancer drugs: towards targeted chemotherapy. Eur. J. Inorg. Chem. 4003–4018 (2006). doi: https://doi.org/10.1002/ejic.200600723

47. Bešker, N., Coletti, C., Marrone, A., Re, N.: Binding of antitumor ruthenium complexes to DNA and proteins: a theoretical approach. J. Phys. Chem. B **111**(33), 9955–9964 (2007). https://doi.org/10.1021/jp072182q

48. Kostova, I.: Ruthenium complexes as anticancer agents. Curr. Med. Chem. **13**(9), 1085–1107 (2006). https://doi.org/10.2174/092986706776360941

49. Bešker, N., Coletti, C., Marrone, A., Re, N.: Aquation of the ruthenium-based anticancer drug NAMI-A: a density functional study. J. Phys. Chem. B **112**(13), 3871–3875 (2008). https://doi.org/10.1021/jp800411g

50. Barresi, E., et al.: A mixed-valence diruthenium (II, III) complex endowed with high stability: from experimental evidence to theoretical interpretation. Dalton Trans. **49**(41), 14520–14527 (2020). https://doi.org/10.1039/D0DT02527E

51. Benedek, T.G.: The history of gold therapy for tuberculosis. J. Hist. Med. Allied Sci. **59**(1), 50–89 (2004). https://doi.org/10.1093/jhmas/jrg042

52. Berners-Price, S.J., Filipovska, A.: Gold compounds as therapeutic agents for human diseases. Metallomics **3**(9), 863–873 (2011). https://doi.org/10.1039/c1mt00062d

53. Checa, S.K., Espariz, M., Audero, M.E.P., Botta, P.E., Spinelli, S.V., Soncini, F.C.: Bacterial sensing of and resistance to gold salts. Mol. Microbiol. **63**(5), 1307–1318 (2007). https://doi.org/10.1111/j.1365-2958.2007.05590.x

54. Checa, S.K., Soncini, F.C.: Bacterial gold sensing and resistance. Biometals **24**(3), 419–427 (2011). https://doi.org/10.1007/s10534-010-9393-2

55. Wei, W., et al.: Structural insights and the surprisingly low mechanical stability of the Au–S bond in the gold-specific protein GolB. J. Am. Chem. Soc. **137**(49), 15358–15361 (2015). https://doi.org/10.1021/jacs.5b09895

56. Tolbatov, I., Re, N., Coletti, C., Marrone, A.: An insight on the gold (I) affinity of golB protein via multilevel computational approaches. Inorg. Chem. **58**(16), 11091–11099 (2019). https://doi.org/10.1021/acs.inorgchem.9b01604

57. Tong, S., Schirnding, Y.E.V., Prapamontol, T.: Environmental lead exposure: a public health problem of global dimensions. Bull. World Health Org. **78**, 1068–1077 (2000)

58. Roane, T.M.: Lead resistance in two bacterial isolates from heavy metal–contaminated soils. Microb. Ecol. **37**(3), 218–224 (1999). https://doi.org/10.1007/s002489900145

59. Tolbert, A.E., et al.: Heteromeric three-stranded coiled coils designed using a Pb (II)(Cys)3 template mediated strategy. Nature Chem. **12**(4), 405–411 (2020). https://doi.org/10.1038/s41557-020-0423-6

60. Borremans, B., Hobman, J.L., Provoost, A., Brown, N.L., van der Lelie, D.: Cloning and functional analysis of the pbr lead resistance determinant of Ralstonia metallidurans CH34. J. Bacteriol. **183**(19), 5651–5658 (2001). https://doi.org/10.1128/JB.183.19.5651-5658.2001

61. Huang, S., et al.: Structural basis for the selective Pb (II) recognition of metalloregulatory protein PbrR691. Inorg. Chem. **55**(24), 12516–12519 (2016). https://doi.org/10.1021/acs.ino rgchem.6b02397
62. Tolbatov, I., Re, N., Coletti, C., Marrone, A.: Determinants of the Lead (II) affinity in pbrR protein: a computational study. Inorg. Chem. **59**(1), 790–800 (2019). https://doi.org/10.1021/ acs.inorgchem.9b03059
63. Tolbatov, I., Marrone, A.: Molecular dynamics simulation of the Pb(II) coordination in biological media via cationic dummy atom models. Theoret. Chem. Acc. **140**(2), 1–12 (2021). https://doi.org/10.1007/s00214-021-02718-z

Long-Range Complex in the HC_3N + CN Potential Energy Surface: Ab Initio Calculations and Intermolecular Potential

Emília Valença Ferreira de Aragão[1,2]($\boxtimes$) (iD), Luca Mancini[2] (iD),
Noelia Faginas-Lago[2] (iD), Marzio Rosi[3] (iD), Nadia Balucani[2] (iD),
and Fernando Pirani[2] (iD)

[1] Master-tec srl, Via Sicilia 41, 06128 Perugia, Italy
emilia.dearagao@master-tec.it
[2] Dipartimento di Chimica, Biologia e Biotecnologie,
Università degli Studi di Perugia, 06123 Perugia, Italy
{emilia.dearagao,luca.mancini2}@studenti.unipg.it,
{noelia.faginaslago,nadia.balucani,fernando.pirani}@unipg.it
[3] Dipartimento di Ingegneria Civile ed Ambientale,
Università degli Studi di Perugia, 06125 Perugia, Italy
marzio.rosi@unipg.it

Abstract. In this work we characterize an initial van der Waals adduct in the potential energy surface of reaction between cyanoacetylene HC_3N and the cyano radical. The geometry of the CN-HC_3N adduct has been optimized through calculations employing ab initio methods. Results show that the energy of the adduct lays below the reactants. Additionally, a saddle point that connects the adduct to an important intermediate of the PES has been localized, with energy below the reactants. Calculations of the intermolecular potential have been performed and results show that the energy of the van der Waals adduct is higher than estimated with the ab initio methods.

Keywords: Astrochemistry · Interstellar medium · Titan atmosphere · Ab initio calculations · Empirical potential energy surface · Improved Lennard-Jones

1 Introduction

To this date, more than 200 molecular species have been detected in the interstellar medium (ISM) [1]. Among the first observed organic molecules is HC_3N, or cyanoacetylene, identified in the early 1970's by Turner [2] towards the galactic radio source SgrB2. In the same decade, new observations have been reported: in 1976 [3] cyanoacetylene has been detected in 17 galactic sources, including dark clouds and a molecular envelope around a carbon star, while later in 1979 Walmsley reported the detection of HC_3N in TMC2 [4]. Later, the detection of HC_5N, HC_7N, HC_9N and $HC_{11}N$ has also been reported [5,6]. These molecules share

© Springer Nature Switzerland AG 2021
O. Gervasi et al. (Eds.): ICCSA 2021, LNCS 12958, pp. 413–425, 2021.
https://doi.org/10.1007/978-3-030-87016-4_31

the same characteristics: they are linear, with alternating carbon-carbon single and triple bonds and have a cyano group. As a whole, this group of molecules is addressed as cyanopolyynes and the members of this group have been detected in a number of environments in the interstellar medium: hot cores, star forming regions, cold clouds and even solar-type protostars [7–11]. In addition, HC_3N has also been detected in low-mass protostars [12], protoplanetary disks [13] and on Titan's atmosphere [14].

It is currently accepted that the synthesis of cyanopolyynes in the ISM is a result of successive chain-elongation reactions involving cyanoacetylene and C_2H radical [15]. However, when cyanoacetylene collides with a CN radical, the reaction might lead to the formation of dicyanoacetylene (NCCCCN). This prevents elongation reactions from occurring, therefore the reaction with cyano radical is considered as a chain-termination reaction. Knowing how effective this reaction is and how fast it proceeds is important to estimate the distribution of nitrogen in the interstellar medium. Yet, the product of the reaction, dicyanoacetylene, is not detectable in the ISM due to the lack of permanent electric dipole moment. Therefore, we need to estimate the rate of formation of this molecule through experiments and using computational tools.

A previous study by Petrie and Osamura [16] reports the results of their investigation on the $HNC + C_3N$ potential energy surface (PES), which share some points in common with the $HC_3N + CN$ PES. At that time they had optimized the geometries at B3LYP/6-311G** level and computed single-point energies at CCSD(T)/aug-cc-pVDZ level. They have reported a channel where, from $HNC + C_3N$, the system has to overcome an energy barrier to form a linear van der Waals adduct, before dissociating into HC_3N and CN. In addition, another channel shows the formation of NCCCCN from HC_3N and CN, but no van der Waals adduct has been reported for this channel. In this work, we report a connection between the linear van der Waals and the intermediate of the channel that forms dicyanoacetylene.

In relation to the kinetics of this reaction, an experimental value and a theoretical estimate of the rate coefficient have been reported by Cheikh et al. [15]. In particular, the theoretical estimate was performed employing a two transition-state model, which implies the formation of a van der Waals adduct. We initially thought that the linear van der Waals adduct could be involved in the estimate of the rate coefficient. However, as it will be shown, another approach between the fragments must be considered. As it will be discussed, the ab initio approach allows us to locate only one of the van der Waals complexes, while the evaluation of the intermolecular potential shows the possibility of more. In particular, the Improved Lennard-Jones (ILJ) [17] function will allow a better description of the long-range interaction within the intermolecular potential. A correct estimation of the weak intermolecular interactions is a key point for an accurate estimate of a reaction rate constant. The ILJ potential can be considered as a refinement of the classical Lennard-Jones potential, which represents the potential as a function of the distance between the two interacting fragments. In particular the ILJ function gives a better reproduction of both the long-range attraction and the short-range repulsion with a simple formulation.

In the present work we investigate the initial approach of the cyanoacetylene and cyano radical at two specific angles. We try to understand how the most stable intermediate of the potential energy surface is formed. We employ two different theoretical methods to identify the formation of a van der Waals adduct. Identifying this type of structure is important for the estimation of the rate constant.

2 Methods

In this section we present two approaches we have employed in this work: the ab initio methods and the semi-empirical method.

2.1 Ab Initio Calculations

The open-shell system HC$_3$N-CN has been investigated following a well established computational strategy [18–24]. Such strategy consists in performing electronic structure calculations for the reactants, intermediates and saddle point on the doublet potential energy surface (PES). Geometry optimizations and harmonic vibrational frequency analysis have been carried out employing density functional theory (DFT), with the Becke-3-parameter exchange and Lee-Yang-Parr correlation (B3LYP) [25,26]. Harmonic frequency analysis serves to estimate the zero-point energy correction and to confirm if an optimized structure is a stationary point. In that case, an optimized geometry is assigned as a minimum if all the frequencies are real and as a saddle point if one single frequency is imaginary. For saddle points, Intrinsic Reaction Coordinate (IRC) calculations [27,28] have also been performed. Frequency analysis was followed by a single-point calculation performed employing coupled-cluster, including single and double excitations as well as perturbative estimate of connected triples (CCSD(T)) [29–31]. The resulting computed energy is combined with the zero-point correction from the frequency calculation to correct it to 0 K. Both B3LYP and CCSD(T) methods have been used along with the correlation consistent valence polarized basis set aug-cc-pVTZ [32]. All electronic structure calculations were performed using the Gaussian09 software [33]. Data on the geometry was collected using the open-source software Avogadro [34].

2.2 Intermolecular Potential

In addition to the ab initio calculations, a semi-empirical study has been done on the evolution of the intermolecular interaction energy as the two reactants approach each other in a specific angle. In the adopted approach, each interacting partner is assumed to be composed of *effective* atoms distributed on the

Table 1. Parameters for the non-electrostatic potential.

Interacting pair	r_m (Å)	ε (meV)
C-C$_{Rad}$	3.80	6.16
N-C$_{Rad}$	3.73	6.07
H-C$_{Rad}$	3.54	2.43
C-N$_{Rad}$	3.71	5.95
N-N$_{Rad}$	3.63	6.07
H-N$_{Rad}$	3.41	2.55

molecular frame. Accordingly, the total intermolecular potential V_{total} has been defined as combination of a non-electrostatic and an electrostatic component:

$$V_{total} = V_{non-elect} + V_{elect} \tag{1}$$

Moreover, each component has been represented as additivity of different atom-atom interaction pair contributions. In particular, each non-electrostatic atom-atom contribution has been provided by the ILJ function, formulated as

$$V_{ILJ}(r) = \varepsilon \left[\frac{m}{n(r) - m} \left(\frac{r_m}{r} \right)^{n(r)} - \frac{n(r)}{n(r) - m} \left(\frac{r_m}{r} \right)^{m} \right] \tag{2}$$

where ε is the depth of the potential well, r_m is its position and r is the atom-atom distance. The parameter $n(r)$ was firstly introduced in a 2004 paper by Pirani et al. [35] as a modification of the Maitland-Smith correction to the Lennard-Jones model [36]. According to the authors, m assumes the value of 6 for neutral-neutral systems, 4 for ion-induced dipole, 2 for ion-permanent dipole, and 1 for ion-ion cases.

Equation 2 is composed by a repulsive term and a term that represents the long-range attraction, both expressed in function of r. To modulate the decline of the repulsion and the strength of the attraction, $n(r)$ takes the following form:

$$n(r) = \beta + 4.0 \left(\frac{r}{r_m} \right)^2 \tag{3}$$

where β is a parameter attributed to the nature and the hardness of the interacting particles. [35,37–39]. In the current system, the value assigned to β is 7. The values for ε and r_m parameters, specific to each atom-atom pair, are reported in Table 1. They have been obtained exploiting the *effective* polarizability of various interacting atoms, whose combinations are consistent with the average polarizability of two molecular partners.   Within the same approach, the electrostatic component V_{elect} is expressed as

$$V_{elect}(r) = \frac{1}{4\pi\varepsilon_0} \sum_{i=1}^{5} \sum_{j=1}^{2} \frac{q_i q_j}{r_{ij}} \tag{4}$$

Table 2. Parameters for the electrostatic potential. The Mulliken partial charges were extracted from the CCSD(T)/aug-cc-pVTZ single-point calculations of the separated reactants.

Atom	Mulliken partial charges (a.u.)
C$_1$	−1.720
C$_2$	1.762
C$_3$	0.088
N	−0.583
H	0.453
C$_{Rad}$	0.152
N$_{Rad}$	−0.152

where ε_0 is the vacuum permittivity, q_i corresponds to the partial charge on an atom of the cyanoacetylene molecule, q_j is the partial charge on an atom of the cyano radical and r_{ij} is the distance between the two atoms involved. In this work, the electrostatic contribution has been computed with charge values extracted from the CCSD(T)/aug-cc-pVTZ single-point calculations of the separated reactants. Those values are reported on Table 2.

3   Results

In this section we present the results of the ab initio calculations and show how the intermolecular potential can provide additional insight into the formation of the van der Waals complex.

3.1   Ab Initio Calculations

The data obtained from electronic structure calculations with the ab initio method shows the formation of a long-range complex as the first step of the reaction between cyanoacetylene and cyano radical. Figure 1 reports a potential energy surface depicting the formation of a bonded intermediate, with energy values relative to the reactants. Four points of the PES were characterized: reactants, a van der Waals complex (MIN1), a saddle point (TS1) and the bonded intermediate (MIN2). The process starts with a barrierless formation of the van der Waals complex MIN1. The system must then overcome a barrier through TS1 to form the bonded intermediate MIN2, in which we can notice the formation of a chemical bond between carbon atoms. This process is exothermic at CCSD(T)/aug-cc-pVTZ level of calculation considering geometries optimized at B3LYP/aug-cc-pVTZ level.

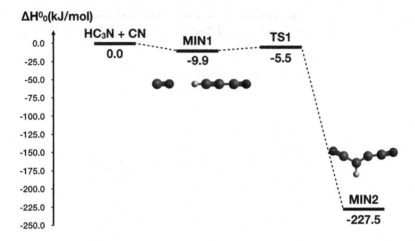

Fig. 1. Potential energy surface of the cyanoacetylene (HC_3N) and cyano radical (CN) reaction. Energies computed at CCSD(T)/aug-cc-pVTZ level with zero-point corrections at B3LYP/aug-cc-pVTZ.

Figure 2 depicts the geometry of the reactants, the van der Waals complex (MIN1), the saddle point (TS1) and the bonded intermediate (MIN2) with labeled atoms, distances in angstroms and angles in degrees. The structure of MIN1 shows the interaction between the hydrogen atom of cyanoacetylene and the nitrogen atom of the radical. As it can be observed, the formation of the complex does not promote significant changes in the bond distances. On the other hand, the transition state TS1 shows a very different geometry: the CN fragment appears to rotate in order to form the carbon-carbon bond between C_1 and C_{Rad}. At last, MIN2 shows the formed carbon-carbon bond and a loss of linearity between the atoms from cyanoacetylene.

3.2   Intermolecular Potential

As it has been discussed in the methods section, the intermolecular potential expression can be decomposed into repulsion and attraction contribution terms. In this section we compare the evolution of the intermolecular potential with variational calculations performed with the ab initio methods when the two reactants approach each other.

In Fig. 3 are displayed the curves of the intermolecular potential, in blue, and of the variational calculation, in black. In the x-axis we chose to represent the distance between carbons C_1 and C_{Rad} since it is the most relevant distance involved in the formation of intermediate MIN2. The curve of the intermolecular potential was built by taking the separate geometries of the reactants and approaching them in a linear way to form MIN1. In every point of the curve, the atom-atom pair distances were calculated and were employed to estimate the non-electrostatic and the electrostatic potential energies using the parameters in tables 1 and 2 respectively. The sum of both terms results in a total

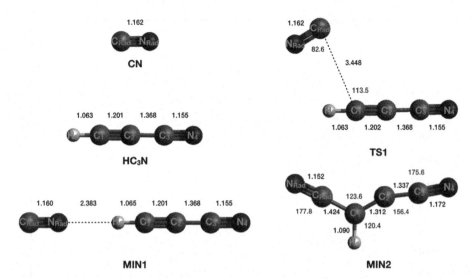

Fig. 2. Structural details of the model representation of cyanoacetylene (HC$_3$N), cyano radical (CN), the van der Waals complex (MIN1), the saddle point (TS1) and the bonded intermediate (MIN2) geometries optimized at the B3LYP/aug-cc-pVTZ level. Bond lengths (black) are shown in Å, while bond angles (blue) are displayed in degrees. Carbon atoms are represented in grey, nitrogen atoms in blue and hydrogen atoms in white. (Color figure online)

intermolecular energy in meV, then converted into kJ/mol after multiplying it by a factor of 0.096487. The variational curve is the result of optimization calculations performed at B3LYP/aug-cc-pVTZ level for fixed C$_1$-C$_{Rad}$ distances using the keyword "Modredundant" in the G09 code. The energies reported in the graph were obtained at CCSD(T)/aug-cc-pVTZ level and were not corrected at 0K. Here, the energy of the separated reactants is set to zero and all other energies are relative to this energy.

Three aspects of this graph must be discussed. First, at long range, the values of the ab initio calculations are underestimated in relation to the ones coming from the semi-empirical method. For instance, at 10 Å we observe the values of V = -0.6 kJ/mol for ab initio and V = -0.004 kJ/mol for the interatomic potential. The long-range interaction seems to be better described by the intermolecular potential. Second, the wells in both curves are located at different distances and have different depths. For the intermolecular potential, the point of the lowest energy value was located at 5.3 Å and had a corresponding V = -1.123 kJ/mol. For the curve of the variational calculation, the geometry with the lowest energy was close to the MIN1 geometry, or at $d_{C_1-C_{Rad}}$ = 4.5 Å and V = -12.03 kJ/mol. If we take the geometry of MIN1 and compute it with the intermolecular potential (red dot on the blue curve), the corresponding energy value is +3.88 kJ/mol. This means that relative to the intermolecular potential, the ab initio calculation seems to be underestimating the effects of the repulsion.

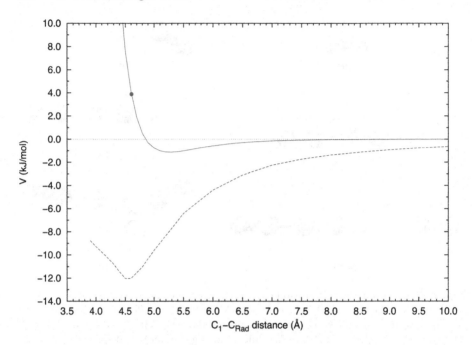

Fig. 3. Curve of the intermolecular potential(blue,full line) and curve of the variational calculation (black, dashed) corresponding to the linear approach between fragments. Energies of the variational curve were computed at CCSD(T)/aug-cc-pVTZ//B3LYP/aug-cc-pVTZ level level. The intermolecular energy of the van der Waals complex MIN1 is also represented (red dot). (Color figure online)

At last, in the intermolecular potential curve, the energy grows exponentially for distances shorter than 4.9 Å, due to the repulsion. In the variational calculation, for distances shorter than 4.4 Å we notice a change in the fragments approach. The fragments start to rotate in order to form the MIN2, and most points in this part of the curve show a geometry closer to TS1.

Previous work by some of the authors of this paper [40] showed that the inclusion of the D3 empirical correction to dispersion in the calculations had no impact on the geometries of the stationary points of this system. By extension, the energies computed at CCSD(T)/aug-cc-pVTZ level were similar. Therefore, variational calculations with geometries optimized either at B3LYP/aug-cc-pVTZ or at B3LYP-D3/aug-cc-pVTZ level would have similar results.

Figure 4, following the same scheme as Fig. 3, corresponds to an attack of 90° degrees between fragments. Unlike the linear approach, the corresponding van der Waals adduct could not be located through calculations employing ab initio methods. Attempts to find this geometry usually ended with the formation of MIN2. However, the curve corresponding to the variational approach shows the

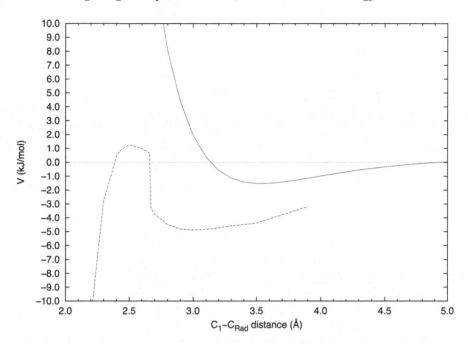

Fig. 4. Curve of the intermolecular potential (blue, full line) and curve of the variational calculation (black, dashed) corresponding to the orthogonal approach between fragments. Energies of the variational curve were computed at CCSD(T)/aug-cc-pVTZ//B3LYP/aug-cc-pVTZ level. (Color figure online)

formation of a minimum around 3.0 Å. In a similar manner, the intermolecular potential curve shows the existence of a minimum around 3.5 Å, with V = −1.52 kJ/mol. At shorter distances, around 2.5 Å, the variational curve shows the presence of a transition state, which also could not be located with ab initio calculations. The subsequent decrease in energy corresponds to the formation of the MIN2. The intermolecular curve shows only an increase in energy since, contrary to the variational calculations, the reactants geometries are frozen.

In Fig. 5, a linear interpolation between the curves from Fig. 4 was made considering values from 2.40 to 2.66 Å of the variational curve and values from 3.3 and 5.2 Å of the intermolecular potential curve. The resulting graph represents the formation of the van der Waals adduct from an attack at 90° degrees and the presence of a barrier that must be overcome to form MIN2.

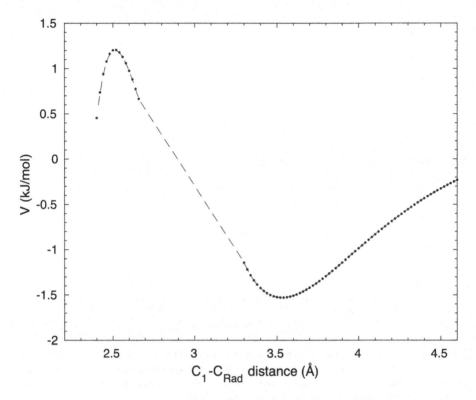

Fig. 5. Linear interpolation (red,dashed) between the curve of the intermolecular potential and curve of the variational calculation corresponding to the orthogonal approach between fragments. The points of the original curves are represented as blue dots. (Color figure online)

4   Conclusions

Though a linear van der Waals adduct has been optimized through ab initio calculations, we cannot conclude with ab initio method alone that this corresponds to the path of formation of the most stable intermediate i.e. MIN2. The approach of the two fragments at an angle of 90° degrees was taken into consideration. The calculations performed employing the semi-empirical method showed that another van der Waals structure can be localised at 3.5 Å. Variational calculations, which employed ab initio methods, shows the presence of a barrier around 2.5 Å. These results characterise better the formation of MIN2.

Acknowledgements. This project has received funding from the European Union's Horizon 2020 research and innovation programme under the Marie Skłodowska Curie grant agreement No 811312 for the project "Astro-Chemical Origins" (ACO). E. V. F. A and N. F.-L. thanks the Herla Project (http://hscw.herla.unipg.it) - Università degli Studi di Perugia for allocated computing time. The authors thank the Dipartimento di Ingegneria Civile e Ambientale of the University of Perugia for allocated computing time within the project "Dipartimenti di Eccellenza 2018-2022". N. F.-L thanks MIUR and the University of Perugia for the financial support of the AMIS project through the "Dipartimenti di Eccellenza" programme. N. F.-L also acknowledges the Fondo Ricerca di Base 2020 (RICBASE2020FAGINAS) del Dipartimento di Chimica, Biologia e Biotecnologie della Università di Perugia for financial support. We thank J. Vekeman, I. García Cuesta and A. Sánchez de Merás for provinding the codes to carry out the fittings. The authors thank S. Meniconi and C. Capponi of the University of Perugia for assistance with the MATLAB code.

References

1. McGuire, B.A.: 2018 census of interstellar, circumstellar, extragalactic, protoplanetary disk, and exoplanetary molecules. Astrophys. J. Suppl. Ser. **239**(2), 17 (2018)
2. Turner, B.E.: Detection of interstellar cyanoacetylene. Astrophys. J. **163**, L35–L39 (1971)
3. Morris, M., Turner, B., Palmer, P., Zuckerman, B.: Cyanoacetylene in dense interstellar clouds. Astrophys. J. **205**, 82–93 (1976)
4. Walmsley, C.M., Winnewisser, G., Toelle, F.: Cyanoacetylene and cyanodiacetylene in interstellar clouds. Astron. Astrophys. **81**, 245–250 (1980)
5. Broten, N.W., Oka, T., Avery, L.W., MacLeod, J.M., Kroto, H.W.: The detection of HC$_9$N in interstellar space. Astrophys. J. **223**, L105–L107 (1978). https://doi.org/10.1086/182739
6. Bell, M., Feldman, P., Travers, M., McCarthy, M., Gottlieb, C., Thaddeus, P.: Detection of HC$_{11}$N in the cold dust cloud TMC-1. Astrophys. J. Lett. **483**(1), L61–L64 (1997)
7. Wyrowski, F., Schilke, P., Walmsley, C.: Vibrationally excited HC$_3$N toward hot cores. Astron. Astrophys. **341**, 882–895 (1999)
8. Takano, S., et al.: Observations of ^{13}C isotopomers of HC$_3$N and HC$_5$N in TMC-1: evidence for isotopic fractionation. Astron. Astrophy. **329**, 1156–1169 (1998)
9. Mendoza, E., et al.: A search for cyanopolyynes in L1157–B1. Mon. Not. R. Astron. Soc. **475**(4), 5501–5512 (2018)
10. Taniguchi, K., Saito, M., Sridharan, T., Minamidani, T.: Survey observations to study chemical evolution from high-mass starless cores to high-mass protostellar objects I: HC$_3$N and HC$_5$N. Astrophys. J. **854**(2), 133 (2018)
11. Jaber Al-Edhari, A., et al.: History of the solar-type protostar IRAS 16293–2422 as told by the cyanopolyynes. A&A **597**, A40 (2017). https://doi.org/10.1051/0004-6361/201629506
12. Bergner, J.B., Öberg, K.I., Garrod, R.T., Graninger, D.M.: Complex organic molecules toward embedded low-mass protostars. Astrophys. J. **841**(2), 120 (2017)
13. Bergner, J.B., Guzmán, V.G., Öberg, K.I., Loomis, R.A., Pegues, J.: A survey of ch3cn and hc3n in protoplanetary disks. Astrophys. J. **857**(1), 69 (2018)
14. Kunde, V., Aikin, A., Hanel, R., Jennings, D., Maguire, W., Samuelson, R.: C$_4$H$_2$, HC$_3$N and CH$_2$NH$_2$ in Titan's atmosphere. Nature **292**(5825), 686–688 (1981)
15. Cheikh Sid Ely, S., Morales, S.B., Guillemin, J.C., Klippenstein, S.J., Sims, I.R.: Low temperature rate coefficients for the reaction CN + HC$_3$N. J. Phys. Chem. A **117**(46), 12155–12164 (2013). https://doi.org/10.1021/jp406842q
16. Petrie, S., Osamura, Y.: NCCN and NCCCCN formation in titan's atmosphere: 2. HNC as a viable precursor. J. Phys. Chem. A **108**(16), 3623–3631 (2004)

17. Pirani, F., Brizi, S., Roncaratti, L.F., Casavecchia, P., Cappelletti, D., Vecchiocattivi, F.: Beyond the Lennard-Jones model: a simple and accurate potential function probed by high resolution scattering data useful for molecular dynamics simulations. Phys. Chem. Chem. Phys. **10**, 5489–5503 (2008). https://doi.org/10.1039/B808524B

18. de Petris, G., Cartoni, A., Rosi, M., Barone, V., Puzzarini, C., Troiani, A.: The proton affinity and gas-phase basicity of sulfur dioxide. ChemPhysChem **12**(1), 112–115 (2011)

19. Leonori, F., et al.: Observation of organosulfur products (thiovinoxy, thioketene and thioformyl) in crossed-beam experiments and low temperature rate coefficients for the reaction $S(^1D) + C_2H_4$. Phys. Chem. Chem. Phys. **11**(23), 4701–4706 (2009)

20. de Petris, G., Rosi, M., Troiani, A.: SSOH and HSSO radicals: an experimental and theoretical study of $[S_2OH]^{0/+/-}$ species. J. Phys. Chem. A **111**(28), 6526–6533 (2007)

21. Rosi, M., Falcinelli, S., Balucani, N., Casavecchia, P., Skouteris, D.: A theoretical study of formation routes and dimerization of methanimine and implications for the aerosols formation in the upper atmosphere of titan. In: Murgante, B., et al. (eds.) ICCSA 2013. LNCS, vol. 7971, pp. 47–56. Springer, Heidelberg (2013). https://doi.org/10.1007/978-3-642-39637-3_4

22. Skouteris, D., et al.: Interstellar dimethyl ether gas-phase formation: a quantum chemistry and kinetics study. Mon. Not. R. Astron. Soc. **482**(3), 3567–3575 (2019)

23. Sleiman, C., El Dib, G., Rosi, M., Skouteris, D., Balucani, N., Canosa, A.: Low temperature kinetics and theoretical studies of the reaction $CN + CH_3NH_2$: a potential source of cyanamide and methyl cyanamide in the interstellar medium. Phys. Chem. Chem. Phys. **20**(8), 5478–5489 (2018)

24. Berteloite, C., et al.: Low temperature kinetics, crossed beam dynamics and theoretical studies of the reaction $S(^1D) + CH_4$ and low temperature kinetics of $S(^1D) + C_2H_2$. Phys. Chem. Chem. Phys. **13**(18), 8485–8501 (2011)

25. Becke, A.D.: Density functional thermochemistry. III. The role of exact exchange. J. Chem. Phys. **98**(7), 5648–5652 (1993). https://doi.org/10.1063/1.464913

26. Stephens, P.J., Devlin, F.J., Chabalowski, C.F., Frisch, M.J.: *Ab Initio* calculation of vibrational absorption and circular dichroism spectra using density functional force fields. J. Phys. Chem. **98**(45), 11623–11627 (1994)

27. Gonzalez, C., Schlegel, H.B.: An improved algorithm for reaction path following. J. Chem. Phys. **90**(4), 2154–2161 (1989)

28. Gonzalez, C., Schlegel, H.B.: Reaction path following in mass-weighted internal coordinates. J. Phys. Chem. **94**(14), 5523–5527 (1990)

29. Bartlett, R.J.: Many-body perturbation theory and coupled cluster theory for electron correlation in molecules. Annu. Rev. Phys. Chem. **32**(1), 359–401 (1981)

30. Raghavachari, K., Trucks, G.W., Pople, J.A., Head-Gordon, M.: A fifth-order perturbation comparison of electron correlation theories. Chem. Phys. Lett. **157**(6), 479–483 (1989)

31. Olsen, J., Jørgensen, P., Koch, H., Balkova, A., Bartlett, R.J.: Full configuration-interaction and state of the art correlation calculations on water in a valence double-zeta basis with polarization functions. J. Chem. Phys. **104**(20), 8007–8015 (1996)

32. Dunning Jr, T.H.: Gaussian basis sets for use in correlated molecular calculations. I. the atoms boron through neon and hydrogen. J. Chem. Phys. **90**(2), 1007–1023 (1989)

33. Frisch, M., et al.: Fox: Gaussian 09, Revision A. 02, 2009, Gaussian. Inc., Wallingford CT (2009)

34. Hanwell, M.D., Curtis, D.E., Lonie, D.C., Vandermeersch, T., Zurek, E., Hutchison, G.R.: Avogadro: an advanced semantic chemical editor, visualization, and analysis platform. J. Cheminform. **4**(1), 1–17 (2012)
35. Pirani, F., Albertí, M., Castro, A., Moix Teixidor, M., Cappelletti, D.: Atom-bond pairwise additive representation for intermolecular potential energy surfaces. Chem. Phys. Lett. **394**(1–3), 37–44 (2004). https://doi.org/10.1016/j.cplett.2004.06.100
36. Maitland, G., Smith, E.: A simplified representation of intermolecular potential energy. Chem. Phys. Lett. **22**(3), 443–446 (1973). https://doi.org/10.1016/0009-2614(73)87003-4
37. Pacifici, L., Verdicchio, M., Faginas-Lago, N., Lombardi, A., Costantini, A.: A high-level ab initio study of the $N_2 + N_2$ reaction channel. J. Comput. Chem. **34**(31), 2668–2676 (2013). https://doi.org/10.1002/jcc.23415
38. Bartolomei, M., et al.: The intermolecular potential in NO-N_2 and (NO-N_2)+ systems: implications for the neutralization of ionic molecular aggregates. Phys. Chem. Chem. Phys. **10**, 5993–6001 (2008). https://doi.org/10.1039/B808200F
39. Cappelletti, D., Pirani, F., Bussery-Honvault, B., Gomez, L., Bartolomei, M.: A bond-bond description of the intermolecular interaction energy: the case of weakly bound N_2-H_2 and N_2-N_2 complexes. Phys. Chem. Chem. Phys. **10**, 4281–4293 (2008). https://doi.org/10.1039/B803961E
40. Valença Ferreira de Aragão, E., Faginas-Lago, N., Rosi, M., Mancini, L., Balucani, N., Skouteris, D.: A computational study of the reaction cyanoacetylene and cyano radical leading to 2-butynedinitrile and hydrogen radical. In: Gervasi, O., et al. (eds.) ICCSA 2020. LNCS, vol. 12251, pp. 707–716. Springer, Cham (2020). https://doi.org/10.1007/978-3-030-58808-3_51

Intermolecular Forces for the Interaction of H_2O–Graphtriyne Membrane: Contribution of Induction Effects

Noelia Faginas-Lago[1,3]($\boxtimes$) (ID), Yusuf Bramastya Apriliyanto[2] (ID),
and Andrea Lombardi[1,3] (ID)

[1] Dipartimento di Chimica, Biologia e Biotecnologie, Università degli Studi di Perugia, 06123 Perugia, Italy
{noelia.faginaslago,andrea.lombardi}@unipg.it
[2] Department of Chemistry, Indonesia Defense University,
Kampus Unhan Komplek IPSC Sentul, 16810 Bogor, Indonesia
[3] Master-tec srl, Via Sicilia 41, 06128 Perugia, Italy

Abstract. Among various carbon allotropes, graphynes are a class of two-dimensional nanosheets, analogous to graphene, that recently have been considered as ideal nanofilters for small gas molecules. In this work, the authors report molecular dynamics (MD) simulations of graphtriyne-H_2O system performed using refined potentials. Intermolecular forces are the key points that govern the adsorption dynamics of gaseous molecules on graphynes surfaces. In order to define the full intermolecular potentials, the Improved Lennard-Jones (ILJ) semi-empirical potential have been subsequently modified by adding an induction term (ind) to take into account the polarizability of H_2O molecules. Evaluation of the computational cost and the distribution of H_2O molecules over graphtriyne membrane have been assessed by comparing the intermolecular forces with and without inclusion of induction potential.

Keywords: Molecular dynamics · Semi-empirical potential energy surface · Gaseous adsorption · Graphynes · DL_POLY software

1 Introduction

Water is one of the most important natural solvent and a by-product of chemical reactions involving energy production either through combustion or respiratory processes. A proper description of H_2O–H_2O intermolecular interactions is essential to study the behaviour of several chemical and biochemical systems towards a better atomistic understanding of a certain system [1,2]. From a chemical point of view, a water molecule can be modeled by a simple point of charge, a tri-atomic system formed by two different atomic constituents, or even higher order site models. These varieties of water models are commonly implemented in the widely used force fields such as UFF and AMBER [3,4]. Despite of this simplicity, H_2O has unusual properties when compared with other similar species.

© Springer Nature Switzerland AG 2021
O. Gervasi et al. (Eds.): ICCSA 2021, LNCS 12958, pp. 426–438, 2021.
https://doi.org/10.1007/978-3-030-87016-4_32

As an example, HF, H$_2$S and NH$_3$ molecules are gaseous at atmospheric pressure and room temperature, whereas water is at liquid phase under the same conditions. Moreover, as a liquid, H$_2$O is rather peculiar because it has a maximum density at about 4 °C and a heat capacity anomalously large. This explains why a considerable research effort is spent to understand water properties (in particular, its ability to form hydrogen bonds, a variety of (H$_2$O)$_n$ type clusters and to rationalize H$_2$O–H$_2$O pairs in terms of intermolecular interactions) [5,6]. Several effective potentials have been developed and implemented in molecular dynamics (MD) calculations with a specific purpose of describing the behaviour of water [7–10].

MD simulations is a theoretical chemistry method for analyzing the movement of atoms and molecules using pre-described potential functions called as force fields. This method can be employed to investigate the structural rearrangement of chemical and biochemical systems such as pure solvents, mixed solutions, gaseous separation and combustion processes [11–14]. However, a generic type of force fields is often limited in its use when studying a particular system, for instance simulation of systems involving water. Aqueous liquid and gaseous phase of H$_2$O are principally not the same in the description of their total potential energy function. Therefore, researchers interested in a particular system frequently have to partly develop or modify the generic force fields [15–17]. The choice of the modifications must be on the basis of available experimental and/or theoretical data from the literature or prior high level quantum chemical calculations. While the parameterization of force fields is not a simple task, it is crucial for defining a system correctly. One particular system that needed force fields refinement is post-combustion flue gas where H$_2$O vapour has a significant role on the dynamics of the system [18]. Besides H$_2$O, post-combustion flue gas contains carbon dioxide which is generally considered as a greenhouse gas. As the emission of carbon dioxide shows an increasing trend during last decades, carbon capture and storage (CCS) attracted global attention in order to mitigate catastrophic effects of global warming [19,20].

In the last few years, various porous materials have been evaluated in their ability to selectively capture gas, especially CO$_2$ [21–28]. In particular, carbon-based membranes have desirable physicochemical properties (e.g. hydrophobic, chemically inert and thermally stable) and are economically suitable and viable for CCS application [29,30]. The authors of this paper have been recently involved in the study of γ-graphynes using MD tools, specifically the development of force fields related to gas adsorption in that class of carbon allotropes and their analogs [31–34]. γ-graphynes are two-dimensional atomic monolayers where the carbon atoms are arranged in a way that two adjacent hexagons are connected through C-C triple bonds forming uniformly distributed and adjustable nanopores [35]. As nanoporous materials, γ-graphynes are interesting candidates for CCS, particularly in a form of graphtriyne. Graphtriyne is a form of graphynes where each of its benzene ring is connected to each of six others through a chain composed by three acetylenic bonds. Recent reports shows that graphtriyne exhibits high carbon uptake with a relatively good selectivity [36].

A number of force fields have been developed for evaluating the adsorption of gas molecules on different porous materials [37–40]. However, a challenge that have been facing is when dealing with gaseous mixture where H_2O molecules are present [41,42]. A H_2O molecule can induct and alter polarizability of other molecules in its vicinity. This phenomenon indeed changes the intermolecular forces description between the molecules. Therefore, an additional term is needed to be included to the total potentials to solve this issue. However, as a consequence, this additional term will increase the computational cost. The incomplete description of the full intermolecular potentials can partially be fixed by the inclusion of an induction term [9,10]. In this work, MD simulations were performed involving a graphtriyne membrane and an amount of H_2O molecules in gas phase in an attempt to evaluate the distribution of H_2O molecules over graphtriyne membrane and the computational cost for system with and without inclusion of induction potential.

In the following section, theoretical methods and construction of the present potential energy functions are outlined. The discussions regarding the results and improvements of the molecular simulations code are presented in the Sect. 3, while in the Sect. 4 the paper brings up concluding remarks.

2   Methods

The intermolecular forces of interest in this work are those occured between H_2O molecules pair and between the H_2O and the graphtriyne membrane. The intermolecular interaction energy is further decomposed in terms of molecule-molecule pair contribution, which are non-electrostatic and electrostatic contributions.

$$V_{tot}(r) = V_{nonelec} + V_{elec} \tag{1}$$

The non-electrostatic contribution ($V_{nonelec}$) is measured by taking into consideration the strength of induced dipoles and the average molecular sizes. This can be done by assigning a value of polarizability to the both interacting centers. On the other hand, the electrostatic contribution (V_{elec}) is evaluated by employing the Coulomb's law. $V_{nonelec}$ is given by the following equation

$$V_{nonelec}(r) = V_{ILJ} + V_{ind} \tag{2}$$

where the non-inductive part of the non-electrostatic contribution is expressed by adopting the Improved Lennard-Jones (ILJ) potential [43–47].

$$V_{ILJ}(r) = \varepsilon \left[\frac{m}{n(r) - m} \left(\frac{r_0}{r} \right)^{n(r)} - \frac{n(r)}{n(r) - m} \left(\frac{r_0}{r} \right)^m \right] \tag{3}$$

In Eq. 3, ε, r_0 and m are parameters specific to the involved molecular pair, and r is the distance between the two interacting centers of the same molecular pair. m indicates the type of interaction where its value is 6 for neutral-neutral pairs, 4 for ion-neutral pair and 1 for ion-ion pairs. In order to control the decline of the repulsion and the strength of the attraction in Eq. 3, the $n(r)$ term is employed (Eq. 4).

$$n(r) = \beta + 4.0 \left(\frac{r}{r_0}\right)^2 \tag{4}$$

In Eq. 4, β is a factor that modulates the hardness of the interacting pair [48, 49]. This newly introduced parameter is what makes ILJ potential (Eq. 3) able to indirectly take into account some effects of atom clustering, induction and charge transfer and to improve the Lennard-Jones function at asymptotic regions. Nevertheless, while ILJ improves the description of the present system, other effects should be included in the intermolecular potential for enhancing the model of the system.

It should be considered that charge transfer and induction effects may be important in the interaction between H_2O–H_2O molecules. The H_2O–H_2O interaction can be well defined by using a single effective dispersion + induction center $(V_{ILJ} + V_{ind})$ as already mentioned in (Eq. 2). A careful separate characterization of each of these contributions was performed. Charge transfer effects in the perturbative limit were taken into account indirectly inside the ILJ part by lowering the value of β as discussed, for instance, in Ref. [31]. As for the induction term (V_{ind}), commonly, its contribution to the total interaction is quite small. However, we decided to include it (Eq. 2) in order to quantify its average contribution to the total intermolecular interaction in the water pair interaction and water-graphtriyne interaction, using the single term (in meV) as follows [50].

$$V_{ind}(r) = -4.0\, C\mu^2\alpha/R^6 \tag{5}$$

In Eq. 5 μ and α are the dipole moment and the polarizability of H_2O expressed in debye (D) and Å^3, respectively. R is the distance between the center of mass of each H_2O pair given in Å. This distance is assumed to be coincident with the Ow–Ow separation (Fig. 1), while C is a constant equal to 316.14 to convert the potential in meV unit.

Figure 1 shows the geometrical details of the molecular models employed in this work. A model taken from Ref. [10] was used to represent the water molecule. In this model, the charge is distributed in a way that corresponds to the dipole moment of water in the gas phase (2.1 D) [9]. Each of these point charges is centered in the atoms composing water molecule. The membrane structure was taken from Ref. [36], and had been previously optimized through periodic DFT calculations. For the MD simulations, the membranes were set as a frozen framework while H_2O molecules were set as rigid structures. The MD simulations were performed in simulation boxes with dimensions $72.210\,\text{Å} \times 62.523\,\text{Å} \times 280.0$ Å. Inside each box, a graphtriyne membrane with dimensions $72.210\,\text{Å} \times 62.523$ Å was placed. Simulations were performed uniquely at the temperature of 333 K. The gas molecules were randomly distributed with equal amount into each region of the box yielding a bulk density of H_2O about 3.1526×10^{-2} mol L^{-1}. Figure 2 shows the relative sizes of H_2O molecules, the graphtryine membrane and the simulation box in a qualitative view.

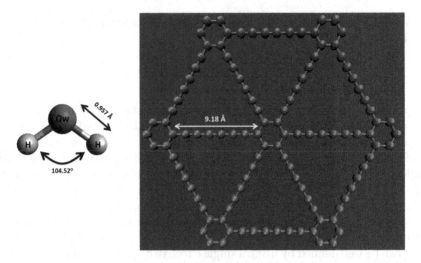

Fig. 1. Structural details of the molecular models of water and graphtryine membrane.

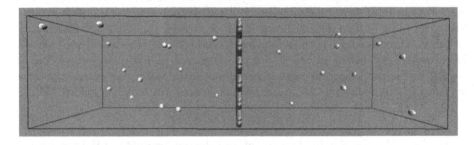

Fig. 2. A screenshot of the simulation box filled with H_2O molecules where the graph-triyne layer is located in the middle of the box.

All MD simulations were performed using the DL_POLY 2 package [51] at canonical NVT ensemble using the Nose-Hoover thermostat and periodic boundary conditions applied in all directions. The ILJ potential and the electrostatic interactions cutoff distances were set to 15 Å, where the electrostatic part was calculated by using the Ewald method. At first, two short simulations were performed by using ILJ and ILJ coupled with induction. Both lasted 2.2 ps after 0.2 ps of equilibration period with a time step of 1 fs. Thereafter, other two longer calculations (2 ns after 0.2 ns equilibration) were run in order to analyze the distribution of H_2O molecules and the corresponding energy contributions. The simulations were performed before and after a modification in some particular routines. Values of relevant parameters are given in Table 1.

Table 1. Parameters for the non-electrostatic interactions (ILJ) of water–water and water–graphtriyne membrane.

Interacting pair	ϵ $(kcal\ mol^{-1})$	r_0 $(\mathring{A})$	β	m
Ow–Ow	0.2089	3.730	6.6	6.0
Ow–C	0.1845	3.712	6.5	6.0

3   Computational Results

We have incorporated some modified routines to include the induction (ind) contribution into the full intermolecular interaction. The modification was done mainly in a routine of the DL_POLY2 package called *forces_modules.f* that handles all interatomic forces using the verlet neighbour list. The *forces_modules.f* is a piece of code that calls other subroutines to calculate the intermolecular forces for each interacting pair of the system. The subsequent subroutines brought by *forces_modules.f* depend on the choice of the predefined potential. *Ewald1* subroutine will be called for ILJ potential, while *ewaldm1* and *induct* subroutines will be called for ILJ+ind potential. The *ewaldm1* and *induct* subroutines were written in order to take into account the electrostatic forces and the induction forces itself, respectively. These subroutines are located in *ewald_module.f* and *coulomb_module.f*. The difference between *ewaldm1* and the original *ewald1* is that the *ewaldm1* subroutine takes into account the point charges distribution which often altered by the induction processes.

A small modification to the above mentioned subroutines had also been done in the previous report [42]. It was reported that the modification had a considerable impact on the total simulation time. As already reported there that, initially, the total CPU time for the ILJ+ind potential took about five times longer than simulation with only the ILJ potential. After a small modification, the difference in total CPU time decreases to about four times between the two potentials. The reported simulations were conducted for 600 fs, accordingly, longer simulation time would has considerable impact on the total CPU time. It was then concluded that something inside the *ewaldm1* and *induct* subroutines that made the simulations took more time than the *ewald1* subroutine applied for ILJ only.

The aim of this work is to evaluate MD simulations codes and results reported in the previous publication [42], thus further improvement of the code can bring us more efficient computational time with reasonable statistical results. At this point, the authors have performed further analysis to the subroutines and simulations results reported in the ICCSA 2019 and 2020 papers [18,42] where a system of $CO_2/N_2/H_2O$ gaseous mixture was simulated without and with induction potential, respectively. The authors find that the most time consuming of the ILJ+ind potential code is the calculation of electrostatic contributions after induction occurs (particularly, inside the *ewaldm1* subroutine), not in the van der Waals (non-electrostatic) part. It should be noted that Refs. [9, 10] indicate that the total dipole moment of H_2O is varying from 2.1 D (H_2O–H_2O pair) to 1.85 D (H_2O–CO_2/N_2 pair). Therefore, the dipole moment of H_2O is not a single value (hence the atomic charges of H_2O are also varying). It's values depend on which molecules interact with H_2O. In order to account for the flexibility of H_2O atomic charges, the authors wrote 3 Fourier cycles inside the *ewaldm1* subroutine.

These 3 Fourier cycles were inspired by the counterpoise method. The authors handled the interchange of H_2O atomic charges (total dipole moment from 1.85 D to 2.1 D) by calculating the electrostatic contribution in *ewaldm1* subroutine as follows:

Fourier 1: total electrostatic term for all interacting pairs, where the atomic charges of H_2O correspond to 1.85 D (as provided in the FIELD input file).

Fourier 2: electrostatic term for interaction involving only H_2O–H_2O pairs, where the atomic charges of H_2O correspond to 1.85 D.

Fourier 3: electrostatic term for interaction involving only H_2O–H_2O pairs, where the atomic charges of H_2O correspond to 2.10 D.

Consequently, the total electrostatic contribution from the *ewaldm1* is Fourier 1 - Fourier 2 + Fourier 3. These Fourier terms are needed only if periodic boundary conditions (PBC) are applied. This approach has proven energetically can recover the interchange of atomic charge as the effect of induction. Unfortunately, this separation of Fourier cycles is the reason why the computational time is quite high for ILJ+ind potential.

Up to this paper is being written, the authors are still searching an alternative way to solve the electrostatic contribution of ILC+ind potential (*ewaldm1*) in a single Fourier cycle without altering too much the original code, while adapting the establihed architecture and workflow of DL_POLY2 package. However, we have made an improvement to *forces_modules.f* in a way that this code can evaluate the simulations systems whether in a form of pure or mixture systems. Furthermore, we present a code modification by introducing conditional statement to only perform a single Fourier transform (*ewald1*) for pure system in order to make the program run more efficient. It is worth to note here that, before modification, the total CPU time is quite high for the case of pure CO_2 system (ILJ+induction) [42]. It is four times longer than the same system with ILJ potential for only 600 steps. For pure CO_2 with ILJ+induction, the CPU time is almost even close to the CPU time for mixture system. We know that since pure systems are not as complex as mixtures, the computational time for pure system should not approach the mixture systems if their total steps are the same. After modification, we report that the total CPU time for simulation of pure H_2O system with and without induction are quite fast and do not significantly different for 2.2 ps (2200 steps) simulations (Table 2). This trend in CPU time will hold for all pure gaseous systems. Moreover, the energy contributions for 2.2 ps simulations are similar and the inclusion of induction potential does not much altering the average of configuration energy (PES). Table 2 shows the comparison of CPU time and statistical analysis of MD simulations results for pure H_2O systems with and without induction.

Table 2. Total CPU time and statistical energy contribution of MD simulations. The energy for the simulations with shorter MD time is reported in unit of 10^{-2} kcal mol^{-1}.

Potential	Time		Energy (*kcal mol*$^{-1}$)		
	MD (ps)	CPU (s)	Configuration	vdW	Coulombic
ILJ	2.2	148.768	-2.637 ± 7.990	-1.234 ± 0.112	-1.403 ± 7.994
	2000	32786.587	-5.266 ± 2.604	-3.865 ± 2.402	-1.402 ± 1.965
ILJ+ind	2.2	151.778	-2.683 ± 7.990	-1.279 ± 0.142	-1.404 ± 7.995
	2000	62725.082	-3.773 ± 7.146	-0.631 ± 2.446	-3.142 ± 6.999

In our case, we are interested in introducing the induction term for the contributions related with the water interaction pairs and water-membrane interactions. Indeed, 2.2 ps simulations are not sufficient in order to describe quantitatively the dynamics of the systems. Therefore, we perform further MD simulations with total simulation time of 2000 ps. From the Table 2 we can see that the CPU time for ILJ+ind is about two times from the ILJ only. Judging from the CPU time, this result is better than the previous reported result [42]. This is a good indication that an improvement of the code's efficiency has been achieved. Although the inclusion of induction potential has fairly small contribution to the total potential (configuration) energy for short time MD simulations (2.2 ps), this small energy contribution is accumulated at much longer simulation (2000 ps), producing quite different statistical energy contributions (see Table 2). As the result, the dynamical process of the system can be considerably affected and induction potential starts to get much more important role to the systems. Furthermore, to assess the impact of induction term to the dynamical process of the system, we also evaluated the distribution of H_2O molecules on graphtriyne as well as the distribution between H_2O molecules. The distribution of H_2O molecules from the surface of graphtriyne is represented by the z-density, in which the density of H_2O as a function of z axis relative to the graphtriyne position is reported. Meanwhile, intermolecular distribution between H_2O molecules is represented by the radial distribution function, which is the probability of a water molecule to have other water molecules as neighbors at a certain distance. The radial distribution functions (RDFs) and z-density profiles for 2000 ps simulation time are presented in Fig. 3.

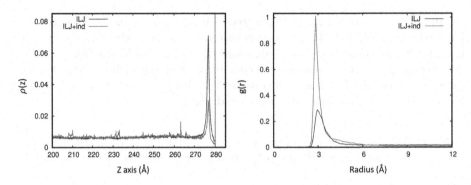

Fig. 3. z-density profiles (left panel) and radial distribution functions of H_2O–H_2O (right panel) for the simulations using ILJ and ILJ+ind potentials. The red vertical line represent the position of graphtriyne layer. The reported values have been normalized. (Color figure online)

Figure 3 shows that the inclusion of induction term has considerably significant impact to the system. The H_2O molecules tend to prefer interacting with each other after the introduction of induction potential. This phenomenon can be seen in the RDFs. The ILJ+ind has higher peak meaning that more H_2O molecules are located near a certain H_2O molecule. As a consequence, the interaction between H_2O–graphtriyne tend to decrease for the case of the ILJ+ind potential, yielding a lower peak in the z-density profile. It should be noted that these results are obtained at 2 ns simulation time. However, running MD simulations for 2 ns is not long enough for estimating quantitative results. In order to yield much more representative data, a simulation higher than five nanoseconds is more adequate. Nevertheless, by introducing some modifications to the code, we improved the performance of ILJ+ind code so that CPU time could be reduced significantly. We also proofed that the induction potential played an important role and contributed to the dynamics of the system. In future works, further improvements are needed to be made to the code to have a faster running simulation using ILJ+ind potential, especially for mixture systems.

4   Conclusions

The induction term has been introduced into the internal DL_POLY2 code in order to improve the description of intermolecular forces and to evaluate H_2O distribution on graphtriyne surface as well as the corresponding computational cost. A considerable impact on the total CPU time has been observed for pure gaseous systems both for ILJ and ILJ+ind potentials after modifications to the existing code. The inclusion of induction potential has fairly small contribution to the total potential energy for short time MD simulations. However, this small energy contribution can be accumulated for much longer simulation time, thus the dynamical process of the system can be considerably affected. Future modifications in the *ewaldm1* subroutine are expected to diminish CPU time even further for calculations with ILJ+ind potential for pure and mixture systems. That way, future MD simulations with larger quantities of molecules and even longer simulation time will be accessible thus the system will be described better than with only ILJ potential.

Acknowledgements. N. F.-L and A. L. thank the MIUR and the University of Perugia for the financial support of the AMIS project through the "Dipartimenti di Eccellenza" program. N. F.-L also acknowledges the Fondo Ricerca di Base 2020 (RICBASE2020FAGINAS) del Dipartimento di Chimica, Biologia e Biotecnologie della Università di Perugia for financial support and the Herla Project for allocated computing time. A. L. acknowledges financial support from MIUR PRIN 2015 (contract 2015F59J3R 002).

References

1. Faginas-Lago, N., Lombardi, A., Albertí, M., Grossi, G.: Accurate analytic intermolecular potential for the simulation of Na^+ and K^+ ion hydration in liquid water. J. Mol. Liq. **204**, 192–197 (2015). https://doi.org/10.1016/j.molliq.2015.01.029
2. Faginas-Lago, N., Albertí, M., Laganà, A., Lombardi, A.: Ion-water cluster molecular dynamics using a semiempirical intermolecular potential. In: Gervasi, O., et al. (eds.) ICCSA 2015. LNCS, vol. 9156, pp. 355–370. Springer, Cham (2015). https://doi.org/10.1007/978-3-319-21407-8_26
3. Rappe, A.K., Casewit, C.J., Colwell, K.S., Goddard, W.A., Skiff, W.M.: UFF, a full periodic table force field for molecular mechanics and molecular dynamics simulations. J. Am. Chem. Soc. **114**(25), 10024–10035 (1992). https://doi.org/10.1021/ja00051a040
4. Pearlman, D., et al.: AMBER, a package of computer-programs for applying molecular mechanics, normal-mode analysis, molecular-dynamics and free-energy calculations to simulate the structural and energetic properties of molecules. Comput. Phys. Commun. **91**, 1–41 (1995). https://doi.org/10.1016/0010-4655(95)00041-D
5. Faginas-Lago, N., Albertí, M., Laganà, A., Lombardi, A.: Water $(H_2O)_m$ or benzene $(C_6H_6))_n$ aggregates to solvate the K^+? In: Murgante, B., Misra, S., Carlini, M., Torre, C.M., Nguyen, H.Q., Taniar, D., Apduhan, B.O., Gervasi, O. (eds.) Computational Science and Its Applications -ICCSA 2013, pp. 1–15. Springer, Berlin Heidelberg (2013). https://doi.org/10.1007/978-3-642-39637-3_1
6. Lago, N.F., Albertí, M., Laganà, A., Lombardi, A., Pacifici, L., Costantini, A.: The molecular stirrer catalytic effect in methane ice formation. In: Murgante, B., et al. (eds.) ICCSA 2014. LNCS, vol. 8579, pp. 585–600. Springer, Cham (2014). https://doi.org/10.1007/978-3-319-09144-0_40
7. Das, A.K., et al.: Development of an advanced force field for water using variational energy decomposition analysis. J. Chem. Theory Comput. **15**(9), 5001–5013 (2019). https://doi.org/10.1021/acs.jctc.9b00478
8. Wang, H., Yang, W.: Force field for water based on neural network. J. Phys. Chem. Lett. **9**(12), 3232–3240 (2018). https://doi.org/10.1021/acs.jpclett.8b01131
9. Albertí, M., Pirani, F., Laganà, A.: Carbon dioxide clathrate hydrates: selective role of intermolecular interactions and action of the SDS catalyst. J. Phys. Chem. A **117**(32), 6991–7000 (2013). https://doi.org/10.1021/jp3126158

10. Albertí, M., Aguilar, A., Cappelletti, D., Laganà, A., Pirani, F.: On the development of an effective model potential to describe water interaction in neutral and ionic clusters. Int. J. Mass Spectrom. **280**, 50–56 (2009). https://doi.org/10.1016/j.ijms.2008.07.018

11. Liu, B., Smit, B.: Molecular simulation studies of separation of CO_2/N_2, CO_2/CH_4, and CH_4/N_2 by ZIFs. J. Phys. Chem. C **114**(18), 8515–8522 (2010). https://doi.org/10.1021/jp101531m

12. Faginas-Lago, N., Albertí, M., Costantini, A., Laganà, A., Lombardi, A., Pacifici, L.: An innovative synergistic grid approach to the computational study of protein aggregation mechanisms. J. Mol. Model. **20**(7), 2226 (2014). https://doi.org/10.1007/s00894-014-2226-4

13. Rampino, S., Faginas-Lago, N., Laganà, A., Huarte-Larrañaga, F.: An extension of the grid empowered molecular simulator to quantum reactive scattering. J. Comput. Chem. **33**(6), 708–714 (2012). https://doi.org/10.1002/jcc.22878

14. Lombardi, A., Faginas-Lago, N., Laganà, A.: Grid calculation tools for massive applications of collision dynamics simulations: carbon dioxide energy transfer. In: Murgante, B., et al. (eds.) ICCSA 2014. LNCS, vol. 8579, pp. 627–639. Springer, Cham (2014). https://doi.org/10.1007/978-3-319-09144-0_43

15. Lombardi, A., Faginas-Lago, N., Pacifici, L., Grossi, G.: Energy transfer upon collision of selectively excited CO_2 molecules: State-to-state cross sections and probabilities for modeling of atmospheres and gaseous flows. J. Chem. Phys. **143**(3), 034307 (2015). https://doi.org/10.1063/1.4926880

16. Faginas-Lago, N., Lombardi, A., Pacifici, L., Costantini, A.: Design and implementation of a grid application for direct calculations of reactive rates. Comput. Theor. Chem. **1022**, 103–107 (2013). https://doi.org/10.1016/j.comptc.2013.08.014

17. DuBay, K.H., Hall, M.L., Hughes, T.F., Wu, C., Reichman, D.R., Friesner, R.A.: Accurate force field development for modeling conjugated polymers. J. Chem. Theory Comput. **8**(11), 4556–4569 (2012). https://doi.org/10.1021/ct300175w

18. Faginas-Lago, N., Apriliyanto, Y.B., Lombardi, A.: Molecular simulations of $CO_2/N_2/H_2O$ gaseous mixture separation in graphtriyne membrane. In: Misra, S., et al. (eds.) ICCSA 2019. LNCS, vol. 11624, pp. 374–387. Springer, Cham (2019). https://doi.org/10.1007/978-3-030-24311-1_27

19. Smit, B.: Carbon capture and storage: introductory lecture. Faraday Discuss. **192**, 9–25 (2016). https://doi.org/10.1039/C6FD00148C

20. Bui, M., et al.: Carbon capture and storage (CCS): the way forward. Energy Environ. Sci. **11**, 1062–1176 (2018). https://doi.org/10.1039/C7EE02342A

21. Srinivas, G., Krungleviciute, V., Guo, Z.X., Yildirim, T.: Exceptional CO_2 capture in a hierarchically porous carbon with simultaneous high surface area and pore volume. Energy Environ. Sci. **7**, 335–342 (2014). https://doi.org/10.1039/C3EE42918K

22. Ghosh, S., Sevilla, M., Fuertes, A.B., Andreoli, E., Ho, J., Barron, A.R.: Defining a performance map of porous carbon sorbents for high-pressure carbon dioxide uptake and carbon dioxide-methane selectivity. J. Mater. Chem. A **4**, 14739–14751 (2016). https://doi.org/10.1039/C6TA04936B

23. Kim, J., Lin, L.C., Swisher, J.A., Haranczyk, M., Smit, B.: Predicting large CO_2 adsorption in aluminosilicate zeolites for postcombustion carbon dioxide capture. J. Am. Chem. Soc. **134**(46), 18940–18943 (2012). https://doi.org/10.1021/ja309818u

24. Lin, L.C., et al.: Understanding CO_2 dynamics in metal-organic frameworks with open metal sites. Angew. Chem. Int. Ed. **52**(16), 4410–4413 (2013). https://doi.org/10.1002/anie.201300446

25. Schrier, J.: Carbon dioxide separation with a two-dimensional polymer membrane. ACS Appl. Mater. Interfaces. **4**(7), 3745–3752 (2012). https://doi.org/10.1021/am300867d

26. Xiang, Z., et al.: Systematic tuning and multifunctionalization of covalent organic polymers for enhanced carbon capture. J. Am. Chem. Soc. **137**(41), 13301–13307 (2015). https://doi.org/10.1021/jacs.5b06266

27. Liu, H., et al.: A hybrid absorption-adsorption method to efficiently capture carbon. Nat. Commun. **5**, 5147 (2014). https://doi.org/10.1038/ncomms6147

28. Apriliyanto, Y.B., Darmawan, N., Faginas-Lago, N., Lombardi, A.: Two-dimensional diamine-linked covalent organic frameworks for co 2/n 2 capture and separation: theoretical modeling and simulations. Phys. Chem. Chem. Phys. **22**(44), 25918–25929 (2020). https://doi.org/10.1039/D0CP04258G

29. Bartolomei, M., Carmona-Novillo, E., Giorgi, G.: First principles investigation of hydrogen physical adsorption on graphynes' layers. Carbon **95**, 1076–1081 (2015). https://doi.org/10.1016/j.carbon.2015.08.118

30. Ganesan, A., Shaijumon, M.: Activated graphene-derived porous carbon with exceptional gas adsorption properties. Microporous Mesoporous Mater. **220**, 21–27 (2015). https://doi.org/10.1016/j.micromeso.2015.08.021

31. Apriliyanto, Y.B., et al.: Nanostructure selectivity for molecular adsorption and separation: the case of graphyne layers. J. Phys. Chem. C **122**(28), 16195–16208 (2018). https://doi.org/10.1021/acs.jpcc.8b04960

32. Faginas-Lago, N., Yeni, D., Huarte, F., Wang, Y., Alcamí, M., Martin, F.: Adsorption of hydrogen molecules on carbon nanotubes using quantum chemistry and molecular dynamics. J. Phys. Chem. A **120**(32), 6451–6458 (2016). https://doi.org/10.1021/acs.jpca.5b12574

33. Yeamin, M.B., Faginas-Lago, N., Albertí, M., García Cuesta, I., Sánchez-Marín, J., Sánchez de Merás, A.: Multi-scale theoretical investigation of molecular hydrogen adsorption over graphene: coronene as a case study. RSC Adv. **4**, 54447–54453 (2014). https://doi.org/10.1039/C4RA08487J

34. Faginas-Lago, N., Apriliyanto, Y.B., Lombardi, A.: Confinement of co2 inside carbon nanotubes. Eur. Phys. J. D **75**(161), 1–10 (2021). https://doi.org/10.1140/epjd/s10053-021-00176-7

35. James, A., et al.: Graphynes: indispensable nanoporous architectures in carbon flatland. RSC Adv. **8**, 22998–23018 (2018). https://doi.org/10.1039/C8RA03715A

36. Bartolomei, M., Giorgi, G.: A novel nanoporous graphite based on graphynes: First-principles structure and carbon dioxide preferential physisorption. ACS Appl. Mater. Interfaces. **8**(41), 27996–28003 (2016). https://doi.org/10.1021/acsami.6b08743

37. Lim, J.R., Yang, C.T., Kim, J., Lin, L.C.: Transferability of CO₂ force fields for prediction of adsorption properties in all-silica zeolites. J. Phys. Chem. C **122**(20), 10892–10903 (2018). https://doi.org/10.1021/acs.jpcc.8b02208

38. Boyd, P.G., Moosavi, S.M., Witman, M., Smit, B.: Force-field prediction of materials properties in metal-organic frameworks. J. Phys. Chem. Lett. **8**(2), 357–363 (2017). https://doi.org/10.1021/acs.jpclett.6b02532

39. Lin, L.C., Lee, K., Gagliardi, L., Neaton, J.B., Smit, B.: Force-field development from electronic structure calculations with periodic boundary conditions: applications to gaseous adsorption and transport in metal-organic frameworks. J. Chem. Theory Comput. **10**(4), 1477–1488 (2014). https://doi.org/10.1021/ct500094w

40. Vekeman, J., García Cuesta, I., Faginas-Lago, N., Wilson, J., Sánchez-Marín, J., Sánchez de Merás, A.: Potential models for the simulation of methane adsorption on graphene: development and CCSD(T) benchmarks. Phys. Chem. Chem. Phys. **20**(39), 25518–25530 (2018). https://doi.org/10.1039/C8CP03652G

41. Faginas-Lago, N., Apriliyanto, Y.B., Lombardi, A.: Carbon capture and separation from $CO_2/N_2/H_2O$ gaseous mixtures in bilayer graphtriyne: a molecular dynamics study. In: Gervasi, O., et al. (eds.) ICCSA 2020. LNCS, vol. 12255, pp. 489–501. Springer, Cham (2020). https://doi.org/10.1007/978-3-030-58820-5_36

42. de Aragão, E.V.F., Faginas-Lago, N., Apriliyanto, Y.B., Lombardi, A.: Gas adsorption on graphtriyne membrane: impact of the induction interaction term on the computational cost. In: Gervasi, O., et al. (eds.) ICCSA 2020. LNCS, vol. 12255, pp. 513–525. Springer, Cham (2020). https://doi.org/10.1007/978-3-030-58820-5_38

43. Pirani, P., Brizi, S., Roncaratti, L., Casavecchia, P., Cappelletti, D., Vecchiocattivi, F.: Beyond the Lennard-Jones model: a simple and accurate potential function probed by high resolution scattering data useful for molecular dynamics simulations. Phys. Chem. Chem. Phys. **10**, 5489–5503 (2008). https://doi.org/10.1039/B808524B

44. Lombardi, A., Laganà, A., Pirani, F., Palazzetti, F., Lago, N.F.: Carbon oxides in gas flows and earth and planetary atmospheres: state-to-state simulations of energy transfer and dissociation reactions. In: Murgante, B., et al. (eds.) ICCSA 2013. LNCS, vol. 7972, pp. 17–31. Springer, Heidelberg (2013). https://doi.org/10.1007/978-3-642-39643-4_2

45. Faginas-Lago, N., Albertí, M., Lombardi, A., Pirani, F.: A force field for acetone: the transition from small clusters to liquid phase investigated by molecular dynamics simulations. Theor. Chem. Acc. **135**(7), 1–9 (2016). https://doi.org/10.1007/s00214-016-1914-9

46. Lombardi, A., Faginas-Lago, N., Gaia, G., Federico, P., Aquilanti, V.: Collisional energy exchange in $CO_2–N_2$ gaseous mixtures. In: Gervasi, O., et al. (eds.) ICCSA 2016. LNCS, vol. 9786, pp. 246–257. Springer, Cham (2016). https://doi.org/10.1007/978-3-319-42085-1_19

47. Albertí, M., Faginas-Lago, N.: Ion size influence on the ar solvation shells of $M^+C_6F_6$ clusters (M = Na, K, Rb, Cs). J. Phys. Chem. A **116**(12), 3094–3102 (2012). https://doi.org/10.1021/jp300156k

48. Pirani, F., Albertí, M., Castro, A., Moix Teixidor, M., Cappelletti, D.: Atombond pairwise additive representation for intermolecular potential energy surfaces. Chem. Phys. Lett. **394**(1–3), 37–44 (2004). https://doi.org/10.1016/j.cplett.2004.06.100

49. Pacifici, L., Verdicchio, M., Faginas-Lago, N., Lombardi, A., Costantini, A.: A high-level ab initio study of the $N_2 + N_2$ reaction channel. J. Comput. Chem. **34**(31), 2668–2676 (2013). https://doi.org/10.1002/jcc.23415

50. Albertí, M., et al.: Small water clusters: the cases of rare gas-water, alkali ion-water and water dimer. In: Gervasi, O., Murgante, B., Laganà, A., Taniar, D., Mun, Y., Gavrilova, M.L. (eds.) ICCSA 2008. LNCS, vol. 5072, pp. 1026–1035. Springer, Heidelberg (2008). https://doi.org/10.1007/978-3-540-69839-5_78

51. Smith, W., Yong, C., Rodger, P.: DL_POLY: application to molecular simulation. Mol. Simul. **28**(5), 385–471 (2002)

International Workshop on Urban Form Studies (UForm 2021)

Some Remarks on Soft Mobility: A New Engineered Approach to the Cycling Infrastructure Design

Mauro D'Apuzzo[1] , Daniela Santilli[1(✉)], Azzurra Evangelisti[1] ,
and Vittorio Nicolosi[2]

[1] Department of Civil and Mechanical Engineering DICEM, University of Cassino and Southern Lazio, Cassino, Italy
{dapuzzo,daniela.santilli}@unicas.it
[2] Department of Enterprise Engineering "Mario Lucertini", University of Rome "Tor Vergata", Rome, Italy
nicolosi@uniroma2.it

Abstract. Worldwide, countries are working to reorganize transport networks by promoting a new form of mobility that is sustainable and healthy for citizens. The task assigned to the designers is to create interconnected, safe, attractive and comfortable routes so that users begin to change their habits by favoring modal shift to sustainable transport. In this paper, a preliminary procedure is defined for the design of the different types of cycling routes based on area's characteristics and, above all, cycling flows. An original estimation method for the cycling flow has been proposed that allows a refined safety-oriented cycling infrastructure design. Once that the design interventions have been defined, through a benefit-cost analysis and with the help of technical guides, it is possible to evaluate optimal cycling infrastructure layouts on the examined urban road network.

Keywords: Sustainable mobility · Cycling flow · Cycling networks

1 Introduction

Sustainable mobility, especially in recent years, is a key topic that has generated numerous debates in international and national context. In fact, governance increasingly needs to promote policies aimed at reducing the environmental impact deriving from the mobility of people and goods. An engaging discussion on sustainable mobility or rather on low environmental impact mobility aimed at maximizing the efficiency and speed of travel has been also undertaken in Italy since the 1990s. Indeed, according to the World Business Council for Sustainable Development [1], this mobility allows people to move freely, communicate and establish relationships without ever losing sight of the human and environmental aspects.

Thanks to a huge amount of research-driven evidences, European countries have now realized that by improving transport systems (focusing above all on public, shared and more eco-sustainable services) it is possible to make cities safe and livable by reducing

© Springer Nature Switzerland AG 2021
O. Gervasi et al. (Eds.): ICCSA 2021, LNCS 12958, pp. 441–456, 2021.
https://doi.org/10.1007/978-3-030-87016-4_33

negative externalities (noise pollution, smog, traffic congestion, accidents, greenhouse gas emissions or fine dust, etc.).

The growing demand for mobility of road transport, especially private, often makes circulation conditions in urban and extra-urban contexts very critical. Due to the unbalanced interaction between supply and demand, the decline in service levels and the increase in emissions of greenhouse gases, nitrogen oxides and fine particles are observed [2].

The spread of Covid-19 in 2020 and the consequent need to implement restrictive measures, as highlighted by National Geographic [3] and the ESA (European Space Agency) [4], emphasized that the reduction of vehicles in circulation and the reduction of the activity of factories have led to an improvement in air quality.

It is, therefore, necessary to change habits, choosing to share a new way of moving, this requires a multidisciplinary approach that involves citizens, car manufacturers, public administrations and politics.

It is, therefore, necessary to make cities smart by implementing strategies to optimize and innovate public services. This would allow for connected and automated multimodal mobility. This intelligent mobility, in addition to reducing congestion and pollution, is likely to improve traffic safety, inducing citizens to travel in a sustainable way [5, 6]. Moreover, developing smarter and more sustainable mobility will allow to:

– *Reduce air pollution*: Europe has set as a goal, by 2050, a 60% reduction in emissions from transport since transport sector consumes about one-third of total energy consumption and produces one-fifth of greenhouse gas emissions. To achieve the set goal, new technologies and the use of the most efficient systems must be encouraged (for example, hydrogen-powered trains, cars with electric motors, technological infrastructures, etc.).
– *Reduce noise pollution*: transport generates excessive noise levels and roads, railways and airports are certainly among the main sources of disturbance. This pollution has consequences on the health and well-being of people (sleep disturbances, increased blood pressure, cardiovascular diseases, etc.) and regulations at national level indicate the exposure thresholds and the measures to be undertaken.
– *Reduce vehicular congestion*: by encouraging the use of shared and public transport to the detriment of private ones, in order to reduce congestion and travel times and to make cities more accessible to vulnerable users.
– *Reduce land use*: due to the growth of transport systems often irrespective of the landscape issues, it is necessary to optimize the collective built-up spaces.
– *Reduce costs and transport efficiency*: by creating innovative, integrated, efficient and connected transport, both individual and collective costs and times are reduced.

To make cities innovative, connected but at the same time sustainable, technology can be used to control and save energy as well as to optimize mobility and safety solutions. To do this, it is essential to make the transport service efficient by focusing on multimodality. Multimodal transport allows using in a combined way different modes (at least two) of transport. So, tailor-made offers must be developed including various ways, such as public transport, shared cars and bicycles, electric scooters, taxis and more, such as Mobility-As-A-Service MAAS sytems that allow simple and safe access to the offers of mobility providers through an app, which becomes visible and bookable; allowing to maximize resources and time by combining the different available means (Fig. 1).

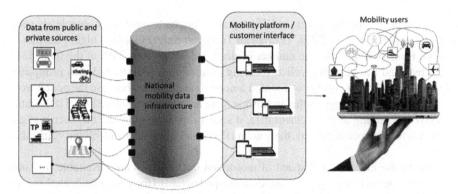

Fig. 1. Operation diagram of a multimodal service

Within this context, more and more often targeted interventions are implemented in the cities, such as:

- the re-design of public transport supply by means of the strengthening of the infrastructure and services both at local (urban) and and national/international level.
- the promotion of preferential lanes intended exclusively for public transport (buses, trams, taxis) or emergency vehicles; this allows to avoid traffic congestion giving an advantage to those who use public transport instead of private transport.
- the creation of cycling paths or pedestrian areas, therefore areas dedicated exclusively to bicycles and pedestrians; giving the feeling of greater safety and protection, which encourages people to walk or pedal for short trips instead of using a car or a motorbike;
- road pricing (urban toll) and park pricing to discourage or limit the access in urban areas to private vehicles (cars, motorcycles, scooters, etc.) in order to reduce traffic congestion, smog and encourage the use of public transport.
- traffic blocking i.e. a temporary and occasional public intervention to partially or totally limit vehicular traffic in urban areas;
- the use of limited traffic areas (ZTL in Italy) as a permanent blocking of traffic in the central or more congested areas of the city;
- car-sharing or bike-sharing i.e. forms of collective mobility based on the rental of a low environmental impact vehicle (electric car or bike) for a few hours or days, that are increasingly adopted in urban areas;
- car-pooling i.e. another form of collective mobility which consists in the use of a private car by several people, often colleagues or acquaintances, who travel the same journey from home to work at the same times.

Despite the idea of moving towards multimodal transport, most European countries and cities have devoted most of resources in the construction and management of infrastructure for motor vehicles, neglecting those for active modes, namely walking and cycling. Among the many European projects implemented, the FLOW project [7] involving the implementation of strategies to promote walking and the use of bicycles, both in large and small cities, on short and medium distance journeys is one of most noticeable.

However, despite the success of EU programs, the roads are still not completely safe, in fact, a report [8] of the ETSC (European Transport Safety Council) highlights that in Europe from 2010 to 2018 the number of dead pedestrians was 21% of the total, 18% of cyclists and 8% of motorcyclists (bearing in mind that pedestrian deaths or injuries of vulnerable users are often not counted among road accidents because the police were not consulted). This suggests that in Europe there are on average more than 5180 deaths every year. Looking at the accident data, it seems that although there has been a slight reduction in fatal road accidents, there are no decreases in accidents involving vulnerable users.

Due to the intensity and speed of motorized traffic, cities are unsuitable for such users but especially for cyclists, since unlike pedestrians (for whom dedicated spaces have been built) they are often forgotten. It is, consequently, necessary to reorganize the road network to promote the use of bicycles as a daily mode of transport for various reasons (home-work/study, recreation, sport and free time).

To accomplish this task, it is necessary to establish rules to reduce the high risk of injury to which cyclists and pedestrians are exposed. This implies the reorganization of the streets which become multifunctional spaces shared equally among all users.

People choose the bicycle as a means of transport [9] based on subjective and objective factors. The former is linked to the sense of security, the feeling of comfort and social acceptance; while the latter ones are related to speed, topography, climate and safety (understood as the absence of obstacles).

Taking these factors into account, a cycle network can be designed, making it an integral part of urban mobility policies (Mobility plans and transport), which deal, among other aspects, to ensure that the journey takes place smoothly and therefore that the structure is:

- safe: the risk of injury due to interactions with other modes is reduced;
- direct: limiting the detours so that the travel time is reduced;
- continuous: so that the movements, between the different origins and destinations, do not have path interruptions (with good connections with other networks, mainly public transport stops and junctions);
- attractive or well integrated with the environment in which it is inserted;
- comfortable: allowing the cyclist to reduce physical effort and discomfort, so as to have a pleasant and relaxed travel experience.

In practice it is not always possible to meet all these requirements, so there is the need to find the right balance based on the environment in which the designer is operating.

2 Cycling Network Design

The design of a short-distance transport network depends on historical characteristics and land use evolution, thus knowledge of the land use layout, topography, climate and lifestyle of the population is required. In addition, it is necessary to have traffic data (flow of motor vehicles, cyclists and pedestrians) and injury rates, highlight the presence of attractions (schools, universities, commercial or recreational activities, tourist areas, etc.) and existing structures with their respective geometric characteristics.

Known the land use characteristics, the different origins and destinations must be taken into consideration to identify the paths that users could choose to meet their needs.

This allows you to hierarchize the network in:

- *Main cycling paths*, for long distances, with city or rural connection function;
- *Secondary streets* that connect adjacent neighbourhoods;
- *Local routes*, for short distances, which allow movement within the neighbourhoods.

2.1 Types of Cycling Path Layouts

Before introducing the proposed methodology for the cycling infrastructure design based on given area characteristics and flows, the most common cycling path layouts are briefly presented.It is worth to be highlighted that this is not a exhaustive review, given the different legal definitions and terminologies used in EU countries.

Depending on whether or not cyclists share the infrastructure with other users, three situations can occur:

- *total sharing of road space* between the bicycle and vehicular traffic; this is usually a one-way lane, but there may be situations in where the bicycle can travel in the opposite direction (for example, zone 30) (Fig. 2).

Fig. 2. Total sharing of road space example

- *visual separation* with simple indication with horizontal signs on the sidewalk of the runway. The space intended for bicycles is an integral part of the carriageway, unidirectional, generally in the direction of the traffic flow (Fig. 3).

Fig. 3. Visual separation example

– *physical separation*: it is a lane, one or two-way, dedicated to bicycles (with the possibility of sharing with not motorized mode) separated by obstacles from the road network for other ways (Fig. 4).

Fig. 4. Physical separation example

By reviewing the different guidelines of European countries [10–18] albeit with different names, the cycle networks can be grouped as follows:

– *Greenway:* it is a "multipurpose" route reserved for non-motorized users, separated from traffic and independent from main roads, which passes trought open spaces, parks, gardens and woods and must respect the surrounding environment. Sharing the lane by different users can cause conflicts so it is recommended to physically separate the different parts intended for different users (Fig. 5).

Fig. 5. Greenway example

– *Cycle lane* is an independent lane, separated from the carriageways, designed for the exclusive use of bicycles (Fig. 6).

Fig. 6. Example of cycle lane

– *Protected cycle path* are protected lanes designed exclusively for bicycles with physical separation from motorized traffic. Usually, neither pedestrians nor skaters are allowed. This can be one-way (one lane on each side of the main road) or two-way (one lane with both directions on one side of the main road) usually near a road with high motorized traffic (Fig. 7).

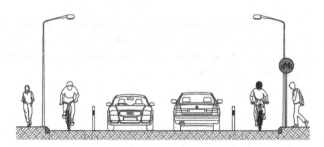

Fig. 7. Example of one-way protected cycle path

– *Cycle path* is reserved for bicycles and it is separated from the rest of the circulation by horizontal signs. It is designed for roads at low speed and with reduced transit of heavy vehicles (Fig. 8).

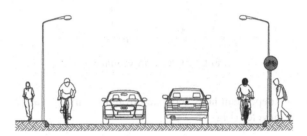

Fig. 8. Example of cycle path

– *Road of 30 km/h zone* where both bicycles and cars share the carriageway without any access restrictions (Fig. 9).

Fig. 9. Example of road of 30 km / h zone

– *Cycle track* in which pedestrians and cyclists share the sidewalk. The part intended for the bicycle must have the relative signs. As there is not always sufficient space, this usually takes place in pedestrian areas or in common routes where the speed limit for cyclists is of 20 km/h (Fig. 10).

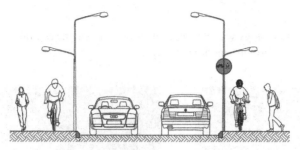

Fig. 10. Example of cycle track

– *Shared-use path* is shared between pedestrians and cars. These roads are also suitable for cycling, but with a speed limit of 20 km/h and with pedestrians always having priority (Fig. 11).

Fig. 11. Shared-use path example

2.2 Choice of the Specific Cycling Path Layout to Be Adopted

Since there is no absolute rule for the application of the different solutions for the choice of cycle path layouts, it is necessary to take into account the density or flow rate and speed of the vehicles (to define the type of protection on the cycle path), the expected number of cyclists (to define the width of the track), the existing space and the urban environment (to identify the type of cycle path and its characteristics).

The information that is hardly known is the density or the flow of cyclists traveling on the examined road network. To this purpose, an original prediction methodology has been developed and implemented in this work to estimate, at a preliminary level, the cycling demand at urban level.

Estimation of Cycling Flows

To evaluate the transport flows loading the network, several models and approaches have been proposed and employed, but while for the vehicular flow there is a solid knowledge, the same cannot be said for the cycling and pedestrian flow [19]. Therefore, a new methodology has been developed to preliminarly estimate the cycle flows, loading a urban road network starting from National commuter mobility data (15th ISTAT census, 2011).

Case Study

The proposed methodology was developed and calibrated in the central area of the Italian town of Cassino (Lazio, Frosinone) (Fig. 12).

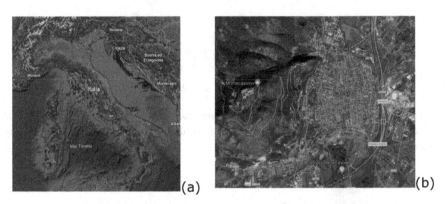

Fig. 12. Position of city of Cassino (a) detail of the study area (b)

The study area was discretized into census sections each represented by a corresponding centroid. Each of these defines an origin and/or destination (o-d) to which the total flow (given by the sum of the movements of students and workers) obtained from the ISTAT microdata has been assigned and an o-d matrix has thus been derived. Once the matrix was imported into QGIS using a plugin (*FlowerMapper*), the desire lines directly connecting each origin centroid with each destination centroid, were obtained (Fig. 13).

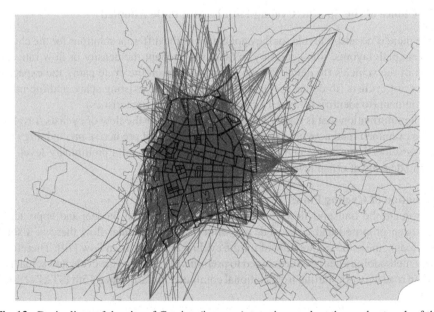

Fig. 13. Desire lines of the city of Cassino (in green) superimposed on the road network of the central area of the city (in blue) (Color figure online)

To apply the proximity function [19]. it was necessary to construct a distance matrix; this made it possible to obtain the real flows.

Once the distance between the different origins and destinations is known, it is possible to evaluate the cycling trip for a specific o-d pair by making use of an modal split impedance function derived from technical literature [20] able to estimate the attractiveness of the cycling mode for a commuter trip as a function of the traveled distance (see Fig. 14).

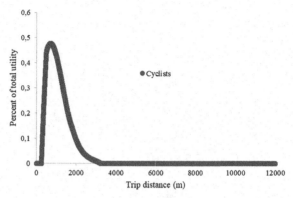

Fig. 14. Cycling impedance function

Therefore, by multiplying the commuting movements with the impedance coefficients, as a function of the distance, the actual flows that are likely to load the different link belonging to the Cassino road network are obtained.

Loading the Cycling Network

Once the road network model was developed and each road section (arc) was uniquely identified, As far as network loading is concerned, it is necessary to take into account that each arc can be affected by the contribution of different o-d pairs; shortest route connecting each o-d pair has been therefore evaluated by using QGIS geoprocessing tools according to a desire line buffer varying from 0 to 45 m (Fig. 15).

Fig. 15. Example of a superimposed buffer on the road network for a some o-d pairs

Buffer size calibration was carried out by a comparison with results provided by a common web-based route planning program. Then, once that the optimal route identification has been evaluated for each o-d pair, each route has been decomposed in its road sections and for each road arc belonging to the examined road network the contribution of all the relevant o-d pair cycling flow has been evaluated and summed (Fig. 16).

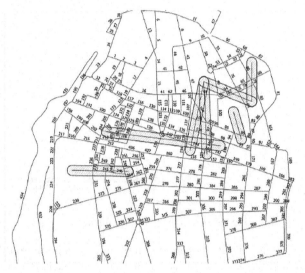

Fig. 16. Intersection of the road network with the buffer

Assigned cycling flows estimated with 0 and 45 m wide buffer approaches were conveniently averaged in order to derive a likely evaluation of cycling flow loading in the study area that is conveniently reported below (Fig. 17).

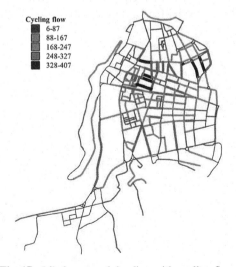

Fig. 17. Likely network loading with cycling flows

A Proposal for Use of Cycling Flows in Cycling Lane Layout Cost-Benefit Analysis
Once that cycling flows have been evaluated as described above, it is possible to use
a cycling path layout decision matrix, such as the one shown below [21] derived from
Dutch Standards and reported in the following table for sake of example, in order to
evaluated optimal cycling path layout solution suitable for each specific road section
(Table 1).

Table 1. Decision matrix for cycling path cross-sectional layout from Dutch Standards [20].

Function traffic road		Speed (Km/h)		Intensity (vehicles/day)	Density of cyclists (bike/day)		
					<750	500-2500	>2000
		Not applicable		0	Greenway		
	Local access road	Walking space or 30 Km/h		1-25000	Shared-use path		Cycle lane or cycle path
				2000-5000			
				>4000	Cycle lane or cycle track		
	Distributor road	50 Km/h	2x1 lanes	not applicable	Cycle track (adjacent or separated)		
			2x2 lanes				
		70 Km/h					

However, in order to choose the optimal solution it is necessary to take into account
the characteristics of the road, the vehicular flows and speeds, the surrounding space,
the hierarchy of the roads together with the available budget.

This means that planners and decision-makers must carry out cost-benefit analyzes
that may represent an effective help to use the funds in a targeted way and to justify the
investment on one choice rather than another. According to Elvik [19], the cost-benefit
analysis of pedestrian and cycle infrastructures should use methodologies similar to those
used for transport projects in general, keeping in mind that the costs associated with the
design and construction of the cycling infrastructure improvements are relatively low
compared to road projects of similar lengths.

Although apparently simple, it is not so straightforward to estimate the costs for the
installation of cycle networks as these are often part of a larger maintenance or retrofitting
project, such as the resurfacing of a road. So while it is quite simple to describe the cost
of purchasing and installing the bike path equipment (vertical signs, paints, etc.), the
other elements are grouped together in the larger project and are difficult to detail.

Each cycling path layout type has a series of possible variable costs, determined by
the different measures implemented, which are related to the design and asset managment. Therefore. the costs presented in this paper, relating to the design of cycle networks
in Italy, are purely representative as they may greatly vary locally and even more nationally. Nevertheless they may represent a reference basis for a refined further engineered
analysis.

It is intuitive to understand that optimizing the existing network by inserting a horizontal and vertical signaling system that delimits the route requires moderate financial resources (400 to 600 €/Km); such as, expanding an existing cycle network involves lower costs than new construction. Similarly, it is more convenient to create multi-purpose cycle paths than dedicated ones.

Many authors [23–27] have dealt with defining the costs of the different solutions, sometimes lacking details on the different components of the project. All the studies analyzed refer to specific manuals to define the costs according to the characteristics of the specific examined layout component (Table 2).

Table 2. Cost estimates for the design of the different solutions

	Type of separator	Cost (€/Km)	
		Unidirectional	Bidirectional
\Cycle path	Road markings	50000	40000
	Coloured bitumen	125000	100000
Protected cycle path	Curbstone	210000	120000
	Creasing	100000	60000
	Flower bed	210000	120000
	Parking stalls	260000	140000
Cycle track	Horizontal signs	170000	120000
	Sidewalk with staggered floors	165000	120000
	No separation on the sidewalk	40000	35000
Road of 30 km/h	No separation on the road	60000	
Cycle lane	Calcestre	\	330000
	Bitumen	\	195000

Once the costs have been defined, the benefits related to a specific cycling path layout must therefore be assessed in terms of reduction of accidents. However, in this connection, there is still a lack of knowledge for specific engineered safety performance functions based on national accident data. Moreover, multi-criteria methods can be effectively employed if the reduction of pollutant emissions, or the improvement of the quality of life and social profitability have to be also evaluated.

3   Conclusions

The use of bicycles as a way of moving on a daily basis is not equally widespread worldwide, although in recent years the idea that promoting cycling as a transport mode able to improve health conditions, support sustainability and facilitate access to different areas, has been increasingly spreading. It has been shown [28] that, by installing bicycle infrastructures, users are able to perceive a greater level of comfort and safety which has encouraged them to use the bicycle as a preferential transport mode in urban areas.

In this paper, an original methodology was suggested able to evaluate cycling flows loading a urban road network that, in turn, may be critical for the design of the optimal cycling path cross-sectional layout within a specific study area. Designing a cycle network involves knowing the characteristics of the area (topographic, climatic, geometric, etc.) but, above all, motorized and non-motorized flows loading the road network. It is now fairly known how to estimate the vehicular flows but the same cannot be said for cycling ones, therefore a preliminary algorithm has been defined that takes into account area topology, commuter o-d matrix derived from National Census Database, based on a proximity criterion. Once that involved cycling flows have been evaluated, it is possible to choose the different cycling cross-sectional layout solutions within a benefits-cost (B-C) framework similarly to what is undertaken in other European Countries.

Hovever, within the proposed methodological framework that is still in his preliminary stage, several future development need to be carried out detailed in the followings:

- the prediction methodology needs to be experimentally calibrated and subsequently validated on-site, by performing a suitable traffic data collection campaign; this will allow a finer tuning of the model parameters;
- the methodology needs to be applied to urban areas other than that specifically examined;
- a huge research effort should be carried out on safety of road vulnerable user with emphasis on cyclists in order to derive engineered National Safety Performance Functions that can help designer in selecting the most appropriate cycling path cross-sectional layout within a B-C analysis.

Nevertheless the proposed methological approach seems promising in helping designer in the development of Sustainable Urban Mobility Plans (SUMP) and it may represent a starting point for a wider design approach to be included in SUMP Guidelines for cycling infrastructures.

References

1. Council, World Business (2020). https://www.wbcsd.org/Programs/Cities-and-Mobility/Transforming-Mobility
2. Fioravanti, G., et al.: Gli indicatori del clima in Italia nel 2019-annoXV. s.l. : ISPRA – Istituto Superiore per la Protezione e la Ricerca Ambientale (2020)
3. Geographic, National. Coronavirus, le misure di contenimento hanno ridotto l'inquinamento (2020). https://www.nationalgeographic.it/ambiente/2020/04/coronavirus-le-misure-di-contenimento-hanno-ridotto-linquinamento-europa
4. Agency, European Space. La chiusura per fronteggiare il Coronavirus ha portato ad una riduzione dell'inquinamento in tutta Europa (2020). https://www.esa.int/Space_in_Member_States/Italy/La_chiusura_per_fronteggiare_il_Coronavirus_ha_portato_ad_una_riduzione_dell_inquinamento_in_tutta_Europa#:~:text=Agency-,La%20chiusura%20per%20fronteggiare%20il%20Coronavirus%20ha%20portato%20ad,dell'inqui

5. Garau, C., Masala, F. e Pinna, F.: Cagliari and smart urban mobility: Analysis and comparison. Cities **56**, 35–46 (2016)

6. Pinna, F., Masala, F. e Garau, C.: Urban policies and mobility trends in Italian smart cities. Sustainability (2017)

7. European Union, (UE). Flow (2020). http://h2020-flow.eu/

8. Council, European TRansport Safety. How safe is walking and cycling in Europe? (PIN Flash 38) (2020). https://etsc.eu/how-safe-is-walking-and-cycling-in-europe-pin-flash-38/

9. European Union, (UE). Cities for Bicicles, Cities of the Future (2009). https://www.ecf.com/sites/ecf.com/files/Future-cities-are-cycling-cities.pdf

10. Meschik, M.: Planungshandbuch radverkehr. Springer-verlag, Wien (2008)

11. Mobility, Brussels. Vademecum Velo en Region de Bruxelles-Capitale Brussels, Belgium : s.n (2006). https://mobilite-mobiliteit.brussels/en/node/265

12. Celis, Consult. Danish handbook for cycle traffic. s.l., Denmark : HÅNDBOG CYKEL-TRAFIK (2014)

13. Julien, A.: Cycling infrastructure design and urban public space- a comparison of cycling design manuals. Association Metropolis . s.l., France: PREDITMELT/DRAST (2000)

14. Ciclável, R.: Princípios de Planeamento e Desenho. COLECÇÃO DE BROCHURAS TÉCNICAS / TEMÁTICAS. s.l.: IMT (2011)

15. Government of Catalonia. Manual for the Design of Cyclepaths in Catalonia (2008)

16. Landsting, Trafikverket / Sveriges Kommuner och. Guideline on configuration, operation and maintenance of pedestrian, cycling and moped traffic. Handbok – Utformning, drift och underhåll med gång-, cykel- och mopedtrafik I fokus (2010)

17. Eidgenossenschaft, Schweizerische. Handbuch Wegweisung für Velos, Mountainbikes und fahrzeugähnliche Geräte (2010)

18. Officials, National Association of City Transportation. Urban Bikeway Design Guide (2014)

19. Gervasi, O., et al. (eds.): ICCSA 2020. LNCS, vol. 12251. Springer, Cham (2020). https://doi.org/10.1007/978-3-030-58808-3

20. Kuzmyak, J.R.: J. W. NCHRP REPORT 770 - Estimating bicycling and walking for planning and project development: a guidebook (2014)

21. Dufour D.: Ligtermoet and the Netherlands Partners. PRESTO Cycling Policy Guide- Cycling Infrastructure (2010)

22. Elvik, R.: Which are the relevant costs and benefits of road safety measures designed for pedestrian and cyclist? Accident Anal. Prevent. **32**, 37–45 (2000)

23. Monsere, C., et al.: Evaluation of innovative bicycle facilities: SW Broadway Cycle Track & SW Stark/Oak Street Buffered Bike Lanes (2014)

24. NACTO: Urban bikeway design guide. New York: National Association of City Transportation Officials (2014)

25. Bushell, M.A., et al.: Costs for Pedestrian and bicyclist infrastructure improvements: a resource for researchers, engineers, planners, and the general public. s.l.: UNC Highway Safety Research Center (2013)

26. Benni, J., Macaraig, M. e Malmo-Laycock, J.: Costing of bicycle infrastructure and programs in Canada. s.l.: Mc Grill, (2019)

27. Nuno Lopez, F., et al.: Linee guida per la progettazione delle reti ciclabili (2006)

28. Weigand, L., McNeil, N. e Dill, J.: Cost Analysis of bicycle facilities: cases from cities in the Portland, OR region (2013)

The Axial Analysis for Defining Neighborhoods' Crime Vulnerability. A Methodological Proposal

Francesca Coppola$^{(\boxtimes)}$ and Isidoro Fasolino

DICIV– Department of Civil Engineering, University of Salerno, Via Giovanni Paolo II, 132, 84084 Fisciano, SA, Italy
{fracoppola,i.fasolino}@unisa.it

Abstract. One major requirement for well-functioning cities, and for their sustainability, is that they have secure streets and public spaces, as also confirmed by the SDG 11. The work presented here deepens an ongoing research that addresses the issue of urban security in terms of risk. The study is carried out at the neighborhood scale aimed at examining the urban space accessibility and its role in the creation of security conditions. The model uses the *Space Syntax Analysis*, the *TOPSIS method* and *zonal statistic*, for the construction of a ranking and comparison between neighborhoods. The *composite security index* constructed (I_{sa}) allows the identification of the critical conditions in the area examined, identifying neighborhoods that, with respect to optimal accessibility conditions, understood in terms of urban security, are configured as better or worse. The application of the model to the Milan case study has highlighted how within the same territorial context individual neighborhoods can have different responses to the urban crime problem by virtue of their accessibility conditions, delineating possible further research developments.

Keywords: Accessibility · Crime risk vulnerability · Neighborhood security · Space Syntax Analysis · TOPSIS method

1 Introduction

One of the main requirements for well-functioning cities, and for their sustainability [9, 15, 17, 19, 29, 30, 36], is that they have secure streets and public spaces [5, 10, 26]. This circumstance is reaffirmed by the *Sustainable Development Goals* (SDG), in particular SDG 11, by which the creation of secure, as well as inclusive, resilient and sustainable cities is promoted.

Security in the city is hindered everyday by the occurrence of predatory crimes (assaults, thefts or other violent acts) or incivility episodes that affect the perception of insecurity, raising fear and creating, consequently, alienation with respect to the surrounding context [34].

The growing demand for security that citizens ask for requires a new perspective with respect to the approaches that have been adopted so far to deal with this problem. A repressive approach is not sufficient to guarantee effective and long-lasting security

© Springer Nature Switzerland AG 2021
O. Gervasi et al. (Eds.): ICCSA 2021, LNCS 12958, pp. 457–473, 2021.
https://doi.org/10.1007/978-3-030-87016-4_34

conditions. It is necessary to focus on an integrated approach in which urban planning plays a fundamental role.

The work presented here deepens an ongoing research that addresses the topic of urban security in terms of risk. In it crime risk is defined as a function of three factors: crime hazard (H_c), crime vulnerability (V_c), crime exposure (E_c) and described through the *Composite Index of crime risk I_{Rc}*, with spatial character [3, 14].

The study starts from an analysis recently developed in which, starting from the crime risk map constructed by applying the model to the city of Milan [14], and adopting a multi-scalar approach, it deepens the link between the accessibility of urban spaces and the vulnerability to crime risk (V_c) [3]. The methodology outlined combines the configurational approach with a multi-criteria method for constructing a ranking at the neighborhood scale and the subsequent comparison between neighborhoods. This allows to identify the neighborhoods that are better or worse compared to optimal accessibility conditions, considered in terms of urban security.

2   Materials and Methods

2.1   Axial Analysis

Space Syntax Analysis [24] allows to describe the accessibility conditions of urban space and simulate the pedestrian movement within it. The focus is on urban space, identified as an intrinsic aspect of human activities and as an essential element in the creation of movement flows [22, 45]. In the configurational theory, the measuring unit is the *visual perspective* connecting two points in space. The preference of one path over another is not based on metric distance but on its articulation.

The analysis of an urban settlement is performed through the urban grid reduction to a system and through the subsequent study of the relationships between its elements. A set of configurational properties assumed as state variables is associated to each of them. The urban grid can be discretized and analysed using a variety of operational techniques: *Linear Analysis*, separated into *Axial Analysis* [21], *Angular Analysis* and *Angular Segment Analysis* [39, 41], *Fragment Angular Analysis* [8]; *Visibility Graph Analysis* (normal and angular) [42]; *Mark Point Parameter Analysis* [7].

Axial Analysis [21] discretizes the urban grid by adopting as an elementary unit of reference the *line* that corresponds to a unit of movement and visual perception. The urban space is schematized and examined by constructing the *axial map*. The latter is composed of the longest axial lines, taken in the smallest number, and it is used as the basic topological map for the calculation of configurational indices: integration index, choice index, connectivity index, controllability index, control value [6].

In detail, the first of them represents the average depth of each line with respect to all the other lines of the axial map and is associated with the *to movement* [20, 22]. The index of choice is a measure of the potential of choice of a line understood as a path in the journey within the system and is associated with the *through movement* [20]. Both parameters are influenced by the axial map size, i.e. the number of lines it consists of. The connectivity index is representative of the number of lines that are directly accessible from the line in question [6].

2.2   TOPSIS Method

The *TOPSIS (Technique for Order Preference by Similarity to Ideal Solution) method* is a multi-criteria method developed by Hwang and Yoon [25, 28, 46] as an alternative to the *ELECTRE method* of which it is a widely used and advantageous variant [2, 44].

Given a sample of alternatives, the method is based on the assumption that the most convenient alternative is at the least distance from the *ideal* alternative (the best), and at the greatest distance from the *anti-ideal* alternative (the worst). The implementation of the method requires the selection of suitable indices (criteria) to evaluate the alternatives and the definition of a weight to be given to each of them [32].

The procedure is structured in different steps that include: the construction and normalization of the decision matrix; the definition of appropriate weights to be attributed to the indices and the construction of the weighted decision matrix; the definition of the two virtual solutions (*ideal* and *anti-ideal*) and the measurement of the relative distance of each real alternative. The procedure concludes by calculating the *relative closeness coefficient* C_i, based on which the alternatives are ranked. More precisely, in the construction of the ranking, the best alternative is characterized by the highest values of C_i.

3   Model

The model outlined aims at analyzing the accessibility conditions of urban space in relation to its influence on crime risk vulnerability (V_c). The analysis is performed at the neighborhood scale, since some key security issues, including accessibility [3] can only be captured through the study of limited-sized areas.

The methodology allows to describe and compare the accessibility conditions of neighborhoods, combining the configurational approach with a multi-criteria method and performing analysis on two spatial levels of reference:

- *Level 1 – accessibility by axial line;*
- *Level 2 – accessibility by neighborhood.*

In particular, it involves the use of Axial Analysis, the TOPSIS method, zonal statistics and is divided into three macro-phases.

The first of these analyzes the accessibility conditions of urban space using Axial Analysis [21] and the calculation of three configurational parameters: integration index (global and local), choice index (global and local), connectivity index. In the context of the analysis, *global* refers to the application to a spatial area containing a defined set of lines, while *local* refers to the measurement related to a surrounding of each line.

Analysis is followed by the systematisation, normalisation and weighing of the index values obtained and a first comparison of the accessibility conditions described by each configurational parameter.

The second macro-phase is dedicated to the implementation of the TOPSIS method [25] to construct a ranking of accessibility values and a first comparison between neighborhoods in relation to Level 1. The selected criteria for the analysis of alternatives are five and correspond to the configurational indices (global and local) calculated in the first macro-phase. For each area are used the normalized values of the indices for each line, weighted by the lines length, in global and local form. The ranking is constructed considering all the lines that constitute the axial maps of the examined neighborhoods.

The third macro-phase is implemented on Level 2, for which the areas examined are ranked using zonal statistics based on the ranking obtained on Level 1. For this purpose, the lines examined are classified into 5 criticality classes, with increasing intensity from very low (1) to very high (5). The classes are constructed according to the values of the relative proximity coefficient C_i, obtained in the previous macro-phase. More precisely, low criticality conditions are associated to lines with high values of C_i coefficient, representing positive conditions of accessibility and security, vice versa for lines in class 5. Indeed, accessibility is closely linked to crime risk vulnerability, since it influences the possibilities of informal control of the territory. Urban spaces with high values of accessibility and visual permeability, combined with a regular urban grid, encourage the presence of people on the street who act as potential "eyes on the street" [3, 26].

Attention then turns exclusively to the lines included in classes 1 and 5. In relation to these last ones, the model evaluates, for each class (c), and referring to the lines length ($l_{j,c}$ with $j = 1,..., m$ and $c = 1, 5$): the minimum value (l_{min}), the maximum value (l_{max}), the average value (l_{av}), the standard deviation (l_{sd}) and the overall sum of the lines lengths (L_c).

Therefore, the study of accessibility conditions is deepened by introducing two security indicators. The first of these represents the density of critical lines, class 5, for each neighborhood under study, D_{cl}:

$$D_{cl_i} = \frac{L_5}{A_i} = \frac{\sum_{j=1}^{m} l_{j,5}}{A_i}$$

with:

- D_{cl_i} = density of critical lines, class 5, in the i neighborhood (with $i = 1,..., n$);
- $L_5 = \sum_{j=1}^{m} l_{j,5}$ = sum of lengths of the m critical lines, class 5, of the i neighborhood;
- A_i = area of the i neighborhood under study.

High values of the indicator are representative of critical conditions. They highlight the presence, in the neighborhood examined, of a high density of lines with very low accessibility values and, therefore, critical regarding security.

The second indicator describes the criticality rate of lines. It is evaluated as ratio between the total length of the critical lines (class 5) and that of the lines with positive values (class 1), R_{cl}:

$$R_{cl_i} = \frac{L_5}{L_1} = \frac{\sum_{j=1}^{m} l_{j,5}}{\sum_{z=1}^{k} l_{z,1}}$$

with:

- R_{cl_i} = criticality rate of lines in the i neighborhood (con $i = 1, ..., n$);

- $L_5 = \sum_{j=1}^{m} l_{j,5}$ = sum of lengths of the m critical lines, class 5, of the i neighborhood;

- $L_1 = \sum_{z=1}^{k} l_{z,1}$ = sum of lengths of the k positive lines, class 1, of the i neighborhood.

High values of the indicator represent critical conditions. They highlight the prevalence of critical lines compared to lines with positive accessibility values in terms of vulnerability and, therefore, security.

The computation of these security indicators is followed, then, by their spatialization and combination into a composite index, with spatial character, I_{sa}:

$$I_{sa} = I_{sa}(D_{cl}; R_{cl})$$

The indicators are combined with each other using a matrix approach. The model involves the use of reclassification and overlay mapping between rasters, fundamental map-algebra operations [38], implemented from the base maps.

To this purpose, for each of the neighborhoods examined, the n values of the two indicators (D_{cl_i} and R_{cl_i} = with i = 1,...,n) are reclassified into 5 classes of criticality, as before. Through the overlay mapping a combination matrix is built in which each cell, defined according to the logical Boolean operator AND, identifies a specific class of criticality according to the accessibility values. Based on this principle and according to risk matrix logic [11–14], it is possible to interpret and reclassify the combination results by constructing 5 criticality classes related to accessibility values: very low (CA1), low (CA2), moderate (CA3), high (CA4), very high (CA5).

The *composite security index* thus constructed, I_{sa}, allows the identification of the critical conditions in the area examined, highlighting the potential of individual neighborhoods to provide an answer to the urban crime problem by virtue of their accessibility conditions. The most problematic conditions, which need attention, are found at class CA5.

4 Application of the Model

The outlined methodology was applied to the case study of Milan. It deepens and integrates a previous study that led to map the risk conditions of the city [14] and study the link between accessibility and crime risk vulnerability [3].

According to the paper's objectives, the application involved 31 neighborhoods selected among the *Nuclei di Identità Locale* (NIL) which correspond to local identity cores, defined by the *Piano di Governo del Territorio* (PGT-Milano 2030) which correspond to the urban Plan of Milan (Fig. 1). The 35 NILs to be analysed were chosen according to the presence of medium (R3), high (R4) and very high (R5) crime risk classes (Fig. 1) and according to land use. Only neighborhoods with a mainly residential land use category, with grid layout and irregular layout, were included in the analysis [3]. In detail: 1-Duomo; 2-Brera; 3-Giardini Pt. Venezia; 4-Guastalla; 5-P.ta Vigentina, P.ta Lodovica; 6-P.ta Ticinese, Conca del Naviglio; 7-Magenta, S. Vittore; 8-Parco Sempione; 9-P.ta Garibaldi, P.ta Nuova; 10-Stazione Centrale, Ponte Seveso; 11-Isola; 12-Maciachini, Maggiolina; 20-Loreto, casoretto, NoLo; 21-Buenos Aires, P.ta

Venezia, P.ta Monforte; 22-Città studi; 25-Corsica; 26-XXII Marzo; 27-P.ta Romana; 28-Umbria, Molise, Calvairate; 44-P.ta Ticinese, Conchetta; 50-P.ta Genova; 51-P.ta Magenta; 52-Bande Nere; 57-San Siro; 58-De Angeli, Monte Rosa; 59-Tre Torri; 68-Pagano; 67-Portello; 69-Sarpi; 70-Ghisolfa; 71-Villapizzone, Cagnola, Boldinasco; 77-Bovisa; 78-Farini; 79-Dergano; 80-Affori. Some areas consist of 2 NILs, due to the continuity of the urban structure.

The area of interest corresponds to the central ring of the Milan consolidated fabric. As stated in the PGT-Milano 2030, it is characterized by a very high urbanization and high accessibility, in some cases equal in size to 100% of the NIL surface.

In the PGT-Milano 2030 zoning it is characterized by the presence of *Nuclei di Antica Formazione* (NAF) which correspond to cores of ancient formation, external historical cores, pedestrian spaces and squares. These are 5 of the 7 squares with high accessibility, for which the PGT-Milano 2030 envisages regeneration interventions aimed at improving design quality, pedestrian accessibility and attractiveness. There are *Ambiti di Rinnovamento Urbano* (ARU) which correspond to urban renewal areas and Environmental Regeneration Areas alongside existing and new urban green spaces. Moreover, the NIL 78-Farini, is characterized by the presence of a railway yard where a new urban park and some social housings are to be built.

Almost all of the selected NILs, in addition, are affected by regeneration and transformation interventions, planned or partially implemented, aimed at increasing urban green areas, services and environmental regeneration of the urban fabric.

Moreover, several changes of land use are foreseen, characterized by a significant increase of the residential land use category and by the introduction of accomodation functions, replacing part of the commercial, tertiary and productive land uses[1].

The application of the model was divided into successive steps. The first of these has regarded the implementation of the Axial Analysis on the selected neighborhoods. For this purpose, for each of the 31 neighborhoods examined, the urban grid was represented, by vector editing functions carried out starting from the basic cartography.

In the construction of the latter, it was chosen to exclude and consider not freely accessible: parks, playgrounds, railway lines, subways and highway connections. Then, through the Depthmap software [40], the topological base map was obtained and configurational indices with global (R = n) and local (R = 3) valence were calculated. In addition, in order to make the accessibility values of the examined neighborhoods comparable, it was necessary to disassociate the integration and choice indexes from the axial maps dimension through a normalization step. The first of them, in particular, was normalised using the concept of Real Relative Asymmetry-RRA, through the Krüger's formulation [27].

The results were systematized in a summary table and weighted according to the lines' length. This allowed an initial evaluation of the accessibility values recorded for each line and helped the next steps to be taken.

The second macro-phase was conducted by implementing the TOPSIS method on the spatial reference Level 1. The five configurational measures used as analysis criteria are: Global Normalised Integration Index, RRA(R = n); Local Normalised Integration

---

[1] For further information please consult the PGT-Milano 2030, available at the link: https://www.pgt.comune.milano.it/ (accessed 21/04/2021).

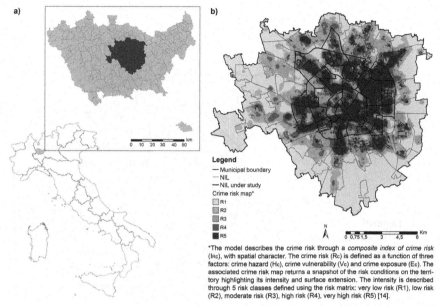

Fig. 1. a) Territorial context of the study area; b) Milan municipality's crime risk map. Source: authors' elaboration.

Index, RRA($R = 3$), Global Normalised Choice Index ($R = n$); Local Normalised Choice Index ($R = 3$); Connectivity Index. The analysis was performed considering for each index (global and local) the values of all lines of the 31 axial maps under study, with 2499 lines in total (Fig .2).

The analysis was conducted with equal weights and the value judgment, representative of ideal and anti-ideal accessibility conditions, was constructed, for each index, according to the relevant performance scale. In detail, the normalization criterion used for the integration index, both global and local, cause its values to range between 0 (ideal accessibility) and values greater than 1 (segregation). Therefore, the minimum value was set as ideal condition and maximum value as anti-ideal. The normalized choice index, both global and local, ranged between 0 (low *through movement*) and 1 (high *through movement*). Consequently, the ideal condition was associated with the maximum value and the anti-ideal with the minimum. The same judgment criterion was used for the connectivity index.

The third macro-phase concerned the realization of zonal statistics in a GIS environment, through the use of ArcGIS software [18], on Level 2, starting from the ranking obtained in Level 1. To this purpose, the lines under study were classified on the basis of the C_i coefficient values into 5 criticality classes, with increasing intensity from very low (1) to very high (5). These classes were constructed using the *Natural Breaks* setting. Among the 2499 values examined, only those belonging to classes 1 and 5 were extracted for each neighborhood. For the latter, with reference to the length of the lines (l), were evaluated: the minimum value (l_{min}), the maximum (l_{max}), the average value (l_{av}), the standard deviation (l_s) and the overall sum of the lines lengths (L_c) (Table 1).

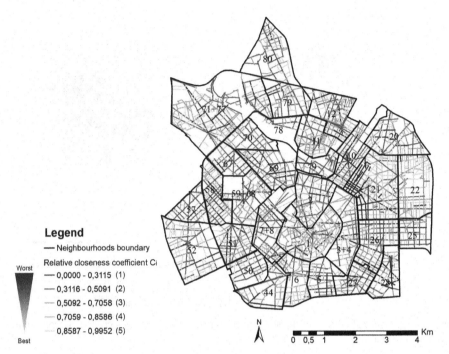

Fig. 2. Ranking of accessibility values for axial line (Level 1). Source: authors' elaboration.

Next, the following were calculated for each of the areas: the density of critical lines (D_{cl_i} with $i = 1,...,31$) and the criticality rate of lines (R_{cl_i}, with $i = 1,...,31$). The values obtained were reclassified into 5 classes of criticality, with increasing intensity from 1 to 5, and spatialized in order to allow their combination (Fig. 3 and 4). The resulting base maps were combined using an overlay mapping operation, and the results were interpreted using the matrix of critical accessibility levels (Fig. 5), structured following the logic of the risk matrix [14]. The criticality classes built through this matrix cannot be generalized but are only valid for the case study of Milan.

The map associated with the composite index of security thus constructed, I_{sa}, is shown in Fig. 6.

Table 1. Results of statistical analysis performed by neighborhood (Level 2). Source: authors' elaboration.

NIL	Area	Lines – class 1				Lines – class 5			
		l_{min}	l_{max}	l_{av}	l_{sd}	l_{min}	l_{max}	l_{av}	l_{sd}
(ID)	(km²)	(m)	(m)	(m)	(m)	(m)	(m)	(m)	(m)
1	2,3	35,2	476,3	130,9	74,7	313,2	881,8	520,8	169,4
2	1,6	36,9	619,7	163,0	110,2	571,6	1074,9	725,7	237,6
3 + 4	1,6	67,6	386,0	178,4	83,6	620,3	1522,4	936,2	347,5

(continued)

Table 1. (*continued*)

NIL	Area	Lines – class 1				Lines – class 5			
		l_{min}	l_{max}	l_{av}	l_{sd}	l_{min}	l_{max}	l_{av}	l_{sd}
5	1,0	10,7	708,3	205,6	149,3	379,6	896,5	673,8	195,4
6	1,2	34,9	976,2	238,9	202,6	181,7	378,7	280,2	139,3
7 + 8	0,5	55,4	753,3	187,7	144,7	440,0	917,5	671,7	159,6
9	0,8	24,4	418,5	178,6	96,7	306,8	648,9	543,2	130,7
10	1,6	10,0	738,6	253,0	162,4	508,3	1624,5	974,9	340,0
11	1,3	24,4	539,2	176,5	131,6	646,7	1132,8	769,5	242,2
12	1,7	63,9	643,6	186,1	112,5	122,2	854,4	508,2	313,4
20	1,8	39,8	469,8	190,5	84,1	478,1	724,7	583,1	127,3
21	2,9	131,2	2016,7	684,9	599,3	95,9	1951,2	543,6	414,7
22	2,1	66,1	1996,2	462,2	406,3	109,7	412,4	242,1	154,9
25	1,0	67,7	503,3	195,2	101,3	892,3	924,0	908,1	22,5
26	1,6	68,1	520,9	242,5	119,9	812,7	1300,6	958,8	192,2
27	0,9	85,5	491,7	232,3	114,7	497,3	706,7	617,8	70,2
28	1,2	68,1	506,3	225,5	123,2	572,9	1034,7	784,8	146,5
44	1,4	25,6	361,1	190,8	89,1	513,2	1073,6	819,0	283,7
50	1,1	15,7	339,9	151,0	85,9	371,4	1140,1	587,5	369,9
51	1,3	58,5	345,3	213,0	72,9	648,3	1239,5	985,8	255,5
52	2,7	81,4	695,2	236,4	129,0	692,7	1465,1	1195,8	436,1
57	1,0	72,4	554,8	212,0	132,0	643,8	1227,7	930,3	259,1
58	1,3	55,9	499,6	208,2	98,0	682,1	1073,1	852,0	147,7
67	0,9	166,4	434,4	303,1	115,7	512,5	831,3	671,9	225,5
59 + 68	1,3	44,2	803,9	197,9	156,1	576,3	901,0	762,7	136,3
69	1,8	74,0	367,5	182,7	77,1	516,9	986,0	782,9	152,3
70	1,0	68,0	512,4	235,1	125,7	0,0	0,0	0,0	0,0
71 + 77	5,4	45,5	948,3	223,3	164,2	542,0	1633,9	959,6	466,9
78	1,1	73,9	322,9	194,6	73,8	0,0	0,0	0,0	0,0
79	1,3	43,6	336,5	196,3	74,0	503,7	864,6	632,1	201,7
80	2,1	57,9	1255,3	271,9	231,4	485,9	485,9	485,9	0,0

5 Discussion of Results

The results obtained from the axial analysis performed at Level 1 show a heterogeneous situation with regard to the accessibility values recorded for the 31 neighborhoods examined.

In detail, the highest values of local and global integration, 0,095 and 0,098, occur in lines belonging to NIL 9 and 21, respectively. The lowest values, equal to 4,788 and 1,212, are identified in lines of NIL 1 and 50. The neighborhoods in which high accessibility conditions are observed, with more than 50% of lines whose global integration values are lower than the average value, correspond to NIL: 1, 2, 3 + 4, 6, 7 + 8, 9, 10, 11, 12, 21, 22, 26, 27, 51, 52, 69. The same situation, in local terms, is noted in all the areas examined, except for NIL 1 and 71 + 77. The values of the choice index range from a minimum of 0, observed in some lines of all the areas examined, to maximum values, in global and local terms, equal to 0,879 and 0,667 measured in lines belonging respectively to NIL 80 and 50. Neighborhoods where conditions of high accessibility are observed, associated with a high potential for through movement, with more than 50% of lines whose overall choice values exceed the mean value, correspond to NIL: 9, 70, 78. The same circumstance, in local terms, is in NIL: 9, 67, 70, 78, 79. As regards connectivity, 16 of the 31 neighborhoods examined (NIL: 2, 3 + 4, 5, 7 + 8, 9, 10, 12, 25, 28, 44, 50, 52, 69, 71 + 77,78, 80) present lines in which a minimum value of 1 is recorded, while the maximum value, equal to 33, is found in NIL 21. High accessibility conditions, with more than 50% of lines whose connectivity values exceed the average value, are found in NIL: 10, 21, 22, 26, 27, 51.

The ranking construction at Level 1 led to the identification of the best and worst lines in relation to accessibility conditions, with reference to urban security [3]. The ranking presents values of the relative closeness coefficient C_i ranging between the minimum value (worst condition) of 0 and the maximum value (best condition) of 0,9952 (Fig. 2). The subsequent construction of 5 criticality classes for the 2499 lines under attention highlights the presence of: 155 lines in class 5, 444 in class 4, 423 in class 3, 551 in class 2 and 926 in class 1. Examining the data globally, lines characterized by positive values appear to predominate, however the effect that poor accessibility generates on neighborhoods, in terms of security, requires an analysis on a neighborhood-by-neighborhood basis.

Starting from this result, the analysis conducted on Level 2 has made it possible to evaluate in greater detail the conditions of accessibility of the areas examined. It highlighted the real incidence of lines with critical values both in relation to the NIL surface extension, and to the presence of lines with positive values (Figs. 3 and 4). In particular, the density of critical lines, D_{cl}, ranges from a minimum of 0 at NIL 70 and 78, where no class 5 lines are present, to a maximum of 0,0086 at NIL 7 + 8. The criticality rate of lines, R_{cl}, has a minimum value of 0, at NILs 70 and 78, for the reasons just stated, and a maximum value of 91,3627 at NIL 69.

The maps obtained from the reclassification and spatialization of the two indicators $(D_{cl}; R_{cl})$ (Figs. 3 and 4) show that, in terms of critical line density, the most critical areas are represented by NIL: 7 + 8, 10, 21 and 28. In relation to the rate of critical lines the most critical areas are NIL 1 and 69.

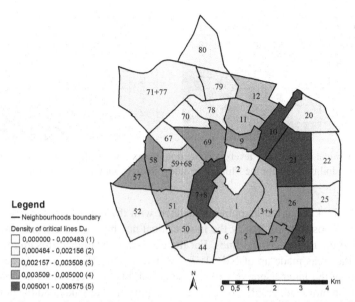

Fig. 3. Spatialization of critical line density values, D_{cl}, by neighborhood (Level 2). Source: authors' elaboration.

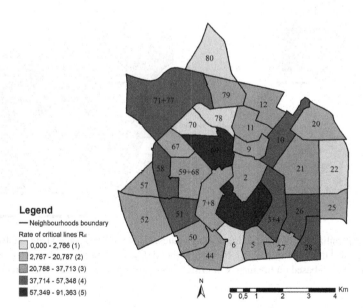

Fig. 4. Spatialization of critical lines rate values, R_{cl}, by neighborhood (Level 2). Source: authors' elaboration.

a)

Critical Accessibiliy classes		D_d classes				
		D_d1	D_d2	D_d3	D_d4	D_d5
R_d classes	R_d1	11	12	13	14	15
	R_d2	21	22	23	24	
	R_d3	31	32	33	34	
	R_d4	41	42	43		
	R_d5	51				

b)

Critical Accessibiliy classes		D_d classes				
		D_d1	D_d2	D_d3	D_d4	D_d5
R_d classes	R_d1	CA1	CA1	CA2	CA3	CA4
	R_d2	CA1	CA2	CA3	CA4	
	R_d3	CA2	CA3	CA3	CA4	
	R_d4	CA3	CA4	CA4		
	R_d5	CA4				

Fig. 5. a) Critical accessibility levels construction matrix for the Milan case study; b) Matrix of critical accessibility levels for the Milan case study. Source: authors' elaboration.

Finally, looking at the mapping associated with the composite security index, I_{sa}, (Fig. 6), it is possible to identify the most critical neighborhoods considering both the density and the rate of critical lines. For the case study examined this circumstance is found in the areas made up of NIL: 1, 7 + 8, 69, 58, 10, 21, 26, 28. The accessibility conditions of the latter negatively affect the possibility of exercising informal control, making them more vulnerable to crime. They require further study and the definition of specific strategies and actions to reduce vulnerability and, consequently, crime risk.

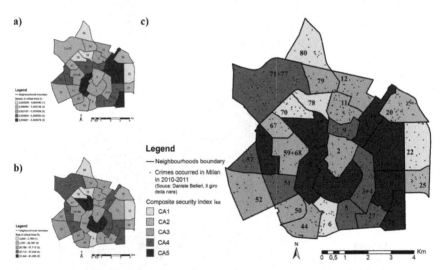

Fig. 6. a) Spatialization of critical line density values, D_{cl}, by neighborhood (Fig. 3); b) Spatialization of critical lines rate values, R_{cl}, by neighborhood (Fig. 4); c) Spatialization of the composite security index, I_{sa}, based on the matrix of critical accessibility levels (Level 2). Source: authors' elaboration.

6 Conclusions and Prospects

The application of the model to the Milan case study has highlighted how within the same territorial context individual neighborhoods can have different responses to the issue of urban crime. In detail, this response was examined considering a physical aspect of urban space, namely accessibility understood in topological terms, as the ease by which a space can be reached by others. This characteristic, as mentioned above, can influence crime vulnerability by affecting the possibility of exercising informal surveillance. Urban spaces with high values of accessibility and visual permeability, combined with a regular urban grid, encourage the presence of people on the street, residents and non-residents, who act as potential "eyes on the street" [3, 26].

The analysis of neighborhood accessibility was performed using a configurational approach combined with a multi-criteria method in order to examine the characteristics of the individual lines under study. The composite security index, I_{sa}, obtained after the implementation of zonal statistics, allows for an assessment on a neighborhood scale. In fact, it describes the critical conditions of the neighborhood examined, considering both the critical lines density and the prevalence (or not) of the latter compared to the lines with positive accessibility values in terms of crime vulnerability and urban security. The mapping associated with it allows for the rapid identification of neighborhoods with greater criticality in relation to the phenomenon studied and in need of attention. The model outlined is also suitable to be applied to different territorial contexts from the one examined.

The results obtained suggest possible further developments of the research. The work presented here is oriented to understand a complex phenomenon that, as such, requires a deepening and the introduction of further analysis and variables of a physical, functional and social nature. In fact, the beneficial effect of accessibility on crime risk vulnerability is influenced by multiple aspects, including: the presence of residential units on both sides of streets; intervisibility between dwellings; a proper, consciously structured functional mix in which the residential function is calibrated to balance the vulnerability created by other uses, etc. [3, 16, 23, 33, 35, 43]. The balance between these factors is fundamental to facilitate the possibility of informal control which, however, will be implemented with more or less relevance depending on the socio-cultural context of the place and the citizens' lifestyle. Informal surveillance is more likely to be practiced where walking is a consolidated habit [31]. In the absence of the aforementioned requirements, high accessibility could have the opposite effect, as it is also correlated to the offender's greater awareness and freedom of action, greater ease of approach to potential victims, and the presence of greater escape routes for criminals [1, 16, 23, 37].

Specifically, in relation to the case study, the overlap between the composite security index, I_{sa}, and the spatial distribution of crimes (Fig. 6) qualitatively highlights a positive effect of accessibility on vulnerability. The presence of higher crime events is perceived at the highest levels of critical accessibility (CA4 and CA5). This observation leads to include, among future research developments, a quantitative analysis of the relationship between the crime level and the spatial configuration of neighborhood units in Milan.

Based on the observations made, it is necessary to emphasize the importance of considering urban security when defining urban planning tools. It appears clear that planning choices can significantly affect the conditions of vulnerability and exposure to crime risk.

With reference to the case study examined, in particular, the PGT-Milano 2030 foresees urban requalification interventions, changes of use, etc., without considering the effects that such choices may have in terms of crime risk. For instance, the *External Istorical Cores* and *Pedestrian Areas*, for which the PGT-Milano 2030 (NTA, art. 15) [4] foresee as a form of regeneration the realization of any urban function or an increase in neighborhood shops, craft activities (with regard to personal services and those in the food and non-food sectors) and service activities (in which are also included basements, semi-basements and mezzanines if functionally and physically connected, located on the ground floor overlooking the public plane and/or public use. Such predictions can alter the functional mix, which is a major factor in security because it can influence the cities' vitality and informal surveillance of urban space [14]. In addition, many of the neighborhoods examined are affected by medium and long term forecasts that will modify the accessibility conditions, as understood in the present contribution, through the increase of paths and pedestrian areas, without taking into account the influence this has on crime vulnerability and, therefore, on urban security [3]. In conclusion, it is observed that the possibility of promoting neighborhood security is closely linked to the definition of a suitable framework of rules to be constructed downstream of the risk scenario simulation resulting from the planning choices. This could be made possible by introducing the crime risk map [14] among the knowledge documents in the ex-ante phase of the urban Plan formation.

References

1. Baran, P.K., Smith, W.R., Toker, U.: The space syntax and crime. In: Kubat, A.S., Ertekin, Ö., Güney, Y.I., Eyüboğlu, E. (eds.) Proceedings of the sixth International Space Syntax Symposium, pp. 119-01–119-06. ITU Faculty of Architecture, Istanbul (2007)
2. Behzadian, M., Khanmohammadi Otaghsara, S., Yazdani, M., Ignatius, J.: A state-of the-art survey of TOPSIS applications. Expert Syst. Appl. **39**(17), 13051–13069 (2012). https://doi.org/10.1016/j.eswa.2012.05.056
3. Coppola, F., Grimaldi, M., Fasolino, I.: A configurational approach for measuring the accessibility of place as an analysis tool for crime risk vulnerability. In: La Rosa, D., Privitera, R. (eds.) INPUT 2021. LNCE, vol. 146, pp. 501–509. Springer, Cham (2021). https://doi.org/10.1007/978-3-030-68824-0_54
4. Comune di Milano: Piano delle Regole, Norme di attuazione. Milano (2019)
5. Cozens, P.: Planning, crime and urban sustainability. WIT Trans. Ecol. Environ. **102**, 187–196 (2007). https://doi.org/10.2495/SDP070181
6. Cutini, V.: La rivincita dello spazio urbano. L'approccio configurazionale allo studio e all'analisi dei centri abitati. Plus-Pisa University Press, Pisa (2010)
7. Cutini, V., Petri, M., Santucci, A.: From axial maps to mark point parameter analysis (Ma.P.P.A.) – A GIS implemented method to automate configurational analysis. In: Laganá, A., Gavrilova, M.L., Kumar, V., Mun, Y., Tan, C.J.K., Gervasi, O. (eds.) ICCSA 2004. LNCS, vol. 3044, pp. 1107–1116. Springer, Heidelberg (2004). https://doi.org/10.1007/978-3-540-24709-8_116

8. Dalton, N.: Fractional configurational analysis and a solution to the Manhattan problem. In: Peponis, J., Wineman, J., Bafna, S. (eds.) Proceedings of the 3rd Space Syntax Symposium, College of Architecture, Georgia Tech, Atlanta, 7–11th May 2001. Georgia Tech, Atlanta (2001)

9. De Mare, G., Nesticò, A., Macchiaroli, M., Dolores, L.: Market prices and institutional values. In: Gervasi, O., et al. (eds.) ICCSA 2017. LNCS, vol. 10409, pp. 430–440. Springer, Cham (2017). https://doi.org/10.1007/978-3-319-62407-5_30

10. Du Plessis, C.: The links between crime prevention and sustainable development. In: Lawrence, R. (ed.) Sustaining Human Settlement: a challenge for the new millennium, pp. 239–270. Urban International Press, North Shields (2002)

11. EC-European Commission: Commission Staff Working Paper Risk Assessment and Mapping Guidelines for Disaster Management; 21/12/2010, SEC (2010) 1626 final. European Commission, Brussels (2010)

12. EC-European Commission: Recommendations for National Risk Assessment for Disaster Risk Management in EU. European Commission (2019). https://doi.org/10.2760/147842

13. ECDC-European Centre for Disease Prevention and Control: Operational guidance on rapid risk assessment methodology. European Centre for Disease Prevention and Control, Stockholm (2011). https://doi.org/10.2900/57509

14. Fasolino, I., Coppola, F., Grimaldi, M.: La sicurezza urbana degli insediamenti. Azioni e tecniche per il piano urbanistico. FrancoAngeli, Milano (2018)

15. Fasolino, I., Coppola, F., Grimaldi, M.: A model for urban planning control of the settlement efficiency. a case study. ASUR – Archivio di Studi Urbani e Regionali, LI, **127**(suppl.), 181–210 (2020). https://doi.org/10.3280/asur2020-127-s1010

16. Friedrich, E., Hillier, B., Chiaradia, A.: Anti-social behaviour and urban configuration using space syntax to understand spatial patterns of socio-environmental disorder. In: Koch, D., Marcus, L., Steen, J. (eds.) Proceedings of the seventh International Space Syntax Symposium, School of Architecture and the Built Environment, KTH Royal Institute of Technology, Stockholm, 8–11th June 2009. KTH, Stockholm (2009)

17. González-Méndez, M., Olaya, C., Fasolino, I., Grimaldi, M., Obregón, N.: Agent-based modeling for urban development planning based on human needs. conceptual basis and model formulation. Land Use Policy **101**, 105110 (2021). https://doi.org/10.1016/j.landusepol.2020.105110

18. Gorr, W.L., Kurland, K.S.: GIS Tutorial for Crime Analysis. Esri Press, Redlands (2011)

19. Grimaldi, M., Sebillo, M., Vitiello, G., Pellecchia, V.: Planning and managing the integrated water system: a spatial decision support system to analyze the infrastructure performances. Sustainability **12**(16), 6432 (2020). https://doi.org/10.3390/su12166432

20. Hillier, B.: Spatial sustainability in cities organic patterns and sustainable forms. In: Koch, D., Marcus, L., Steen, J. (eds.) Proceedings of the seventh International Space Syntax Symposium, School of Architecture and the Built Environment, KTH Royal Institute of Technology, Stockholm, 8–11th June 2009. KTH, Stockholm (2009)

21. Hillier, B., Hanson, J.: The Social Logic of Space. Cambridge University Press, Cambridge (1984)

22. Hillier, B., Iida, S.: Network and psychological effects in urban movement. In: Cohn, A.G., Mark, D.M. (eds.) COSIT 2005. LNCS, vol. 3693, pp. 475–490. Springer, Heidelberg (2005). https://doi.org/10.1007/11556114_30

23. Hillier, B., Sahbaz, O.: Safety in numbers: high-resolution analysis of crime in street networks. In: Ceccato, V. (ed.) The Urban Fabric of Crime and Fear, pp. 111–137. Springer, Dordrecht (2011). https://doi.org/10.1007/978-94-007-4210-9_5

24. Hillier, B., Leaman, A., Stansall, P., Bedforf, M.: Space syntax. Environ. Plann. B Plann. Des. **3**(2), 147–185 (1976). https://doi.org/10.1068%2Fb030147

25. Hwang, C.L., Yoon, K.: Multiple attribute decision making: methods and applications. Lecture Notes in Economics and Mathematical Systems, vol. 186. Springer-Verlag, Berlin (1981). https://doi.org/10.1007/978-3-642-48318-9
26. Jacobs, J.: The Death and Life of Great American Cities. Random House, New York (1961)
27. Krüger, M.J.T.: On node and axial grid maps, distance measures and related topics. In: Proceedings of the European Conference on the Representation and Management of Urban Change. Unit for Architectural Studies, UCL-University College London, London (1989)
28. Lai, Y.-J., Liu, T.-Y., Hwang, C.-L.: TOPSIS for MODM. Eur. J. Oper. Res. **76**(3), 486–500 (1994)
29. Macchiaroli, M., Pellecchia, V., D'Alpaos, C.: Urban water management in Italy: An innovative model for the selection of water service infrastructures. WSEAS Trans. Environ. Dev. **15**, 463–477 (2019). ISSN:1790–5079
30. Nesticò, A., Macchiaroli, M., Maselli, G.: An innovative risk assessment approach in projects for the enhancement of small towns. Valori e Valutazioni **25**, 91–98 (2020). ISSN: 20362404
31. Nubani, L., Wineman, J.: The role of space syntax in identifying the relationship between space and crime. In: van Nes, A. (ed.) 5th International Space Syntax Symposium. Proceedings, vol. 1, pp. 413–422. Techne Press, Delft (2005)
32. Olson, D.L.: Comparison of weights in TOPSIS models. Math. Comput. Model. **40**(7–8), 721–727 (2004). https://doi.org/10.1016/j.mcm.2004.10.003
33. Reis, A.T., Rosa, C.G.: Configuration, land use, perception, and security: an analysis of residential Burglary. In: Greene, M., Reyes, J., Castro, A. (eds.) Proceedings of the eighth international space syntax Symposium, pp. 8130:1–8130:14. PUC, Santiago (2012)
34. Scialdone, A., Giuliano, G.A.: Percezioni di insicurezza e bisogno di protezione. Un'esplorazione della domanda sociale. Sinappsi, X, **2**, 43–56 (2020). https://doi.org/10.1485/2532-8549-202002-4
35. Shu, S.C.F.: Spatial configuration of residential area and vulnerability of burglary: case studies from UK and Taiwan. In: Koch, D., Marcus, L., Steen, J. (eds.) Proceedings of the seventh International Space Syntax Symposium, School of Architecture and the Built Environment, KTH Royal Institute of Technology, Stockholm, 8–11th June 2009. KTH, Stockholm (2009)
36. Sebillo, M., Vitiello, G., Grimaldi, M., De Piano, A.: A citizen-centric approach for the improvement of territorial services management. ISPRS Int. J. Geo Inf. **9**(4), 223 (2020). https://doi.org/10.3390/ijgi9040223
37. Summers, L., Johnson, S.D.: Does the configuration of the street network influence where outdoor serious violence takes place? Using space syntax to test crime pattern theory. J. Quant. Criminol. **33**(2), 397–420 (2017). https://doi.org/10.1007/s10940-016-9306-9
38. Tomlin, D.C.: GIS and Cartographic Modeling. Prentice Hall, Upper Saddle River (1990)
39. Turner, A.: Angular Analysis. In: Peponis, J., Wineman, J., Bafna, S. (eds.): Proceedings of the 3rd Space Syntax Symposium, College of Architecture, Georgia Tech, Atlanta, 7–11th May 2001. Georgia Tech, Atlanta (2001)
40. Turner, A.: Depthmap 4. A Researcher's Handbook. Bartlett School of Graduate Studies. UCL-University College London, London (2004)
41. Turner, A.: From axial to road-centre lines: a new representation for space syntax and a new model of route choice for transport network analysis. Environ. Plann. B. Plann. Des. **34**, 539–555 (2007). https://doi.org/10.1068/b32067
42. Turner, A., Doxa, M., O'Sullivan, D., Penn, A.: From isovists to visibility graphs: a methodology for the analysis of architectural space. Environ. Plann. B Plann. Des. **28**, 103–121 (2001). https://doi.org/10.1068%2Fb2684
43. van Nes A., Lo´pez M.J.J.: Macro and micro scale spatial variables and the distribution of residential burglaries and theft from cars. J. Space Syntax **1**(2), 296–314 (2010)
44. Velasquez, M., Hester, P.T.: An analysis of multi-criteria decision making methods. Int. J. Oper. Res. **10**(2), 56–66 (2013)

45. Yamu, C., van Nes, A., Garau, C.: Bill Hillier's legacy: space syntax-a synopsis of basic concepts, measures, and empirical application. Sustainability **13**, 3394 (2021). https://doi.org/10.3390/su13063394
46. Yoon, K., Hwang, C.L.: Multiple Attribute Decision Making: An Introduction. Sage, Thousand Oaks (1995)

Resilient Urban Form Assessment – Burgage Cycle and Morphometry

Malgorzata Hanzl$^{(\boxtimes)}$ and Kamil Kowalski$^{(\boxtimes)}$

Lodz University of Technology, Lodz, Poland
malgorzata.hanzl@p.lodz.pl, kamil.kowalski@dokt.p.lodz.pl

Abstract. Over the years, cities and urban districts undergo constant transformations. Some areas are in their prime; others experience stagnation or, in the extreme case, collapse. We aim to contribute to the definition of the concept of urban resilience. Our goal is to expand its understanding from the normative perspective of urban design. We propose the method based on contemporary research in morphometrics. Our starting point is the Conzenian process of the burgage cycle. We begin with the approach developed by Marek Koter for several streets in Lodz. We expand the method further and relate it to the well-recognised attributes of urban resilience, i.e. diversity, connectivity, redundancy and modularity. Moreover, the key issue of this study was the proper relationship between the front width, plot area and Building Coverage Ratio (BCR). The case study showcases the method applying it to the case study of Zachodnia Street in Lodz, Poland.

Keywords: Urban resilience · Urban morphology · Urban form · Urban morphometry · Burgage cycle · Urban block · Urban design

1 Introduction

Urban areas undergo continuous transformations. The specific form of urban settings is the outcome of a given historical moment, stage of economic development and socio-political situation (Parysek 2015, p. 46). The development sine wave shows the periods of prosperity followed by stagnation and collapse (ibid. p. 47).

Sudden events left their mark on an urban system, its spatial, social, economic and environmental aspects. Cities able to restore functioning soon after major disruptions feature high resilience. Urban resilience gains researchers' attention, particularly concerning current climate change and sudden violent natural phenomena that degrade urban systems. In urban morphology, this concept has been increasingly applied to the analysis of physical urban form. Feliciotti et al. (2016, p. 2) claim that resilient urban form can be achieved at the architectural and urban design stage. Despite numerous studies, the issue has not been fully explored yet. Particularly the methodology that might support the objective assessment of the resilience level still welcomes new insights. The growth of mathematical and statistical methods for urban form assessment, as shown in publications describing the urban morphometry, opens new avenues for future research. Moreover, the search for relationships between specific elements of urban fabric becomes the subject of evaluation of resilient urban form.

© Springer Nature Switzerland AG 2021
O. Gervasi et al. (Eds.): ICCSA 2021, LNCS 12958, pp. 474–489, 2021.
https://doi.org/10.1007/978-3-030-87016-4_35

2   The Purpose of the Research

This article intends to supplement the definition of urban resilience with additional elements stemming from urban design. The analysis of physical form enables us to verify whether the evolutions of urban tissue can positively influence resilience in the long period perspective. The starting point is urban morphology and morphometry; we use and develop the current research framework in this field. Our goal is to enhance the current set of indicators to assess the resilience of urban form. For this purpose, we have performed a quantitative evaluation of selected 19th-century urban block. We measure elements such as front width, plot area, front-to-plot ratio and Building Coverage Ratio (BCR). The parameters mentioned above determine the quality of city centre tissue and its efficiency (Romice et al. 2020, p.47). Therefore, determining the proper relationships between them is necessary for the working urban system.

The parcels proportions, and the active fronts of buildings, have been researched before (e.g., Bobkova 2019; Dovey et al. 2017). The results show a clear relationship between active fronts and the FAR and BCR values. It also turns out that street fronts play a vital role in adding land value and shaping a resilient urban form. In order to verify this, we analyse the evolution of urban blocks located in the city centre, at Zachodnia Street in Lodz, Poland. We pay particular attention to the changing proportions between the front width, plot area, front-to-plot ratio and BCR. Scope of analysis is consistent with the research carried out in the 1990s by Professor Marek Koter (1990), who statistically and mathematically assessed the evolution of the urban form of the city centre of Lodz. In his research, he addressed plots located along the historical route and main transport axis of the city of Lodz, i.e. Piotrkowska Street. Therefore, this article continues the former local research on urban resilience with more contemporary urban morphometry.

3   Research Background

The concept of urban resilience is rooted in the theory of systems, described by the Austrian biologist and philosopher Ludwig von Bertalanffy (Van Assche 2019). Initially, this term was used in ecosystem research and means ability to keep essential functional characteristics, especially in the face of sudden threats and disruptions. Later it found its application in research on social-ecological systems. No less important is that, according to Bertalanfy's theory, complex systems, which are constantly changing, must also be resilient to violent and unexpected events. Therefore, building the resilience of complex systems is inevitable for a system to work without disruptions or, at least, to minimise the impact of adverse events.

Various definitions of resilience focus on continuity of urban systems (Meerow et al. 2016; Fuller and Quine 2016; Folke et al. 2010; Walker and Salt 2006, p. 1; Holling 1986, p. 296; Tobin 1999; Adger 2000; Zhou et al. 2008; Garschagen 2013). The concept changed since it was brought in the 1970s into ecology (Walker et al., 2004; Walker and Salt, 2006; Carter et al. 2015, Hanzl et al. 2021, Hanzl and Maldonado 2021). Holling (1973), who introduced the term to ecology from the engineering domain (Alexander 2013), highlighted the time needed by a system to return to the original after the disturbance. His definition assumes that at least some parts of the system continue. In the ecological understanding of resilience, the system might accept some disruption before approaching a threshold (Holling 1996, p. 33; Wallington et al. 2005), although these are citizens who carry the weight of adaptation. The social-ecological perspective assumes that the local society is behind the ongoing transformations (Adger 2000; Tobin 1999).

The researchers pay attention to the ability of cities to adapt to rapid demographic changes, both depopulation, sudden population growth or the threat of terrorism. Resilience term is a part of a broader discourse on the concept of sustainable development (Davis 2013). The ambiguity also stems from its broad application since urban resilience also relates to other significant scientific issues such as sustainability, adaptability and system vulnerability. A wide field of interpretation may mean that it is a fluid term and should not constitute a basis for scientific considerations (Merrow et al. 2016). They propose to define the concept as follows: '*Urban resilience refers to the ability of an urban system and all its constituent socio-ecological and socio-technical networks across temporal and spatial scales to maintain or rapidly return to desired functions in the face of a disturbance, to adapt to change, and to quickly transform systems that limit current or future adaptive capacity.*' (Merrow et al. 2016).

Resilience has also been implemented into urban morphology research; we find a comprehensive description in the work of Romice, Porta and Feliciotti (Feliciotti et al. 2016; Romice et al. 2020; Venerandi et al. 2017). The authors distinguish the five most important attributes that define a resilient urban form: diversity, connectivity, redundancy, modularity, efficiency. The same researchers popularise the concept of urban morphometry to assess the resilience of an urban form.

Morphometry is a method that has been developing recently in research on urban form. Nevertheless, the term has its origin in biology, where it means the quantitative characterisation, analysis and comparison of biological forms (Dibble et al. 2015). According to Roth and Mercer (2000), morphometry is a way to obtain information about biological material and biological processes (Dibble et al. 2019). Thanks to the quantitative evaluation employing statistical methods, biologists determine the degree of similarity and the relationship between elements taking into account form evolutions. Thanks to many groundbreaking scientific articles and publications in urban morphology (e.g. Berghauser Pont and Haupt 2021; Dibble et al. 2015; Dibble et al. 2019; Venerandi et al. 2017), the research perspective is already well recognised.

Nevertheless, the methodology is still evolving, and there is no single objective and commonly accepted way to quantify urban form (Venerandi et al. 2017). This paper contributes to developing a mathematical and statistical method to assess the resilience of urban form. In order to use morphometry, it is necessary to properly define elemental objects for quantitative assessment (Dibble et al. 2019). Therefore, an exercise was carried out in which the main aim was to an appropriate variable that could define individual proxies using the quantitative method.

4 Methodology

A starting point in our efforts to analyse urban form from the perspective of resilient thinking has been the concept of the burgage cycle developed by M.R.G. Conzen (1960). This theory describes five phases of transforming urban form, namely: institutive, repletive, climax, recessive and fallow. The first of them covers the gradual filling of the original morphological plots – changes concern increasing FAR. The second repletive phase is the creation of new morphological units through the subdivision of existing ones. The third transformation phase often entails a complex reconstruction of existing spatial structures. It aims to create new, more efficient, more functional and aesthetic forms and usually has a chiefly qualitative dimension (Pireveli 2011, p. 511). The last two phases are strictly related to the erosion of city substance. Conzen's method has been recognised in the scientific literature as an appropriate tool to describe the evolution of spatial structures. In Poland, this method was popularised by Koter (1970). Continuing the research of M.R.G. Conzen, Koter (1990) presents the evolution of urban fabric adjacent to the principal street in Łódź, i.e. Piotrkowska Street. Based on historical cartographic data, Koter (ibid.) assesses basic features such as the BCR of an entire urban block, the minimum and maximum BCR values for individual lots, numbers of new streets and derivative cut lots. The results supplied a quantitative evaluation of the diachronic transformations of urban blocks. Koter (ibid.) concludes that BCR depends on the phase of the burgage cycle and the proportion between plot front and plot depth. His research should be seen as one of the first Polish quantitative analyses defining urban form. It might also be considered a precursory example of a morphometry study.

In order to verify assumptions concerning the evaluation of urban form, we based our approach on the research by Feliciotti et al. (2020, 2016). As mentioned earlier, they indicate five elemental proxies of resilient urban form. After reviewing over forty scientific publications, authors pick up a few of the essential attributes that best suit urban form and explain how these concepts can be reflected in the urban tissue. The attributes of the resilient urban form include (Feliciotti et al. 2016):

- Diversity is understood in an urban form as heterogeneity of function within one building or a variety of function within an urban block. Moreover, diversity can also be considered in the context of transport. Differentiating transport may improve accessibility and quality of life. The well-designed facades also positively affect diversity in urban form.
- Connectivity is conditioned by a level of connections between elements of an urban system. In this context, we shall consider streets, their length (which results from the size of the block) and the number of intersections per square kilometre. Well-developed connectivity allows for the free flow of people, which contributes to the greater intensity of activities. Small and compact urban blocks improve connectivity.
- The redundancy of an urban layout means an excessive number of streets or connections. This feature proves useful, notably when a sudden failure or traffic incident on one road cuts it off. From the point of view of urban resilience, redundancy protects against sudden damage or failure.
- Modularity is defined by the presence of all essential morphological elements in the appropriate scale: the higher modularity, the higher resilience of urban form. For instance, if an urban block consists of one lot, it is less resilient than an urban block with many plots.
- The efficiency of the urban structure is determined by small urban blocks, proper street scale, the suitable number of streets with pedestrian priority, and easy access to public transport and services.

Resilient thinking spans across scales, from a district through an urban block, street and down to a single lot. Urban resilience can occur at the architectural and urban design level. Since transformations of urban tissue are slow, proper solutions need to be implemented at the early stage to avoid time-consuming and costly works and to minimise disruptive events in future. Feliciotti (2016) claims that the designer might improve resilience by proposing proper configurations and relations between individual morphological urban elements. In this sense, the author admits that the above provisions should become principles of urban design. These research assumptions should be examined empirically. This might be done through the analysis of past transformations and the impacts of disruptive events.

We aim to quantify and objectively assess the resilience of the urban form. The primary assumption is to isolate a few essential elements, i.e. front width, plot area, front-to-plot ratio and BCR and to measure these features at each stage of the burgage cycle. This approach stems from the literature review, which shows that the width of the front of the plot located along the streets directly affects the plot's attractiveness and land value. Moreover, buildings located along an attractive street are more susceptible to changes (Le Fort and De Vissher 2020; Torma et al. 2017; Dovey et al. 2017). Besides, researchers observe the relationship between the width of the frontage and the intensity of plot development (Bobkova 2019). It turns out that the relations between these elements influence accessibility (Oliveira 2013, p. 25; Sharifi and Yamagata 2018, p. 175), which Feliciotti et al. (2016) interpret as affecting the resilience of the urban form. In turn, double access to the street front in the case of a through plot or a wide frontage available from the street favours diversification. Plots with narrow fronts and greater depth are more exposed to structural changes under high economic pressure (Törmä et al. 2017). In the current study, we have investigated all the above assumptions. The research has used the available cartographic data:

1. 1823 – The original plan of Łódź by F. De Viebig (https://atlas.ltn.lodz.pl/)
2. 1849 – Map by J. Lenartowski (https://atlas.ltn.lodz.pl/)
3. 1873 – Map by R. Miciński (https://atlas.ltn.lodz.pl/)
4. 1907 – Map by W. Starzyński (https://atlas.ltn.lodz.pl/)
5. 1989 – Satellite imagery (https://lodz.retromapy.pl/)
6. 2021 – Satellite imagery (https://lodz.retromapy.pl/)

The Quantum GIS software has been applied as a tool supporting the use of the method described above. The following parameters have been included in the table of attributes and measured. The Front-to-plot ratio was calculated using the equation:

$$\frac{Front\ width}{Plot\ Area} = Front - to - plot\ ratio \qquad (1)$$

The BCR values have been calculated using the equation.

$$\frac{Summary\ Building\ Area\ in\ one\ plot}{Plot\ Area} \times 100\% = BCR \qquad (2)$$

Based on this material, the stages of spatial development were traced, and the socio-economic situation at various stages of transformation of plots was also considered.

5   Case Study Selection

Continuing the study by Koter (1990) we have chosen a site located in Lodz, in central Poland. Founded back in the Middle Ages, Lodz went through rapid economic and spatial growth during the industrial revolution, i.e. the turn of the 19th and 20th centuries. Initially planned as a handicraft settlement, Lodz was one of the pilot planning activities of the then authorities of the Kingdom of Poland. Its spatial arrangement stands out as a typical street village, i.e. short fronts and deep plots (21,5 m × 285 m). In the second half of the nineteenth century, handicraft gave way to mechanised industry, and violent and uncontrolled urbanisation and poor administration became the main factors in the lack of coordinated planning. The city has characteristic large quarters reaching 180 × 230 m. Besides, as a result of raging urbanisation processes, the city has relatively scarce public space, which negatively affects accessibility. The first attempt to repair the spatial structure of Lodz took place when the general plan was developed in 1915, the principal designer of which was Christoph Ranck (Olenderek 2004, p. 23). One of the essential planning decisions was the decrease of the proportion of urban blocks and the creation of local nodal points and city squares. The latter, due to the specific nature of a handicraft settlement, were not initially planned. The bold design decisions were aimed at "healing" the dense inner-city tissue of the agricultural origin. The elaboration of the plan lasted until 1935 when the City Council adopted the General Development Plan for the City of Lodz in a limited version. The essential alteration covered resignation from changing the proportions of urban blocks to increase the length of the fronts and from punching the streets through the middle of the quarter.

The enlarging of the streets right of way was proposed as a substitute along with the demolition of the street facade on one side. Christoph Ranck, who was the designer of the original version of the General Plan, opposed such an idea; he considered destroying the entire frontage an action contradicting rational urban management (Holcgreber et al. 1930, p. 311–314). Wacław Ostrowski, after a careful analysis of potential breakthroughs and street widening, concluded that both options are burdened with too much risk and uncertainty in the implementation, even assuming the support of private and public capital (Ostrowski 1935b, p. 365). However, he pointed out factors that might have had a decisive influence on the success of street widening. These observations remain valid. Not only is the success of the widening scheme determined by creating a new communication route enabling active fronts. Another condition is defining the proper intensity ratio and the frontages height (Ostrowski 1935a, p. 321). An indisputable benefit is the increase of real estate value located on the new street. Despite several decades of discussion conducted by town planners and architects in Lodz, finally, in the 1960s, a decision was made to demolish the entire street frontage of Zachodnia Street in the New Town. This street was delineated in the original plan from 1823.

The demolition belongs to the category of sudden events in the face of which urban form should be capable of efficient adaptation and reorganisation. In the free market economy, the high value of plots located in the city centre contributes to a gradual increase in rent, which has a significant impact on the variability of functions and form; in Lodz, however, this was not the case. Unfortunately, the centrally planned economy in the years after the Second World War hindered the development of the frontage of Zachodnia Street.

6   Analysis of the Urban Blocks Transformations

6.1   1821–1827 – the Original Plan of Lodz by F. De Viebig – Institutive Phase

The analysed part of the city of Lodz was originally planned as a handicraft settlement. Its core was the octagonal market square of the new city. The dimensions of the analysed block are 172 × 215 m, the minimum dimensions of a single lot are 21.5 m × 43.0 m, and the maximum dimensions are 21.5 m × 86 m. The settlement outlined in this way was to form the basis of a later development model, which assumed the construction of a front one-story building and the use of the remaining part of the lot for production.

6.2   1849 – Map by J. Lenartowski – Repletive Phase

Until 1849, the filling of the analysed blocks with buildings proceeded relatively slowly (see Fig. 1). It is possible to distinguish twelve masonry buildings and thirty-six wooden buildings, the average BCR of a single lot was from 9% to 22.2%. Notably, some lots were not built on at all. There was no division or merger of the lots. There is no setback; all buildings facades were placed on the edge of the street. Most probably, most of the buildings were single-story buildings. The following Table 1. gives a summary of all measures and calculations.

6.3   1873 – Map by R. Miciński – Repletive Phase

There is a noticeable tendency to develop the plot deeper (see Fig. 1). It could have resulted from the development of handicraft processes and the need to build farm buildings. Significantly, new buildings are usually placed along one border; they are single-bay buildings with a depth of about 5 m, lit only from the inside of the plot. These structures are often independent, not connected to the front building. Despite various depths, most lots are developed up to a depth of forty meters, even lots that are 86 m deep. This is also the stage of the construction of the first urban tenement houses.

We can observe the most prominent construction activity near the new market and along the main road, i.e. Piotrkowska Street. The front tenement houses have two outbuildings leading into the plot with an average depth of 5 m. The bias towards the exterior of the lots closest to the edge of the street is still noticeable. As an outcome, the central areas of the analysed blocks are undeveloped because they do not fulfil any active urban function. The following Table 1 gives a summary of all measures and calculations.

6.4   1907 – Map by W. Starzyński – Climax Phase

The turn of the nineteenth and twentieth century is a moment of intensive urbanisation, which is reflected in a significant increase in the built-up area of plots. At this stage, the urban development in the form of two wings of four-storey outbuildings fills in the rest of the plots (see Fig. 1). The front buildings often remain intact. This results in a one-story front building adjacent to the four-storey outbuildings at the back of the plot. Moreover, there are several changes in the proportions and sizes of plots (plots A6, A23, A25 and A7). The time just before First World War marked an evident slowdown

Table 1. Table with measures and calculation of urban block from 1849 on the left and from 1873 on the right.

Plot number	Front width (meters)	Plot Area (square meters)	Front-to-plot ratio	BCR %	Plot number	Front width (meters)	Plot Area (square meters)	Front-to-plot ratio	BCR %
A1	21,5	1849	0,01116	9,5	A1	21,5	1849	0,0116	23,4
A2	21,5	1849	0,0116	0	A2	21,5	1849	0,0116	16,7
A3	21,5	1849	0,0116	9,5	A3	21,5	1849	0,0116	18,2
A4	21,5	1849	0,0116	9,5	A4	21,5	1849	0,0116	21
A5	21,5	1849	0,0116	9,5	A5	21,5	1849	0,0116	25
A6	21,5	1849	0,0116	9,5	A6	21,5	1849	0,0116	30,2
A7	21,5	1849	0,0116	0	A7	21,5	1849	0,0116	10,4
A8	21,5	1849	0,0116	9,5	A8	21,5	1849	0,0116	30,6
A9	21,5	1849	0,0116	0	A9	21,5	1849	0,0116	15,4
A10	21,5	1849	0,0116	9,5	A10	21,5	1849	0,0116	19,9
A11	64,5	924,5	0,0698	0	A11	64,5	924,5	0,0698	42,8
A12	21,5	924,5	0,0233	0	A12	21,5	924,5	0,0233	40,6
A13	21,5	924,5	0,0233	0	A13	21,5	924,5	0,0233	32
A14	21,5	924,5	0,0233	19	A14	21,5	924,5	0,0233	35
A15	21,5	924,5	0,0233	19	A15	21,5	924,5	0,0233	23,1
A16	64,5	924,5	0,0698	19	A16	64,5	924,5	0,0698	49,54
A17	21,5	924,5	0,0233	19	A17	21,5	924,5	0,0233	36,9
A18	21,5	924,5	0,0233	19	A18	21,5	924,5	0,0233	19
A19	21,5	924,5	0,0233	19	A19	21,5	924,5	0,0233	44,5
A20	21,5	924,5	0,0233	19	A20	21,5	924,5	0,0233	37,6
A21	64,5	924,5	0,0698	19	A21	64,5	924,5	0,0698	45
A22	21,5	924,5	0,0233	7,8	A22	21,5	924,5	0,0233	37,1
A23	53,75	1213,4	0,0443	21,8	A23	53,75	1213,4	0,0443	53,3
A24	53,75	1213,4	0,0443	22,2	A24	53,75	1213,4	0,0443	67,7
A25	22,8	1300	0,0175	15,8	A25	22,8	1300	0,0175	34,3
A26	22,8	1300	0,0175	15,8	A26	22,8	1300	0,0175	45,3

in urban development, but this was also the moment when lots gained the maximum level of investment (BCR). The First World War left an imprint on the development dynamics of the city, and from that moment on, the recession started. In the analysed area, the structures start gradually degrading. The following Table 2. gives a summary of all measures and calculations.

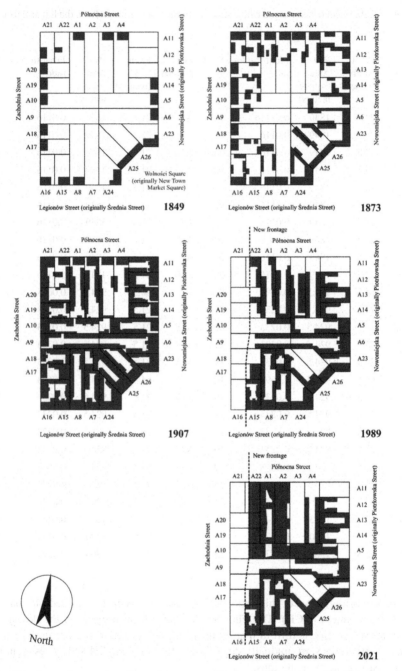

Fig. 1. This figure shows urban tissue drawn up on the basis of Lenartowski's Map from 1849, on the basis of Miciński's Map from 1873, on the basis of Starzyński's Map from 1907, on the basis of Satellite imagery from 1989 and on the basis of Satellite imagery from 2021.

Table 2. Table with measures and calculation of urban block from 1907 on the left and from 1989 on the right. Cells with outlines shows plots whose proportions changed as a result of the demolition of the eastern frontage of Zachodnia Street.

Plot number	Front width (meters)	Plot Area (square meters)	Front-to-plot ratio	BCR %	Plot number	Front width (meters)	Plot Area (square meters)	Front-to-plot ratio	BCR %
A1	21,5	1849	0,0116	51,6	A1	21,5	1849	0,0116	48,6
A2	21,5	1849	0,0116	49,5	A2	21,5	1849	0,0116	49,8
A3	21,5	1849	0,0116	34	A3	21,5	1849	0,0116	51,2
A4	21,5	1849	0,0116	26,8	A4	21,5	1849	0,0116	42,7
A5	21,5	1849	0,0116	57,1	A5	21,5	1849	0,0116	45,9
A6	28,3	2190	0,0129	61	A6	28,3	2190	0,0129	62,2
A7	21,5	1574	0,0137	62,5	A7	21,5	1574	0,0137	63,8
A8	21,5	1849	0,0116	63,7	A8	21,5	1849	0,0116	59,2
A9	21,5	1849	0,0116	59,2	A9	21,75	1304	0,0167	52,77
A10	21,5	1849	0,0116	53,8	A10	21,5	1268	0,017	21,21
A11	64,5	924,5	0,0698	71	A11	64,5	924,5	0,0698	0
A12	21,5	924,5	0,0233	66,5	A12	21,5	924,5	0,0233	39,4
A13	21,5	924,5	0,0233	69,7	A13	21,5	924,5	0,0233	72
A14	21,5	924,5	0,0233	63,3	A14	21,5	924,5	0,0233	41,1
A15	21,5	924,5	0,0233	71,3	A15	64,5	924,5	0,0698	74
A16	64,5	924,5	0,0698	69,6	A16	–	–	–	–
A17	21,5	924,5	0,0233	65,5	A17	21,5	462	0,0465	71,4
A18	21,5	924,5	0,0233	65,9	A18	21,5	924,5	0,0233	–
A19	21,5	924,5	0,0233	62,3	A19	21,5	343,8	0,0625	22,7
A20	21,5	924,5	0,0233	44,5	A20	21,5	343,8	0,0233	36,36
A21	64,5	924,5	0,0698	71,2	A21	–	–	–	–
A22	21,5	924,5	0,0233	49,6	A22	59	687,9	0,0857	58,6
A23	46,95	872,4	0,0538	75,2	A23	46,95	872,4	0,0538	67,2
A24	53,75	1213,4	0,0443	78,8	A24	53,75	1213,4	0,0443	50,8
A25	22,8	1575	0,0145	80,5	A25	22,8	1575	0,0145	54,5
A26	22,8	1300	0,0175	64,2	A26	22,8	1300	0,0175	22,8

6.5 1989 – Satellite Imagery – Recessive Phase and Fallow

Having survived two world wars and changes of spatial development directions of Lodz in line with the spirit of the era and modernist ideals, the analysed area entered a period of a deep recession. Poor technical conditions, abandonment of conservation and technical activities contributed to the erosion of the urban substance. The deep transformations in this part of the city, including the demolition of the eastern frontage of Zachodnia Street, enhanced the process (see Fig. 1). This disruption became the spiritus movens of the subsequent degradation of this part of the city. The organised undertaking of demolishing the frontage was to be a cure for the growing spontaneous movement and, in a sense, also to heal the urban tissue. However, this did not happen; the changes in the proportions of the lots of the eastern frontage of Zachodnia Street would not happen over the next 50 years. This stems partly from the abandonment of further construction activities by the city authorities before 1989 and insufficient efforts to develop this part of the city after 1989 in the realities of a free market economy. The following Table 2 gives a summary of all measures and calculations.

6.6 2021 – Satellite Imagery – Fallow and Repletive Phase

The current condition indicates changes towards the revival of the urban form. There is a clear attempt to repair the degraded tissue of city quarters. The city, regaining its development dynamics, fills up empty plots again (see Fig. 1). At the same time, steps have been taken to create new communication routes while reducing the size of the urban blocks. Thus, the city gained new public spaces and a chance to develop new fronts. The intensification of redevelopment processes is also, in a way, caused by the implementation of new investments in the vicinity of the analysed quarter, among others, revitalisation of the factory complex of Izrael Poznański. The following Table 3. gives a summary of all measures and calculations.

Table 3. Table with measures and calculation of urban block from 2021.

Plot number	Front width (meters)	Plot Area (square meters)	Front-to-plot ratio	BCR %
A1 + A2 + A22 + A20 + A19 + A10	166,5	6342	0,0262	87
A2	–	–	–	–
A3	21,5	1849	0,0116	0
A4	21,5	1849	0,0116	42,7
A5	21,5	1849	0,0116	36,7
A6	28,3	2190	0,0129	62,2
A7	21,5	1574	0,0137	63,8
A8	21,5	1849	0,0116	59,2
A9	21,75	1304	0,0167	22,6
A10	–	–	–	–
A11	64,5	924,5	0,0698	0
A12	21,5	924,5	0,0233	39,4
A13	21,5	924,5	0,0233	72

(continued)

Table 3. (*continued*)

Plot number	Front width (meters)	Plot Area (square meters)	Front-to-plot ratio	BCR %
A14	21,5	924,5	0,0233	41,1
A15	64,5	924,5	0,0698	74
A16	–	–	–	–
A17	21,5	462	0,0465	71,4
A18	21,5	924,5	0,0233	–
A19	–	–	–	–
A20	–	–	–	–
A21	–	–	–	–
A22	–	–	–	–
A23	46,95	872,4	0,0538	67,2
A24	53,75	1213,4	0,0443	50,8
A25	22,8	1575	0,0145	54,5
A26	22,8	1300	0,0175	22,8

7 Results

This article aims to assess urban resilience based on urban plot transformation analysis and urban morphometry. Basic calculations were made with Quantum GIS software for each of the development stages of the site based on available cartographic data. From this study, we have drawn several conclusions:

1. The analysis shows a relationship between the front width and BCR. There is a clear rule that plots with more elongated fronts also feature a higher BCR. The practice to enlarge the front contributes to increasing profits from the real estate for the commercial premises.
2. Plots with a lower ratio of the front length to the plot area develop much slower (A1-A10). The shape of the lot was adjusted to the land use in the initial phase of the development. When the activity changed, such deep lots were no longer needed.
3. Plots with a higher front-to-plot ratio (A11, A16, A21, A23, A24) are more susceptible to changes than deeper plots with a shorter front. We can refer to this as the penetration of lots by active urban life. Smaller quarters are more susceptible to urban activity, i.e. their penetration rate with urban activity is higher.
4. Anomalies - despite alleged actions leading to a reduction in the proportion of plots and the entire quarter, plots along Zachodnia Street were not developed for a long time. A probable explanation of this situation may be the fact that the reality of the centrally planned economy did not create favourable conditions for this restoration after this disruption. It also means that the dimensions of the plots are not the only factor determining the city's resilience. In the case of some lots, this improved the

accessibility, efficiency and penetration of the plot by urban activity. However, it did not bring any effects that would affect the replacement of depleted buildings. This was partly because the shortening of plots with a proportion of 43 m to 15 m made it impossible, from an architectural point of view, to construct two-bay residential buildings (with light from both the west and the east). In other words, the replacement of buildings was uneconomical and unprofitable.

5. Anomalies - even though after 1989, conditions of the market economy made it possible to invest in empty plots of land, nothing changed. The situation improved when some plots were joined together. It was then that the interest in new investments appeared. The reason is as follows: the deep plot 21.5 m large does not allow for implementing an economically profitable investment. It is related not only to the available FAR and BCR but also to the possibility of arranging good-quality and well-litten premises. Moreover, we observe that corner plots are relatively more attractive and more susceptible to changes and market activities. While regarding the modularity of the urban form, the consolidation of plots should be assessed negatively, the outcome indicates that this remains the only possibility of healing this part of the city.

6. Extensive urban development projects are much more prone to failure than smaller-scale individual projects. In theory, reducing the quarter's dimensions by demolishing the frontage should positively affect the accessibility, efficiency, and connectivity of the urban form (Oliveira, 2013, p.25; Sharifi, Yamagata, 2018, p.175). Despite these actions that should bring a more resilient urban form, it was impossible to complete and implement all the assumptions. At the same time, it means that point actions seem essential for chain reactions in the market economy realities (the case of consolidation of plots).

7. The case of plot A3, A9, A10, A5 shows that deep plots with a short front take much longer to return to the repletive phase, i.e. refilling after fallow.

8. The buildings in the back of the plot react more slowly to the market, which means that marking a new street in the middle of the quarter (as an alternative to demolishing the street frontage) would be a driving force for changes. This intervention shall simultaneously shape two new street frontages, doubling the length of the fronts for plot owners. The key is access to public space and greater penetration with urban activity.

9. The improvements in car traffic did not increase the attractiveness of the site.

10. The current size of plots is too tiny to revive the city's functioning, which means that one should strive to consolidate smaller plots into larger ones, bearing in mind the architectural design aspects (availability of light and conditions of not obscuring the development).

11. In order to fully reflect the architectural issues and the quality of the urban form, it is also necessary to track changes in the intensity of development over time. The intensity of development is probably higher in the case of longer fronts, as shown by the conclusions from the last 30 years.

The analysed example of Zachodnia Street confirms that streets and organised transformations of spatial structures have varied potential to support or reduce urban resilience. Depending on the specific factors, the level of immunity can be positively or negatively affected. In retrospect, the nineteenth-century activities led to the creation of a unique, multifunctional spatial structure, which at the same time was not free from defects. Even though the procedure of demolishing entire street frontages was commonly practised during Modernism, our case shows that such action can significantly weaken the city's spatial structure for many years. The realities of the centrally planned economy hindered the reconstruction, and market mechanisms could not have positively impacted the rapid reconstruction of the frontage. However, there was a noticeable change in the development of smaller plots.

In conclusion, in the light of the presented analyses, applying the concept of resilience in urban design has a strong foundation. For this reason, an attempt should be made to prepare broader analyses on this topic. This approach will help define the design framework. It is also reasonable to take all measures to minimise adverse events in the future. From the perspective of the urban system, making the right decisions at the design stage seems to be the easiest and least costly way to obtain a resilient urban form. Moreover, as our case shows, organised urban planning activities often leave permanent scars on the urban tissue.

8 Summary Conclusions

The current research proves the need to continue analysing urban resilience using computational and quantitative methods. The study based on the indicated attributes enabled an assessment of how the resilience changed at each stage of development. The proposed method shows significant dependencies between the width of the plot front, the plot area and the plot development area. These dependencies and the analyses of FAR and BCR can be the basis for the quantitative assessment of the resilience of the urban form. The mutual influence and proportions between the individual morphological elements of the city determine the pace and nature of the changes taking place in the urban form. The analyses on urban resilience might help to recommend good development directions.

References

1. Adger, W.N.: Social and ecological resilience: are they related? Prog. Hum. Geogr. **24**, 347–364 (2000)
2. Alexander, D.E.: Resilience and disaster risk reduction: an etymological journey. Nat. Hazards Earth Syst. Sci. **13**(11), 2707–2716 (2013)
3. Berghauser Pont, Meta & Haupt, Per.: Spacematrix - Space, Density and Urban Form (2021)
4. Bobkova, E.: Towards a theory of natural occupation. Developing theoretical, methodological and empirical support for the relation between plot systems and urban processes (Thesis for the degree of Doctor of Philiosophy), Chalmers University of Technology, Gothenburg, Sweden (2019)
5. Carter, J.G., et al.: Climate change and the city: building capacity for urban adaptation. Prog. Plan. **95**, 1–66 (2015)
6. Conzen, M. R. G.: Alnwick, Northumberland. A study in town-plan analysis. In: Publications, Institute of British Geographers, vol. 27 (1960)
7. Czachor, R.: Koncepcja urban resilience: założenia, treść, możliwości implementacji. In: Społeczności Lokalne. Studia Interdyscyplinarne (3) (2019)

8. Davis, J.: Evolving Cities. Exploring the relations between urban form resilience and the governance of urban form, London School of Economics and Political Science (2013)
9. Dibble, J., Prelorendjos, A., Romice, O., Zanella, M., Strano, E., Pagel, M., Porta, S.: On the origin of spaces: morphometric foundations of urban form evolution. Environ. Plann. B Urban Anal. City Sci. **46**(4) (2019)
10. Dibble, J., Prelorendjos, A., Romice, O., Zanella, M., Strano, E., Pagel, K., Porta, S.: Urban Morphometrics: towards a science of urban evolution. In: Strappa, G, Amato, AR., Camporeale, A.: City as organism. New visions for urban life, Rome, IT: U+D edition, 22–26 September 2015
11. Dovey, K., Pike, L., Woodcock, I.: Incremental urban intensification: transit-oriented redevelopment of small-lot corridors. Urban Policy .Res. **35**(3), 261–274 (2017). https://doi.org/10.1080/08111146.2016.1252324
12. Feliciotti, A., Romice, O., Porta, S.: Design for change: five proxies for resilience in the urban form, Open House Int. **41**(4). 23–30 (2016). ISSN 0168–2601
13. Folke, C., et al.: Resilience thinking: integrating resilience, adaptability and transformability. Ecol. Soc. **15**(10) (2010)
14. Fuller, L., Quine, C.P.: Resilience and tree health: a basis for implementation in sustainable forest management. Forestry **89**(1) (2016)
15. Garschagen, M.: Resilience and organisational institutionalism from a cross-cultural perspective: an exploration based on urban climate change adaptation in Vietnam. Nat. Hazards **67**, 25–46 (2013)
16. Hanzl, M., Geerse, A., Guschl, L., Dewan, R.: Urban metabolism and land use optimization: In quest for modus operandi for urban resilience. In Understanding Disaster Risk, pp. 109–130. Elsevier (2021). https://doi.org/10.1016/B978-0-12-819047-0.00007-X
17. Hanzl, M., Fernández-Maldonado, A.M.: Editorial to the Special issue on planning resilient cities and region. Cities **114**, 103190 (2021). https://doi.org/10.1016/j.cities.2021.103190
18. Holcgreber, J., et al.: Księga pamiątkowa dziesięciolecia samorządu miasta Łodzi, Nakładem Magistratu Łódzkiego (1930)
19. Holling, C.S.: Resilience and stability of ecological systems. Annu. Rev. Ecol. Syst. **4**, 1–23 (1973)
20. Holling, C.S.: The resilience of terrestrial ecosystems; local surprise and global change. In: Clark, W.C., Munn, R.E. (eds.) Sustainable Development of the Biosphere, pp. 292–317. Cambridge University Press, Cambridge, UK (1986)
21. Holling, C.S.: Engineering resilience versus ecological resilience. In: Schulze, P. (ed.) Engineering Within Ecological Constraints, vol. 31, pp. 32–43. National Academy of Engineering, Washington (1996)
22. Koter, M.: Geneza układu przestrzennego Łodzi przemysłowej (Origin of the spatial pattern of industrial Lodz) (Warszawa) (1970)
23. Koter, M.: The morphological evolution of a nineteenth-century city Centre: Łódź, Poland, 1825–1973. In: Slater, T.R. (ed.): The Built Form of Western Cities. Essays for M. R. G. Conzen on the Occasion of his Eightieth Birthday. Leicester University Press, Leicester–London (1990)
24. Le Fort, B., De Visscher, J.P.: Typo-morphological diversity and urban resilience: a comparative study of three heterogeneous blocks in Brussels. Urban Morphol. **24**(1) (2020)
25. Meerow, S., Newell, J.P., Stults, M.: Defining urban resilience: A review. In: Landscape and Urban Planning, (2016).
26. Meerow, S., Newell, J.P.: Urban resilience for whom, what, when, where, why? In: Urban Geography (2016)
27. Olenderek, J.: Proces kształtowania przestrzeni w Łodzi II Rzeczypospolitej a awans administracyjny miasta. W poszukiwaniu przesłanek rozwoju Łodzi III Rzeczypospolitej, Łódź (2004)

28. Oliveira, V.: Morpho: A methodology for assessing urban form. Urban Morphol. **17**, 149–161 (2013)
29. Ostrowski, W.: Poszerzenia i przebicia ulic (I). In: Architektura i Budownictwo, nr 11 (1935a)
30. Ostrowski, W.: Poszerzenia i przebicia ulic (II). In: Architektura i Budownictwo, nr 12 (1935b)
31. Parysek, J.J.: Miasto w ujęciu systemowym. In: Ruch prawniczy, ekonomiczny i socjologiczny, Rok LXXVII – zeszyt 1 (2015)
32. Pireveli, M.: Od morfologii przez urbomorfologię do morfoznaku. In: Przegląd Geograficzny, vol. 83, p. 4, (2011)
33. Romice, O., Porta, S., Feliciotti, A.: Master Planning for Change. RIBA Publishing, Designing the Resilient City (2020)
34. Roth, V.L., Mercer, J.M.: Morphometrics in development and evolution. Am. Zool. **40**(5), 801–810 (2000)
35. Sharifi, A., Yamagata, Y.: Resilient urban form: a conceptual framework. In: Yamagata, Y., Sharifi, A. (eds.) Resilience-Oriented Urban Planning. LNE, vol. 65, pp. 167–179. Springer, Cham (2018). https://doi.org/10.1007/978-3-319-75798-8_9
36. Tobin, G.A.: Sustainability and community resilience: the holy grail of hazards planning? Global Environ. Change B Environ. Hazards **1**, 13–25 (1999)
37. Törmä, I., Griffiths, S., Vaughan, L.: High street changeability: the effect of urban form on demolition, modification, and use change in two south London suburbs. Urban Morphol. **21**(1), (2017)
38. Van Assche, K., Verschraegen, G., Valentinov, V., Gruezmacher, M.: The social, the ecological, and the adaptive. Von Bartalanffy's general systems theory and the adaptive governance of social-ecological systems. In: Systems Research and Behavioral Science, Volume 36, Issue 3, (2019).
39. Venerandi, A., Zanella, M., Romice, O., Dibble, J., Porta, S.: Form and urban change – an urban morphometric study of five gentrified neighbourhoods in London. Environ. Plann. B Plann. Des. **44**(6) (2017)
40. Walker, B., Salt, D.: Resilience Thinking: Sustaining Ecosystems and People in a Changing World. Island Press, Washington (2006)
41. Walker, B., Holling, C.S., Carpenter, S.R., Kinzig, A.: Resilience, adaptability and transformability in social–ecological systems. Ecol. Soc. **9**(2) 5, (2004)
42. Wallington, T.J., Hobbs, R.J., Moore, S.A.: Implications of current ecological thinking for biodiversity conservation: a review of the salient issues. Ecol. Soc. **10**(1) (2005)
43. Zhou, H., Wang, J., Wan, J., Jia, H.: Resilience to natural hazards: a geographic perspective. Nat. Hazards **53**, 21–41 (2008)
44. Historical atlas of the city of Lodz. https://atlas.ltn.lodz.pl/. Accessed 01 May 2021
45. Satellite imagery of the city of Lodz. https://lodz.retromapy.pl/. Accessed 01 May 2021

International Workshop on Urban Space Accessibility and Safety (USAS 2021)

Towards the Definition of a Comprehensive Walkability Index for Historical Centres

Barbara Caselli[1](✉) , Silvia Rossetti[1](✉) , Matteo Ignaccolo[2] ,
Michele Zazzi[1] , and Vincenza Torrisi[2](✉)

[1] Department of Engineering and Architecture, University of Parma, 43124 Parma, Italy
{barbara.caselli,silvia.rossetti}@unipr.it
[2] Department of Civil Engineering and Architecture, University of Catania, 95125 Catania, Italy
vtorrisi@dica.unict.it

Abstract. Historical centres are crucial areas where urban and transport planners should aim at enhancing adequate walkability conditions. This should be considered a priority in order to allow all users, including the most vulnerable ones, to access the activities they wish to engage in.

Based on this premises, the paper aims at defining a methodological approach to comprehensively assess the existing pedestrian network infrastructure within historical centres, considering safety, comfort and enjoyment factors of the walking experience.

In-field inspections have been carried out for the main pedestrian paths and crossings within the historical centre of Parma and data have been georeferenced in a GIS database. The indicators considered in the walkability analysis are: sidewalks width, change of levels, bottlenecks, coloured ground signs, protection level, presence of seats, maintenance level and presence of tactile flooring. A comprehensive walkability index has been developed to assess the quality of each pedestrian link and crossing. The results have been represented in GIS-based thematic maps, that can support local authorities in defining priorities of intervention.

Keywords: Pedestrian mobility · Paths · Crossings · Walkability · Historical Centres · Sustainable Mobility

1 Introduction

Even if historical centres have extremely different characteristics depending on their origins, evolution, size and geographical location, in the historical city the primary type of movement has always been the pedestrian one: city centres were from the very beginning planned and designed to support and foster walkability.

The authors jointly designed and contributed to the paper. Conceptualization: B.C., S.R., M.I., M.Z., V.T.; Methodology: B.C., S.R., V.T.; Data curation: B.C., S.R..; Data elaboration: V.T.; Writing: B.C (chapter 3.1; 4.1; 4.2; 5.2), S.R. (chapter 1; 2; 4.2; 5.1; 6), V.T. (chapter 1; 2; 3.2; 3.3; 6). Supervision and funding acquisition: M.I, M.Z.

© Springer Nature Switzerland AG 2021
O. Gervasi et al. (Eds.): ICCSA 2021, LNCS 12958, pp. 493–508, 2021.
https://doi.org/10.1007/978-3-030-87016-4_36

But nowadays, except for pedestrian areas closed to motorised vehicles, historical centres are often affected by different types of traffic: this determines a promiscuity of circulation that is managed, in most cases, with horizontal and vertical signs and which with difficulty integrates within the historical-monumental fabric and its spaces [1].

However, it is still crucial to consider walking as the main modal component within city centres and consequently adopt measures that do not limit the pedestrian movement by providing a high-quality design of pedestrian paths provisions to maximise accessibility and safety for the weakest road users [2].

Within this framework, the paper aims at presenting a methodology to comprehensively assess the existing pedestrian network infrastructure within historical centres, where walkability conditions should be particularly enhanced. This can be considered as comprehensive assessment for evaluating pedestrian paths provisions and prioritise possible maintenance, renewal and regeneration interventions, rooting on detailed in-field inspections of pedestrian paths and crossings.

The reminder of the paper is organised as follows: Sect. 2 describes the literature and the research framework in which the paper roots; Sect. 3 focuses on the materials and methods adopted to conduct the assessment, starting from data collection based on in-filed inspections of pedestrian paths and the construction of a GIS-based model (Sect. 3.1); then describing the variables considered in the study (Sect. 3.2) and the walkability index calculation (Sect. 3.3); Sect. 4 presents the case study of the historical centre of Parma; Section 5 presents the results and the assessment maps obtained, providing a discussion; Finally, Sect. 6 will conclude by presenting future research steps.

2 The Theoretical Framework on Walkability and Pedestrian Friendly Environments

The research on how to create pedestrian friendly environments, to improve walkability and to proper design pedestrian paths is nowadays still dense and articulated [3–12], providing also focuses on specific aspects of the pedestrian movement, like road safety [13, 14]; accessibility to urban functions [15, 16]; universal design or pedestrian accessibility for specific vulnerable users group [17–20] and urban planning legal tools to support this form of sustainable mobility [21, 22].

In this respect, the Pedestrian Environment Review System (PERS) developed by TRL (Transport Research Laboratory) [23] constitutes a walkability audit tool to assess the level of service and quality provided for pedestrians across a range of pedestrian environments.

In addition, in the literature there are many walkability indices and measures, generally based on urban form features like density, land use mix and street connectivity, used to describe the overall walkability level of a city, or of a given area [24, 25]. Those indices are mainly based on evaluations made through GIS-based applications and geoprocessing tools that process different datasets allowing to measure and assess the spatial walkability conditions.

Starting from this theoretical framework, the proposed methodology bases on in-field inspections that allow a very detailed and punctual approach to comprehensively assess the existing pedestrian network infrastructure within historical centres.

3   Materials and Method

3.1   GIS-Based Model

In the proposed study, the walkability of pedestrian paths has been assessed using a Territorial Information System created by implementing and enriching a model previously adopted for other studies carried out at the University of Parma [26]. This model provided for a survey methodology and a detailed filing and mapping of pedestrian paths and crossings in a GIS environment.

The GIS database has been built on a vector basis as a network data structure (link-node graph) and allowed the analysis of the existing pedestrian network system.

All the selected pedestrian paths available in the public space, sidewalks and pedestrian crossings have been mapped in the database, associating each link with a series of qualitative and quantitative attributes.

The processing of these data has resulted, firstly, in a series of thematic maps that identify the main critical issues related to the degree of walkability of each link and crossing, secondly, in the calculation of a walkability index, detecting whether the pedestrian network is able to meet the needs of all users, even the most vulnerable ones.

3.2   Selected Attributes for Evaluating Walkability

To perform a comprehensive assessment of the walkability associated with the analysed pedestrian paths, a selection of qualitative and quantitative attributes has been made referring to the literature analysis and the territorial context. In fact, in addition to attributes strictly related to the road infrastructure, which can affect the operational performance of the path and pedestrian safety, in consideration of the analysed context represented by a historical centre, attributes related to comfort and attention to users with special needs have also been included.

From an operational point of view, the attributes to be measured have been identified both for the links in which the route is divided and for the pedestrian crossings. Furthermore, it is important to highlight that an in-depth analysis has been carried out, distinguishing the values assumed by these parameters for both directions, that is, for each side of the road.

Table 1 summarises the selected attributes to perform the walkability assessment: those underlined have been detected both for links and for pedestrian crossings.

Table 1. Selected attributes and assessment correspondance

Attribute	Qualitative assessment	Quantitative assessment
A_1 - Sidewalk width	< 90 cm; 90 cm-150 cm; > 150 cm	−1; 1; 2
A_2- Change of levels	Access with steps; with ramps; None	−1; 1; 2
A_3 - Bottlenecks	Present; Absent	−1; 1
A_4- Coloured ground signs	Absent; Present	−1; 1
A_5- Protection level	None; Low; Medium- High	−1; 1; 2
A_6 - Presence of seats	Absent; Present	−1; 1
A_7- Maintenance level	Poor; Good; Excellent	−1; 1; 2
A_8- Presence of tactile flooring	Absent; Present	−1; 1

3.3 Index Calculation

Following the detailed in-field survey, in addition to a specific evaluation of each individual attribute, in order to have a comprehensive assessment of the analysed area, global indices have been calculated, both for links and pedestrian crossings. The formulation of the indicators considers, in an aggregate way, all the attributes and the calculation is shown by the following equations (Eq. 1 and Eq. 2):

$$I_{link} = A_1 * \left(1 + \frac{\sum_1^n A_n}{12}\right) \tag{1}$$

$$I_{crossing} = A_2 * \left(1 + \frac{\sum_1^n A_n}{8}\right) \tag{2}$$

where n indicates the number of considered attributes and the denominator of the fraction corresponds to the sum obtained considering the maximum values assumed by these attributes.

Afterward to the link calculation and crossing calculation indices, to realise their graphic representation through a chromatic scale map, a normalisation of these indices has been performed.

The normalisation have been consisted in calculating the ratio between the two absolute values respectively obtained as (i) the difference between the index value and the minimum value and (ii) the difference between the maximum value and the minimum value of the index.

4   Case Study

4.1   Territorial Framework

The proposed analytic method has then been applied to the case of Parma's historic centre. Parma is a medium-sized city, with a population constantly growing of about 198.200 inhabitants. About 24,500 reside in the historic centre, which has an extension of 272 hectares and a population density of about 90 inhabitants per hectare.

In the historic city there are functions with the highest rank, a wide range of cultural, commercial, and institutional services that project the entire city on a national and international scale. The historic centre has a strongly characterising plural nature. It is crossed in an east-west direction by the historical route Via Emilia and it is organised in two districts, *Parma Centro* and *Oltretorrente*, separated on the north-south axis by a stream with its wide natural green corridor. The historical urban fabric hosts monumental buildings with a strong identity and a wide range of cultural heritage, museums and theatres. Noteworthy is the Ducal Park, an extensive historical open space surrounded by cultural functions, schools and research institutions, covering a large portion of the district *Oltretorrente*.

A valid premise for the analysis of the pedestrian infrastructure accessibility requirements is the consistent presence of the elderly which, on average, constitute the 20% of the population residing in the historic centre, with peaks of over 30% in many urban sectors. Moreover, the city has been nominated "Capital of Culture 2020 + 21" and it is assumed that over the next few years, regardless of the health emergency, the influx of people in the city, especially in the historic centre, may increase. Major urban events generally represent, for cities in which they take place, an opportunity of verification, redevelopment, and urban re-organisation. The city government, therefore, in addition to responding to the daily needs of its citizens, should be able to manage the increased flow of tourists, especially in the historic centre.

The enhancement of pedestrian mobility is one of the strategic issues for Parma city government, which is committed in collaboration with the University of Parma in identifying criteria, methods and guidelines for planning pedestrian accessibility for people with special needs or disabilities.

4.2   In-Field Survey Campaign

The proposed methodology has been tested with an initial focus on the investigation of the main distribution axes that connect the main cultural sites within the historical city centre (*Oltretorrente* and *Parma Centro* neighbourhoods). The surveyed paths are the north-south axis connecting the train station - recently involved in a regeneration intervention (2015) - with the city centre, and the east-west axis corresponding to the path of the Via Emilia, a historic road which provides a connection with *Piazza del Duomo* (Fig. 1).

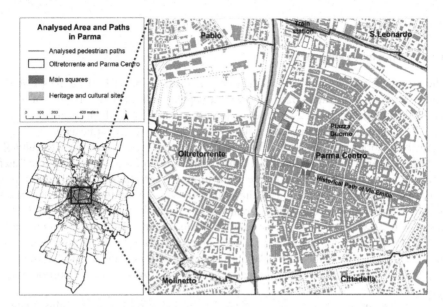

Fig. 1. In field surveyed pedestrian paths within the historic centre of Parma (*Oltretorrente* and *Parma Centro* neighbourhoods)

In order to build the cognitive framework for the application of the proposed methodology, in-field investigations have been carried out, involving direct survey operations and the filling of inspection sheets. The in-field survey campaign has been conducted in 2020.

The proposed inspection sheet, described in [27], is an essential tool for highlighting both the quantitative and qualitative features of each homogeneous link of a pedestrian path. The inspection sheet has been filled in for each pedestrian path section and for each pedestrian crossing along the analysed routes.

The outcomes have been georeferenced and returned into the GIS database for the calculation of the walkability index. By querying the database, it has been possible to draw up thematic maps that identify the potentialities and criticalities of the analysed pedestrian infrastructures.

5   Results and Discussion

5.1   Thematic Maps Representing Individually Attributes

The following figures (Figs. 2, 3, 4, 5, 6, 7 and 8) represent the detailed maps of the inspected Attributes which have been used to calculate the walkability indices. The maps consider the pedestrian path width, the presence of changes in level (ramps and steps), bottlenecks, coloured ground signs the protection, seats and the maintenance level of each analysed pedestrian path link.

Figure 2 highlights that only few of the analysed pedestrian links have a critical width of less than 90 cm, while the majority are more than 150 cm large.

Figure 3 shows where paths or crossing with changes in level are located. In a few sidewalks and in some crossings the presence of steps has been detected, although steps should be avoided to ensure a comprehensive accessibility for all the users. Anyway, the map highlights that most of the crossings have proper ramps and the majority of paths do not have level changes.

Figure 4 shows the presence of some bottlenecks along the analysed paths, where the width presents narrowing points. Those bottlenecks are usually caused by street furniture, lamps, garbage bins, etc. and may represent critical points for the pedestrian flow.

Figure 5 highlights an overall lack of coloured ground signs for the pedestrian paths, except for some links.

Figure 6 shows the protection level provided to pedestrians with regard to the motorised traffic; the map highlights some paths and crossing where the protection level should be increased.

Figure 7 shows that seats along the paths are rare and, in fact, many sidewalks are not equipped with seats.

Figure 8 highlights an overall excellent or good maintenance level of the pedestrian infrastructure, except for some critical points.

Finally, Fig. 9 shows that there are few links and crossings where tactile flooring is available for visually impaired pedestrians.

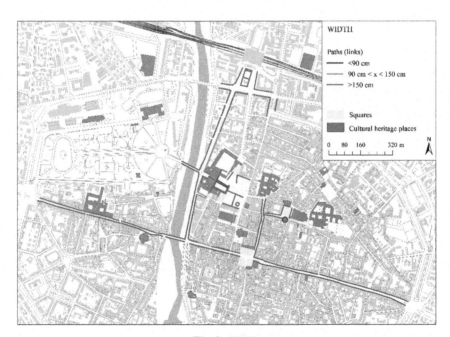

Fig. 2. Width

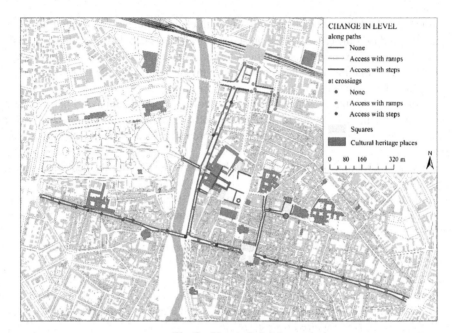

Fig. 3. Change in level

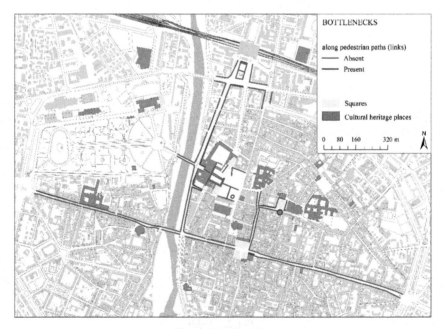

Fig. 4. Bottlenecks

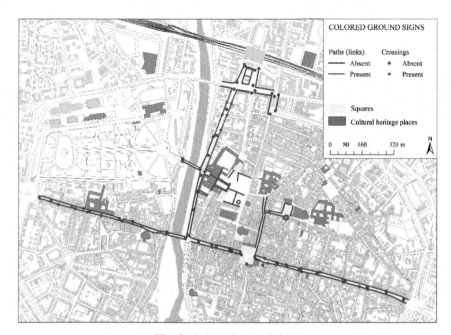

Fig. 5. Coloured ground signs

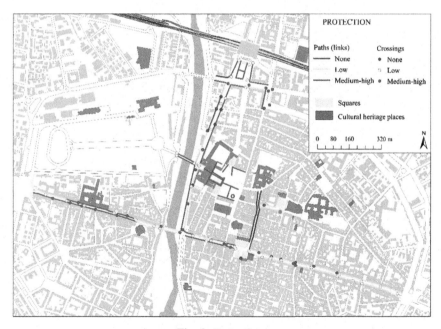

Fig. 6. Protections

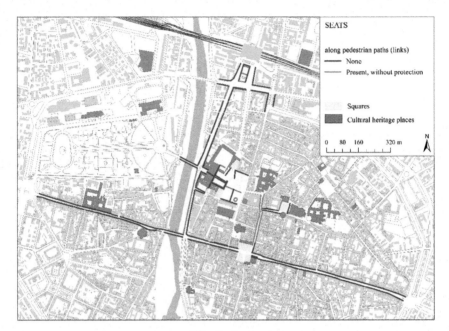

Fig. 7. Seats

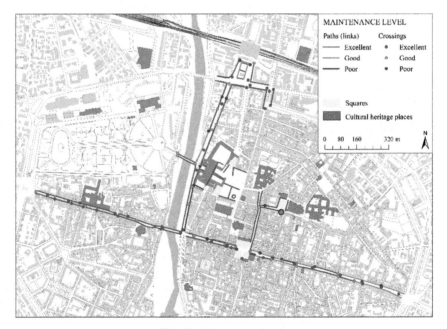

Fig. 8. Maintenance level

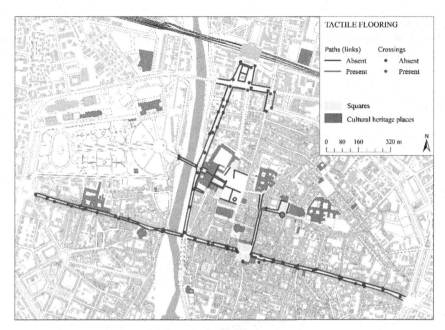

Fig. 9. Presence of tactile flooring

5.2 Global Index

Finally, the considered parameters have been calculate the walkability index, as explained in paragraph 3.3. The results are mapped in Fig. 10 that shows the assessment index for each analysed link and crossing belonging to the pedestrian paths.

It is noticeable that the obtained analytical results showed a close correspondence of the index to the real physical configuration of the paths.

Links with a very low walkability index along Viale Bottego, in front of the station, are characterised by the absence of the sidewalk. In this case, the transit of pedestrians takes place in the maneuvering area of parking areas.

Similarly, the links with a low walkability along Viale Toschi near the Pilotta, have a sidewalk with an insufficient width. The path is often mixed pedestrian-cycle and the presence of very crowded bus stops significantly restricts the passage.

In addition, many pedestrian crossings have a low or very low index due to the absence of adequate road markings and colour signs, the poor state of maintenance or the low/absent level of protection, i.e. they are not raised or are characterised by poor visibility and lack of life-saving islands.

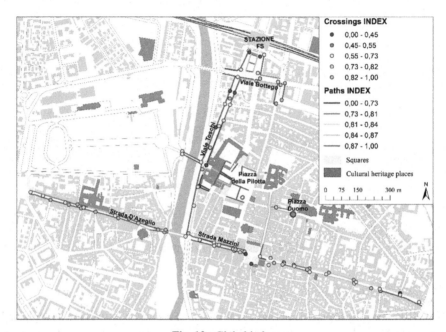

Fig. 10. Global index

However, apparent inconsistencies may also be highlighted. The index value of some links is low despite they are mainly in pedestrian areas e.g., in *Piazza Duomo*. The square is characterised by a paving made of cobblestones or "*san pietrini*" which make the transit difficult especially for weak road users. Therefore, only the sidewalks along the edges of the square have been detected, considering them the only paths potentially accessible to all. However, these sidewalks often have an insufficient width (i.e. definitely less than 90 cm) often aggravated by the presence of fixed obstacles that hinder the passage. For these reasons, what is shown by the indices is once again consistent.

Similarly in the case of *Piazza della Pilotta*, due to the cobbled paving, only the sections with a stone slabs paving have been detected (Fig. 11).

Fig. 11. The stone slabs pedestrian sections considered in Piazza della Pilotta

6   Conclusions and Further Research

The renewal of historic centres, intended as an improvement in accessibility and safety for the weakest and most vulnerable road users, can play a fundamental role in the development of cultural itineraries.

The performed analysis can provide the Public Administration with a useful tool for assessing the walkability of pedestrian mobility in the historical centre. The proposed methodology, initially applied only to the main road axes (e.g. to evaluate accessibility on the occasion of major cultural events), can then also be applied in the management practice, extending the survey to the entire historical centre. In this way, the proposed model can provide a complete cognitive framework of the pedestrian network, highlighting the criticalities, and suggesting possible solutions.

The processing of a complete walkability map, in fact, can provide support for the decision-makers in selecting the relevant urban policies and related planning, ordering the implementation phases and defining the priority interventions. Furthermore, the availability of a representation characterised by specific and detailed information on the walkability of pedestrian paths would allow local administrations to identify which areas need interventions to ensure accessibility for all users, thus implementing localised improvement interventions and avoiding the insertion of invasive solutions.

Among the identifiable criticalities of the presented analysis model, it is possible to highlight the onerousness associated with the in-field survey of all the analysed paths as well as the need for periodic updating of the data to ensure its effectiveness. For these updating and monitoring activities, it could be very useful to provide forms of community involvement (e.g., crowdsourcing methodologies for data collection), in order to highlight the main criticalities of public spaces, also related to the different types of disabilities or needs. A perceptive rating approach could also be developed, including utility-based information, such as the presence of amenities or commercial activities capable of enhancing the route attractiveness. Also, surveys among a sample of pedestrian paths users could be carried out, and then correlated with the aggregate walkability index.

Furthermore, as the visual inspections conducted are subjected to bias, more accurate measuring methods could be preferred, perhaps having them performed by more than one person to allow a more precise auditing procedure.

The GIS based database containing all the information collected during the on-site inspections may be enriched including measured or foreseeable pedestrian flows, to assess the Level of Service and capacity of each pedestrian connection. Geo-tagged photos of the analysed paths and of the main criticalities observed may also be added in the informative layers, as well as maintenance planning information.

Further improvements of the applied index may also consider among the indicators:

– the presence of pedestrian areas restricted to traffic, that allow a wider use of the public space for pedestrians, not strictly limited to sidewalks;
– the paving materials of each link, to assess the limits it imposes on the transit of certain types of road users.

The proposed methodological approach could be useful in the drafting and implementation of the Sustainable Urban Mobility Plans (SUMPs) and the Urban Furniture Plans. About the last one, it is also necessary to identify the presence or absence of street furniture along the pedestrian paths and whether it constitute a risk or impediment for the correct use of the public space by citizens.

Finally, the model developed could also be used as a support for the drafting of the Plans for the Elimination of Architectural Barriers (PEBA), in the different steps of urban analysis, classification of walkability and accessibility levels and identification of architectural barriers. Therefore, future research developments will foresee the extension of the study to the entire historical centre and the inclusion of other indicators within the calculation of the global index.

Acknowledgments. In field inspections of the pedestrian paths were carried out within a research project on pedestrian accessibility to the historical centre of Parma financed by Parma Municipality (scientific responsible prof. Michele Zazzi). The authors wish to thank Maddalena Moretti for conducting the inspections.

This study was also supported by the MIUR (Ministry of Education, Universities and Research [Italy]) through a project entitled WEAKI TRANSIT: WEAK-demand areas Innovative TRANsport Shared services for Italian Towns (Project code: 20174ARRHT), financed with the PRIN 2017 (Research Projects of National Relevance) programme. We authorise the MIUR to reproduce and distribute reprints for Governmental purposes, notwithstanding any copyright notations thereon. Any opinions, findings and conclusions or recommendations expressed in this material are those of the authors, and do not necessarily reflect the views of the MIUR.

References

1. Tiboni, M., Ventura, V.: Mobilità pedonale e spazi pubblici urbani nella città storica, vol. unico, pp. 1–205. Tipografia Camuna, Brescia (2002). ISBN: 9788898027088
2. El Saied, H.M.H., El Gezawi, L.S.E.D., El Sayad, N.A.E.H.: The role of cycling and walkability on revitalizing the historic urban areas in Egypt case study: El Galaa Street-Damietta City. Bulletin of the Faculty of Engineering. Mansoura University, vol. 43, no. 3, pp. 1–10 (2020)
3. Tolley R. (ed.): Sustainable Transport. Planning for walking and Cycling in Urban Environments. Woodhead Publishing, Sawston (2003)
4. Forsyth, A.: What is a walkable place? The walkability debate in urban design. Urban Design Int. **20**(4), 274–292 (2015)
5. Global Designing Cities Initiative: Global Street Design Guide. Island Press (2016)
6. Giuliani, F., Maternini, G. (eds): Percorsi Pedonali. Progettazione e tecniche di itinerari ed attraversamenti. Egaf, Forlì (2017)
7. Ignaccolo, C., Giuffrida, N., Torrisi, V.: The queensway of New York city. a proposal for sustainable mobility in queens. Town Infrastruct. Plann. Saf. Urban Qual. 69–76 (2018)
8. Tira, M., Pezzagno, M., Richiedei, A. (eds): Pedestrians, urban spaces and health. In: Proceedings of the XXIV International Conference on Living and Walking in Cities (LWC, 12–13 September 2019, Brescia, Italy), pp. 88–92. CRC Press, London (2020). ISBN 9781003027379
9. Annunziata, A., Garau, C.: A literature review on walkability and its theoretical framework. emerging perspectives for research developments. In: Gervasi, O., et al. (eds.) ICCSA 2020. LNCS, vol. 12255, pp. 422–437. Springer, Cham (2020). https://doi.org/10.1007/978-3-030-58820-5_32
10. Campisi, T., Basbas, S., Tesoriere, G., Trouva, M., Papas, T., Mrak, I.: How to create walking friendly cities. a multi-criteria analysis of the central open market area of Rijeka. Sustainability **12**, 9470 (2020). https://doi.org/10.3390/su12229470
11. Tiboni, M., Rossetti, S., Vetturi, D., Torrisi, V., Botticini, F., Schaefer, M.D.: Urban policies and planning approaches for a safer and climate friendlier mobility in cities: strategies Initiatives and Some Analysis. Sustainability **13**, 1778 (2021). https://doi.org/10.3390/su13041778
12. Ignaccolo, M., Inturri, G., Giuffrida, N., Le Pira, M., Torrisi, V., Calabrò, G.: A step towards walkable environments: spatial analysis of pedestrian compatibility in an urban context. Eur. Transp. Trasporti Europei **76**(6), 1–12 (2020)
13. ITF: Pedestrian Safety. ITF Research Reports, OECD Publishing, Paris, Urban Space and Health (2012)
14. Garau, C., Annunziata, A., Coni, M.: A methodological framework for assessing practicability of the urban space: the survey on conditions of practicable environments (SCOPE) procedure applied in the case study of Cagliari (Italy). Sustainability **10**(11), 4189 (2018)
15. Rossetti, S., Tiboni, M., Vetturi, D., Zazzi, M., Caselli, B.: Measuring pedestrian accessibility to public transport in urban areas: a GIS-based discretisation approach, European Transport, Issue no. 76, May 2020, Paper no. 2 (2020). ISSN 1825–3997
16. Carpentieri, G., Guida, C., Masoumi, H.E.: Multimodal accessibility to primary health services for the elderly: a case study of naples Italy. . Sustainability **12**, 781 (2020). https://doi.org/10.3390/su12030781
17. Marzi, L.: Esperienze nell'ambito della pianificazione dell'accessibilità in ambito urbano. I casi dei centri storici delle città di Arezzo e Pisa, Ingenio (2021)
18. Campisi, T., Ignaccolo, M., Inturri, G., Tesoriere, G., Torrisi, V.: Evaluation of walkability and mobility requirements of visually impaired people in urban spaces. Res. Transp. Busin. Manage. 100592 (2020). ISSN 2210-5395. https://doi.org/10.1016/j.rtbm.2020.100592

19. Gargiulo, C., Zucaro, F., Gaglione, F.: A set of variables for the elderly accessibility in urban areas. TeMA – J. Land Use Mobil. Environ. 53–66 (2018)
20. Alves, F., Cruz, S., Rother, S., Strunk, T.: An application of the walkability index for elderly health—WIEH. The Case of the UNESCO Historic Centre of Porto, Portugal. Sustainability, vol. 13, p. 4869 (2021)
21. Torrisi, V., Garau, C., Ignaccolo, M., Inturri, G.: "Sustainable Urban Mobility Plans": key concepts and a critical revision on SUMPs guidelines. In: Gervasi, O., et al. (eds.) ICCSA 2020. LNCS, vol. 12255, pp. 613–628. Springer, Cham (2020). https://doi.org/10.1007/978-3-030-58820-5_45
22. Torrisi, V., Garau, C., Inturri, G., Ignaccolo, M.: Strategies and actions towards sustainability: encouraging good ITS practices in the SUMP vision. In: International Conference of Computational Methods In Sciences And Engineering ICCMSE 2020 (2021). https://doi.org/10.1063/5.0047897
23. Allen, D., Clark, S.: New directions in street auditing: lessons from the PERS audits. In: International Conference on Walking and Liveable Communities, 8th, Toronto, Ontario, Canada (2007)
24. Conticelli, E., Maimaris, A., Papageorgiou, G., Tondelli, S.: Planning and designing walkable cities: a smart approach. In: Papa R., Fistola R., Gargiulo C. (eds) Smart Planning: Sustainability and Mobility in the Age of Change. Green Energy and Technology. Springer, Cham (2018). https://doi.org/10.1007/978-3-319-77682-8_15
25. Garau, C., Annunziata, A., Yamu, C.: A walkability assessment tool coupling multi-criteria analysis and space syntax: the case study of Iglesias, pp. 1–23. European Planning Studies, Italy (2020)
26. Zazzi, M., Ventura, P., Caselli, B., Carra, M.: GIS-based monitoring and evaluation system as an urban planning tool to enhance the quality of pedestrian mobility in Parma. In: Tira, M., Pezzagno, M. (eds.) Town and Infrastructure Planning for Safety and Urban Quality: Proceedings of the XXIII International Conference on Living and Walking in Cities, pp. 87–94. CRC Press, Taylor and Francis group, London (2018)
27. Rossetti, S., Zazzi, M.: In field assessment of existing pedestrian paths: a comprehensive approach towards pedestrian oriented neighbourhoods. In: Tira, M., Pezzagno, M., Richiedei, A. (eds), Pedestrians, Urban Spaces and Health. Proceedings of the XXIV International Conference on Living and Walking in Cities (LWC, 12–13 September 2019, Brescia, Italy), pp. 88–92. CRC Press, London (2020). ISBN 9781003027379

Urban Accessibility and Social Equity in Covid-19 Era: A Spatial Analysis in Two Neighbourhoods of the City of Naples

Carmela Gargiulo, Federica Gaglione$^{(\boxtimes)}$, and Floriana Zucaro

Department of Civil, Building and Environmental Engineering, University of Naples Federico II, Naples, Italy
{gargiulo,federica.gaglione,floriana.zucaro}@unina.it

Abstract. The academic debate has been turn the attention on pedestrian accessibility to urban services, as walking allow to solve several issues ranging from social and health problems also accentuated by the ongoing pandemic. The innovation in geospatial field has encouraged the development of accessibility and walkability measures and indicators oriented to measure the main physical and functional characteristics of the built environment related to the accessibility of urban services at the neighbourhood scale. According to these premises, this research work, aimed at improving pedestrian accessibility and guaranteeing equal access to neighbourhood-scale services, proposes a seven-steps GIS method based on an Accessibility Indicator that integrates the main aspects of walkability indexes relating to connectivity, sense of security, geometry and amenity of urban built environment. This Accessibility Indicator defines the areas of easy accessibility to the local essential services, by referring to two different maximum distances: the first relates to the distance of 700 m defined in the literature as the distance that a user is willing to walk to use a neighborhood service and the second relates to the regulatory restrictions adopted in the most difficult periods of the pandemic (500 m).

Keywords: Social equity · Urban accessibility · Covid-19

1 Trends and Research Perspectives of Walkability

1.1 Walking as Opportunity to Improve the Urban Quality

The World Health Organization in the Action Plan for the prevention and control of communicable diseases 2013–2020 invites governments and local decision makers to promote active mobility (walking and cycling) in local government policies to help reduce various health diseases such as obesity, diabetes, etc. and therefore favour healthier lifestyles and behaviors [1]. Some authors investigated the link between urban mobility

---

Despite being a joint study, Carmela Gargiulo elaborated Sect. 3, Federica Gaglione Sect. 2 and Floriana Zucaro Sect. 1.

O. Gervasi et al. (Eds.): ICCSA 2021, LNCS 12958, pp. 509–524, 2021.
https://doi.org/10.1007/978-3-030-87016-4_37

habits and health conditions and found that the odds of obesity increase by 6% for each additional hour spent in a car and conversely decline by 4,8% for each additional km walked per [2]. The economic burden of this situation has been estimated to be around 80.4 billion euro per year for Europe and 400 million dollars per year for USA, due to the costs related to the healthcare system [3] and [4]. This cost could be avoided if all segments of population were to achieve an average of 20 min per day of simple and inexpensive activities such as walking [3]. Until before the pandemic in Italy fewer and fewer people choose to move using a means of transport other than the car to go to the workplace but, at the same time, the number of journeys on foot and by bicycle was increasing: the distances on foot increased by more than 5%, while the bike doubles (and more) its share while still occupying a small segment of the modal distribution of urban journeys (2.7%) [5]. This slow growth occurred in the period 2017–2018 and had a remarkably raised during and post lockdown conditions, as the Covid-19 made walking and cycling even more appealing. In fact, sidewalks are open spaces where pedestrians can usually avoid crowding and keep a safe distance of at least 1 m. Nonetheless, these trends seem not to fully correspond to the results expected from the implementation of strategies and actions that for 15 years have been referring to the Smart City paradigm and more recently to the Age Friendly City model. If on the one hand through the Smart Mobility approach the technological solutions and innovations can encourage people to walk by supporting them in planning the paths and overcoming immaterial barriers, [6, 7] and [8], on the other hand the diffusion of the principles of Universal Design favour re-organising the physical and functional structure of urban systems, in order to increase urban accessibility to the main urban services, mainly by walking, for all population segments [9–11] and [12]. Therefore, the aims of smartness and improvement of the urban accessibility both of open spaces (built and not) and activities, involves increasing the walkability. Recently a few policy options to promote active mobility in urban areas have been proposed by different government institutions. The UN Agenda 2030 for Sustainable Development [13] has claimed how in the transition to a low-carbon society a radical modal shift towards soft mobility is required to reach most goals, in particular the ones related to well-being (goal n. 3), urban sustainability (goal n. 11) and climate (goal n. 13). In 2020, the UN and the WHO highlighted how cities must adapt to the new health crisis such as the Covid-19 by increasing the quality of urban spaces and the accessibility options to reach the primary services such as food and health [14].

According to what has just been described, it results that local decision makers intend to adapt and reorganize built and open spaces according to the renewed needs of pedestrian accessibility to essential urban places and services that reveal to be more pressing during a pandemic crisis. In this perspective, this study aims to support local policymakers in improving pedestrian accessibility and guaranteeing equal access to neighbourhood-scale services.

The paper is structure as follows: the two next sub-sections provide the scientific framework of walkability issue and the review of its main indexes respectively; Sect. 2 illustrates the methodology developed in GIS environment; Sect. 3 discusses the results for two municipalities of the city of Naples; Sect. 4 draws the conclusions by providing causes of reflections.

1.2 Walkability and Urban Built Environment

Walking is currently an intense topic of discussion in academic debate, as researchers have been focusing on it as a mean to solve a variety of issues from social ills and health problems relating to global warming and air pollution. Measuring the friendliness of the urban settlements to the pedestrian users commits the scientific community in identifying the urban characteristics that influence walking behaviours. In fact, urban settlement features can perform both as facilitators and impediments to walkability, that can be defined as "the extent to which the built environment supports and encourages walking by providing for pedestrian comfort and safety, connecting people with varied destinations within a reasonable amount of time and effort, and offering visual interest in journeys throughout the network" [15]. Cervero and Kockelman [16] before and Ewing and Cervero [17] after, suggested the five main features of the built environment influencing walkability: the greater buildings Density and better accessibility to public transport are accompanied by a smaller amount of kilometres travelled (shorter Distances); in the same way, the greater Diversity in Land Uses and in the mix of functions (Destination accessibility) is accompanied by a greater level of pedestrianization of the spaces (Design) and therefore a more limited use of motorized vehicles. These famous "5Ds" have been linked to basic or neighbourhood services to highlight the importance of their proximity for social inclusion and access opportunities. Promoting pedestrian accessibility can make urban societies more inclusive by allowing easier access to relevant services even for people with limited mobility. Several authors found that quality and attractiveness of a neighbourhood were strongly related to walkability levels [18] and [19] and this correlation depends also on the socio-economic conditions of the community. For instance, gentrification processes and associated displacement of disadvantaged groups worsen social inequity of those who could potentially benefit the most from highly walkable urban environments. The disadvantaged are likely to include socially vulnerable groups such the elderly, minorities, and those with low education and/or low-skill occupations that have limited resources and are often mobility-restricted [20] and [21]. Furthermore, if the Covid-19 era increased the need of walking, it also exposed the spatial inequalities in moving through the different urban districts. The innovation in geospatial technology field, such as the Geographical Information Systems (GIS), has enabled the development of walkability measures. Some studies used a "place-based" approach, as their main aim was measuring the walkability levels of territorial unit like census tracts or catchment areas by reason of the presence of local services (i.e. green areas, recreational activities, health assistance) [22]. Other works employs "network-based" approach, as they aimed at measuring the accessibility to nearby service by focusing on the features of pedestrian network and on the identification of the best paths for users [23]. Both the lines of research aggregate different variables and indicators into a walkability index helping to measure various dimensions of built environment that cannot be captured completely by individual indicators alone [24].

1.3 Reviewing Walkability Indexes

According to Vale et al. [25] approximately 80 or more walkability indexes have been developed from different perspectives such as urban studies, public health and transport planning, to measure the pedestrian friendliness at neighbourhood and city levels.

Among all these indexes, this work takes into consideration the nine most consolidated and wide used ones by providing a compared reading of them: Walkshed,
Neighbourhood Destination Accessibility Index (NDAI), Moveability Index, Pedshed,
Walk Opportunity Index, Walk Score®, Walkability Index (WI), Pedestrian Environment
Index (PEI) and Pedestrian Index of the Environment (PIE). They were selected after
an extensive literature review and all of them can represent a level-headed overview of
the current main methods for measuring walkability. According to the method described
in the next section, the review of the walkability indexes was a preliminary and necessary step to develop the method described in the next section, as it allowed defining the
features of walkability to take into consideration and the most suitable way to measure
them. Data collection, methods and spatial level of analysis represented the key aspects
of the review supplied.

In 2006 Frank et al. [26] lead the foundations for the development of walkability
methods oriented to capture the influence of urban form on walkability. Frank et al. [26]
and [27] developed the Walkability Index that integrates land-use mix, connectivity,
and residential density. Their values are first measured in a network buffer around each
participant's residence and then normalized (z-score) by assigning a double weight to the
connectivity of the street network as the higher density of intersections, the easier of travel
to destinations is. These normalized variables are combined to calculate the WI [27] that
has been used in numerous studies related to travel behavior too, by defining different
ranges of weights for the three components of the index. As the WI was developed
in USA where cities are characterized by lower population density, degree of land-
use mix, and connectivity than European cities, Grasser et al. [28] adapted Frank's
Walkability Index adapting it to them: population density, household density, an entropy
index for land-use mix and three-way intersection density were considered and weighted
in a different way. As far as the use of the kernel density method is concerned and
regarding the concentration of recreational facilities or playgrounds, the Moveability
Index differs from the WI whose inspiration took from. In fact, the aim of Moveability
Index was to measure opportunities for physical activity of children in urban areas
[29] and [30]. Walkability Index inspired the development of another index taken into
consideration that is Walk Score. It rates the proximity of daily life activities to specific
addresses in USA, Canada, Australia, and New Zealand. Walk Score® measure is based
on an algorithm that calculates the points according to the distance of an origin to each
category of urban opportunities within 30 min on foot. Distances are transformed in
0–100 "amenity scores" through a polynomial distance decay function. If the closest
facility in a category is within 0.4 km, the maximum number of points is assigned and
no points are allocated to facilities further away than 1.6 km. Further elements such as
weather and crime allow to calculate the add-on scores. All the scores are first weighted
and then summed to the final Walk Score® on a 0–100 scale. This commercial web-
tool is used by users mainly to assess their home-buying decisions and by researchers to
measure built environment characteristics in transport and health research. Nevertheless,
the complete algorithm is proprietary and some aspects of the methodology remain
unavailable, many researchers agree that the Walk Score® metric is an overall measure
of walkability that does not take into account the aspects of space design and street
furniture that can influence the quality and the choice pf a path, such as the width of a

sidewalk, the presence of obstacles to the walk, or the visual quality of the space [31] and [32]. Some of these aspects related to the street layout, together with safety and sidewalk connectivity, are considered in the Pedshed index that is based on walking catchment approach as it measures the area accessible through the street network within a defined Euclidean distance. In addition to Walk Score that has a calculation procedure proprietary, also Walkshed index works through a DecisionTree® Avencia's geographic planning and prioritization software that scores a location based on the quantity and diversity of amenities within a 1-mile radius. Walkshed allows users to customize the weight of the variables according to their preferences, to calculate the walkability of Philadelphia neighborhoods to reach shops, stops and other services. Like the previous, the Walk Opportunities Index (WOI) developed by Kuzmyak et al. [33] mainly refer to residential density, mix of functions and completeness of pedestrian network. The WOI calculates the walking distance to each opportunity in 0.25-mile buffers. Distance, size and importance of each destination determine WOI weight. Instead of summing the values of the variables composing the index, the Pedestrian Environment Index (PEI), multiplying each of them to avoid influences between components and that the final value can be zero because of one single component. The PEI formula requires data that are mostly available publicly, such as population density, land use, buildings, street network features [34]. The Pedestrian Index of the Environment (PIE) differ from this last index and from the others for the more elaborated procedure to calculate it. PIE variables, referring to the 5 D's of urban form, are calculated through the kernel density method to consider the decreasing impact of urban features on walking behavior as distance increases [35]. The variables are then weighed by using a single-variable binary logit models and their sum is normalized on a 20–100 scale. The last index is the neighborhood destination accessibility index (NDAI) whose final score was calculated by summing the eight weighted domain scores (education, transport, recreation, social and cultural, food retail, financial, health, and other retail), obtaining a value between 0 and 31, with a higher score representing better walking access to services and amenities [36]. To provide an effective and worthy representation of the outputs of the compared review of the walkability indexes taken into account a radar diagram was elaborated (Fig. 1). Pedshed and PEI count more built environment characteristics than the other indexes, by requiring a wider set of data to be collected. Thus, can be explained by considering that data gathering phase can reveal onerous for the calculation of an indicator, as it depends on the accessibility and availability of databases available for the study area [37] and [38]. However, the measurement of the susceptibility of the built environment to be walked cannot take place without working at a level of detail that is as accurate as possible, compatibly with the resources available. Features related to connectivity, land use and presence of amenities are shared by most walkability indexes, as the localization and distribution of services and places influence the choice of possible walking paths [39]. Moving to the methodological aspects, except of the Walkshed index, the others use compensatory methods by summing (unless PEI) and standardizing characteristics of the built environment related to the 5Ds. All the indexes' outputs refer to an area and Walkscore, Walkshed and Moveability refer to a deeper level of detail by referring to sub-sections of streets or to pixels.

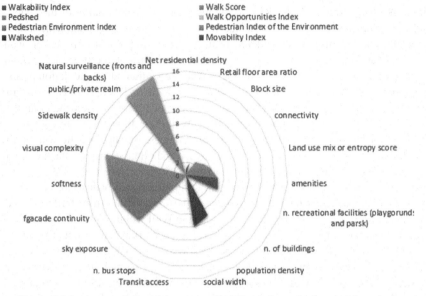

■ Walkability Index   ■ Walk Score
■ Pedshed   ▩ Walk Opportunities Index
▩ Pedestrian Environment Index   ■ Pedestrian Index of the Environment
■ Walkshed   ■ Movability Index

Fig. 1. Main characteristics of the nine walkability indexes (authors' elaboration).

2 Methodology

The renewed needs for pedestrian accessibility to urban places and services, also resulting from the pandemic crisis, constitute the starting point to rethink the physical and functional organization of urban systems.

In this perspective, this study aims to support local policymakers in improving pedestrian accessibility and guaranteeing equal access to neighborhood-scale services through a GIS-based method integrating the main characteristics of indexes of walkability. Nine indexes were considered to identify and measure in a quali-quantitative way numerous physical features of the pedestrian network and the built environment that influence the accessibility of urban services. The main goal is the measurement of pedestrian accessibility to services which are essential during pandemics, according to the restrictive distance imposed by national regulations too. These two central aspects related to Covid-19 were considered due to the assumption that the new Covid-19 Virus Variants and the still-uncertain ways of transmission require to ensure equal access to urban activities and places to all population segments. Besides, the organization of the urban system affects the accessibility and the use of services and urban spaces, as well as their localization and distribution. Therefore, they are key elements to avoid further forms of inequality and marginalization in those parts of the city which, due to their socio-economic level and quality of life, are normally disadvantaged compared to others and whose gap tends to worsen in times of crisis such as the pandemic.

The study is in continuity with previous works by the authors who, adopting a systemic approach that integrates the pedestrian network, the demand and supply of services, aimed at improving pedestrian accessibility by the elderly to services, also through the definition of optimal pedestrian paths that facilitate the achievement of services by the elderly.

In this perspective, during the research work presented in these pages, aimed at improving pedestrian accessibility to urban services, especially at the neighborhood scale, a six-phase method in a GIS environment was developed. The first phase consisted of measuring pedestrian accessibility to services identified as essential in the Covid-19 lockdown period or identifying areas equipped with necessary services that can be easily reached on foot by the inhabitants of those areas.

To this end, the significant characteristics of the urban system have been selected such as: (i) the geomorphological characteristics and those relating to safety, amenities and pleasantness of both the pedestrian network and the urban fabric, (ii) the socio-economic characteristics of the population, (iii) the location of services. Furthermore, reference was taken at two different distances: the first relates to the distance of 700 m, defined in the literature as the distance a user is willing to travel on foot to use a neighborhood service, while the second relates to regulatory restrictions adopted in the most difficult periods of the pandemic in Italy (500 m). With this in mind, 19 variables have been identified to measure pedestrian accessibility which also include those relating to the walkability indicators derived from the review which refer to the topological and geometric aspects of the network (connectivity) and the supply of proximity services (Table 1).

Table 1. The characteristics of urban system useful to measure pedestrian accessibility.

ID	Variable	Measure	Source
Socio-economic characteristics			
1	Population divided by age groups (30–39;40–49;50–59;60–69; +70)	Inhabitant	ISTAT
2	Population density	Inhabitant	ISTAT
Characteristics of the pedestrian network and the built environment			
3	Network connectivity	$n°/m$	GIS
4	Slope of the network link	$> 5\% = 0 < 5\% = 1$	GIS
5	Sidewalk width	$< 1{,}5\ m = 0 > 1{,}5\ m = 1$	Google maps
6	State of the flooring	$0 = poor\ good = 1$	Google maps
7	Crossroad	$No = 0\ Yes = 1$	Google maps
8	Traffic light intersection	$No = 0\ Yes = 1$	Google maps
9	Speed of vehicular traffic	$> max\ 50\ km/h = 0 < 30\ km/h = 0$	Openstreet map

(continued)

Table 1. (*continued*)

ID	Variable	Measure	Source
10	Volume of vehicular traffic	> 17,5 m = 0 < 9 m = 1	GIS
11	Presence of benches	No = 0 Yes = 1	Google maps
12	Presence of shaded paths	No = 0 Yes = 1	Google maps
13	Noise pollution	< 55 dBA = 0 > 55 dBA = 1	Acoustic zoning plan
Functional characteristics			
14	Pharmacies	n°	Google my maps
15	Banks	n°	Google my maps
16	Post office	n°	Google my maps
17	Neighborhood food	n°	Google my maps
18	Supermarket	n°	Google my maps
19	Neighborhood green	n°	Google my maps

The second phase concerned the parameterization and geolocation of the variables.

The socio-economic and functional variables were parameterized using the ISTAT database and the Google Mymaps platform, respectively.

The variables, relating to both the characteristics of the pedestrian network and the built urban environment, were detected through direct surveys in the study area. They were parameterized afterward concerning a qualitative scale, through the presence/absence, or by identifying threshold values (based on regulatory or planning documents), explaining conditions that are favorable (or not) to the practicability of each arch of the pedestrian network. In other words, in the first case for the definition of the state of the pavement, for example, pedestrian paths with pavement in a poor state of maintenance were defined as "poor"; in the second case, the speed of vehicular traffic, the Highway Code was consulted, since in Article 142 it governs the maximum speeds on each type of road permitted for traffic safety and protection of human life by identifying the roads passable even by pedestrians with speeds below < 30 km/h. Similarly, for the variable linked to noise pollution, the reference values of the decibels were taken from the acoustic zoning plan of the Municipality of Naples. The coexistence of qualitative and quantitative variables made it necessary, in phase three, to normalize the values. Normalization was also useful to calculate the sum of the walk score scores for each arc of the pedestrian network from generic node i to node j, on a scale from 1 to 13 due to the characteristics of the routes and the urban context considered. The choice of this method is due to the different nature of the considered variables, which do not allow to objectively define a differential "weight" without the use of statistical methods and local surveys as was performed in the authors' previous works [40].

Based on the walk scores obtained and the reading of the walkability indicators, the following accessibility indicator was developed in phase four:

$$\text{Accessibility Index} = D_{ij} + \left(D_{ij} \times \sum_{ij}^{1} W_{ij} \right) \tag{1}$$

where:

D_{ij} is the distance of each arc of the pedestrian network that can be traveled from node i to node j;

$(\sum_{ij}^{1} W_{ij})$ the relevance of the weight of each characteristic of the pedestrian network from node i to node j.

The indicators outlined within the literature review take into account the characteristics relating to connectivity, land use and the presence of services and the relative distances from them. Distance, size and relevance of each destination determine its weight by assigning a pedestrian score for the achievement of urban services.

Compared to the indicators reported in the review, the indicator developed in this study takes into account not only the characteristics of the pedestrian network linked to its connectivity but also those relating to its geometry, the sense of safety perceived by users and the context of the urban area of reference, components considered essential in defining the degree of usability of the routes and the level of accessibility to neighborhood services. More specifically, the proposed Accessibility indicator relates the distance to be traveled to reach a certain service on each arc of the pedestrian network with the weighted average of its characteristics, on a scale of values from 0 to 1.

In phase five, on the basis of the distances that a user can or is willing to travel, respectively in times of pandemics and not, urban areas have been classified in terms of pedestrian accessibility to essential services through the use of a Network Analysis tool in GIS environment. Starting from the services present within the study area and defined the areas accessible to them, it was possible to identify the number of users served [32]. In phase six, in relation to these two distances, the population served in five age groups (30–39, 40–49, 50–59,60–69, +70) was calculated to understand if there is social equity between different areas of the same city and between the different age groups of the population.

3 Results

The proposed methodology was tested in the V and VIII Municipalities of Naples that have profound differences in terms of the socio-economic, settlement, geomorphological and functional characteristics, although characterized by the same number of inhabitants. More in detail, the V municipality is characterized by central districts that developed between the nineteenth and twentieth centuries (Vomero) or by ancient small villages that have succumbed to the intense settlement expansion of the 60s–70s of the last century (Arenella), endowed with the functional characteristics of the city center; the VIII instead includes peripheral districts, which once represented the rich and fertile Neapolitan agricultural reservoir but which, the myopic expansion policy (Scampia) or the spontaneous and uncontrolled expansion (Chiaiano and Piscinola) of the last 50 years, have relegated to areas substantial economic, social and settlement discomfort leaving them deprived of both essential and general services that constitute the basic elements on which to build the "community effect". Figure 2 shows two examples of the application of the Indicator to two categories of different services: healthcare (pharmacies) and economic (post offices) in the two different periods considered. As can be seen, both types of services have a consistent diffusion in the 5th municipality and consequently the areas served by these cover ordinarily almost the entire territory of the Municipality. On the other hand, the situation in the VIII municipality is different since the conditions of discomfort and poor accessibility are perceptible due to the reduced number of equipment, the consequent scarce extension of the areas ordinarily served, to be further reduced in periods of restriction. Furthermore, in the VIII Municipality, the situation is further aggravated considering that the areas identified by the Accessibility Index must be built by contemplating not only the elements considered above but also the conditions of the pedestrian network, which in this part of the city is lacking in safety, comfort, and amenities (Fig. 2).

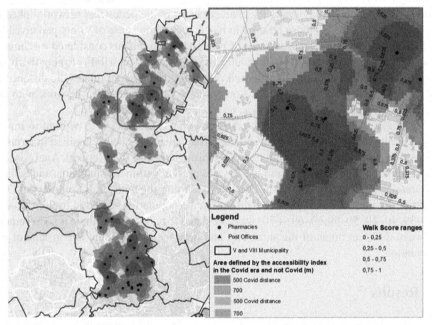

Fig. 2. Accessibility Index results and walk scores of pedestrian network links for the V and VIII municipalities of City of Naples (authors' elaboration).

The Index applied to the two Municipalities show the distribution of services and their accessibility, highlights the gap that differentiates the two study areas which is not only physical, functional and organizational (as already mentioned at the beginning of this paragraph) but also refers to services accessibility.

In detail, the Vomero district, characterized by a high population density and a hilly orographic conformation, has a compact urban fabric designed on a rather orderly and regular design, with a strong presence of commercial activities and a good endowment

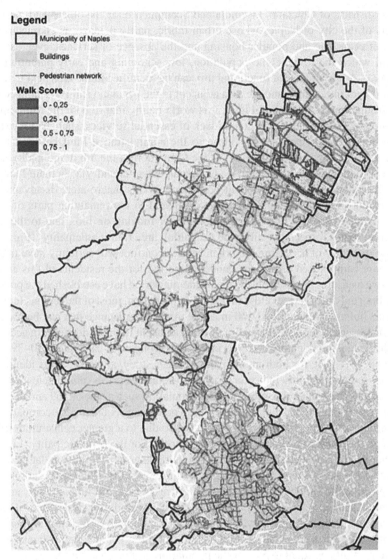

Fig. 3. Classification of pedestrian network according to Walk Score calculated (authors' elaboration).

and a variety of neighborhood services and general services, especially in some areas such as those adjacent to Piazza Vanvitelli, Piazza Bernini and Piazza Medaglie d'Oro. The Arenella district, on the other hand, is more recent than the Vomero district and includes areas such as that of the Rione Alto, adjacent to the hospital area, the Policlinico and via Domenico Fontana, characterized by an unplanned fabric that has extended as a consequence of the building saturation of the Vomero.

The districts of Chiaiano, Piscinola and Scampia are, on the other hand, peripheral districts of the city of Naples whose urban fabric, partly planned, is characterized by blocks of economic and popular housing and the absence of services, even assistance ones, in which the low-income population, low schooling and early parenting found their place. A fair amount of functional mix can be identified in the area next to the Ciro Esposito Park in Scampia and the area adjacent to the Chiaiano and Pisci-nola-Scampia underground line 1. Regarding Fig. 2, it is worth noting that in both the Municipalities there are areas characterized by a total lack of essential services, such as, for example, the portion of municipal territory close to the administrative limit between the two municipalities. This is the hilly area of the Camaldoli in the 5th municipality and the area next to the Cotugno hospital, Via Comunale Guantai and Via Vicinale Margherita in the 8th municipality. The resident population in this macro-area, disadvantaged in terms of the supply of essential services compared to the remaining parts of the two Municipalities, also has limited opportunities for moving on foot, due to the lack of pedestrian routes, especially -all in the Camaldoli area (5th municipality) (Fig. 3). The extreme difficulty of accessing the urban services on foot will certainly have made life even more complicated during the pandemic period for the residents of this area. The restrictive measures imposed during the pandemic period have established the possibility of reaching only the services close to homes. In particular, most of the regions (e.g. Friuli Venezia Giulia) have identified 500 m as the maximum distance that can be traveled to reach the essential services present in the area adjacent to the residences. In accordance with this value, the population served in five age groups was calculated (30–39, 40–49, 50–59.60–69, +70), for both municipalities under study, all of the areas identified by the proposed Accessibility Indicator. For health-related services (pharmacies) the results (Fig. 4) show that vulnerable groups of the population such as the 60–69 and the over 70 are better served in the 5th municipality, with a percentage equal to 35% compared to the other groups of the population. This figure is also due to a greater concentration of this service in the more consolidated urban fabric areas. For the V municipality (Fig. 5), on the other hand, a social marginalization of vulnerable groups of the population emerges (60–69; +70), served only for 12% compared to 26% of the other population groups. For the economic services (banks and post offices) of the 5th municipality, an almost uniform distribution of about 11% is seen for banks, while for post offices it is about 6%, however, constituting a very low rate of the population of the entire municipality. The rates drop further for the VIII municipality, with a percentage for banks equal to 3% and post offices equal to 5% for the population groups considered.

Finally, compared to commercial services (supermarket and grocery stores), in the 5th municipality, the over 70s are better served within a radius of 500 m, with a percentage equal to 13% and 12% compared to other groups of the population, who can more easily travel a greater distance. The scenario is completely opposite for the VIII Municipality where the most disadvantaged groups of the population are those of the 60–69 and over 70. Among the overall population served by all the services considered, a substantial disparity emerges between the two Municipalities. For the V, about 50% of the population is served within 500 m (except for the age group 30–39 minors equal to about 40%). In the VIII municipality, 27% of the population aged between 30 and 59 is served within 500 m, while the percentage drops to 22% for the over 60s.

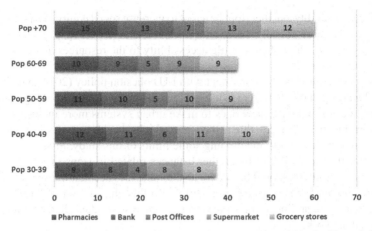

Fig. 4. Percentage of segments of population accessing to services within the V municipality of Naples.

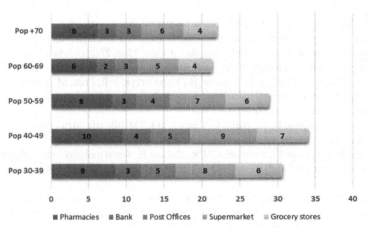

Fig. 5. Percentage of segments of population accessing to services within the VIII municipality of Naples.

4   Conclusions

The results just outlined underline how the measure of pedestrian accessibility can efficiently support local decision-makers in localizing, distributing and integrating urban services, by improving the walking network quality. In particular, the physic and functional organization of the urban system should be equity-oriented towards all the population segments, according to the different socio-economic backgrounds. In line with age-friendly city principles, local decision-makers should guarantee equally accessible urban services to all citizens, independently from their social, economic and physical conditions, to avoid "states of crisis" of the urban system when subjected to external agents like pandemics.

Urban accessibility can therefore be a tool to increase social equity even in peripheral neighborhoods, more socially disadvantaged and characterized by physical and functional marginality, where there is little accessibility to the resources and opportunities that a city can offer.

This consideration is also consistent with EU cohesion policy (2014) which recommends planners and policymakers to use the "lens of social equity" to change old development strategies and write new ones to make urban systems more inclusive, resilient and sustainable provide accessible and connected jobs, health care and recreation.

Nevertheless, it is worth mentioning some limits of this study. Firstly, for the measurement of the Accessibility Index the distances related to stops of public transport and the cycling mobility could be added, also to take into account the spread of micromobility consequent to post pandemic period. To this aim, the set of variables could be increased by regarding further proximity services and other characteristics of the multimodal network.

References

1. WHO News. https://www.unscn.org/en/news-events/. Accessed 21 Jan 2021
2. Frank, L.D., Andresen, M.A., Schmid, T.L.: Obesity relationships with community design, physical activity, and time spent in cars. Am. J. Prev. Med. **27**(2), 87–96 (2004)
3. ISCA News. https://inactivity-time-bomb.nowwemove.com/. Accessed 10 Jan 2021
4. Ding, D., Kolbe-Alexander, T., Nguyen, B., Katzmarzyk, P.T., Pratt, M., Lawson, K.D.: The economic burden of physical inactivity: a systematic review and critical appraisal. Br. J. Sports Med. **51**(19), 1392–1409 (2017)
5. Donati A., Petracchini F., Gasparini C. Tomassetti L.: Mobilitaria 2019 - Politiche di mobilità e qualità dell'aria nelle 14 città e aree metropolitane 2017–2018
6. Battarra, R., Gargiulo, C., Tremiterra, M.R., Zucaro, F.: Smart mobility in Italian metropolitan cities: a comparative analysis through indicators and actions. Sustain. Urban Areas **41**, 556–567 (2018)
7. Battarra, R., Zucaro, F., Tremiterra, M.R.: Smart mobility: an evaluation method to audit Italian cities. In: 5th IEEE International Conference on Models and Technologies for Intelligent Transportation Systems (MT-ITS), pp. 421–426 (2017)
8. Pinna, F., Masala, F., Garau, C.: Urban policies and mobility trends in Italian smart cities. Sustainability **9**(4), 494 (2017)
9. Gargiulo, C., Zucaro, F., Gaglione, F.: A set of variables for the elderly accessibility in urban areas. TeMA - Journal of Land Use, Mobility and Environment, 53–66 (2018)
10. Carpentieri, G., Guida, C., Masoumi, E.H.: Measuring multimodal accessibility to urban services for elderly. An application at primary health services in the city of Naples. In: Gargiulo, C., Zoppi, C., (eds.) Planning, Nature and Ecosystem Services, pp. 810–825 (2019)
11. Cottrill, C., Gaglione, F., Gargiulo, C., Zucaro, F.: Defining the characteristics of walking paths to promote an active ageing. In: Pedestrians, Urban Spaces and Health: Proceedings of the XXIV International Conference on Living and Walking in Cities, pp. 209–213 (2020)
12. Rossetti, S., Zazzi, M.: In field assessment of existing pedestrian paths: a comprehensive approach towards pedestrian oriented neighbourhoods. In: Pedestrians, Urban Spaces and Health: Proceedings of the XXIV International Conference on Living and Walking in Cities, pp. 88–92 (2020)
13. UN Publications. https://www.un.org.com. Accessed 29 Dec 2020
14. WHO Publications. https://www.who.org.com. Accessed 20 Feb 2021

15. Southworth, M.: Designing the walkable city. J. Urban Plann. Dev. **131**(4), 246–257 (2005)
16. Cervero, R., Kockelman, D.: Travel demand and the 3Ds: density, diversity, and design. Transp. Res. Part D **2**(3), 199–219 (1997)
17. Ewing, R., Cervero, R.: Travel and the built environment: a meta-analysis. J. Am. Plann. Assoc. **76**(3), 265–294 (2010)
18. Garau, C., Annunziata, A., Yamu, C.: A walkability assessment tool coupling multi-criteria analysis and space syntax: the case study of Iglesias, Italy. Eur. Plann. Stud. 1–23 (2020)
19. Motamed, B., Bitaraf, A.: An empirical assessment of the walking environment in a megacity: case study of Valiasr Street, Tehran. Archnet-IJAR: Int. J. Architectural Res. **10**(3), 76–99 (2016)
20. Kim, S.: Assessing mobility in an aging society: environmental factors associated with older people's subjective transportation deficiency in the US. Transp. Res. Part F Traffic Psychol. Behav. **14**(5), 422–429 (2011)
21. Cutts, B.B., et al.: City structure, obesity, and environmental justice: an integrated analysis of physical and social barriers to walkable streets and park access. Soc. Sci. Med. **69**(9), 1314–1322 (2009)
22. Boulange, C., Pettit, C., Giles-Corti, B.: The walkability planning support system: an evidence-based tool to design healthy communities. In: Geertman, S., Allan, A., Pettit, C., Stillwell, J. (eds.) CUPUM 2017. LNGC, pp. 153–165. Springer, Cham (2017). https://doi.org/10.1007/978-3-319-57819-4_9
23. Su, S., Zhou, H., Xu, M., Ru, H., Wang, W., Weng, M.: Auditing street walkability and associated social inequalities for planning implications. J. Transp. Geogr. **74**, 62–76 (2019)
24. Yamu, C., Van Nes, A.: An integrated modeling approach combining multifractal urban planning with a space syntax perspective. Urban Sci. **1**, 37 (2017)
25. Vale, D.S., Saraiva, M., Pereira, M.: Active accessibility: a review of operational measures of walking and cycling accessibility. J. Transp. Land Use **9**, 209–235 (2015)
26. Frank, L.D., Sallis, J.F., Conway, T.L., Chapman, J.E., Saelens, B.E., Bachman, W.: Many pathways from land use to health: associations between neighborhood walkability and active transportation, body mass index, and air quality. J. Am. Plann. Assoc. **72**(1), 75–87 (2006)
27. Frank L.D., et al.: The development of a walkability index: application to the neighborhood quality of life study. Brit. J. Sports Med. **44**(13), 924–933 (2010)
28. Grasser, G., Van Dyck, D., Titze, S., Stronegger, W.: Objectively measured walkability and active transport and weight-related outcomes in adults: a systematic review. Int. J. Public Health **58**, 615–625 (2013)
29. Buck, C., Pohlabeln, H., Huybrechts, I., et al.: Development and application of a moveability index to quantify possibilities for physical activity in the built environment of children. Health Place **17**, 1191–1201 (2011)
30. Buck, C., et al.: Objective measures of the built environment and physical activity in children: from walkability to moveability. J. Urban Health **92**(1), 24–38 (2015)
31. Kim, H.J., Heinrich, K.M.: Built environment factors influencing walking to school behaviors: a comparison between a small and large US city. Front. Public Health **4**, 77 (2016)
32. Frank, L.D., Appleyard, B.S., Ulmer, J.M., Chapmanm, J.E., Fox, E.H.: Comparing walkability methods: creation of street smart walk score and efficacy of a code-based 3D walkability index. J. Transp. Health **21**, 101005 (2021)
33. Kuzmyak, J.R., Baber, C., Savory, D.: Use of walk opportunities index to quantify local accessibility. Transp. Res. Rec. **1977**(1), 145–153 (2006)
34. Peiravian, F., Derrible, S., Ijaz, F.: Development and application of the pedestrian environment index (PEI). J. Transp. Geogr. **39**, 73–84 (2014)
35. Duncan, G.E., et al.: Genetic and environmental influences on residential location in the US. Health Place **18**(3), 515–519 (2012)

36. Witten, K., et al.: Neighborhood built environment and transport and leisure physical activity: Findings using objective exposure and outcome measures in New Zealand. Environ. Health Perspect. **120**, 971–977 (2012)

37. Gargiulo, C., Sforza, A., Sterle, C., Zucaro, F.: An optimization model fitting the neighborhood sustainability assessment tools. Sustainability **10**(10), 3365 (2018)

38. Blečić, I., Congiu, T., Fancello, G., Trunfio, G.A.: Planning and design support tools for walkability: a guide for urban analysts. Sustainability **12**(11), 4405 (2020)

39. Gaglione, F., Gargiulo, C., Zucaro, F. Elders' quality of life. A method to optimize pedestrian accessibility to urban services. TeMA – J. Land Use Mobility Environ. **12**(3), 295–312 (2019)

40. Gaglione, F., Cottrill, C., Gargiulo, C.: Urban services, pedestrian networks and behaviors to measure elderly accessibility. Transp. Res. Part D Transp. Environ. **90**, 102687 (2021)

A Literature Review on Urban Usability and Accessibility to Investigate the Related Criteria for Equality in the City

Francesco Pinna⊙, Chiara Garau$^{(\boxtimes)}$ ⊙, and Alfonso Annunziata⊙

Department of Civil and Environmental Engineering and Architecture, University of Cagliari, 09129 Cagliari, Italy
cgarau@unica.it

Abstract. The environmental issues and, in recent years, the Covid-19 pandemic determined an increasing consensus around the need for urban policies aimed at re-shaping the urban realm. The issue of equality and the related conditions of accessibility and usability emerge as critical requirements in the re-shaping of the urban landscape and mobility. As a consequence, the proposed article discusses a comprehensive literature review on the topics of usability and accessibility and of the complementary notions of disability and exclusion. The objectives of the literature review are to define a taxonomy of the different dimensions of usability and accessibility, to assess the relevance of the different forms of usability and accessibility across disciplinary fields related to urban and transportation studies, to identify the co-relations among specific aspects of urbanity and mobility and conditions of accessibility and usability. The proposed literature review is the preliminary stage of a study aimed at defining a methodological framework for quantitatively describing the urban environment in terms of its accessibility and usability. The proposed defines the theoretical framework of an analysis method for evaluating inequality incorporated into the urban environment and for facilitating smart decisions and holistic design in the context of urban planning.

Keywords: Usability · Accessibility · Urban equality · Vitality · Urbanity · Morphology

1 Introduction

The concept of sustainability emerges as a central aspect of the development and transformation of urban areas. The increasing consensus on the need for a sustainable development of the city, formalized in the intersecting images of the city as smart, resilient,

---

This paper is the result of the joint work of the authors. 'Abstract' 'Methodology' and 'Results' with its subparagraphs were written jointly by all authors. Francesco Pinna wrote the 'Introduction', Chiara Garau wrote 'Discussion and Conclusions' and Alfonso Annunziata the 'Theoretical framework'.

© Springer Nature Switzerland AG 2021
O. Gervasi et al. (Eds.): ICCSA 2021, LNCS 12958, pp. 525–541, 2021.
https://doi.org/10.1007/978-3-030-87016-4_38

anti-fragile, walkable, is reinforced by the recognition of limits of the current organization of urban areas, underlined by the Covid-19 Pandemic and by emerging environmental issues [1–3]. In particular, land-use distribution and configuration of transport
systems and of public open spaces determine patterns of mobility incompatible with
needs of social distancing, local-scale movements and soft mobility engendered by the
Covid-19 pandemic and by environmental issues. Moreover, the notion of sustainability incorporates a social dimension and embodies the ethical implication of equality.
In social terms, a relevant aspect of sustainability is the construction of a public space
conceptualized as a convivial place and as the place of the exposure to difference [4–7].
These dimensions partially overlap and embody two fundamental ethical implications:
on the one hand, the idea of the public space as a place where the encounter of diversity
facilitates recognition and acceptance of difference [6, 8, 9]; on the other hand, the idea
of the public space as an inclusive place, accessible and usable by all people, builds on
the concepts of the just city and of the right to the city [10, 11]. Inclusion and equality
incorporate the components of usability and accessibility. Usability is herein defined
as the potential of public spaces to enable users with different individual abilities to
engage in different activities [12]. Accessibility refers to the distribution of financial,
spatial, cultural, social capital determining opportunities and constraints to access urban
facilities, cultural services, and to engage in sociality [13–16].

The notions of usability and accessibility are thus related to the conditions of disability (different social participation caused by difficulty to develop personal activities) [13]
and exclusion. The proposed article presents a literature review on the topics of usability
and accessibility. The objectives of the literature review include: i) the definition of a
taxonomy of the dimensions of usability and accessibility, based on the different forms
of disability and exclusion; ii) the evaluation of the relevance of specific dimensions of
usability and accessibility across disciplinary fields related to urban and transportation
studies; iii) the determination of co-relations among specific aspects of urbanity and
mobility and the different dimensions of usability/disability and accessibility/exclusion.

The proposed literature review is the preliminary stage of a study aimed at defining
a method for the quantitative analysis of accessibility and usability in the urban environment. The relevance of the proposed study is twofold: the definition of a taxonomy of
co-relations between dimensions of accessibility and usability and aspects of urbanity
and mobility; and the usefulness of analytic methods for supporting smart decisions and
holistic design in the context of urban planning.

The article is structured on five sections: After the introduction, notions of usability
and accessibility are presented. Then, in Sect. 3, the methodology and the case study are
presented. In Sect. 4 the results from the literature review are presented and discussed.
Finally, in the Sect. 5, Discussion and Conclusions summarise the findings of the study
and illustrates hypotheses for the future development of the research.

2   Theoretical Framework

Usability and accessibility are central aspects of the discourse on the re-structuring of
the contemporary city [17, 18]. Moreover, the existing literature reveals the multidimensional character of these concepts, thus underlining the risk of overlooking the compound

effects of different, yet intertwined, components of usability and accessibility. Accessibility is primarily conceptualized within the discourse on mobility; it refers to the extent to which a space can be approached, entered or used, or to the extent to which land use distribution, configuration of the urban layout and transport systems enable individuals to reach different destinations [16, 19, 20]. This conceptualization hence focuses on the spatial dimension of exclusion of specific group of users. Yet, spatial segregation reflects and reproduces patterns of social, cultural, technological marginalization. More precisely, social exclusion, can be defined as a multi-dimensional process, in which various forms of marginalization are combined, including marginalization from decision-making and political processes, employment and material resources, and common cultural processes; these processes, when combined, determine acute forms of exclusion in particular districts [21–23]. Technological exclusion, encompasses the notion of digital divide and refers to the uneven distribution of information and communication technologies in society, resulting in inequalities in terms of political engagement, access to service, knowledge and information [24]. Spatial exclusion, refers to spatial segregation and to inequal distribution of spatial resources, including infrastructures and facilities, limiting engagement in sociality, cultural activities and employment and reproducing combined forms of social marginalization [15]. Consequently, accessibility is herein defined as the extent to which the distribution of spatial, social, cultural and financial capital enables individuals to engage in interpersonal relations, sociality, political, cultural and economic activities. On the other hand, usability is related to the concept of Universal Design and partially replaces accessibility within the discourse on disability: usability, in fact, encompasses an activity component and refers to the extent to which a space, product or service can be meaningfully utilised by users with different individual abilities [12, 25]. Universal Design, furthermore, encompasses a design paradigm focused on the project of spaces inclusive and meaningful for all users. As a consequence, universal design embodies the concept of usable, imageable, and understandable spaces, designed taking into consideration the needs of the greatest number of people [25–27]. In particular, Universal Design prefigures spaces whose material, geometric, perceptual properties are modulated taking into account the different forms of impairment - including physical, emotional, cognitive/developmental, visual, auditory, mental, and situational disability. Moreover, the concept of situational disability, introduces in the design of public space, the notion that all individuals can experience in a particular moment, a condition of temporary or permanent disability. Two considerations emerge: first, the refusal of strategies of spatial distinction that relegate particular categories of users in specific spaces, 'designed for'; Secondly, the need to take into account a comprehensive conceptualization of disability, that encompasses the different dimensions of impairment, and that underlines also the need of users affected by mental health issues - including bipolar disorder, psychosis, schizophrenia, anxiety, attention deficit - by emotional disability - including depression, anxiety or stress - or by the impairment of specific cognitive functions, including autism [28]. The discourse on disability, as well as the discourse on exclusion, thus underlines the ethical dimension of planning and design of the contemporary city. More precisely, the concepts of usability and accessibility involve the ethical notion of equality and its formalization in the claims for the 'right to the city' and for the construction of the just or the good city [7, 11, 29]. The analysis of the impact and centrality of the concepts of usability and accessibility within the existing literature on the planning and design of the urban environment is presented in the following sections.

3 Methodology

This study investigates the existing literature on usability and accessibility to identify components of urban form involved in the reproduction of patterns of exclusion of vulnerable users. The literature review is articulated on six stages: i) retrieving articles related to the complementary concepts of accessibility/ exclusion and disability/usability, via the queries (("urban design" OR" public spac*") AND "disability")); (("universal design" OR "public spac*") AND "disabilit*"))); (("exclusion" OR "access*") AND ("injustic*" OR "inequalit*") AND ("urban" OR "city") AND ("servic*" OR "facilit*"))); the time span considered ranges from 2012 to 2021; ii) refining sets retrieved in stage i via the criteria Categories: (Social Sciences Interdisciplinary OR Architecture OR Geography OR Green Sustainable Science Technology OR Environmental Sciences OR Urban Studies OR Environmental Studies OR Sociology OR Engineering Civil OR Transportation Science Technology OR Regional Urban Planning OR Transportation); iii) definition of criteria for retrieving articles, from set defined in stage ii, related to specific dimensions of usability these criteria, are: "visual", "auditory", "situational", "physical", "mental", "emotional" and "Intellectual" or "Developmental" or "Learning", individuating specific dimensions of disability and, consequently, specific set of needs informing design for usability; iv) definition of criteria for retrieving sub-sets of articles related to different dimension of access and exclusion. These criteria are "cultural" "social" "spatial" and "digital"; v) evaluation of relevance of the concepts identified in stage i, iii and iv, via indicators retrieved from the WoS database and including Number of Items, Total Number of Citations (N_CIT), Number of Citations per item (AV_CIT) and H-index (H); vi) comparative analysis of most relevant articles from sets defined in stage ii aimed at investigating dimensions of usability and accessibility considered, related components of the urban environment, independent variables, forms of inequality considered, related dependent variables and co-relations among independent and dependent variables. The comparative analysis focuses on articles available from open access journals and repositories. Open access Journals, in fact, are considered as an optimal solution for the dissemination of research findings, thus maximizing their impact on the evolution of decision-making processes in the fields of urban and transport planning. The findings from the literature review and from the comparative analysis of the most relevant articles, is discussed in the sub-sequent section.

4 Results

4.1 Universal Design, Usability and Disability

The Web of Science (WoS) database contains 86 items, respondent to the queries (("urban design" OR "public spac*") AND "disability")); (("universal design" OR "public spac*") AND "disabilit*")), and related to the categories pertinent to the disciplines of urban and transport planning. The impact and centrality of the retrieved items is measured via the indicators Total number of citations (N_CIT), Average citations per item (AV_CIT) and H-index (H). Within this collection of articles, 42 items are available on Open Access OA journals or platforms. For these, the Number of total citations is equal to 186, the average number of citations per item to 4.43, determining an H-index of 8. The distribution of citations and publications per year, moreover, reveals an increasing centrality of the topics of usability, disability and universal design. Moreover, with respect to articles available from Open Access repositories, a significant increase in the number of publications is observed in 2018 and in 2020. This collection of articles is then refined utilizing criteria denoting specific forms of impairment (Table 1). Developmental disability emerges as a central topic of articles investigating usability, disability and universal design in the context of urban and transport planning. On the other hand, no direct references to auditory disability are retrieved. The comparative content analysis reveals the centrality of geometric and material conditions as factors influencing the usability of public open spaces: Geometric factors include the presence of obstacles, slope and width of pedestrian surfaces, the ergonomics of urban furniture components, presence and density of formal and informal seats, the continuity of pedestrian surfaces and the degree of separation between pedestrian spaces and vehicular lanes (Table 2) [17, 25, 27, 30, 31].

Table 1. Results of the analysis of the Relevance and impact of the set of articles retrieved from the WoS database and related to the topic of Universal Design, Usability and Disability

Category	N results (NR)	Sum of times cited (N_CIT)	Average citations per item AV_CIT)	H-index (HI)
Total set of pertinent articles	86	565	6.57	13
OA_pertinent articles	42	186	4.43	8
Developmental Disability	24	247	10.29	9
OA_Developmental_Disability	8	80	10	4
Emotional disability	3	45	15	2
OA_Emotional_Disability	1	9	9	1
Mental disability	7	103	14.71	3
OA_Mental_Disability	5	50	10	1
Physical disability	9	38	4.22	5
OA_Physical_Disability	4	23	5.75	3
Visual disability	1	0	0	0
OA_Visual_Disability	1	0	0	0
Auditory disability	0	0	0	0
OA_Auditory_Disability	0	0	0	0

Table 2. Results of the comparative analysis of the articles retrieved from the WoS

Papers	Total citations	Average per Year	Dimension of disability	Determinants
[17]	11	1.83	Functional impairment: Situational/ Physical/Visual disability	Absence of Obstacles (PO); Presence of perceptible Information Devices (PID); Condition of Ped Surface (CPS); Slope (S); Section (W); Doors Opening Functioning (DOF); Pavement Continuity (PEDC); Degree of pedestrian motorized movement separation (PMSEP); Ergonomics of components of Furniture (EFC); Density of Seats (DOS); Negative Impact of vegetation on pavements usability (NIVU)
[18]	10	1.43	Functional/ Situational disability	Implementation of Regulatory Standards on Universal Design (REGS)
[30]	6	1.5	Situational disability	Absence of Obstacles (PO); Presence of perceptible Information Devices (PID); Condition of Ped Surface (CPS); Slope (S); Presence/Size of Platform along Ramps (PLRAMP); Section (W); Doors Opening Functioning (DOF); Negative Impact of vegetation on pavements usability (NIVU); Degree of pedestrian motorized movement separation (PMSEP); Pavement Continuity (PEDC);
[25]	6	1.5	Situational/Visual/ Auditory/Bodily disability	Absence of Obstacles (PO); Presence of perceptible Information Devices (PID); Condition of Ped Surface (CPS); Slope (S); Presence/Size of Platform along Ramps (PLRAMP); Section (W); Doors Opening Functioning (DOF); Negative Impact of vegetation/Furniture on pavements usability (NIVU); Degree of pedestrian motorized movement separation (PMSEP); Pavement Continuity (PEDC); Presence of Supports at transit nodes (SUPNOD); Reflectance Levels (LRV); Absence of Lamps under pedestrians eye level (LSUND); Presence of Understandable information Devices (PUD); Colour Contrast among spatial components (CCOL); Accessible Areas from Transit Node (ACCTN);
[31]	6	0.86	Visual disabilities	Absence of Obstacles (PO); Reverberating Noise (RN); Persistent Noise (PLN); Condition of Ped Surface (CPS); Level of luminous comfort (LUMCOM); Presence of perceptible Information Devices (PID)

(*continued*)

Table 2. (*continued*)

Papers	Total citations	Average per Year	Dimension of disability	Determinants
[26]	4	1.33	Cognitive/ Mental disabilities	Shared Purpose (SPUR); Built-in Boundaries (BIB); Presence of Spatial Interfaces (SPINT)
[27]	3	0.75	Physical disability	Condition of Ped Surface (CPS); Slope (S); Absence of Obstacles (PO); P_Lots for Disabled (PLOTS); Ergonomics of Formal seats (EFC); Density of Seats (DOS); Density of Informal Seats (DOIS); Presence of anti-social Practices (ASOCP)
[33]	2	1	Physical disability	Utilization of IM Strategies [Video (V) or Images (I) or Interactive Games (IG)]

Material conditions refer to the properties of surfaces: slipperiness, stability, regularity and roughness of pavements are widely recognized as basic and central aspects of usable spaces [17, 25, 27, 30, 32]. Moreover, requirements related to the material conditions of surfaces affect the selection and arrangement of other components, including vegetation [17, 30]. The tendency towards the holistic design of public spaces, and the comprehensive consideration of the dimensions of disability, emphasize the relevance of perceptual properties [17, 25]. Within this perspective, the presence of perceptible information and the understandability of information conveyed by tactile, visual and auditive stimuli emerge as conditions for public space usability.

Understandability, in particular, embodies the issue of the disorientation engendered by incomplete, ambiguous information or by the conflict/interference among sensory inputs embodied in the built environment - and intended to assist impaired users - and context sensory stimuli engendered by activities across spaces. More precisely, reflectance levels, position of lights in relation to the line of sight, colour contrast, levels of reverberating noise and of persistent noise are factors that influence the legibility and understandability of spaces [25, 31]. Further aspects concern the governance and normative dimensions: in particular, the need to implement Regulatory Standards on Universal Design, emphasizes the demand for a paradigm shift from visitability/accessibility to usability, thus focusing on the multiplicity of opportunities – or affordances – for emotional, social interactions and activities incorporated into the built environment [18]. Lastly, the design of convivial places, hence of spaces of convivial encounter, highlights three social and configurational factors that affect the probability of shared activities: shared purpose, built-in boundaries, and the presence of spatial interfaces. Shared purpose refers to the promotion of group activities, focused on a common goal, that activate non-competitive interactions among different individuals. Built-in boundaries refer to social roles and rules enabling encounters and concurrently defining the limits in the time, place, and intensity of the interactions. Spatial interfaces refer to semi-public spaces along built edges that enable frequent, informal social contacts while ensuring the freedom to disengage [26].

4.2 Accessibility and Exclusion

The Web of Science database contains 318 items respondent to criteria incorporated into the query ((("exclusion" OR "access*") AND ("injustic*" OR "inequalit*") AND ("urban" OR "city") AND ("servic*" OR "facilit*"))) and related to the categories Urban Studies, Environmental Studies, Sociology, Engineering Civil, Transportation Science Technology, Regional Urban Planning and Transportation. The total number of citations is 3372, the average number of citations per item is equal to 10.6, determining an h-index of 28. The values of the indicators N_CIT, AV_CIT and H-index, and the distribution of the number of publications and of citations per year, reveal the relevance of the topics of accessibility and exclusion, and the increasing impact of pertinent studies (see Table 3).

Table 3. Results of the analysis of the relevance and impact of the set of articles retrieved from the WoS database and related to the topic of Accessibility and exclusion

Category	N results (NR)	Sum of times cited (N_CIT)	Average citations per item (AV_CIT)	H-index (HI)
Access	318	3372	10,6	28
OA_Access	129	916	7,1	15
Cultural exclusion	21	253	12,05	8
OA_Cultural exclusion	8	56	7	5
Digital exclusion	12	185	15,42	5
OA_Digital exclusion	6	74	12,33	4
Social exclusion	149	1879	12,61	21
OA_Social exclusion	62	434	7	11
Spatial exclusion	151	1548	10,25	19
OA_Spatial exclusion	60	383	6,38	10

Furthermore, 129 articles are available from open access repositories. The total number of citations, calculated for this sub-set, is equal to 916, the average number of citation per item to 7.1, and the H-index to 15. The number of publications and of citations per year, reveals the increasing relevance and impact of the topics of accessibility and exclusion.

Table 4. Results of the comparative analysis of the articles retrieved from the WoS database

Paper	Sum of total citations	Average citations per year	Dim. of access	Indicators (Independent variable)	Indicator dependent variable
[35]	47	5.88	Digital	Urban/ Rural Classification (URC); Indicator of Multiple Deprivation (IMD)	Average Download Speed (ADS); Distance to nearest node (DNN)
[36]	36	5.14	Spatial/Social	Educational Level (EDU); Activity Status (JOB); Political Status (CIT); Residential Stability (RES); Build Density (BD); Green/Pedestrian Areas Accessed [Density/Area] Indicator (APGS); Cultural, Leisure, Public Facilities Density Indicator (DPOI); Diversity of LU (DVLU); Density of Transport Nodes (DTRANS); Frequency of Social Disorder (ASOC); F of Signs of Neglect (PDIS); F of Violent Crimes (VCRM); F of Vandalism (VAND)	Consumption of Anti-depressants (CADEP)
[37]	33	5.5	Social/ Spatial	Social and Material Deprivation Ind (SMDI); Population Density (DPOP); Age (AGE); Gender (GND);	Distance to PGS (PPGS); PGS Area (APGS); Distance to PGS U Sport Facilities (PPGSPORT); PGS Dist to Transport Nodes (PGS_TRAN)
[38]	21	2.63	Spatial	Relative Proportion of Abandoned Lands (R-PDL); Env. Deprivation (MEDIX); Social and Material Deprivation Ind (SMDI/ TAIND); Educational Level (EDU); Activity Status (JOB); Ethnical Composition (ETCOMP); Residential Tenure (RES); Car Tenure (CAR)	Standardised Morbidity Ratio (SMR); Standardised Premature Mortality Ratio (SPMR)

(continued)

Table 4. (*continued*)

Paper	Sum of total citations	Average citations per year	Dim. of access	Indicators (Independent variable)	Indicator dependent variable
[39]	19	4.75	Spatial	Miles Traveled Car (VMT); Average Body Mass ind (BMI), F of Violent Crimes (VCRM); Air Quality Ind (AQUAL); Smoking (SBEV); Population Density (DPOP); Age (AGE); Gender (GND); Social and Material Deprivation Ind (SMDI); Ethnical Composition (ETCOMP); County Compact Ind (CCI)	Standardised Premature Mortality Ratio (SPMR)
[22]	15	5	Social/Spatial/Social	SES Ind (SECIN) f [Activity Status [Inverse] Unemployment Rate (UR); Log of median after-tax HH Income (LN_MHI); L income measure (LIM); L income cut-off (LICO)]	Location i access to employment by Transit (ALT); Location i access to employment by Driving (ALD); Access to labour force from employment location (LJ);
[40]	15	3.75	Social/Spatial	Street Tree Density (STRED); Green Areas Accessed Indicator (APGS); PGS Quality (PGSQ)	Social Deprivation (HHD); Ethnical Composition/ Concentration of Minorities (ETCOMP/AS); Ethnical Composition/ Concentration of W Residents (ETCOMP/WH);
[41]	13	4.33	Spatial/Social	Ratio of Res under 14 (AGE_14); ratio of Res Over 65 (AGE_65); Ethnical Composition/ Concentration of Minorities (ETCOMP/AS); Educational Level (EDU); L Income Measure (LIM); Street Density Ind (RDI)	Ecosystem Services Ind (ESERV) f [Air Purification Ind (AIR); Run-off Mitigation Ind (WAT); Urban Temperature Regulation Ind (TEMP)]; UGI Coverage (NDVI)

(*continued*)

Table 4. (*continued*)

Paper	Sum of total citations	Average citations per year	Dim. of access	Indicators (Independent variable)	Indicator dependent variable
[23]	13	2.17	Spatial	Green Areas Accessed [Ratio of PGS over Census Area] Indicator (APGS); Green Areas Available (Ratio of PGS per Resident in district] (AVPGS); Distance to HCF (DISTHCF); Medical Density (D_HCF); Environmental Negative Exposure [Ratio of Buildings in Area Buffer from Infrastructure] Indicator (ENVNEG); Social and Material Deprivation Ind (SMDI);	Neonatal mort Rate (NNMR); Infant Mortality Rate (IMR); R of Neonatal Mortality (RRNN); R of Infant Mortality (RRI)
[42]	12	4	Social/Spatial	Social and Material Deprivation Ind (SMDI);	Distance to PGS (PPGS); Green Areas Accessed Indicator (APGS); Population Density in Service Area (D_POP/GS); PGS Quality (PGSQ); Presence of Prov for Young People (YOUNG)

Within these collections of articles, spatial and social exclusion emerge as central topics. On the other hand, only 6 items focus on digital divide. Yet, the average number of citations per item, equal to 15.42, demonstrates the significant impact of studies on digital exclusion. The comparative analysis focuses on a sub-set of relevant articles selected depending on the pertinence to the discipline of transport and urban planning and on their impact. The first finding concerns the centrality of the access to green public spaces (PGS) and to urban green infrastructure (UGI) as an indicator of spatial and social inequality [36, 37, 40–45]. UGIs are considered, in fact, as a component of the built environment providing significant ecosystem services (see Table 4); Ecosystem services refer to conditions and processes through which natural ecosystems sustain and fulfil human life. [46, 47]. Consequently, equality in terms of access to the cultural, provisioning and regulatory services provided by urban green infrastructure emerges as a central component of the discourse on social and spatial justice in the contemporary city. In particular, a relevant part of the articles investigated (29%) investigates the co-relations between socio-economic status, deprivation, social marginalization and access to UGIs or PGS. Moreover, a clear negative co-relation between social and material deprivation and access to UGIs does not emerge. Nevertheless, a clearer negative co-relation between social and material deprivation and access to ecosystem services provided by UGIs emerges when the quality, level of maintenance and equipment of green spaces are considered [37, 42]. Moreover, the issue of green gentrification identifies the relation between social marginalization and access to Urban green infrastructure and facilities as a process resulting from urban greening agendas and interventions [48, 49]. The WoS database contains 34 items, published in the 2017–2021 time-span, cited 311 times by 229 articles. A further condition of spatial inequality concerns the co-relation between social marginalization, defined in terms of occupational, education status and income, and access to transport systems, which in turn affects individuals' opportunities to access employment, basic services and to engage in sociality and cultural activities. Further aspects of spatial inequalities concern the positive co-relation between deprivation and proximity to brownfields [38] and large road infrastructures [23], the negative co-relation between deprivation and access to healthcare facilities and services, and the negative co-relations between urbanity and premature mortality [39] and digital marginalization, measured by Average Download Speed and Distance to nearest node [35]. Lastly, a relevant consideration concerns the relation between spatial access and exclusion and the cultural, socio-economic and technological dimensions of marginalization: spatial exclusion, defined as a condition of marginality determined by inequality in the distribution of urban facilities and infrastructures, emerges both as result and as a determinant of exclusion from decision-making, cultural activities, employment. Hence, spatial structures reflect and reproduce socio-cultural patterns [15, 50, 51]. A discussion of the findings from the literature review is presented in the following section.

5 Discussion and Conclusions

The findings presented in the previous section led to different for the development of the research on accessibility and usability. In particular, the analysis of the different forms of marginalization, reveals that the inequalities in the distribution of cultural, social and financial capital manifest in specific spatial patterns; these are, hence, both a result and a co-determinant of exclusion and poverty. Within this perspective, the analysis of the configurational properties of the urban environment emerges as a central aspect for the understanding of exclusion [52, 53]. Configuration, in fact, is the aspect of space where the spatial implications of social and cultural patterns can be observed. Configuration refers to the set of topological relations and interdependencies among components comprising a spatial system. Thus, the concept of configuration focuses on the inner formal logic of space: the potential of space to form patterns constitutes, in turn, the means through which social logic and meanings can be expressed [13, 50, 51, 54, 55]. In particular, patterns of segregation, integration and centrality can be described in quantitative, objective terms through the analysis of configurational properties based on space syntax techniques and theories. As a consequence, the marginal consideration of configurational properties as a central aspect of processes of marginalization represents a significant gap in the existing literature [56]. The Web of Science database contains, in fact, only seven articles, published in the 2012–2021 time-span, pertinent to the topics "space syntax" "social exclusion" and "inequality". On the other hand, the analysis of factors of usability focuses on intrinsic material, geometric, and perceptual properties of spaces, and on the structure of decision-making processes, with respect to the mobilization of information related to intrinsic physical qualities of spaces. Hence, the existing literature on usability focuses on the environmental factors that determine opportunities and constraints for individuals' activities. Yet, the emotional and social aspects of individuals' engagement with the public space are only marginally considered. The Web of Science database returns 27 results, related to the disciplines of urban and transport planning and to the 2012–2021 time-span, which refer to the topics of "usability" or "universal design" or "disability" and "social" or "emotional" opportunities. Consequently, the concept of affordance emerges as a central aspect of a comprehensive theoretical framework for the understanding of the relationship between built environment factors and usability.

Affordances, in fact, refer to the functional, social and emotional opportunities and constraints embodied in a setting and resulting from the set of relations – situated in space and time – between environmental factors and individual abilities, needs and interests [57–60]. Furthermore, the concept of usability could be expanded in order to consider both the inner qualities and the extrinsic properties of a space. Extrinsic properties refer to the qualities determined by contextual factors, including land use patterns, configuration of the transport system, and configuration and morphology of the built fabric.

Finally, both dimensions of equality in the urban context, encompassed by accessibility and usability, can be comprehensively analysed through the concept of capability. In Sen's words [61] capability is defined as the ability of an individual to achieve a specific condition or "functioning" considered as meaningful. Capabilities depend both on specific abilities of the person and on opportunities embodied in the spatial and social environment. This opportunity dimension, which is more comprehensively understood through the concept of affordance, thus constitutes a relevant object of studies on equality in the built environment: in this context, equality can be reframed as the potential of the built environment to provide all individual with the opportunities for the achievement and exercise of central capabilities. This study presents three limits: first, the comparison among studies that adopt different conceptualizations of usability and accessibility results in the heterogeneity of perspectives in the analysis of factors related to disability and exclusion; Second, the context-specificity of cultural aspects related to disability and exclusion and the diversity of methodological frameworks can result in the incommensurability of built environmental factors considered as determinants of marginalization. A further limit concerns the scarceness of statistical analyses measuring the co-relation among built-environment factors and patterns of independent activities of impaired individuals. The aspects affect the understanding of the relative importance of intrinsic compositional and of extrinsic configurational-functional qualities of spaces in determining patterns of exclusion of impaired individuals. As a result, the findings from the literature review, are relevant to the definition of a theoretical and methodological framework for describing the urban environment in terms of equality. Yet, the future development of the research should address three issues: first, the investigation of the effects of configurational properties of the urban structure on marginalization of vulnerable individuals; the investigation of the effect of extrinsic qualities of urban spaces on patterns of independent activities of people affected by different forms of disability; and, lastly, the formulation of a method that integrates spatial analysis, space syntax techniques and qualitative assessment for individuating patterns of spatial exclusion, and for evaluating the potential of the urban environment to equally assist all individuals in achieving and exercising their central capabilities.

Acknowledgments. This study was supported by the MIUR through the project "WEAKI TRAN-SIT: WEAK-demand areas Innovative TRANsport Shared services for Italian Towns (Project protocol: 20174ARRHT_004; CUP Code: F74I19001290001), financed with the PRIN 2017 (Research Projects of National Relevance) programme. We authorize the MIUR to reproduce and distribute reprints for Governmental purposes, notwithstanding any copyright notations thereon. Any opinions, findings and conclusions or recommendations expressed in this material are those of the authors, and do not necessarily reflect the views of the MIUR. This study was developed within the Interdepartmental Center of the University of Cagliari "Cagliari Accessibility Lab". This study was also supported by a project founded by the Foundation of Sardinia and Autonomous Region of Sardinia (Fondazione di Sardegna): 'Investigating the relationships between knowledge-building and design and decision-making in spatial planning with geodesign', (Convenzione triennale tra la Fondazione di Sardegna e gli Atenei Sardi Regione Sardegna 2018).

References

1. Garau, C., Annunziata, A.: Supporting children's independent activities in smart and playable public places. Sustainability **12**, 8352 (2020)
2. Low, S., Smart, A.: Thoughts about public space during Covid-19 Pandemic. City Soc (Wash). **32** (2020). https://doi.org/10.1111/ciso.12260
3. Lai, K.Y., Webster, C., Kumari, S., Sarkar, C.: The nature of cities and the covid-19 pandemic. Curr. Opin. Environ. Sustain. **46**, 27–31 (2020). https://doi.org/10.1016/j.cosust.2020.08.008
4. Annunziata, A.: Spazi urbani praticabili. Franco Angeli, Milano (2020)
5. Annunziata, A., Garau, C.: A literature review on walkability and its theoretical framework. emerging perspectives for research developments. In: Gervasi, O., et al. (eds.) ICCSA 2020. LNCS, vol. 12255, pp. 422–437. Springer, Cham (2020). https://doi.org/10.1007/978-3-030-58820-5_32
6. Chan, J.: Urban Ethics in the Anthropocene. The Moral Dimensions of Six Emerging Conditions in Contemporary Urbanism. Palgrave Macmillan, London (2019)
7. Barrett, B.F., Horne, R., Fien, J.: The ethical city: a rationale for an urgent new urban agenda. Sustainability **8**, 1197 (2016)
8. Ignatieff, M.: The Ordinary Virtues. Harvard University Press, Cambridge (2017)
9. Jacobs, J.: The Death and Life of Great American Cities. Vintage Books, New York (2016)
10. Fainstein, S.S.: The just city. Int. J. Urban Sci. **18**, 1–18 (2014). https://doi.org/10.1080/12265934.2013.834643
11. Lefebvre, H.: The Right to the City, Writings on Cities. Trans. Eleonore Kofman and Elizabeth Lebas. Blackwell, Oxford (1996)
12. Pinna, F., Garau, C., Maltinti, F., Coni, M.: Beyond architectural barriers: building a bridge between disability and universal design. In: Gervasi, O., et al. (eds.) ICCSA 2020. LNCS, vol. 12255, pp. 706–721. Springer, Cham (2020). https://doi.org/10.1007/978-3-030-58820-5_51
13. Garau, C., Annunziata, A., Yamu, C.: A walkability assessment tool coupling multi-criteria analysis and space syntax: the case study of Iglesias, Italy. Eur. Plann. Stud. 1–23 (2020). https://doi.org/10.1080/09654313.2020.1761947
14. Sennett, R.: Costruire e abitare. Etica per la città. Milano: Feltrinelli (ed. or, 2018, Building and Dwelling. Ethics for the City. London: Penguin Books) (2018)

15. Secchi, B.: La città dei ricchi e la città dei poveri. Editori Laterza, Bari, Italy (2013)
16. Geurs, K.T., van Wee, B.: Accessibility evaluation of land-use and transport strategies: review and research directions. J. Transp. Geogr. **12**, 127–140 (2004). https://doi.org/10.1016/j.jtr angeo.2003.10.005
17. Meshur, H.F.A,: Evaluation of urban spaces from the perspective of universal design principles: the case of Konya/Turkey. TeMA. **9**, 191-208 (2016). https://doi.org/10.6092/1970-9870/3786
18. Larkin, H., Hitch, D., Watchorn, V., Ang, S.: Working with policy and regulatory factors to implement universal design in the built environment: The Australian experience. Int. J. Environ. Res. Public Health. **12**, 8157–8171 (2015). https://doi.org/10.3390/ijerph120 708157.
19. Canale, A., Campisi, T., Tesoriere, G., Sanfilippo, L., Brignone, A.: The evaluation of home-school itineraries to improve accessibility of a university campus trough sustainable transport modes. In: Gervasi, O., et al. (eds.) ICCSA 2020. LNCS, vol. 12250, pp. 754–769. Springer, Cham (2020). https://doi.org/10.1007/978-3-030-58802-1_54
20. Leonardi, S., Tesoriere, G., Distefano, N., Pulvirenti, G., Canale, A., Campisi, T.: Crossing conditions and kerb delay assessment for better safety and accessibility of road pedestrian crossings at urban intersections. In: La Rosa, D., Privitera, R. (eds.) INPUT 2021. LNCE, vol. 146, pp. 623–632. Springer, Cham (2021). https://doi.org/10.1007/978-3-030-68824-0_66
21. Silver, H.: Social exclusion. In: The Wiley Blackwell Encyclopedia of Urban and Regional Studies, pp. 1–6. American Cancer Society (2019). https://doi.org/10.1002/9781118568446. eurs0486
22. Allen, J., Farber, S.: Sizing up transport poverty: a national scale accounting of low-income households suffering from inaccessibility in Canada, and what to do about it. Transp. Policy **74**, 214–223 (2019). https://doi.org/10.1016/j.tranpol.2018.11.018
23. Padilla, C.M., Kihal-Talantikit, W., Perez, S., Deguen, S.: Use of geographic indicators of healthcare, environment and socioeconomic factors to characterize environmental health disparities. Environ. Health **15**, 79 (2016). https://doi.org/10.1186/s12940-016-0163-7
24. Reddick, C.G., Enriquez, R., Harris, R.J., Sharma, B.: Determinants of broadband access and affordability: an analysis of a community survey on the digital divide. Cities **106**, 102904 (2020). https://doi.org/10.1016/j.cities.2020.102904
25. Borowczyk, J.: Sustainable urban development: spatial analyses as novel tools for planning a universally designed city. Sustainability. **10**, 1407 (2018). https://doi.org/10.3390/su1005 1407.
26. Bredewold, F., Haarsma, A., Tonkens, E., Jager, M.: Convivial encounters: conditions for the urban social inclusion of people with intellectual and psychiatric disabilities. Urban Stud. **57**, 2047–2063 (2019). https://doi.org/10.1177/0042098019869838
27. Bates, C.: Conviviality, disability and design in the city. Sociol. Rev. **66**, 984–999 (2018). https://doi.org/10.1177/0038026118771291
28. Leonardi, M., Bickenbach, J., Ustun, T.B., Kostanjsek, N., Chatterji, S.: The definition of disability: what is in a name? Lancet **368**, 1219–1221 (2006). https://doi.org/10.1016/S0140-6736(06)69498-1
29. Connolly, J.J.T.: From Jacobs to the just city: a foundation for challenging the green planning orthodoxy. Cities **91**, 64–70 (2019). https://doi.org/10.1016/j.cities.2018.05.011
30. Yılmaz, M.: Public Space and Accessibility. ICONARP. **6**, 1–14 (2018). https://doi.org/10. 15320/ICONARP.2018.46
31. Jenkins, G.R., Yuen, H.K., Vogtle, L.K.: Experience of multisensory environments in public space among people with visual impairment. Int. J. Environ. Res. Public Health. **12**, 8644–8657 (2015). https://doi.org/10.3390/ijerph120808644
32. Sungur, A., Czaplinska, P.: Designing Playgrounds for All. Megaron. **13**, (2018)

33. Labbé, D., Mahmood, A., Miller, W.C., Mortenson, W.B.: Examining the impact of knowledge mobilization strategies to inform urban stakeholders on accessibility: a mixed-methods study. Int. J. Environ. Res. Public Health. **17**, 1561 (2020). https://doi.org/10.3390/ijerph17051561

34. Auger, C., et al.: Mobile applications for participation at the shopping mall: content analysis and usability for persons with physical disabilities and communication or cognitive limitations. Int. J. Env. Res. Public Health. **11**, 12777–12794 (2014). https://doi.org/10.3390/ijerph 111212777

35. Riddlesden, D., Singleton, A.D.: Broadband speed equity: a new digital divide? Appl. Geogr. **52**, 25–33 (2014). https://doi.org/10.1016/j.apgeog.2014.04.008

36. Melis, G., Gelormino, E., Marra, G., Ferracin, E., Costa, G.: The effects of the urban built environment on mental health: a cohort study in a large Northern Italian City. Int. J. Env. Res. Public Health **12**, 250 (2015). https://doi.org/10.3390/ijerph121114898

37. Ngom, R., Gosselin, P., Blais, C.: Reduction of disparities in access to green spaces: their geographic insertion and recreational functions matter. Appl. Geogr. **66**, 35–51 (2016). https://doi.org/10.1016/j.apgeog.2015.11.008

38. Bambra, C., et al.: Healthy land? An examination of the area-level association between brownfield land and morbidity and mortality in England. Environ Plan A. **46**, 433–454 (2014). https://doi.org/10.1068/a46105

39. Hamidi, S., Ewing, R., Tatalovich, Z., Grace, J.B., Berrigan, D.: Associations between urban sprawl and life expectancy in the United States. Int. J. Environ. Res. Public Health. **15**, 861 (2018). https://doi.org/10.3390/ijerph15050861

40. Ferguson, M., Roberts, H.E., McEachan, R.R.C., Dallimer, M.: Contrasting distributions of urban green infrastructure across social and ethno-racial groups. Landsc. Urban Plan. **175**, 136–148 (2018). https://doi.org/10.1016/j.landurbplan.2018.03.020

41. Baró, F., Calderón-Argelich, A., Langemeyer, J., Connolly, J.J.T.: Under one canopy? Assessing the distributional environmental justice implications of street tree benefits in Barcelona. Environ. Sci. Policy **102**, 54–64 (2019). https://doi.org/10.1016/j.envsci.2019.08.016

42. Mears, M., Brindley, P., Maheswaran, R., Jorgensen, A.: Understanding the socioeconomic equity of publicly accessible greenspace distribution: the example of Sheffield, UK. Geoforum **103**, 126–137 (2019). https://doi.org/10.1016/j.geoforum.2019.04.016

43. Crouse, D.L., et al.: Urban greenness and mortality in Canada's largest cities: a national cohort study. Lancet Planet. Health **1**, e289–e297 (2017). https://doi.org/10.1016/S2542-519 6(17)30118-3

44. Yao, L., Liu, J., Wang, R., Yin, K., Han, B.: Effective green equivalent—A measure of public green spaces for cities. Ecol. Ind. **47**, 123–127 (2014). https://doi.org/10.1016/j.ecolind.2014.07.009

45. De Sousa Silva, C., Viegas, I., Panagopoulos, T., Bell, S.: Environmental justice in accessibility to green infrastructure in two European cities. Land **7**, 134 (2018). https://doi.org/10.3390/land7040134

46. Garau, C., Annunziata, A.: Smart city governance and children's agency: an assessment of the green infrastructure impact on children's activities in Cagliari (Italy) with the tool "opportunities for children in urban spaces (OCUS)." Sustainability **11**, 4848 (2019)

47. Reid, W.V.: Millennium ecosystem assessment (2005)

48. Anguelovski, I., Connolly, J.J., Garcia-Lamarca, M., Cole, H., Pearsall, H.: New scholarly pathways on green gentrification: what does the urban 'green turn' mean and where is it going? Prog. Hum. Geogr. **43**, 1064–1086 (2018). https://doi.org/10.1177/0309132518803799

49. Talen, E., Menozzi, S., Schaefer, C.: What is a "great neighborhood"? An analysis of APA's top-rated places. J. Am. Plann. Assoc. **81**, 121–141 (2015). https://doi.org/10.1080/01944363.2015.1067573

50. Hillier, B., Hanson, J.: The Social Logic of Space. Cambridge University Press, Cambridge (1984). https://doi.org/10.1017/CBO9780511597237

51. Hillier, B.: Space is the Machine: a Configurational Theory of Architecture. Space Syntax. University College of London, London (2007)
52. Scorza, F., Fortunato, G., Carbone, R., Murgante, B., Pontrandolfi, P.: Increasing Urban walkability through citizens' participation processes. Sustainability **13**, 5835 (2021). https://doi.org/10.3390/su13115835
53. Scorza, F., Fortunato, G.: Cyclable cities: building feasible scenario through urban space-morphology assessment. J. Urban Plann. Dev. **147**(4), 05021039 (2020)
54. Yamu, C., van Nes, A., Garau, C.: Bill Hillier's legacy: space syntax—a synopsis of basic concepts, measures, and empirical application. Sustainability **13**, 1–25 (2021)
55. Garau, C., Annunziata, A., Yamu, C.: The multi-method tool 'PAST' for evaluating cultural routes in historical cities: evidence from Cagliari, Italy. Sustainability. **12**, (2020). https://doi.org/10.3390/su12145513
56. Hidayati, I., Yamu, C., Tan, W.: The emergence of mobility inequality in greater Jakarta, Indonesia: a socio-spatial analysis of path dependencies in transport-land use policies. Sustainability **11**, 5115 (2019)
57. Kyttä, M., Oliver, M., Ikeda, E., Ahmadi, E., Omiya, I., Laatikainen, T.: Children as urbanites: mapping the affordances and behavior settings of urban environments for Finnish and Japanese children. Children's Geographies. **16**, 319–332 (2018). https://doi.org/10.1080/14733285.2018.1453923
58. Heft, H.: Affordances and the perception of landscape. Innov. Approaches Res. Landscape Health Open Space People Space **2**, 9–32 (2010)
59. Chemero, A.: An outline of a theory of affordances. Ecol. Psychol. **15**, 181–195 (2003). https://doi.org/10.1207/S15326969ECO1502_5
60. Heft, H.: Affordances of children's environments: A functional approach to environmental description. Children's Environments Quarterly, 29–37 (1988)
61. Sen, A.: Capability and well-being. In: The Quality of Life, pp. 30–54. Oxford University Press, New York (1993)

A Conceptual Framework for Risk Assessment in Road Safety of Vulnerable Users

Mauro D'Apuzzo[1] , Daniela Santilli[1](✉), Azzurra Evangelisti[1] ,
and Vittorio Nicolosi[2]

[1] Department of Civil and Mechanical Engineering DICEM,
University of Cassino and Southern Lazio, Cassino, Italy
{dapuzzo,daniela.santilli}@unicas.it

[2] Department of Enterprise Engineering "Mario Lucertini", University of Rome "Tor Vergata",
Rome, Italy
nicolosi@uniroma2.it

Abstract. The risk-based engineering analyzes, created mainly to activate forecasting and prevention measures in response to the damage generated by natural disasters, have been extended to many other sectors. One of these is that relating to road safety. Over the last few decades, the European Union has pushed towards a noticeable improvement in road safety (EU roads are the safest in the world), but there are still too many deaths and injuries. It must be said that all the procedures and measures implemented so far in the road sector are aimed at reducing the hazard of the motorized component. In fact, the advent of ITS onboard devices has enormously improved the safety of drivers and passengers, but almost nothing has been done to protect vulnerable users. Although car manufacturers are recently pay more attention to this latter issue, road safety engineers can play a critical role in identifying and evaluating the various accident scenarios and then selecting optimal countermeasures. In this paper, following a review of risk based methodologies, an original risk-based methodological approach is proposed for pedestrian. The ultimate goal is to bring, as requested by the European Community, a drastic reduction in the number and consequences of accidents involving vulnerable users.

Keywords: Vulnerable user · Road safety · Hazard · Vulnerability

1 Risk Definition

Due to climate change and global warming, natural disasters involving transport infrastructures is recently increasing. These are significant damage to both the natural and built environment with deaths and injuries, and long-term damage to communities as well as to the social aspects linked to the reconstruction and restoration of the functionality of structures and infrastructures. This requires long recovery times to return to "pre-disaster" conditions, therefore countries are moving towards a risk reduction policy with the aim of predicting the effects, on the most relevant territorial assets, to

© Springer Nature Switzerland AG 2021
O. Gervasi et al. (Eds.): ICCSA 2021, LNCS 12958, pp. 542–556, 2021.
https://doi.org/10.1007/978-3-030-87016-4_39

minimize their impact. This allows stakeholders (planners, public administrators, service managers, emergency departments, private investors, insurance companies, etc.) to take mitigation actions [1, 2].

However, it is necessary to clarify because in common language the terms "hazard" and "risk" are used as synonyms, even if from a technical point of view they express different concepts. In fact, according to the legislation [3], the hazard is the potential of a specific entity (machine, equipment, plant, substance, process, system, etc.) to cause damage. The hazard can, therefore, be defined as a "source of potential damage".

While, the risk depends on the interaction between the source of danger and the person. Unlike the hazard that is characterized by its physical objectivity, the risk is linked to the hypothesis that a future event could cause damage.

The first risk assessment strategies were developed in the 1970s, when the international community began to emphasize the need to plan and prevent natural phenomena that were becoming an obstacle to settlement development. Therefore, the effects of natural disasters began to be considered in humanitarian and social terms as well as economic and developmental ones, especially for those countries where urbanization involves areas subject to natural events (earthquakes, floods, tsunamis, fires, etc.). After years of research on the main natural hazards (phenomena) of meteorological, geological and geophysical origin in 1979, the conference of the United Nations Disaster Relief Office [4] defined risk as the predicted number of lives lost, injured, property damage and business disruption due to a particular natural phenomenon. Therefore, risk was defined as the product of a specific risk (i.e. the degree of expected loss due to a natural phenomenon, a function of both danger and vulnerability) and elements at risk.

$$Risk = Hazard \cdot Consequences \tag{1}$$

The UNDRO Committee also highlighted that in order to assess the potential loss due to a given natural hazard, the following must be taken into consideration:

- The randomness of natural hazards at a given site;
- The role of existing structures which have their intrinsic vulnerability;
- The importance of the elements (population, housing, economic activities, etc.) possibly affected, called "elements at risk";
- The definition of the expected risk over a period of time.

So to emphasize both the concept of chance or possibility (for example, the risk of an accident) of potential losses, for a given cause, place and period, the risk can simply be expressed as the product of three integral components, namely danger, vulnerability (of buildings, infrastructures and population) and exposure of these resources present in the study area. It is a probabilistic estimate that can be evaluated as:

$$R_0 = H \cdot V \cdot E \tag{2}$$

where is it:

R_0 is the risk referred to the assets displayed in the area of interest, expressed as far as possible in terms of probability or frequency of occurrence of predefined consequences;

H expresses the danger of the area of interest (as it increases, the risk increases); "A potentially damaging physical event, phenomenon and/or human activity, which may cause loss of life or injury, property damage, social and economic disruption or environmental degradation. Hazards can be single, sequential or combined in their origin and effects" [5];

E expresses the exposure in the area of interest (as it increases, the risk increases); is the measure of possible future losses that may arise from an activity or event or as reported by Kolluru et al. [6] exposure is the process by which an organism comes into contact with a hazard;

V expresses the vulnerability of the goods exposed (as it increases, the risk increases); "The characteristics of a person or a group in terms of their capacity to anticipate, cope with, resist and recover from the impact of a natural or man-made disaster - noting that vulnerability is made up of many political-institutional, economic and socio-cultural factors" [7, 8].

This expression of risk is very broad both because it can refer to any type of hazard and because for a certain type of hazard there is no single risk assessment.

It can be generalized by considering x the effects of natural phenomena on the site, whose distribution is the function $\phi(x)$ which represents the probability of exceeding each value of x within the reference period. It is therefore possible to define the functions $F(x) = 1 - \phi(x)$ or $p(x) = dF/dx$ which respectively represent the probability that x is not exceeded or the probability density function. Since vulnerability represents the expected damage on an entity (structure or population) induced by a phenomenon of a given magnitude, it can be written as $\alpha = \alpha(x)$. To evaluate the probability of failure (df) associated with the risk probability x between x and $x + dx$ can be written as (Fig. 1a):

$$df = p_H F_s dx \tag{3}$$

Where

$p_H(x)$ the probability density function;
F_S the probability of exceeding.

Similarly, from Fig. 1b, the probability of failure (*df*) associated with the probability of the strength x ranging between x and $x + dx$ is:

$$df = p_s \phi_H dx \tag{4}$$

Where

p_S density function of distribution of the mechanical properties of the structure;
ϕ_H the probability of exceedance.

The elementary specific risk associated with the probability of the entity of the event between x and $x + ds$ is:

$$\frac{dr}{(er)} = \alpha(x) F_s p_H dx = \alpha(x) \Phi_H p_s dx \tag{5}$$

where (er) are the elements at risk (all the other parameters are described previously).

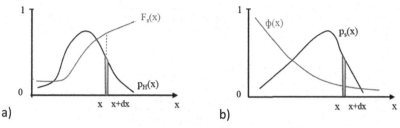

Fig. 1. Functional forms of the hazard and structural strength probabilities: a) probability densi-ty function pH (x) and probability of non-exceedance a level of structural strength FS(x) for a given value of the magnitude x; b) probability of exceedance ϕH(x) and probability density function of a structural strength ps(x) for a given value of the magnitude x (modified after [4]).

Following the UNDRO Conference, from 1 January 1990, the International Framework of Action for the International Decade for Natural Disaster Reduction (IDNDR) initiated the Yokohama strategy with the aim of reducing loss of life, damage to property, the social and economic hardships caused by "natural disasters", especially in developing countries. This strategy identified gaps related to governance, risk identification, assessment, monitoring and early warning, knowledge management and education, reduction of underlying risk factors, preparation for effective response and recovery. Starting from these shortcomings, the Hyogo action was then launched (2005–2015) aimed at making countries aware of their primary role in the prevention and reduction of the risk of disasters. This has pushed them towards international cooperation policies and the development of regional strategies with the creation of global and regional platforms for disasters. While in the past the protection of social and economic development from external shocks was considered, now the goal is growth and development planning to manage risks holistically; which means the establishment of multidisciplinary approaches to promote sustainable economic and social growth, protect environmental health conditions and strengthen resilience (i.e. take proactive behaviours, ready to survive disasters and maintain economic competitiveness) and stability. This gave rise to the Sendai Framework 2015–2030 plan [9] which is aimed at strengthening risk governance by developing risk prevention, mitigation and management activities, in order to reduce the risk of catastrophes and loss of life, human resources, livelihoods and health, and the economic, physical, social, cultural and environmental assets of people, businesses, communities and countries.

1.1 Risk Analysis

Therefore, starting from a mainly geotechnical risk definition, risk assessment processes (or risk analysis) are being tested in various sectors.

The risk assessment consists of a set of activities that make it possible to identify and quantify the risk, to then put in place the appropriate prevention and protection measures, to activate all those activities measures of a technical, organizational and procedural nature that make up the so-called process of "risk treatment" and more generally "risk management" (Fig. 2).

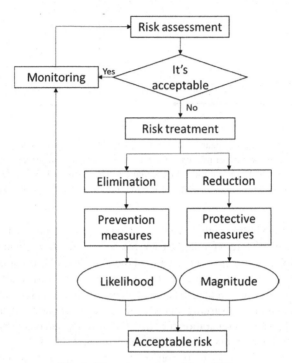

Fig. 2. Flow chart adapted from [10].

In general, the process starts with the identification of risk factors and then estimates the identified risks. To do this, probabilistic approaches can be used that evaluate both the probability of occurrence (Pr) and the magnitude of the damage (M).

These approaches can be grouped into two macro-categories:

– quantitative or semi-quantitative approach;
– qualitative approach.

The first is based on the use of mathematical models, which use inferential statistical methods; it is used in specific contexts, where the analysis of safety standards must be very precise and accurate. Quantitative analyzes provide a more objective understanding, however, their effectiveness is fundamentally based on the quality of the information available, that is the number and accuracy of the data, which represent various possible situations.

Whenever possible, a quantitative approach should be preferred to be more objective and examine the system in more detail, but supplementation with qualitative analysis should be considered. An appropriate combination to sum the advantage of both approaches becomes crucial when not all factors can be parameterized.

While the qualitative approach is also called "subjective" as it is based on the "expert judgment" of the risk analyst, whose level of competence and the quality of the data acquired in the preliminary phase must be reliable. Qualitative methods offer analysis without detailed information, are performed with intuitive and subjective processes and can lead to different results/conclusions depending on who uses them. Although suspected of leading to subjective conclusions, they offer the possibility of considering factors that are difficult to quantify, such as those related to human behavior, and sometimes lead to an adequate risk assessment. There are several theories that allow you to transform qualitative into quantitative assessment (e.g., probability of imprecise interval, possibility and theories of evidence), an overview is provided by Tesfamariam and Goda [11].

In qualitative estimation, the definition of scales is used, in which both the probability and magnitude of graduation are explicitly defined (table 1).

Table 1. Qualitative estimation scale relationship between probability and damage.

Likelihood	Magnitude
Very low	Negligible
Medium low	Moderate
Medium high	Remarkable
High	Huge

Based on this estimate, the analyst identifies three classes of risk: HIGH RISK, MEDIUM RISK, LOW RISK which determine different levels and priorities of intervention (Table 2).

Table 2. Levels and priorities of intervention definitions.

Likelihood	Magnitude	Risk	Intervention
High	Huge	High	The measures are urgent. The intervention plan goes beyond cost/benefit assessments
High	Remarkable		
Medium high	Huge		
High	Moderate	Medium	Plan and apply prevention and protection measures; these must be checked to assess the effectiveness of the risk reduction process
High	Negligible		
Medium high	Remarkable		
Medium high	Moderate		
Medium high	Negligible		
Medium low	Huge		

(*continued*)

Table 2. (*continued*)

Likelihood	Magnitude	Risk	Intervention
Medium low	Remarkable		
Medium low	Moderate		
Very low	Huge		
Very low	Remarkable		
Medium low	Negligible	Low	No interventions are necessary but it is necessary to continue to monitor by evaluating possible future improvements
Very low	Moderate		
Very low	Negligible		

Once the probability and magnitude have been estimated, graphical representations have used that highlight the assessment carried out for each risk. Among the most used is the "risk matrix" which is obtained by plotting in a Cartesian graph, the probability scale in the ordinate and the magnitude scale in the abscissa (Fig. 3).

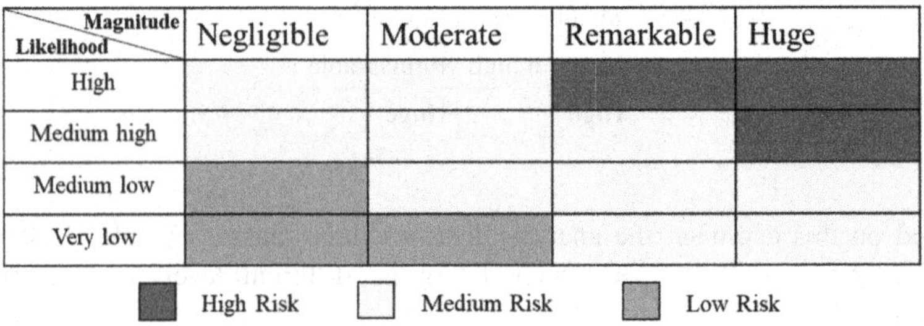

Magnitude / Likelihood	Negligible	Moderate	Remarkable	Huge
High				
Medium high				
Medium low				
Very low				

High Risk   Medium Risk   Low Risk

Fig. 3. Risk matrix (Color figure online)

The next step is the "risk weighting" phase which serves to determine whether the risk is acceptable and to what extent. That is, it is necessary to establish for each risk its limit of acceptability, beyond which it must be reduced with prevention and protection measures. The acceptability of the risk depends on several factors, including the phenomenon (whether or not controllable), the type and nature of the consequences, the short and long-term effects, the benefits obtained, the preparedness for natural hazards and the influence of individual and total risk. The definition of acceptability limits depends on legal constraints, rather than on technical standards or improvement practices. Therefore it is required that, in order to satisfy the safety conditions, the measured risk is to a lesser extent equal to the acceptable one. Therefore, once the pre-mitigation risk R0 has been assessed, a benefit-cost analysis must be carried out to assess the suitability of the mitigation. In general terms, it can include risk reduction (active mitigation), vulnerability reduction (passive mitigation) or both options (active and passive mitigation).

Regardless of the type, assuming a mitigation cost equal to U_d, the residual risk R'_d can be calculated:

$$R'_d = H' \cdot V' \cdot E' + U_d \tag{6}$$

Where:

H', V' and E' represent the new terms of Hazard, Vulnerability and Exposure respectively after mitigation.

Starting from the same risk level R0, there are two different scenarios:

- R'd < R0 there is a convenient situation that justifies the adoption of countermeasures;
- R'd > R0 a situation of non-economic convenience emerges. While effective countermeasures reduce hazard or vulnerability, their cost has resulted in a residual risk greater than pre-mitigation.

At the end of this phase, a risk map is obtained which highlights the unacceptable risks that must be reduced by adopting measures that will be programmed and planned with a prioritization process. The general criterion is based on the entity of the risk, i.e. the higher the estimated risk level, the higher the priority of intervention.

So the priority is divided into three categories:

- High Priority: urgent interventions to be implemented in the short term, for unacceptable risk situations according to previous regulations.
- Medium Priority: interventions to be implemented in the medium term, for risk situations to be reduced to acceptable values within the terms set by the regulations.
- Low Priority: interventions to be implemented in the long term for situations of acceptable risk, but aimed at the continuous improvement of safety (further reduction of the risk).

The last phase of risk management is the monitoring or the periodic process of control and measurement of the risk parameters, review and weighting of new and/or modified risks following the changes made to the environments.

2 Road Safety Risk

The risk arising from the evaluation of the protection and prevention measures to be adopted in the event of natural disasters can actually be applied in various fields. Precisely from the understanding and application of risk estimation techniques it is possible to evaluate road safety[12]. The main task in the road safety audit is to identify the elements of danger that could cause death or injury. So usually when we talk about road risk we implicitly refer to accidents (the severity and frequency of which must be defined) [13, 14].

These, in fact, represent a problem of absolute priority for public health since in addition to the loss of human life they generate enormous social and human costs, to which are added high economic costs, which make the issue of road safety a topic of enormous importance for the prevention departments and health systems of all countries.

There is talk of a social scourge that causes almost 10 deaths and about 700 people with injuries every day.

The causes can be attributed to numerous risk factors:

- related to the person or health conditions, age, the intake of compromising drugs, attention, balance and reflexes;
- lifestyles that involve the consumption of alcohol and psycho-altering substances, and incorrect driving behavior (use of cell phones, inattention, excessive speed, failure to use protection systems);
- safety of roads and vehicles;
- social: the poor socio-economic conditions have less access to training and information resources on prevention measures and more generally to the acquisition of a culture of safety on the roads.

To obtain a good reduction in the number and severity of road accidents, a program of prevention interventions is required that considers the multiple factors that underlie a certain type of accident and that simultaneously weigh on the risk.

Globally, the World Health Organization (WHO) through the World report on road traffic injury prevention [15] encourages countries to plan a multi-sector strategy for road safety, which takes into consideration the needs of each one by implementing specific intervention projects.

In Europe, therefore, the European Commission has promoted a road safety program which identifies some areas of intervention such as: encouraging road users to behave more responsibly, making vehicles safer thanks to technological innovations, improving road infrastructures through information and communication technologies, collect and analyze data relating to physical injuries due to road accidents.

In Italy, according to Istat estimates, since 2007 [16] there has been an average reduction in accidents with injured people of about 3% every year. This reduction is explained by the fact that users have begun to use alternative means of transport to private vehicles.

It has been understood that, in order to reduce the risk of an accident and know the result that can be obtained in terms of safety, it is necessary to go beyond simple compliance with the Highway Code or awareness of potential damage. It is essential to focus on techniques and tools for forecasting events on the road. Therefore, by systematically analyzing the information of "near miss" accident situations, it is possible to implement the related corrective actions.

Some researchers who have dealt with the evaluation of road safety [17, 18] have defined the risk as:

$$Risk = Exposure \cdot Hazard \cdot Vulnerability \qquad (7)$$

where:
Exposure: quantifies the exposure of road users to potential road hazards;
Hazard: quantifies the possibility that a vehicle or user is involved in a collision;
Vulnerability: quantifies the severity level resulting from potential collisions.

It can therefore be observed that, with respect to the risk defined previously for natural phenomena, there is an inversion of the terms, but the assessment procedure remains the same.

Basing on this approach a conceptual framework has been proposed to evaluate the road safety risk for vulnerable user, namely pedestrian. The risk thus defined is therefore a function of multiple variables whose correlations are outlined in the following flow chart (Fig. 4).

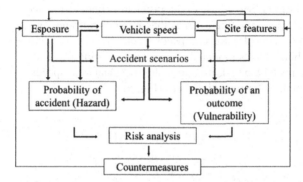

Fig. 4. Summary scheme of the procedure.

Therefore, once the global risk has been quantified, it is possible to arrange interventions that will improve exposure, vehicle speed and site conditions.

In order to being assessing the risk of having an accident in the study area, it is necessary to know the history of accidents and their characteristics, in order to bring them back to a typical scenario.

Once the accident scene has been identified, the three key parameters of the risk begin to be assessed.

2.1 Exposure

To identify the factors that best predict where and when accidents are likely to occur, exposure needs to be assessed. This is understood as the assessment of potential arrests under sudden conditions. When it comes to exposure, both vehicular and pedestrian flows are involved. The first requires knowledge of the traffic in transit on the section of the road network to be analyzed; this can be obtained from survey-based models or from simplified or forecast models. While for the estimation of cycle-pedestrian flows, there are no consolidated models, therefore direct (based on socio-economic and demographic variables) or forecast models (configurational or four-stage, similar to vehicular ones) are used.

Vehicular Flows Exposure
One of the factors that influence the exposure linked to vehicular flows is the speed held by the vehicles, which in turn is a function of both the characteristics of the site and the flows themselves. Many studies link road safety to speed, but the relationships between

risk (intended for example as the number of deaths on the road per distance travelled) and speed are almost absent.

The underlying problem is the lack of data collected or their poor quality, i.e. in the databases or in the reports of the law enforcement agencies there is an underestimation of the reports of accidents according to the severity, the number of victims, the number of vehicles involved, location, etc. This indicates that the relationship between speed and risk of collision is based on the number of collisions observed with serious injuries and in strategic locations, but little or nothing is known about accidents with minor injuries or localized in little-known areas, so the problem is underestimated. To overcome the problem of localization relating to areas that are neither urban nor rural, an alternative method could be to consider the real speeds recorded on a road section by extrapolating them from the black boxes mounted on cars (the Floating Car Data, FCD) [19]. Once these data have been obtained, it is possible to evaluate the speeds also in areas other than urban or rural, or for transition areas (Fig. 5).

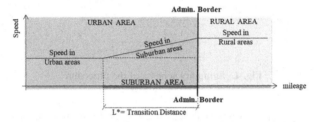

Fig. 5. The transition length concept.

This area represents the space of passage between a rural to an urban area in which, however, the user is still unable to realize the passage and therefore may not adopt a suitable speed. Formally, the transition between the rural and the urban environment is highlighted by warning signs that are displayed at the entrance to urban areas. Often these signs are associated with specific urban speed limits. However, it must be recognized that "official" administrative boundaries do not always express the real boundary between the urban environment and the surrounding areas.

Therefore it is possible to apply a generalized predictive model that starts from the re-calibration and readjustment of the literature models.

Pedestrian Flows

The estimation of the exposure of pedestrian flows can be approached starting from the use of configurational methodological tools [20] which will then be enriched with "demand-driven" models (four-stage) which will also allow obtaining estimates of the cycle flow. The configurational analysis considers only the connectivity of the network, so the more this is connected, the greater the connectivity of the sections. This exemplified approach has been enriched by integrating the analysis with behavioural models deriving from the transport analysis. The results of the hybrid approach obtained can then be correlated to the pedestrians observed on the network in order to understand the goodness of the estimate.

In order to improve the estimation of pedestrian flows and to evaluate cycling flows, the hybrid configurational model can be enriched using the four-stage model (similar to vehicular) starting from literature models. This allows to obtain an estimate of the flows and distribute them on the network so as to be able to understand where it is necessary to intervene to redevelop the area.

Hazard

Whenever the user enters a road, he is exposed to accept the danger and therefore the risk of being injured. In order to evaluate the hazard it is necessary to understand if the user correctly perceives the environment crossed, this requires an analysis of the site.

So first of all, it must be understood in what administrative environment you are, then let's talk about urban or rural context. The urban area is that set of buildings, delimited along the access roads by the appropriate start and end signs [21]. In which the set of buildings includes a continuous grouping, albeit interspersed with streets, squares, gardens or the like, consisting of no less than twenty-five buildings and areas of public use with vehicular or pedestrian accesses on the street. Anything that does not fit this definition is rural. It should be emphasized that the boundaries between the two areas are never clearly defined; however, formally, in most Western countries, urban limits or "administrative boundaries" are identified with vertical entry warning signs usually associated with speed limits.

Depending on the context, there is a greater chance of coming into conflict with other users, therefore it is necessary to take into account the presence of local attractions, such as schools, hospitals, shopping centers or any other activity that may generate greater crowding.

In addition to other users, further sources of danger are linked to the presence of obstacles on the route which are often not correctly displayed due to poor visibility conditions. Visibility is defined as the minimum stopping distance, this depends on many factors such as speed, the conditions of the road surface (the type of road surface, maintenance status, etc.), the condition and pressure of the tires, the characteristics and condition of the vehicle's braking system, the weather conditions as well as the geometric characteristics of the site (considering the road as the sum of straights and curves, number of lanes, longitudinal and transverse slope, etc.).

Vulnerability

To assess the risk, vulnerability remains to be defined. This is the probability, conditioned by the type of accident, that a vulnerable user suffers damage (injured or dead) or that the driver suffers damage (uninjured, injured or deceased).

In addition to a security point of view, vulnerability is seen as a problem of reduced accessibility that occurs for various reasons. In general, accessibility is understood as "ease of access", or the opportunity provided by the transport system for users to carry out an activity [22]. Improving accessibility means increasing the number of routes or the quantity of services considering low costs.

Estimating vulnerability means studying all those events, of a more or less sudden and/or unpredictable nature, which cause circulation problems. These events depend on adverse weather conditions, rather than physical breakdowns or road accidents, or planned road works, etc. Depending on the event and the category, there is a variation in terms of frequency, predictability, geographical extension, etc. To achieve a reduction in vulnerability it is necessary to limit the risks involved in various incidents; this implies the need to identify a spectrum of accidents, collect data on the probabilities and consequences of these, having done this it will be possible to establish experiments to identify acceptability values, as well as investigate and evaluate the effects of possible mitigation measures and strategies for improvement.

Numerous relationships are reported in the literature that considers the links between stress characteristics, kinematic or mechanical magnitudes of the impact of the occupants, but there are still few of them regarding vulnerable users. The basic problem is that the existing ones are based on simulations with corpses or with limited data-sets in terms of location, severity and number of accidents, necessary for the calibration and validation of the models.

Hence the need to create a virtual laboratory that through multibody numerical simulations, as the position (front, side), age, weight and height of the pedestrian, vehicle fronts and travel speed vary, allows obtaining objective kinematic parameters (acceleration, speed, etc.) or mechanical (moments, shear, normal stresses, etc.) with which to enrich the vulnerability functions.

Studies on head injuries are being launched at a preliminary phase, since it is the part of the body that has a high probability of death, using the scale based on damage, disability and social cost, in which the long-term consequences are assessed and the influence that injuries have on the patient's quality of life.

The most used criterion is the Head Injury Criterion (HIC) [2, 23] which is estimated with an iterative process. Then to identify the level of damage, the HIC was correlated with the Abbreviated Injury Scale (AIS) [25–27] which assigns a score from 0 to 6 and using logistic functions from the literature, the probability of fatality was obtained.

In collisions between vehicle and pedestrian, there is different kinematics according to the impact speed, the pedestrian position, the different height and length of the bumper and the bonnet inclination angles; this means that the pedestrian impacts the various regions of the human body (e.g. head and thorax) in a different way also based on his build. From the simulations, it is observed that among pedestrians the age group most likely to die from a blow to the head are adults, while young people and children are more likely to be injured.

3 Conclusions

Despite the large number of deaths and injuries due to road accidents, there is still no clear regulation according to which the safety assessment for vulnerable users is reported. The goal of this study is to identify a procedure for estimating the main risk factors starting from microscopic analyzes. The results of these analyzes can then be integrated at a macroscopic level to define and predict safety performance as well as predict the probability of collision.

Starting from the traffic and cycling-pedestrian data, from the accident data and from the speed estimates, it is possible to identify blackspots i.e. those points or section of the road network that present anomalous concentrations of accidents. Once the risk of each road section has been identified, it is necessary, before implementing the proposed interventions, to evaluate the benefits that these would bring and the respective costs. Until now, road safety analysts have relied on personal experience in order to make reliable forecasts, thus working subjectively; to avoid this, analysis methodologies have been developed that take into account the correlations between "cause" (man - road - environment) and "effect" (occurrence of the accident). These methodologies, typical of the engineering field, try to identify links of an empirical nature between the occurrence of the generic accident and the multiplicity of factors that make up the road environment, to the point of proposing mathematical models for forecasting purposes. In the Italian context, such models do not yet exist, so it is intended to apply macroscopic models calibrated in the international scientific literature (cf. Highway Safety Manual recently released in United States [28]) to transpose them to Italian context and calibrate corresponding Safety Performance Functions (SPFs). These latter mathematical tools, based on statistical analysis, evaluate the impact in terms of the number of accidents, as a function of the characteristics of the site and of the exposure. SPFs, refer to basic conditions but can be applied to different study conditions with the use of accident modification factors (Crash Modification Factor - CMF) that take into account specific local site-conditions.

Once the procedure will be developed and applied, it will be possible to evaluate, depending on the characteristics of the site and the type of risks present in the area, the countermeasures to be adopted to increase safety.

References

1. D'Apuzzo, M., Evangelisti, A., Santilli, D., Rasulo, A., Zullo, M., Nicolosi, V.: Strategies for the assessment of risk induced by seismic liquefaction on road networks. In: Beer, M., Zio, E. (eds.) Proceedings of the 29th European Safety and Reliability Conference, pp. 3277–3285 (2019). https://doi.org/10.3850/978-981-11-2724-3. 0592-cd. Copyright © 2019 European Safety and Reliability Association. Published by Research Publishing, Singapore. ISBN: 978-981-11-2724-3
2. D'Apuzzo, M., et al.: Simplified approach for liquefaction risk assessment of transportation systems: preliminary outcomes. In: Gervasi, O., et al. (eds.) ICCSA 2020. LNCS, vol. 12255, pp. 130–145. Springer, Cham (2020). https://doi.org/10.1007/978-3-030-58820-5_10
3. UNI11230. Gestione del rischio: Vocabolario (2007)
4. UNDRO, O. o.-o. Natural disasters and vulnerability analysis. Report of expert group meeting (1979)
5. UN/ISDR. Glossary. Basic Terms of Disaster Risk Reduction (2004). http://www.unisdr.org/ unisdr/eng/library/lib-terminology-eng%20home.htm<viewed2004>
6. Kolluru, R., Bartell, S.: Risk Assessment and Management Handbook. McGraw-Hill, New York (1996)
7. IFRC. Vulnerability and Capacity Assessment. An International Federation Guide, Geneva (1999). http://www.proventionconsortium.org/files/vca.pdf
8. Wolfensohn, J., Cherpitel, D.: Why we need to do what we are doing, Washington DC (2002). http://www.proventionconsortium.org/articles/whyweneed.htm
9. UN General Assembly. The Sendai Framework for Disaster Risk Reduction 2015–2030 (2015). www.unisdr.org/we/inform/publications/43291
10. D.Lgs n°81. modulo B8 (2008)

11. Tesfamariam, S., Goda, K.: Seismic risk analysis and management of civil infrastructure systems: an overview. In: Tesfamariam, S., Goda, K. (eds.) Handbook of Seismic Risk Analysis and Management of Civil Infrastructure Systems, pp. 141–174. Woodhead Publishing Limited (2013)

12. Bonera, M., Maternini, G.: Methodology for the application of predictive method for road safety analysis in urban areas: the case study of Brescia. Paper presented at the Transportation Research Procedia, vol. 45, pp. 659–667 (2020)

13. Porcu, F., Olivo, A., Maternini, G., Barabino, B.: Evaluating bus accident risks in public transport. Transp. Res. Procedia **45**, 443–450 (2020)

14. Porcu, F., Olivo, A., Maternini, G., Coni, M., Bonera, M., Barabino, B.: Assessing the risk of bus crashes in transit systems. Eur. Transp. **81**, 4 (2021)

15. Peden, M., Scurfield, R.: World report on road traffic injury prevention. World Health Organization, Geneva (2004)

16. ISTAT. Dati ISTAT (2018). http://dati.istat.it

17. Hadden, W.: Advances in the epidemiology of injuries as a basis for public policy. Public Health Rep. **95**(5), 411–421 (1980)

18. Koornstra, M.J.: The evolution of road safety and mobility. IATSS Res. **16**(2), 129–148 (1992)

19. D'Apuzzo, M., et al.: Towards the development of a hybrid approach to speed estimation in urban and rural areas. Traffic Injury Prev. (2021). https://doi.org/10.1080/15389588.2021.1935904

20. D'Apuzzo, M., Santilli, D.: An exploratory step to evaluate the pedestrian exposure in urban environment. In: Computational Science and Its Applications – ICCSA 2020 VII, Cagliari, Italy, pp. 645–657. Springer, Heidelberg (2020)

21. Ministero delle infrastrutture e dei trasporti. Art. 3. Definizioni stradali e di traffico. Nuovo codice della strada. D.lgs 30 aprile 1992 n. 285 (1992)

22. Jones, S.R.: Accessibility Measures: A Literature Review. Rapporto TRRL 967. Transport and Road Research Laboratory, Crowthorne, Berkshire (1981)

23. Mizuno, Y.: Summary Of IHRA pedestrian safety WG activities (2005) -proposed test methods to evaluate pedestrian protection afforded by passenger cars. In: The 19th International Technical Conference on the Enhanced Safety of Vehicles, Washington D.C. (2005)

24. Yang, J.: Review of injury biomechanics in car-pedestrian collisions. Int. J. Vehicle Saf. **1**(1/2/3), 100–117 (2005)

25. Virzì, M., Golfo, S.: Determination and analysis of the head and chest parameters by simulation of a vehicle– teenager impact. Proc. Inst. Mech. Eng. J. Automobile Eng. Part D **228**(1), 3–20 (2014)

26. Battaglia S., Damiani, I.: La bicicletta sportiva. Caratteristiche geometriche ed inerziali. Simulazione dinamica, Aracne (2006). ISBN 88-548-0801-6

27. Bellavia, G., Virzi'Mariotti, G.: Multibody numerical simulation for vehicle – pedestrian crash test. In: Ingegneriadell'autoveicolo ATA Vol. 62, 11/12. XXI Science and Motor Vehicles 2007, JUMV International Conference with Exhibition, Belgrade, Serbia, pp. 40–49 (2009). ISSN: 0001-2661

28. AASHTO. The Highway Safety Manual, American Association of State Highway Transportation Professionals, Washington, D.C (2010). http://www.highwaysafetymanual.org

Towards a Better Understanding of Vulnerability in Pedestrian-Vehicle Collision

Mauro D'Apuzzo[1] , Daniela Santilli[1(✉)], Azzurra Evangelisti[1] , Luca Di Cosmo[1], and Vittorio Nicolosi[2]

[1] Department of Civil and Mechanical Engineering DICEM, University of Cassino and Southern Lazio, Cassino, Italy
{dapuzzo,daniela.santilli}@unicas.it
[2] Department of Enterprise Engineering "Mario Lucertini", University of Rome "Tor Vergata", Rome, Italy
nicolosi@uniroma2.it

Abstract. The road is a transport infrastructure intended for the movement of users, such as vehicles and pedestrians. These interact with each other following rules that guarantee safety and security. Unfortunately, however, traffic safety does not depend solely on compliance with the rules but is affected by a series of factors, such as inattention by users or malfunctioning due to a particular environmental condition, etc. Although the accident data in Italy show a reduction in the mortality of motorists, thanks to the new on-board technologies, an increase in the number of victims among pedestrians is observed. To increase the safety of vulnerable users, several projects have been developed in order to define the correlation between the severity of the accident, the response of the vehicle and the stresses that can be tolerated without serious risks to the occupant's life. However, this requires detailed accident and user injury data. Often without this information, it is not possible to predict the accident situations of a site and the related consequences. The aim of this study is to enrich the existing vulnerability functions by correlating the objective kinematic parameters (acceleration, speed, etc.) with user injuries through multi-body simulations.

Keywords: Head Injury Criterion · Pedestrian injury · AIS

1 Introduction

In recent decades, the need to improve road safety has been increasingly felt both on vehicles equipped with innovative technological means (in terms of active and passive safety) and on the infrastructure. In fact, the European Union has drawn up a set of laws to obtain a coherent and complete system of measures aimed at improving road safety (cf. the recent European Directive 2008/96/EC); but also by promoting and financing programs and initiatives that have fostered both greater awareness and, consequently, consumer demand for safer vehicles (thanks to the EuroNCAP scoring system). Road safety requires an articulated approach capable of integrating multiple aspects, from

© Springer Nature Switzerland AG 2021
O. Gervasi et al. (Eds.): ICCSA 2021, LNCS 12958, pp. 557–572, 2021.
https://doi.org/10.1007/978-3-030-87016-4_40

the most purely technical to the psychological ones that govern user behaviour. The adoption of measures in favour of safety presupposes that one is able to recognize and evaluate the risk conditions that accompany a specific infrastructural configuration. The preventive safety analyzes of existing infrastructures (defined internationally with the term Road Safety Review) can help to identify, in a road layout, the presence of situations of potential risk for traffic, addressing the problem from the point of view of users and trying to investigate how they perceive, interpret and use street space. During the examination of the infrastructure, it is necessary to apply the principles of road safety according to a multidisciplinary perspective; that is, taking into account all types of users: motorists, motorcyclists, cyclists, pedestrians, the elderly, children, etc.

Especially in urban areas, a very important aspect is to make roads safe, especially for vulnerable users (pedestrians and cyclists), who often shared the space with motorized vehicle traffic, in order to encourage sustainable mobility (zero pollution). To focus attention on this type of user, it is advisable to identify the points or sections of the road network where it is most urgent to proceed with engineering investigations and safety analyzes for the assessment of risk factors. Talking about a risk factor means considering an event, or a condition, which intervenes in the Vehicle-Driver-Environment (VDE) system and modifies its correct functioning, thus constituting a probable trigger for a possible accident. Once the risk factors have been identified, it is necessary to evaluate the number, severity and recurrence of accidental events [1, 2] as well as the severity of the consequences to people. The objective is to determine the priorities of the interventions to be implemented, maximizing their effectiveness and optimizing the financial resources available.

To do this, it is necessary to have detailed data on the localization and dynamics of the accident as well as the harmful/fatal consequences that are encountered on users. Such data are often difficult to find and the ISTAT database is not useful since it does not provide a detailed location of the accident or a precise description of the dynamics.

In many European countries, in-depth accident databases [3, 4] are already available to help understand the mechanisms of injury and tolerance of the human body so as to provide an operational framework for investigating pedestrian accident scenarios in the real world [5–9].

These data together with the biomechanical knowledge (with which it is possible to know the tolerance of the human body to stresses and to attribute criteria that classify the injuries suffered by the occupants of the vehicle) have allowed starting studies whose purpose was to define the vulnerability prediction functions [10].

Evaluating vulnerability means defining the results of an impact, this means examining what in the reconstruction of an accident is called the post-impact phase. Numerical analyzes based on empirical formulations are usually used for the reconstruction of accidents involving pedestrians, even if the use of software that makes use of multi-body simulation is increasingly widespread. By means of the multi-body simulation codes, once the initial conditions have been imposed, it is possible to describe the motion of the bodies involved and, as a function of the dynamics, allowing to evaluate induced damage.

In this paper a new methodology aimed at enriching the existing pedestrian vulnerability prediction functions by the information on kinematic (acceleration, speed, etc.)

and mechanical (moments, cuts, normal stresses, etc.) outcomes provided by multi-body simulation codes is proposed.

2 Dynamic Vehicle-Pedestrian Collisions

Reconstructing the dynamics of the pedestrian-vehicle collision is not a simple task. In fact this depends on the concatenation of many factors such as: physical ones of the vehicle (type, speed, etc.), physical ones of the pedestrian (size, a position assumed at the moment of impact, age, etc.), the atmospheric, urban, legislative, psycho-physical ones of the driver etc.

2.1 Pedestrian Vehicle Collisions

Kinematics and pedestrian injuries in vehicle accidents are affected by numerous factors such as impact speed, vehicle type, stiffness and shape of the vehicle front (such as bumper height, hood height and length, windshield frame), age and build of pedestrians, as well as the pedestrian's initial posture relative to the front of the vehicle [11].

In this work for the reconstruction of accidents, reference was made to "free trajectories". These allow to model the collision between vehicle-pedestrian and the subsequent motion of the pedestrian in a series of successive phases (contact, acceleration, loading, projection, rolling or sliding on the ground).

Basically, it is possible to distinguish two types of free trajectories:

– *Forward projection:* in which the height of the centre of gravity of the pedestrian "hcg" is placed below the height of the upper edge of the front of the vehicle "Hc". It is substantially realized in all those cases in which the pedestrian is hit in full, or the impact occurs in the central area of the front of the vehicle.
– *Wrap* o with wrapping: which has three sub-categories (Fender Vault, Roof Vault and Somersoult). The centre of gravity of the pedestrian is greater than that of the height of the upper edge of the front of the vehicle. By schematizing the pedestrian as a rigid body, the motion that is given to it following the impact is a horizontal translation and a rotation around the centre of mass. Consequently, the pedestrian wraps around the hood of the vehicle with a subsequent impact of the head on it or on the windscreen. In this regard, a fundamental parameter is introduced, the WAD (Wrap Around Distance).

The WAD is defined as the distance from the point of contact with the front of the bumper to any point on the front structure of the vehicle. This parameter is influenced by the impact speed of the vehicle, the length of the hood and the height of the pedestrian. With the same shape of the front of the vehicle and the height of the pedestrian, the higher the speed, the greater the WAD.

Given the variability of each influencing parameter in each phase, it is more convenient to classify the types of impact on the basis of the overall trajectories (pre-impact, impact, post-impact). As already mentioned, this work mainly dealt with the post-impact phase which is influenced by the characteristics of the impact phase such as: the geometry of the front of the vehicle related to the height, position and motion of the pedestrian in the pre-impact phase, the braking characteristics of the vehicle and the impact speed.

2.2 Vehicle Characteristics

As far as the vehicles characteristics are concerned, three fundamental geometric parameters are used to define the shape of the vehicle's front (Fig. 1):

Fig. 1. Geometric parameters for defining the front of the vehicle

- γ = "Lead Angle" loading angle which determines the amount of vertical thrust on the pedestrian in the primary impact;
- β = "Bonnet Angle" influences both the loading and the launch direction of the pedestrian, as well as the way in which the pedestrian hits the bonnet in the secondary impact;
- Hc = Height of the front edge of the "Lead Edge" hood which together with the height of the centre of gravity of the pedestrian determines the arm of the rotary moment (ω).

According to the relationship between the height of the pedestrian and the front of the vehicle, three types of front are identified:

- *Low Front Vehicles,* which the height h of the frontal is less than 0.55 m, that is the value corresponding to the 50% percentile of the knee height of the adult population;
- *High Front Vehicles,* such as the height of the front h is between 0.55 m and 1.05 m; that is the value corresponding to the 50% percentile of the height of the center of gravity of the adult population;
- *Vertical front vehicles,* whose front height h is greater than 1.05 m.

The height of the front edge of the hood and its combination with other parameters affect the head or torso injuries of the vulnerable user. In fact, increasing the height of the front edge of the hood can potentially reduce the risk of head injuries.

Further consideration should be made on the profile of the front of the vehicle seen from above which can be rectangular, triangular or arched.

This latter classification has a considerable influence on the speed component of the pedestrian positioned transversely with respect to the direction of the vehicle. In fact, for rectangular type fronts, the speed remains unchanged, with a consequent variation of the momentum of the pedestrian in the direction of advancement of the vehicle itself, neglecting the friction during contact. While for triangular or arched fronts, the transverse motion of the pedestrian can undergo a deceleration or acceleration depending on the area in which the impact occurs. According to Han et al. [12] the hood therefore affects:

- the loading phase;
- the extent of the vaulting during the loading phase, since it depends on the height from the ground of the upper edge of the bonnet (this is greater for low edges, lower for high edges);
- the parts of the body that impact the front of the vehicle vary according to the height from the ground of the front edge of the bonnet and the length of the bonnet.

2.3 Pedestrian's Characteristics

Pedestrians are characterized according to their age, their size, but a not marginal factor is their position relative to the vehicle at the moment of impact. In fact, based on the position and the angle of impact there is a different sequence of the parts of the body that collide with the vehicle and therefore of the related injuries [13, 14].

As regards the pedestrian rest position, if the vehicle starts braking immediately after the primary impact, it is placed in front of the stop position of the same, otherwise, it is placed in a rearward and lateral position (Fig. 2).

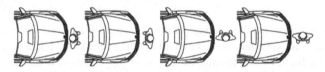

Fig. 2. Different position of the pedestrian relative to the vehicle

By further increasing the vehicle's impact speed, i.e. greater than 60 km/h, the somersault-like trajectory of the is passed, which differs from the Roof Vault in that the secondary impact does not occur since the pedestrian undergoes a greater vertical thrust with a flight phase and vehicle moves much faster under the pedestrian in flight. In this case, the final resting position of the pedestrian is always behind the vehicle stop position.

In fact, many studies [15, 16] confirm that the frontal position is more dangerous than the lateral one because the contact of the head and the thorax occurs directly on the hood; while the pedestrian in the lateral position hits the hood with the shoulder, this limits the injuries to the fatal parts. The above is confirmed by the analysis of the data on accidents.

3 Proposed Methodology for Pedestrian Injuries Evaluation

To determine the pedestrian injuries, both in terms of location and severity, following an impact, several factors must be considered. They never occur individually but combined with each other.

In order to identify the outcomes of the impact, vulnerability functions are often used. These, however, consider only two parameters, not allowing to take into account the mechanical behavior of the bodies during the impact. To make the results of the analyzes more realistic, once the various factors have been defined, a model can be built and then multi-body simulations can be started, from which the mechanical or kinematic parameters useful for defining the lesions will be obtained (Fig. 3).

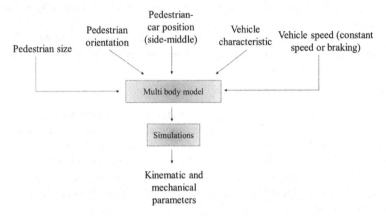

Fig. 3. Conceptual scheme adopted in the numerical simulations

The vehicle-pedestrian collision generates damages of a different nature, due to the primary impact, the secondary impact and finally those due to the impact on the ground. In this work, the focus was on the injuries suffered by a pedestrian in the primary impact. Usually, in these cases, there are bruises, fractures, or trauma and they vary according to the speed of the vehicle and the pedestrian and whether it is an adult or a child (Fig. 4).

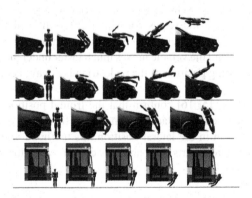

Fig. 4. Pedestrian kinematics after various vehicle impacts

This is easily found by observing the different frames of the multibody simulations. In fact, in these, it is clearly visible that when the front of the vehicle and the respective shape vary, there are impact conditions and therefore different outcomes and injuries in the different parts of the body.

Nowadays pedestrian-vehicle impact outcome in terms of injury level can be evaluated by means of vulnerability prediction functions employing a logistic approach [32]. Logistic models are stochastic models that do not allow us to know the outcome of an accident but only to estimate the probability of a certain degree of injury and they are calibrated on detailed accident data collected within in-depth accident databases [3, 4]. Unfortunately, most of the existing vulnerability logistic models (VLM) is based on few statistically significant explanatory variables (namely, vehicle speed and pedestrian age) since the size of the in-depth accident database is very limited.

However, in order to analyses pedestrian safety according to a risk-based approach a better understanding of how pre-impact conditions (in term of pedestrian, vehicle and site characteristics and possible evasive maneuvres) may affect accident outcome is needed. The basic idea underlining this work is therefore to develop and calibrate a multi-body pedestrian-vehicle model. The aim is to provide an additional analysis tool that may complement the prediction yield by VLM by producing reliable synthetic accident data to enrich VLM with additional and new explanatory variables.

In order to accomplish this task, the following procedure has been pursued:

1) review of existing relationships between kinematic and mechanical quantities provided by multibody/fem accident numerical simulations and pedestrian injury scales;
2) assessment of numerical reliability of the developed multibody model by calibration with scientific literature data;
3) experimental calibration of the proposed methodology by comparison with results provided by existing VLM based on real accident data.

3.1 Injury Scales

Based on the type and severity of the lesions, they are classified with different scales based on the area of use. The main ones can be grouped into three sets:

• anatomical scales: classify the lesion in terms of anatomical location, type and severity. These scales assess the extent of the injury rather than the long-term consequences. The most famous and widespread of these scales is the "Abbreviated Injury Scale" (AIS);
• physiological scales: they describe the physiological state of the patient based on the change in function caused by the lesion. The status and its numerical rating may vary during the period of care. This type of scale is widely used in the clinical setting;
• scales based on damage, disability and social cost. In this case, the long-term consequences and the influence that the injuries have on the patient's quality of life are assessed.

The first two types are medical, biomechanics is concerned with the scales that belong to the third group.

Abbreviated Injury Scale

The most common injury scale worldwide is the Abbreviated Injury Scale (AIS). This is commonly used to assess the severity and describe types of injuries. Starting from the patients' medical records assigns a score from 0 to 6 [17] as a function of injury severity, as described in international literature [16, 18–20].

For each level, there is [21] different damage to different parts of the body.

In reality, other scales are used to take into account the injuries involving the different parts of the body, including the Injury Severity Score (ISS) [22–24]. To determine the ISS it is necessary to evaluate the AIS of six body regions (head, face, chest, abdomen, upper and lower limbs) and then sum the squares of the three highest AIS indices. The ISS score, therefore, assumes values ranging from 0 to 75 (where 1 represents the presence of moderate injuries while 75 represents a fatal injury). By definition, if a region of the body has an AIS of 6, it automatically has an ISS of 75.

This is an anatomical scoring system that correlates linearly with mortality, hospital stay, and other measures of severity [25].

To define these scales it is, so, appropriate to estimate the lesions for the different parts of the body with the corresponding parameters.

Head Injury Criterion

In this report, statistical data was used to identify relationships between the injury criteria and the probability that it will occur. Several studies [26–28] have shown that the parts of the body that are most injured following an accident are the head and legs.

It is difficult to define a criterion that is able to take into account all the different modes of injury. But the international literature comes in support by providing various risk criteria [16, 19].

The most used criterion for head injuries in impact with the various areas of the vehicle is the Head Injury Criterion (HIC), also known as Head Performance Criterion (HPC).

The modification of the formula leads to the definition of the Head Injury Criterion:

$$\mathrm{HIC} = \max\{(t_2 - t_1)[\frac{1}{(t_2 - t_1)} \int_{t_1}^{t_2} a(t)dt]^{2.5}\} \tag{1}$$

where:

– $a(t)$ is the resultant of the acceleration evaluated in the center of gravity of the head[g];
– t_1 and t_2 are two points on the time axis which, during impact, maximize the HIC[seconds];
– the exponent 2.5 is the slope of the curve in bilogarithmic coordinates.

Therefore the Head Injury Criterion indicates the threshold beyond which the individual undergoes fatal injuries by inversely correlating the intensity of the acceleration and its duration; but the HIC does not provide any information regarding the extent of the injury. This is precisely why the HIC-AIS correlation is used.

Thoracic Trauma Index

For the evaluation of thoracic trauma, one of the most common injury criteria, especially for lateral impact cases, is the Thoracic Trauma Index (TTI). This is evaluated as expressed in the following Eq. (2):

$$\text{TTI} = 1.4 * \text{age} + 0.5 * (\text{RIBy} + \text{T12y}) * \frac{m_c}{M_{std}} \tag{2}$$

where:

age is the age of the pedestrian;

RIB_y is the maximum lateral acceleration of the abdominal spine (12th spinal segment) [g];

T_{12y} is the maximum lateral acceleration of the 12th thoracic vertebra [g];

mc is the mass of the pedestrian [Kg];

Mstd is the standard mass equal to 75 kg.

In the case under examination, having a simplified model of a dummy, the vertebral and thoracic accelerations are hypothesized to be similar to the resulting acceleration in the chest.

Spine Injury Criterion

Another injury found recurrently in accidents is that of the spine; although the injured in most cases make a full recovery within short periods, there are prolonged medical problems. So the socio-economic cost of these injuries is enormous.

The part of the spine most involved in collisions is the cervical one. In this, the stresses are due to the contact forces acting on the head or to inertial forces related to the mass of the same. Therefore, several combined loads must be considered to estimate neck injuries [29, 30] between them so that these do not exceed certain limits.

In this preliminary phase, the spinal injuries are assimilated to those of the torso.

Conversion of Injury Thresholds to AIS Scale

Not having available complete data that would allow evaluating the precise AIS values, starting from the relationship between AIS and the different lesion parameters present in the literature, the level of the lesion was assessed. For example, I notice that the HIC has entered the range and assigned an AIS level [31] (Table 1)

Table 1. HIC-AIS relationship

HIC	AIS	Brain and head injury level
135–519	1	Headache or dizziness
520–899	2	Loss of consciousness for less than 1 h - linear fracture
900–1254	3	Loss of consciousness from 1 to 6 h - depressed fracture
1255–1574	4	Loss of consciousness from 1 to 24 h - open fracture
1575–1859	5	Loss of consciousness for more than 25 h - diffuse hematoma
>1860	6	Not survivable

Similarly it is done for the other injury parameters. After evaluating the AIS for the different parts of the body, the three maximum values are taken and the ISS is estimated (3):

$$ISS = AIS_1^2 + AIS_2^2 + AIS_3^2 \tag{3}$$

The next step is to define the probability of having an injury using both deterministic and stochastic models.

3.2 Calibration of Numerical Multi-body Model for the Reconstructions of Vehicle-Pedestrian Impacts

In order to reconstruct the vehicle-pedestrian collision phenomena, numerical analyzes are started using a pedestrian model based on the multibody system, while the vehicle is schematized as a rigid body.

In order to start the simulations, the initial conditions of the vehicle (speed, trajectory, braking), the pedestrian (age, height, weight, position with respect to the car) and the type of simulation to be started (kinetics or kinematics).

Starting from the study conducted by Corallo F. et al. [16] which considers the reconstruction of an impact with multibody modelling between a teen pedestrian and an SUV/sedan, the model is calibrated. Having known the pedestrian's positions, its physical characteristics as well as the dimensions and speeds of the vehicle, the simulations are started from which the maximum acceleration values to the head and chest are extrapolated (Fig. 5).

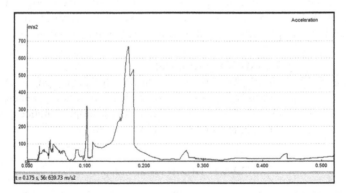

Fig. 5. Graphic-analytical determination of the head's accelerations provided by the numerical simulation

Once these maximum accelerations relating to the primary impact are obtained, the injury parameters are evaluated.

These simulation parameters are then compared with those in [16] and it can be observed a fairly good correlation with Pearsons values equal to 0.93 with the SUV and to 0.88 for the sedan, whereas those for HICs seems lower (0.77 for the SUV and 0.87 for the sedan) (Figs. 6 and 7).

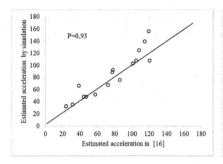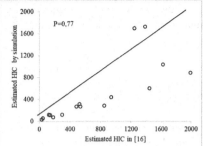

Fig. 6. Comparison of data from simulation and those reported in [16] (teenager-SUV)

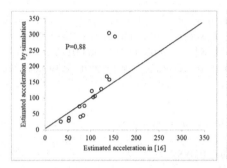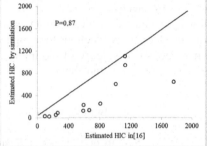

Fig. 7. Comparison of the simulation results with those reported in [16] (teenager-sedan)

This allows to say that the results obtained are not very dissimilar from each other, therefore it follows that the model has been calibrated correctly and the differences can be attributed to the different software used.

Once the software is calibrated, numerous simulations are carried out in which the following are varied:

– vehicle speed between 20 and 50 km/h (with a step of 10 km/h, as proposed by EuroNCAP) assuming both the absence and the presence of braking;
– different vehicles: suv, sedan, coupé, van and bus;
– pedestrians of different age groups and different sizes (30-year-old adult with normal build, strong 50-year-old adult, 15-year-old teenager and 6-year-old child);
– position of the front or side pedestrian with respect to the bonnet of the vehicle.

From the various simulations, the acceleration parameters are obtained with which the extent of the injury suffered by the pedestrian is assessed, therefore the corresponding AIS and ISS are evaluated for the various scenarios.

3.3 Evaluation of Injury Level by Existing Prediction Function

To define the injury risk functions, logistic models are used, obtained as a result of laboratory experiments, with which it is possible to determine the biomechanical response and the level of tolerance to injuries. Logistic regression models, which are used to estimate the effect of one or more factors on the probability of injury, are binary.

$$Pi = \frac{1}{1 + \exp(a + b \cdot Y_{ped} + c \cdot V)} \tag{4}$$

where:

Pi, probability of a specific injury level;
a, b, c are the calibration parameters;
Y_{ped} is the age of the pedestrian;
V the speed of the car (considered constant).

Therefore by means of these function it is possible to estimate the probability that following an injury the pedestrian can reach or exceed a certain level of severity. Starting from the vulnerability functions for assigned ISS [32], implemented on GIDAS data [3], the five degrees of severity of the injury and the respective probability estimates are identified, as shown in the Table 2.

Table 2. Probability of injury based on severity

Severity of the injury	ISS range	P (ISS)
Minor	0–8	1 - P (ISS$_{9+}$)
Mild	9–15	P (ISS$_{9+}$) - P (ISS$_{16+}$)
Moderate	16–25	P (ISS$_{16+}$) - P (ISS$_{25+}$)
Serious	26–75	P (ISS$_{25+}$)
Not survivable	>75	P (fatalities)

These models estimate the probability of an injury considering two explanatory variables, namely the age of the pedestrian and the speed of the car.

Starting from these models, the probabilities associated with the different levels of injury were assessed (Fig. 8).

From this for each age-speed pair the expected value is obtained as:

$$ISS_{\text{vulnerability model}} = \sum P(ISS) * ISS_{\text{average of the interval}} \tag{5}$$

Then different input parameters such as the age of the pedestrian and the travel speed of the car (steady mode), the position of the pedestrian (front or side with respect to the bonnet of the car) and the type of car (SUV, sedan, cabrio) have been changed. Then a overall ISS average value, ISS_{average} has been evaluated to be compared with that provided by the vulnerability prediction functions, $ISS_{\text{vulnerability model}}$. The comparison between the two ISS, taking into consideration an adult pedestrian of 30 years and a 15-year-old teenager is reported below for several vehicle (steady) speed values (Table 3 and Fig. 9).

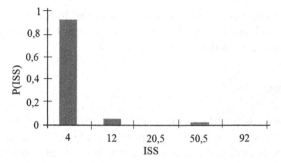

Fig. 8. Example of ISS probability distribution derived from vulnerability prediction functions

Table 3. ISS vulnerability model-ISS average comparison

Pedestrian's age	V (Km/h)	ISS vulnerability model	ISSaverage
15	20	5.16	3.07
	30	6.40	5.4
	40	8.84	12.3
	50	13.44	27.72
30	20	5.76	0.85
	30	7.35	1.9
	40	10.79	7.35
	50	17.32	25.075

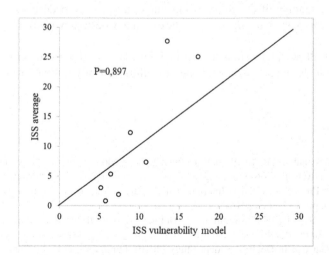

Fig. 9. ISS vulnerability model-ISSaverage comparison (teenager-adult pedestrian)

The agreement between the average outcome provided by the simulation models and that derived from vulnerability prediction functions seem fairly acceptable. However further simulations are needed in order to improve it.

4 Conclusions

The aim of the work is to analyze the vehicle-pedestrian impact dynamics, as recent national and international accident reports provide evidence for an increase of crashes involving pedestrians. In this connection, refined pedestrian vulnerability prediction tool are needed to help road safety engineers. It is believed that multibody accident reconstruction models may offer a significant contribution in improving existing pedestrian vulnerability predictions functions.

To this purpose, a multibody pedestrian vehicle impact model has been developed. Following an initial calibration by a comparison with data provided by technical and scientific literature, a parametric analysis has been carried out by varying several pedestrian and vehicle related impact parameters. From kinematic and mechanical results obtained by numerical simulations, injury level evaluation has been performed and an estimation of an average values of ISS has been derived. This value obtained for several vehicle speed and pedestrian type has been compared with an average ISS value derived from existing pedestrian vulnerability prediction functions that have been calibrated on real accident data collected in a German in-depth accident database (GIDAS).

The comparison is fairly acceptable and more simulations are needed in order improve the modelling framework. However, basing on these preliminary results, the multibody pedestrian-vehicle impact developed seems to be able to capture the complexity of this accident scenario and to provide a reliable estimation of possible outcomes. By an extensive use of this model it is believed that it will be possible to add a better understanding of the complex kinematic of impacted pedestrians and provide more significant explanatory variables in the existing pedestrian vulnerability prediction functions.

This will allow safety engineers to highlight site conditions affecting the initial pedestrian-vehicle impact parameters and therefore to study mitigations countermeasures.

References

1. Ebner, A., Samaha, R.R., Scullion, P., Helmer, T.: Methodology for the development and evaluation of active safety systems using reference scenarios: application to preventive pedestrian safety. In: Proceedings of the International Research Council on Biomechanics of Injury (IRCOBI), pp. 155–168 (2010)
2. Ebner, A., Samaha, R.R., Scullion, P., Helmer, T.: Identifying and analyzing reference scenarios for the development and evaluation of preventive pedestrian safety systems (2010)
3. GIDAS. German In-Depth Accident Study (2010). http://www.gidas.org/files/GIDAS_eng.pdf
4. UMTRI. 1994–1998 NASS pedestrian crash data study (PCDS) codebook. s.l.: UMTRI Transportation Data Center., Version 03 Mar01 (2005)

5. Bahman, S.R., Charles, N.M., Robert, K.: An evaluation of the association between vehicle type and the source and severity of pedestrian injuries. Traffic Inj. Prev. **6**, 185–192 (2005)
6. Kong, C.Y., Yang, J.K.: Logistic regression analysis of pedestrian casualty risk in passenger vehicle collisions in China. Accid. Anal. Prev. **42**, 987–993 (2010)
7. Naif, A.S., Salaheddine, B., Saad, A.G.: In-depth analysis of pedestrian crashes in Riyadh. Traffic Inj. Prev. **10**, 552–559 (2009)
8. Olukoga, I.A.: Pedestrian casualties and fatalities in road traffic crashes in a South African municipality. Traffic Inj. Prev. **4**, 355–357 (2003)
9. Otte, D., Krettek, C., Brunner, H., Zwipp, H.: Scientific approach and methodology of a new in-depth-investigation study in Germany so called GIDAS. Paper presented at: ESV Conference, Nagoya, Japan (2003)
10. Helmer, T., Ebner, A., Huber, W.: Präventiver Fußgängerschutz - Anforderungen und Bewertung. Aechen:18. Aechener Kolloquium Fahrzeug- und Motorentechnik (2009)
11. Yang, J.K.: Injury biomechanics in car-pedestrian collisions: development, validation and application of human-body mathematical models. Doctoral dissertation, Department of Injury Prevention, Chalmers University of Technology, Sweden (1997)
12. Han, Y., Peng, Y., Peng, Q., Huang, H., Mizuno, K.: A study on kinematic behavior and head injury rick in vehicle to pedestrian collisions. In: Fifth International Conference on Measuring Technology and Mechatronics Automation, Hong Kong, China (2013)
13. Chen, H., Poulard, D., Crandall, J.R., Panzer, M.B.: Pedestrian response with different initial positions during impact with a mid-sized sedan. Paper presented at: 24th International Technical Conference on the Enhanced Safety of Vehicles (ESV) (2015)
14. Yang, J.K., Lovsund, P.: Development and validation of a human body mathematical model for simulation of car pedestrian collisions. In: Proceedings of IRCOBI Conference, pp. 133–149 (1997)
15. Carollo, F., Virzì Mariotti, G., Naso, V., Golfo, S.: Head, chest and femur injury in teenage pedestrian – SUV crash; mass influence on the speeds. J. Automobile Eng. Part D **233**(4), 790–809 (2018)
16. Virzi, G., Golfo, S.: Determination and analysis of the head and chest parameters by simulation of a vehicle-teenager impact. J. Automobile Eng. Part D **228**(1), 3–20 (2014). https://doi.org/10.1177/0954407013501487
17. AAAM (Association for Advancement of Automotive Medicine). The Abbreviated Injury Scale (AIS) 2005 (2008)
18. States, J.D., Huelke, D.F.: The abbreviated injury scale. 1980 revision. American Association for Automotive Medicine (AAAM) (1980)
19. Bellavia, G., Virzì Mariotti, G.: Multibody numerical simulation for vehicle - pedestrian crash test. In: Motor Vehicle Engineering ATA. XXI Science and Motor Vehicles 2007, JUMV International Conference with Exhibition, vol. 62, 11/12, pp. 40–49 (2009). ISSN: 0001–2661
20. Bellavia, G., Virzì Mariotti, G.: Development of an anthropomorphic model for vehicle - pedestrian crash test. In: Automotive Engineering. XXI Science and Motor Vehicles 2007, JUMV International Conference with Exhibition, Belgrade, Serbia, s.n., vol. 62, pp. 48–56, 3/4 (2009). ISBN 978-86-80941-31-8
21. Shojaati, M.: Correlation between injury risk and impact severity index ASI. In: Proceedings of the 3rd Swiss Transport Research Conference, pp. 19–21 (2003)
22. Restrepo-Álvarez, C.A., et al.: Trauma severity scores. Revista Co-lombiana de Anestesi-ología Colombian J. Anesthesiol. **44**(4), 317–323 (2016)
23. States, J.D., Huelke, D.F.: The abbreviated injury scale. 1980 revision. s.l.: Des Plaines: American Association for Automotive Medicine (AAAM) (1980)
24. States, J.D.: Abbreviated and the comprehensive research injury scales. In: Proceedings of Thirteenth Stapp Car Crash Conference, 2–4 December 1969 (1969). Society of Automotive Engineers, New York, 13, pp. 282–294

25. Baker, S.P., O'Neil, B.: The injury severity score: an update. J. Trauma. **16**, 882–885 (1976)
26. Mizuno, Y.: Summary of IHRA pedestrian safety WG activities - proposed test methods to evaluate pedestrian protection afforded by passenger cars. In: The 19th International Technical Conference on the Enhanced Safety of Vehicles, Washington, DC (2005)
27. Yang, J.: Review of injury biomechanics in car-pedestrian collisions. Int. J. Vehicle Saf. **1**(1/2/3), 100–117 (2005)
28. Martin, J.L., Lardy, A., et al.: Pedestrian injury patterns according to car and casualty characteristics in France. Ann. Adv. Automot. Med. **55**, 137–46 (2011)
29. Myers, B., et al.: Improved assessment of lumbar vertebral body strength using spine lateral dual-energy X-ray absorptiometry. J. Bone Min Res. **9**(5), 687–693 (1994)
30. Belwadi, A., Yang, K.: Response of the cadaveric lumbar spine to flexion with and without anterior shear displacement. In: Proceedings of IRCOBI Conference, pp. 397–410 (2008)
31. National Highway Traffic Safety Administration. Report: Issue 9. Vol. Part 2 (1981)
32. Helmer, T.: Development of a methodology for the evaluation of active safety using the example of preventive pedestrian protection (2015). Doctoral Thesis accepted by Technische Universität, Berlin, Germany https://doi.org/10.1007/978-3-319-12889-4

A New Framework to Evaluate Crash Risk for Road Traffic Safety Management System

Fabio Porcu[1] , Francesca Maltinti[2(✉)] , Nicoletta Rassu[2(✉)] , Francesco Pili[1] ,
Michela Bonera[3] , and Benedetto Barabino[3]

[1] SPIVA Srl - Technological Start Up, Cagliari, Italy
[2] Department of Civil and Environmental Engineering and Architecture, University of Cagliari,
09129 Cagliari, Italy
{maltinti,nicoletta.rassu}@unica.it
[3] Department of Civil Engineering, Environment and Mathematics, University of Brescia,
25123 ArchitectureBrescia, Land, Italy

Abstract. Road safety issue is becoming increasingly important for both public administrations and road users. Therefore, tools for assessing and managing safety performance take on even more relevance.

Previous research has proposed different types of Road Safety Management Systems but, to the best of our knowledge, only a few of these studies have focused on recent road safety regulations such as the ISO 39001:2012.

This paper proposes a new framework that evaluates the crash risk for administrative areas according to ISO39001:2012. First, this framework identifies the safety factors. Next, it specifies the risk components in terms of frequency, severity and exposure factors that may affect road crashes. Then, combining these components in a risk crash function, it is possible to build a safety performance ranking for each administrative areas.

The viability of the proposed methodology was tested on the administrative areas of all Italian provinces, using over 500,000 road crashes data recorded by the Italian National Institute of Statistics ISTAT between 2015 and 2017, which were merged for the 107 Italian provinces. The results helped ranking the road safety of the Italian provinces according to a scale with four risk scores: maximum, high, medium and low.

The findings show how the implementation of the proposed framework could help public administrations in managing the safety performance of their road networks and, also, qualify them according to the recent safety norms.

Keywords: Road Safety · Smart city · Safety regulations · Risk · Safety performance

1 Introduction

During the last decade, road safety issue has assumed considerable importance for public administrations all over the world. Although considerable differences still remain

© Springer Nature Switzerland AG 2021
O. Gervasi et al. (Eds.): ICCSA 2021, LNCS 12958, pp. 573–587, 2021.
https://doi.org/10.1007/978-3-030-87016-4_41

among regions, more and more countries are adopting restrictive measures and international guidelines to reduce road traffic deaths and injuries [1]. The ISO 39001 [2] is one of the most important international norms for road safety of recent years and it is directed to all the organizations operating in and with the road traffic environment. The aim of this norm is the reduction of death and serious injuries caused by road traffic crashes by improving safety performance. According to [2], the improvement of the safety performance may be pursued by implementing a Road Traffic Safety Management System (RTSMS) organized in a Plan, Do, Check and Act (PDCA) cycle. In the Plan stage, the organization plans the goal, establishes roles and responsibilities, and identifies safety factors as well as risk exposure factors for the safety assessment. In the Do stage, the organization commits to achieve the safety objectives. In the Check stage, the organization establishes procedures to record crashes to monitor safety performance and periodically revises it. In the Act stage, the organization works towards a continuous improvement of its RTSMS. A key crucial point of ISO 39001 [2] is the implementation of a method to evaluate the crash risk, but no specific method is suggested.

Nevertheless, despite the literature is quite rich about road safety management systems, as far as we know, there are still few studies related to the ISO 39001 [2] and risk assessment methods in the domain of road safety.

During the last ten years, studies focused on three approaches to perform RTSMS models. The first approach is based on the conflict points assessment as safety management models. Many of these studies follow the Swedish Traffic Conflict Technique [3] and were implemented with new technologies (i.e. [4–8]). The second approach assesses the crash risk as a function of traffic flows ([9–11]). The last approach uses crash data to assess the risk associated within the reference context, and it is adopted in this study. Indeed, it is the most common in the road safety literature. Moreover, two different sub-approaches may be considered according to the size of the context: the former is focused on large administrative area as countries or regions ([12–19]), the latter tries to evaluate road safety performance on more restricted areas such as routes, intersection or districts ([20–24]). Despite this literature and as far as we know, no study has proposed a solid RTSMS that assesses road risk in terms of probability, consequence ad exposure of crashes. Therefore, there is not a mature scientific treatment about the implementation of ISO 39001 [2] on safety management models. Even outside of the scope of private transport (i.e., car based), there are few contributions. Porcu et al. ([25, 26]) focused on the evaluation of accident risk in public transport companies, whereas [27] in transport of dangerous good.

The objective of this paper is to develop a framework for the evaluation of the road safety encompassing the requirements of ISO 39001 [2] that combines safety factors of crash frequency and severity and exposure in one function. The proposed methodology adjusts the well-known risk index first introduced by [28] who considered the following three components: the potential crash consequence, the exposure factor and the probability factor. However, unlike [28] who used predefined numerical ratings for these components, our index is expressed by a mathematical relation among these components and uses real crashes data. Moreover, our index links together frequency and severity prediction models (or functions) to the exposure factors.

The viability of this framework was tested in Italy, using over 500,000 road crashes recorded by the Italian National Institute of Statistics (ISTAT), merged by province, between 2015 and 2017. More precisely, the results are provided in an aggregate form for each province and a focus is also reported for the Sardinian road safety performance situation, being the origin of most of the authors.

This paper aim to contribute to both theory and practice. From a theoretical perspective, this paper covers a research area that has not been fully addressed and provides useful outcomes for many applications. On the practical side, this framework helps implement a RTSMS for each administration interested in the monitoring of road safety performance and in the safety certification process according to [2].

The remaining paper is organized as follows. Section 2 presents a general framework to evaluate the crash risk. Section 3 illustrates the experimentation of this framework in all the Italian provinces and briefly discusses the results. Finally, Sect. 4 draws conclusions and research perspectives.

2 Methodology

The proposed framework builds on ([25, 26]) for the public transport and it describes each step for the crash risk assessment of the private transport, according to the safety factors introduced by the ISO 39001 [2]. A scheme of the framework is shown in Fig. 1.

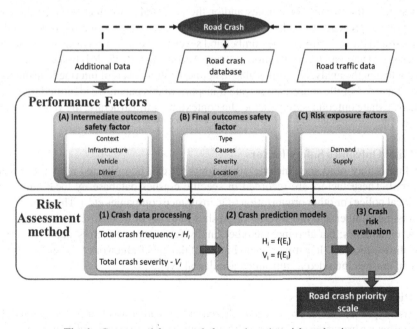

Fig. 1. Conceptual framework for road crashes risk evaluation

2.1 Performance Factors

According to [2], a performance factor is "*a measurable factor, element and criterion to the road traffic safety identified to cause road traffic crashes and road traffic incidents that lead, or have the potential to lead, to death and serious injuries of road users*". Other studies have already focused on identifying these factors, usually called variables or safety factors but their deepening is not the subject of this study (i.e., [26, 29–32]). From a practical viewpoint, there is no standard variable within each crash database. Moreover, usually the available database has a limited number of variables and it may contain factors that are difficult to implement in the methodology. Therefore, it is important to identify the different types of factors to better understand the available variable and its usefulness within the methodology.

Following the ISO39001 [2] directives, three classes of factors are distinguished: (A) intermediate outcome safety factors, (B) final outcome safety factors and (C) risk exposure factors.

(A) Intermediate Outcomes Safety Factors

The intermediate outcome safety factors are related to safe planning design and use of the road network, vehicle type, user safety equipment, fitness of drivers and so on. They are described by the ISO 39001 [2] as the condition or interventions that improve the final road traffic safety performance both in terms of occurrence and severity of crashes. In other words, intermediate outcome safety factors are the elements that can reduce (or increase) the number of crashes and/or the potential consequence of crashes. For example, the presence of well-signalized pedestrian crossings along the road could be the reason to the reduction of the number and severity of crashes because drivers tend to reduce speed and pay more attention to them. According to ([25, 26]) based on the scale and context of the analysis, it is possible to define different class of intermediate outcome safety factors. For the analysis of private transport, in this paper, we identified four types of intermediate outcome safety factor: the context, the infrastructure, the vehicle and the driver.

(B) Final Outcomes Safety Factors

The final safety outcomes include all factors that can be collected after a crash has occurred. These factors are recorded in specific crashes database by local authorities (i.e. local police) or other organization (e.g. insurance companies etc.). This class largely reflects the number and the severity of crashes in terms of deaths, serious injuries, and property damages; but also include other final safety outcome factors such as the crash type, the location etc. It is important to highlight that this framework focuses exclusively on road crashes intended as unwanted accidental events.

(C) Risk Exposure Factors

The risk exposure factors are related to the supply of road network and user demand. For this reason, we group the risk exposure factors into supply-oriented and demand-oriented factors. Supply oriented factors concern road characteristics (e.g., the length of the road) while demand oriented factors concern the use of the road network by users (e.g. the annual average daily traffic). However, despite the importance of such factors, they are usually not recorded in the crash databases. Indeed, crashes will result by the interaction between the intermediate safety outcome factors and the risk exposure factors.

2.2 Risk Assessment Method

The methodology exposed in this paper is inspired by the well-known risk index introduced by [28], where the risk is computed as a combination of three components: Probability, Exposure and Consequence (or Vulnerability). Let R be the risk score, C the consequence, E the exposure factor and P the probability factor.

$$R = C \times E \times P \tag{1}$$

The consequences refer to the most probable results of a potential crash; exposure is described as the frequency of occurrence of the hazard-event (unsafe condition or potential source of an accident) while probability is the likelihood that an accidental event may arise from the hazard-event [28].

However, unlike [28] who assigned default values for the risk components, our index introduced a mathematical relation among these components which are evaluated through analytical functions as already applied in public transport ([25, 26]). Nevertheless, in this study, a methodology is proposed for the calculation of a risk index on homogeneous administrative areas, intended as a part of the road network where each contextual, infrastructural, vehicular and user characteristics remain constant.

Let:

- l be the homogeneous administrative area of interest;
- i be the index of the intermediate outcome factor (or the associated sub-factor);
- n be the total number of intermediate outcome factors;
- $H_{i,l}$ be the frequency of crashes occurrence on homogeneous administrative area l that can be evaluated as the total number of crashes in a predefined time interval (e.g., a year) in which factor i manifests itself;
- $V_{i,l}$ be the potential consequence of crash (in terms of severity of crashes) on homogeneous administrative area l, that can be evaluated as the total cost of crashes in a predefined time interval (e.g., a year) in which factor i manifests itself;
- $E_{i,l}$ be the exposure factor on homogeneous administrative area l associated with factor i.

The crash risk index on homogeneous administrative area l (R_l) may be defined as:

$$R_l = \sum_{i=1}^{n} (H_{i,l} * V_{i,l} * E_{i,l}) \tag{2}$$

Each individual component of (2) is better explained in the following steps.

(1) Crash Data Processing

The estimate of $H_{i,l}$ and $V_{i,l}$ needs a preliminary crash data processing, in which the total number of crashes and the severity are computed from the raw crashes database. More precisely, for each intermediate outcome safety factor i, the occurrence frequencies and associated economic costs are counted.

Let:

- j be the index of the crash;
- m be the total of number of crashes;
- h_{ijl} be a binary variable related to the crash occurrence, which is 1 if crash j occurred on homogeneous administrative area l, due to factor i, 0 otherwise.
- v_{ijl}^{dm}, v_{ijl}^{f}, v_{ijl}^{d} be ordered variables related to the crash severity due to damages (dm), injuries (f) and dead (d), respectively, according to a numerical scale. Although several scales may be adopted for this purpose (e.g., [33]), in this paper we adopt the average cost related to the severity of damage computed as sum of costs for material damage (C_m), injured (C_f) or dead (C_d).

Thus, the total frequency of crashes and the associated severities may be computed as follows:

$$H_{i,l} = \sum_{j=1}^{m} h_{ijl} \ \forall i = 1, \ldots, n; \ \forall l = 1, \ldots, L \tag{3}$$

$$V_{i,l} = \sum_{j=1}^{m} (v_{ijl}^{dm} * C_m + v_{ijl}^{f} * C_f + v_{ijl}^{d} * C_d) \ \forall \ i = 1, \ldots, n; \ \forall \ l = 1, \ldots, L \tag{4}$$

(2) Crash Prediction Models

In the second step the frequency and the severity of crashes are computed by bivariate models, one for each intermediate safety outcome factor i, where $H_{i,l}$ and $V_{i,l}$ are the response variables, and the predictors are represented only by the exposure factor $E_{i,l}$. Although this choice impedes analysis of the correlations between intermediate safety outcome factors, the simple formulation of bivariate models enables to easily evaluate the impact on risk assessment of each factor singularly. Thus, differently from multivariate models, this choice helps compute the risk exposure factors value for each i. In other words, each bivariate model can have a different risk exposure factor according to the intermediate safety outcome factor. For instance, if i is daylight, then the exposure factor could be the average daily traffic during the daylight hours.

According to [34], road crashes are random, rare and non-negative integer events. Therefore, we decide to use the Generalized Linear Modelling approach that assumes a negative binomial structure to predict the frequency of crashes. However, there is a non-linear relationship between the frequency of crashes and traffic exposure factors (e.g., [35]). Moreover, exposure $E_{i,l}$ refers to a variable that when it assumes zero value, the frequency of crashes and severities must be zero. Therefore, according to (e.g., [35, 36]), a power function regression is a viable solution. Let:

- α_{1i}, α_{2i}, β_{1i}, β_{2i} be the coefficients to be estimated in the model.

The prediction of $\widehat{H_{i,l}}$ and $\widehat{V_{i,l}}$ is performed as follows:

$$\widehat{H_{i,l}} = \alpha_{1,i,l} * E_{i,l}^{\alpha_{2,i,l}} \tag{5}$$

$$\widehat{V_{i,l}} = \beta_{1,i,l} * E_{i,l}^{\beta_{2,i,l}} \tag{6}$$

(3) Crash Risk Calculation and Risk Priority Scale

The estimation of crash prediction models $\widehat{H_{i,l}}$ and $\widehat{V_{i,l}}$ enables us to computing the crash risk index for each homogeneous road section by adjusting Eq. (1) as follows:

$$R_l = \sum_{i=1}^{n}\left(\widehat{H_{i,l}}(E_{i,l}) + \widehat{V_{i,l}}(E_{i,l})\right) = \sum_{i=1}^{n}\left(\left(\alpha_{1,i,l} * E_{i,l}^{\alpha_{2,i,l}}\right) * \left(\beta_{1,i,l} * E_{i,l}^{\beta_{2,i,l}}\right)\right) \ \forall\, l$$
$$= 1, \ldots, L \tag{7}$$

Results of Eq. (7) enables us to classify roads according to a predefined risk scale to prioritize the road safety improving actions. In this paper, a simple risk priority scale for homogeneous administrative area l is proposed according to the following criterion: we divide the range lower, middle and upper quartiles ($Q_1 = $ 25th percentile, $Q_2 = $ 50th percentile and $Q_3 = $ 75th percentile) and classify each road as follows:

- $R_1 \rightarrow R > Q_3$ - Maximum risk (8)
- $R_2 \rightarrow Q_2 > R > Q_3$ - High risk (9)
- $R_3 \rightarrow Q_1 > R > Q_2$) - Average risk (10)
- $R_4 \rightarrow (R < Q_1)$ - Low risk. (11)

This risk classification helps identify the roads that require greater safety measures to apply the risk mitigation measures. First, it is important to understand the reasons for poor performance safety on this road sections by using a detailed analysis of the crashes and the severity; next, the actions to for the risk mitigation should be searched. This may be pursued by prevention and/or protection actions that act on the terms of Eq. (7). Prevention actions aim to reduce level $\widehat{H_{i,l}}(E_{i,l})$, whereas protection actions aim to reduce the level of $\widehat{V_{i,l}}(E_{i,l})$.

3   Real World Experiment

This section shows the application of the methodology. The crash database was acquired by ISTAT. This database contains crashes data occurred on Italian roads (from 2015 to 2017), which are merged for the 107 Italian provinces for this experiment. The characteristics which have been analyzed and processed are shown in Table 1.

ISTAT only collects road crashes data recorded by law enforcement agencies in which at least one person is injured or dead. Therefore, property damage only road crashes are missing.

Moreover, since the data on accidents provided by ISTAT are aggregated by province, the risk index was calculated at the provincial level, considering all the roads of the single province- together. The Automobile Club Italia (ACI) and other ISTAT databases (not crashes) are used for the computation of exposure factors data.

Table 1. Intermediate outcome factor

Factors	Sub-factors	Exposure factors
Type of vehicle	Passengers car [C] – Bus [B] - Commercial Vehicles [CV] – Motorcycles [M] – other [O]	N° of vehicles by province
Type of road	Motorway [Mw] - State Road [Sr] - Provincial Road [Pr]	Km of road typology by province
Gender of the driver	Male [gM] – Female [gF]	N° of male and female drivers by province
Age class of the driver	14/17 [a1] - 18/29 [a2] – 30/54 [a3] – 55/64 [a4] - + 65 [a5]	N° of drivers for age classes by province

In brackets the acronyms of the sub-factors are reported. They help reading results in Table 2

Therefore, following the steps indicated in Fig. 1, the total frequency of crashes and the associated severities are calculated by applying Eqs. (3) and (4). It should be noted that for the calculation of the latter, the average cost associated with each event was taken from [37]. The reference values are: € 1,503,990.00 for the average annual cost for road deaths and € 42,219 for the injured.

Next, by Eqs. (5) and (6) we predicted $\widehat{H_{i,l}}$ and $\widehat{V_{i,l}}$ for each Italian province. More precisely, the frequency and the severity of crashes are computed by bivariate models, one for each intermediate safety outcome factor i, where $H_{i,l}$ and $V_{i,l}$ are the response variables, and the predictors are represented only by the exposure factor $E_{i,l}$. Coefficients α_i e β_i were estimated by a power function regression. In addition, estimating a vulnerability value for the type of vehicle factors was not possible owing to the aggregated data provided by ISTAT.

Next, each model was evaluated by different goodness-of-fit measures: F-test, the Pearson correlation coefficient (R), R^2 and the adjusted-R^2. In addition, the sign and the significance of the coefficient are evaluated for each model.

Table 2 reports the results of these estimations. Generally speaking, all models provide a good data fit.

As expected, all models give evidence that by increasing exposure factor $E_{i,l}$, $\widehat{H_{i,l}}$ and $\widehat{V_{i,l}}$ increase as well.

As for vehicles, motorcycles have the highest H compared to the other types of vehicles. This result is probably related to the high speeds and the relatively poor safety conditions of motorcyclists, who are still considered as vulnerable road users for their few protection devices.

Focusing on infrastructure factors, the motorway is the safest type for high exposure values. This unexpected result can be explained as follows: at the same traffic volumes, the high standards of highway design provide the highest levels of safety.

Lastly, as for the driver factors, males aged 18 to 29 have the highest values of $\widehat{H_{i,l}}$ and $\widehat{V_{i,l}}$. Inexperience and recklessly behavior may have significantly influenced this result.

Table 2: Regression coefficients

Pattern	F-Test	R	R^2	Adjusted R2	t-stat (p value)
Type of vehicle					
$H_C = 0,002E_C^{1.097}$	483,271	0,906	0,822	0,820	$\alpha_2 = 21.983\ (<.001)$
$H_B = 0.019E_B^{0.967}$	83,051	0,666	0,444	0,439	$\alpha_2 = 9.113\ (<.001)$
$H_{CV} = 0.002E_{CV}^{1.062}$	150,621	0,768	0,589	0,585	$\alpha_2 = 12.273\ (<.001)$
$H_M = 0.0001E_M^{1.393}$	881,235	0,945	0,894	0,893	$\alpha_2 = 29.686\ (<.001)$
$H_O = 0.0005E_O^{1.282}$	263,450	0,846	0,715	0,712	$\alpha_2 = 16.231\ (<.001)$
Type of road					
$H_{Mw} = 0.00003E_{Mw}^{0.915}$	213,768	0,843	0,711	0,707	$\alpha_2 = 14.621\ (<.001)$
$V_{Mw} = 7.749E_{Mw}^{0.863}$	109,805	0,747	0,558	0,553	$\beta_2 = 10.479\ (<.001)$
$H_{Sr} = 0.002E_{Sr}^{0.698}$	139,680	0,757	0,573	0,569	$\alpha_2 = 11.819\ (<.001)$
$V_{Sr} = 382.920E_{Sr}^{0.668}$	108,489	0,715	0,511	0,506	$\beta_2 = 10.416\ (<.001)$
$H_{Pr} = 0.00004E_{Pr}^{0.911}$	151,729	0,770	0,593	0,589	$\alpha_2 = 12.318\ (<.001)$
$V_{Pr} = 4.785E_{Pr}^{0.907}$	131,084	0,747	0,558	0,553	$\beta_2 = 11.449\ (<.001)$
Gender of the driver					
$H_{gM} = 0.002E_{gM}^{1.092}$	652,176	0,929	0,863	0,861	$\alpha_2 = 25.538\ (<.001)$
$V_{gM} = 316.365E_{gM}^{1.008}$	699,106	0,933	0,871	0,869	$\beta_2 = 26.441\ (<.001)$
$H_{gF} = 0.002E_{gF}^{1.050}$	460,165	0,903	0,816	0,814	$\alpha_2 = 21.451\ (<.001)$
$V_{gF} = 92.673E_{gF}^{1.044}$	435,729	0,899	0,807	0,806	$\beta_2 = 20.874\ (<.001)$
Age class of the driver					
$H_{a1} = 0.012E_{a1}^{0.907}$	242,745	0,837	0,700	0,697	$\alpha_2 = 15.580\ (<.001)$
$V_{a1} = 423.802E_{a1}^{0.944}$	197,782	0,810	0,655	0,652	$\beta_2 = 14.063\ (<.001)$
$H_{a2} = 0.003E_{a2}^{1.070}$	552,234	0,917	0,842	0,8400	$\alpha_2 = 23.500\ (<.001)$
$V_{a2} = 316.141E_{a2}^{1.028}$	492,398	0,909	0,826	0,8239	$\beta_2 = 22.190\ (<.001)$
$H_{a3} = 0.001E_{a3}^{1.090}$	601,736	0,923	0,853	0,8512	$\alpha_2 = 24.530\ (<.001)$
$V_{a3} = 110.376E_{a3}^{1.073}$	561,478	0,919	0,844	0,8422	$\beta_2 = 23.696\ (<.001)$
$H_{a4} = 0.002E_{a4}^{1.049}$	394,841	0,890	0,792	0,7895	$\alpha_2 = 19.871\ (<.001)$
$V_{a4} = 268.136E_{a4}^{0.978}$	286,069	0,856	0,733	0,7308	$\beta_2 = 16.914\ (<.001)$
$H_{a5} = 0.001E_{a5}^{1.040}$	355,403	0,880	0,774	0,7714	$\alpha_2 = 18.852\ (<.001)$
$V_{a5} = 299.085E_{a5}^{0.971}$	309,698	0,865	0,749	0,7462	$\beta_2 = 17.598\ (<.001)$

Finally, by Eq. (7), for each province has been calculated the crash risk index R_l. Since the index values are very high, the scale was obtained considering their logarithm. The results are ranked in decreasing order of risk and are shown in Figs. 2, 3, 4 and 5. They show the general risk scale (Fig. 2) and the detailed scale for each R_l risk classification (Figs. 3, 4, 5 and 6, respectively). For sake of clarity, the black lines in Fig. 2 represent the threshold of the lower, middle and upper quartiles, which define the risk classes.

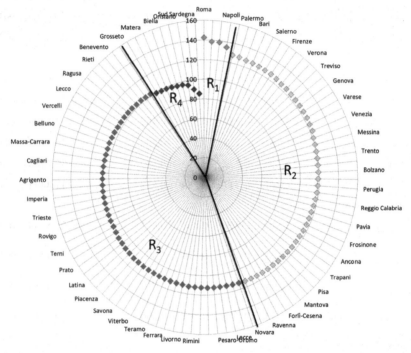

Fig. 2. Risk scale

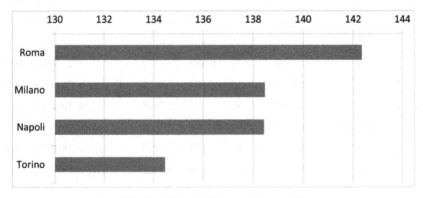

Fig. 3. Risk scale R_1 – maximum risk

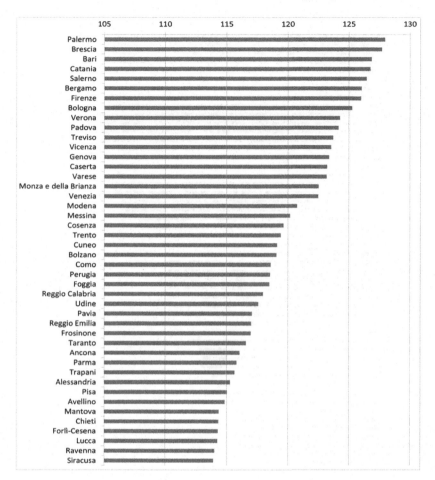

Fig. 4. Risk scale R_2 – high risk

Considering the results at the national context, the provinces ranked as R_1 (i.e., Roma, Milano, Napoli and Torino – Fig. 3) are also four of the largest and important Italian cities, which have very high population densities and a large number of road links. Therefore, due to these conditions, the exposure values are higher than in the other provinces. Conversely, the risk index classifies the Sardinian provinces (marked in yellow) at a medium (Fig. 5) - low risk (Fig. 6). This can be explained in absolute terms by considering the low demand values of the provinces of the island compared to the levels of the remaining Italian provinces.

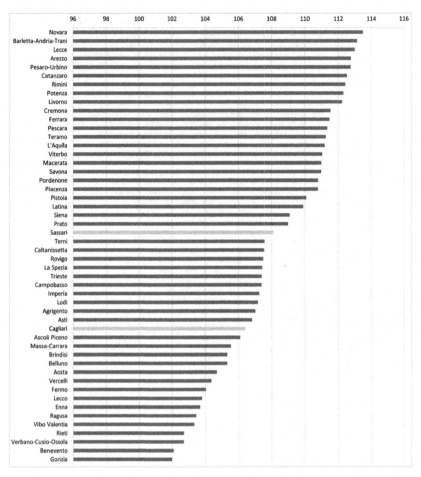

Fig. 5. Risk scale R_3 – average risk

A small-scale analysis, such as the road section, with a disaggregate crashes database, will enable to carry out a more detailed analysis and will enable to look for prevention and/or protection actions for risk mitigation. However, this case study was developed for testing the methodology according to the available data.

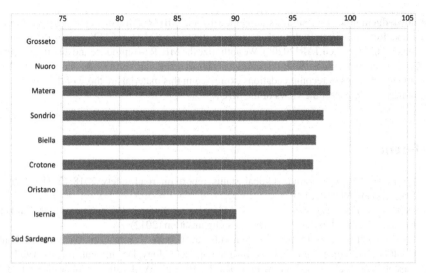

Fig. 6. Risk scale R_4 – low risk

4 Conclusions

In recent years, road safety issue is becoming increasingly important for both public administrations and road users. In this context, the tools for assessing and managing safety performance become even more important. However, to our knowledge, there is a gap in the literature on the assessment of the crash risk in private transport encompassing the requirements of ISO 39001 [2] by considering the frequency and the severity of the crash as a function of exposure factors.

This paper covers this gap by proposing a framework to assess the crash risk in the private transport by integrating safety factors, prediction models of frequency and severity to exposure factors and a risk assessment method. This framework was experimented in a real case study using over 500,000 road crashes data recorded by the Italian National Institute of Statistics ISTAT between 2015 and 2017, which were merged for the 107 Italian provinces. These results helped ranking the road safety of the Italian provinces from a maximum risk score (4 provinces) to a lower risk one (9 provinces) passing through intermediate values of high risk (44 provinces) and average risk (50 provinces). Indeed, this was helpful in identifying areas that require further attention in terms of road safety so that specific strategies can be developed.

Further developments of this research may follow: first, it could be of interest the evaluation of the risk of crashes for road sections using a disaggregate road crashes database, to better analyse the criticalities of this road network. Second, a complex bivariate (frequency and severity) risk model with all intermediate outcome factors and exposure factors will be developed. This model could help derive a compact set of significant factors to explain the frequency and severity of crashes to measure the crash risk for each administrative area, road, or road section.

Acknowledgements. This study is supported by the MIUR (Ministry of Education, Universities and Research [Italy]) through project entitled: the SMART CITY framework (project: PON04a2_00381 "CAGLIARI2020"). We authorize the MIUR to reproduce and distribute reprints for Governmental purposes, notwithstanding any copyright notations thereon. Any opinions, findings and conclusions or recommendations expressed in this material are those of the authors, and do not necessarily reflect the views of the MIUR.

References

1. World Health Organization. Global status report on road safety 2018 (2018). Geneva, Switzerland, WHO (2019)
2. ISO 39001. Road Traffic Safety (RTS) Management Systems: Requirements with Guidance for Use. Geneva: International Standards Organisation (2012)
3. Hydén, C.: The development of a method for traffic safety evaluation: The Swedish Traffic Conflicts Technique. Bulletin Lund Institute of Technology, Department, vol. 70 (1987)
4. Vasconcelos, L., Neto, L., Santos-Pólo, R.L.R., II., Seco, Á.M., Silva, A.B.: Validation of the ssam technique for the assessment of intersections safety. Meet. Transp. Res. Board **38**, 39 (2014)
5. So, J., Hoffmann, S., Lee, J., Busch, F., Choi, K.: A prediction accuracy-practicality tradeoff analysis of the state-of-the-art safety performance assessment methods. Transp. Res. Procedia **15**, 794–805 (2016)
6. Giuffrè, T., Trubia, S., Canale, A., Persaud, B.: Using microsimulation to evaluate safety and operational implications of newer roundabout layouts for European Road networks. Sustainability **9**(11), 2084 (2017)
7. Astarita, V., Festa, D.C., GiofrÃ, V.P.: Microsimulation and the evaluation of safety levels in the presence of roadside obstacles. Eur. Transp. Trasp. Eur. **77**, 1–12 (2020)
8. Tesoriere, G., Campisi, T., Canale, A., ZgrabliÄ, T.: The surrogate safety appraisal of the unconventional elliptical and turbo roundabouts. J. Adv. Transp. **2018**, 1–9 (2018)
9. Yannis, G., et al.: Road safety performance indicators for the interurban road network. Accid. Anal. Prev. **60**, 384–395 (2013)
10. Lynam, D, Sutch, T., Broughton, J, and Lawson, S.D.: European road assessment programme, pilot phase technical report. AA Foundation for Road Safety Research, Farnborough, UK (2003).
11. Lynam, D., Hummel, T., Barker, J., Lawson, S.D.: European road assessment programme, EuroRAP! Technical report. AA Foundation for Road Safety Research, Farnborough, UK (2004)
12. Jamroz, K.: The impact of road network structure and mobility on the national traffic fatality rate. Procedia Soc. Behav. Sci. **54**, 1370–1377 (2012)
13. Khorasani, G., Yadollahi, A., Rahimi, M., Tatari, A.:.Implementation of MCDM methods in road safety management. In: International Conference on Transport, Civil, Architecture and Environment engineering (ICTCAEE'2012), pp. 26–27 (2012)
14. Jamroz, K., & Smolarek, L.: Road safety management tools for country strategic level. In: 16th International Conference Road Safety on Four Continents. Beijing, China (RS4C 2013), 15–17 May 2013 (2013)
15. Gitelman, V., Vis, M., Weijermars, W., Hakkert, S.: Development of road safety performance indicators for the European countries. Adv. Soc. Sci. Res. J. **1**(4), 138–158 (2014)
16. Hughes, B.P., Anund, A., Falkmer, T.: System theory and safety models in Swedish, UK, Dutch and Australian road safety strategies. Accid. Anal. Prev. **74**, 271–278 (2015)

17. Persia, L., et al.: Management of road infrastructure safety. Transp. Res. Procedia **14**, 3436–3445 (2016)
18. Sakhapov, R.L., Nikolaeva, R.V., Gatiyatullin, M.H., Makhmutov, M.M.: Risk management model in road transport systems. J. Phys. Conf. Ser. **738**(1) 012008 (2016)
19. Wegman, F., Berg, H.Y., Cameron, I., Thompson, C., Siegrist, S., Weijermars, W.: Evidence-based and data-driven road safety management. IATSS Res. **39**(1), 19–25 (2015)
20. Sumaila, A.F.: Road crashes trends and safety management in Nigeria. J. Geogr. Regional Plan. **6**(3), 53 (2013)
21. Costescu, D., Raicu, S., Rosca, M., Burciu, S., Rusca, F.: Using intersection conflict index in urban traffic risk evaluation. Procedia Technol. **22**, 319–326 (2016)
22. Bonera, M., Maternini, G.: Methodology for the application of predictive method for road safety analysis in urban areas the case study of Brescia. Transp. Res Procedia **45**, 659–667 (2020)
23. Mahmud, S.S., Ferreira, L., Hoque, M.S., Tavassoli, A.: Micro-level safety risk assessment model for a two-lane heterogeneous traffic environment in a developing country: a comparative crash probability modeling approach. J. Safety Res. **69**, 125–134 (2019)
24. Wu, P., Meng, X., Song, L., Zuo, W.: Crash Risk Evaluation and crash severity pattern analysis for different types of urban junctions: fault tree analysis and association rules approaches. Transp. Res. Rec. **2673**(1), 403–416 (2019)
25. Porcu, F., Olivo, A., Maternini, G., Barabino, B.: Evaluating bus accident risks in public transport. Transp. Res. Procedia **45**, 443–450 (2020)
26. Porcu, F., Olivo, A., Maternini, G., Coni, M., Bonera, M., Barabino, B.: Assessing the risk of bus crashes in transit systems. Eur. Transp. **81**, 4 (2021)
27. Conca, A., Ridella, C., Sapori, E.: A risk assessment for road transportation of dangerous goods: a routing solution. Transp. Res. Procedia **14**, 2890–2899 (2016)
28. Fine, W.T.: Mathematical evaluations for controlling hazards. J. Safety Res. **3**, 157–166 (1971)
29. Ma, J., Kockelman, K.M., Damien, P.: A multivariate Poisson-lognormal regression model for prediction of crash counts by severity, using Bayesian methods. Accid. Anal. Prev. **40**(3), 964–975 (2008)
30. Moghaddam, F.R., Khiavi, M.P., Moghaddam, T.R., Ghorbani, M.A.: Crash severity modeling in urban highways using backward regression method. J. Civil Eng. Arch. **4**(6), 43–49 (2010)
31. Rosolino, V., et al.: Road safety performance assessment: a new road network risk index for info mobility. Procedia. Soc. Behav. Sci. **111**, 624–633 (2014). https://doi.org/10.1016/j.sbs pro.2014.01.096
32. Casado-Sanz, N., Guirao, B., Attard, M.: Analysis of the risk factors affecting the severity of traffic accidents on Spanish crosstown roads: the driver's perspective. Sustainability **12**(6), 2237 (2020)
33. AAAM.: The Abbreviated Injury Scale, 1990 revision. Des Plaines, IL: Association for the Advancement of Automotive Medicine (1990)
34. Mannering, F.L., Bhat, C.R.: Analytic methods in accident research: methodological frontier and future directions. Anal. Methods Accid. Res. **1**, 1–22 (2014)
35. Cheung, C., Shalaby, A., Persaud, B., Hadayeghi, A.: Models for safety analysis of road surface transit. Transp. Res. Rec. **2063**, 168–175 (2008)
36. D'Agostino, C.: Reliability-based assessment of benefits in roadway safety management. Transp. Res. Rec. J. Transp. Res. Board **2513**, 1–10 (2015)
37. Ministero delle Infrastrutture e dei Trasporti, M.D.I.: Studio di valutazione dei Costi Sociali dell'incidentalità stradale (2010)

Urban Accessibility to Healthcare Facilities for the Elderly: Evolution of the Time-Based 2SFCA Methodology for the Nice Case Study (France)

Carmen Guida[1], Carmela Gargiulo[1], Matteo Caglioni[2], and Gerardo Carpentieri[1]([✉])

[1] Department of Civil, Building and Environmental Engineering,
University of Naples Federico II, Naples, Italy
gerardo.carpentieri@unina.it

[2] Department of Geography, Urban Planning and Sustainable Environment,
CNRS, UMR 7300 ESPACE, Université Côte d'Azur, Nice, France

Abstract. This study proposes a GIS-based methodology to measure accessibility to urban services, from the elderly perspective to support urban planning processes. In the light of a significant demographic change, policymakers should promote age-friendly urban planning approaches in order to guarantee equal opportunities to access to services and activities. We developed a methodology to measure accessibility to healthcare provision services, which considers urban characteristics and mobility features, as well as behavioral traits of older adults. The method belongs to the family of 2SFCA (Two-Steps Floating Catchment Area), which evaluates accessibility as the combination of both supply and demand of urban services; thus, we introduce innovative elements to shape actual mobility opportunities for the elderly and their travel choices within three different timeslots. The methodology was applied to the city of Nice (France), to measure accessibility to proximity services managed by Healthcare Regional Agency (l'Agence Régionale de Santé – ARS) of Provence, Alpes and Côte d'Azur. The outputs allow to quantify elderly people accessibility to primary health services and the application to the French case study has shown that the methodology could be effective to identify critical issues to support urban planning process.

Keywords: Urban accessibility · Elderly · Proximity healthcare facilities · GIS

1 Introduction

In Europe the share and number of older people will increase. The proportion of population aged 65 and over is expected to increase to 30.3% by 2070, compared to 20.3% in 2019, and 13.2% is projected to be aged 80 years or older, compared to 5.8% in 2019 [1]. Although Europe is by no means the only continent with an ageing population, the process is most advanced here. It is driven by a significant increase in life expectancy and lower birth rates, which is affecting EU countries in a variety of ways. For instance,

© Springer Nature Switzerland AG 2021
O. Gervasi et al. (Eds.): ICCSA 2021, LNCS 12958, pp. 588–602, 2021.
https://doi.org/10.1007/978-3-030-87016-4_42

in 2018, life expectancy at birth increased to 78.2 years for men and 83.7 for women and this growth is projected to continue: men born in 2070 are expected to live 86 years, and women 90 [2]. Hence, on average, Europeans will enjoy longer lives.

This trend is having a significant impact on people's everyday lives and on our societies. It has implications for economic growth, fiscal sustainability, health and long-term care, well-being and social cohesion [3, 4]. Thus, the Covid-19 pandemic has disproportionately impacted on older people – in terms of hospitalizations and deaths – and it has highlighted some of the vulnerabilities, and consequent challenges, that an ageing population poses on health and social care. Moreover, social isolation, loneliness, and depression due to age-associated limitations may affect the opportunities that can potentially arise within 'silver' age: elderly people are fundamental resources for their families and for the communities in which they live [5].

Healthy and active ageing is a personal choice and responsibility, but it depends heavily on the environment in which people live and public policies can play a significant supporting role [6]. Along with an increasing interest, age-friendly urban planning interventions have emerged as an urgent need on national, regional and local agendas. Within these issues, living near services has been shown to be important for older adults in performing activities to meet daily needs, including access to food shopping, healthcare provision, public transportation, banking, social and sportive clubs [7, 8]. As essential service within the supply of urban areas, healthcare facilities may play a key role to ensure a good level of spatial equity and quality of life for the elderly [9]. These issues span multiple fields: social sciences, urban and regional planning, transport planning, health geography, information and communication technologies (ICTs) [10].

The evaluation of accessibility to essential services provides a spatial analytical perspective to assess whether or not, and to what degree, the distribution of urban public facilities is equitable [11]. Accessibility measures reflect the potential availability of healthcare facilities, if based on solid theoretical ground, by revealing the ability of different people to overcome spatial, physical, temporal and socioeconomic barriers to healthcare provision [12, 13].

Studies over the past two decades have provided significant development for measuring spatial accessibility to public services. The two-step floating catchment area (2SFCA) method, based in GIS (Geographical Information System) environment, is the most widely applied measure of spatial accessibility due to its operability [14]. A growing body of cross-sectional research has enhanced and improved the theoretical foundation and applicability of 2SFCA. Although many researchers have provided several gateways to the accessibility paradigm, there has been no reasonable mechanism to integrate results of urban public facility measures into an overall evaluation scheme suitable for easy and intuitive use by planners. Moreover, far too little attention has been paid to develop methodologies that should be easily applied and interpreted to heterogeneous urban contexts.

This paper traces the development of an enhanced 2SFCA method to evaluate accessibility to healthcare facilities and provides the results of its application to Nice, France. This work is part of a wider research project, whose partners are the Department of Civil, Building and Environmental Engineering at University of Naples Federico II (Naples, Italy), the research laboratory UMR ESPACE at Université Côte d'Azur (Nice, France) and Energent S.p.A. (Rome, Italy), that aims at providing a decision-making support tool for facing elderly people's needs in ordinary conditions as well as other operating scenarios. Hence, the primary aims of this paper are: (i) to apply and, hence, validate the methodology for a case study in Nice, France; (ii) to demonstrate that results can be translated into takeaways for practice, according to a holistic approach.

This paper has been divided into five paragraphs. Following this introduction, we present a literature review, in order to highlight how the accessibility paradigm has evolved in urban planning, how it has been introduced in assessment methodologies and, finally, which are the main traits of research design. The third paragraph focuses on the proposed method. Following, the results of the application to the city of Nice are discussed. In the final paragraph the key features of the methodology evolutions, according to the results of its applications to Naples, Milan (Italy) and Nice (France), and the conclusions of the work are presented.

2 Literature Review

Ensuring good health and promoting well-being are among the sustainable development goals of the United Nations Agenda 2030 program [15]. Hence, equal accessibility to healthcare is recognized as a universal key for improving quality of life and should drive decision-making processes for urban and transport planners, as well as for healthcare providers [16, 17]. Due to the increasing political and scientific interest on the topic, several methods and approaches were produced to determine healthcare accessibility at different levels. At the same time, since geographical analyses of spatial equity rely on different measures, the conceptualization of accessibility is a key issue to understand their results and sensitivity [18, 19].

The earliest studies of the topic defined accessibility as the count of facilities within a geographical unit. Thus, spatial accessibility also refers to the relative ease by which people can reach the locations of facilities and activities, from a given location. This approach implicitly considers factors such as spatial externalities, physical and natural barriers, the structure of transport network, the frictional effect of distance, properties of the supply side, safety and socioeconomic issues [20]. According to this approach, in our research, we understand accessibility as an inherent feature of urban environment, which may explain the competitiveness and social justice of a territorial unit, compared to another.

Thanks to the availability of reliable big data and the processing capabilities of GIS-based technologies, researchers are developing advanced quantitative methods and procedures to evaluate accessibility to urban services, according to this holistic approach. However, there have been very few reasonable mechanisms to integrate academic results of urban public services measure into an overall evaluation scheme, suitable for intuitive and easy use by planners [21, 22].

The simplest way to assess healthcare accessibility is to use contour measures (or opportunity measures), which define catchment areas by drawing one or more travel time contours around a node of interest and measuring the number of opportunities (facilities, services and activities) within each contour. This measure is easy to compute and understand, but suffers of a poor theoretical basis, since it is not possible to weight different distances within the same area in evaluating accessibility. Moreover, in a metropolis where many alternatives exist the distance to the nearest primary care service does not match the people's demand.

In order to define catchment areas by measuring travel impediment on a continuous scale, gravity measures were introduced: even though they are more accurate representations of travel resistance than contour measures, they tend to be less readable and neglect the variation across individuals living in the same area [23]. The Two-Steps Floating Catchment Area (2SFCA) is among the most widely used gravity-based methodologies to evaluate accessibility. In order to fill the gap between scientific theories and real practices, it takes into account the main urban, individual and mobility variables within a user-friendly procedure. It is a special application of a gravity model and it was proposed for the first time by Luo and Wang in 2003 [24]. From its first application, the method has been further developed and enhanced. Scientific literature proposes many examples of 2SFCA application to evaluate accessibility to services at different territorial scales and according to different social and age perspectives. For instance, researchers investigated spatial accessibility to urban public facilities, such as parks [25, 26], physicians [27], compulsory schools [28], but also to rural green areas [29], hospitals [30–32] and eldercare centers [25]. The latter facilities tend to have larger service areas, crossing the administrative boundaries of a city or a region. Hence, when designing 2SFCA methods researchers have to answers preliminary questions: the first refers to the demand point (population) of public facilities, which usually is the smallest census area. The smaller the research unit, the more detailed accessibility differences can be obtained. The second question concerns the extent of study area, which has to take into account several issues: firstly, the actual catchment area size of the service and its temporal modification, between weekdays and holydays, or throughout the day; secondly, in order to support decision-making processes with reliable academic findings, the study area should match the administrative domain of policymakers and involved stakeholders (e.g., transport companies and healthcare providers).

Our work aims at contributing to both methodological and practical terms within the debate of urban accessibility. Hence, we answered the previous questions with an enhanced research design, in order to evaluate spatial and temporal accessibility to proximity healthcare services, from the elderly perspective, and systematically consider features from both supply and demand sides.

3 Research Design

We propose an enhanced method to evaluate accessibility to urban services and facilities, and to point out spatial and temporal inequalities among elderly population. This paragraph summarizes the newest advancement of a wider research project, whose aim is to develop an operational methodology to support decision-making processes in order to turn cities into *age-friendly* environments [33]. As highlighted in the previous paragraph, the methodology has been designed and applied in a GIS environment to take advantage of its storing, analyzing, and visualizing capabilities. What we are describing now is the third phase of a wider research design: starting from a methodological hypothesis, we enhanced and modified it through consecutive validation steps, by applying the methodology to heterogeneous case studies. We measured accessibility to primary healthcare facilities from the elderly perspective for Naples, Milan (Italy) and Nice (France), which differ from each other for territorial and orographic contexts, socioeconomic issues and administrative rules. Moreover, while designing the methodology, we considered the availability of open and reliable data as a key issue, in order to turn the results of our research into real-world practices.

At the same time, we paid attention to the theoretical bases of the methodology that takes cue from the 2SFCA procedure, described in previous paragraph. The method developed by Luo and Wang in 2003 only represents the starting point of our research. In fact, it was enhanced with additional variables and steps to address the actual mobility capital for people aged 65 and over and improved following the findings of each case study application [34, 35].

As concerns the components of urban and mobility systems, both supply and demand-side features were considered, since the level of accessibility in an urban environment depends on the interactions between supply and demand. In particular, the demand for healthcare provisions consists of population distribution P_i, where i refers to the smallest territorial unit, a 50-m-side hexagonal cell [36, 37]. The use of hexagonal grid (rather than a square one or census track) is preferred when dealing with problems related to the connectivity of different space units and identifying shorter paths for calculating travel distances [38]. Due to geometric issues, the hexagonal grid provides a substantially better match between distances measured in grid units and straight line (Euclidean) distances, which might make a coarse hexagonal grid more acceptable for modelling dispersal than a square or rectangular grid. Another advantage of the hexagonal grid is its greater clarity when used for visualization.

On the supply-side, the land-use component is described by the combination of healthcare structures (j) locations and their resources $– S_j –$ described, for instance, by the number of working physicians, available beds or surface of buildings (m^2).

In order to include features on the supply-side of transport facilities, we developed a multimodal network to run time travel analyses. The network is made of walkable roads and transit (bus and metro) lines. The residential locations of dwellers, approximated to the barycenter of hexagonal cells $– i –$ were considered as origins of multimodal travel journeys to reach healthcare facilities.

The most innovative aspect of the developed study is the introduction of variables and feature that take into account the behaviors of the elderly population, such as their dependence on public transport and their reduced use of private cars. In other words, the study introduced characteristics linked to the behavior of the population, considering them essential to improve accessibility to places and services of the urban system.

We introduced Gaussian distance-decay functions $– W_{i,j} –$ [39], one per age group, in order to consider the degressive mobility capital of elderly people while ageing. Moreover, we attributed decreasing walking speeds by age group (65–69; 70–74; $\geq$ 75) to the links of pedestrian network, to measure travel time $t_{i,j}$ to get from origins i to healthcare facilities j. The computation of travel time is the second innovative feature of the methodology: in order to evaluate travel times from each hexagonal cell to the main local health buildings, we created a multimodal transport network. We considered the network as the combination of both walkable streets and local public transport lines (bus and metro) in order to better simulate elderly mobility habits.

$$W_{ij} = e^{-t_{ij}^2/\beta} \tag{1}$$

According to Lindemann *et al.* [40] and Rydwik *et al.* [41], we introduced decreasing walking speed for each age group: 0.8 m/s for those aged 65–69; 0.7 m/s for people aged between 70–74; 0.6 m/s for the oldest (≥ 75). As far as for the Gaussian distance-decay functions, their main characteristic is that they quickly decrease when time travel increases and gets close to the maximum time that each elderly age category manages to hold (according to their physical capabilities) to access health services. Moreover, as people age, their mobility capital decreases; hence, the inverse of impedance coefficients β were set equal to 180 for people aged between 65–69, 160 for those between 70–74 and 140 for those aged 75 and over, to best represent mobility attitudes of different elderly age categories according to outcomes in the scientific literature [42]. The last component relates to the variable accessibility perceived by dwellers due to temporal issues. The transport network model is based on GTFS (General Transit Feed Specification) data to run separate temporal analyses and evaluate accessibility variations during a weekday. The input data described above are essential features to process the method, which consists of two consecutive steps, described by the following formulas.

$$R_j = \frac{S_j \cdot \left(\frac{S_j}{S}\right)}{\sum_{65-69} P_i \cdot W_{ij}^{65-69} + \sum_{70-74} P_i \cdot W_{ij}^{70-74} + \sum_{>75} P_i \cdot W_{ij}^{>75}} \tag{2}$$

$$A_i = \sum_{65-69} R_j \cdot W_{ij}^{65-69} + \sum_{70-74} R_j \cdot W_{ij}^{70-74} + \sum_{>75} R_j \cdot W_{ij}^{>75} \tag{3}$$

R_j is the supply-demand ratio of each healthcare structure, while Ai refers to the overall accessibility to each i hexagonal cell's primary healthcare provision. For the representation of results by the GIS in maps and tables, the proposed method implements a quantile classification of measured accessibility in ten levels, from level 1 (low accessibility) to level 10 (high accessibility). The quantile classification is defined as cumulated accessibility values considering the three age categories [43].

4 The Case Study

Nice is the fifth French city for number of inhabitants (over 340,000) and population density of 4.762 inh./Km^2 (INSEE, 2017). The city is close to the France-Italian border, 20 km away the Monaco Principality. The city stretches from the sea to the Alpes, with a 71.92 Km^2 surface, and 520 m total ascent. It is divided into nine urban administrative districts, which are named cantons. The share of elderly people in Nice, in the 2017, is over 24% (48,102 women and 32,819 men). Table 1 shows the distribution of elderly people in the nine city cantons, and Fig. 1 displays in detail the localization of the elderly. The highest shares of people aged 65 and over live in T2, T4, T6, T5 and T9 cantons.

Like other European Welfare States, France provides to citizens a system of universal health care, which is largely financed by the government through a system of national

Table 1. Elderly people distribution and primary health center in the city districts of Nice.

Districts		Number of Primary health center		
	Elderly	Morning	Afternoon	Evening
T1 - Plaine du Var	6,823	2	2	0
T2 - Ouest Littoral & Coteaux	12,100	1	0	0
T3 - Collines niçoises	9,159	2	2	1
T4 - Centre Ouest	11,045	3	3	0
T5 - Centre Nord	10,081	3	3	0
T6 - Centre Est Trois Collines	10,254	4	4	1
T7 - Rives du Paillon	4,824	0	0	0
T8 - Coeur de Paillon	6,550	3	3	0
T9 - Est Littoral	10,085	2	2	1
	80,921	20	19	3

health insurance. However, there are some major differences in the structure of the French healthcare system and in its financing, versus its EU peers. Most crucially, France spends over 11% of GDP on health care, much higher than the EU average. The French healthcare provision is based on a Social Security system, which is available to all and comprises a fully integrated and capillary network of public hospitals, private clinics, doctors and other health professionals. It is a multi-payer system which provides medical care for all citizens regardless of age, income or social status.

In a recent document published by the French Ministry of Healthcare and Solidarity, it turns out that 99,9% of French citizens access to a physician within 20 min. At the same time, the ministry highlights that, because of healthcare supply distribution, it fails to meet the demand for care, in some territories. The Healthcare Regional Agency (l'Agence régionale de santé – ARS) of Provence, Alpes and Côte d'Azur developed in 2018 a regional strategy to strengthen and assure equal accessibility to territorial services, through the Territorial Plan of Accessibility (PTAS – Plan Territorial d'Accès aux Soins). The plan is mostly focused on the increasing share of people aged 65 and over, promoting higher accessibility to proximity healthcare facilities, in particular to polyclinic centers (Maisons de Santé Pluriprofessionnelles, Centre de Santé and Communauté Professionnelle Territorial de Santé).

The healthcare system of such services for the city of Nice and dedicated to elderly people is made of 20 facilities. They were selected from France OpenData database (2021). Each center offers a variable number of primary health services, from 10 to 1. The data of health services located in each structure was collect consulting the open-access information available on the websites. Also, the opening hours are different for each center, and this feature was taken into account to assess temporal variation of accessibility, within a weekday. Table 1 compares the number of open centers for each timeslot in the districts. For this application, we consider only the public primary health centers located in the city of Nice.

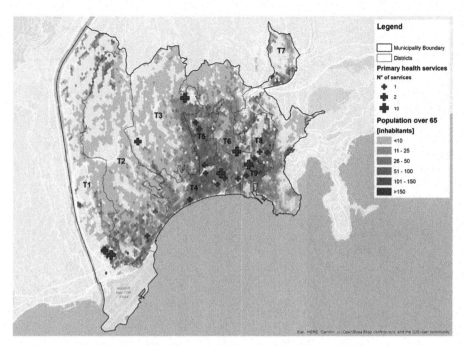

Fig. 1. The elderly people location in the city of Nice.

For the mobility component, we created a multimodal network of Nice, using ArcGIS tools to connect the walking roads network and GTFS (General Transit Feed Specification) data into a network dataset and to evaluate the total travel times. First, Open-StreetMap data was used to create the walking network, taking into account only pedestrian roads and their slope. For this application, we consider the pedestrian network's slope because it is a significant aspect in Nice that influences the readiness to walk, especially for the elderly people. Then, GTFS data of 2020 from the Transit Company of Nice (Lignes d'Azur) were used to add bus and tram lines and stops in the local transport network. Since public transport is not a continuous service in space and time, additional modelling operations were needed to join the pedestrian system to the public transit system (Fig. 2). Once the multimodal network was ready, the ArcGIS Network Analyst tool was used to compute an OD (Origin and Destination) matrix, showing the total travel time to get from a generic hexagonal cell to the city healthcare centers.

For the application to the city of Nice, we evaluated the level of urban accessibility to 20 ambulatories that serve over 80,000 old people in three different timeslots (Morning, Afternoon and Evening). The available health services of each healthcare center were addressed as the number of surgeons of interest to the elderly, that are: cardiology, dentistry, urology, otolaryngology, ophthalmology, dermatology, orthopedics, pulmonology, diabetology, rehabilitation, neurology.

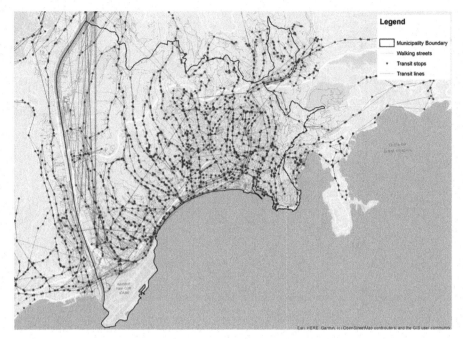

Fig. 2. The walking and transit network in the city of Nice.

5 Results and Discussion

In this paragraph, we present the outcomes of EM2SFCA methodology application in the city of Nice. We considered three different age groups (young elderly, medium elderly and old elderly) and three timeslots (morning, afternoon and evening). Figure 3 presents the results of evaluating the total accessibility for elderly people at primary health services in the selected city for the three-time scenarios. According to scientifically established and widespread practices (PTAL – Transport for London), ten accessibility levels' thresholds were chosen though a quantile classification. These accessibility values are represented in ten classes following a color gradient from the red (very poor accessibility) to the green (very good accessibility). The primary health services are added to the three different maps in Fig. 3 following their opening and closing timetables. As morning time, we considered 6 am to 12 pm, afternoon time from 12 pm to 6 pm, and evening time after 6 pm. Hence, the GIS analyses were run for a 9 am scenario, 4 pm and 8 pm scenarios.

In the three maps in Fig. 3, we can easily recognize some specific spatial patterns. The historical center of Nice always shows a good accessibility during the day (characterized by green color independently by the timeslot). In the morning and afternoon also the two main valleys in Nice are show a high accessibility towards the primary health services: the one in the middle with the Magnan river and the one on the west with the Var river. The hills of Nice are permanently characterized by lower values of accessibility to the primary health services, due to the distinctive street network configuration and the difficulty for the public transport system to serve all low-density subdivisions on the separate hills.

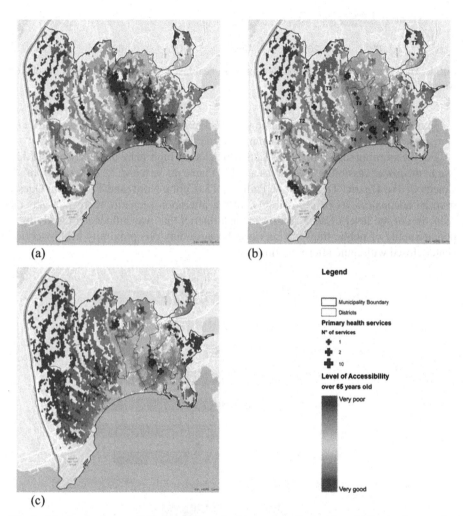

Fig. 3. The level of accessibility at primary health services in the city of Nice in the morning scenario (a), in the afternoon scenario (b) and in the evening scenario (c).

Figure 4 shows the comparison between the three-time scenarios (morning, afternoon and evening) in the city of Nice. The frequency of each one of the ten accessibility levels is represented in a proportional staked bar histogram. In the morning time, the first five worst classes (from red to yellow) correspond only to 20% of the total values, which augment to 30% in the afternoon and to 70% in the evening. It is interesting to note that the worst class do not increase significatively during the day: The travel time to join an open service increase, but nevertheless this one remains accessible.

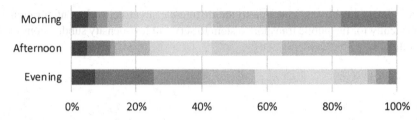

Fig. 4. The comparison of accessibility at primary health services for the elderly in the city of Nice for the three-time scenarios.

Figures 5, 6 and 7 show the variation of accessibility levels in each urban district of Nice in the morning, afternoon and evening scenarios.

For the morning scenario, the districts which have a high share of elderly people that live in the low accessibility level areas are T1 (Plaine du Var) and T2 (Ouest Littoral & Coteaux). The District T8 (Coeur de Paillon), T5 (Centre Nord) and T4 (Centre Ouest) have an adequate level of accessibility. In the afternoon scenario, there is a general reduction of the level of accessibility in each district that was influenced mostly by a poorer supply of public transport services, because only one proximity health service center closed within the afternoon timeslot.

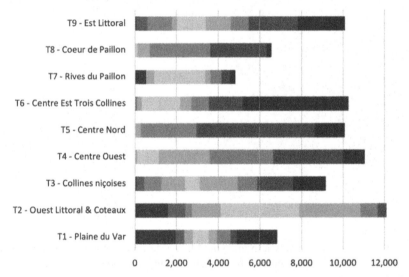

Fig. 5. The levels of accessibility for the three elderly categories in the morning scenario for the city of Nice.

There is a diffuse reduction of perceived accessibility, due to a reduced provision of healthcare services during the evening timeslot: the number of available centers is only three.

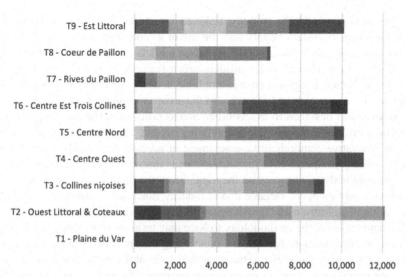

Fig. 6. The levels of accessibility for the three elderly categories in the afternoon scenario for the city of Nice.

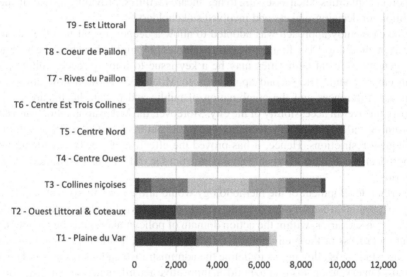

Fig. 7. The levels of accessibility for the three elderly categories in the evening scenario for the city of Nice.

6   Conclusion

In the last decades, the growth of elderly people in industrialized nations and in urban areas increased the needs for specific services for this group of inhabitants. So, the proximity services need to be properly designed: structures' locations, the types of services, the transport system supply and the urban morphology are some of the main features influencing users' accessibility to urban services. This study developed a GIS-based 2SFCA methodology that considers urban features, both from the supply and demand side. Hence, the proposed measure for evaluating urban accessibility considers the balance between needs and resources of the urban environment. Moreover, since the methodology was designed to assess urban accessibility from the elderly perspective, we consider this age category's limited mobility capital. The present methodology provides an innovative comprehensive assessment of accessibility in urban environment, from the elderly perspective. In particular, it adds innovative and practical takeaways to the growing body of literature on the topic. From the methodological point of view, the current study employs variable distance-decay functions, walking speeds and the combination of pedestrian and transit networks to assess elderly mobility capital.

The application of the methodology to Nice may be affected by some limits due the lack of available and more recent data, concerning transport and healthcare provision features. Hence, the results refer to the measured accessibility only to a share of a wider healthcare provision system, in particular to proximity facilities which are the focus of ARS for the elderly dwelling in Provence, Alpes and Cote d'Azur Region. At the same time, the results show the effectiveness of the methodology to evaluate spatial and temporal inequalities when assessing to healthcare facilities, providing a state-of-the-art condition for decision-makers and involved stakeholders.

The case-study approach was adopted to allow a deeper insight into the enhanced 2SFCA methodology. The first application to Naples [34] highlighted how the healthcare management by local authorities may be a key issue to improve accessibility within urban environment. The second application to Milan [35] showed how almost zero altimetric differences and the combination of public and private healthcare facilities improve the overall accessibility of the city. Moreover, the Milan application was run for an ordinary and an emergency scenario, due to the outbreak of Covid-19 infection and consequent restrictions. Hence, it has proved the effectiveness of the methodology to support decision-makers in urban planning practices in ordinary as well as in emergency scenarios.

Further development of the methodology would allow not only to evaluate accessibility to essential urban services from the elderly perspective, but also to identify possible intervention scenarios, within the action domain of policymakers and stakeholders. The evolution process of the methodology, throughout the applications of three representative case studies, is allowing us to define the administrative and territorial limits of that domain of intervention, in order to build an innovative and efficient accessibility-oriented tool, to support policymakers' decisions and finally fill the hiatus between real-world practices and academic knowledge.

References

1. European Commission: Green Paper on Ageing. Fostering solidarity and responsibil-ity between generations. European Commission, Brussells (2021). https://ec.europa.eu/info/sites/info/files/1_en_act_part1_v8_0.pdf
2. Eurostat: Ageing Europe — 2019 edition. Eurostat, Brussels (2020)

3. Ilinca, S., Rodrigues, R., Schmidt, A., Zólymi, E.: Gender and social class inequali-ties in active ageing: policy meets theory. European Centre for Social Welfare Policy and Research, Wien (2016)
4. Sadana, R., Blas, E., Budhwani, S., Koller, T., Paraje, G.: Healthy ageing: raising awareness of inequalities, determinants, and what could be done to improve health equity. Gerontologist **56**(Suppl_2), 178–193 (2016)
5. Melo, L.A.D., Ferreira, L.M.D.B.M., Santos, M.M.D., Lima, K.C.D.: Socioeco-nomic, regional and demographic factors related to population ageing. Revista Bra-sileira de Geriatria e Gerontologia **20**(4), 493–501 (2017)
6. Mouratidis, K.: Compact city, urban sprawl, and subjective well-being. Cities **92**, 261–272 (2019)
7. Tijeras, E., González-García, L., Postigo, S.: The relationship between social support, basic psychological needs satisfaction and well-being in elderly adults. Europ. J. Health Res. **6**(2), 133–143 (2021)
8. Sazali, M.F., Zainol, H., Ab Dulhamid, H., Yetti, A.E.: Urban green open space as a health resilience catalyst for the elderly. Environ. Behav. Proc. J. **6**(16) (2021)
9. Yamada, T., Chen, C.C., Murata, C., Hirai, H., Ojima, T., Kondo, K.: Access disparity and health inequality of the elderly: unmet needs and delayed healthcare. Int. J. Environ. Res. Public Health **12**(2), 1745–1772 (2015)
10. Guida, C., Caglioni, M.: Urban accessibility: the paradox, the paradigms and the measures. A scientific review. TeMA – J. Land Use Mobility Environ. **13**(2), 149–168 (2020)
11. Rossetti, S.: Planning for Accessibility and Safety. Theoretical Framework and Research Methodologies to Address People Friendly Mobility, Maggioli, Rimini (2020), ISBN 978-88-916-4311-7
12. Bhat, C., Handy, S., Kockelman, K., Mahmassani, H., Chen, Q., Weston, L.: Accessibility measures: formulation considerations and current applications. University of Texas at Austin, Center for Transportation Research (2000)
13. Banister, D.: Transport for all. Transp. Rev. **39**(3), 289–292 (2019)
14. Silva, C., Bertolini, L., te Brömmelstroet, M., Milakis, D., Papa, E.: Accessibility instruments in planning practice: bridging the implementation gap. Transp. Policy **53**, 135–145 (2017)
15. United Nations: Transforming Our World: The 2030 Agenda for Sustainable Devel-opment. United Nations, New York (2015). http://bit.ly/TransformAgendaSDG-pd
16. Ko-Wan, T., Yu-Ting, H., Yao-Lin, C.: An accessibility-based integrated measure of relative spatial equity in urban public facilities. Cities **22**, 424–435 (2005)
17. Baudet-Michel, S., Chouraqui, J., Conti, B., Guiraud, N., Le Neindre, C., Toutin, G.: The shrinkage of justice and hospital facilities in small French cities (200–2016). Geografiska Annaler: Series B, Human Geography, 1(23) (2021)
18. Geurs, K.T., Van Wee, B.: Accessibility evaluation of land-use and transport strat-egies: review and research directions. J. Transp. Geography **12**(2), 127–140 (2004)
19. Cui, M., Levinson, D.: Full cost accessibility. J. Transport Land Use **11**(1), 661–679 (2018)
20. Cui, M., Levinson, D.: Full cost accessibility. J. Transport Land Use **11**(1), 661–679 (2019)
21. Geurs, K.T., Van Wee, B.: Accessibility evaluation of land-use and transport strategies: review and research directions. J. Transp. Geogr. **12**(2), 127–140 (2004)
22. Farrington, J., Farrington, C.: Rural accessibility, social inclusion and social justice: towards conceptualisation. J. Transp. Geogr. **13**(1), 1–12 (2005)
23. Scheurer, J., Curtis, C.: Accessibility Measures: Overview and Practical Applications. Impacts of Transit Led Development in a New Rail Corridor, Working Paper No. 4 (2007)
24. Luo, W., Wang, F.: Measures of spatial accessibility to health care in a GIS environment: synthesis and a case study in the Chicago region. Environ. Plann. B. Plann. Des. **30**(6), 865–884 (2003)

25. Guo, S., et al.: Accessibility to urban parks for elderly residents: perspectives from mobile phone data. Landscape Urban Planning **191**, 103642 (2019)
26. Hu, L., Zhao, C., Wang, M., Su, S., Weng, M., Wang, W.: Dynamic healthy food accessibility in a rapidly urbanizing metropolitan area: socioeconomic inequality and relative contribution of local factors. Cities **105**, 102819 (2020)
27. Stentzel, U., Piegsa, J., Fredrich, D., Hoffmann, W., van den Berg, N.: Accessibility of general practitioners and selected specialist physicians by car and by public transport in a rural region of Germany. BMC Health Serv. Res. **16**(1), 1–10 (2016)
28. Gao, Y., He, Q., Liu, Y., Zhang, L., Wang, H., Cai, E.: Imbalance in spatial accessibility to primary and secondary schools in china: guidance for education sustainability. Sustainability **8**(12), 1236 (2016)
29. Shi, L., Halik, Ü., Abliz, A., Mamat, Z., Welp, M.: Urban green space accessibility and distribution equity in an arid oasis city: Urumqi. China. Forests **11**(6), 690 (2020)
30. Cheng, G., et al.: Spatial difference analysis for accessibility to high level hospitals based on travel time in Shenzhen. China. Habitat Int. **53**, 485–494 (2016)
31. Yang, Y., Mueller, N.J., Croes, R.R.: Market accessibility and hotel prices in the Caribbean: the moderating effect of quality-signaling factors. Tour. Manage. **56**, 40–51 (2016)
32. Nakamura, T., Nakamura, A., Mukuda, K., Harada, M., Kotani, K.: Potential accessibility scores for hospital care in a province of Japan: GIS-based ecological study of the two-step floating catchment area method and the number of neighborhood hospitals. BMC Health Serv. Res. **17**(1), 1–7 (2017)
33. Carpentieri, G., Gargiulo, C., Guida, C.: The elderly and urban accessibility before and during the Covid-19 lockdown: a comparative analysis of Mediterranean cities with a focus on Naples and Milan. In: Mediterranean Economies 2020, 215–246 (2020). ISBN:978-88-15-29082
34. Carpentieri, G., Guida, C., Masoumi, H.E.: Multimodal accessibility to primary health services for the elderly: a case study of Naples. Italy. Sustainability **12**(3), 781 (2020)
35. Guida, C., & Carpentieri, G.: Quality of life in the urban environment and primary health services for the elderly during the Covid-19 pandemic: an application to the city of Milan (Italy). Cities, **110,** 103038 (2021)
36. Papa, E., Carpentieri, G., & Guida, C.: Measuring walking accessibility to public transport for the elderly: the case of Naples. TeMA – J. Land Use Mob. Environ. 105–116 (2018)
37. Rossetti, S., Tiboni, M.: In Field Assessment of Safety, Security, Comfort and Accessibility of Bus Stops: a Planning Perspective, European Transport, Issue n. 80, December 2020, Paper n° 8, ISSN 1825–3997 (2020)
38. Kibambe Lubamba, J.P., Radoux, J., Defourny, P.: Multimodal accessibility modeling from coarse transportation networks in Africa. Int. J. Geogr. Inf. Sci. **27**(5), 1005–1022 (2013)
39. Kwan, M.P.: Space-time and integral measures of individual accessibility: A comparative analysis using a point-based framework. Geographical Analysis **30**(3). Ohio State University Press, (1998).
40. Lindemann, U., et al.: Distance to achieve steady state walking speed in frail elderly persons. Gait Posture **27**(1), 91–96 (2008)
41. Rydwik, E., Bergland, A., Forsen, L., Frändin, K.: Investigation into the reliability and validity of the measurement of elderly people's clinical walking speed: a systematic review. Physiother. Theory Pract. **28**(3), 238–256 (2012)
42. Bauer, J., & Groneberg, D. A.: Measuring spatial accessibility of health care providers–introduction of a variable distance decay function within the floating catchment area (FCA) method. PloS One **11**(7), e0159148 (2016)
43. Zhu, X., Tong, Z., Liu, X., Li, X., Lin, P., Wang, T.: An improved two-step floating catchment area method for evaluating spatial accessibility to urban emergency shelters. Sustainability **10**(7), 218 (2018)

A New Vision on Smart and Resilient Urban Mobility in the Aftermath of the Pandemic: Key Factors on European Transport Policies

Tiziana Campisi[1](✉) ⓘ, Chiara Garau[2](✉) ⓘ, Matteo Ignaccolo[3] ⓘ, Mauro Coni[2] ⓘ, Antonino Canale[1] ⓘ, Giuseppe Inturri[4] ⓘ, and Vincenza Torrisi[3](✉) ⓘ

[1] Faculty of Engineering and Architecture, University of Enna Kore, 94100 Enna, Italy
tiziana.campisi@unikore.it
[2] Department of Civil and Environmental Engineering and Architecture, University of Cagliari, 09129 Cagliari, Italy
cgarau@unica.it
[3] Department of Civil Engineering and Architecture, University of Catania, 95125 Catania, Italy
vtorrisi@dica.unict.it
[4] Department of Electric Electronic and Computer Engineering, University of Catania, Cittadella Universitaria, 95125 Catania, Italy

Abstract. Recent events related to the COVID-19 pandemic event highlighted some criticalities of transport systems, especially the public sector. The respect for social distancing and a widespread fear of contagion have reduced travel on public transport. In addition, the new trend to reduce daily long-range mobility needs due to the increase in teleworking is present. Following the pandemic, there has been a paradigm shift, from smart cities to smart and sustainable cities (SSCs) in which a new concept of resilience is contemplated. Among the various changes, a reversal of the trend has occurred with respect to the transition to the use of public transport. The growing density of car traffic causes an increase in external costs, in terms of atmospheric pollution and waste of time, with negative consequences also for the balance between private life and work. In this regard, the focus of this paper is to analyse the European policies promoted in the aftermath of the pandemic in the field of urban and suburban mobility. An exploratory analysis of key factors for active mobility, public transport and shared services has been carried out highlighting possible actions and strategies to be implemented in the light of the recent pandemic and the defined restrictions. Among the European policies implemented, the redevelopment of public spaces for the promotion of various forms of active mobility, such as cycling and walking, are considered. Among the possible transport solutions, which allow medium and long-range travel, demand responsive transport (DRT) services can reduce the use of private vehicles. In fact, they are implemented for two purposes: both to connect the centres with

This paper is the result of the joint work of the authors. 'Abstract' and 'Conclusions' were written jointly by all authors. Chiara Garau wrote "Introduction". Tiziana Campisi wrote "Promoting "active mobility" in urban areas". Vincenza Torrisi wrote "Materials and Methods" and "The impact on public transport and future scenarios". Tiziana Campisi and Vincenza wrote the paragraph titled "Research Framework: European Transport Policies towards SSCs". Matteo Ignaccolo, Mauro Coni, Giuseppe Inturri and Antonino Canale supervised and Matteo Ignaccolo founded the work.

© Springer Nature Switzerland AG 2021
O. Gervasi et al. (Eds.): ICCSA 2021, LNCS 12958, pp. 603–618, 2021.
https://doi.org/10.1007/978-3-030-87016-4_43

low demand for transport often lacking an adequate supply of travel choices and to cope with the pandemic, strengthening the service on the routes with greater demand for transport.

Keywords: Urban Mobility · Transport Policies · COVID-19 · DRT · Key factors · PUMS · SUMP

1 Introduction

The pandemic has significantly transformed the concept of spaces, wellbeing, relationships and it is no longer possible to hypothesize a city without analysing the new paradigms that look at respect for the environment, accessibility, inclusion, health, and the future in general [1]. This has led policy makers to define more focused objectives, designing short- and long-term strategies in an attempt to achieve an urban sustainability associated with a new concept of resilience [2]. This new concept of resilience overlaps with the concept of smartness and, despite having different roots and missions, they have many similarities and present key characteristics to both concepts, some of which are: efficiency, sustainability, flexibility, learning and innovation skills, participation, awareness, etc.

In this regard, the literature has highlighted how the smartest cities are sustainable and resilient cities [3], because the monitoring of the city through smart infrastructures leads to the acquisition of deep knowledge and the timely decision-making process and the execution of actions, particularly considering the new strategies to be adopted with the pandemic. With this new meaning, in this article the authors consider the concept of Smart and Sustainable Cities (SSCs) [4, 5]. As far as the development of sustainable cities is concerned, in the eleventh Sustainable Development Goal (SDGs) named "Sustainable Cities and Communities" it is specified that most of the urban challenges not only related to environmental issues, but also to social and economic issues, making that the success of the implementation of the SDGs depends on the local authorities [6]. The connection between a smart city and sustainability requires smart city approaches to produce sustainable and liveable places in urban centers [7, 8]. Cities can be considered smart if investments ensure sustainability in urban areas through the use of modern technologies [9] that allow access to more and smarter solutions based on knowledge and innovation [10]. Particularly in recent years, the SSC has been focusing on the transformation of conventional cities and their processes into resilient and smart cities, by considering the interdisciplinary challenges that involve different scientific fields, at the level of urban growth [6], modelling, design and implementation [11–13]. An analysis on SSCs revealed a human centered approach [14, 15] and most of the services focused mainly on the dimensions of mobility, compared to the rest (environment, economy, governance and living) [16]. In fact, particularly with the pandemic, a high quality of life in cities is wanted to ensure, trying to make the same cities more accessible, clean and competitive. The authors will focus in this paper on transport field, by analysing a necessary modal change, and by also considering the shift to sustainable modes of transport.

Based on these premises, the aim of this paper is the understanding and investigation of how cities have made themselves smart and sustainable, starting from an analysis of European policies promoted in the aftermath of the pandemic in the field of urban mobility. This paper is divided into 5 sections: Sect. 2 considers the methodological framework based on European Transport policies towards SSCs. Section 3 and Sect. 4 focus on identifying the key factors for the promotion of strategies and actions respectively in favour of active mobility and public transport with shared services; finally, Sect. 5 concludes the paper with some remarks and laying the basis for further research.

2   Materials and Methods

As stated in the previous section, the research area of this paper is on SSCs, particularly focusing on European policies that both at the local and international level that have been promoted also following the pandemic.

The work focuses on a methodological framework based on a detailed examination of case studies and literature review characterized by 3 steps (Fig. 1): the preliminary phase is of the research is fundamental in order to be able to clearly identify the key objectives related to the Sustainable and Smart Mobility Strategy; then, is it possible to focus on the main strategies promoted in the aftermath of the pandemic in the field of urban mobility, in particular regarding active mobility and public transport innovations; finally the key factors for the promotion of these strategies and actions are highlighted.

Fig. 1. Methodological framework – Research steps (Our elaboration)

2.1   Research Framework: European Transport Policies Towards SSCs

One of the aspects that most affect cities and the transport sector is addressing the decarbonization of urban areas in the long run [17]. Among the main European strategies, the Green Deal Commission includes as a main target to reduce transport-related greenhouse gas emissions by 90% by 2050. The European Commission intends to adopt a comprehensive strategy to achieve this and ensure that the EU transport sector is fit for a clean, digital and modern economy. The objectives include:

– increasing the uptake of zero-emission vehicles;
– making sustainable alternative solutions available to the public and businesses;
– supporting digitisation and automation;
– improving connectivity and access.

The Sustainable and Smart Mobility Strategy is structured around three key objectives (Fig. 2). These targets will enable a 90% reduction in greenhouse gas emissions from transport by 2050 as defined in the European Green Deal [17].

Through the implementation of 10 action areas defined as flagships, the European Commission has proposed concrete policies for 2030 and 2050:

- at least 30 million zero-emission cars will be in operation on European roads;
- 100 European cities will be climate neutral;
- collective trips planned for less than 500 km should be carbon neutral;
- automated mobility will be widespread.

By 2050:

- almost all cars, vans, buses and new heavy-duty vehicles will be zero-emission. Emissions;
- a fully operational multimodal trans-European transport network (TEN-T) for sustainable and intelligent transport with high-speed connectivity.

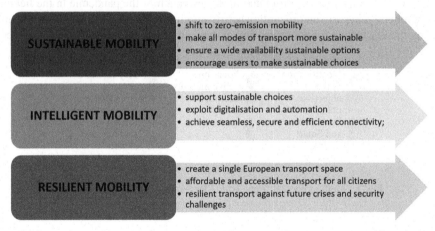

Fig. 2. Key objectives of the Sustainable and Smart Mobility Strategy (Our elaboration)

The development of digitisation and technologies (i.e. IoT or the Cloud) with the development of ITS systems [18] and also the implementation of digital mobility platforms MaaS (Mobility As a Service) [19] can be a best practice for upgrading the whole system, making it even more efficient. This will enable the EU to maintain its leadership in transport equipment production and services and improve our global competitiveness [20]. Unfortunately, the recent COVID-19 pandemic has affected several economic sectors including transport, and the crisis has caused healthy companies to lose jobs and revenue. To stem the crisis, several strategies have been promoted in accordance with the above-mentioned targets and to implement the recommendations for reducing contagion such as social distancing and limitation of seats on board [21]. Several studies in the literature show the need for more sustainable and resilient policies and strategies to reduce the impacts of catastrophic events such as climate change and pandemics [22, 23].

To ensure a rapid recovery, a series of bottom-up actions have been disseminated that directly involve citizens and administrations. These actions allow to have a better analysis of critical issues and travel habits so that strategies can be implemented that are best suited to the urban realities under investigation. The EU works with cities to develop a sustainable urban mobility policy, including efficient public transport systems and good connectivity at national level [24, 25]. It also aims to improve the quality of life in cities by promoting active mobility solutions, such as walking and cycling, and ensuring good accessibility for residents and commuters [26, 27]. Therefore, the next two sections will present the policies that EU has promoted and implemented in various cities regarding soft/active mobility and local public transport with the integration of shared services.

3   Promoting "Active Mobility" in Urban Areas

Several strategies have been implemented by European countries to promote active (soft) mobility. This includes all ways of getting around under one's own steam (cycling, walking, skating, etc.). These options are often faster and cleaner and make short-distance travel easier [28–32]. The modal choice of transport has been widened by the advent of e-scooters, bikes and car sharing. In congested urban centres and on blocked main highways, many road users are opting for alternatives to single occupancy vehicles. After individual cars and public transport, soft/active mobility is the third most used mode of transport for daily travel [33]. This form of mobility is increasing, especially in urban centres, and has many advantages: it saves time, often money, and of course reduces the overall environmental impact. Many cities and communities are encouraging these new modes of transport with the aim of reducing emissions and freeing main roads from traffic congestion.

In general terms, active mobility is part of the ecological transition, with a clear trend: fewer internal combustion engine cars and more electric cars [34]. Several studies have focused on the dissemination of good practices and the analysis of the impact on users [35].Different forms of mobility other than ownership have spread over the last decade, including both renting [36] and sharing [37–39]. The distribution of vouchers for the purchase of micro mobility has recently been one of the European practices respecting the social distancing due to the pandemic together with the encouragement of new design and improvement of cycling and walking infrastructure [40]. Several research studies investigate transport demand habits and the frequency of use of different modes through surveys and interviews [41–43] in order to foster a bottom-up view and in several cases the democratic participation of people in urban planning activities [44–47]. The dissemination of good practices that encourage walking for short distances (<1km) [48] and at the same time reduce the gender gap [49] and limitations of people with disabilities [50] will increase the demand for mobility in urban areas, allowing everyone to move around easily.

At the urban planning level, the drafting and revision of Sustainable Urban Mobility Plans (SUMPs) should be a strategic priority [51, 52], considering the recent Italian

Recovery Plan strategies, encouraging the construction of cycle paths and the opening of new construction sites for metro and tram lines. The spread of the new urban planning with the development of 15-min and compact cities favours sociality and short-distance travel, ensuring the concentrated location of services and an increase in Wi-Fi technology for greater connectivity [53, 54]. Therefore, it will be necessary to build a new local welfare system that includes individual mobility, in communities, with schools, universities, companies, public bodies and communities (neighbourhoods, apartment blocks) becoming places where environmentally and socially sustainable mobility is defined. For each macro area, i.e. the transport offer (service and infrastructure), the transport demand (the user) and the environment, it is therefore necessary to define the key factors in order to improve the impacts by defining ad hoc strategies and actions. In Leipzig (Germany), for example, bicycle parking spaces were created instead of car parking spaces, thus reducing the availability of car parking spaces and making cycling more convenient [55]. In several cases, however, parking policies were not coherent with policies for sustainable urban mobility: in Poland, and especially in Warsaw, the fine for not paying for a parking space is lower than the fine for not paying a ticket on public transport; and in Poland, even where parking on the side of the road is prohibited, it is still possible to park on the pavement, thus reducing the space available for pedestrians [56].

Other ways to discourage the use of private vehicles include the creation of pedestrian zones and the use of the congestion charge as happened in 2018 in Madrid which introduced a 472-hectare restricted traffic zone resulting in a reduction in NO2 pollution. Barcelona has removed cars from the streets by creating "superbills" (macro isolates), which include nine residential blocks, with an area of 400 m x 400 m, surrounded by streets where traffic, including bus traffic, is concentrated. In the inner streets, cars are banned or speeds are limited [57]. "Supertiles" are an example of how cities can give priority to pedestrians and cyclists, taking public space away from parking and giving it back to citizens. In Italy, pedestrian zones of 4 hectares have been established in Palermo and the local administration plans to double the size. It also intends to reduce the space available for cars to extend the tram network. Table 1 summarizes the above the key factors to be taken under consideration to propose strategies and actions related to active mobility:

4   The Impact on Public Transport and Future Scenarios

The adopted strategy by Europe proposes a roadmap towards sustainable mobility and a series of targets to be achieved: among the main objectives defined by the new plan is the increase in the efficiency of the transport system through the enhancement of digital technologies and intelligent systems [58–60]. The European Commission also intends to accelerate the distribution of sustainable mobility alternatives, favouring elements such as advanced biofuels, electricity, hydrogen and renewable synthetic fuels and removing the obstacles in the transport electrification. [61]. In addition, several strategies have been implemented by various European countries to reduce the use of private vehicles. A series of incentives have been implemented for the use of electric mobility, encouraging the dismantling of cars with traditional power supply and in some cases eliminating toll

Table 1. Key factors linked to discourage the use of private vehicle and promote active mobility (Our elaboration).

Areas	Key factors	Strategies and actions
Road pavement	Greenways, Pedestrian area or ZTL, Shared space, Bike and micro mobility parking, Road pavement	Reduction of road space for cars (parking and carriageways) Dedicated lanes Electric charging station Route hierarchy Regularizing and restoring the road surface
Service	Frequency, Shared service type	Incentive to transport multimodality Special rates Green-vehicle (e-mobility) Gender equity/equality
User	Behaviour, Habits, Economical aspects, Barriers	Incentives single user Democratic planning Survey and interview campaign
Environment	Reuse of spaces, New urban planning	Ensuring respect for historical and cultural diversity present on the territory Promoting cross-border cooperation at local and regional level Define and implement policies on landscape also through the involvement of communities Consistency with policies traffic and transport policies Enhancing the urban centre by improving its usability, safety and accessibility Incentives for buying bikes and micro mobility Promoting slow tourism Compact cities and 15min cities development

road costs and Limited Traffic Zones costs [62]. But one of the major innovations is the advent of sharing mobility, which is a phenomenon in constant expansion and which continues to change the world of traditional transport, making it more innovative and eco-friendlier. The sharing mobility represents a choice: each person can decide not to travel with their own private vehicle (i.e. car, bicycle, scooter, etc.) and use shared vehicles. Thanks to the development of technology, sharing mobility makes it possible to share both vehicles and journeys, making transport more interactive and efficient and significantly reducing costs and consumption related to the vehicle ownership [63]. The sharing mobility is characterized by numerous transport services based on the use of different modes. Among these, the most well-known type is the car sharing, that allows to rent a car, alone or with others, to make a trip by paying only the linked travel costs. It can present different forms of service, such as traditional or electric power supply, station based, free floating and peer-to peer [64, 65]. Electric car sharing has also become an integral part of urban landscapes and thanks to the increasing spread of charging areas, it will be possible to reduce the number of combustion engine vehicles in the coming years [66]. Instead, carpooling is not configured as a transport service realized by organizations or companies, but it is made available by private individuals. In fact, carpooling is a shared service based on the use of private cars between two or more passengers who must perform the same journey. The driver makes the vehicle available and the passengers contribute financially to fuel and travel costs. The carpooling model currently most used is the real-time one, realized thanks to digital platforms and apps for smartphones that allow to connect the driver and passengers [67]. It is possible to mention the so-called On-demand Transport Services, which are characterized by shared journeys that take place at the specific request of one or more users. Taxis, for example, belong to this transport category, but there are also the most innovative services (e.g. the American Uber) that allow to book a ride in just a few minutes via smartphone. The implementation of this type of service, also identifiable with the term of Demand Responsive Transit (DRT), is envisaged in areas with low mobility demand to replace low-utilization scheduled services and characterized by considerable dispersion spatial and temporal. In this context, the need that emerges is to identify innovative solutions capable of offering a widespread coverage of the territory, guaranteeing the movement of citizens from their residences to the main "transportation hubs" (main bus and train stations) or to the main point of interests (schools, hospitals, urban centres, sports centres, etc.) [68].

Furthermore, the changed transport conditions resulting from the need to cope with the pandemic caused by COVID-19, make it essential to strengthen the service on the routes with greater demand for transport [69]. Its main features are:

– user-oriented (flexibility/adaptability of the route, times and frequency based on transport demand);
– accessibility to the service via web, through specific platforms available for smartphones, apps, PCs;
– versatility of use with reference to the areas and users to be served (more calibrated vehicles and mileage).

In a post-COVID scenario, the availability of resources and technological innovations seem to create the ideal situation to lay the foundations for a new model of mobility, which intercepts the strong social interest in the issues of safety and environmental sustainability. In this sense, close collaboration between private actors and the public sector becomes essential, which constitutes an enabling and coordinating role in the functional planning processes of cities with a view to intermodality between the different transport solutions. This full integration between different mobility services is achievable through the MaaS platforms: the idea is to integrate various forms of transport services into a single access point for mobility services [70]. Thanks to the availability of new digital technologies, users can plan their journeys in real time, taking advantage of mobility services provided by different operators (public and private) using a single platform and a single payment method. With the technological platforms for DRTs it is possible to achieve: the travel optimization; the use of cashless payment systems; the possibility of integrating booking and payment systems through MaaS for a better synchronization of the modal interchange. Similarly, to what has already been studied for the strategies and policies aimed at active mobility, with reference to the different macro areas, it is essential to highlight the key factors that allow to identify and implement strategies and actions for the improvement of public transport and discourage the use of private vehicles, thanks to technologies and new forms of shared mobility. For example, in the city of Copenhagen a model was developed to study the accessibility of the metro network. Considering the simultaneous choice of residential location and car ownership by households, the impact of an extension of the metro network has been studied. he results showed that with an extension of the metro network in the Greater Copenhagen Area, the car ownership decreases by 2–3% [71].

Another important aspect is represented by the presence of an appropriate electric charging infrastructure. In Turin, a model to study the performance and costs of fleet charging management, with reference to an Electric Free-Floating Car Sharing. To maximize the number of trips of users, and at the same time minimize the cost of relocating cars for charging, it emerged that the better solution is represented by a distributed set of charging poles around the most-used zones, where users can eventually contribute to plug cars [72]. Regarding the type of service, many cities have investigated the propensity of users to share the means of transport [73–75] and, also in light of the new mobility needs deriving from the pandemic, innovative mobility services have been implemented such as the DRT in the city of Ragusa (Italy) [76]; the fully flexible and true door-to-door DRT experiment implemented in Oberharz (Germany) [77] and the e-mobility bus fleet application in Sorrento (Italy) [78]. In these cases, the complementary extension of the existing public transport service through the DRT should meet mobility needs of rural areas to redeem car dependency and improve mobility for all population groups. In this regard, it is important to implement strategies and actions shared with the population, through bottom-up procedures, which take into account the preferences of users and stakeholders, as implemented for example in the city of Enna (Italy) [79, 80] and Manchester (UK) [81] and in rural areas of the Netherlands [82]. However, the use of sensors and simulation models also constitutes a valid support for comparing different scenarios and monitoring the effects of certain strategies [83]. In Italy, the city of Catania implemented a traffic monitoring and forecasting system equipped with radar sensors [84, 85]; while in France, the city of Marseilles realized a machine learning model to estimate driving behaviour as a function of traffic conditions and road infrastructure coupled with a physics-based microscopic emissions model [86].

Following the analysis of these case studies and the literature review, Table 2 summarizes the emerging key factors linked to the strategies and actions to discourage the use of private vehicle and promote the use of shared transport services.

Unlike the analysis carried out in the previous section, referred to transport modes with a single user, in this case it is possible that the shared vehicles are also used by

Table 2. Key factors linked to discourage the use of private vehicle and promote the use of shared transport services (Our elaboration).

Areas	Key factors	Strategies and actions
Infrastructure	Parking areas, Bus stop location, Recharge infrastructure, ICT infrastructure	Redesign of parking areas Identification of virtual stops Location of recharge infrastructure Clear identification of the delimitation of areas
Service	Frequency of the service, Type of service, Number of users, Social distancing, Load factor	Digital platform to transport multimodality Integrated ticketing Encourage the E-mobility Innovative shared transport services (DRT) Territorial network planning
User	Behaviour, Travel habits, Economical aspects, Incentives for safety	Democratic planning User preferences investigation Awareness campaigns Establishment of the Green pass
Environment	Continuous monitoring, Reuse of spaces, Environmental emissions, Acoustic emissions, Travel time optimization	Implementation of sensor networks (smart road) Use of green vehicles Big-data applications Charges to discourage the use of private vehicle

several users simultaneously. They are all alternatives to single occupancy vehicles and enable the development of sustainable mobility in line with decarbonization policies.

5 Conclusions

Sustainable urban mobility under the SSC recent paradigm is one of the main challenges that European cities have been facing for the past decade, although recently the pandemic has overturned the concept of mobility and imposed various restrictions. It is necessary to conceive solutions designed not for a transitory phase, but rather to offer a vision and tools that are inspired by a completely new perspective. It would not be correct and extremely insufficient to face only to immediate financial and sectoral needs and not making the effort to propose a systemic approach. Therefore, it is necessary to rethink the mobility system through an integrated and human centered oriented design.

In this perspective, various considerations and strategies for the decarbonization of mobility up to 2030 and 2050 have been disseminated through the definition of the Horizon 2020 and Green Deal strategies. Cities are adopting a series of initiatives to encourage "active mobility" by combining with the creation of models (i.e. 5 min city) and to increase the quality and availability of public transport in order to meet the new transport demand mobility needs. In view of a trend that could be lasting, the preparation of SUMPs is essential for planning adequate strategies and actions.

This work, through a detailed examination of case studies and literature review, has made possible to identify the key factors, strategies and actions aimed in these directions. The results will constitute the basis for future research aimed at the critical analysis of the drafting of SUMPs at both National and European level, focusing on the topics about the regeneration of urban spaces and the use of technologies for the promotion of innovative shared forms of mobility.

Acknowledgments. This study was supported by the MIUR (Ministry of Education, Universities and Research [Italy]) through a project entitled WEAKI TRANSIT: WEAK-demand areas Innovative TRANsport Shared services for Italian Towns (Project code: 20174ARRHT/CUP Code: E44I17000050001), financed with the PRIN 2017 (Research Projects of National Relevance) programme. We authorize the MIUR to reproduce and distribute reprints for Governmental purposes, notwithstanding any copy-right notations thereon. Any opinions, findings and conclusions or recommendations expressed in this material are those of the authors, and do not necessarily reflect the views of the MIUR.

References

1. Kim, H.M.: Smart cities beyond COVID-19. In: Smart Cities for Technological and Social Innovation, pp. 299–308. Academic Press (2021)
2. DeWit, A., Shaw, R., Djalante, R.: An integrated approach to sustainable development, National Resilience, and COVID-19 responses: the case of Japan. Int. J. Disaster Risk Reduction **51**, 101808 (2020)
3. Zhou, Q., Zhu, M., Qiao, Y., Zhang, X., Chen, J.: Achieving resilience through smart cities? evidence from China. Habitat Int. **111**, 102348 (2021)
4. Lim, H.S.M., Taeihagh, A.: Autonomous vehicles for smart and sustainable cities: an in-depth exploration of privacy and cybersecurity implications. Energies **11**(5), 1062 (2018)
5. Allam, Z., Jones, D.S.: Future (post-COVID) digital, smart and sustainable cities in the wake of 6G: Digital twins, immersive realities and new urban economies. Land Use Policy **101**, 105201 (2021)
6. Poon, L.: What the UN's New Sustainable Development Goals Will (and Won't) Do for Cities. https://www.bloomberg.com/news/articles/2015-09-29/what-the-un-s-new-sustainable-development-goals-will-and-won-t-do-for-cities. Accessed 21 Mar 2021
7. Monfaredzadeh, T., Krueger, R.: Investigating social factors of sustainability in a smart city. Procedia Eng. **118**, 1112–1118 (2015)
8. Leem, Y., Han, H., Lee, S.H.: Sejong Smart City: on the road to be a city of the future. In: Lecture Notes in Geoinformation and Cartography. Springer International Publishing: New York, NY, USA, pp. 17–33 (2019)
9. Bifulco, F., Tregua, M., Amitrano, C.C., D'Auria, A.: ICT and sustainability in smart cities management. Int. J. Public Sect. Manag. **29**, 132–147 (2016)
10. Romanelli, M.: Analysing the role of information technology towards sustainable cities living. Kybernetes **49**, 2037–2052 (2020)
11. Bibri, S.E.: A novel model for data-driven smart sustainable cities of the future: the institutional transformations required for balancing and advancing the three goals of sustainability. Energy Inf. **4**(1), 1–37 (2021)

12. Garau, C., Nesi, P., Paoli, I., Paolucci, M., Zamperlin, P.: A Big Data Platform for Smart and Sustainable Cities: Environmental Monitoring Case Studies in Europe. In: International Conference on Computational Science and Its Applications, pp. 393–406. Springer, Cham (2020). doi: https://doi.org/10.1007/978-3-030-58820-5_30

13. Garau, C., Pavan, V.M.: Evaluating urban quality: Indicators and assessment tools for smart sustainable cities. Sustainability **10**(3), 575 (2018)

14. Maltinti, F., et al.: Vulnerable users and public transport service: analysis on expected and perceived quality data. In: International Conference on Computational Science and Its Applications (pp. 673–689). Springer, Cham (2020). Doi: https://doi.org/10.1007/978-3-030-58820-5_49

15. Garau, C., Desogus, G., Zamperlin, P.: Governing Technology-based Urbanism: Degeneration to Technocracy or Development to Progressive Planning? (2020)

16. Garau, C., Annunziata, A., Coni, M.: A methodological framework for assessing practicability of the urban space: the survey on conditions of practicable environments (SCOPE) procedure applied in the case study of Cagliari (Italy). Sustainability **10**(11), 4189 (2018)

17. Garau, C., Masala, F., Pinna, F.: Cagliari and smart urban mobility: analysis and comparison. Cities **56**, 35–46 (2016)

18. Urrutia-Azcona, K., Tatar, M., Molina-Costa, P., Flores-Abascal, I.: Cities4ZERO: overcoming carbon lock-in in municipalities through smart urban transformation processes. Sustainability **12**(9), 3590 (2020)

19. Coni, M., Garau, C., Pinna, F.: How has Cagliari changed its citizens in smart citizens? Exploring the influence of ITS technology on urban social interactions. In: International Conference on Computational Science and Its Applications, pp. 573–588. Springer, Cham (2018). Doi: https://doi.org/10.1007/978-3-319-95168-3_39

20. European Commission: Sustainable and Smart Mobility Strategy – putting European transport on track for the future (2020). https://ec.europa.eu/transport/sites/default/files/legislation/com 20200789.pdf

21. Canale, A., Tesoriere, G., Campisi, T.: The MAAS development as a mobility solution based on the individual needs of transport users. In AIP conference proceedings, vol. 2186, No. 1, p. 160005). AIP Publishing LLC, December 2019

22. Moslem, S., Campisi, T., Szmelter-Jarosz, A., Duleba, S., Nahiduzzaman, K.M., Tesoriere, G.: Best–worst method for modelling mobility choice after COVID-19: evidence from Italy. Sustainability **12**(17), 6824 (2020)

23. Campisi, T., Basbas, S., Skoufas, A., Akgün, N., Ticali, D., Tesoriere, G.: The Impact of COVID-19 Pandemic on the Resilience of Sustainable Mobility in Sicily. Sustainability **12**(21), 8829 (2020)

24. Moraci, F., Errigo, M.F., Fazia, C., Campisi, T., Castelli, F.: Cities under pressure: strategies and tools to face climate change and pandemic. Sustainability **12**(18), 7743 (2020)

25. Barabino, B., Coni, M., Olivo, A., Pungillo, G., Rassu, N.: Standing passenger comfort: a new scale for evaluating the real-time driving style of bus transit services. IEEE Trans. Intell. Transp. Syst. (2019). https://doi.org/10.1109/TITS.2019.2921807

26. Coni, M., et al.: On-board comfort of different age passengers and bus-lane characteristics. In: Gervasi, O., et al. (eds.) ICCSA 2020. LNCS, vol. 12255, pp. 658–672. Springer, Cham (2020). https://doi.org/10.1007/978-3-030-58820-5_48

27. Annunziata, A., Garau, C.: A literature review on walkability and its theoretical framework. emerging perspectives for research developments. In: Gervasi, O., Murgante, B., Misra, S., Garau, C., Blečić, I., Taniar, D., Apduhan, B.O., Rocha, A.M.A.C., Tarantino, E., Torre, C.M., Karaca, Y. (eds.) ICCSA 2020. LNCS, vol. 12255, pp. 422–437. Springer, Cham (2020). https://doi.org/10.1007/978-3-030-58820-5_32

28. Garau, C., Annunziata, A., Yamu, C.: A walkability assessment tool coupling multi-criteria analysis and space syntax: The case study of Iglesias, Italy. European Planning Studies, 1–23 (2020)
29. Tiboni, M., Rossetti, S., Vetturi, D., Torrisi, V., Botticini, F., Schaefer, M.D.: Urban policies and planning approaches for a safer and climate friendlier mobility in cities: strategies. Initiatives and Some Analysis. Sustainability **13**(4), 1778 (2021). https://doi.org/10.3390/su1304 1778
30. Ignaccolo, C., Giuffrida, N., Torrisi, V.: The queensway of New York city. A proposal for sustainable mobility in queens. Town and Infrastructure Planning for Safety and Urban Quality, 69–76 (2018). doi:https://doi.org/10.1201/9781351173360-12
31. Rossetti, S., Tiboni, M., Vetturi, D., Zazzi, M., Caselli, B.: Measuring pedestrian accessibility to public transport in urban areas: a GIS-based discretisation approach. European Transport, Issue n. 76, May 2020, Paper n° 2 (2020). ISSN 1825–3997, SCOPUS ID 2-s2.0–85087331889.
32. Ignaccolo, M., Inturri, G., Giuffrida, N., Le Pira, M., Torrisi, V., Calabrò, G.: A step towards walkable environments: spatial analysis of pedestrian compatibility in an urban context. Europ. Transport Trasporti Europei **76**(6), 1–12 (2020)
33. European Environment Agency: Transport and environment report 2019 The first and last mile — the key to sustainable urban transport (2019)
34. Mądziel, M., Campisi, T., Jaworski, A., Tesoriere, G.: The development of strategies to reduce exhaust emissions from passenger cars in rzeszow city—poland a preliminary assessment of the results produced by the increase of E-Fleet. Energies **14**(4), 1046 (2021)
35. Tesoriere, G., Campisi, T.: The benefit of engage the "crowd" encouraging a bottom-up approach for shared mobility rating. In: Gervasi, O., Murgante, B., Misra, S., Garau, C., Blečić, I., Taniar, D., Apduhan, B.O., Rocha, A.M.A.C., Tarantino, E., Torre, C.M., Karaca, Y. (eds.) ICCSA 2020. LNCS, vol. 12250, pp. 836–850. Springer, Cham (2020). https://doi.org/10.1007/978-3-030-58802-1_60
36. Campisi, T., Akgün, N., Ticali, D., Tesoriere, G.: Exploring public opinion on personal mobility vehicle use: a case study in Palermo. Italy. Sustainability **12**(13), 5460 (2020)
37. Nikiforiadis, A., Paschalidis, E., Stamatiadis, N., Raptopoulou, A., Kostareli, A., & Basbas, S.: Analysis of attitudes and engagement of shared e-scooter users. Transp. Res. Part D: Transport and Environment **94**, 102790 (2021)
38. Torrisi, V., Ignaccolo, M., Inturri, G., Tesoriere, G., Campisi, T.: Exploring the factors affecting bike-sharing demand: evidence from student perceptions, usage patterns and adoption barriers. Trans. Res. Procedia **52**, 573–580 (2021)
39. Campisi, T., Nahiduzzaman, K.M., Ticali, D., Tesoriere, G.: Bivariate analysis of the influencing factors of the upcoming personal mobility vehicles (PMVs) in Palermo. In: Gervasi, O., Murgante, B., Misra, S., Garau, C., Blečić, I., Taniar, D., Apduhan, B.O., Rocha, A.M.A.C., Tarantino, E., Torre, C.M., Karaca, Y. (eds.) ICCSA 2020. LNCS, vol. 12250, pp. 868–881. Springer, Cham (2020). https://doi.org/10.1007/978-3-030-58802-1_62
40. Campisi, T., Acampa, G., Marino, G., Tesoriere, G.: Cycling master plans in Italy: the I-BIM feasibility tool for cost and safety assessments. Sustainability **12**(11), 4723 (2020)
41. Rassu, N., Maltinti, F., Coni, M., Garau, C., Barabino, B., Pinna, F., Devoto, R.: (2020) Elderly people and local public transport - a focus on their travel behavior - the case of Cagliari. In International Conference on Computational Science and Its Applications (pp. 690–705). Springer, Cham
42. Maltinti, F., Rassu, N., Coni, M., Garau, C., Pinna, F., Devoto, R., Barabino, B.: Vulnerable users and public transport service: analysis on expected and perceived quality data. In: Gervasi, O., Murgante, B., Misra, S., Garau, C., Blečić, I., Taniar, D., Apduhan, B.O., Rocha, A.M.A.C., Tarantino, E., Torre, C.M., Karaca, Y. (eds.) ICCSA 2020. LNCS, vol. 12255, pp. 673–689. Springer, Cham (2020). https://doi.org/10.1007/978-3-030-58820-5_49

43. Ignaccolo, M., Inturri, G., Giuffrida, N., Pira, M.L., Torrisi, V.: Public engagement for designing new transport services: investigating citizen preferences from a multiple criteria perspective. Transp. Res. Procedia **37**, 91–98 (2019). https://doi.org/10.1016/j.trpro.2018. 12.170
44. Garau, C.: Processi di Piano e Partecipazione [Planning Processes and Citizen Participation]; Gangemi Editore: Rome, Italy (2013)
45. Garau, C.: Citizen participation in public planning: a literature review. Int. J. Sci. **1**(12), 21–44 (2012)
46. Garau, C.: Focus on citizens: public engagement with online and face-to-face participation—a case study. Future Internet **4**(2), 592–606 (2012)
47. Ignaccolo, M., Inturri, G., Giuffrida, N., Le Pira, M., Torrisi, V.: Structuring transport decision-making problems through stakeholder engagement: The case of Catania metro accessibility. Transport Infrastructure Syst., 19–926 (2017). doi:https://doi.org/10.1201/978131528189 6-118
48. Campisi, T., Basbas, S., Tesoriere, G., Trouva, M., Papas, T., Mrak, I.: How to create walking friendly cities. a multi-criteria analysis of the central open market area of rijeka. Sustainability **12**(22), 9470 (2020)
49. Al-Rashid, M.A., Nahiduzzaman, K.M., Ahmed, S., Campisi, T., Akgün, N.: Gender-responsive public transportation in the dammam metropolitan region. Saudi Arabia. Sustainability **12**(21), 9068 (2020)
50. Campisi, T., Ignaccolo, M., Inturri, G., Tesoriere, G., Torrisi, V.: Evaluation of walkability and mobility requirements of visually impaired people in urban spaces. Research in Transportation Business & Management, 100592 (2020)
51. Torrisi, V., Garau, C., Ignaccolo, M., Inturri, G.: "Sustainable urban mobility plans": key concepts and a critical revision on SUMPs guidelines. In: Gervasi, O., et al. (eds.) ICCSA 2020. LNCS, vol. 12255, pp. 613–628. Springer, Cham (2020). https://doi.org/10.1007/978-3-030-58820-5_45
52. Torrisi, V., Garau, C., Inturri, G., Ignaccolo, M.: Strategies and actions towards sustainability: Encouraging good ITS practices in the SUMP vision. In: International Conference of Computational Methods in Sciences and Engineering ICCMSE 2020 (2021). doi:https://doi.org/10.1063/5.0047897
53. Metre, K., Baghel, H., Suman, G., Batra, M., Ghodmare, S.D.: Compact city and related impact on sustainable development in urban areas. In: Advances in Civil Engineering and Infrastructural Development, pp. 523–530 (2021)
54. Nadeem, M., Aziz, A., Al-Rashid, M.A., Tesoriere, G., Asim, M., Campisi, T.: Scaling the potential of compact city development: the case of lahore, Pakistan. Sustainability **13**(9), 5257 (2021). https://doi.org/10.3390/su13095257
55. Keidel, T.: Mobility Concepts in a large new housing estate in eastern Germany. The Example of Leipzig-Grünau. In Urban Ecology, pp. 547–550. Springer, Heidelberg (1998)
56. Turoń, K., Czech, P., Juzek, M.: The concept of a walkable city as an alternative form of urban mobility. Zeszyty Naukowe. Transport/Politechnika Śląska (2017)
57. Rueda Palenzuela, S.: Les superilles per al disseny de noves ciutats i la renovació de les existents: el cas de Barcelona. Papers: Regió Metropolitana de Barcelona: Territori, estratègies, planejament, (59), 0078–93 (2017)
58. Torrisi, V., Ignaccolo, M., Inturri, G.: Innovative transport systems to promote sustainable mobility: developing the model architecture of a traffic control and supervisor system. In: Gervasi, O., et al. (eds.) ICCSA 2018. LNCS, vol. 10962, pp. 622–638. Springer, Cham (2018). https://doi.org/10.1007/978-3-319-95168-3_42
59. Monzer, J.V., Qader, H.I.: Using digital technology to help users of public transportation to cope when experiencing lack of control (2020)

60. Torrisi, V., Ignaccolo, M., Inturri, G.: Analysis of road urban transport network capacity through a dynamic assignment model: validation of different measurement methods. Transp. Res. Procedia **27**, 1026–1033 (2017). https://doi.org/10.1016/j.trpro.2017.12.135

61. Pavić, I., Pandžić, H., Capuder, T.: Electric vehicle based smart e-mobility system–Definition and comparison to the existing concept. Appl. Energy **272**, 115153 (2020)

62. Carteni, A., Henke, I., Molitierno, C., Errico, A.: Towards E-Mobility: Strengths and Weaknesses of Electric Vehicles. In: Barolli, L., Amato, F., Moscato, F., Enokido, T., Takizawa, M. (eds.) WAINA 2020. AISC, vol. 1150, pp. 1383–1393. Springer, Cham (2020). https://doi.org/10.1007/978-3-030-44038-1_126

63. Smorto, G., & Vinci, I. M. (2020). The Role of Sharing Mobility in Contemporary Cities. Legal, Social and Environmental Issues.

64. Campisi, T., Ignaccolo, M., Tesoriere, G., Inturri, G., Torrisi, V.: The evaluation of car-sharing to raise acceptance of electric vehicles: evidences from an Italian survey among university students. SAE Technical Paper Series (2020). doi:https://doi.org/10.4271/2020-24-0021

65. Campisi, T., Ignaccolo, M., Inturri, G., Tesoriere, G., Torrisi, V.: The growing urban accessibility: a model to measure the car sharing effectiveness based on parking distances. In: Gervasi, O., et al. (eds.) ICCSA 2020. LNCS, vol. 12255, pp. 629–644. Springer, Cham (2020). https://doi.org/10.1007/978-3-030-58820-5_46

66. Kaya, Ö., Alemdar, K.D., Campisi, T., Tortum, A., Çodur, M.K.: The development of decarbonisation strategies: a three-step methodology for the suitable analysis of current EVCS locations applied to Istanbul. Turkey. Energies **14**(10), 2756 (2021)

67. Tomás, R., Fernandes, P., Macedo, J., Coelho, M.C.: Carpooling as an immediate strategy to post-lockdown mobility: a case study in University Campuses. Sustainability **13**(10), 5512 (2021)

68. Ronald, N., Yang, J., Thompson, R.G.: Exploring co-modality using on-demand transport systems. Transp. Res. Procedia **12**, 203–212 (2016)

69. Ahangari, S., Chavis, C., Jeihani, M.: Public Transit Ridership Analysis during the COVID-19 Pandemic. medRxiv (2020)

70. Brezovec, P., Hampl, N.: Electric vehicles ready for breakthrough in MaaS? consumer adoption of E-car sharing and E-scooter sharing as a part of mobility-as-a-service (MaaS). Energies **14**(4), 1088 (2021)

71. Mulalic, I., Rouwendal, J.: Does improving public transport decrease car ownership? Evidence from a residential sorting model for the Copenhagen metropolitan area. Regional Science and Urban Economics, 83, 103543 (2020)

72. Ciociola, A., Markudova, D., Vassio, L., Giordano, D., Mellia, M., Meo, M.: Impact of charging infrastructure and policies on electric car sharing systems. In: 2020 IEEE 23rd International Conference on Intelligent Transportation Systems (ITSC), pp. 1–6. IEEE, September 2020

73. Torrisi, V., Inturri, G., Ignaccolo, M.: Introducing a mobility on demand system beyond COVID-19: Evidences from users' perspective. In: International Conference of Computational Methods in Sciences and Engineering ICCMSE 2020 (2021). doi:https://doi.org/10.1063/5.0047889

74. Abdullah, M., Ali, N., Dias, C., Campisi, T., Javid, M.A.: Exploring the traveler's intentions to use public transport during the COVID-19 pandemic while complying with precautionary measures. Appl. Sci. **11**(8), 3630 (2021)

75. Torrisi, V., Campisi, T., Inturri, G., Ignaccolo, M., Tesoriere, G.: Continue to share? an overview on Italian travel behavior before and after the COVID-19 lockdown. In: International Conference of Computational Methods in Sciences and Engineering ICCMSE 2020 (2020). doi:https://doi.org/10.1063/5.0048512

76. Inturri, G., et al.: Taxi vs. demand responsive shared transport systems: an agent-based simulation approach. Transp. Policy **103**, 116–126 (2021)

77. Sörensen, L., Bossert, A., Jokinen, J.P., Schlüter, J.: How much flexibility does rural public transport need?–Implications from a fully flexible DRT system. Transp. Policy **100**, 5–20 (2021)

78. Cartenì, A., Henke, I., Molitierno, C., Di Francesco, L.: Strong sustainability in public transport policies: An e-mobility bus fleet application in Sorrento Peninsula (Italy). Sustainability **12**(17), 7033 (2020)

79. Campisi, T., Torrisi, V., Ignaccolo, M., Inturri, G., Tesoriere, G.: University propensity assessment to car sharing services using mixed survey data: the Italian case study of Enna city. Transp. Res. Procedia **47**, 433–440 (2020). https://doi.org/10.1016/j.trpro.2020.03.155

80. Campisi, T., Canale, A., Ticali, D., Tesoriere, G.: Innovative solutions for sustainable mobility in areas of weak demand. Some factors influencing the implementation of the DRT system in Enna (Italy). In: AIP Conference Proceedings, vol. 2343, No. 1, p. 090005. AIP Publishing LLC, March 2021

81. Matyas, M., Kamargianni, M.: Investigating heterogeneity in preferences for Mobility-as-a-Service plans through a latent class choice model. Travel Behav. Soc **23**, 143–156 (2021)

82. Bronsvoort, K.A., Alonso González, M.J., van Oort, N., Molin, E.J.E., Hoogendoorn, S.P.: Preferences towards Bus Alternatives in Rural Areas of the Netherlands (PPT). In Transportation Research Board (TRB) 99th Annual Meeting (2020)

83. Torrisi, V., Ignaccolo, M., Inturri, G.: Toward a sustainable mobility through a dynamic real-time traffic monitoring, estimation and forecasting system: the RE.S.E.T. project. In: Town and Infrastructure Planning for Safety and Urban Quality - Proceedings of the 23rd International Conference on Living and Walking in Cities, LWC 2017, pp. 241–247 (2018). doi:https://doi.org/10.1201/9781351173360-32

84. Calabrò, G., Torrisi, V., Inturri, G., Ignaccolo, M.: Improving inbound logistic planning for large-scale real-world routing problems: a novel ant-colony simulation-based optimization. European Transport Research Review, 12(1). (2020). https://doi.org/10.1186/s12544-020-00409-7

85. Torrisi, V., Ignaccolo, M., Inturri, G.: Estimating travel time reliability in urban areas through a dynamic simulation model. Transp. Res. Procedia **27**, 857–864 (2017). https://doi.org/10.1016/j.trpro.2017.12.134

86. De Nunzio, G., Laraki, M., Thibault, L.: Road traffic dynamic pollutant emissions estimation: from macroscopic road information to microscopic environmental impact. Atmosphere **12**(1), 53 (2021)

International Workshop on Virtual and Augmented Reality and Applications (VRA 2021)

Motion and Interaction Tracking Tool
for Virtual Reality Environments

Marcelo de Paiva Guimarães[1,2]([✉]) [iD], Diego Roberto Colombo Dias[3] [iD],
Leonardo Chaves Dutra da Rocha[3] [iD], Elvis Hernandes Ribeiro[3],
Rogério Luiz Iope[4,5], and José Remo Brega[4,5] [iD]

[1] Rectory, Federal University of São Paulo (UNESP), São Paulo, Brazil
`marcelo.paiva@unifesp.br`
[2] Computer Science Master Program (Unifaccamp), Campo Limpo, Paulista, Brazil
[3] Computer Science, Federal University of São João del Rei (UFSJ), São João del Rei, Brazil
`{diegodias,lcrocha}@ufsj.edu.br`, `elvishribeiro@aluno.ufsj.edu.br`
[4] São Paulo State University (UNESP), São Paulo, Brazil
`{rogerio.iope,remo.brega}@unesp.br`
[5] Computer Science Department, São Paulo State University (UNESP), Bauru, Brazil

Abstract. Evaluating user behavior in virtual reality environments is a challenging task, requiring leading with spatial user freedom and with non-conventional visualization and interaction devices. By gathering and analyzing user movements and interactions, researchers and even game designers can notice important behavioral patterns and correlations. This paper aims to present an automatic motion and interaction tracking tool for virtual reality environments that allows researchers and game developers to move from the pure observational paradigm, such as video recording and questionnaires, to one that considers quantitative data. After gathering users' data, the tool automatically generates charts to assist the analysis process and also allows the replaying of all user behavior executed in the application. A case study case is shown in which a user navigates and interacts in a virtual reality city performing instrumental activities of daily living (IADL). Using the tool presented here, we conclude that tracking user behavior automatically in a virtual reality environment is possible. To facilitate the software development process, we have developed a Unity Asset, allowing developers to use the tool easily by importing our asset into their projects.

Keywords: User behavior · Tracking · Virtual reality

1 Introduction

Virtual reality environments in which users are inserted into 3D worlds with a high degree of freedom of movement and interaction now have new ways to evaluate user behavior. Moreover, these virtual environments can deliver stimulus and create situations in a controlled mode that are nearly impossible with any other means, building a large and practical data source of user behavior. As such, new approaches to test and verify hypotheses in a realistic and scalable manner can be executed in virtual environments that were previously infeasible. Understanding user behavior in these virtual environments is

© Springer Nature Switzerland AG 2021
O. Gervasi et al. (Eds.): ICCSA 2021, LNCS 12958, pp. 621–630, 2021.
https://doi.org/10.1007/978-3-030-87016-4_44

fundamental to scaling up this technology's use and identifying correlations and patterns in user movements and interactions.

User behavior analysis evaluates how users move and interact with the virtual reality environment and what obstacles they experience during the navigation, which requires to collect, combine, and analyze user data. Behavioral analysis of users has already been investigated in several applications, including virtual reality applications [1–4]. The results of these analysis are fundamental, such as to verify whether the user is performing a similar behavior as demonstrated previously during skills training.

Considering virtual reality applications, which use non-conventional devices (e.g., a head-mounted display and data gloves), behavioral analysis is more complex than in common applications like web applications. Notably, users' degree of freedom and interaction levels in a virtual environment are immense, as they can walk and look freely in any direction. Recently, the possibilities for tracking users using devices such as Oculus, PlayStation VR, HTC Vive, and Kinect Azure have considerably increased. These devices have been used for behavioral observation of users in virtual reality environments.

In this paper, we present an automated tool to gather information about user behavior during virtual reality application use. The collected data can be utilized to improve virtual environment design and to identify points where users have difficulty performing a task, allowing, for example, an instructor to identify a user's difficulties and to investigate the user's attitudes. This tool logs [5, 6] users' movements and interactions while they are interacting with the virtual environment. The data are combined, and charts are generated automatically. These charts provide valuable insight, such as how long a user spent going from one place to another and how long a user stayed in one place. Moreover, this tool allows the researcher/user to replay user behavior in the virtual environment. Furthermore, via such replay, recreating the user's playing experience in detail is possible. To facilitate the software development process, we developed a Unity Asset, allowing developers to use the tool easily by importing our asset into their projects.

Several areas tend to benefit from using our approach, such as the activities employed in virtual neuromotor rehabilitation applications [7], when a patient must perform several tasks during a physical therapy session. Currently, health professionals write down everything that occurs during the virtual session, depending purely on their cognitive senses; however, using this paper's proposed solution, this annotation will be done automatically, employing milestones defined in the application. Another benefit of using this type of automated annotation is the metadata creation that enriches the data generated and stored in a medical database, facilitating the data pre-processing phase, usually necessary when using machine learning techniques.

This study is structured as follows. Section 2 discusses work related to this research. Section 3 presents the motion and interaction tracking tool developed. Section 4 offers a case study of our motion and interaction tracking. Finally, Sect. 5 presents our conclusion and suggests future work.

2   Related Work

Users' data behavior in space is a valuable source of information about their activities. Moreover, such data allows identification of correlations and patterns in user movements and interactions, corresponding with their activity patterns. Simkovic, Hajtmanek, and Zajicek [4] tracked users of Barcelona Pavilion by Mies van der Rohe from Expo 1929 using an HTC Vive. They compared the user's heatmap with photoshoot positions, concluding that users' movements influence their activity in space and vice versa. Hurst [5] examined user behavior when they interacted with websites. Ivory [8] showed automatic data logging to analyze web application users. Mellon [9] evaluated user behavior in digital games. Drachen and Canossa [10] discussed spatial analysis methods for user behavior and presented case studies involving data from thousands of users. Southgate [11] captured videos to analyze a student learning environment. Kim et al. [3] examined game users by combining behaviors recorded in logs with visualizations and hierarchically organized reports.

Behavior analyses have usually been made based on tools such as questionnaires [12], direct interviews [13], and screen recorders [11]. For example, Deb et al. [14] used a questionnaire to measure the general attitudes of people while crossing in front of autonomous vehicles. Additionally, Tussyadiah, Wang, and Jia [15] also used a questionnaire to understand how the virtual environment influences users' travel decision-making. These analysis tools are powerful, but they create difficulties in use because they are time-consuming and laborious, requiring extended research time to ensure proper collection and data interpretation.

Research methods have tailored and combined techniques for each context to overcome their limitations [16, 17]. Therefore, relatively few solutions exist for integrating user behavior with the virtual environment in an automatic way. Although the idea of automatically tracking what users are doing while interacting with the environment seems simple, this task is complicated regarding virtual reality applications that use non-conventional devices, where the quantity of movement and interaction is immense. Our tool is integrated with the game engine Unity in that it was not originally designed to grab information about user behavior [18].

3   Motion and Interaction Tracking Tool

Depending on the research field, several interpretations exist when discussing human interaction. According to Edwin Hutchins [19], from the artificial intelligence viewpoint, interaction with humans is performed through the strings exchanged with an artificially intelligent agent. From the conversational analyst perspective, interaction is performed through speech. In ethnography, interaction can be characterized by face-to-face interplay, highlighting facial interactions and verbal behavior. However, human interaction goes beyond the social interaction between people and also includes user interaction with a virtual environment. With immersive virtual environments interaction can happen in several ways if we consider the interaction form and time between actions. User´s interaction is different for each individual. Thus, ways to identify and represent user environmental interactions are of great value to understanding user behavior within virtual environments.

Figure 1 depicts the workflow of our solution. Initially, the virtual environment is developed using the Unity game engine. Subsequently, a specific script is added to the main camera, and the hotspots are defined. User movements and interactions are recorded via triggers with colliders that were added on hotspots spread over the virtual environment. When the application is running, the log files are recorded. Finally, charts are generated, and the application can be replayed according to data registered in the log files.

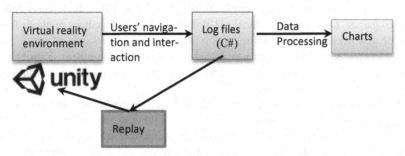

Fig. 1. Tracking tool workflow

Colliders are meant to represent the hotspot's physical properties. We register data about the user's camera, hotspots name, timestamp, and interaction with the environment while the application is running. Collecting this data enables monitoring of the time spent in each spot, how many times the user goes through each location, and the user's head movements, allowing a complete replaying of user behavior.

The tool was designed to be easy to use, without writing code. Developers simply must do the following:

- **Create hotspots:** When the user goes through a hotspot, the tool saves users' behavior data (e.g., timestamp and hotspot name) about the event. The quantity of hotspots depends on the research/user interest and is unlimited.
- **Add the script TrackingTool:** Developers must add this script to the main camera to gather all information. During interaction with the virtual environment, users are free to move and interact.

Figure 2 presents a code snippet showing the TrackingTool script created to gather information about user behavior. When running, this script records (1) when a user collides with a hotspot; (2) when a user stops touching a hotspot; (3) quaternions that represent the camera rotation; and (4) vector3, which represents camera position. TrackingTool script has functions to generate chart images on-the-fly[1] and to replay user behavior. Furthermore, TrackingTool script also maps physical keys on the keyboard to functions, such as "S" to call the function to save data in a file. TrackingTool script can be extended easily to monitor any conventional or non-conventional input device (e.g., data glove, biomechanics sensor nodes, mouse, and keyboard).

---

[1] We use QuickChart (https://quickchart.io/) service to generate chart images on-the-fly. Charts are rendered by Chart.js on web browsers.

```
...
public class TrackingTool : Monobehavior{
    private Vector3 obj_pos;
    private Quaternion obj_rot;
    ...
    // Users collided with a hotspot
    private void OnTriggerEnter(Collider col)
    //Replay users' behavior
    private IEnumerator Replay()
    // Save  users' behavior
    public void WriteToLogFile(string message)
    // chart to show time period in each hotspot
    private void Chart_period()
    // chart to show how many times crossed the hotspot
     private void Chart_crossed()
        ...
}
```

Fig. 2. Code snippet of the TrackingTool script added to the camera

4   Case Study

The activities of daily living (ADL) are extremely important for a person's daily life. ADL includes feeding, using the toilet, choosing clothes, dressing, personal hygiene, and keeping continent, among others. ADL activities are learned during childhood. Instrumental activities of daily living (IADL) also exist, which are more complex than ADL because they also include actions performed outside and activities necessary for a person's autonomy. Unlike ADL, IADL activities are learned during adolescence. Examples of IADL are managing finances, dealing with traffic, handling public transportation, shopping, preparing meals, managing medications, and maintaining household chores, among others. We can simulate most of these activities in virtual environments, allowing users to perform training in controlled and safe environments.

In this work, we defined as a use case the activities of a user's interaction with city artifacts. The user interacts with streets, sidewalks, and crosswalks. Our solution allows all the user's activities to be described regarding chronological order and duration, allowing a better understanding because of the visual metaphor employed (graph).

The purpose of the virtual reality environment presented is to simulate user behavior while walking in a city. Then, we are interested if the user utilizes the pedestrian crossings properly when navigating to some place, such as the gas station or bus stop. We added motion and tracking functionalities to the 3D city model called "City package."[2]. Figure 3 (a) depicts the 3D city, and Fig. 3(b) depicts the 3D city with the hotspots visible on the crosswalks and over the gas station.

---

[2] https://assetstore.unity.com/packages/3d/environments/urban/city-package-10722.

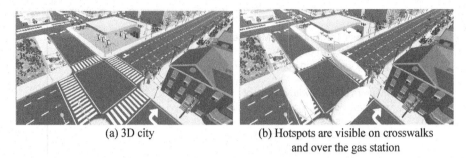

(a) 3D city

(b) Hotspots are visible on crosswalks and over the gas station

Fig. 3. 3D city model

Figure 4 depicts the hotspots created in the chosen 3D city. The colliders of each hotspot are enabled and set as a trigger, then the hotspots detect external interaction from the user's camera and execute code that is within the OnTriggerEnter and OnTriggerExit from the TrackingTool script. Then, the application can monitor when users collide or stop touching a hotspot.

Fig. 4. Hotspots

To evaluate our tool, a user navigated in the 3D city. We gave him the task of going to a variety store and returning to the starting point. He had unlimited time to accomplish the task. Once all data were recorded, we transformed, analyzed, and interpreted the results. All charts were created automatically. Figure 5(a) depicts how long the experience took, and Fig. 5(b) illustrates how many times the experiment was executed.

(a) Period of time

(b) How many times

Fig. 5. Period of time and quantity

Figure 6 depicts the user's routes during navigation represented by a graph. Each node is a hotspot, and the edge label shows how long the user took to move from one hotspot to another (a) and how many times the user traveled between two hotspots (b).

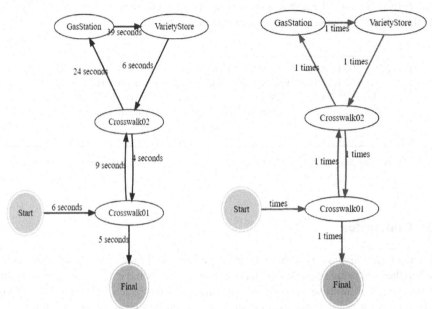

(a) How many times the user spent in each travel

(b) How many times each route has been travelled.

Fig. 6. The user's routes

Figure 7 depicts how long the user stayed inside the hotspot area during each crossing. For example, the user spent 6 s walking the pedestrian Crossing01 the first time, and 2 s the second time.

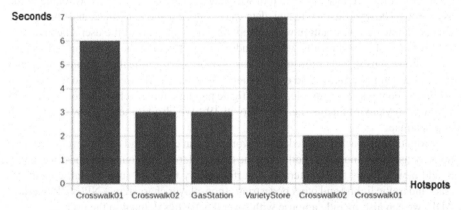

Fig. 7. How long the user stayed inside the hotspot area during each crossing.

After walking in the 3D city, the researcher/user also had the opportunity to replay users' movements and interactions, including the gazing behavior that can reflect the user's attention to spatial objects. Thus, a log file (Fig. 8) is generated while users' movements and interactions with the virtual environment. From the observed results, the performance of the application was not be considerably affected by the Tracking tool, being able to maintain the user experience in real time.

```
09/06/2021 13:48:17 Position: (-150.6, 71.2, 2.5) Rotation: (0.0, 0.0, 0.0, 1.0)
09/06/2021 13:48:17 Position: (-150.6, 71.2, 2.5) Rotation: (0.0, 0.0, 0.0, 1.0)
09/06/2021 13:48:17 Position: (-150.6, 71.2,2.5) Rotation: (0.0, 0.0, 0.0, 1.0)
09/06/2021 13:48:17 Position: (-150.6, 71.2, 2.5) Rotation: (0.0, 0.0, 0.0, 1.0)
...
```

Fig. 8. Log file snipped while a user moves and interacts with the virtual environment.

5   Conclusion

User behavior analysis is commonly employed to identify patterns related to individuals when they are using applications. Understanding user behavior in a virtual reality environment is not intuitive and depends on various factors, such as interaction and visualization devices used and world complexity. Even though there are several behavior studies available, automatic tools to gather user behavior in virtual reality environments remain an open issue.

This paper presented a tool that gathers information about user behavior, including motion and interaction in virtual reality worlds, and combines these data to generate charts. The tool also allows the researcher/user to replay all user behavior. This tool, integrated with virtual reality environments, tracks user behavior, allowing instructors, designers, developers, and researchers to reduce errors and save significant time. We also presented a case study that used our tool, where a user explored a virtual reality environment in several ways. The tool was added easily to the 3D city available in the asset store. The user then navigated, data were collected and combined, and charts were created, allowing investigation with quantitative data analysis of the user's behavior.

From the observed results, we conclude that our tracking tool has achieved its purpose, allowing us to gather information easily about users while they are navigating and interacting with a virtual world environment. As future work, we intend to use our tool in specific contexts, for example, to investigate patients' motor rehabilitation sessions in virtual reality environments (i.e., after Covid-19). We also aim to add new charts, such as a heatmap.

From the approach proposed in this work, we can extend and create several applications focused on simulation. Following the theme addressed in our case study, we intend to add new artifacts to the interaction performed by the user, such as traffic elements (cars and traffic lights) and other pedestrians (non-player characters—NPCs). Regarding ADL, we can also include a house with several activities defined to the user.

As for behavioral study applications, the data generated by our tool can be used to infer treatments and training aimed at ADL and AIDL. Going further, the tool can help health professionals understand the actions performed in virtual environments and generate data for use in the automatic inference of information by machine learning approaches.

Acknowledgments. This project has been partially supported by Huawei do Brasil Telecomunicações Ltda (Fundunesp Process # 3123/2020).

References

1. Stadler, S., Cornet, H., Novaes Theoto, T., Frenkler, F.: A tool, not a toy: using virtual reality to evaluate the communication between autonomous vehicles and pedestrians. In: tom Dieck, M.C., Jung, T. (eds.) Augmented Reality and Virtual Reality. PI, pp. 203–216. Springer, Cham (2019). https://doi.org/10.1007/978-3-030-06246-0_15
2. Loomis, J.M., Blascovich, J.J., Beall, A.C.: Immersive virtual environment technology as a basic research tool in psychology. Behav. Res. Methods Instrum. Comput. **31**, 557–564 (1999). https://doi.org/10.3758/BF03200735
3. Kim, J.H., Gunn, D.V., Schuh, E., Phillips, B., Pagulayan, R.J., Wixon, D.: Tracking real-time user experience (TRUE): a comprehensive instrumentation solution for complex systems (2008). https://doi.org/10.1145/1357054.1357126
4. Šimkovič, V., Zajíček, V., Hajtmanek, R.: User tracking in VR environment. In: 2019 International Conference on Engineering Technologies and Computer Science (EnT), pp. 80–84 (2019). https://doi.org/10.1109/EnT.2019.00022
5. Hurst, A., Hudson, S.E., Mankoff, J.: Dynamic detection of novice vs. skilled use without a task model. In: Proceedings of the SIGCHI Conference on Human Factors in Computing Systems. pp. 271–280. Association for Computing Machinery, New York (2007). https://doi.org/10.1145/1240624.1240669
6. Hilbert, D.M., Redmiles, D.F.: Extracting usability information from user interface events. ACM Comput. Surv. **32**, 384–421 (2000). https://doi.org/10.1145/371578.371593
7. Brandão, A.F., et al.: Biomechanics sensor node for virtual reality: a wearable device applied to gait recovery for neurofunctional rehabilitation. In: Gervasi, O., et al. (eds.) ICCSA 2020. LNCS, vol. 12255, pp. 757–770. Springer, Cham (2020). https://doi.org/10.1007/978-3-030-58820-5_54
8. Ivory, M.Y., Hearst, M.A.: The state of the art in automating usability evaluation of user interfaces. ACM Comput. Surv. **33**, 470–516 (2001). https://doi.org/10.1145/503112.503114
9. Mellon, L.: Applying metrics driven development to MMO costs and risks. Versan Corporation. 9 (2009)
10. Canossa, A., Drachen, A.: Evaluating motion: spatial user behaviour in virtual environments MindTrek 2009 // Everyday Life in the Ubiquitous Era // Ambient Media + Social Media + Games. International Journal of Arts and Technology (2010)
11. Southgate, E.: Using screen capture video to understand learning in virtual reality. In: 2020 IEEE Conference on Virtual Reality and 3D User Interfaces Abstracts and Workshops (VRW), pp. 418–421 (2020). https://doi.org/10.1109/VRW50115.2020.00089
12. Rea, L.M., Parker, R.A.: Designing and conducting survey research: a comprehensive guide. Jossey-Bass, San Francisco, CA (2014)
13. Crundall, D.: Driving experience and the acquisition of visual information. http://eprints.nottingham.ac.uk/13917/. Accessed 25 Mar 2021

14. Deb, S., Strawderman, L., Carruth, D.W., DuBien, J., Smith, B., Garrison, T.M.: Development and validation of a questionnaire to assess pedestrian receptivity toward fully autonomous vehicles. Transp. Res. Part C: Emerging Technol. **84**, 178–195 (2017). https://doi.org/10.1016/j.trc.2017.08.029
15. Tussyadiah, I.P., Wang, D., Jia, C.(: Virtual reality and attitudes toward tourism destinations. In: Schegg, R., Stangl, B. (eds.) Information and Communication Technologies in Tourism 2017, pp. 229–239. Springer, Cham (2017). https://doi.org/10.1007/978-3-319-51168-9_17
16. Davis, J., Steury, K., Pagulayan, R.: A survey method for assessing perceptions of a game. Int. J. Comput. Game Res. 5 (2005)
17. Karwowski, W.: A Gameplay-Centered Design Framework for Human Factors in Games. CRC Press (2006). https://doi.org/10.1201/9780849375477-283
18. Brookes, J., Warburton, M., Alghadier, M., Mon-Williams, M., Mushtaq, F.: Studying human behavior with virtual reality: the unity experiment framework. Behav. Res. Methods **52**(2), 455–463 (2019). https://doi.org/10.3758/s13428-019-01242-0
19. Hutchins, E.: The Distributed Cognition Perspective on Human Interaction. Routledge (2006). https://doi.org/10.4324/9781003135517-19

Augmented Reality in Medical Education, an Empirical Study

Imre Zsigmond$^{(\boxtimes)}$ and Alexandru Buhai

Faculty of Mathematics and Computer Science, Babeş-Bolyai University,
1 Mihail Kogălniceanu, 400084 Cluj-Napoca, Romania
`imre@cs.ubbcluj.ro`

Abstract. Even though we live in a high tech world some of the learning techniques used in medical schools are outdated or are not taking advantage of the latest technologies available. This is partially due to the cost associated with adopting new and ever-changing technologies in emerging economies and lacking awareness of their existence. We created an application that has the potential to help students train themselves better by using Augmented Reality and gamification techniques. It detects the student's face through the laptop or phone camera and maps realistic skin conditions on the detected face, prompting the student to recognize them. With the overwhelmingly positive response from the surveys, the application should deepen student knowledge of pathologies.

Keywords: Augmented Reality · Medical · Education · Face detection · Gamification

1 Introduction

Medical education has been the subject of much research ever since its inception. Different technologies and techniques, for example simulation have appeared throughout the years. [5] Classical, physical simulation while becoming more sophisticated with advances in engineering and new materials, had an offshoot in the form of digital simulation. Virtual Reality and Augmented Reality becoming more sophisticated as 3D technology matured. On the teaching side technology takes an ever increasing role, for example in ontologies based eLearning [7]. In the last decade a new approach to education, namely gamification, has been gaining ground. The goal of gamification is to engage and motivate students to learn by using video game design elements in their learning environments [27].

Nowadays, both preclinical and clinical training have to grow well beyond the traditional approaches, with new ways of learning, new techniques and with the introduction of the media into the academic curriculum [18]. One of the new interactive ways to enhance normal environments or situations is Augmented Reality. Augmented Reality (AR) refers to a series of technologies that overlay CGI (Computer Generated Images), text and video on the real world. Ronald Azuma [1], defined the implementation of AR by three characteristics [33]:

© Springer Nature Switzerland AG 2021
O. Gervasi et al. (Eds.): ICCSA 2021, LNCS 12958, pp. 631–640, 2021.
https://doi.org/10.1007/978-3-030-87016-4_45

1. the combination of the real world and virtual elements
2. which are interactive in real time
3. which are registered in 3D

Augmented Reality (AR) is closer to the real world than its counterpart virtual reality, where both the generated objects as well as the world are computer generated. Even so Augmented Reality is still closely tied to Virtual Reality (VR) since the core concept of AR evolved as an extension or variation of VR. According to [33] AR represents the cutting edge of modern society's technological development. The information presented to the user in Augmented Reality is seamlessly added to their surroundings. The simulation can be either constructive (i.e. will build on the surrounding environment), or destructive (i.e. will mask the surrounding environment).

Since the price of most AR devices can be prohibitive for most medicine students, we were interested to know weather we can enhance their study with smartphones/laptops which they are likely to posses. Section 3 details how we merged AR with Gamification to enhance the study experience for medical students. The approach overlays the likeness of various pathologies (more in Sect. 3.2) on the face of anybody it is pointed towards (more in Sect. 3.1). The student then has various choices to identify the condition. In turn, they get to gain points and compete for high scores with their peers (Sect. 3.3). Not only do the students get more varied exposure to pathologies but it also incentivizes repetition through game mechanics. We conducted a small scale study with third-year medical students on a working prototype with positive results (Sect. 4). We conclude in Sect. 5 our hope that this new approach will promote self-learning and be more advantageous for both the students and the faculty, increasing the desire to learn.

2 Related Works

Virtual reality as a precursor to Augmented Reality has been and continues to be the subject of research in medical education [14]. Applications using VR have managed to increase learning outcomes for various medical specialties in different training procedures [3,24,25,29]. While the case for VR has been made an equal if not greater case for AR can also be made. AR's strength is combining a physical simulation in the form of mannequins or laparoscopy equipment for example, with virtual overlays to give better feedback and make the learning experience more immersive [2].

Literature reviews agree that a well-designed AR system has the potential for improving healthcare education [2,13,17,34]. The authors from [2] claim that there are relatively few AR apps in medicine, it is worth mentioning that ProMIS [4] seems over-represented in the literature. [34] found that 2/3 of papers focused on surgery, primarily laparoscopic surgery. Other uses include a navigation tool during surgery [6] or as a therapeutic tool for the patients [15].

Gamification is most commonly defined as the "use of game design elements in non-game contexts" [9]. Shorter attention spans among students, and ever more potent distractions has prompted research into the gamification of learning, in an attempt to capture their engagement, and to inspire learning [[35]]. The concept is relatively recent and it has already been used to enhance graduate medical education. Kaizen-IM software developed by [20] have used daily questions and leaderboards to facilitate acquisition of new knowledge and engaged a large number of residents. In [19] authors used "Top Gun" and "Jeopardy" style contests to motivate thoracic surgery students to study more, which they did. There are a lot of interesting experiments with gamification in the literature, applied to many fields. For example [[36]] found 19 reports of gamified systems pertaining to health and well-being, with 59% positive and 41% mixed results. Physical health related behaviors were positive, while the cognitive behaviors were mixed.

On the intersection of AR and gamification [21] argues strongly for the potential use. [11] sees a huge possibility for AR and gamification, though clarifies that more study is warranted on gamification's side. In studies not related to learning, [26] proposes a AR and Gamification solutions to alleviate boredom for adolescent drivers. [12] and [26] mention gamification as applied in their AR game systems.

3   AR for Medical Education

3.1   Face Detection

The Human face is a very difficult object to detect since it comes in many forms and colors, is highly dynamic and a lot of times the features are not regular. In order for our idea to be practical we had to opt for a marker-less AR in the classical sense, and use the human face itself as a marker. Although a lot of algorithms exist in order to detect faces, a lot of them are too computationally expensive to work in real time [32]. The core of our application is the Open Computer Vision Library (OpenCV) together with the Unity3D cross-platform game engine[1]. We chose unity to be able to run it on both PC and Android so it can reach a wider audience. The classification algorithm used in this project for object and face detection is AdaBoost, with a machine learning approach proposed by Paul Viola and Michael Jones, based on Haar Feature cascade classifiers [30].

OpenCV is an open-source library computer vision, image processing, video processing, and object detection[2]. In order to use it inside Unity3D, we needed a third party plugin that lets you use OpenCV inside Unity3D by translating OpenCV into C# provided by Enox Software[3]. The AdaBoost Classifier cascades, are based on Haar-like features and not on pixels. A Haar-like feature is a weak classifier and will be used for face recognition [8]. The Viola-Jones face detection also uses an important concept of a rejection cascade. This allows the algorithm to be fast and to discard photos were no face is recognized with little

---

[1] https://unity.com/.

[2] https://opencv.org/.

[3] https://enoxsoftware.com/.

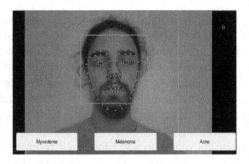

Fig. 1. Face tracking visualization

computational cost. It works by having layers of classifiers. The first test with a classifier in the cascade is designed to discard as many negative windows as possible, and if one of the features does not appear in the windows the whole process is stopped. Then a new window is tested and the process is repeated. After checking the last window, the scale of the window is increased and the detection process begins again. In the end, every face detected in the different windows, are merged and are considered as one at the closure of the process. Therefore, using weak classifiers we are capable to detect faces fast and with reasonable accuracy. An example of the real-time highlighted face features can bee seen in Fig. 1.

3.2 Considered Skin Diseases

For the study, we have chosen 3 types of diseases and skin conditions that have really specific characteristics: xanthelasma, herpes, malignant melanoma.

The xanthelasma is typically present in middle-aged and senior adults, most often around the eyelids. Xanthelasma is composed of xanthoma cells, which are foamy, lipid-laden histiocytes [23]. They are characterized by a macroscopic yellow hue. We chose this condition because it is usually found around the eyes and its yellowish color, which makes it instantly recognisable to medical students.

Malignant melanoma is a malignant tumor of melanocytes, which are the cells that make the pigment melanin and are derived from the neural crest. It mostly appears on the skin, but also rarely on mucosal surfaces. Melanoma represents a fraction (5%) of skin cancers but results in the highest mortality rate [16]. Some signs of melanoma are a darker or variable discoloration, itching, increase in size or development of satellites and later even ulceration or bleeding. It's easily identifiable by its color and can be found everywhere on the skin of a person, including the face. It also is the most dangerous type of skin cancer [28], therefore is extremely important to be recognised, so medical students should pay close attention to it. To mimic reality, pictures from various melanomas were used, two can be seen in Fig. 2.

Herpes simplex virus 1 is a member of the Herpesviridae family. It is known from ancient times and it frequently infects human beings [31]. Many of those

Fig. 2. Melanoma examples, used in the application.

infected do not have any visible signs or symptoms of the virus, but for some, the infection can even be life-threatening. Some of the symptoms of herpes include, but not limited to, itching, burning sensation, pain around the infected area, cold sores, blisters and redness in close proximity of the lesion point. Around 67% of the world population under 50 years old is infected with Herpes (HSV-1) [22]. In depicting the disease we focused on oral herpes, represented with redness, blisters, and cold sores. Being that common, a lot of people have seen herpes in real life, so it is easily discernible.

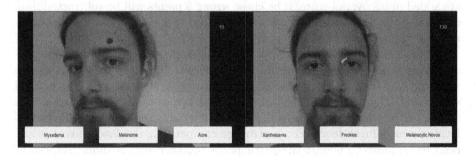

Fig. 3. Rendered Melanoma(left), and Xanthelasma(right)

Photos of the mentioned maladies as they appear in the application can be seen in Fig. 3. The original background was set to transparent in order to eliminate the clutter of the picture and to be accurate for any skin color of the subject. After every picture was cropped and adapted according to our needs, a normal map and a specular map of them was created, using ShaderMap4[4]. The normal map is a way to imitate the texture of an object (i.e. the indentation, coarseness, smoothness, the way it reflects light) by using shading. The specular map uses white and black values to create zones that have different reflectivity percentages. Meaning that some surfaces will appear shinier than the others. We can also increase the contrast of the surface to make it more recognisable in relation to its neighbours.

---

[4] https://shadermap.com/home/.

The 3D models of the diseases were made using the Unity in-game editor. We created a plane object and a material from an image of the skin condition. The material is a Specular Bump Transparent material. Transparent material implies that the transparent parts of the image will not show, leaving only the excrescence. The bump or normal material allows us to create variations in the way light bounces off the surface of the picture. It creates the illusion of 3d and improves low-polygon models making them appear more detailed.

3.3 Gamification Elements

The number of game design elements in gamification can be vast. For example [20] a number of elements: points, badges, levels, leaderboards and instant feedback. These in turn can be used to motivate participants towards desired outcomes. The aforementioned study reported that leaderboards were the most important motivator of participation amongst the residents.

When we designed our system we opted for an instant feedback approach for a positive feedback loop together with auditory feedback. Buttons were added to the bottom of the screen such that the player can choose what disease they believe is showing on the subject's face. If the player guesses correctly 10 points are added to his overall score. If he chose wrong 5 points will be subtracted from the final score. This together with a leaderboard is meant to foster competition amongst the students. Leaderboards serve as a social comparison tool.

As the primary gameplay loop a disease is mapped on the subject once the algorithm detects a face in the live video stream. The first disease is chosen randomly and stays until the user makes its choice. The diseases are randomised each round. The position of the melanoma and herpes changes so that the users can be better trained since in real life both afflictions could be found in various locations on human faces. For a stronger competition the leaderboard would need to be shared amongst the participants together with a timer. As well as some kind of progression mechanic, possibly in the form of leveling.

4 Discussion of Results

A study was conducted on third-year Medical Students with ages between 21–23. The sample size is low, only 9 participants. When our application is further developed the study should be redone on a larger sample, the overwhelmingly positive results are a strong indicator of the approach. The study consisted of explaining to the students the concept of the application and letting them use it for 5–10 min. While this was taking place we left the room. At the end of their trial usage, they were asked to complete a survey. All of them correctly recognised the diseases, validating that the diseases resemble their real-life counterpart/medical book description. Third-year medical students in Romania already had to study Semiology/Symptomatology, Anatomical Pathology and Physiology, all of which helped them with the identification task. It must be mentioned again that the

Table 1. Likert scale survey results

Concept of interest	Very negative	Negative	Neutral	Positive	Very positive
Visual accuracy compared to medical textbook	0%	0%	0%	66.67%	33.33%
Visual accurate compared to real life	0%	0%	0%	0%	100%
Perceived usefulness	0%	0%	0%	33.33%	66.67%
Willingness to compete with peers?	0%	0%	0%	66.67%	33.33%
Likeliness to recommend	0%	0%	0%	0%	100%

diseases were specifically chosen to be easily identifiable by people with medical training (Table 1).

Subsequently, some of them were interested if we could add more gamified elements to the application, like the concept of "combo", winning streaks or timers. The fact that our application is not static and you can examine the diseases from different angles made them curious because until then they were only exposed to pictures/descriptions of some of the pathologies, never seeing them in real life. This feature allowed the students to get a new point of view for the diseases.

Since all responses were purely positive, the demonstration of statistical significance is not warranted. The discrepancy between the first 2 questions, although the sample size is small, revealed that the medical textbook description and representation of disease differ with real-life diseases. Further studies are needed to verify the accuracy with medical professionals.

5   Conclusion and Further Work

The goal of this study was to review the usefulness of an application that combines Augmented Reality with gamification, in the context of a medical university. Even with the small sample size, the responses suggest potential in our approach. Students are willing and excited about using new technologies and they are ready to accept new learning methodologies like gamification in their day-to-day lives. Most of the students agreed that an application like this would be useful with their studies and that it presents an interesting complement to textbooks.

The study also shows that the models were realistic enough and that the students could quickly identify the signs of the disease and make an assumption based on their previous knowledge. Further work is needed to refine the techniques of simulation and broaden the symptoms. As stated in [10], gamification in education is an emerging trend. Even though early adopters of gamification are Computer Science professors, we think that it is well designed and used correctly, it has the potential to improve the learning conditions of the students in the medical field.

The application can be further enhanced by moving away from multiple choice questions towards personalized testing and suggestion along the lines of Developing Ontology-Grounded Methodology and Applications [7]. The gamification aspect of the application could also be improved and tested with game mechanics other than points, progress bar, and leaderboard. Some students could benefit from specific or immediate goals, visible progression systems, and digital badges. This could be a follow-up study with significantly increased sample size, and a control group. On a technical level, detecting other parts of the body and to have more skin conditions and diseases added in would be important.

References

1. Azuma, R.T.: A survey of augmented reality. Presence Teleoper. Virtual Environ. **6**(4), 355–385 (1997)
2. Barsom, E.Z., Graafland, M., Schijven, M.P.: Systematic review on the effectiveness of augmented reality applications in medical training. Surg. Endoscopy **30**(10), 4174–4183 (2016)
3. Bharathan, R., Vali, S., Setchell, T., Miskry, T., Darzi, A., Aggarwal, R.: Psychomotor skills and cognitive load training on a virtual reality laparoscopic simulator for tubal surgery is effective. Eur. J. Obstet. Gynecol. Reprod. Biol. **169**(2), 347–352 (2013)
4. Botden, S.M.B.I., Jakimowicz, J.J.: What is going on in augmented reality simulation in laparoscopic surgery? Surg. Endoscopy **23**(8), 1693 (2009)
5. Bradley, P.: The history of simulation in medical education and possible future directions. Med. Educ. **40**(3), 254–262 (2006)
6. Chu, M.W.A., et al.: Augmented reality image guidance improves navigation for beating heart mitral valve repair. Innovations **7**(4), 274–281 (2012)
7. Ciuciu, I., Tang, Y.: A Personalized and Collaborative eLearning Materials Recommendation Scenario Using Ontology-Based Data Matching Strategies. In: Meersman, R., Dillon, T., Herrero, P. (eds.) OTM 2010. LNCS, vol. 6428, pp. 575–584. Springer, Heidelberg (2010). https://doi.org/10.1007/978-3-642-16961-8_81
8. Delbiaggio, N., et al.: A comparison of facial recognition's algorithms (2017)
9. Deterding, S., Dixon, D., Khaled, R., Nacke, L.: From game design elements to gamefulness: defining gamification, vol. 11, pp. 9–15 (2011)
10. Dicheva, D., Dichev, C., Agre, G., Angelova, G., et al.: Gamification in education: a systematic mapping study. Educ. Technol. Soc. **18**(3), 75–88 (2015)
11. Dunleavy, M.: Design principles for augmented reality learning. TechTrends **58**(1), 28–34 (2014)
12. Eleftheria, C.A., Charikleia, Iason, C.G., Athanasios, T., Dimitrios, T.: An innovative augmented reality educational platform using gamification to enhance lifelong learning and cultural education. In: IISA 2013, pp. 1–5. IEEE (2013)
13. Ferrer, V., Perdomo, A., Rashed-Ali, H., Fies, C., Quarles, J.: How does usability impact motivation in augmented reality serious games for education? In: 2013 5th International Conference on Games and Virtual Worlds for Serious Applications (VS-GAMES), pp. 1–8. IEEE (2013)

14. Holden, C.: The local games lab abq: homegrown augmented reality. TechTrends **58**(1), 42–48 (2014)
15. Hondori, H.M., Khademi, M., Dodakian, L., Cramer, S.C., Lopes, C.V.: A spatial augmented reality rehab system for post-stroke hand rehabilitation. In: MMVR, vol. 184, pp. 279–285 (2013)
16. National Cancer Institute. Melanoma treatment'for health professionals (pdq®)2015
17. Kamphuis, C., Barsom, E., Schijven, M., Christoph, N.: Augmented reality in medical education? Persp. Med. Educ. **3**(4), 300–311 (2014)
18. McCoy, L., Lewis, J.H., Dalton, D.: Gamification and multimedia for medical education: a landscape review. .J. Am. Osteopath. Assoc **116**(1), 22–34 (2016)
19. Mokadam, N.A., et al.: Gamification in thoracic surgical education: using competition to fuel performance. J. Thor. Cardiovasc. Surg. **150**(5), 1052–1058 (2015)
20. Nevin, C.R., et al.: Gamification as a tool for enhancing graduate medical education. Postgrad. Med. J. **90**(1070), 685–693 (2014)
21. Noor, N.M., Yusoff, F.H., Yussof, R.L., Ismail, M.: The potential use of augmented reality in gamification. In: 5th International Conference on Computing and Informatics Proceedings, Istanbul, Turkey, pp. 159–167 (2015)
22. World Health Organization. Herpes simplex virus (2017)
23. Rohrich, R.J., Janis, J.E., Pownell, P.H.: Xanthelasma palpebrarum: a review and current management principles. Plastic Reconstruct. Surg. **110**(5), 1310–1314 (2002)
24. Schout, B.M.A., et al.: Transfer of cysto-urethroscopy skills from a virtual-reality simulator to the operating room: a randomized controlled trial. BJU Int. **106**(2), 226–231 (2010)
25. Schreuder, H.W.R., Oei, G., Maas, M., Borleffs, J.C.C., Schijven, M.P.: Implementation of simulation in surgical practice: minimally invasive surgery has taken the lead: the Dutch experience. Med. Teach. **33**(2), 105–115 (2011)
26. Schroeter, R., Oxtoby, J., Johnson, D.: Ar and gamification concepts to reduce driver boredom and risk taking behaviours. In Proceedings of the 6th International Conference on Automotive User Interfaces and Interactive Vehicular Applications, pp. 1–8 (2014)
27. Shatz, I.: Using gamification and gaming in order to promote risk taking in the language learning process. In: Proceedings of the 13th Annual MEITAL National Conference, Haifa, Israel, pp. 227–232 (2015)
28. Stewart, B.W.K.P., Wild, C.P., et al.: World cancer report 2014 (2014)
29. Vanderbilt, A.A., et al.: Randomized controlled trials: a systematic review of laparoscopic surgery and simulation-based training. Global J. Health Sci. **7**(2), 310 (2015)
30. Viola, P., Jones, M., et al.: Rapid object detection using a boosted cascade of simple features. CVPR **1**(1), 511–518 (2001)
31. Whitley, R.J., Roizman, B.: Herpes simplex virus infections. The Lancet **357**(9267), 1513–1518 (2001)
32. Phillip Ian Wilson and John Fernandez: Facial feature detection using haar classifiers. J. Comput. Sci. Coll. **21**(4), 127–133 (2006)
33. Yuen, S.C.Y., Yaoyuneyong, G., Johnson, E.: Augmented reality: an overview and five directions for ar in education. J. Educ. Technol. Dev. Exchange (JETDE) **4**(1), 11 (2011)
34. Zhu, E., Hadadgar, A., Masiello, I., Zary, N.: Augmented reality in healthcare education: an integrative review. PeerJ **2**, e469 (2014)

35. Jenni, M., Jonna, K., Juho, H.: Gamification of education and learning: a review of empirical literature. In: Proceedings of the 2nd International GamiFIN Conference, GamiFIN 2018 (2018)
36. Johnson, D., Deterding, S., Kuhn, K.-A., Staneva, A., Stoyanov, S., Hides, L.: Gamification for health and wellbeing: a systematic review of the literature. Internet Intervent. **6**, 89–106 (2016)

Evaluation Methods Applied to Virtual Reality Educational Applications: A Systematic Review

Daniel Bueno Domingueti[1]([✉])(iD), Diego Roberto Colombo Dias[1](iD),
Marcelo de Paiva Guimarães[2](iD), and Dárlinton Barbosa Feres Carvalho[1](iD)

[1] Universidade Federal de São João del-Rei, São João del-Rei, Brazil
danieldomingueti@aluno.ufsj.edu.br,
{diegodias,darlinton}@ufsj.edu.br
[2] Universidade Federal de São Paulo/UNIFACCAMP, Campo Limpo Paulista, Brazil
marcelo.paiva@unifesp.br

Abstract. Evaluation is an important activity in software development since it allows detecting issues like design flaws under different analysis perspectives. However, conducting a satisfactory assessment is challenging, especially considering new interactive technologies such as virtual reality (VR). This paper presents a systematic review revealing the most used evaluation methods in this context to deepen the understanding of the evaluation of educational applications employing VR. Considering a search in the ACM database with a filter for the last six years, we selected 1351 initial studies and 81 for analysis. The results show that the tests of usability, flow, and technology acceptance model are the most common, as well as the methods used in many articles present weaknesses due to the lack of an adequate theoretical foundation. Accordingly, we strengthen the relevance of using well-defined support theories in all stages of an evaluation.

Keywords: Evaluation · Virtual Reality · Systematic review

1 Introduction

Evaluation is a crucial stage in software development, being considered in various methodologies and development processes [31]. At this stage, it is possible to assess the product value and quality, and in the case of research projects, it enables us to check the hypothesis and draw conclusions. An evaluation can be executed based on different perspectives, each having its principles and methods.

From another perspective, the interplay between users and software applications has been studied by the Human-Computer Interaction (HCI). This field considers a set of elements for analysis in a software evaluation, but mainly regarding user experience and design alternatives.

Each evaluation perspective and the different kinds of software interactions bring a variety of methods and techniques available to perform the evaluation stage. There are numerous approaches in the literature for such purposes.

© Springer Nature Switzerland AG 2021
O. Gervasi et al. (Eds.): ICCSA 2021, LNCS 12958, pp. 641–657, 2021.
https://doi.org/10.1007/978-3-030-87016-4_46

Nevertheless, multiple perspectives are relevant when analyzing a software product to get a better quality assessment. However, building an evaluation instrument is not a trivial task, requiring many steps and deliberations to be performed. For instance, related to actions to conduct an evaluation, the *DECIDE Framework* establishes a formal structure to create and execute a user evaluation [29] in six steps.

Defining an evaluation instrument can be even more challenging when dealing with new (or unique) interaction styles such as mixed reality systems—a concept that joins Virtual Reality (VR) with Augmented Reality (AR). The challenge concerning those peculiar evaluations includes the greater need for specialized resources as well as concerning the definition of the task for analysis—mainly due to the unusual interaction style adopted by the advanced applications [2].

Notwithstanding, the new interaction styles provided by VR brought a set of significant innovations to many research areas and commercial applications. Notably, VR is scoring remarkable results in the context of educational software. For example, it can help with medical training and education [25], and even providing new experiences on education [33].

Accordingly, this paper presents research with the objective of providing a better understanding of how educational software applications based on VR have been evaluated through a systematic review. This study seeks to identify and characterize the most popular research approaches and evaluation methods. Thus, we expect to promote a better comprehension of how evaluation methods have been used in research considering VR applications aimed at education. Consequently, we hope it nurtures better practices in dealing with the evaluation of new technologies.

2   Background

The experimental evaluation stage plays a vital role in software development and scientific research. Experiments are conducted to reveal the influences of intervention in such a way as to allow varying input parameters and learn possible causes, effects, and causal relations [28]. This stage has evolved over time based on scientific thinking: a post-positivist philosophy that involves the exam and interpretation of pieces of evidence into a theoretical structure molding all the scientific research stages ([16] *apud* [17]).

Four main elements define the experimental evaluation, as depicted in Fig. 1: support theories, method, data collection tools, and results. Determined by the practiced method, the research type (or approach) fixes the range of possible data collection tools. Moreover, data collection tools dictate how the data will be analyzed. According to scientific thinking and method, the whole process should be anchored at well-defined support theories.

A method defines a structured process and guides researchers through the whole evaluation performance. That is, it determines how the evaluation (and the research) will be conducted, which steps will be performed, and the order of their execution [12]. The chosen method is related to the study objective

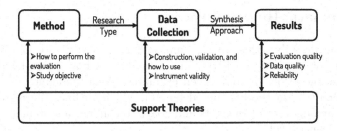

Fig. 1. The four main elements used to characterize an experimental evaluation and their relationships.

and must be based on a well-defined academic grounding. Thus, as long as the selected method counts on reliable supporting theories, the experiment results deliver scientific value. That is, the extent to which the results are valuable and contributing to the body of knowledge, especially from the current experiment scenario to other contexts [8] *apud* [1].

Therefore, the chosen method, along with the study objectives, establishes an approach qualifying the experiment. The paradigm adopted by the researcher (i.e., the primary research approach) refers to how the researcher perceives and interprets the world. The research approach may be qualified as quantitative, qualitative, mixed, or, as defined in this study, combined. The following paradigm guides the researcher in defining or building the data collection tools based on the data types to be collected further.

The mixed approach uses both classical approaches (i.e., quantitative and qualitative) in order to provide a better comprehension of the evaluated phenomena through a complementary (or even a different) point of view [10]. In our study, however, we use the concept of combined approach: the research uses both classical approaches, although it is not necessarily based on the mixed method theory, as described in the literature.

The use of well-defined support theories is also desirable to set the data collection process. The gold standard is to validate the data collection through statistical methods besides establishing specific instructions about its usage in experiments. Performing the validation through statistics provides a better internal quality of the test - the condition in which the variables can be related to each other, not representing measurement errors [28]. In the case of more than one possible way of analysis, each one must also be validated [8].

With support theories ensuring internal and external qualities, that is, the validity of methods, tools, and analysis view, a greater sense of scientific rigor backs the experiment, besides the whole research. Thereby, the study conclusions are not merely assigned to the hypothesis and conceptions created by the researchers but based on substantial evidence that answer - positively or negatively - the well-defined assumptions supported by the backing theories. Thus, it is also possible to ensure the experiment and research reliability, allowing its replication and confident use of the obtained results in a similar context [28].

3 Systematic Review Process

This section describes the process employed in this study to conduct a systematic review to provide a better understanding of how educational software applications based on VR have been evaluated. As a guideline for this study, we considered the method proposed by [15], which outlines the required steps and ideas, among a set of elements and goals, to conduct a systematic review in computer science studies.

3.1 Research Questions

Five research questions (RQ) were set and considered in this study based on the main elements used to characterize an experimental evaluation. It is worth mentioning, the presence of support theories is also considered, but as a feature of methods and tools.

- **RQ1**: What are the most popular methods used to evaluate educational software based on VR?
- **RQ2**: How the methods that had been used in researches were conceived?
- **RQ3**: What are the most popular data collection tools that have been used?
- **RQ4**: How the data collection tools were conceived?
- **RQ5**: What is the most common research approach which has been used by authors?

3.2 Search Strategy

The search string was constructed incrementally, combining search terms and verifying their results. Search terms from three research domains were taken into consideration (i.e., VR, evaluation, and education). These terms were selected according to know keywords presented in the literature and related to the explored domains. In particular, the evaluation domain keywords had been extracted and adapted from [7] article, since it was needed to refine and limit the results. Finally, the search string used in this article was built using *AND* and *OR* operations, as defined in the following box.

> ((virtual AND (reality OR environment)) OR (immersive AND
> environment)) **AND** (test OR validation OR analysis OR
> (user AND (evaluation OR study OR studies)) OR experiment
> OR (pilot AND study) OR participant OR subject) **AND**
> (education OR teaching OR learning OR schooling)

This review explored studies recently published in a six-year window, that is, articles published in January 2014 and June 2020.

Initially, a variety of portals and digital libraries have been considered in the paper retrieval process regarding the proposed search string, such as IEEE[1], ACM Digital Library[2], Scopus[3] and Web of Science[4]. However, due to the high number of results, only the ACM Digital Library portal was used to set papers for analysis.

3.3 Selection Criteria

The whole set of articles retrieved through the search string has been considered for analysis. Going forward in the revision processes, the following inclusion criteria were considered:

– Studies that have developed a VR application considering education as the main objective; and,
– Studies that have been peer-reviewed.

Studies that fill at least one of the following (exclusion) criteria have been excluded from the analysis:

– Studies related to education, but that has not developed a VR application;
– Studies that developed a VR application, which is not related to education;
– Studies that has an evaluation, which is not related to education nor VR;
– Gray literature, for example, resumed articles, posters, thesis, and others.

For each analyzed article, the selection criteria were first applied considering its abstract. Later, if it still fulfills the selection criteria, the whole paper was thoroughly analyzed.

3.4 Data Extraction

We created a report to summarize the studies and their metadata to answer our research questions. This report contains topics about the article's metadata (e.g., title, publishing date, and others) and questions related to the research questions, such as the presence of an evaluation or assessment stage, how it was done, among other relevant issues. The report was built with the online tool Google Forms[5] to ease the data collection and management. The form also contains a field to enumerate the possible research results, according to the authors, which will also be analyzed further. The extraction data was executed by one researcher, and the data was stored in a digital spreadsheet.

---

[1] https://ieeexplore.ieee.org/Xplore/home.jsp.
[2] https://dl.acm.org/.
[3] https://www.scopus.com/search/form.uri?display=basic.
[4] https://apps.webofknowledge.com/.
[5] https://www.google.com/forms/about/.

3.5   Data Synthesis

The studies included in the analysis through the acceptance criteria were then summarized and analyzed. The data collected on the previous step is synthesized with a detailed report based on statistics [15]. Then, we summarized the data according to the fields that have been defined in the report: publish year, type of event, the number of studies that have an evaluation stage, and others. Regarding evaluation, we defined a set of categories relating to the base elements described by Fig. 1 in Sect. 2, being how the method was built, how the data collection tool was built, and the approach used by the authors.

4   Results

We found 1351 articles in the ACM repository. We excluded 23 because of the lack of access. From 1328 left, we excluded 1246 by the exclusion criteria. The amount of studies accepted and excluded in each stage is depicted in Fig. 2. As shown in Fig. 2, 81 articles were accepted in this revision, being six were published in magazines or journals, and 75 in conference papers. Notably, there has been a rise in the number of publications through the years (Table 1). The selected articles are listed in Table 4.

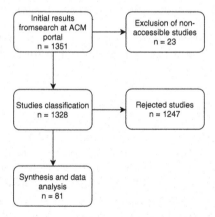

Fig. 2. Articles accepted and excluded in each stage of the systematic review

The accepted studies were classified according to the employed method, research approach, and data collection used. The classification below is applied for the method and data collection instrument of each study that includes an evaluation stage:

Table 1. Number of accepted papers grouped by year of publication

2014	2015	2016	2017	2018	2019	2020
1	3	8	13	19	28	9

- Validated: the study used a method or a data collection instrument, which is found in the literature; the study used all the rules and recommendations regarding the original authors related to the use and experimental evaluation.
- Adapted: the study used a method or data collection instrument adapted from some paper or validated research. The study may be or not be validated.
- Created: the study used a method created by the authors. As adapted studies, it may be or not be validated.

We found 61 studies that performed an evaluation stage. Only three studies have applied validated methods, 38 choose have adapted other methods (or they have some similarities with the classical ones), and 18 created their way. The validated method employed was the Quasi-Experiment method and a Mixed-method approach. However, most of the adapted evaluations were based on HCI principles. In particular instances, it is worth mentioning several studies using statistical hypothesis testing to validate the results. One used an approach based on design methodology—called interactive design by the authors—and the other article used a mixed-method approach.

Regarding the methods based on HCI principles, it is relevant to point out that the analysis was performed considering the basic experiment structure defined by the Decide Framework and the theory presented in Sect. 2. The classification was listed in Table 2.

Table 2. Articles classified by the method type

Studies	Method type	Base method
1, 3, 6, 7, 9, 11, 12, 18, 19, 21, 22, 24, 25, 35, 36, 39 ,41 ,43	Created	None
3, 5, 17, 20, 23, 28, 30, 34, 44, 46, 47, 48, 50, 52, 54,55, 57, 60, 62, 63, 65, 66, 68, 69, 72, 74, 75, 78, 81	Adapted	HCI principles
14, 31, 56, 59, 64, 71, 73, 80	Adapted	HCI principles and hypothesis test
29	Adapted	Iterative design
8, 33	Validated	Quasi-experiment
49	Validated	Mixed-method design

Relating to the 61 articles which performed an evaluation stage, we classified the approach used by the authors. The quantitative approach is the most common, with 38 studies, while only nine articles opted for a qualitative app-roach. The combined method—mixing both qualitative and quantitative—has been employed by 13 articles. From all of the 60 studies that performed an evaluation stage, only two have not involved users in the experiment: study 7 has performed an experiential analysis from its authors regarding the technolo-gies involved; and study 39 has modified the 3D environment with algorithms, describing the effects of that intervention.

Accordingly to the Data Synthesis process (Sect. 3), the evaluations were clas-sified into two categories: simple (i.e., use only one data collection instrument); and complex (i.e., use more than one data collection instrument). Regarding these two categories, 28 articles belong to the simple type, and the rest 33 belong to the other group, the complex evaluations.

In the group of studies with simple evaluations, 22 created their data collec-tion tool, three opted for an adapted tool, and only three used a validated tool. Only one adapted tool (43) and one created tool (8) were validated, as seen in Table 3.

Table 3. Studies grouped by tool's type and the number of validated tools considering simple evaluation studies

Tool's type	Studies	Amount of validated tools
Validated	12, 33, 78	3
Adapted	24, 28, 44	1
Created	4, 5, 6, 7, 8, 11, 17, 20, 22, 23, 35, 39, 43, 46, 55, 63, 65, 68, 71, 75	2

Studies that used validated or adapted tools have employed the following data collection tools: User Experience Questionnaire [23], Technology Accep-tance Model [6], and a questionnaire extracted from a previous article [24]. Related to the created instruments, the authors used questionnaires to mea-sure usability and user learning after the intervention, data provided for sensors (such as EEG), and statistical analysis along with their form to gauge the answer quality.

Studies performing complex evaluations employ two to five different data col-lection instruments. Thus, each study used a combination of validated, created, and adapted instruments, though most studies created at least one, and 11 arti-cles changed an existing one(Fig. 3). From the adapted tools, study 18 validated a tool with the statistical process, and both studies 59 and 60 validated a tool with experts. Only one study validated a created tool (study 21).

Table 4. Primary studies selection list

ID	Title
1	Teaching Case: Applying Gamification Techniques and Virtual Reality for Learning Building Engineering 3D Arts
2	A student project experience: a virtual campus tour
3	Development and Evaluation of a Virtual Reality Driving Simulator
4	Immersive virtual reality to enhance the spatial awareness of students
5	Ogma. A Virtual Reality Language Acquisition System
6	A High-fidelity Virtual Training System for Myoelectric Prostheses Using an Immersive HMD
7	Immersive visualization anatomical environment using virtual reality devices
8	How Does Web-based Virtual Reality Affect Learning: Evidences from a Quasi-experiment
9	Passive haptics based MR system for geography teaching
10	VR biology, an interdisciplinary and international student project towards an inquiry-based pedagogy
11	Design insights into embedding virtual reality content into life skills training for people with intellectual disability
12	User perception on 3D stereoscopic cultural heritage ancient collection
13	A Virtual Experience: Benefits of Extracurricular Group Projects
14	A study on improving performance in gesture training through visual guidance based on learners' errors
15	360 Vision Applications for Medical Training
16	An Implementation of VR Chemistry Experiment System
17	Teaching-Learning Process through VR Applied to Automotive Engineering
18	Getting up your nose: a virtual reality education tool for nasal cavity anatomy
19	Behavioral Intention of Using Virtual Reality in Learning
20	Design and evaluation of multiple role-playing in a virtual film set
21	Train in virtual court: Basketball tactic training via virtual reality
22	Enhancing learning through virtual reality and neurofeedback
23	Teaching Language and Culture with a Virtual aReality Game
24	A VR Simulator for Emergency Management in Endodontic Surgery
25	Experimenting with PlayVR, a virtual reality experience for the world of theater
26	Simulator of the Glycolytic Pathway in a Virtual Reality Environment as a Learning Resource for Teaching Cellular Respiration
27	Holobody galleries: blending augmented and virtual reality displays of human anatomy
28	Exploring the potential of a 360 video application for foreign language learning
29	LearnDNA: An interactive VR application for learning DNA structure
30	Designing a virtual environment for teacher training: Enhancing presence and empathy
31	Study of self-avatar's influence on motor skills training in immersive virtual environments
32	Incorporating Virtual Reality in an Embodied Interaction Course
33	Integration of Speech Recognition into Virtual Classroom to Enhance Learning Achievement
34	A Movement Analysis System based on Immersive Virtual Reality and Wearable Technology for Sport Training
35	Drawing in a Virtual 3D Space - Introducing VR Drawing in Elementary School Art Education
36	Innovation in Urban Design Education
37	Personal Basketball Coach: Tactic Training Through Wireless Virtual Reality
38	Geometrical Hong Kong: An Immersive and Interactive Virtual Reality Tour
39	Visualizing the tape of life: exploring evolutionary history with virtual reality
40	Virtual Reality Training System for Surgical Anatomy

(*continued*)

Table 4. (*continued*)

41	Eyestrain impacts on learning job interview with a serious game in virtual reality
42	Using Immersive Visualization Environments to Engage Students in Hands-On Learning
43	VR Application for Technology Education in a Public Library
44	Development of a model for explaining the learning outcomes when using3D virtual environments in informal learning settings
45	DAVEE : A Deaf Accessible Virtual Environment for Education
46	Keep the Ball Rolling : Designing Game-Based Tangible VR for Spatial Penetrative Thinking Ability
47	Virtual Reality Fire Disaster Training System for Improving Disaster Awareness
48	Usability of gamified knowledge learning in VR and desktop-3D
49	Supporting Anatomy Education with a 3D Puzzle in a VR Environment - Results from a Pilot Study
50	LIVE: the Human Role in Learning in Immersive Virtual Environments
51	Virtual Reality as a Means of Teaching Contemporary Chemistry
52	Do Low Cost Virtual Reality Devices Support Learning Acquisition?: A comparative study of two different VR devices
53	To Survive in a CBRN Hostile Environment: Application of CAVE AutomaticVirtual Environments in First Responder Training
54	Developing a virtual reality game for manufacturing education
55	Juggling in VR: Advantages of Immersive Virtual Reality in Juggling Learning
56	Virtual Reality Forge: Pattern-Oriented Authoring of Virtual Reality Nuggets
57	Investigating Representation of Text and Audio in Educational VR using Learning Outcomes and EEG
58	Evaluating Virtual Reality as a Medium for Vocational Skill Training
59	The Difficulties and Countermeasures of Applying Virtual Reality to Industrial Design Education
60	Improving Accessibility to Intangible Cultural Heritage Preservation Using Virtual Reality
61	Research on 3D Virtual Training Courseware Development System of Civil Aircraft Based on Virtual Reality Technology
62	Virtually the Same Experience?: Learning from User Experience Evaluation of In-vehicle Systems in VR and in the Field
63	Virtual Reality and Collaborative Interdisciplinary Work in the Development of Competences
64	The Effect of Presence and Appearance of Guides in Virtual Reality Exhibitions
65	Multi-user Virtual Training Assistant for Maintenance on Energized Medium-Voltage Lines
66	Embodying the homunculus in virtual reality: creating an interactive laboratory procedure for brain mapping and visualization
67	Design and Implementation of Virtual Simulation Experiment for Generation, Transmissionand Application of Electric Power
68	Visual Technologies for Urban Design Competences in Architecture Education
69	The Effects of VR Environments on the Acceptance, Experience, and Expectations of Cultural Heritage Learning
70	Towards Designing Agent Based Virtual Reality Applications for Cybersecurity Training
71	Blended Learning Supports in Chinese Architectures with 360 Degree VR Contents and 3D Modelling VR Contents
72	How Important is Immersion for Learning in Computer Science Replugged Games?
73	Design and Evaluation of a VR Training Simulation for Pump Maintenance
74	X-Road: Virtual Reality Glasses for Orientation and Mobility Training of People with Visual Impairments

(*continued*)

Table 4. (*continued*)

75	The Constructing and Application Case of Online Virtual Exhibits Arrangement System for Museum Learning
76	A Virtual Reality Training Tool to Improve Weight-Related Communication Across Healthcare Settings
77	Virtual Simulation of Palletizing Training for Industrial Robots
78	Multi-User System for Virtual Interaction of a Pasteurization Process
79	Virtual simulation of glue coating training for industrial robots
80	How to VizSki: Visualizing Captured Skier Motion in a VR Ski Training Simulator
81	Web-Portal-Based Repurposing of VR Scenarios for TEFL Applications

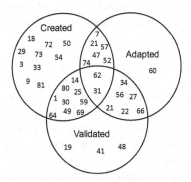

Fig. 3. Studies with complex evaluation grouped by classification regarding the kind of data collection instrument.

The created instruments usually were based on interviews, experiment observation, and use of experiment data, usability questionnaires, and learning outcomes surveys. Among the validated or adapted instrument, we can cite:

- Presence questionnaires: Witmer Presence [34], Igroup presence questionnaire[6], Multimodal Presence Scale [21] and ITC-Sense of presence inventory [19], a presence questionnaire adapted from [27] and translated in french;
- Usability and technology acceptance questionnaires: TAM [6], System Usability Scale [4], UTAUT [32], USE [20], AttrackDiff questionnaire[7], Depth of presence [30];
- Flow and discomfort questionnaires: Flow Short Scale [9], Visual Discomfort [35] and Simulator Sickness Questionnaire[14]; and
- Other tools: NASA-Task Load Index questionnaire [11], User Experience Questionnaire [18], a questionnaire extracted from [26], a questionnaire to measure the uncanny valley effect[13], an adaption from the questionnaire presented by [5], Think Aloud method [22] and Delphi Method to list the application requirements.

---

[6] http://www.igroup.org/index.php.
[7] http://attrakdiff.de/index-en.html.

Several studies used the following statistical tools to validate the adapted or created questionnaires: structural equation modeling, Cronbach Alpha test, double-sided T-test, and one study validated the data through scientific software[8]. It is also noted that some authors used other statistical methods, such as the Friedman test, independent sample T-test, and Wilcoxon signed-rank test, to discuss the obtained results.

We also collected the main statement presented as the conclusion of the study expressed regarding the experiment effects. First, it is important to point out that not every study is assertive about its outcome. However, most studies reports getting positive effects from the conducted evaluation: 4, 5, 12, 17, and 18. Study number 14 has also presented positive effects, yet the authors pointed out a difficulty in learning how to manipulate the new system interface.

5   Discussion

To better understand how educational software applications based on VR have been evaluated, we performed a systematic review in which 81 articles were analyzed. This study aimed to answer the five research questions (RQ), listed in Sect. 3, through the data collection step using a form. The questions are answered in the following subsections.

(**RQ1 - RQ2**) Based on the data presented in Table 2, the presence of studies employing a validated method is limited, whereas the typical approach is to adjust some method or create its own. In addition to the created methods, we can point to three approaches used in the analyzed studies:

1. adapted methods, that somehow follows the theory defined in HCI;
2. methods that use statistical analysis and hypothesis testing; and,
3. other approaches, such as design method and mixed-method.

A method must be based on a well-defined theory to provide reliability. More discretion is needed when using results from articles that created their evaluation without proper validation: studies without a well-defined method do not provide sufficient reliability to be generalized to other situations due to the lack of internal and external qualities [28].

The use of an adapted method, or at least structured in HCI and experimentation theories, can provide better results. Well-defined methods set up tasks, workgroups, questionnaire appliances, and data analysis, but only a few studies validate the collected data and point out outcome limitations. Thus, this also affects their reliability. There were only five articles that have validated their methods and tools by statistical analysis.

The lack of a well-defined experimentation structure can light problems regarding data validation. For instance, in studies 4 and 23, the users answered the same questionnaire before and after the intervention stage. In this case, the user can influence the results better or worse by remembering the previous

---

[8] https://www.ibm.com/br-pt/analytics/spss-statistics-software.

answer or question. This way, the results may reflect the person's memory, not the real intervention effects.

Despite the reasons and importance regarding the experimentation design, only one study has formally used them. The lack of an explicit definition could mean that the authors are unaware of it or do not take it for granted. This conclusion may also be extended to mixed methods since we noted studies that used more than one research approach and were not necessarily grounded upon a theoretical framework.

(RQ3) We can point out the lack of specific instrumentation to evaluate a VR application. The authors prefer to use usability, technology acceptance, and presence questionnaires to assess the new application. These are standard methods that can be used in general applications, not only VR-based.

This result is correlated to a previous systematic review, which had the objective of assessing how AR applications were evaluated with users [7]. Similar tools were found, such as usability assessments, interviews, and the measurement of tasks and data sensors. Even though the interactions with these domains—AR and VR—are different, they are analyzed nearly with the same methods listed in this article. Most of the methods listed by [7] were also not validated. Thus, they present an informal evaluation. Nevertheless, new research can change the scenario towards the tools' validation since its publication.

The lack of specific tools for performing VR and AR application evaluations may be due to the complexity of its interactions besides the required resources. Notwithstanding, 33 studies employed a more complex evaluation design composed of more than one data collection tool to perform such evaluation. Although it was not selected to further analysis due to the exclusion criteria, a study found during the search of this systematic review presents an evaluation measuring the application flow using the user's physiological data [3]. A similar approach was used by studies 22 and 30, which used EEG data to analyze some perspective of user experience. Thus, methods based on physiological sensors may be a possible solution to evaluate a VR application. However, it needs more resources to evaluate the system using this type of tool.

(RQ4) We classified the evaluation process of studies based on the number of data collection tools they had used: simple (i.e., used only one tool); and complex (i.e., used more than one instrument). The most common practice in studies belonging to the simple evaluation group is creating their instrument, which the only one that proceeded with a validation process of an adapted tool. As with all new methods, extra caution is required when analyzing and drawing conclusions since the experiment's internal quality is unsure.

The lack of support theories can not provide sufficient reliability; that is, there is no assurance when relating the variables and the interpretation. Thus, the analysis is based on the authors' not declared assumptions, hypothesis, and conceptions [28] and may not have sufficient formal pieces of evidence to support the analysis. In brief, the results will be limited and not accurately reflect the effects of the intervention.

It is also observed the choice for creating tools in complex evaluation studies. Figure 3 illustrates that most studies built their experiment using both created and validated tools. In contrast, few studies used an adapted tool composing the research - and only one adapted tool was validated. The use of non-validated tools among validated tools can provide better reliability of the interpretations and analysis - despite the discussion limitations due to lack of reliability. This article mentions that data supplied by sensors was also classified as a created tool, yet it may present accurate data. The qualitative tools were also classified as created tools in most cases. However, we can cite the Think Aloud method and Delphi method to develop the application requirements in two separate studies.

(RQ5) The predominant research classification signs the methodological principles considered by the studies, such as quantitative, qualitative, or even a combination of both approaches. An evaluation may use different tools (e.g., data collection instruments) accordingly to its paradigm, as observed in the results obtained through this study. Still, the tools are acknowledged through a predominant perspective or a specific method involving both aspects based on a mix-method theory. Regarding the research design, this study reveals the quantitative approach as favorite, with 38 articles, followed by some combined approach (13), and the least likely the qualitative approach (9).

6   Threats to Validity

The factors that can threaten this study's validity are presented following the concepts defined by [28]: construct, internal, and external validity. Construct validity involves the correct interpretation of concepts and if the results obtained are relevant or not. Despite evaluation concepts are well defined, there is a problem regarding the VR general concept: we eliminated studies that have not used a specific VR interface such as Oculus VR[9] and Google Cardboard[10]. This way, some relevant studies may be eliminated.

Internal validity implies that the relation between two desired variables, A and B, is consistent and not a measurement error. The limited amount of primary studies analyzed is a limitation of this study. We only used one source in our research, ACM Digital Library, and more sources would provide us a better broader understanding. Moreover, there was only one extractor, and another person did not validate the studies to find different assumptions and results.

External validity stands for the degree to which the results and interpretation can be generalized to other similar scenarios. The use of only one scientific repository is a concern about external validity. As noted before, more studies would be possible to find more accurate results. However, the results from this study provide a compilation of approaches and methods to evaluate a VR educational application. We also point out issues concerning the analyzed experiments, which serve as a guideline to help with setting evaluation in further research.

---

[9] https://www.oculus.com.

[10] https://arvr.google.com/cardboard/.

7   Conclusion

The obtained results show that most studies conduct evaluations based on their crafted procedures. That is, researchers created their methods or tools to investigate the effect of the intervention. Most of the analyzed studies have used adapted tools such as usability, user experience, flow questionnaires, task load questionnaire, the acceptance level of technology questionnaires, and other tools summarized. Moreover, many studies have used a method based on HCI theory related to experiment conduction. In contrast, only a few have handled more rigorous experimental designs, such as the Quasi-Experiment method and analysis through statistical hypothesis testing. Lastly, most studies employed quantitative approaches to synthesize and analyze the data to answer the research questions and hypotheses defined rather than qualitative or combined methods.

Although some studies reported a positive effect on the intervention of a VR educational application, more discretion is required to compare and generalize those results. The observed lack of support theories in many reviewed cases suggests high risks of evaluation flaws affecting data integrity, analysis, and, ultimately, the study's reliability.

Finally, we strengthen the relevance of using well-defined support theories in all stages of an evaluation. As future work, we propose expanding this research by exploring other fields such as VR in health and analyzing other scientific repositories.

Acknowledgments. This project has partially supported by Huawei do Brasil Telecomunicações Ltda (Fundunesp Process # 3123/2020), and CAPES.

References

1. American Educational Research Association, American Psychological Association, N.C.o.M.i.E.: Standards for Educational and Psychological Testing. Amer Educational Research Assn (2014)
2. Bach, C., Scapin, D.L.: Obstacles and perspectives for evaluating mixed reality systems usability. In: Acte du Workshop MIXER, IUI-CADUI, vol. 4. Citeseer (2004)
3. Bian, Y., Yang, C., Gao, F., Li, H., Zhou, S., Li, H., Sun, X., Meng, X.: A framework for physiological indicators of flow in vr games: construction and preliminary evaluation. Pers. Ubiq. Comput. **20**(5), 821–832 (2016)
4. Brooke, J., et al.: Sus-a quick and dirty usability scale. Usab. Eval. Ind. **189**(194), 4–7 (1996)
5. Csikszentmihalyi, M., Larson, R.: Validity and reliability of the experience-sampling method. In: Flow and the Foundations of Positive Psychology, pp. 35–54. Springer, Dordrecht (2014). https://doi.org/10.1007/978-94-017-9088-8_3
6. Davis, F.D.: Perceived usefulness, perceived ease of use, and user acceptance of information technology. MIS Q., 319–340 (1989)
7. Dünser, A., Grasset, R., Billinghurst, M.: A survey of evaluation techniques used in augmented reality studies. Human Interface Technology Laboratory New Zealand (2008)

8. Elmore, P.B.: Reporting standards for research publications. Couns. Outcome Res. Eval. **1**(2), 19–29 (2010)
9. Engeser, S., Rheinberg, F.: Flow, performance and moderators of challenge-skill balance. Motiv. Emot. **32**, 158–172 (2008). https://doi.org/10.1007/s11031-008-9102-4
10. Greene, J.C., Caracelli, V.J., Graham, W.F.: Toward a conceptual framework for mixed-method evaluation designs. Educ. Eval. Policy Anal. **11**(3), 255–274 (1989)
11. Hart, S.G.: Nasa-task load index (nasa-tlx); 20 years later. In: Proceedings of the Human Factors and Ergonomics Society Annual Meeting, vol. 50, pp. 904–908. Sage Publications Sage CA, Los Angeles (2006)
12. Hevner, A.R., March, S.T., Park, J., Ram, S.: Design science in information systems research. Manag. Inf. Syst. Q. **28**, 75–105 (2004)
13. Ho, C.C., MacDorman, K.F.: Measuring the uncanny valley effect. Int. J. Soc. Rob. **9**(1), 129–139 (2017)
14. Kennedy, R.S., Lane, N.E., Berbaum, K.S., Lilienthal, M.G.: Simulator sickness questionnaire: an enhanced method for quantifying simulator sickness. Int. J. Aviat. Psychol. **3**(3), 203–220 (1993)
15. Kitchenham, B.: Procedures for performing systematic reviews. Keele, UK, Keele Univ. **33**(2004), 1–26 (2004)
16. Kitcher, P.: The Advancement of Science: Science without Legend, Objectivity without Illusions. Oxford University Press, Oxford (1995)
17. Kuhn, D., Pearsall, S.: Developmental origins of scientific thinking. J. Cogn. Dev. **1**(1), 113–129 (2000)
18. Laugwitz, B., Held, T., Schrepp, M.: Construction and evaluation of a user experience questionnaire. In: Holzinger, A. (ed.) USAB 2008. LNCS, vol. 5298, pp. 63–76. Springer, Heidelberg (2008). https://doi.org/10.1007/978-3-540-89350-9_6
19. Lessiter, J., Freeman, J., Keogh, E., Davidoff, J.: A cross-media presence questionnaire: the itc-sense of presence inventory. Pres. Teleoper. Virtual Environ. **10**(3), 282–297 (2001)
20. Lund, A.M.: Measuring usability with the use questionnaire12. Usab. Interface **8**(2), 3–6 (2001)
21. Makransky, G., Lilleholt, L., Aaby, A.: Development and validation of the multimodal presence scale for virtual reality environments: a confirmatory factor analysis and item response theory approach. Comput. Human Behav. **72** (2017). https://doi.org/10.1016/j.chb.2017.02.066
22. Nielsen, J.: Thinking aloud: The# 1 usability tool. Nielsen Norman Group 16 (2012)
23. Rauschenberger, M., Schrepp, M., Pérez Cota, M., Olschner, S., Thomaschewski, J.: Efficient measurement of the user experience of interactive products. How to use the user experience questionnaire (ueq). example: Spanish language version. Int. J. Interact. Multimedia Artif. Intell. (2013)
24. Roberts, P.G., Guyver, P., Baldwin, M., Akhtar, K., Alvand, A., Price, A.J., Rees, J.L.: Validation of the updated arthros simulator: face and construct validity of a passive haptic virtual reality simulator with novel performance metrics. Knee Surg. Sports Traumatol. Arthrosc. **25**(2), 616–625 (2017)
25. Ruthenbeck, G.S., Reynolds, K.J.: Virtual reality for medical training: the state-of-the-art. J. Simul. **9**(1), 16–26 (2015)
26. Rutten, N., Van Joolingen, W.R., Van Der Veen, J.T.: The learning effects of computer simulations in science education. Comput. Educ. **58**(1), 136–153 (2012)
27. Schubert, T., Friedmann, F., Regenbrecht, H.: The experience of presence: factor analytic insights. Pres. Teleoper. Virt. Environ. **10**(3), 266–281 (2001)

28. Shadish, W.R., Cook, T.D., Campbell, D.T., et al.: Experimental and quasi-experimental designs for generalized causal inference/William R. Shedish, Thomas D. Cook, Donald T. Campbell. Houghton Mifflin, Boston (2002)
29. Sharp, H., Rogers, Y.J.P.: Design de Interação: Além da interação humano computador. Bookman (2005)
30. Slater, M., Usoh, M., Steed, A.: Depth of presence in virtual environments. Pres. Teleoper. Virt. Environ. 3(2), 130–144 (1994)
31. Sommerville, I.: Engenharia de software. PEARSON BRASIL (2011). https:// books.google.com.br/books?id=H4u5ygAACAAJ
32. Venkatesh, V., Morris, M.G., Davis, G.B., Davis, F.D.: User acceptance of information technology: toward a unified view. MIS Q., 425–478 (2003)
33. Villagrasa, S., Fonseca, D., Durán, J.: Teaching case: applying gamification techniques and virtual reality for learning building engineering 3d arts. In: Proceedings of the Second International Conference on Technological Ecosystems for Enhancing Multiculturality, pp. 171–177 (2014)
34. Witmer, B.G., Singer, M.J.: Measuring presence in virtual environments: a presence questionnaire. Presence 7(3), 225–240 (1998)
35. Zeri, F., Livi, S.: Visual discomfort while watching stereoscopic three-dimensional movies at the cinema. Ophthal. Physiol. Opt. 35 (2015). https://doi.org/10.1111/ opo.12194

IoT to Monitor People Flow in Areas of Public Interest

Damiano Perri[1,2]([✉]) [ID], Marco Simonetti[1,2] [ID], Alex Bordini[2] [ID],
Simone Cimarelli[2], and Osvaldo Gervasi[2] [ID]

[1] Department of Mathematics and Computer Science,
University of Florence, Florence, Italy
`damiano.perri@unifi.it`
[2] Department of Mathematics and Computer Science,
University of Perugia, Perugia, Italy

Abstract. The unexpected historical period we are living has abruptly pushed us to loosen any sort of interaction between individuals, gradually forcing us to deal with new ways to allow compliance with safety distances; indeed the present situation has demonstrated more than ever how critical it is to be able to properly organize our travel plans, put people in safe conditions, and avoid harmful circumstances. The aim of this research is to set up a system to monitor the flow of people inside public places and facilities of interest (museums, theatres, cinemas, etc.) without collecting personal or sensitive data. Weak monitoring of people flows (i.e. monitoring without personal identification of the monitored subjects) through Internet of Things tools might be a viable solution to minimize lineups and overcrowding. Our study, which began as an experiment in the Umbria region of Italy, aims to be one of several answers to automated planning of people's flows in order to make our land more liveable. We intend to show that the Internet of Things gives almost unlimited tools and possibilities, from developing a basic information process to implementing a true portal which enables business people to connect with interested consumers.

Keywords: IOT · Sensors · Image processing · Augmented reality · Virtual reality

1 Introduction

One of the characteristics related to the pandemic of COVID19 as a result of social distancing is that it has forced institutions to reduce the maximum acceptable number of simultaneous visitors. This situation generated difficulties from the organisational point of view of both the structures and the tourists who wanted to visit certain areas of cultural and tourist interest. The words "Internet of Things" (IoT) refer to a collection of objects that gain intelligence through the internet, exchanging data about themselves and gaining access to information from other sources [1,2].

© Springer Nature Switzerland AG 2021
O. Gervasi et al. (Eds.): ICCSA 2021, LNCS 12958, pp. 658–672, 2021.
https://doi.org/10.1007/978-3-030-87016-4_47

The goal of this research is to maximize the potential of IoT devices to collect particular data by combining privacy with useful information, simplicity of use with usefulness, economy with power, and versatility with accuracy. This project will aim at leveraging existing infrastructure to develop the concept of indoor tracking, i.e. the ability to provide information on the number of people presently inside a building, public or private, and selectively providing the details publicly available.

The system we are proposing is made up of three major components: acquisition devices, which deal with understanding how the flow varies over time based on the impulses they receive, coordination devices, which deal with managing all of the information received, and presentation devices, which make the previously acquired information available to the public.

2   Related Works

The effort to automate work and manufacturing processes that began in the nineteenth century has never truly ended, due to the assistance of increasingly efficient and performing technology. Today's strategy is to make machines increasingly autonomous and intelligent [3–5], rather than highly reliant on human supervision [6,7]. This has required interaction with a complex world, which necessitates the development of numerous external inputs on which to take decisions [8,9]. As a result, the Internet of Things has become a significant paradigm in a variety of fields, including manufacturing [10,11], remote control [12,13] and monitoring [14,15], home automation [16,17], gaming [18] and Virtual and Augmented Reality [19,20]. Our concept is based on the basic requirement to track the flow of individuals moving through restricted settings for a variety of reasons, including real-time monitoring and control to minimize congestion, and statistical assessment for economic and logistical considerations. Although the goal is the same, the methodologies used over time have been the most varied: RFID techniques [21], ultrasound sensors [22], PIR sensors [23], closed-circuit TV (CCTV) [24], face recognition by Artificial Intelligence [25–27], post-processed data local memories or in Cloud Services [28].

The use of IoT has always proven to be a simple answer, given the low cost of the components, which certainly favors the implementation of a do-it-yourself solution. The method we presented is intended to be simple, both in terms of design and implementation, as well as in terms of simplicity of use and with a low learning curve.

3   The Architecture of the System

Our system is tasked with monitoring and tracing the movement of people passing through a *location*, which is a confined environment such as a public or private structure. This data is very useful in ensuring the safety and security of people in the area, and it is controlled differently by those who have the information, and decides what to publish, and those who utilize it, i.e. the end user.

To ensure the generic collection of data, useful for guaranteeing service, and to realize the anonymity of individual people, a scalable stack architecture, as shown in Fig. 1, is divided into three logical levels: *data acquisition layer, data coordination layer* which has the function to improve a correct exchange of information across devices, and *presentation layer* needed to allow the flexible use of information in manageable formats.

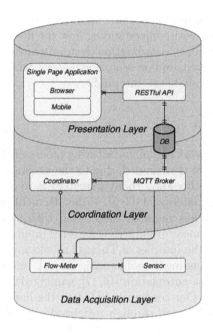

Fig. 1. System architecture scheme

3.1 Data Acquisition Layer

This layer contains every object related to the collection and conversion of sensor data into processable information from higher layers.

The first critical component of our research is a collection of flow acquisition devices known as *Flow-Meters*. They can be heterogeneous or homogeneous: in some situations, using different sensors may be convenient to get a wide overview; in others, using sensors of the same kind may enhance overall accuracy or area detection. The first scenario entails the employment of numerous sensors of various sorts to improve detection possibilities, utilizing the plurality of signals received to manage the complexity of the surrounding environment. In the second case, the detection system is implemented using a single type of sensor, like an emitter and a receiver photo-diode; such a simple structure was initially considered but later rejected because it is incapable of effectively describing contingent situations, as the direction of the person.

To prevent issues with correctly recognizing the passing of one or more persons, we ultimately choose a thermal camera sensor, best known as *Grid-EYE matrix sensor*, shown in Fig. 2a. This is one of the most common option in the field of Indoor Localization. It is a tiny detector, less than a centimeter in size, that creates a two-dimensional 8×8 matrix, able to detect the average temperature for the section of the plane that is projected to the ground using lasers similar to those used in thermoscanners - Fig. 2c.

The size of the detectable plane sections is obviously determined by the distance between the device and the ground: the higher the device's positioning height, the larger the effect on the single viewing angle measurements, i.e. the incidence of each laser sensor on the ground. The area covered by sensor and relative geometrical distortion is shown in Fig. 2b.

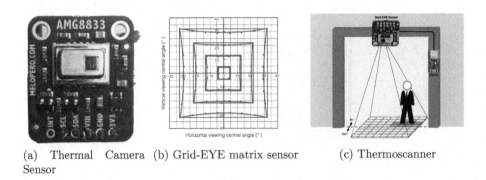

(a)   Thermal   Camera   (b) Grid-EYE matrix sensor   (c) Thermoscanner
Sensor

Fig. 2. GRID-EYE matrix sensor

To manage the incoming flow from the different sensors, we utilize an ESP32 micro-controller, which is responsible for processing the raw data and creating a version suitable for control devices. It continually interrogates the sensor and extracts all of the information about the flow. The huge amount of RAM memory required for the management of our matrices needed a sophisticated micro-controller.

The sensor's output signal is a low-resolution thermal image. It is accompanied with a lot of noise, which has been reduced by using interpolation techniques and filtering matrices. Initially, we sought a method that attempted to make these passages less apparent, incorporating filters to tackle the problem; these filters are known as *convolutive* in the context of digital image processing. A convolutive filter is a kernel matrix that is applied to another matrix, in this case the one from the sensor, to produce an effect based on the values it assumes. The initial working hypothesis was to blur the image; however, after implementing the algorithm, it was discovered that the benefits were minimal because the system was limited by the few pixels available. As a result, the originally expected homogeneity would not have been achieved, and some information would have been lost, eliminated by the convolutive filter. This indicated to us that the primary requirement was not to mix the pixels we already had, but to dilute them over a broader region. Interpolation is a method that involves adding new pixels to existing ones and calculating their value using a reconstruction algorithm. The technique we have chosen is one of the most often used tools for upscaling in photo editing, *bicubic interpolation*, whereas the technique to filter pixels has been *Background Subtraction* [29].

Only when the noise has been adequately attenuated, the instrument's sensitivity can be modified using a threshold value. This allows you to maintain the highest values of the matrix unchanged while attenuating the minimums and clearly identifying the individual clusters as shown in Fig. 3a. We called *cluster* a submatrix with variable shape and size, that numerically represents the area which the person can be projected on.

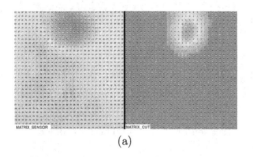 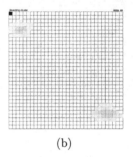

(a)   (b)

Fig. 3. Image processing

The matrix is then scanned to determine the size of the clusters. The objective is to minimize these regions to a single point. This point is their center of gravity, and acquire one for each individual in order to work on data distribution uniformity. To do this, a Flood-Fill algorithm is used to extrapolate the individual clusters, and then their centers of gravity are computed using a weighted average ah shown in Fig. 3b.

To convey the results of this level's computations to higher levels, the device requires a communication logic, capable of being simple and reliable. Physical communication in binary form is used to support this, with increments and decrements communicated to the relevant pins through the electrical potential difference. In this way a proper electrical diagram can help us to quickly provide feedback on functioning and faults as shown in Fig. 4.

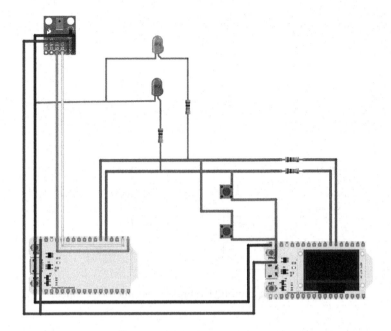

Fig. 4. Wiring diagram for the circuit

3.2   Coordination Layer

At this level, we can locate all of the equipment that deal with coordinating the data from the Flow-Meters. They are classified into two kinds:

- within the infrastructure
- outside of the infrastructure.

The former are *microcontrollers that manage data synchronization* from many sorts of sensors. The latter are servers (called **brokers**) that *communicate with the former* through the MQTT protocol and ensure the consistency of infrastructure acquisitions. Microcontrollers have the responsibility to manage this data in accordance with the standards of the linked devices and to act as an interface with the MQTT broker as shown in Fig. 5a.

Our infrastructure must be a closed system in order for the broker to be aware of the full flow. This enables the broker to ensure that the incoming data is consistent and to store it in a database. The broker and the coordinator use the MQTT protocol to interact safely and reliably, and they take particular actions based on the messages they receive as shown in Fig. 5b.

The connection initialization and initial configuration are performed during the first start, and the device is resumed once done. During this phase, the device runs in WIFI_STA[1] modality and provides a setup web page via the *Autocon-*

---

[1] The possible working states are: WIFI_AP (Access Point mode), WIFI_STA (Client only), WIFI_AP_STA (dual mode), WIFI_OFF (disabled).

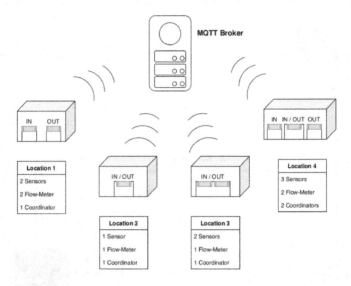

(a) Interface among the MQTT broker and microcontrollers

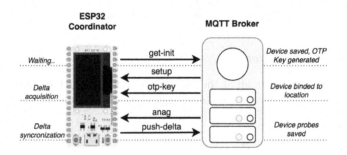

(b) Data communication between MQTT broker and a coordinator

Fig. 5. Coordination between microcontroller and broker

nect library, where the connection credentials may be entered. On the server side, there is a validation and registration phase during the initial connection; from then on, at each successive start, the device requests the server for its personal data, publishing on the specific topic of the MQTT protocol. The server responds with the device type, location information, and any setup constants, which are collected by three distinct callbacks. If a single coordinator is responsible for managing large number of sensors, a first coordination is necessary. The influx of data from these sensors must be coordinated based on their characteristics; hence, the several Flow-Meters employ a common standard to transmit the specifications and results of their processing. One of their parameters is the region the sensor can cover: the objective is to broaden the range of action of certain types of sensors while keeping the system scalable, since signal processing and identification are delegated to a lower level, the Flow-Meter. The coordinator then assigns a difference value to each of the sensors and updates it at each state change with the increase or reduction. Another thread is responsible for posting the updated value to the server.

At this level, coordination is based on an overview of the sites and we expect that our sensors have mapped at least all of the entrance and exit areas. The coordinators function as repeaters in the interaction with the Broker. As a result, all coordinators within the location must be linked with it. The broker must be aware of the whole flow, which occurs only if our site is a closed system; at that point, it has visibility of what comes in and what comes out.

Essentially, the protocol implemented provides us with channels to publish and receive messages among the various clients via callbacks. As a result, this paradigm does not provide intellectual ability for those that manage the messages, the broker, which is only limited to coordinating communication. It was necessary to build an additional layer on top of an existing broker that would allow intercepting messages passing through the network and triggering server-side actions. These activities include retrieving data, storing and maintaining information, and performing tasks based on the kind of message provided to the subjects, which are used as API endpoints. At this stage, the server relays the message exchange, which does not just send the message but also applies predefined logic to it: an example might be the phase of adding a new device, which merely registers on the server. Following the authentication and authorization stages, the server verifies and tells the device about the place which it is allocated to, and then informs the other devices connected.

One of the challenges we faced throughout the project's execution was how to maintain the quantity of information arriving from the coordinators synced and the quality on a high level, because these devices, as previously said, are not so reliable when they perform this kind of tasks. To address this issue, it was therefore decided to adopt the MQTT protocol, which has a very high degree of reliability in handling the transmission of information across various devices and equipment.

Security deserves a separate mention, as there are two "by design" vulnerabilities of the MQTT protocol: protection against unwanted subscription/publication and encryption of packets exchanged between client and broker. Unwanted subscription protection can be achieved through a *whitelist*. Each device is provided with a unique key and the subscription is made possible only if the key is valid. In the event that the key is compromised, a new one can be generated, as the device is capable of receiving updates via OTA (Over-The-Air). By default, even to keep the protocol light, no encryption is applied to the packets.

There are several methods for securing message exchange and each of them should be chosen based on the device's power. According to RFC 7228, these devices are classified into three types: our microcontroller belongs to the class 2 devices, capable of managing the overhead of the SSL/TLS protocol; additionally, because it is dual-core, it is possible to delegate the server update to a separate process that manages the queue, without slowing down the data acquisition process.

3.3 Presentation Layer

This level has the purpose of making the information stored to the user accessible through the devices located at the underlying levels, and to manage the access mode for single users, guaranteeing the separation of responsibilities for any of them. So, main actions for this layer are:

- make the information acquired by the devices located at the underlying levels available to the user
- manage access methods
- separate the responsibilities relating to the user profile

The first evident distinction is between the external user, called *standard user*, who reads the information, and the internal user, called *business*, who owns the information and determines how to display it. The latter, unlike the former, must be registered in the system, in order to manage an activity.

This level's structure has been extensively tested in various environments; there is a Docker container which virtualizes the data archived in the MySQL database in a secure environment, and the server, which runs on a virtual machine and externally exposing only the endpoints of the APIs that the application calls as shown in Fig. 6.

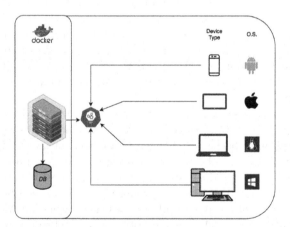

Fig. 6. Presentation layer and docker container

The presentation system is made up of two parts: the web server and the client. Infrastructure services manage main database activities (CRUD) using

APIs accessible to the application client. These APIs are classified into three categories (authentication, task management, and device management), corresponding to a different set of entities in the database.

The development scheme we have chosen provides the *Model View Controller* (MVC) pattern is an approach that involves categorizing the elements of an application into three distinct parts in order to make their modification and management autonomous, thereby increasing maintainability and portability. These three categories are the *Model*, the *View*, and the *Controller*, in that order as shown in Fig. 7.

- *Model*: contains the data access methods
- *View*: takes care of viewing the data to the user and manages the interaction between the latter and the underlying infrastructure
- *Controller*: receives user commands through the View and reacts by performing operations that may affect the Model and which generally lead to a change in the View state

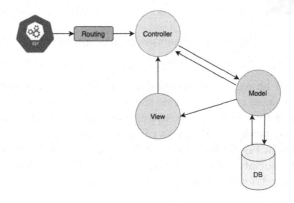

Fig. 7. Scheme of MVC pattern

Therefore, the *Model level* is responsible for managing the data that the application must manipulate. The term Model implies its nature that is a representation of the object, which will subsequently be mapped to the database according to rules set by the programmer, abstracting the structure of the data within the database.

In the MVC framework, the *Controller level* is the most crucial. The Controller level contains all of the classes that allow you to validate user requests and process them in order to return a response. It is able of intercepting user requests, choosing the components capable of processing them, mapping the result into an object, and returning it to the caller.

To allow the user to interact with the system, we created a Progressive Web Application that can run within the browser and so adapt to any operating system or device, with a responsive UI. The application's Home screen greets the user with a map that shows nearby areas of interest as well as associated information. By picking the point of interest, you will have access to extra information that the management has decided to make available for the specific user as shown in Fig. 8.

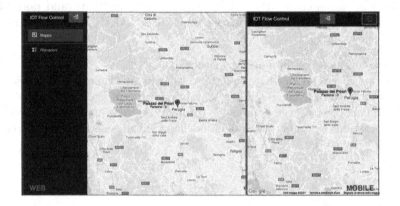

Fig. 8. App responsive graphic interface

The user must be registered and enabled in order to utilize the application's functions as a business role. Every time the user takes an action, a request is sent to the server, and the request is successful if the formal check is accurate. After an user has been verified and approved, he/she may manage their corporate profiles as shown in Fig. 9. To publish updates on their activity, the user has to enter them and associate the devices with them too. The localization information about the site is retrieved through a *Geocoding* service. When the insertion is

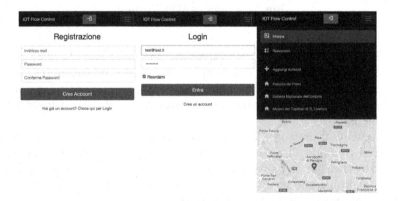

Fig. 9. Registration, login and modification authorization phases

finished, the server changes the tables and notifies the other clients via *RPC* and so the device is completely associated with the support of an *OTP Key*.

The application has also been enriched with an additional module that allows the visitor to obtain information on artifacts where appropriate (museums, exhibitions, etc.). With the help of virtual reality techniques, the user can take a guided tour of the facility and view the main works of art. Furthermore, a series of QR codes have been created inside the structure that allow the user to view the artifact through augmented reality technologies.

4   Discussion of Results

We proceeded with the verification of the overall correctness of the system after completing all of the steps mentioned in the previous chapters. All testing were carried out on a precised room within the University area with a single entrance and exit door, with a setup consisting of a single Grid-EYE sensor, a Flow-Meter, and a Coordinator. We tested the system in its entirety after performing all of the tests required to ensure the system's correct operation and, later, those required to refine the functionality of the individual components. The following operations were then performed:

1. Positioning of the Grid-EYE sensor on the door jamb, at a height of about two meters
2. Connection of the sensor to the acquisition microcontroller, which in turn is connected to the coordinator
3. Connecting the microcontrollers to the network
4. Configuration of Coordination Layer (Broker MQTT) and Presentation Layer (database and web server) on two separate machines
5. Installing the application on an Android device
6. Registration via email and password
7. Authentication and authorization within the system
8. Insertion of a fictitious activity so that it can appear on the map and be selected from the context menu
9. Association of the coordinator via the OTP Key. The correct name for a business role appeared on the microcontroller display and the device appeared on the proper page.

At this point, the activity and the device had been properly setup, and the fifteen-day testing period could begin. We turned on the detector at the start of the first day, when all staff (professors, students, and so on) members were not yet in the room. We found that every time a person went in, the counter was incremented and when he/she went out, the number was decremented. At the conclusion of the test period, late in the last day's evening, the counter was correctly returned to zero.

5 Conclusions and Future Works

The testing revealed that our system has a strong basic detection capacity, as we discovered a result of zero for eight days, a value of one for four days, and a value of two for the remaining three days on 42 average daily passes. The detections were monitored using the program, which checked that the inputs and outputs were appropriately synchronized whenever a state change happened. It was also able to examine the logs, which revealed that the mistakes were caused by erroneous assessments by the acquisition tools. The different test phases have demonstrated how, although being in an experimental phase, our technology seems to be adequate for creating a reliable infrastructure. It has been shown that the Internet of Things provides nearly limitless tools and potential, both in terms of opportunities and future extensions, ranging from the development of a simple information process to the implementation of a real portal capable of allowing those who do business to communicate with interested customers. An exciting future use might be to make available, in addition to the actual survey summary, booking systems capable of sending the flow of people, which, when combined with the information status signals, allows customers to have direct contact with who provides the service in real time.

Acronyms

The following acronyms are used in this manuscript:

OTP	One Time Password
RPC	Remote Procedure Call
CRUD	Create, Read, Update, Delete
MVC	Model View Controller
UI	User Interface
CCTV	closed-circuit TV
PIR	Passive InfraRed
IOT	Internet of Things
RAM	Read Only Memory
CPU	Central Processing Unit
OTA	Over The Air
API	Application Program Interface
MQTT	MQ Telemetry Transport or Message Queue Telemetry Transport

References

1. Atzori, L., Iera, A., Morabito, G.: The Internet of Things: a survey. Comput. Netw. **54**(15), 2787–2805 (2010). https://doi.org/10.1016/j.comnet. 2010.05.010. ISSN 1389–1286. https://www.sciencedirect.com/science/article/pii/S1389128610001568

2. Mainetti, L., Patrono, L., Vilei, A.: Evolution of wireless sensor networks towards the Internet of Things: a survey. In: SoftCOM 2011, 19th International Conference on Software, Telecommunications and Computer Networks, pp. 1–6. IEEE (2011)

3. Benedetti, P., Perri, D., Simonetti, M., Gervasi, O., Reali, G., Femminella, M.: Skin cancer classification using inception network and transfer learning. In: Gervasi, O., et al. (eds.) ICCSA 2020. LNCS, vol. 12249, pp. 536–545. Springer, Cham (2020). https://doi.org/10.1007/978-3-030-58799-4_39

4. Perri, D., Simonetti, M., Lombardi, A., Faginas-Lago, N., Gervasi, O.: Binary classification of proteins by a machine learning approach. In: Gervasi, O., et al. (eds.) ICCSA 2020. LNCS, vol. 12255, pp. 549–558. Springer, Cham (2020). https://doi.org/10.1007/978-3-030-58820-5_41

5. Perri, D., Sylos Labini, P., Gervasi, O., Tasso, S., Vella, F.: Towards a learning-based performance modeling for accelerating deep neural networks. In: Misra, S., et al. (eds.) ICCSA 2019. LNCS, vol. 11619, pp. 665–676. Springer, Cham (2019). https://doi.org/10.1007/978-3-030-24289-3_49

6. McFarlane, D., Sarma, S., Chirn, J.L., Wong, C., Ashton, K.: Auto ID systems and intelligent manufacturing control. Eng. Appl. Artif. Intell. **16**(4), 365–376 (2003)

7. Zhong, R.Y., Xu, X., Klotz, E., Newman, S.T.: Intelligent manufacturing in the context of industry 4.0: a review. Engineering **3**(5), 616–630 (2017)

8. Franzoni, V., Tasso, S., Pallottelli, S., Perri, D.: Sharing linkable learning objects with the use of metadata and a taxonomy assistant for categorization. In: Misra, S., et al. (eds.) ICCSA 2019. LNCS, vol. 11620, pp. 336–348. Springer, Cham (2019). https://doi.org/10.1007/978-3-030-24296-1_28

9. Laganà, A., Gervasi, O., Tasso, S., Perri, D., Franciosa, F.: The ECTN virtual education community prosumer model for promoting and assessing chemical knowledge. In: Gervasi, O., et al. (eds.) ICCSA 2018. LNCS, vol. 10964, pp. 533–548. Springer, Cham (2018). https://doi.org/10.1007/978-3-319-95174-4_42

10. Yao, X., Zhou, J., Zhang, J., Boër, C.R.: From intelligent manufacturing to smart manufacturing for industry 4.0 driven by next generation artificial intelligence and further on. In: 2017 5th International Conference on Enterprise Systems (ES), pp. 311–318. IEEE (2017)

11. Wang, Y.: Industrial structure technology upgrade based on 5G network service and IoT intelligent manufacturing. Microprocess. Microsyst. **81**, 103696 (2021)

12. Adhya, S., Saha, D., Das, A., Jana, J., Saha, H.: An IoT based smart solar photovoltaic remote monitoring and control unit. In: 2016 2nd International Conference on Control, Instrumentation, Energy & Communication (CIEC), pp. 432–436. IEEE (2016)

13. Pallavi, S., Mallapur, J.D., Bendigeri, K.Y.: Remote sensing and controlling of greenhouse agriculture parameters based on IoT. In: 2017 International Conference on Big Data, IoT and Data Science (BID), pp. 44–48. IEEE (2017)

14. Ghosh, A.M., Halder, D., Alamgir Hossain, S.K.: Remote health monitoring system through IoT. In: 2016 5th International Conference on Informatics, Electronics and Vision (ICIEV), pp. 921–926. IEEE (2016)

15. Na, A., Isaac, W., Varshney, S., Khan, E.: An IoT based system for remote monitoring of soil characteristics. In: 2016 International Conference on Information Technology (InCITe)-The Next Generation IT Summit on the Theme-Internet of Things: Connect your Worlds, pp. 316–320. IEEE (2016)

16. Kodali, R.K., Jain, V., Bose, S., Boppana, L.: IoT based smart security and home automation system. In: 2016 International Conference on Computing, Communication and Automation (ICCCA), pp. 1286–1289. IEEE (2016)

17. Pavithra, D., Balakrishnan, R.: IoT based monitoring and control system for home automation. In: 2015 Global Conference on Communication Technologies (GCCT), pp. 169–173. IEEE (2015)

18. Santucci, F., Frenguelli, F., De Angelis, A., Cuccaro, I., Perri, D., Simonetti, M.: An immersive open source environment using godot. In: Gervasi, O., et al. (eds.) ICCSA 2020. LNCS, vol. 12255, pp. 784–798. Springer, Cham (2020). https://doi.org/10.1007/978-3-030-58820-5_56

19. Hu, M., Luo, X., Chen, J., Lee, Y.C., Zhou, Y., Wu, D.: Virtual reality: a survey of enabling technologies and its applications in IoT. J. Netw. Comput. Appl. **178**, 102970 (2021)

20. Simonetti, M., Perri, D., Amato, N., Gervasi, O.: Teaching math with the help of virtual reality. In: Gervasi, O., et al. (eds.) ICCSA 2020. LNCS, vol. 12255, pp. 799–809. Springer, Cham (2020). https://doi.org/10.1007/978-3-030-58820-5_57

21. Gervasi, O., Fortunelli, M., Magni, R., Perri, D., Simonetti, M.: Mobile localization techniques oriented to tangible web. In: Misra, S., et al. (eds.) ICCSA 2019. LNCS, vol. 11619, pp. 118–128. Springer, Cham (2019). https://doi.org/10.1007/978-3-030-24289-3_10

22. Therib, M.A., Marzog, H.A., Mohsin, M.J.: Smart digital bi-directional visitors counter based on IoT. J. Phys. Conf. Ser. **1530**, 012018 (2020)

23. Sruthi, M.S.: IoT based real time people counting system for smart buildings. Int. J. Emerg. Technol. Innov. Eng. **5**(2), 83–86 (2019)

24. Saon, S., Hashim, H., Ahmadon, M.A., Yamaguchi, S., et al.: Cloud-based people counter. Bull. Electr. Eng. Inform. **9**(1), 284–291 (2020)

25. Nag, A., Nikhilendra, J.N., Kalmath, M.: IoT based door access control using face recognition. In: 2018 3rd International Conference for Convergence in Technology (I2CT), pp. 1–3. IEEE (2018)

26. Biondi, G., Franzoni, V., Gervasi, O., Perri, D.: An approach for improving automatic mouth emotion recognition. In: Misra, S., et al. (eds.) ICCSA 2019. LNCS, vol. 11619, pp. 649–664. Springer, Cham (2019). https://doi.org/10.1007/978-3-030-24289-3_48

27. Othman, N.A., Aydin, I.: A face recognition method in the Internet of Things for security applications in smart homes and cities. In: 2018 6th International Istanbul Smart Grids and Cities Congress and Fair (ICSG), pp. 20–24. IEEE (2018)

28. Cai, H., Xu, B., Jiang, L., Vasilakos, A.V.: IoT-based big data storage systems in cloud computing: perspectives and challenges. IEEE Internet Things J. **4**(1), 75–87 (2016)

29. Kallur, D.C.: Human localization and activity recognition using distributed motion sensors (2014)

International Workshop on Advanced and Computational Methods for Earth Science Applications (WACM4ES 2021)

Digital Twins of Hydrocarbon Reservoir

Vladimir Cheverda[1,2]($\boxtimes$) (iD), Vadim Lisitsa[1,2](iD), Maksim Protasov[1],
and Galina Reshetova[2,3](iD)

[1] Institute of Petroleum Geology and Geophysics, Novosibirsk 630090, Russia
`cheverdava@ipgg.sbras.ru`
[2] Mathematical Centre in Akademgorodok, Akademgorodok, Russia
[3] Institute of Computational Mathematics and Mathematical Geophysics,
Novosibirsk 630090, Russia

Abstract. The construction of a detailed geological model of the object under study is necessary to ensure the successful conduct of seismic exploration and the subsequent development of a hydrocarbon reservoir. This stage is crucial concerning fields in a carbonate environment, widespread in the north of Eastern Siberia, particularly for the Yurubcheno-Tokhomskaya zone. Indeed, such hydrocarbon reservoirs are characterized by an extremely complex internal structure represented by the presence of multiple accumulations of subseismic objects, such as caverns, fractures and fracture corridors. A definition is given in this work, and technology for constructing a digital twin of a geological object is provided. The digital twin of a geological object in our understanding is a set of data that determine its geometric and physical properties in conjunction with the corresponding synthetic geophysical fields. In this work, a seismic digital twin of one of the Yurubcheno-Tokhomskaya zone objects is constructed.

This work describes the technology for constructing a digital twin of one of the most complex geological objects - a cavernous-fractured hydrocarbons reservoir, complicated by geological faults. At this stage, we are interested in this object's elastic characteristics, which affect its interaction with seismic waves. Three-dimensional seismic data and borehole observations are used as input information. We pay special attention to faults' construction, given their thin internal structure filled with fractured breccias. To do this, we use discrete element modelling of fault formation, which allows us to take into account the fragmentation of the geological rock. The constructed multi-scale model destination performs full-scale numerical simulation; the main goal is to obtain an accurate description of the scattered waves. We use the previously developed finite-difference methods using grids with local refinement in time and space to describe their occurrence and propagation processes. As a result, we got a digital twin of a specific geological object. By this term, we mean a detailed full-scale elastic model together with the calculated seismic wave field.

Keywords: Numerical modelling · Seismic waves ·
Cavernous-fractured reservoir · Geological faults · Caves · Fracture
corridors

© Springer Nature Switzerland AG 2021
O. Gervasi et al. (Eds.): ICCSA 2021, LNCS 12958, pp. 675–688, 2021.
https://doi.org/10.1007/978-3-030-87016-4_48

1   Introduction

The construction of a detailed geological model of the hydrocarbon reservoir is necessary to ensure the successful conduct of seismic exploration. This stage is especially crucial concerning fields in a carbonate environment, widespread in the north of Eastern Siberia, particularly for the Yurubcheno-Tokhomskaya zone. Indeed, such hydrocarbon reservoirs are characterized by an extremely complex internal structure represented by the presence of multiple accumulations of subseismic objects, such as caverns, fractures and fracture corridors.

This work describes the technology for constructing a digital twin of one of the most complex geological objects - a cavernous-fractured hydrocarbons reservoir, complicated by geological faults. At this stage, we are interested in this object's elastic characteristics, which affect its interaction with seismic waves. Three-dimensional seismic data and borehole observations are used as input information. We pay special attention to faults' construction, given their thin internal structure filled with fractured breccias. To do this, we use discrete element modelling of fault formation, which allows us to take into account the fragmentation of the geological rock. The constructed multi-scale model destination performs full-scale numerical simulation; the main goal is to obtain an accurate description of the scattered waves. We use the previously developed finite-difference methods using grids with local refinement in time and space to describe their occurrence and propagation processes. As a result, we got a digital twin of a specific geological object. By this term, we mean a detailed full-scale elastic model together with the calculated seismic wave field.

The successful development of hydrocarbon deposits requires a deep understanding of the multi scale features of its geological structure. Recently, scattered/diffracted waves have become more and more widely used for solving such problems. One of the main problems here is the need to perform reliable testing of the developed approaches. The most reliable way to do this is to build a digital geological model of the field, its digital twin, which describes the studied object's main geological elements: its geometry, stratigraphy, lithological and facies characteristics of reservoir layers, net thicknesses, reservoir properties, and others. Knowledge of these features is of particular importance in the development of carbonate reservoirs, which, as a rule, have a very complex structure of void space. When developing deposits of this type, it is necessary to consider the uneven distribution of cracks and caverns. They form a storage space (caves) and act as the main ways of fluid filtration (fractures) in carbonate reservoirs. Such deposits are distinguished by their diversity and concentrate a significant part of the world's hydrocarbon reserves.

For a detailed study of carbonate reservoirs, it is necessary to use a wide range of geological and geophysical information, in which seismic exploration plays an important role. It should give an idea of the reservoir's internal structure and changes in reservoir properties in the interwell space. However, fundamental physical properties of seismic wave fields impose very severe limitations on the resolution of methods based on the use of reflected waves. Therefore, when it comes to fractured and fractured-cavernous reservoirs, standard seismic methods based on the use of reflected waves are not as effective as in classical terrigenous ones. A distinctive feature of carbonate reservoirs is the absence of a sharp acoustic boundary on their top, which is associated with the diffuse nature of the voids formed during the dissolution and leaching of rocks. A significant expansion and deepening of information obtained using seismic methods can be achieved by attracting scattered/diffracted waves. Indeed, their presence indicates the presence of singular objects in the medium, such as faults, cracks, accumulations of caverns, and others. Consequently, the use of such waves opens up the possibility of a significant increase in the information content and resolution of seismic methods for studying the medium's internal structure.

In this paper, we present a technology for simulation of three-dimensional seismic data, focused on identifying hydrocarbon deposits in carbonate reservoirs and based on the use of scattered waves. These waves are formed on geological inhomogeneities, the characteristic dimensions of which is at least for one direction significantly less than the seismic wavelength. Usually, they associated with fracturing and cavernous rocks.

Let us mention, that we have developed technology using Gaussian beams for the separation of scattered waves. A Gaussian beam is a special kind of elastic waves, concentrated in a narrow neighbourhood of a preselected beam [Babich and Buldyrev 2009; Popov, 2002]. The imaging is performed at a fixed point from which a pair of beams is started - one towards the sources and the other towards the receivers (Fig. 1). Then, for these rays, we introduce the corresponding Gaussian beams. Then, on the receivers and sources' apertures, the traces of these beams are calculated, which are used as the summation weights of the initial multiple overlapping data to build an image at the selected point. As a result, a detailed three-dimensional image of the reservoir is obtained in scattered waves. Using the pair of P-rays one constructs the PP-scattered images, P- and S-rays waves give the PS-ones. It should be emphasized that neither for the construction of images in scattered PP nor in PS waves is necessary to perform preliminary separation of the total wavefield into longitudinal and transverse waves (see (Protasov et al. 2016, 2019)).

2   Building a Digital Twin of a Geological Object

The construction of a three-dimensional model was based on the known structure of one of the fields in the north of Eastern Siberia, the main object of which is the exposed carbonate reservoir of the Riphean age, containing massive deposits screened tectonically and lithologically.This reservoir has a complex structure with two types of voids - caverns and fractures and is characterized by strong heterogeneity and anisotropy of properties. It also combines low capacity (on average 1–2%) and high permeability (up to 4000 mD), mainly due to natural fracturing. The initial stage of the formation of the model consisted of constructing its skeleton, describing the interfaces between layers, built as a result of processing and interpreting 3D seismic data. Well log data determine the elastic medium parameters between these layers.

An important feature of the studied area is the presence of faults that break the reservoir into a series of blocks with displacement amplitudes reaching hundreds of meters. It should be emphasized here that at present, it is becoming generally accepted to understand a geological fault as a complex three-dimensional geological object [Kolyukhin et al. 2017; Vishnevsky et al. 2017]. Therefore, we treat the faults as 3D geological bodies consisting of rocks deformed due to tectonic movements [Faulkner et al. 2010]. Such movement's main characteristics are determined by a wide range of parameters, including the tectonic regime, the magnitude of the displacement of the layers, the mechanical properties of the surrounding rocks and others [Hardy and Finch, 2005; 2007].

Numerical modelling of a complex nonlinear process forming of geological faults was carried out using discrete elements approach. It treats the geological media as a set of "discrete elements/particles" of a simple geometric shape. In particular, here we use discrete elements in the form of various radii spheres, interacting with each other according to a certain set of physical laws.

When considering tectonic processes, one of the main types of interaction is friction between elements, which determines the so-called angle of rocks' internal friction. Simultaneously, it is convenient to separate the forces that determine the normal and tangential interactions.

Tangential forces, in particular friction, mainly determine the properties of the medium at the macro-level [Duan et al. 2017]. Coulomb's law is most often used to describe internal friction. According to this law, static friction determines the interaction between discrete elements/particles until it exceeds a certain threshold value, after which sliding friction becomes dominant. For most geomaterials, the static friction coefficient is 0.9, and this value we used in our computations. Another important quantity is the coefficient of dynamic friction. It usually ranges from 0.0 to 0.4. It is this coefficient that determines such a significant parameter as the angle of internal friction. In this work, we used a dynamic coefficient of friction that changes with depth, and this change was set in the range from 0.1 to 0.3.

The main goal of numerical modelling of the formation of a fault is to determine and analyze the distribution of deformations in its vicinity, especially for a fault with displacement. The computational area is a parallelepiped $2000\,\text{m} \times 2000\,\text{m} \times 500\,\text{m}$ (Fig. 1). The size of the discrete elements (balls) varied from 2.5 to 15 m. The stiffness module is equal to 16 GPa, regardless of the layer. To consider the variability of the medium (layers)' geomechanical properties (layers), we changed the coefficient from layer to layer, which controlled the intensity of the tangential forces. To simulate tectonic movements on fault banks, horizontal and vertical displacements were set as boundary conditions. Figure 2 shows the distribution of deformations in the vicinity of the fault with a fault amplitude of 100 m and a displacement in the positive Y direction equal to 50 m. The performed numerical experiments made it possible to estimate the distribution of deformations in the faults' vicinity. Further, following the empirical law describing the relationship between the variability of the relative volumetric deformation and the variations in the P-wave velocities [Botter et al. 2014], we determine the variations in the elastic parameters in the vicinity of the faults 2.

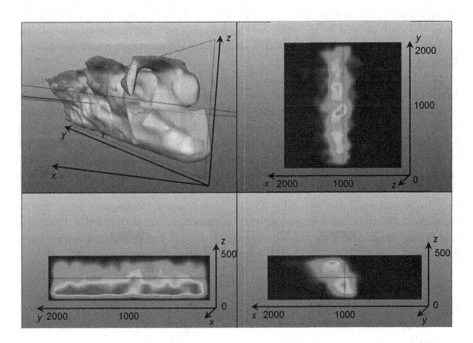

Fig. 1. Volumetric deformations in the vicinity of the fault: general view and projections.

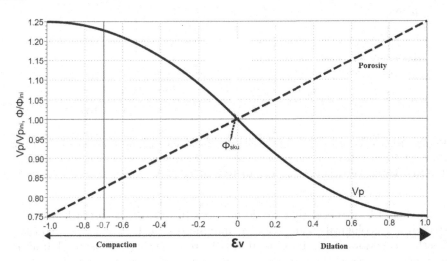

Fig. 2. The laboratory derived empirical dependence of volumetric deformations and P-wave propagation velocity.

To simulate the faults' internal structure, we used the data of geophysical studies in a horizontal well, opening the fault in the studied field (see Fig. 3). Of course, we know that the data from one well is not enough to describe the tectonic breccia in detail. However, the P and S wave velocities and densities set in the well allowed us to calibrate the parameters used in the geomechanical modelling, which provided a close to a realistic description of the tectonic breccia filling the geological faults (Fig. 4).

In addition to faults, the studied carbonate reservoir contains fracture corridors and caverns in various proportions: the main reservoir (caves) and transport routes (cracks) of the fluid. We introduced fracture zones in the form of two multidirectional systems of subvertical fractures obtained by statistical modelling using the spectral decomposition of random fields. This allowed the generation of fractures from 5 to 300 m long, forming realistic fracture corridors. Additionally, the model has been added to the intervals of intense cavities, which are regularly encountered in the field. According to core studies, these intervals have increased voidness reaching 15–20 % and small thicknesses from one to ten meters. To determine these cavities' parameters, we performed a statistical analysis of ten digital core models constructed by X-ray computed tomography [Bazaikin et al. 2017].

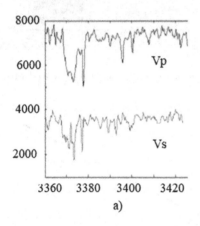 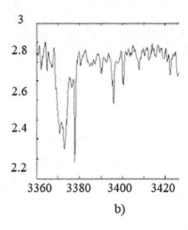

a)   b)

Fig. 3. Seismic velocity (a) and density (b) behaviour along a horizontal well bore. Horizontal axis - distance along well bore. The fault zone corresponds to distances of 3370 m–3380 m. Vertical axis: a) m/s b) 1000 kg/m^3.

It should be stressed that we do not seek to describe each crack when constructing a geological model, several millimetres thick. Instead, we construct fracture corridors [Questiaux et al. 2010], representing a cluster of fractures with one or more selected orientations. Fracture corridors can extend for several hundred meters, have a height of the first tens of meters and a thickness of the first meters. When constructing them in the geological model, direct observations on outcrops and data from borehole measurements are used. In this work, we relied on the results obtained earlier (see [Kolyukhin et al. 2017]), describing the structure of such objects based on a statistical analysis of the results of field observations, including outcrops and UIB formation micro scanner observation data.

Figure 5 shows a general view of the constructed 3D model's skeleton with faults and other small-scale irregularities. The framework is defined as a set of reflective boundaries, geological faults, fracture corridors and zones of increased cavernosity. To determine the medium filling this frame's elastic properties, we used the results of velocity analysis, well data, and laboratory measurements of the core material.

3   Seismic Synthetic Data

3.1   Finite-Difference Scheme with Locally Refined Grids

The next step completes development of a digital twin of the object under study by finite-difference modelling of three-dimensional seismic data. Let us emphasize that it is on this basis that it opens the possibility of a detailed analysis of the

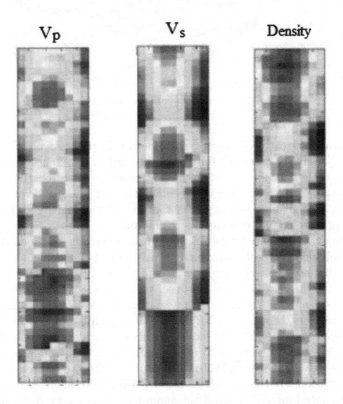

Fig. 4. Variations in elastic parameters of tectonic breccia filling the faults.

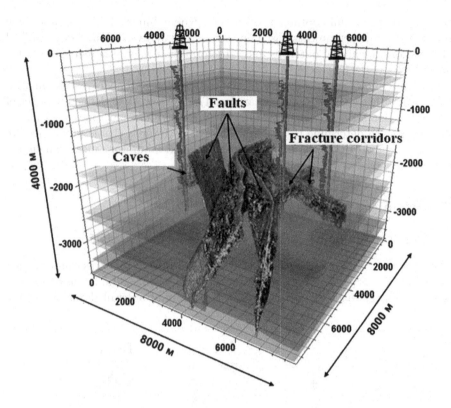

Fig. 5. 3D view of synthetic test model.

specific features of scattered waves generation within the reservoir. On this way, it becomes possible to carry out fully controlled numerical experiments to verify the developed methods for reconstructing the structure of hydrocarbon reservoirs on a sub-seismic scale to localize the accumulations of cracks and caves. It is the distribution of such micro-heterogeneity that provides a strategy for the optimal development of reservoirs in a carbonate environment.

However, the currently existing numerical modelling methods of seismic waves for solving such problems cannot consistently be implemented even with the use of the most powerful high-performance computing systems today. The fact is that, as a rule, for this purpose, people use explicit finite-difference schemes, based on uniform grids with a spatial cell size equal to 0.1–0.2 of the dominant wavelength, which, as a rule, is 5–10 m, while the typical size of the inhomogeneities is 0.01–0.1 m. To model seismic wavefields' interaction with such inhomogeneities, it is necessary to use a spatial step comparable to their size. However, using a grid step of 0.05 m across the entire target area will require huge computational resources - terabytes of RAM and teraflops of performance. To avoid the need for such unrealistic computer resources, we developed finite-difference schemes with local space-time refinement of the grid in the areas filled with clusters of subseismic heterogeneities (Kostin et al. 2015; Landa et al. 2018). In this case, grids with varying spatial steps correctly represent various components of the model: relatively large steps - to describe a three-dimensional heterogeneous reference medium and much smaller ones - inside the reservoir and fault zones (see 6). The computations are doing to ensure the uniform load of processor elements involved. This approach significantly reduces the requirements for the amount of RAM and the number of computing processes.

3.2   Communication Between Groups of Processor Units

The computational area for full multiscale elastic simulation is parallelepiped $8\,km \times 10\,km \times 6\,km$. To carry out numerical simulation, we divided the elastic model into two classes:

- the reference medium containing reflective borders and smoothly changing elastic parameters between them;
- with small-scale heterogeneities, such as faults with tectonic breccias, as well as accumulations of caves and fractures.

In the reference medium, we use a grid step of five meters. Inside the target reservoir, we choose a grid of $0.25\,m$, which made it possible to describe the medium's elastic properties' with acceptable accuracy.

Thus, the entire studied medium is represented as a superposition of the enclosing medium (coarse grid), and the reservoir contained in it (fine mesh) and all processing elements are divided into two groups, performing computations on coarse and fine grids, respectively. Consider the organization exchanges between these groups.

From Coarse Mesh to Fine Mesh. First of all, the first group's processor elements are determined (coarse mesh), covering the reservoir (see Fig. 7, left), and are grouped along each of the faces contacting the parallelepiped on the fine mesh. A particular master processor is defined for each face (abbreviation MP in Fig. 7), which collects the solution's current values and sends them to the corresponding MP on a fine grid. All subsequent processing of this data, which ensures the matching of the grids by interpolation based on the FFT (Fast Fourier Transform), is performed by the MP for the fine grid, sending data to the corresponding processors from the second group (fine grid). Interpolation in place significantly reduces the amount of the data transferred and, hence the time of unproductive waiting.

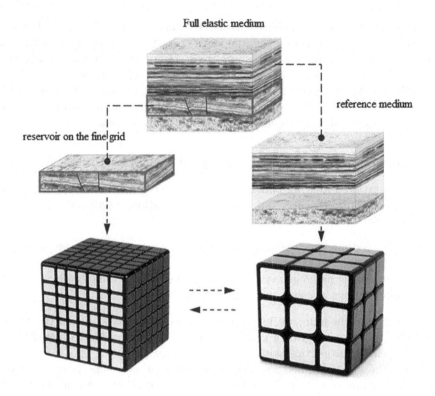

Fig. 6. Decomposition of the full elastic model in two components and loading them onto different groups of Processor Units.

From the Fine Mesh to the Coarse Mesh. As in the previous case we define processor elements performing computations on the faces of the fine-mesh parallelepiped that encloses the reservoir, and for each face is determined by a master processor (MP). It collects data from each of the faces for transmission to the corresponding master processor operating on a coarse grid. In this case, not all the data obtained is needed to calculate the solution values for the next moment in time with a small step, but only those that correspond to the coarse grid nodes. Formally, these data can be thinned out, but, as our experience has shown, noticeable artefacts arise, associated with the loss of smoothness of the solution. Therefore, FFT-based interpolation is also used here to restore values with a high accuracy. Performing such a thinning procedure in place by a master processor operating on a fine mesh significantly reduces the amount of data transferred and therefore reduces the unproductive waiting time.

3.3   Acquisition

The 3D acquisition is on the surface $z = 0$ within an $8\,\text{km} \times 10\,\text{km}$ rectangle filled by three-component receivers evenly spaced over a 25×25-meter grid. The volumetric sources are set with $50\,\text{m}$ along lines parallel to the X-axis at a distance of $300\,\text{m}$. This geometry provided the fold factor equal to 100 at most points of the observation area. We use Ricker wavelet with a dominant frequency $40\,\text{Hz}$ as a source function.

In the Fig. 8, we present the vertical component of the displacement for a volumetric point source located in the centre of the acquisition, along with two mutually orthogonal profiles. As one can see, there are, along with reflected many scattered waves also.

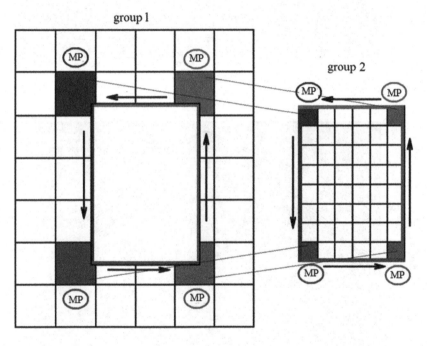

Fig. 7. Data exchange between groups of processing elements on coarse (left) and fine (right) meshes.

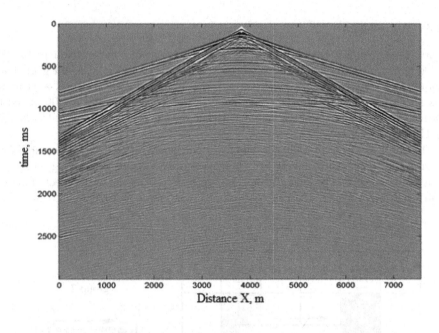

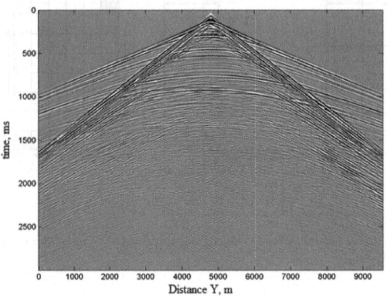

Fig. 8. Data exchange between groups of processing elements on coarse (left) and fine (right) meshes.

4   Conclusion

In this work, we focus on the development of the data sets for verifying various techniques for constructing images of multiscale geological objects. That is why we have created a digital twin of some real geology in the north of the East Siberia. Also, to enhance testing capabilities, we have added several specific features to this twin, such as fractured corridors and areas of high cavernosity. For the constructed digital object, numerical modelling was performed to synthesize seismic data were obtained. Thus, we got the opportunity to conduct a fully controlled numerical experiment. Having made sure that the developed procedures correctly restore the digital model structure, we carried out processing of real data, which also gave results that fully correspond to those previously obtained using other approaches and carry additional, essential geological information.

Acknowledgement. The work is supported by Mathematical Center in Akademgorodok, the agreement with Ministry of Science and High Education of the Russian Federation number 075-15-2019-1613.

References

Babich V.M., Buldyrev V.D.: Asymptotic methods in short-wavelength diffraction theory. Alpha Science International (2009)

Bazaikin, Y., et al.: Effect of CT image size and resolution on the accuracy of rock property estimates. J. Geophys. Res. Solid Earth. **122**(5), 3645–3647 (2017)

Botter, C., Cardozo, N., Hardy, S., Lecomte, I., Escalona, F.: From mechanical modeling to seismic imaging of faults: a synthetic workflow to study the impact of faults on seismic. Mar. Petrol. Geol. **57**, 187–207 (2014)

Duan, K., Kwok, C.Y., Ma, X.: DEM simulations of sandstone under true triaxial compressive tests. Acta Geotechnica **12**(3), 495–510 (2017)

Faulkner, D.R., et al.: A review of recent developments concerning the structure, mechanics and fluid flow properties of fault zones. J. Struct. Geol. **32**, 1557–1575 (2010)

Hardy, S., Finch, E.: Discrete-element modelling of detachment folding. Basin Res. **17**(4), 507–520 (2005)

Hardy, S., Finch, E.: Mechanical stratigraphy and the transition from trishear to kink-band fault-propagation fold forms above blind basement thrust faults: a discrete-element study. Marine Petrol. Geol. **24**, 75–90 (2007)

Kolyukhin, D.R., et al.: Seismic imaging and statistical analysis of fault facies models. Interpretation 5(4), SP71– SP82 (2017)

Kostin, V.I., Lisitsa, V.V., Reshetova, G.V., Tcheverda, V.A.: Local time-space mesh refinement for simulation of elastic wave propagation in multi-scale media. J. Comput. Phys. **281**, 669–689 (2015)

Landa, E., Reshetova, G., Tcheverda, V.: Modeling and imaging of multiscale geological media: exploding reflectors revisited. Geosciences **8**(12), 486 (2018)

Popov, M.M.: Ray theory and Gaussian beam method for geophysicists. Efuba, Salvador-Bahia (2002)

Protasov, M.I., Reshetova, G.V., Tcheverda, V.A.: Fracture detection by Gaussian beam imaging of seismic data and image spectrum analysis. Geophys. Prospect. **64**(1), 68–82 (2016)

Protasov, M.I., Tcheverda, V.A., Pravduhin, A.P.: 3D true-amplitude anisotropic elastic Gaussian beam depth migration of 3D irregular data. J. Seis. Explorat. **28**(2), 121–146 (2019)

Questiaux, J.-M., Gary, D., Couples, G.D., Ruby, N.: Fractured reservoirs with fracture corridors. Geophys. Prospect. **58**, 279–295 (2010)

Vishnevsky, D.M., et al.: Correlation analysis of statistical facies fault models. Doklady Earth Sci. **473**(2), 477–481 (2017)

Author Index

Printed in the United States
by Baker & Taylor Publisher Services

Printed in the United States
by Baker & Taylor Publisher Services